RIEMANNIAN GEOMETRIC STATISTICS IN MEDICAL IMAGE ANALYSIS

THE ELSEVIER AND MICCAI SOCIETY BOOK SERIES

Advisory Board

Nicholas Ayache
James S. Duncan
Alex Frangi
Hayit Greenspan
Pierre Jannin
Anne Martel
Xavier Pennec
Terry Peters
Daniel Rueckert
Milan Sonka
Jay Tian
Kevin Zhou

Titles:

Balocco, A., et al., Computing and Visualization for Intravascular Imaging and Computer Assisted Stenting, 9780128110188

Dalca, A.V., et al., Imaging Genetics, 9780128139684

Depeursinge, A., et al., Biomedical Texture Analysis, 9780128121337

Pennec, X., et al., Riemannian Geometric Statistics in Medical Image Analysis, 9780128147252

Wu, G., and Sabuncu, M., Machine Learning and Medical Imaging, 9780128040768

Zhou K., Medical Image Recognition, Segmentation and Parsing, 9780128025819

Zhou, K., et al., Deep Learning for Medical Image Analysis, 9780128104088

Zhou, K., et al., Handbook of Medical Image Computing and Computer Assisted Intervention, 9780128161760

MICCAI

RIEMANNIAN GEOMETRIC STATISTICS IN MEDICAL IMAGE ANALYSIS

Edited by

XAVIER PENNEC
STEFAN SOMMER
TOM FLETCHER

ACADEMIC PRESS
An imprint of Elsevier

ELSEVIER

Academic Press is an imprint of Elsevier
125 London Wall, London EC2Y 5AS, United Kingdom
525 B Street, Suite 1650, San Diego, CA 92101, United States
50 Hampshire Street, 5th Floor, Cambridge, MA 02139, United States
The Boulevard, Langford Lane, Kidlington, Oxford OX5 1GB, United Kingdom

Notices

Knowledge and best practice in this field are constantly changing. As new research and experience broaden our understanding, changes in research methods, professional practices, or medical treatment may become necessary.

Practitioners and researchers must always rely on their own experience and knowledge in evaluating and using any information, methods, compounds, or experiments described herein. In using such information or methods they should be mindful of their own safety and the safety of others, including parties for whom they have a professional responsibility.

To the fullest extent of the law, neither the Publisher nor the authors, contributors, or editors, assume any liability for any injury and/or damage to persons or property as a matter of products liability, negligence or otherwise, or from any use or operation of any methods, products, instructions, or ideas contained in the material herein.

Library of Congress Cataloging-in-Publication Data
A catalog record for this book is available from the Library of Congress

British Library Cataloguing-in-Publication Data
A catalogue record for this book is available from the British Library

ISBN: 978-0-12-814725-2

For information on all Academic Press publications
visit our website at https://www.elsevier.com/books-and-journals

Publisher: Mara Conner
Acquisition Editor: Tim Pitts
Editorial Project Manager: Leticia M. Lima
Production Project Manager: Kamesh Ramajogi
Designer: Miles Hitchen

Typeset by VTeX

Working together
to grow libraries in
developing countries

www.elsevier.com • www.bookaid.org

Contents

Stephen M. Pizer, Junpyo Hong, Jared Vicory, Zhiyuan Liu, J.S. Marron,
Hyo-young Choi, James Damon, Sungkyu Jung, Beatriz Paniagua,
Jörn Schulz, Ankur Sharma, Liyun Tu, Jiyao Wang

Chapter 9   Bias on estimation in quotient space and correction methods........343

Nina Miolane, Loic Devilliers, Xavier Pennec

Chapter 10   Probabilistic approaches to geometric statistics.........377

Stefan Sommer

Contributors

Martin Bauer
Florida State University, Department of Mathematics, Tallahassee, FL, United States

Rudrasis Chakraborty
University of Florida, CISE Department, Gainesville, FL, United States

Benjamin Charlier
IMAG, Univ. Montpellier, CNRS, Montpellier, France
Institut du Cerveau et de la Moëlle Épinière, ARAMIS, Paris, France

Nicolas Charon
Johns Hopkins University, Center of Imaging Sciences, Baltimore, MD, United States

Hyo-young Choi
UNC, Chapel Hill, NC, United States

James Damon
UNC, Chapel Hill, NC, United States

Loic Devilliers
Université Côte d'Azur and Inria, Epione team, Sophia Antipolis, France

Aasa Feragen
University of Copenhagen, Department of Computer Science, Copenhagen, Denmark

Tom Fletcher
University of Virginia, Departments of Electrical & Computer Engineering and Computer Science, Charlottesville, VA, United States

Joan Glaunès
MAP5, Université Paris Descartes, Paris, France

Polina Golland
Massachusetts Institute of Technology, Computer Science and Artificial Intelligence Lab, Cambridge, MA, United States

Pietro Gori
Télécom ParisTech, LTCI, équipe IMAGES, Paris, France

Junpyo Hong
UNC, Chapel Hill, NC, United States

Sarang Joshi
University of Utah, Department of Bioengineering, Scientific Computing and Imaging Institute, Salt Lake City, UT, United States

Sungkyu Jung
Seoul National University, Seoul, Republic of Korea

Zhiyuan Liu
UNC, Chapel Hill, NC, United States

Marco Lorenzi
Université Côte d'Azur and Inria, Epione team, Sophia Antipolis, France

J.S. Marron
UNC, Chapel Hill, NC, United States

Stephen Marsland
Victoria University of Wellington, School of Mathematics and Statistics, Wellington, New Zealand

Nina Miolane
Université Côte d'Azur and Inria, Epione team, Sophia Antipolis, France
Stanford University, Department of Statistics, Stanford, CA, United States

Jan Modersitzki
Institute of Mathematics and Image Computing, University of Lübeck, Lübeck, Germany
Fraunhofer MEVIS, Lübeck, Germany

Klas Modin
Chalmers University of Technology and the University of Gothenburg, Department of Mathematical Sciences, Göteborg, Sweden

Marc Niethammer
Department of Computer Science, University of North Carolina at Chapel Hill, Chapel Hill, NC, United States
Biomedical Research Imaging Center (BRIC), Chapel Hill, NC, United States

Tom Nye
Newcastle University, School of Mathematics, Statistics and Physics, Newcastle upon Tyne, United Kingdom

Beatriz Paniagua
UNC, Chapel Hill, NC, United States

Xavier Pennec
Université Côte d'Azur and Inria, Epione team, Sophia Antipolis, France

Stephen M. Pizer
UNC, Chapel Hill, NC, United States

Thomas Polzin
Institute of Mathematics and Image Computing, University of Lübeck, Lübeck, Germany

Laurent Risser
Institut de Mathématiques de Toulouse, CNRS, Université de Toulouse, UMR CNRS 5219, Toulouse, France

Pierre Roussillon
ENS Cachan, CNRS, Université Paris-Saclay, CMLA, Cachan, France

Jörn Schulz
Arctic University of Norway, Tromsø, Norway

Ankur Sharma
UNC, Chapel Hill, NC, United States

Stefan Sommer
University of Copenhagen, Department of Computer Science, Copenhagen, Denmark

Anuj Srivastava
Florida State University, Tallahassee, FL, United States

Liyun Tu
UNC, Chapel Hill, NC, United States

Baba C. Vemuri
University of Florida, CISE Department, Gainesville, FL, United States

François-Xavier Vialard
Laboratoire d'informatique Gaspard Monge, Université Paris-Est Marne-la-Vallée, UMR CNRS 8049, Champs sur Marne, France

Jared Vicory
UNC, Chapel Hill, NC, United States

Jiyao Wang
UNC, Chapel Hill, NC, United States

William M. Wells III
Harvard Medical School, Department of Radiology, Boston, MA, United States

Miaomiao Zhang
Washington University in St. Louis, Computer Science and Engineering, St. Louis, MO, United States

Ruiyi Zhang
Florida State University, Tallahassee, FL, United States

Introduction

Introduction

Over the last two decades, there has been a growing need in the medical image computing community for principled methods to process nonlinear geometric data. Typical examples of data in this domain include organ shapes and deformations resulting from segmentation and registration in computational anatomy, and symmetric positive definite matrices in diffusion imaging. In this context, Riemannian geometry has gradually been established as one the most powerful mathematical and computational paradigms.

This book aims at being an introduction to and a reference on Riemannian geometric statistics and its use in medical image analysis for researchers and graduate students. The book provides both descriptions of the core methodology and presentations of state-of-the-art methods used in the field. We wish to present this combination of foundational material and current research together with examples, applications, and algorithms in a volume that is edited and authored by the leading researchers in the field. In addition, we wish to provide an overview of current research challenges and future applications.

Beyond medical image computing, the methods described in this book may also apply to other domains such as signal processing, computer vision, geometric deep learning, and other domains where statistics on geometric features appear. As such, the presented core methodology takes its place in the field of *geometric statistics*, the statistical analysis of data being elements of nonlinear geometric spaces. We hope that both the foundational material and the advanced techniques presented in the later parts of the book can be useful in domains outside medical imaging and present important applications of geometric statistics methodology.

Contents

Part 1 of this edited volume describes the foundations of Riemannian geometric computing methods for statistics on manifolds. The book here emphasizes concepts rather than proofs with the goal of providing graduate students in computer science the mathematical background needed to start in this domain. Chapter 1 presents an introduction to differential, Riemannian and Lie group geometry, and chapter 2 covers statistics on manifolds. Chapters 3–5 present introductions to geometry of SPD matrices, shape analysis through the action of the diffeomorphism group, and geometry and statistical analysis beyond the Riemannian setting when an affine connection, not a metric, is available.

Part 2 includes contributions from leading researchers in the field on applications of statistics on manifolds and shape spaces in medical image computing. In chapter 6, Stephen Pizer, Steve Marron, and coauthors describe shape representation via skeletal models and how this allows application of nonlinear statistical methods on shape spaces. Chapter 7 by Rudrasis Chakraborty and Baba Vemuri concerns estimation of the iterative Riemannian barycenter, a candidate for the generalization of the Euclidean mean value on selected manifolds. In chapter 8, Aasa Feragen and Tom Nye discuss the statistics on stratified spaces that generalize manifold by allowing variation of the topological structure. Estimation of templates in quotient spaces is the topic of chapter 9 by Nina Miolane, Loic Devilliers, and Xavier Pennec. Stefan Sommer discusses parametric statistics on manifolds using stochastic processes in chapter 10. In chapter 11, Ruiyi Zhang and Anuj Srivastava consider shape analysis of functional data using elastic metrics.

Part 3 of the book focuses on diffeomorphic deformations and their applications in shape analysis. Nicolas Charon, Benjamin Charlier, Joan Glaunès, Pierre Roussillon, and Pietro Gori present currents, varifolds, and normal cycles for shape comparison in chapter 12. Numerical aspects of large deformation registration is discussed in chapter 13 by Thomas Polzin, Marc Niethammer, François-Xavier Vialard, and Jan Modersitzki. Francois-Xavier and Laurent Risser present spatially varying metrics for large deformation matching in chapter 14. Chapter 15 by Miaomiao Zhang, Polina Golland, William M. Wells, and Tom Fletcher presents a framework for low-dimensional representations of large deformations and its use in shape analysis. Finally, in chapter 16, Martin Bauer, Sarang Joshi, and Klas Modin study densities matching in the diffeomorphic setting.

We are extremely grateful for this broad set of excellent contributions to the book by leading researchers in the field, and we hope that the book in its entirety will inspire new developments and research directions in this exciting intersection between applied mathematics and computer science.

The editors:
Xavier Pennec
University Côte d'Azur and Inria, Sophia Antipolis, France
Stefan Sommer
DIKU, University of Copenhagen, Copenhagen, Denmark
Tom Fletcher
University of Virginia, Charlottesville, VA, United States
February, 2019

1

Foundations of geometric statistics

Introduction to differential and Riemannian geometry

Stefan Sommer[a], Tom Fletcher[b], Xavier Pennec[c]

[a]*University of Copenhagen, Department of Computer Science, Copenhagen, Denmark.* [b]*University of Virginia, Departments of Electrical & Computer Engineering and Computer Science, Charlottesville, VA, United States.* [c]*Université Côte d'Azur and Inria, Epione team, Sophia Antipolis, France*

1.1 Introduction

When data exhibit nonlinearity, the mathematical description of the data space must often depart from the convenient linear structure of Euclidean vector spaces. Nonlinearity prevents global vector space structure, but we can nevertheless ask which mathematical properties from the Euclidean case can be kept while still preserving the accurate modeling of the data. It turns out that in many cases, local resemblance to a Euclidean vector space is one such property. In other words, up to some approximation, the data space can be linearized in limited regions while forcing a linear model on the entire space would introduce too much distortion.

The concept of local similarity to Euclidean spaces brings us exactly to the setting of manifolds. Topological, differential, and Riemannian manifolds are characterized by the existence of local maps, charts, between the manifold and a Euclidean space. These charts are structure preserving: They are homeomorphisms in the case of topological manifolds, diffeomorphisms in the case of differential manifolds, and, in the case of Riemannian manifolds, they carry local inner products that encode the non-Euclidean geometry.

The following sections describe these foundational concepts and how they lead to notions commonly associated with geometry: curves, length, distances, geodesics, curvature, parallel transport, and volume form. In addition to the differential and Riemannian structure, we describe one extra layer of structure, Lie groups that are manifolds equipped with smooth group structure. Lie groups and their quotients are examples of homogeneous spaces. The group structure provides relations between distant points on the group and thereby additional ways of constructing Riemannian metrics and deriving geodesic equations.

Riemannian Geometric Statistics in Medical Image Analysis
https://doi.org/10.1016/B978-0-12-814725-2.00008-X

Topological, differential, and Riemannian manifolds are often covered by separate graduate courses in mathematics. In this much briefer overview, we describe the general concepts, often sacrificing mathematical rigor to instead provide intuitive reasons for the mathematical definitions. For a more in-depth introduction to geometry, the interested reader may, for example, refer to the sequence of books by John M. Lee on topological, differentiable, and Riemannian manifolds [17,18,16] or to the book on Riemannian geometry by do Carmo [4]. More advanced references include [15], [11], and [24].

1.2 Manifolds

A manifold is a collection of points that locally, but not globally, resembles Euclidean space. When the Euclidean space is of finite dimension, we can without loss of generality relate it to $\mathbb{R}^d$ for some $d > 0$. The abstract mathematical definition of a manifold specifies the topological, differential, and geometric structure by using charts, maps between parts of the manifold and $\mathbb{R}^d$, and collections of charts denoted atlases. We will discuss this construction shortly, however, we first focus on the case where the manifold is a subset of a larger Euclidean space. This viewpoint is often less abstract and closer to our natural intuition of a surface embedded in our surrounding 3D Euclidean space.

Let us exemplify this by the surface of the earth embedded in $\mathbb{R}^3$. We are constrained by gravity to live on the surface of the earth. This surface seems locally flat with two dimensions only, and we use two-dimensional maps to navigate the surface. When traveling far, we sometimes need to change from one map to another. We then find charts that overlap in small parts, and we assume that the charts provide roughly the same view of the surface in those overlapping parts. For a long time, the earth was even considered to be flat because its curvature was not noticeable at the scale at which it was observed. When considering the earth surface as a two-dimensional restriction of the 3D ambient space, the surface is an embedded submanifold of $\mathbb{R}^3$. On the other hand, when using maps and piecing the global surface together using the compatibility of the overlapping parts, we take the abstract view using charts and atlases.

1.2.1 Embedded submanifolds

Arguably the simplest example of a two-dimensional manifold is the sphere $\mathbb{S}^2$. Relating to the previous example, when embedded in $\mathbb{R}^3$, we can view it as an idealized model for the surface of the earth. The sphere with radius 1 can be described as the set of unit vectors in $\mathbb{R}^3$, that is, the set

$$\mathbb{S}^2 = \{(x^1, x^2, x^3) \in \mathbb{R}^3 \mid (x^1)^2 + (x^2)^2 + (x^3)^2 = 1\}. \qquad (1.1)$$

Notice from the definition of the set that all points of $\mathbb{S}^2$ satisfy the equation $(x^1)^2 + (x^2)^2 + (x^3)^2 - 1 = 0$. We can generalize this way of constructing a manifold to the following definition.

Definition 1.1 (Embedded manifold). Let $F : \mathbb{R}^k \to \mathbb{R}^m$ be a differentiable map such that the Jacobian matrix $dF(x) = (\frac{\partial}{\partial x^j} F^i(x))^i_j$ has constant rank $k - d$ for all $x \in F^{-1}(0)$. Then the zero-level set $\mathcal{M} = F^{-1}(0)$ is an embedded manifold of dimension d.

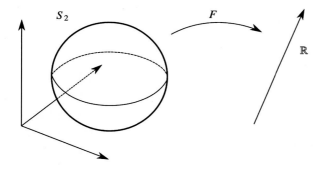

Figure 1.1. An embedded manifold arises as the zero-level subset $\mathcal{M} = F^{-1}(0)$ of the map $F : \mathbb{R}^k \to \mathbb{R}^m$. Here $F : \mathbb{R}^3 \to \mathbb{R}$ is given by the sphere equation $x \mapsto (x^1)^2 + (x^2)^2 + (x^3)^2 - 1$, and the manifold $\mathcal{M} = \mathbb{S}^2$ is of dimension $3 - 1 = 2$.

The map F is said to give an implicit representation of the manifold. In the previous example, we used the definition with $F(x) = (x^1)^2 + (x^2)^2 + (x^3)^2 - 1$ (see Fig. 1.1).

The fact that $\mathcal{M} = F^{-1}(0)$ is a manifold is often taken as the consequence of the submersion level set theorem instead of a definition. The theorem states that with the above assumptions, $\mathcal{M}$ has a manifold structure as constructed with charts and atlases. In addition, the topological and differentiable structure of M is in a certain way compatible with that of $\mathbb{R}^k$ letting us denote M as *embedded* in $\mathbb{R}^k$. For now, we will be somewhat relaxed about the details and use the construction as a working definition of what we think of as a manifold.

The map F can be seen as a set of m constraints that points in $\mathcal{M}$ must satisfy. The Jacobian matrix $dF(x)$ at a point in $x \in \mathcal{M}$ linearizes the constraints around x, and its rank $k - d$ indicates how many of them are linearly independent. In addition to the unit length constraints of vectors in $\mathbb{R}^3$ defining $\mathbb{S}^2$, additional examples of commonly occurring manifolds that we will see in this book arise directly from embedded manifolds or as quotients of embedded manifolds.

Example 1.1. *d-dimensional spheres* $\mathbb{S}^d$ embedded in $\mathbb{R}^{d+1}$. Here we express the unit length equation generalizing (1.1) by

$$\mathbb{S}^d = \{x \in \mathbb{R}^{n+1} \mid \|x\|^2 - 1 = 0\} . \tag{1.2}$$

The squared norm $\|x\|^2$ is the standard squared Euclidean norm on $\mathbb{R}^{d+1}$.

Example 1.2. *Orthogonal matrices* $\mathrm{O}(k)$ on $\mathbb{R}^k$ have the property that the inner products $\langle U_i, U_j \rangle$ of columns U_i, U_j of the matrix $U \in \mathrm{M}_{(k,k)}$ vanish for $i \neq j$ and equal 1 for $i = j$. This gives k^2 constraints, and $\mathrm{O}(k)$ is thus an embedded manifold in $\mathrm{M}_{(k,k)}$ by the equation

$$\mathrm{O}(k) = \left\{ U \in \mathrm{M}_{(k,k)} \mid UU^\top - \mathrm{Id}_k = 0 \right\} \tag{1.3}$$

with Id_k being the identity matrix on $\mathbb{R}^k$. We will see in Section 1.7.3 that the rank of the map $F(U) = UU^\top - \mathrm{Id}_k$ is $\frac{k(k+1)}{2}$ on $\mathrm{O}(k)$, and it follows that $\mathrm{O}(k)$ has dimension $\frac{k(k-1)}{2}$.

1.2.2 Charts and local euclideaness

We now describe how charts, local parameterizations of the manifold, can be constructed from the implicit representation above. We will use this to give a more abstract definition of a differentiable manifold.

When navigating the surface of the earth, we seldom use curved representations of the surface but instead rely on charts that give a flat, 2D representation of regions limited in extent. It turns out that this analogy can be extended to embed manifolds with a rigorous mathematical formulation.

Definition 1.2. A chart on a d-dimensional manifold $\mathcal{M}$ is a diffeomorphic mapping $\phi : U \to \tilde{U}$ from an open set $U \subset \mathcal{M}$ to an open set $\tilde{U} \subseteq \mathbb{R}^d$.

The definition exactly captures the informal idea of representing a local part of the surface, the open set U, with a mapping to a Euclidean space, in the surface case $\mathbb{R}^2$ (see Fig. 1.2).

When using charts, we often say that we work *in coordinates*. Instead of accessing points on $\mathcal{M}$ directly, we take a chart

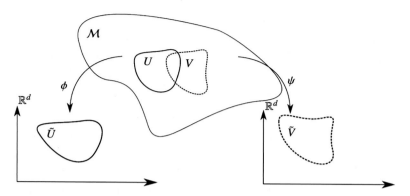

Figure 1.2. Charts $\phi : U \to \tilde{U}$ and $\psi : V \to \tilde{V}$, members of the atlas covering the manifold $\mathcal{M}$, from the open sets $U, V \subset \mathcal{M}$ to open sets $\tilde{U}, \tilde{V}$ of $\mathbb{R}^d$, respectively. The compatibility condition ensures that ϕ and ψ agree on the overlap $U \cap V$ between U and V in the sense that the composition $\psi \circ \phi^{-1}$ is a differentiable map.

$\phi : U \to \tilde{U}$ and use points in $\phi(U) \subseteq \mathbb{R}^d$ instead. This gives us the convenience of having a coordinate system present. However, we need to be aware that the choice of the coordinate system affects the analysis, both theoretically and computationally. When we say that we work in coordinates $x = (x^1, \ldots, x^d)$, we implicitly imply that there is a chart ϕ such that $\phi^{-1}(x)$ is a point on $\mathcal{M}$.

It is a consequence of the implicit function theorem that embedded manifolds have charts. Proving it takes some work, but we can sketch the idea in the case of the implicit representation map $F : \mathbb{R}^k \to \mathbb{R}^m$ having Jacobian with full rank m. Recall the setting of the implicit function theorem (see e.g. [18]): Let $F : \mathbb{R}^{d+m} \to \mathbb{R}^m$ be continuously differentiable and write $(x, y) \in \mathbb{R}^{d+m}$ such that x denotes the first d coordinates and y the last m coordinates. Let $d_y F$ denote the last m columns of the Jacobian matrix dF, that is, the derivatives of F taken with respect to variations in y. If $d_y F$ has full rank m at a point (x, y) where $F(x, y) = 0$, then there exists an open neighborhood $\tilde{U} \subseteq \mathbb{R}^d$ of x and a differentiable map $g : \tilde{U} \to \mathbb{R}^m$ such that $F(x, g(x)) = 0$ for all $x \in \tilde{U}$.

The only obstruction to using the implicit function theorem directly to find charts is that we may need to rotate the coordinates on $\mathbb{R}^{d+m}$ to find coordinates (x, y) and a submatrix $d_y F$ of full rank. With this in mind, the map g ensures that $F(x, g(x)) = 0$ for all $x \in \tilde{U}$, that is, the points $(x, g(x)), x \in \tilde{U}$ are included in $\mathcal{M}$. Setting $U = g(\tilde{U})$, we get a chart $\phi : U \to \tilde{U}$ directly by the mapping $(x, g(x)) \mapsto x$.

1.2.3 Abstract manifolds and atlases

We now use the concept of charts to define atlases as collections of charts and from this the abstract notion of a manifold.

Definition 1.3 (Atlas). An atlas of a set $\mathcal{M}$ is a family of charts $(\phi_i)_{i=1,\ldots,N}$, $\phi_i : U_i \to \tilde{U}_i$ such that

- ϕ_i cover $\mathcal{M}$: For each $x \in \mathcal{M}$, there exists $i \in \{1, \ldots, N\}$ such that $x \in U_i$,
- ϕ_i are compatible: For each pair $i, j \in \{1, \ldots, N\}$ where $U_i \cap U_j$ is nonempty, the composition $\phi_i \circ \phi_j^{-1} : \phi_j(U_i \cap U_j) \to \mathbb{R}^d$ is a differentiable map.

An atlas thus ensures the existence of at least one chart covering a neighborhood of each point of $\mathcal{M}$. This allows the topological and differential structure of $\mathcal{M}$ to be given by a definition from the topology and differential structure of the image of the charts, that is, $\mathbb{R}^d$. Intuitively, the structure coming from the Euclidean spaces $\mathbb{R}^d$ is pulled back using ϕ_i to the manifold. In order for this construction to work, we must ensure that there is no ambiguity in the structure we get if the domain of multiple charts cover a given point. The compatibility condition ensures exactly that.

Definition 1.4 (Manifold). Let $\mathcal{M}$ be a set with an atlas $(\phi_i)_{i=1,\ldots,N}$ with $\phi_i : U_i \to \tilde{U}_i$, $\tilde{U}_i \subseteq \mathbb{R}^d$. Then $\mathcal{M}$ is a manifold of dimension d.

Remark 1.1. Until now, we have been somewhat loose in describing maps as being "differentiable". The differentiability of maps on a manifold comes from the differential structure, which in turn is defined from the atlas and the charts mapping to $\mathbb{R}^d$. The differential structure on $\mathbb{R}^d$ allows derivatives up to any order, but the charts may not support this when transferring the structure to $\mathcal{M}$. To be more precise, in the compatibility condition, we require the compositions $\phi_i \circ \phi_j^{-1}$ to be C^r as maps from $\mathbb{R}^d$ to $\mathbb{R}^d$ for some integer r. This gives a differentiable structure on $\mathcal{M}$ of the same order. In particular, when $r \geq 1$, we say that $\mathcal{M}$ is a differentiable manifold, and $\mathcal{M}$ is *smooth* if $r = \infty$. We may also require only $r = 0$, in which case $\mathcal{M}$ is a *topological* manifold with no differentiable structure.

Because of the implicit function theorem, embedded submanifolds in the sense of Definition 1.1 have charts and atlases. Embedded submanifolds are therefore particular examples of abstract manifolds. In fact, this goes both ways: The Whitney embedding theorem states that any d-dimensional manifold can be embedded in $\mathbb{R}^k$ with $k \leq 2d$ so that the topology is induced by the one of the embedding space. For Riemannian manifolds defined later on, this theorem only provides a local C^1 embedding and not a global smooth embedding.

Example 1.3. *The projective space* P_d *is the set of lines through the origin in* $\mathbb{R}^{d+1}$. Each such line intersects the sphere $\mathbb{S}^d$ in two points that are antipodal. By identifying such points, expressed by taking the quotient using the equivalence relation $x \sim -x$, we get the representation $P_d \simeq \mathbb{S}^d / \sim$. Depending on the properties of the equivalence relation, the quotient space of a manifold may not be a manifold in general (more details will be given in Chapter 9). In the case of the projective space, we can verify the above abstract manifold definition. Therefore the projective space cannot be seen as an embedded manifold directly, but it can be seen as the quotient space of an embedded manifold.

1.2.4 Tangent vectors and tangent space

As the name implies, derivatives lies at the core of differential geometry. The differentiable structure allows taking derivatives of curves in much the same way as the usual derivatives in Euclidean space. However, spaces of tangent vectors to curves behave somewhat differently on manifolds due to the lack of the global reference frame that the Euclidean space coordinate system gives. We here discuss derivatives of curves, tangent vectors, and tangent spaces.

Let $\gamma : [0, T] \to \mathbb{R}^k$ be a differentiable curve in $\mathbb{R}^k$ parameterized on the interval $[0, T]$. For each t, the curve derivative is

$$\frac{d}{dt}\gamma(t) = \dot{\gamma} = \begin{pmatrix} \frac{d}{dt}\gamma^1(t) \\ \vdots \\ \frac{d}{dt}\gamma^k(t) \end{pmatrix}. \tag{1.4}$$

This tangent or velocity vector can be regarded as a vector in $\mathbb{R}^k$, denoted the tangent vector to γ at t. If $\mathcal{M}$ is an embedded manifold in $\mathbb{R}^k$ and $\gamma(t) \in \mathcal{M}$ for all $t \in [0, T]$, we can regard γ as a curve in $\mathcal{M}$. As illustrated on Fig. 1.3, the tangent vectors of γ are also tangential to $\mathcal{M}$ itself. The set of tangent vectors to all curves at $x = \gamma(t)$ span a d-dimensional affine subspace of $\mathbb{R}^k$ that approximates $\mathcal{M}$ to the first order at x. This affine space has an explicit realization as $x + \ker dF(x)$ where $x = \gamma(t)$ is the foot-point and $\ker dF$ denotes the kernel (null-space) of the Jacobian matrix of F. The space is called the tangent space $T_x\mathcal{M}$ of $\mathcal{M}$ at the point x. In the embedded manifold case, tangent vectors thus arise from the standard curve derivative, and tangent spaces are affine subspaces of $\mathbb{R}^k$.

On abstract manifolds, the definition of tangent vectors becomes somewhat more intricate. Let γ be a curve in the abstract

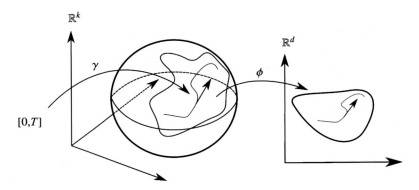

Figure 1.3. The curve γ maps the interval $[0, T]$ to the manifold. Using a chart ϕ, we can work in coordinates with the curve $\phi \circ \gamma$ in $\mathbb{R}^d$. If $\mathcal{M}$ is embedded, then γ is in addition a curve in $\mathbb{R}^k$. The derivative $\dot{\gamma}(t)$ is a tangent vector in the linear tangent space $T_{\gamma(t)}\mathcal{M}$. It can be written in coordinates using ϕ as $\dot{\gamma} = \dot{\gamma}^i \partial_{x^i}$. In the embedding space, the tangent space $T_{\gamma(t)}\mathcal{M}$ is the affine d-dimensional subspace $\gamma(t) + \ker dF(\gamma(t))$ of $\mathbb{R}^k$.

manifold $\mathcal{M}$, and consider $t \in [0, T]$. By the covering assumption on the atlas, there exists a chart $\phi : U \to \tilde{U}$ with $\gamma(t) \in U$. By the continuity of γ and openness of U, $\gamma(s) \in U$ for s sufficiently close to t. Now the curve $\tilde{\gamma} = \phi \circ \gamma$ in $\mathbb{R}^d$ is defined for such s. Thus we can take the standard Euclidean derivative $\dot{\tilde{\gamma}}$ of $\tilde{\gamma}$. This gives a vector in $\mathbb{R}^d$. In the same way as we define the differentiable structure on $\mathcal{M}$ by definition to be that inherited from the charts, it would be natural to let a tangent vector of $\mathcal{M}$ be $\dot{\tilde{\gamma}}$ by definition. However, we would like to be able to define tangent vectors independently of the underlying curve. In addition, we need to ensure that the construction does not depend on the chart ϕ.

One approach is to define tangent vectors from their actions on real-valued functions on $\mathcal{M}$. Let $f : \mathcal{M} \to \mathbb{R}$ be a differentiable function. Then $f \circ \gamma$ is a function from $\mathbb{R}$ to $\mathbb{R}$ whose derivative is

$$\frac{d}{dt} f \circ \gamma(t) . \tag{1.5}$$

This operation is clearly linear in f in the sense that $\frac{d}{dt}((\alpha f + \beta g) \circ \gamma) = \alpha \frac{d}{dt}(f \circ \gamma) + \beta \frac{d}{dt}(g \circ \gamma)$ when g is another differentiable function and $\alpha, \beta \in \mathbb{R}$. In addition, this derivative satisfies the usual product rule for the derivative of the pointwise product $f \cdot g$ of f and g. Operators on differentiable functions satisfying these properties are called *derivations*, and we can define tangent vectors and tangent spaces as the set of derivations, that is, $v \in T_x\mathcal{M}$ is a tangent vector if it defines a derivation $v(f)$ on functions

$f \in C^1(\mathcal{M}, \mathbb{R})$. It can now be checked that the curve derivative using a chart above defines derivations. By the chain rule we can see that these derivations are independent of the chosen chart.

The construction of $T_x\mathcal{M}$ as derivations is rather abstract. In practice, it is often most convenient to just remember that there is an abstract definition and otherwise think of tangent vectors as derivatives of curves. In fact, tangent vectors and tangent spaces can also be defined without derivations using only the derivatives of curves. However, in this case, we must define a tangent vector as an equivalence class of curves because multiple curves can result in the same derivative. This construction, although in some sense more intuitive, therefore has its own complexities.

The set $\{T_x\mathcal{M} \mid x \in M\}$ has a structure of a differentiable manifold in itself. It is called the tangent bundle $T\mathcal{M}$. It follows that tangent vectors $v \in T_x\mathcal{M}$ for some $x \in \mathcal{M}$ are elements of $T\mathcal{M}$. $T\mathcal{M}$ is a particular case of a fiber bundle (a local product of spaces whose global topology may be more complex). We will later see other examples of fiber bundles, for example, the cotangent bundle $T^*\mathcal{M}$ and the frame bundle $F\mathcal{M}$.

A local coordinate system $x = (x^1, \ldots x^d)$ coming from a chart induces a basis $\partial_x = (\partial_{x^1}, \ldots \partial_{x^d})$ of the tangent space $T_x\mathcal{M}$. Therefore any $v \in T_x\mathcal{M}$ can be expressed as a linear combination of $\partial_{x^1}, \ldots \partial_{x^d}$. Writing v^i for the ith entry of such linear combinations, we have $v = \sum_{i=1}^d v^i \partial_{x^i}$.

Remark 1.2 (Einstein summation convention). We will often use the Einstein summation convention that dictates an implicit sum over indices appearing twice in lower and upper position in expressions, in particular, in coordinate expressions and tensor calculations. For example, in the coordinate basis mentioned above, we have $v = v^i \partial_{x^i}$, where the sum $\sum_{i=1}^d$ is implicit because the index i appears in upper position on v^i and lower position on ∂_{x^i}.

Just as a Euclidean vector space V has a dual vector space V^* consisting of linear functionals $\xi : V \to \mathbb{R}$, the tangent spaces $T_x\mathcal{M}$ and tangent bundle $T\mathcal{M}$ have dual spaces, the cotangent spaces $T_x^*\mathcal{M}$, and cotangent bundle $T^*\mathcal{M}$. For each x, elements of the cotangent space $T_x^*\mathcal{M}$ are linear maps from $T_x\mathcal{M}$ to $\mathbb{R}$. The coordinate basis $(\partial_{x^1}, \ldots \partial_{x^d})$ induces a similar coordinate basis $(dx^1, \ldots dx^d)$ for the cotangent space. This basis is defined from evaluation on ∂_{x^i} by $dx^j(\partial_{x^i}) = \delta_i^j$, where the delta-function δ_i^j is 1 if $i = j$ and 0 otherwise. The coordinates v^i for tangent vectors in the coordinate basis had upper indices above. Similarly, coordinates for cotangent vectors conventionally have lower indices such that $\xi = \xi_i dx^i$ for $\xi \in T_x^*\mathcal{M}$ again using the Einstein summation convention. Elements of $T^*\mathcal{M}$ are called covectors. The evaluation $\xi(v)$ of a covector ξ on a vector v is sometimes written $(\xi|v)$ or $\langle \xi, v \rangle$. Note that the latter notation with brackets is similar to the notation for inner products used later on.

1.2.5 Differentials and pushforward

The interpretation of tangent vectors as derivations allows taking derivatives of functions. If X is a vector field on $\mathcal{M}$, then we can use this pointwise to define a new function on $\mathcal{M}$ by taking derivatives at each point, that is, $X(f)(x) = X(x)(f)$ using that $X(x)$ is a tangent vector in $T_x\mathcal{M}$ and hence a derivation that acts on functions. If instead f is a map between two manifolds $f : \mathcal{M} \to \mathcal{N}$, then we get the differential $df : T\mathcal{M} \to T\mathcal{N}$ as a map between the tangent bundle of $\mathcal{M}$ and $\mathcal{N}$. In coordinates, this is $df(\partial_{x^i})^j = \partial_{x^i} f^j$ with f^j being the jth component of f. The differential df is often denoted the pushforward of f because it uses f to map, that is, *push*, tangent vectors in $T\mathcal{M}$ to tangent vectors in $T\mathcal{N}$. For this reason, the pushforward notation $f_* = df$ is often used. When f is invertible, there exists a corresponding pullback operation $f^* = df^{-1}$.

As a particular case, consider a map f between $\mathcal{M}$ and the manifold $\mathbb{R}$. Then $f_* = df$ is a map from $T\mathcal{M}$ to $T\mathbb{R}$. Because $\mathbb{R}$ is Euclidean, we can identify the tangent bundle with $\mathbb{R}$ itself, and we can consider df a map $T\mathcal{M} \to \mathbb{R}$. Being a derivative, $df|_{T_x\mathcal{M}}$ is linear for each $x \in \mathcal{M}$, and $df(x)$ is therefore a covector in $T_x^*\mathcal{M}$. Though the differential df is also a pushforward, the notation df is most often used because of its interpretation as a covector field.

1.3 Riemannian manifolds

So far, we defined manifolds as having topological and differential structure, either inherited from $\mathbb{R}^k$ when considering embedded manifolds, or via charts and atlases with the abstract definition of manifolds. We now start including geometric and metric structures.

The topology determines the local structure of a manifold by specifying the open sets and thereby continuity of curves and functions. The differentiable structure allowed us to define tangent vectors and differentiate functions on the manifold. However, we have not yet defined a notion of how "straight" manifold-valued curves are. To obtain such a notion, we need to add a geometric structure, called a connection, which allows us to compare neighboring tangent spaces and characterizes the parallelism of vectors at different points. Indeed, differentiating a curve on a manifold gives tangent vectors belonging at each point to a dif-

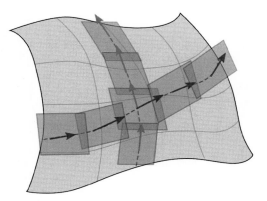

Figure 1.4. Tangent vectors along the red (light gray in print version) and blue (dark gray in print version) curves drawn on the manifold belong to different tangent spaces. To define the acceleration as the difference of neighboring tangent vectors, we need to specify a mapping to connect a tangent space at one point to the tangent spaces at infinitesimally close points. In the embedding case, tangent spaces are affine spaces of the embedding vector space, and the simplest way to specify this mapping is through an affine transformation.

ferent tangent vector space. To compute the second-order derivative, the acceleration of the curves, we need a way to map the tangent space at a point to the tangent space at any neighboring point. This is the role of a connection $\nabla_X Y$, which specifies how the vector field $Y(x)$ is derived in the direction of the vector field $X(x)$ (Fig. 1.4). In the embedding case, tangent spaces are affine spaces of the embedding vector space, and the simplest way to specify this mapping is through an affine transformation, hence the name affine connection introduced by Cartan [3]. A connection operator also describes how a vector is transported from a tangent space to a neighboring one along a given curve. Integrating this transport along the curve specifies the parallel transport along this curve. However, there is usually no global parallelism as in Euclidean space. As a matter of fact, transporting the same vector along two different curves arriving at the same point in general leads to different vectors at the endpoint. This is easily seen on the sphere when traveling from north pole to the equator, then along the equator for 90 degrees and back to north pole turns any tangent vector by 90 degrees. This defect of global parallelism is the sign of curvature.

By looking for curves that remain locally parallel to themselves, that is, such that $\nabla_{\dot\gamma}\dot\gamma = 0$, we define the equivalent of "straight lines" in the manifold, geodesics. We should notice that there exists many different choices of connections on a given manifold,

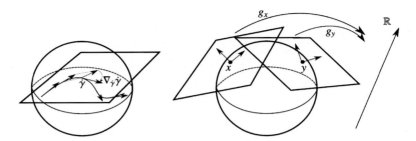

Figure 1.5. (Left) Vectors along a curve, here velocity vectors $\dot{\gamma}$ along the curve γ live in different tangent spaces and therefore cannot be compared directly. A connection ∇ defines a notion of transport of vectors along curves. This allows transport of a vector $\dot{\gamma}(t - \Delta t) \in T_{\gamma(t-\Delta t)}\mathcal{M}$ to $T_{\gamma(t)}\mathcal{M}$, and the acceleration $\nabla_{\dot{\gamma}}\dot{\gamma}$ arises by taking derivatives in $T_{\gamma(t)}\mathcal{M}$. (Right) For each point $x \in \mathcal{M}$, the metric g defines a positive bilinear map $g_x : T_x\mathcal{M} \times T_x\mathcal{M} \to \mathbb{R}$. Contrary to the Euclidean case, g depends on the base point, and vectors in the tangent space $T_y\mathcal{M}$ can only be compared by g evaluated at y, that is, the map $g_y : T_y\mathcal{M} \times T_y\mathcal{M} \to \mathbb{R}$.

which lead to different geodesics. However, geodesics by themselves do not quantify how far away from each other two points are. For that purpose, we need an additional structure, a distance. By restricting to distances that are compatible with the differential structure, we enter into the realm of Riemannian geometry.

1.3.1 Riemannian metric

A *Riemannian metric* is defined by a smoothly varying collection of scalar products $\langle \cdot, \cdot \rangle_x$ on each tangent space $T_x\mathcal{M}$ at points x of the manifold. For each x, each such scalar product is a positive definite bilinear map $\langle \cdot, \cdot \rangle_x : T_x\mathcal{M} \times T_x\mathcal{M} \to \mathbb{R}$; see Fig. 1.5. The inner product gives a norm $\|\cdot\|_x : T_x\mathcal{M} \to \mathbb{R}$ by $\|v\|^2 = \langle v, v \rangle_x$. In a given chart we can express the metric by a symmetric positive definite matrix $g(x)$. The ijth entry of the matrix is denoted $g_{ij}(x)$ and given by the dot product of the coordinate basis for the tangent space, $g_{ij}(x) = \left\langle \partial_{x^i}, \partial_{x^j} \right\rangle_x$. This matrix is called the *local representation of the Riemannian metric* in the chart x, and the dot product of two vectors v and w in $T_x\mathcal{M}$ is now in coordinates $\langle v, w \rangle_x = v^\top g(x)w = v^i g_{ij}(x)w^j$. The components g^{ij} of the inverse $g(x)^{-1}$ of the metric defines a metric on covectors by $\langle \xi, \eta \rangle_x = \xi_i g^{ij} \eta_j$. Notice how the upper indices of g^{ij} fit the lower indices of the covector in the Einstein summation convention. This inner product on $T_x^*\mathcal{M}$ is called a cometric.

1.3.2 Curve length and Riemannian distance

If we consider a curve $\gamma(t)$ on the manifold, then we can compute at each t its velocity vector $\dot{\gamma}(t)$ and its norm $\|\dot{\gamma}(t)\|$, the instantaneous speed. For the velocity vector, we only need the differential structure, but for the norm, we need the Riemannian metric at the point $\gamma(t)$. To compute the length of the curve, the norm is integrated along the curve:

$$\mathcal{L}(\gamma) = \int \|\dot{\gamma}(t)\|_{\gamma(t)} \, dt = \int \left(\langle \dot{\gamma}(t), \dot{\gamma}(t) \rangle_{\gamma(t)} \right)^{\frac{1}{2}} dt \ .$$

The integrals here are over the domain of the curve, for example, $[0, T]$. We write $\mathcal{L}_a^b(\gamma) = \int_a^b \|\dot{\gamma}(t)\|_{\gamma(t)} \, dt$ to be explicit about the integration domain. This gives the length of the curve segment from $\gamma(a)$ to $\gamma(b)$.

The distance between two points of a connected Riemannian manifold is the minimum length among the curves γ joining these points:

$$\text{dist}(x, y) = \min_{\gamma(0)=x, \gamma(1)=y} \mathcal{L}(\gamma). \tag{1.6}$$

The topology induced by this Riemannian distance is the original topology of the manifold: open balls constitute a basis of open sets.

The Riemannian metric is the intrinsic way of measuring length on a manifold. The extrinsic way is to consider the manifold as embedded in $\mathbb{R}^k$ and compute the length of a curve in $\mathcal{M}$ as for any curve in $\mathbb{R}^k$. In section 1.2.4 we identified the tangent spaces of an embedded manifold with affine subspaces of $\mathbb{R}^k$. In this case the Riemannian metric is the restriction of the dot product on $\mathbb{R}^k$ to the tangent space at each point of the manifold. Embedded manifolds thus inherit also their geometric structure in the form of the Riemannian metric from the embedding space.

1.3.3 Geodesics

In Riemannian manifolds, locally length-minimizing curves are called metric geodesics. The next subsection will show that these curves are also autoparallel for a specific connection, so that they are simply called geodesics in general. A curve is locally length minimizing if for all t and sufficiently small s, $\mathcal{L}_t^{t+s}(\gamma) = \text{dist}(\gamma(t), \gamma(t+s))$. This implies that small segments of the curve realize the Riemannian distance. Finding such curves is complicated by the fact that any time-reparameterization of the curve is authorized. Thus geodesics are often defined as critical points of the energy functional $\mathcal{E}(\gamma) = \frac{1}{2}\int \|\dot{\gamma}\|^2 dt$. It turns out that critical points for the energy also optimize the length functional. Moreover, they are parameterized proportionally to their arc length removing the ambiguity of the parameterization.

We now define the Christoffel symbols from the metric g by

$$\Gamma^k{}_{ij} = \frac{1}{2}g^{km}\left(\partial_{x^i}g_{jm} + \partial_{x^j}g_{mi} - \partial_{x^m}g_{ij}\right).\tag{1.7}$$

Using the calculus of variations, it can be shown that the geodesics satisfy the second-order differential system

$$\ddot{\gamma}^k + \Gamma^k{}_{ij}\dot{\gamma}^i\dot{\gamma}^j = 0.\tag{1.8}$$

We will see the Christoffel symbols again in coordinate expressions for the connection below.

1.3.4 Levi-Civita connection

The fundamental theorem of Riemannian geometry states that on any Riemannian manifold, there is a unique connection which is compatible with the metric and which has the property of being torsion-free. This connection is called the Levi-Civita connection. For that choice of connection, shortest curves have zero acceleration and are thus geodesics in the sense of being "straight lines". In the following we only consider the Levi-Civita connection unless explicitly stated.

The connection allows us to take derivatives of a vector field Y in the direction of another vector field X expressed as $\nabla_X Y$. This is also denoted the covariant derivative of Y along X. The connection is linear in X and obeys the product rule in Y so that $\nabla_X(fY) = X(f)Y + f\nabla_X Y$ for a function $f : \mathcal{M} \to \mathbb{R}$ with $X(f)$ being the derivative of f in the direction of X using the interpretation of tangent vectors as derivations. In a local coordinate system we can write the connection explicitly using the Christoffel symbols by $\nabla_{\partial_{x^i}}\partial_{x^j} = \Gamma^k{}_{ij}\partial_{x^k}$. With vector fields X and Y having coordinates $X(x) = v^i(x)\partial_{x^i}$ and $Y(x) = w^i(x)\partial_{x^i}$, we can use this to compute the coordinate expression for derivatives of Y along X:

$$\nabla_X Y = \nabla_{v^i\partial_{x^i}}(w^j\partial_{x^j}) = v^i\nabla_{\partial_{x^i}}(w^j\partial_{x^j}) = v^i(\partial_{x^i}w^j)\partial_{x^j} + v^i w^j\nabla_{\partial_{x^i}}\partial_{x^j}$$

$$= v^i(\partial_{x^i}w^j)\partial_{x^j} + v^i w^j\Gamma^k{}_{ij}\partial_{x^k} = \left(v^i(\partial_{x^i}w^k) + v^i w^j\Gamma^k{}_{ij}\right)\partial_{x^k}$$

$$= \left(X(w^k) + v^i w^j\Gamma^k{}_{ij}\right)\partial_{x^k}.$$

Using this, the connection allows us to write the geodesic equation
(1.8) as the zero acceleration constraint:

$$0 = \nabla_{\dot{\gamma}}\dot{\gamma} = \left(\dot{\gamma}(\dot{\gamma}^k) + \dot{\gamma}^i\dot{\gamma}^j\Gamma^k{}_{ij}\right)\partial_{x^k} = \left(\ddot{\gamma}^k + \dot{\gamma}^i\dot{\gamma}^j\Gamma^k{}_{ij}\right)\partial_{x^k}.$$

The connection also defines the notion of parallel transport along
curves. A vector $v \in T_{\gamma(t_0)}\mathcal{M}$ is parallel transported if it is extended to a t-dependent family of vectors with $v(t) \in T_{\gamma(t)}\mathcal{M}$ and
$\nabla_{\dot{\gamma}(t)}v(t) = 0$ for each t. Parallel transport can thereby be seen as
a map $P_{\gamma,t} : T_{\gamma(t_0)}\mathcal{M} \to T_{\gamma(t)}\mathcal{M}$ linking tangent spaces. The parallel transport inherits linearity from the connection. It follows from
the definition that γ is a geodesic precisely if $\dot{\gamma}(t) = P_{\gamma,t}(\dot{\gamma}(t_0))$.

It is a fundamental consequence of curvature that parallel
transport depends on the curve along which the vector is transported: With curvature, the parallel transports $P_{\gamma,T}$ and $P_{\phi,T}$ along
two curves γ and ϕ with the same end-points $\gamma(t_0) = \phi(t_0)$ and
$\gamma(T) = \phi(T)$ will differ. The difference is denoted holonomy, and
the holonomy of a Riemannian manifold vanishes only if $\mathcal{M}$ is flat,
that is, has zero curvature.

1.3.5 Completeness

The Riemannian manifold is said to be *geodesically complete* if
the definition domain of all geodesics can be extended to $\mathbb{R}$. This
means that the manifold has neither boundary nor any singular
point that we can reach in a finite time. For instance, $\mathbb{R}^d - \{0\}$
with the usual metric is not geodesically complete because some
geodesics will hit 0 and thus stop being defined in finite time.
On the other hand, $\mathbb{R}^d$ is geodesically complete. Other examples of complete Riemannian manifolds include compact manifolds implying that $\mathbb{S}^d$ is geodesically complete. This is a consequence of the Hopf–Rinow–de Rham theorem, which also states
that geodesically complete manifolds are complete metric spaces
with the induced distance and that there always exists at least one
minimizing geodesic between any two points of the manifold, that
is, a curve whose length is the distance between the two points.

From now on, we will assume that the manifold is geodesically complete. This assumption is one of the fundamental properties ensuring the well-posedness of algorithms for computing
on manifolds.

1.3.6 Exponential and logarithm maps

Let x be a point of the manifold that we consider as a local reference point, and let v be a vector of the tangent space $T_x\mathcal{M}$ at

that point. From the theory of second-order differential equations, it can be shown that there exists a unique geodesic $\gamma_{(x,v)}(t)$ starting from that point $x = \gamma_{(x,v)}(0)$ with tangent vector $v = \dot{\gamma}_{(x,v)}(0)$. This geodesic is first defined in a sufficiently small interval around zero, but since the manifold is assumed geodesically complete, its definition domain can be extended to $\mathbb{R}$. Thus the points $\gamma_{(x,v)}(t)$ are defined for each t and each $v \in T_x\mathcal{M}$. This allows us to map vectors in the tangent space to the manifold using geodesics: the vector $v \in T_x\mathcal{M}$ can be mapped to the point of the manifold that is reached after a unit time $t = 1$ by the geodesic $\gamma_{(x,v)}(t)$ starting at x with tangent vector v. This mapping

$$\mathrm{Exp}_x \quad : \quad \begin{array}{ccc} T_x\mathcal{M} & \longrightarrow & \mathcal{M} \\ v & \longmapsto & \mathrm{Exp}_x(v) = \gamma_{(x,v)}(1) \end{array}$$

is called the *exponential map* at point x. Straight lines passing 0 in the tangent space are transformed into geodesics passing the point x on the manifold, and the distances along these lines are conserved (Fig. 1.6).

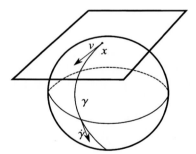
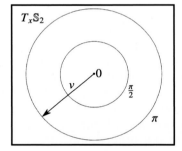

Figure 1.6. (Left) Geodesics starting at x with initial velocity $v \in T_x\mathcal{M}$ are images of the exponential map $\gamma(t) = \mathrm{Exp}_x(tv)$. They have zero acceleration $\nabla_{\dot{\gamma}}\dot{\gamma}$, and their velocity vectors are parallel transported $\dot{\gamma}(t) = P_{\gamma,t}(\dot{\gamma}(t_0))$. Geodesics locally realize the Riemannian distance so that $\mathrm{dist}(x, \gamma(t)) = t\,\|v\|$ for sufficiently small t. (Right) The tangent space $T_x\mathbb{S}^2$ and Exp_x give an exponential chart mapping vectors $v \in T_x\mathbb{S}^2$ to points in $\mathbb{S}^2$ by $\mathrm{Exp}_x(v)$. The cut locus of x is its antipodal point, and the injectivity radius is π. Note that the equator is the set $\{\mathrm{Exp}_x(v) \mid \|v\| = \frac{\pi}{2}\}$.

When the manifold is geodesically complete, the exponential map is defined on the entire tangent space $T_x\mathcal{M}$, but it is generally one-to-one only locally around 0 in the tangent space corresponding to a local neighborhood of x on $\mathcal{M}$. We denote by $\overrightarrow{xy}$ or $\mathrm{Log}_x(y)$ the inverse of the exponential map where the inverse is defined: this is the smallest vector as measured by the Riemannian metric such that $y = \mathrm{Exp}_x(\overrightarrow{xy})$. In this chart the geodesics going through x are represented by the lines going through the origin: $\mathrm{Log}_x \gamma_{(x, \overrightarrow{xy})}(t) = t\,\overrightarrow{xy}$. Moreover, the distance with respect to the base point x is preserved:

$$\mathrm{dist}(x, y) = \|\overrightarrow{xy}\| = \sqrt{\langle \overrightarrow{xy}, \overrightarrow{xy} \rangle_x}\,.$$

Thus the *exponential chart at* x gives a local representation of the manifold in the tangent space at a given point. This is also called a *normal coordinate system* or *normal chart* if it is provided with an orthonormal basis. At the origin of such a chart, the metric reduces to the identity matrix, and the Christoffel symbols vanish. Note again that the exponential map is generally only invertible locally around $0 \in T_x\mathcal{M}$, and $\mathrm{Log}_x y$ is therefore only locally defined, that is, for points y near x.

The exponential and logarithm maps are commonly referred to as the Exp and Log maps.

1.3.7 Cut locus

It is natural to search for the maximal domain where the exponential map is a diffeomorphism. If we follow a geodesic $\gamma_{(x,v)}(t) = \mathrm{Exp}_x(t\,v)$ from $t = 0$ to infinity, then it is either always minimizing for all t, or it is minimizing up to a time $t_0 < \infty$. In this last case the point $z = \gamma_{(x,v)}(t_0)$ is called a *cut point*, and the corresponding tangent vector $t_0 v$ is called a *tangential cut point*. The set of all cut points of all geodesics starting from x is the *cut locus* $C(x) \in \mathcal{M}$, and the set of corresponding vectors is the *tangential cut locus* $\mathcal{C}(x) \in T_x\mathcal{M}$. Thus we have $C(x) = \mathrm{Exp}_x(\mathcal{C}(x))$, and the maximal definition domain for the exponential chart is the domain $\mathcal{D}(x)$ containing 0 and delimited by the tangential cut locus.

It is easy to see that this domain is connected and star-shaped with respect to the origin of $T_x\mathcal{M}$. Its image by the exponential map covers the manifold except the cut locus, and the segment $[0, \overrightarrow{xy}]$ is transformed into the unique minimizing geodesic from x to y. Hence, the exponential chart has a connected and star-shaped definition domain that covers all the manifold except the cut locus $C(x)$:

$$\begin{array}{ccc} \mathcal{D}(x) \subseteq \mathbb{R}^d & \longleftrightarrow & \mathcal{M} - C(x) \\ \overrightarrow{xy} = \mathrm{Log}_x(y) & \longleftrightarrow & y = \mathrm{Exp}_x(\overrightarrow{xy}) \end{array}.$$

From a computational point of view, it is often interesting to extend this representation to include the tangential cut locus. However, we have to take care of the multiple representations: Points in the cut locus where several minimizing geodesics meet are represented by several points on the tangential cut locus as the geodesics are starting with different tangent vectors (e.g. antipodal points on the sphere and rotation of π around a given axis for 3D rotations). This multiplicity problem cannot be avoided as the set of such points is dense in the cut locus.

The size of $\mathcal{D}(x)$ is quantified by the *injectivity radius* $i(\mathcal{M}, x) = \mathrm{dist}(x, \mathcal{C}(x))$, which is the maximal radius of centered balls in $T_x\mathcal{M}$ on which the exponential map is one-to-one. The injectivity radius of the manifold $i(\mathcal{M})$ is the infimum of the injectivity over the manifold. It may be zero, in which case the manifold somehow tends toward a singularity (e.g. think of the surface $z = 1/\sqrt{x^2 + y^2}$ as a submanifold of $\mathbb{R}^3$).

Example 1.4. On the sphere $\mathbb{S}^d$ (center 0 and radius 1) with the canonical Riemannian metric (induced by the ambient Euclidean space $\mathbb{R}^{d+1}$), the geodesics are the great circles, and the cut locus of a point x is its antipodal point $\underline{x} = -x$. The exponential chart is obtained by rolling the sphere onto its tangent space so that the great circles going through p become lines. The maximal definition domain is thus the open ball $\mathcal{D} = \mathcal{B}_d(\pi)$. On its boundary $\partial\mathcal{D} = \mathcal{C} = \mathbb{S}^{d-1}(\pi)$, all the points represent $\underline{x}$; see Fig. 1.6.

For the real projective space P_d (obtained by identification of antipodal points of the sphere $\mathbb{S}^d$), the geodesics are still the great circles, but the cut locus of the point $\{x, -x\}$ is now the equator of the two points, with antipodal points identified (thus the cut locus is P_{d-1}). The definition domain of the exponential chart is the open ball $\mathcal{D} = \mathcal{B}_d(\frac{\pi}{2})$, and the tangential cut locus is the sphere $\partial\mathcal{D} = \mathbb{S}^{d-1}(\frac{\pi}{2})$ where antipodal points are identified.

1.4 Elements of analysis in Riemannian manifolds

We here outline further constructions on manifolds relating to taking derivatives of functions, the intrinsic Riemannian measure, and defining curvature. These notions will be used in the following chapters of this book, for instance, for optimization algorithms.

1.4.1 Gradient and musical isomorphisms

Let f be a smooth function from $\mathcal{M}$ to $\mathbb{R}$. Recall that the differential $df(x)$ evaluated at the point $x \in \mathcal{M}$ is a covector in $T_x^*\mathcal{M}$. Therefore, contrary to the Euclidean situation where derivatives are often regarded as vectors, we cannot directly interpret $df(x)$ as a vector. However, thanks to the Riemannian metric, there is a canonical way to identify the linear form $df \in T_x^*\mathcal{M}$ with a unique vector $v \in T_x\mathcal{M}$. This is done by defining $v \in T_x\mathcal{M}$ to be a vector satisfying $df(w) = \langle v, w \rangle_x$ for all vectors $w \in T_x\mathcal{M}$. This mapping corresponds to the transpose operator that is implicitly used in Euclidean spaces to transform derivatives of functions (row vectors) to column vectors. On manifolds, the Riemannian metric must be specified explicitly since the coordinate system used may not be orthonormal everywhere.

The mapping works for any covector and is often denoted the *sharp* map $\sharp : T^*\mathcal{M} \to T\mathcal{M}$. It has an inverse in the *flat* map $\flat : T\mathcal{M} \to T^*\mathcal{M}$. In coordinates, $(\xi^\sharp)^i = g^{ij}\xi_j$ for a covector $\xi = \xi_j dx^j$, and $(v^\flat)_i = g_{ij}v^j$ for a vector $v = \partial_{x^j}v^j$. The maps $\sharp$ and $\flat$ are denoted musical isomorphisms because they raise or lower the indices of the coordinates.

We can use the sharp map to define the Riemannian gradient as a vector:

$$\operatorname{grad} f = (df)^\sharp.$$

This definition corresponds to the classical gradient in $\mathbb{R}^k$ using the standard Euclidean inner product as a Riemannian metric. Using the coordinate representation of the sharp map, we get the coordinate form $(\operatorname{grad} f)^i = g^{ij}\partial_{x^j}f$ of the gradient.

1.4.2 Hessian and Taylor expansion

The covariant derivative of the gradient, the *Hessian*, arises from the connection ∇:

$$\operatorname{Hess} f(X, Y) = \nabla_X \nabla_Y f = (\nabla_X(df))Y = \langle \nabla_X \operatorname{grad} f, Y \rangle.$$

Here the two expressions on the right are given using the action of the connection on the differential form df (a covector) or the vector field $\operatorname{grad} f = (df)^\sharp$. Its expression in a local coordinate system is

$$\operatorname{Hess} f = \nabla df = (\partial_{x^i x^j} f - \Gamma^k{}_{ij}\partial_k f)dx^i dx^j.$$

Let now f_x be the expression of f in a normal coordinate system at x. Its Taylor expansion around the origin in coordinates is

$$f_x(v) = f_x(0) + df_x v + \frac{1}{2}v^\top H_{f_x}v + O(\|v\|^3),$$

where $df_x = (\partial_{x^i}f)$ is the Jacobian matrix of first-order derivatives, and $H_{f_x} = (\partial_{x^i x^j}f)$ is the Euclidean Hessian matrix. Because the coordinate system is normal, we have $f_x(v) = f(\operatorname{Exp}_x(v))$.

Moreover, the metric at the origin reduces to the identity: $df_x = (\text{grad } f)^T$, and the Christoffel symbols vanish so that the matrix of second derivatives H_{f_x} corresponds to the Hessian Hess f. Thus the Taylor expansion can be written in any coordinate system:

$$f\left(\text{Exp}_x(v)\right) = f(x) + \text{grad } f(v) + \frac{1}{2}\text{Hess } f(v, v) + O(\|v\|^3). \quad (1.9)$$

1.4.3 Riemannian measure or volume form

In a vector space with basis $\mathcal{A} = (a_1, \ldots a_n)$ the local representation of the metric is given by $g = A^\top A$, where $A = [a_1, \ldots a_n]$ is the matrix of coordinates change from $\mathcal{A}$ to an orthonormal basis. Similarly, the measure or the infinitesimal volume element is given by the volume of the parallelepiped spanned by the basis vectors: $dV = |A|\, dx = \sqrt{|g|}\, dx$ with $|\cdot|$ denoting the matrix determinant. In a Riemannian manifold $\mathcal{M}$, the Riemannian metric $g(x)$ induces an infinitesimal volume element on each tangent space, and thus a measure on the manifold that in coordinates has the expression

$$d\mathcal{M}(x) = \sqrt{|g(x)|}\, dx.$$

The cut locus has null measure, and we can therefore integrate indifferently in $\mathcal{M}$ or in any exponential chart. If f is an integrable function of the manifold and $f_x(v) = f(\text{Exp}_x(v))$ is its image in the exponential chart at x, then we have

$$\int_{x \in \mathcal{M}} f(x)d\mathcal{M}(x) = \int_{v \in \mathcal{D}(x)} f_x(v)\sqrt{|g(\text{Exp}_x(v))|}\, dv.$$

1.4.4 Curvature

The curvature of a Riemannian manifold measures its deviance from local flatness. We often have a intuitive notion of when a surface embedded in $\mathbb{R}^3$ is flat or curved; for example, a linear subspace of $\mathbb{R}^3$ is flat, whereas the sphere $\mathbb{S}^2$ is curved. This idea of curvature is expressed in the Gauss curvature. However, for high-dimensional spaces, the mathematical description becomes somewhat more intricate. We will further on see several notions of curvature capturing aspects of the nonlinearity of the manifold with varying details. It is important to note that whereas vanishing curvature implies local flatness of the manifold, this is not the same as the manifold being globally Euclidean. An example is the torus $\mathbb{T}_2$, which can both be embedded in $\mathbb{R}^3$ inheriting nonzero curvature and be embedded in $\mathbb{R}^4$ in a way in which it inherits a flat geometry. In both cases the periodicity of the torus remains, which prevents it from being a vector space.

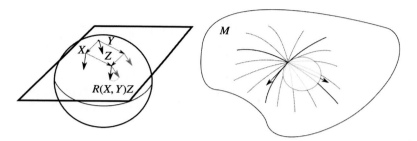

Figure 1.7. (Left) The curvature tensor describes the difference in parallel transport of a vector Z around an infinitesimal parallelogram spanned by the vector fields X and Y (dashed vectors). (Right) The sectional curvature measures the product of principal curvatures in a 2D submanifold given as the geodesic spray of a subspace V of $T_x\mathcal{M}$. The principal curvatures arise from comparing these geodesics to circles as for the Euclidean notion of curvature of a curve.

The curvature of a Riemannian manifold is described by the curvature tensor $R : T\mathcal{M} \times T\mathcal{M} \times T\mathcal{M} \to T\mathcal{M}$. It is defined from the covariant derivative by evaluation on vector fields X, Y, Z:

$$R(X, Y)Z = \nabla_X \nabla_Y Z - \nabla_Y \nabla_X Z - \nabla_{[X,Y]} Z. \qquad (1.10)$$

The bracket $[X, Y]$ denotes the anticommutativity of the fields X and Y. If f is a differentiable function on $\mathcal{M}$, then the new vector field produced by the bracket is given by its application to f: $[X, Y]f = X(Y(f)) - Y(X(f))$. The curvature tensor R can intuitively be interpreted at $x \in \mathcal{M}$ as the difference between parallel transporting the vector $Z(x)$ along an infinitesimal parallelogram with sides $X(x)$ and $Y(x)$; see Fig. 1.7 (left). As noted earlier, parallel transport is curve dependent, and the difference between transporting infinitesimally along $X(x)$ and then $Y(x)$ as opposed to along $Y(x)$ and then $X(x)$ is a vector in $T_x\mathcal{M}$. This difference can be calculated for any vector $z \in T_x\mathcal{M}$. The curvature tensor when evaluated at X, Y, that is, $R(X, Y)$, is the linear map $T_x\mathcal{M} \to T_x\mathcal{M}$ given by this difference.

The reader should note that two different sign conventions exist for the curvature tensor: definition (1.10) is used in a number of reference books in physics and mathematics [20,16,14,24, 11]. Other authors use a minus sign to simplify some of the tensor notations [26,21,4,5,1] and different order conventions for the tensors subscripts and/or a minus sign in the sectional curvature defined below (see e.g. the discussion in [6, p. 399]).

The curvature can be realized in coordinates from the Christoffel symbols:

$$R(\partial_{x^i}, \partial_{x^j})\, \partial_{x^k} = R^m{}_{kij}\, \partial_{x^m}$$
$$= (\Gamma^l{}_{jk}\Gamma^m{}_{il} - \Gamma^l{}_{ik}\Gamma^m{}_{jl} + \partial_i\Gamma^m{}_{jk} - \partial_j\Gamma^m{}_{ik})\, \partial_{x^m}\,. \tag{1.11}$$

The sectional curvature κ measures the Gaussian curvature of 2D submanifolds of $\mathcal{M}$, the Gaussian curvature of each point being the product of the principal curvatures of curves passing the point. The 2D manifolds arise as the geodesic spray of a 2D linear subspace of $T_x\mathcal{M}$; see Fig. 1.7 (right). Such a 2-plane can be represented by basis vectors $u, v \in T_x\mathcal{M}$, in which case the sectional curvature can be expressed using the curvature tensor by

$$\kappa(u, v) = \frac{\langle R(u, v)v, u\rangle}{\|u\|^2\|v\|^2 - \langle u, v\rangle^2}\,. \tag{1.12}$$

The curvature tensor gives the notion of Ricci and scalar curvatures, which both provide summary information of the full tensor R. The Ricci curvature Ric is the trace over the first and last indices of R with coordinate expression

$$R_{ij} = R_{kij}{}^k = R^k{}_{ikj} = g^{kl}\, R_{ikjl}\,. \tag{1.13}$$

Taking another trace, we get the scalar valued quantity, the scalar curvature S:

$$S = g^{ij}\, R_{ij}\,. \tag{1.14}$$

Note that the cometric appears to raise one index before taking the trace.

1.5 Lie groups and homogeneous manifolds

A Lie group is a manifold equipped with additional group structure such that the group multiplication and group inverse are smooth mappings. Many of the interesting transformations used in image analysis, translations, rotations, affine transforms, and so on, form Lie groups. We will in addition see examples of infinite-dimensional Lie groups when doing shape analysis with diffeomorphisms as described in chapter 4. We begin by reviewing the definition of an algebraic group.

Definition 1.5 (Group). A *group* is a set G with a binary operation, denoted here by concatenation or group product, such that

1. $(xy)z = x(yz)$ for all $x, y, z \in G$,
2. there is an *identity* element $e \in G$ satisfying $xe = ex = x$ for all $x \in G$,
3. each $x \in G$ has an *inverse* $x^{-1} \in G$ satisfying $xx^{-1} = x^{-1}x = e$.

A Lie group is simultaneously a group and a manifold, with compatibility between these two mathematical concepts.

Definition 1.6 (Lie Group). A *Lie group* G is a smooth manifold that also forms a group, where the two group operations,

$$
\begin{array}{llll}
(x, y) \mapsto xy & : & G \times G \to G & \textit{product} \\
x \mapsto x^{-1} & : & G \to G & \textit{inverse}
\end{array}
$$

are smooth mappings of manifolds.

Example 1.5. The space of all $k \times k$ nonsingular matrices forms a Lie group called the *general linear group*, denoted GL(k). The group operation is matrix multiplication, and GL(k) can be given a smooth manifold structure as an open subset of $\mathbb{R}^{k^2}$. The equations for matrix multiplication and inverse are smooth operations in the entries of the matrices. Thus GL(k) satisfies the requirements of a Lie group in Definition 1.6. A *matrix group* is any closed subgroup of GL(k). Matrix groups inherit the smooth structure of GL(k) as a subset of $\mathbb{R}^{k^2}$ and are thus also Lie groups.

Example 1.6. The $k \times k$ rotation matrices form a closed matrix subgroup of GL(k) and thus a Lie group. This group is called the *special orthogonal group*. It is defined as SO(k) = $\{R \in$ GL(k) : $R^T R = \mathrm{Id}_k$ and $\det(R) = 1\}$. This space is a closed bounded subset of $\mathbb{R}^{k^2}$ and thus compact.

Example 1.7. Classical geometric transformation groups used in image registration such as rigid-body transformations, similarities, and affine transformations can also be looked upon as matrix groups via their faithful representation based on homogeneous coordinates.

For each y in a Lie group G, the following two diffeomorphisms of G are denoted left- and right-translations by y:

$$
\begin{array}{ll}
L_y : x \mapsto yx & (\textit{left multiplication}) \\
R_y : x \mapsto xy & (\textit{right multiplication})
\end{array}
$$

The differential or pushforward $(L_y)_*$ of the left translation maps the tangent space $T_x G$ to the tangent space $T_{yx} G$. In particular, $(L_y)_*$ maps any vector $u \in T_e G$ to the vector $(L_y)_* u \in T_y G$ thereby giving rise to the vector field $\tilde{u}(y) = (L_y)_* u$. Such a vector field is said to be *left-invariant* since it is invariant under left multiplication: $\tilde{u} \circ L_y = (L_y)_* \tilde{u} = \tilde{u}$ for every $y \in G$. *Right-invariant* vector fields are defined similarly. A left- or right-invariant vector field is uniquely defined by its value $T_e G$ on the tangent space at the identity.

Recall that vector fields on G can be seen as derivations on the space of smooth functions $C^\infty(G)$. Thus two vector fields u and v can be composed to form another operator uv on $C^\infty(G)$, but the operator uv is not necessarily a derivation as it includes second-order differential terms. However, the operator $uv - vu$ is a vector field on G. Indeed, we can check by writing this expression in a local coordinate system that the second-order terms vanish. This leads to a definition of the *Lie bracket* of vector fields u, v on G, defined as

$$[u, v] = uv - vu. \tag{1.15}$$

This is also sometimes called the Lie derivative $\mathcal{L}_u v = [u, v]$ because it is conceptually the derivative of the vector field v in the direction $u(x)$ generated by u at each point $x \in G$.

Definition 1.7 (Lie algebra). A *Lie algebra* is a vector space V equipped with a bilinear product $[\cdot, \cdot] : V \times V \to V$, called a *Lie bracket*, that satisfies
1. $[u, v] = -[v, u]$ (skew symmetry) for all $u, v \in V$,
2. $[[u, v], w] + [[v, w], u] + [[w, u], v] = 0$ (Jacobi identity) for all $u, v, w \in V$.

The tangent space $T_e G$ of a Lie group G at the identity element, typically denoted $\mathfrak{g}$, forms a Lie algebra. The Lie bracket on $\mathfrak{g}$ is induced by the Lie bracket on the corresponding left-invariant vector fields. For two vectors u, v in $\mathfrak{g}$, let $\tilde{u}$, $\tilde{v}$ be the corresponding unique left-invariant vector fields on G. Then the Lie bracket on $\mathfrak{g}$ is given by

$$[u, v] = [\tilde{u}, \tilde{v}](e).$$

The Lie bracket provides a test for whether the Lie group G is commutative. A Lie group G is commutative if and only if the Lie bracket on the corresponding Lie algebra $\mathfrak{g}$ is zero, that is, $[u, v] = 0$ for all $u, v \in \mathfrak{g}$.

Example 1.8. The Lie algebra for Euclidean space $\mathbb{R}^k$ is again $\mathbb{R}^k$. The Lie bracket is zero, that is, $[X, Y] = 0$ for all $X, Y \in \mathbb{R}^k$.

Example 1.9. The Lie algebra for GL(k) is $\mathfrak{gl}(k)$, the space of all real $k \times k$ matrices. The Lie bracket operation for $X, Y \in \mathfrak{gl}(k)$ is given by

$$[X, Y] = XY - YX.$$

Here the product XY denotes actual matrix multiplication, which turns out to be the same as composition of the vector field operators (compare to (1.15)). All Lie algebras corresponding to matrix groups are subalgebras of $\mathfrak{gl}(k)$.

Example 1.10. The Lie algebra for the rotation group SO(k) is $\mathfrak{so}(k)$, the space of skew-symmetric matrices. A matrix A is skew-symmetric if $A = -A^T$.

1.5.1 One-parameter subgroups

Let $\tilde{u}(y) = (L_y)_* u$ be a left-invariant vector field. The solution $x(t)$ to the initial value problem

$$\dot{x}(t) = \tilde{u}(x(t)), \ x(0) = e,$$

is called a one-parameter subgroup because it is a morphing of Lie groups: $x(s + t) = x(s)x(t)$. The Lie exponential map $\exp : \mathfrak{g} \to G$ is then given by the value of $x(t)$ at $t = 1$, that is, $\exp(u) = x(1)$. For matrix groups where the Lie group algebra consists of ordinary matrices, exp corresponds to the matrix exponential. The group exponential should not be confused with the Riemannian exponential as they usually differ, unless the group is provided with a biinvariant Riemannian metric.

1.5.2 Actions

Let $\mathcal{M}$ be a manifold, and let G be a Lie group. The elements of the group can often be used to produce variations of elements of the manifold, for example, elements of GL(k) linearly transform elements of the manifold $\mathbb{R}^k$. Similarly, affine transformations apply to change images in image registration. These are examples of actions of G on $\mathcal{M}$. Such actions are usually denoted $g.x$ where $g \in G, x \in \mathcal{M}$. Because the action involves two manifolds, G and $\mathcal{M}$, we will use x, y to denote elements of $\mathcal{M}$ and g, h to denote elements of G.

Definition 1.8 (Action). A left action of a Lie group G on a manifold $\mathcal{M}$ is a smooth mapping $. : G \times \mathcal{M} \to \mathcal{M}$ satisfying
1. $e.x = x, \forall x \in \mathcal{M}$,
2. $h.(g.x) = (hg).x, \forall x \in M$,

3. the map $x \mapsto g.x$ is a diffeomorphism of M for each $g \in G$.

We will see examples of Lie group actions throughout the book. For example, Chapter 4 on shape analysis relies fundamentally on actions of the group $\text{Diff}(\Omega)$ of diffeomorphisms of a domain Ω on shape spaces $\mathcal{S}$.

Through the action, a curve $g(t)$ on the group G acts on a point $x \in \mathcal{M}$ to give a curve $g(t).x$ in $\mathcal{M}$. In particular, one-parameter subgroups define the curves $x_v(t) = \exp(tv).x$ in $\mathcal{M}$ for Lie algebra elements $v \in \mathfrak{g}$. The derivative

$$v_{\mathcal{M}}(x) := \frac{d}{dt} \exp(tv).x$$

in $T_{x_v(t)}\mathcal{M}$ is denoted the infinitesimal generator associated with v.

Some particularly important actions are the actions of G on itself and on the Lie algebra $\mathfrak{g}$. These include the actions by left translation $g.h := L_g(h) = gh$ and the action by conjugation $g.h := L_g(R_{g^{-1}})h = ghg^{-1}$. The pushforward of the conjugation gives the adjoint action $g.v = (L_g \circ R_{g^{-1}})_* v$ of G on $\mathfrak{g}$. The adjoint action is also denoted $\text{Ad}_g v$.

From the adjoint action, we get the adjoint operator $\text{ad}_u v = \frac{d}{dt}\text{Ad}_{\exp(tu)} v$ for $v, u \in \mathfrak{g}$. This operator is sometimes informally denoted "little ad", and it is related to the Lie bracket by $\text{ad}_u v = [u, v]$.

The actions on the Lie algebra have dual actions as well, denoted coactions: the coadjoint action $G \times \mathfrak{g}^* \to \mathfrak{g}^*$, $g.\xi := \text{Ad}^*_{g^{-1}}\xi$ for $\xi \in \mathfrak{g}^*$, where the dual of the adjoint is given by $\text{Ad}^*_{g^{-1}}\xi(v) = \xi(\text{Ad}_{g^{-1}}v)$ for all $v \in \mathfrak{g}$. Using the notation $(\xi|v)$ for evaluation $\xi(v)$ of ξ on v, the definition of the dual of the adjoint is $(\text{Ad}^*_{g^{-1}}\xi|v) = (\xi|\text{Ad}_{g^{-1}}v)$. The coadjoint operator $\text{ad}^* : \mathfrak{g} \times \mathfrak{g}^* \to \mathfrak{g}^*$ is similarly specified by $(\text{ad}^*_v \xi|u) = (\xi|\text{ad}_v u)$ for $v, u \in \mathfrak{g}$ and $\xi \in \mathfrak{g}^*$.

1.5.3 Homogeneous spaces

Let the group G act on $\mathcal{M}$. If, for any $x, y \in \mathcal{M}$, there exists $g \in G$ such that $g.x = y$, then the action is said to be transitive. In this case the manifold $\mathcal{M}$ is homogeneous. For a fixed $x \in \mathcal{M}$, the closed subgroup $H = \{g \in \mathfrak{g} \,|\, g.x = x\}$ is denoted the isotropy subgroup of G, and $\mathcal{M}$ is isomorphic to the quotient G/H. Similarly, a closed subgroup H of G leads to a homogeneous space G/H by quotienting out H. Examples of homogeneous spaces are the spheres $\mathbb{S}^n \equiv \text{SO}(n + 1)/\text{SO}(n)$ and the orbit shape spaces described in Chapter 4, for example, the manifold of landmark configurations.

1.5.4 Invariant metrics and geodesics

The left- and right-translation maps give a particularly useful way of defining Riemannian metrics on Lie groups. Given an inner product $\langle \cdot, \cdot \rangle_{\mathfrak{g}}$ on the Lie algebra, we can extend it to an inner product on tangent spaces at all elements of the group by setting

$$\langle u, v \rangle_g := \left\langle (L_{g^{-1}})_* u, (L_{g^{-1}})_* v \right\rangle_{\mathfrak{g}}.$$

This defines a left-invariant Riemannian metric on G because $\langle (L_h)_* u, (L_h)_* v \rangle_{hg} = \langle u, v \rangle_g$ for any $u, v \in T_g G$. Similarly, we can set

$$\langle u, v \rangle_g := \left\langle (R_{g^{-1}})_* u, (R_{g^{-1}})_* v \right\rangle_{\mathfrak{g}}$$

to get a right-invariant metric. In the particular case where the metric is invariant to both left- and right-translations, it is called biinvariant.

Geodesics for biinvariant metrics are precisely one-parameter subgroups, and the Lie group exponential map exp therefore equals the Riemannian exponential map Exp_e. For metrics that are left- or right-invariant, but not biinvariant, the ordinary geodesic equation (1.8) can be simplified using, for example, Euler–Poincaré reduction. The resulting Euler–Poincaré equations are discussed further in Chapter 4 in the case of right-invariant metrics on the group $\mathrm{Diff}(\Omega)$.

1.6 Elements of computing on Riemannian manifolds

The Riemannian Exp and Log maps constitute very powerful atomic functions to express most geometric operations for performing statistical computing on manifolds. The implementation of Log_x and Exp_x is therefore the algorithmic basis of programming on Riemannian manifolds, as we will further see.

In a Euclidean space, exponential charts are nothing but orthonormal coordinates systems translated to each point: In this case $\overrightarrow{xy} = \mathrm{Log}_x(y) = y - x$ and $\mathrm{Exp}_x(v) = x + v$. This example is more than a simple coincidence. In fact, most of the usual operations using additions and subtractions may be reinterpreted in a Riemannian framework using the notion of *bipoint*, an antecedent of vector introduced during the 19th century. Indeed, vectors are defined as equivalent classes of bipoints, oriented couples of points, in a Euclidean space. This is possible using the canonical way to compare what happens at two different points by translating. In a Riemannian manifold we can compare vectors using the parallel transport along curves, but the curve dependence on the parallel transport prevents global comparison of vectors as in Euclidean space. This implies that each vector has to remember at which point of the manifold it is attached, as is the case for tangent vectors, which relates back to the Euclidean notion of a bipoint.

Conversely, the logarithm map may be used to map almost any bipoint (x, y) into a vector $\overrightarrow{xy} = \mathrm{Log}_x(y)$ of $T_x\mathcal{M}$. This reinterpretation of addition and subtraction using logarithm and exponential maps is very powerful when generalizing algorithms working on vector spaces to algorithms on Riemannian manifolds. This is illustrated in Table 1.1 and in the following sections.

Table 1.1 Reinterpretation of standard operations in a Riemannian manifold.

	Euclidean space	Riemannian manifold
Subtraction	$\overrightarrow{xy} = y - x$	$\overrightarrow{xy} = \mathrm{Log}_x(y)$
Addition	$y = x + v$	$y = \mathrm{Exp}_x(v)$
Distance	$\mathrm{dist}(x, y) = \|y - x\|$	$\mathrm{dist}(x, y) = \|\overrightarrow{xy}\|_x$
Mean value (implicit)	$\sum_i (x_i - \bar{x}) = 0$	$\sum_i \overrightarrow{\bar{x}x_i} = 0$
Gradient descent	$x_{t+\varepsilon} = x_t - \varepsilon \nabla f(x_t)$	$x_{t+\varepsilon} = \mathrm{Exp}_{x_t}(-\varepsilon\,\mathrm{grad}\,f(x_t))$
Geodesic interpolation	$x(t) = x_0 + t\,\overrightarrow{x_0x_1}$	$x(t) = \mathrm{Exp}_{x_0}(t\,\overrightarrow{x_0x_1})$

The Exp and Log maps are different for each manifold and for each metric. They must therefore be determined and implemented on a case-by-case basis. In some cases, closed-form expressions are known, examples being the spheres $\mathbb{S}^d$, rotations and rigid body transformations with left-invariant metric [22], and covariance matrices (positive definite symmetric matrices, so-called tensors in medical image analysis) [23] and Chapter 3. In cases where closed-form solutions are not known, geodesics with given initial velocity can be obtained by numerically solving the geodesic ODE (1.8) or by solving the variational problem of finding a minimum energy curve between two points. Thus computing $\mathrm{Exp}_x(v)$ may be posed as a numerical integration problem (see e.g. [10,9]) and computing $\overrightarrow{xy} = \mathrm{Log}_x(y)$ as an optimal control problem. This opens the way to statistical computing in more complex spaces than the spaces we have considered up to now, such as spaces of curves, surfaces, and diffeomorphic transformations, as we will see in the following chapters. Geometric computation frameworks such as Theano Geometry[1] [12] and Ge-

[1]http://bitbucket.org/stefansommer/theanogeometry/.

omstats[2] provide numerical implementations of geometric operations on some commonly used manifolds. Theano Geometry uses automatic differentiation to express and compute the derivatives that are essential for differential geometric computations. This results in a convenient code for computing Christoffel symbols, curvature tensors, and fiber bundle operations using the parallel transport.

1.7 Examples

We further survey ways to express the Exp and Log maps on selected manifolds, at the same time exemplifying how particular structure of the spaces can be used for computations.

1.7.1 The sphere

Let x be a point in $\mathbb{S}^d$. From the embedding of $\mathbb{S}^d$ in $\mathbb{R}^{d+1}$, the tangent space $T_x\mathbb{S}^d$ can be identified with the d-dimensional vector space of all vectors in $\mathbb{R}^{d+1}$ orthogonal to x. The inner product between two tangent vectors is then equivalent to the usual Euclidean inner product. The exponential map is given by a 2D rotation of x by an angle given by the norm of the tangent, that is,

$$\mathrm{Exp}_x(v) = \cos\theta\, x + \frac{\sin\theta}{\theta}\, v, \quad \theta = \|v\|. \tag{1.16}$$

The log map between two points x, y on the sphere can be computed by finding the initial velocity of the rotation between the two points. Let $\pi_x(y) = x\,\langle x, y\rangle$ denote the projection of the vector y onto x. Then

$$\mathrm{Log}_x(y) = \frac{\theta\,(y - \pi_x(x))}{\|y - \pi_x(y)\|}, \quad \theta = \arccos(\langle x, y\rangle). \tag{1.17}$$

1.7.2 2D Kendall shape space

The Kendall shape space [13] represents a shape as an equivalence class of all translations, rotations, and scalings of a set of k points, landmarks, in the plane. A configuration of k points in the 2D plane is considered a complex k-vector $z \in \mathbb{C}^k$. Removing translation by requiring the centroid to be zero projects this point to the linear complex subspace $V = \{z \in \mathbb{C}^k : \sum z_i = 0\}$, which is isomorphic to the space $\mathbb{C}^{k-1}$. Next, points in this subspace are deemed equivalent if they are a rotation and scaling of each other,

[2]http://geomstats.ai.

which can be represented as multiplication by a complex number $\rho e^{i\theta}$, where ρ is the scaling factor, and θ is the rotation angle. The set of such equivalence classes forms the complex projective space $\mathbb{C}P^{k-2}$.

We think of a centered shape $p \in V$ as representing the complex line $L_p = \{z\, p : z \in \mathbb{C}\backslash\{0\}\}$, that is, L_p consists of all point configurations with the same shape as p. A tangent vector at $L_p \in V$ is a complex vector $v \in V$ such that $\langle p, v \rangle = 0$. The exponential map is given by rotating the complex line L_p within V by the initial velocity v:

$$\mathrm{Exp}_p(v) = \cos\theta\; p + \frac{\|p\| \sin\theta}{\theta}\, v, \quad \theta = \|v\|. \qquad (1.18)$$

Likewise, the log map between two shapes $p, q \in V$ is given by finding the initial velocity of the rotation between the two complex lines L_p and L_q. Let $\pi_p(q) = p\, \langle p, q \rangle / \|p\|^2$ denote the projection of the vector q onto p. Then the log map is given by

$$\mathrm{Log}_p(q) = \frac{\theta\,(q - \pi_p(q))}{\|q - \pi_p(q)\|}, \quad \theta = \arccos\frac{|\langle p, q \rangle|}{\|p\|\,\|q\|}. \qquad (1.19)$$

In Chapter 4 we will see an example of a different landmark space equipped with a geometric structure coming from the action of the diffeomorphism group.

1.7.3 Rotations

The set of orthogonal transformations $\mathrm{O}(k)$ on $\mathbb{R}^k$ discussed in section 1.2.1 is the subset of linear maps of $\mathbb{R}^k$, square matrices $U \in \mathrm{M}_{(k,k)}$, that preserve the dot product: $\langle Ux, Uy \rangle = \langle x, y \rangle$. In particular, they conserve the norm of a vector: $\|Ux\|^2 = \|x\|^2$. This means that $x^\top (U^\top U - \mathrm{Id})x = 0$ for all vectors $x \in \mathbb{R}^k$, which is possible if and only if the matrix U satisfies the quadratic constraint $U^\top U = \mathrm{Id}$. Thus the inverse transformation is $U^{-1} = U^\top$. The composition of two such maps obviously also preserves the dot product, so this forms the group of orthogonal transformations with the identity matrix Id_k as neutral element e:

$$\mathrm{O}(k) = \left\{ U \in \mathrm{M}_{(k,k)} \mid U^\top U = \mathrm{Id}_k \right\}.$$

Because the quadratic constraint is smooth and differentiable, $O(k)$ constitute a Lie group, submanifold of the linear space of square matrices. However, it is not connected: Taking the determinant of the constraint gives $\det(U)^2 = \det(\mathrm{Id}_k)$, so that $\det(U) = \pm 1$. We see that there are two disconnected components of determinants $+1$ and -1 that cannot be joined by any continuous curve on the space of matrices. Such a curve would have to go through matrices with determinants between -1 and 1 since the determinant is a continuous function. The component of the negative determinant includes symmetries that reverse the orientation of the space. It is not a subgroup because the composition of two such transformations of a negative determinant has a positive determinant.

The component of a positive determinant preserves the orientation of the space and is a subgroup, the group of rotations, or special orthogonal transformations:

$$\mathrm{SO}(k) = \left\{ R \in \mathrm{M}_{(k,k)} \mid R^\top R = \mathrm{Id}_k,\ \det(R) = 1 \right\}.$$

Let $R(t) = R + t\dot{R} + O(t^2)$ be a curve drawn on $\mathrm{SO}(k)$, considered as an embedded manifold in the vector space of matrices $\mathrm{M}_{(k,k)}$. The constraint $R^\top R = \mathrm{Id}_k$ is differentiated into

$$\dot{R}R^\top + \left(\dot{R}R^\top\right)^\top = 0 \quad \text{or} \quad R^\top \dot{R} + \left(R^\top \dot{R}\right)^\top = 0,$$

which means that $\dot{R}R^\top$ and $R^\top \dot{R}$ are skew-symmetric matrices. Thus the tangent space $T_e\mathrm{SO}(k)$ at identity is the vector space of skew-symmetric matrices, and the tangent space at rotation $R \in \mathrm{SO}(k)$ is its left or right translation:

$$T_R\mathrm{SO}(k) = \{X \in \mathrm{M}(k,k) \, / \, R^\top X = -(R^\top X)^\top\}$$
$$= \{X \in \mathrm{M}(k,k) \, / \, XR^\top = -(XR^\top)^\top\}$$

Since $k \times k$ skew-symmetric matrices have $k(k-1)/2$ free components, we also obtain that the dimension of the special orthogonal group is $k(k-1)/2$.

To put a metric on this Lie group, we may take a metric on the tangent space at the identity and left translate it to any other point resulting in a left-invariant metric. We may similarly right translate it to obtain a right-invariant metric. Since $\mathrm{SO}(k)$ is a submanifold of the Euclidean space of matrices $\mathrm{M}_{(k,k)}$, we may also consider the restriction of the embedding Frobenius dot product $\mathrm{Tr}(X^\top Y)$ to the tangent spaces at all points. It is common to rescale the Frobenius metric by $1/2$ to compensate the fact that we are counting twice each off diagonal coefficient of the skew-symmetric matrices. This induces the metric

$$\langle X, Y \rangle_R = \frac{1}{2}\mathrm{Tr}(XY^\top)$$

on the tangent space $T_R\mathrm{SO}(k)$.

This metric is invariant by left and right translation. The existence of this biinvariant metric is a particular case due to the compactness of the SO(k) group. Biinvariant metrics on Lie groups have very special properties, which will be described in Chapter 5. In particular, as mentioned earlier, geodesics passing the identity are one-parameter subgroups whose equations are given by the matrix exponential: $\mathrm{Exp}_e(X) = \exp(X) = \sum_{k=0}^{+\infty} \frac{X^k}{k!}$. This series is absolutely convergent, so that the matrix exponential always exists. Its inverse, the logarithm, may however fail to exist and is also generally not unique when it exists.

For rotations, the exponential of skew symmetric matrices covers the whole rotation group so that the log always exists, but it is not unique: For $k = 2$, rotating of an angle θ is the same as rotating of an angle $\theta + 2l\pi$, where l is an integer. To understand the structure of rotations in higher dimensions, we may look at the spectral decomposition of a rotation matrix R: The characteristic polynomial $P(\lambda) = \det(R - \lambda\ \mathrm{Id}_k)$ is a real polynomial of degree k. Thus the k complex eigenvalues are real or conjugate by pairs, and the polynomial can be factored into at most $\lfloor k/2 \rfloor$ quadratic terms, potentially with multiplicity, and real linear terms. The conservation of the norm by the rotation $\|Rx\| = \|x\|$ shows that the modulus of all the eigenvalues is 1. Thus eigenvalues are $e^{\pm i\theta_j}$ or 1. Since a rotation is a normal matrix, it can be diagonalized, and we conclude that every rotation matrix, when expressed in a suitable coordinate system, partitions into $\lfloor k/2 \rfloor$ independent 2D rotations, called Givens rotations [8]:

$$R(\theta_j) = \begin{pmatrix} \cos(\theta_j) & -\sin(\theta_j) \\ \sin(\theta_j) & \cos(\theta_j) \end{pmatrix} = \exp\left(\theta_j \begin{pmatrix} 0 & -1 \\ 1 & 0 \end{pmatrix}\right).$$

Conversely, each skew symmetric matrix $\Omega = -\Omega^\top$ decomposes the space $\mathbb{R}^k$ in a direct sum of mutually orthogonal subspaces, which are all invariant under Ω [8]. The decomposition has l (possibly equal to zero) two-dimensional vector subspaces E_j on which Ω acts nontrivially, and one single subspace F of dimension $k - 2l$, the orthogonal complement of the span of other subspaces, which is the kernel of Ω. For any E_j, there exists an orthonormal basis of E_j such that Ω restricted to E_j is in this basis of the following matrix form: $\theta_j \begin{pmatrix} 0 & -1 \\ 1 & 0 \end{pmatrix}$ where θ_j $(\neq 0)$ is the jth angle of rotation of the n-dimensional rotation $\exp\Omega$.

We can now come back to the uniqueness of the Log: When the angles of the above $\lfloor k/2 \rfloor$ 2D rotations decomposing the rotation R are within $]-\pi, \pi[$, the logarithm of R is well-defined. Otherwise, we cannot define a unique logarithm. This is only the case for 2D

rotations of 180 degrees, whose two "smallest" real logarithms are
$\begin{pmatrix} 0 & -\pi \\ \pi & 0 \end{pmatrix}$ and $\begin{pmatrix} 0 & \pi \\ -\pi & 0 \end{pmatrix}$.

Geodesics starting at any point in the group are left, or right, translation of geodesics starting at identity. For instance, $\gamma_{(R,Y)}(t) = R\exp(t\,R^\top Y)$ is the unique geodesic starting at R with tangent vector Y. The following reasoning underlies this: To find the geodesic starting at R with tangent vector Y, we first left translate Y by $R^\top$ to the tangent space at identity, compute the geodesic starting at e with tangent vector $R^\top Y$, and left translate back the result by R. Since the metric is biinvariant, the same mechanism can be implemented with right translation. The formula for the exponential map $\mathrm{Exp}_R : T_R\mathrm{SO}(k) \mapsto \mathrm{SO}(k)$ at point R is thus

$$\mathrm{Exp}_R(X) = R\,\mathrm{Exp}_e(R^\top X) = R\exp(R^\top X) = \exp(XR^\top)\,R. \quad (1.20)$$

Likewise, to compute the log map of rotation U at rotation R, we first left translate both rotations by $R^\top$, take the log map of $R^\top U$ at e, and left translate back to result:

$$\mathrm{Log}_R(U) = R\,\mathrm{Log}_e(R^\top U) = R\log(R^\top U) = \log(UR^\top)\,R. \quad (1.21)$$

1.8 Additional references

This very compact introduction to differential geometry, Riemannian manifolds, and Lie groups provides only a brief overview of the underlying deep theory. We here provide some references to further reading. There are many excellent texts on the subjects. The following lists are therefore naturally nonexhaustive.

Introductory texts on differential and Riemannian geometry
- J. M. Lee: Introduction to topological manifolds [17]; Introduction to smooth manifolds [18]; Riemannian manifolds [16].
- M. do Carmo: Riemannian geometry [4].
- J. Gallier: Notes on differential geometry manifolds, Lie groups and bundles, Chapter 3, http://www.cis.upenn.edu/~jean/gbooks/manif.html, [6].
- S. Gallot, D. Hulin, J. Lafontaine; Riemannian geometry [5].
- W. M. Boothby: An Introduction to differentiable manifolds and Riemannian geometry [2].
- C. Small: Statistical theory of shapes [25].

Advanced differential and Riemannian geometry
- J. Jost: Riemannian geometry and geometric analysis [11].
- M. Berger: A panoramic view of Riemannian geometry [1].

- I. Kolář, J. Slovák, P. W. M.: Natural operations in differential geometry [15].
- P. W. Michor: Topics in differential geometry [19].
- M. M. Postnikov: Geometry VI: Riemannian geometry [24].

Lie groups

- S. Helgason: Differential geometry, Lie groups, and symmetric spaces [7].
- J. Gallier: Notes on differential geometry manifolds, Lie groups and bundles, Chapters 2 and 4, http://www.cis.upenn.edu/~jean/gbooks/manif.html, [6].

References

1. Marcel Berger, A Panoramic View of Riemannian Geometry, Springer, Berlin, Heidelberg, 2003.
2. William M. Boothby, An Introduction to Differentiable Manifolds and Riemannian Geometry, Revised, vol. 120, 2 edition, Academic Press, Amsterdam, York New, August 2002.
3. Elie Cartan, Sur les variétés à connexion affine et la théorie de la relativité généralisée (première partie), Annales scientifiques de l'École normale supérieure 40 (1923) 325–412.
4. M. do Carmo, Riemannian Geometry. Mathematics, Birkhäuser, Boston, Basel, Berlin, 1992.
5. Sylvestre Gallot, Dominique Hulin, Jacques Lafontaine, Riemannian Geometry, 2nd edition, Springer, 1993.
6. Jean Gallier, Jocelyn Quaintance, Notes on Differential Geometry and Lie Groups, 2016.
7. Sigurdur Helgason, Differential Geometry, Lie Groups, and Symmetric Spaces, Graduate Studies in Mathematics, vol. 34, American Mathematical Society, Providence, RI, 2001, Corrected reprint of the 1978 original.
8. Roger A. Horn, Charles R. Johnson, Matrix Analysis, Cambridge University Press, 1990.
9. Ernst Hairer, Ch. Lubich, Gerhard Wanner, Geometric Numerical Integration: Structure Preserving Algorithm for Ordinary Differential Equations, Springer Series in Computational Mathematics, vol. 31, Springer, 2002.
10. Uwe Helmke, J.B. Moore, Optimization and Dynamical Systems, Communication and Control Engineering Series, Springer, 1994.
11. Jürgen Jost, Riemannian Geometry and Geometric Analysis, 6th ed. 2011 edition, Springer, Heidelberg, New York, August 2011.
12. Line Kühnel, Stefan Sommer, Alexis Arnaudon, Differential geometry and stochastic dynamics with deep learning numerics, Applied Mathematics and Computation 356 (1 September 2019) 411–437.

13. David G. Kendall, Shape manifolds, procrustean metrics, and complex projective spaces, Bulletin of the London Mathematical Society 16 (2) (March 1984) 81–121.
14. W. Klingenberg, Riemannian Geometry, Walter de Gruyter, Berlin, New York, 1982.
15. Ivan Kolář, Jan Slovák, Peter W. Michor, Natural Operations in Differential Geometry, Springer, Berlin, Heidelberg, 1993.
16. John M. Lee, Riemannian Manifolds, Graduate Texts in Mathematics, vol. 176, Springer, New York, 1997.
17. John M. Lee, Introduction to Topological Manifolds, Graduate Texts in Mathematics, vol. 202, Springer, New York, 2000.
18. John M. Lee, Introduction to Smooth Manifolds, Graduate Texts in Mathematics, vol. 218, Springer, New York, 2003.
19. Peter W. Michor, Topics in Differential Geometry, American Mathematical Society, 2008.
20. Charles W. Misner, Kip S. Thorne, John Archibald Wheeler, Gravitation, W.H. Freeman, San Francisco, 1973.
21. Barrett O'Neill, Semi-Riemannian Geometry: With Applications to Relativity, Pure and Applied Mathematics, vol. 103, Academic Press, New York, 1983.
22. Xavier Pennec, Jean-Philippe Thirion, A framework for uncertainty and validation of 3D registration methods based on points and frames, International Journal of Computer Vision 25 (3) (1997) 203–229.
23. Xavier Pennec, Pierre Fillard, Nicholas Ayache, A Riemannian framework for tensor computing, International Journal of Computer Vision 66 (1) (2006) 41–66, a preliminary version appeared as INRIA Research Report 5255, July 2004.
24. Mikhail Mikhailovich Postnikov, Geometry VI: Riemannian Geometry, Springer, Berlin, 2010, OCLC: 743337505.
25. Christopher Small, The Statistical Theory of Shape, Springer, 1996.
26. Michael David Spivak, Differential Geometry, vol. 1, 2nd edition, Publish or Perish, Inc., 1979.

Statistics on manifolds

Tom Fletcher

University of Virginia, Departments of Electrical & Computer Engineering and Computer Science, Charlottesville, VA United States

2.1 Introduction

This chapter provides a review of basic statistics for data on Riemannian manifolds, including generalizations of the concepts of a mean, principal component analysis (PCA), and regression. Definitions for these statistics in Euclidean space all somehow rely on the vector space operations in $\mathbb{R}^d$. For example, the arithmetic mean is defined using vector addition and scalar multiplication. The inherent difficulty in defining statistics on general Riemannian manifolds is the lack of vector space operations in these spaces.

One avenue for analyzing manifold-valued data is through geometry. Because a Riemannian manifold has a distance metric, we can think of model fitting as a least-squares problem, that is, minimizing the sum-of-squared distances from our data to the model. Whereas least-squares problems in Euclidean space often have closed-form solutions, for example, linear regression, solving least-squares problems in Riemannian manifolds typically requires some form of iterative optimization.

For PCA and regression analysis, a further complication arises in that the underlying models in $\mathbb{R}^d$ are defined as linear subspaces, which are also not available in Riemannian manifolds. In these cases, geodesic curves provide the natural generalization of straight lines to manifolds. Therefore, the natural generalization of linear regression to manifolds is *geodesic regression*, in which a geodesic curve is fit to data with an associated real-valued explanatory variable. In the case of PCA the first principal component may now be replaced with a *principal geodesic* that best fits the data using just one dimension. Higher-order principal components are defined as *principal geodesic subspaces*, which are generated as the image under the exponential map of linear subspaces of a tangent space.

In addition to the geometric perspective, another avenue to define manifold statistics is through probability. In traditional Euclidean statistics, least-squares fitting is equivalent to maximum

Riemannian Geometric Statistics in Medical Image Analysis
https://doi.org/10.1016/B978-0-12-814725-2.00009-1

likelihood estimation under a Gaussian distribution assumption of the errors. Such a probabilistic interpretation is also possible on manifolds through the definition of a Riemannian normal distribution law. We show how this distribution provides a unifying framework for probabilistic interpretation of several models of manifold data, including the Fréchet mean, geodesic regression, and principal geodesic analysis.

Throughout this chapter, let $y_1, \ldots, y_N \in M$ denote a set of data on a Riemannian manifold. From a statistical viewpoint, we will consider these data as coming from a realization of a random sample, that is, draws from a set of N independent identically distributed (i.i.d.) random variables. However, we will often consider data points and their statistical analysis from a purely geometric perspective, without referring to random variables.

2.2 The Fréchet mean

For Euclidean data, the sample mean is the de facto point estimate of the center of a data set. It is the simplest statistic to define, yet also perhaps the most fundamentally important one. The sample mean of a set of points $y_1, \ldots, y_N \in \mathbb{R}^d$ is given by their arithmetic average

$$\bar{y} = \frac{1}{N} \sum_{i=1}^{N} y_i. \tag{2.1}$$

This definition for the mean depends on the vector space operations of Euclidean space. In general, a Riemannian manifold will not be a vector space, and this definition for the mean will not be directly applicable. For data on a manifold embedded in Euclidean space, $\mathcal{M} \subset \mathbb{R}^d$, we could consider applying the linear mean equation using the vector operations of the ambient space $\mathbb{R}^d$. However, the resulting mean point may not land on $\mathcal{M}$. The following two examples demonstrate how the arithmetic mean of data on an embedded manifold can fail to be on the manifold.

Example 2.1 (Linear mean for the sphere). The 2D sphere has a natural embedding in $\mathbb{R}^3$ as the set of all unit-length vectors, that is, $S^2 \equiv \{y \in \mathbb{R}^3 : \|y\| = 1\}$. Given a set of points on the sphere $y_1, \ldots, y_N \in S^2$, their linear average in $\mathbb{R}^3$, $\bar{y}$, will not in general be a point on S^2. Take, for example, the points $y_1 = (1, 0, 0)$ and $y_2 = (0, 1, 0)$. Their mean, $\bar{y} = (0.5, 0.5, 0)$, has norm $\|\bar{y}\| = \sqrt{2}/2$, and thus does not lie on S^2.

Example 2.2 (Linear mean for GL(k)). The space of $k \times k$ matrices with nonzero determinant form a Lie group known as the general linear group, denoted GL(k). This is a connected open subset of $M_{(k,k)}$. However, averaging under the usual vector space operations of $M_{(k,k)} \equiv \mathbb{R}^{k \times k}$ does not preserve the nondegeneracy of GL(k). Take, for example, the two matrices

$$y_1 = \begin{pmatrix} 1 & 2 \\ 0 & 1 \end{pmatrix}, \qquad y_2 = \begin{pmatrix} 1 & 0 \\ 2 & 1 \end{pmatrix}.$$

Both y_1 and y_2 have determinant equal to one and are thus in GL(2), but their linear average $\bar{y} = \begin{pmatrix} 1 & 1 \\ 1 & 1 \end{pmatrix}$ has determinant zero.

Given that formula (2.1) is not defined for general Riemannian manifolds, we may then ask if there are defining properties of the mean point in Euclidean space that can be generalized to the manifold setting. The equation for the Euclidean mean can be derived from several different principles:

1. **Algebraic:** The arithmetic mean is the unique point such that the *residuals sum to zero*:

$$(y_1 - \bar{y}) + \cdots + (y_N - \bar{y}) = 0.$$

Note that this definition uses only the vector space properties of $\mathbb{R}^d$.

2. **Geometric:** It is a *least-squares* centroid of the data points. That is, it minimizes the sum-of-squared distances to the data,

$$\bar{y} = \arg \min_{y \in \mathbb{R}^d} \sum_{i=1}^{N} \| y_i - y \|^2.$$

3. **Probabilistic:** If the y_i are realizations of i.i.d. multivariate normal random variables $Y_i \sim N(\mu, \Sigma)$, then $\bar{y}$ is a *maximum-likelihood estimate* of the mean parameter μ:

$$\bar{y} = \arg \max_{\mu \in \mathbb{R}^d} \prod_{i=1}^{N} p(y_i; \mu, \Sigma),$$

where $p(\cdot; \mu, \Sigma)$ is the pdf for the multivariate normal distribution, $N(\mu, \Sigma)$.

The algebraic characterization of the mean point does not generalize to Riemannian manifolds, again because it is dependent on a vector space structure. However, the geometric and probabilistic characterizations can be generalized. In this section we consider the geometric characterization of the mean point on a Riemannian manifold. This concept of a mean point is due to Maurice

Fréchet [18] and is thus known as the *Fréchet mean*. Later, in Section 2.5 we will see how this is related to a probabilistic interpretation. Now consider a set of data $y_1, \ldots, y_N$ on a Riemannian manifold M. The geometric characterization of the Euclidean sample mean can be generalized to Riemannian manifolds as the *sample Fréchet mean*, which is the minimizer of the sum-of-squared distances to the data,

$$\bar{y} = \arg\min_{y \in M} \sum_{i=1}^{N} d(y, y_i)^2, \qquad (2.2)$$

where d denotes the geodesic distance on M. Fréchet actually introduced a much more general concept of expectation of a probability measure on a metric space, of which the sample Fréchet mean on a manifold is a particular case.

2.2.1 Existence and uniqueness of the Fréchet mean

Because the Fréchet mean is defined via an optimization, the first natural questions are whether a solution to this optimization exists and if it is unique. We begin by giving an example where the Fréchet mean does not exist.

Example 2.3. The "punctured plane" is $\mathbb{R}^2$ with the origin $(0, 0)$ removed. As an open set of $\mathbb{R}^2$, this is a manifold, and it is a Riemannian manifold when given the same Euclidean metric as $\mathbb{R}^2$. However, it is not a complete manifold, as geodesics (which are still straight lines) cannot pass through the missing point at the origin. Any set of points where the Fréchet mean in $\mathbb{R}^2$ would be $(0, 0)$ does not have a Fréchet mean in the punctured plane, for example, $y_1 = (1, 0)$, $y_2 = (-1, 0)$.

It turns out that the key ingredient missing for the punctured plane is the completeness of the metric. In fact, the completeness of a distance metric is sufficient to guarantee the existence of the Fréchet mean, as shown in the next theorem. Note that this holds for *any* complete metric space, not only for those that are Riemannian manifolds.

Theorem 2.1 (Existence of the Fréchet mean). *Let M be a complete metric space. Then the Fréchet mean of any finite set of points $y_1, \ldots, y_N \in M$ exists.*

Proof. Define the sum-of-squared distance function $F(y) = \sum_{j=1}^{N} d(y_i, y_j)^2$. We show that a global minimum of F exists (but it may not be unique). Denote the diameter of the point set by

$r = \max_{i,j} d(y_i, y_j)$. Let $K = \cup_{i=1}^N \bar{B}_r(y_i)$, where $\bar{B}_r(y_i)$ is the closed metric ball of radius r centered at x_i. By the completeness of X, K is a closed set, bounded in diameter by $2r$, and so is a compact set. Therefore the restriction of the sum-of-squared distance function to the set K attains a minimum within K. Now consider a point $y \in X$ such that $y \notin K$. Then $F(y) > nr^2$. However, this must be larger than the minimum within K because $F(y_i) = \sum_{j=1}^N d(y_i, y_j)^2 \le nr^2$.   □

Even when a Fréchet mean of a set of data exists, it may not be unique. That is, there may be multiple points that achieve the minimum in (2.2). A simple example of this is given on the 2D sphere.

Example 2.4 (Nonuniqueness of the Fréchet mean on S^2). Consider the unit sphere S^2 embedded in $\mathbb{R}^3$ with two data points at the north and south pole, $y_1 = (0, 0, 1)$ and $y_2 = (0, 0, -1)$. Then the Fréchet mean is the set of points on the equator $\bar{y} = \{(\cos\theta, \sin\theta, 0) : \theta \in [0, 2\pi)\}$.

Conditions for the uniqueness of the Fréchet mean were given by Karcher [27] and later refined by Kendall [29]. The following result is due to Asfari [1].

Theorem 2.2 (Uniqueness of the Fréchet mean). *Let M be a complete Riemannian manifold with sectional curvature bounded above by Δ, and let $\mathrm{inj}(M)$ denote the injectivity radius of M. If data $y_1, \ldots, y_N \in M$ are contained in a geodesic ball of radius*

$$r = \begin{cases} \frac{1}{2}\min\left\{\mathrm{inj}(M), \frac{\pi}{\sqrt{\Delta}}\right\} & \text{if } \Delta > 0, \\ \frac{1}{2}\mathrm{inj}(M) & \text{if } \Delta \le 0, \end{cases}$$

then the Fréchet mean $\bar{y}$ is unique.

Example 2.5 (2D constant curvature manifolds). To better understand this uniqueness theorem, we consider examples of constant curvature manifolds of dimension two.

- ($\Delta = 0$) For the Euclidean plane $\mathbb{R}^2$, the injectivity radius is infinite, and sectional curvature is equal to 0. Therefore the theorem states that any set of data in $\mathbb{R}^2$ has a unique Fréchet mean.
- ($\Delta = 1$) For the 2-sphere S^2, the injectivity radius is π, and sectional curvature is equal to 1. The theorem then gives a bound of $r = \frac{\pi}{2}$, meaning any set of data contained in an open hemisphere of S^2 will have a unique Fréchet mean.
- ($\Delta = -1$) For the hyperbolic plane H^2, the injectivity radius is infinite, and the sectional curvature is -1. Then the theorem

states that, like Euclidean space, any set of data in H^2 will have a unique Fréchet mean.

Further theoretical results of the sample Fréchet mean were developed by Bhattacharya and Patrangenaru [4,5]. They established the asymptotic consistency of the sample Fréchet mean and proved a central limit theorem.

2.2.2 Estimation of the Fréchet mean

The Fréchet mean is defined by the minimization problem (2.2). The squared-distance function from a point $y \in M$ on a Riemannian manifold is smooth away from the cut locus of y. As such, a natural strategy for computing the Fréchet mean is using gradient descent optimization, first proposed by Pennec [36]. This gradient descent algorithm also appeared in [2] for the case of spheres and in [31] for the case of rotations.

First, consider the squared-distance function from a single point $x \in M$,

$$F_x(y) = d(y, x)^2.$$

As a consequence of the Gauss lemma (see [8]), the gradient of the squared-distance function is given by

$$\operatorname{grad} F_x(y) = -2\operatorname{Log}_y(x).$$

Then the gradient descent, with some step size $\tau > 0$, proceeds as follows:

Algorithm 2.1 Fréchet mean.

Input: $y_1, \ldots, y_N \in M$
Output: $\bar{y} \in M$, the Fréchet mean
Initialize: $\bar{y}_0 = x_1$
while $\|v\| > \epsilon$ **do**
$\quad v = \frac{\tau}{N} \sum_{i=1}^{N} \operatorname{Log}_{\bar{y}_j} y_i$
$\quad \bar{y}_{j+1} = \operatorname{Exp}_{\bar{y}_j} v$

2.3 Covariance and principal geodesic analysis

The covariance of a vector-valued random variable y in $\mathbb{R}^d$ is defined as

$$\operatorname{Cov}(y) = E\left[(y - E[y])(y - E[y])^T\right].$$

This definition clearly relies on the vector space structure of $\mathbb{R}^d$, that is, vector transpose and matrix multiplication operations. Therefore, it does not apply directly as written to a manifold-valued random variable. However, we can rewrite this equation by recalling that the Riemannian log map in Euclidean space is given by $\text{Log}_y x = (x - y)$. Then the covariance of y is equivalently

$$\text{Cov}(y) = E\left[\left(\text{Log}_{E[y]}y\right)\left(\text{Log}_{E[y]}y\right)^T\right].$$

This equation can now be directly generalized to a Riemannian manifold by replacing the Euclidean expectation $E[y]$ with Fréchet expectation. For a random sample $y_1, y_2, \ldots, y_n \in M$, the sample covariance matrix is given by

$$S = \sum_{i=1}^{n}\left(\text{Log}_{\bar{y}}y_i\right)\left(\text{Log}_{\bar{y}}y_i\right)^T. \tag{2.3}$$

2.3.1 Principal component analysis

The covariance matrix encodes the variability of multivariate data; however, it is often difficult to interpret or make use of it directly. A more convenient breakdown of the variability of high-dimensional data is given by principal component analysis (PCA), a method whose origins go back to Pearson [35] and Hotelling [21]. See the book [25] for a comprehensive review of PCA. The objectives of principal component analysis are (1) to efficiently parameterize the variability of data and (2) to decrease the dimensionality of the data parameters. In this section we review PCA for Euclidean data $y_1, \ldots, y_N \in \mathbb{R}^d$ with mean $\bar{y}$ before describing how it can be generalized to manifolds in the next section.

There are several different ways to describe PCA. The definitions given here may not necessarily be standard, but they are helpful as the basis for the generalization to Riemannian manifolds. The goal of PCA is to find a sequence of nested linear subspaces $V_1, \ldots, V_d$ through the mean that best approximates the data. This may be formulated in two ways, both resulting in the same answer. The first is a least-squares approach, where the objective is to find the linear subspaces such that the sum-of-squares of the residuals to the data are minimized. More precisely, the linear subspace V_k is defined by a basis of orthonormal vectors, that is, $V_k = \text{span}(\{v_1, \ldots, v_k\})$, which are given by

$$v_k = \arg\min_{\|v\|=1} \sum_{i=1}^{N} \|y_i^k - \langle y_i^k, v\rangle v\|^2, \tag{2.4}$$

where the y_i^k are defined recursively by

$$y_i^1 = y_i - \bar{y},$$
$$y_i^k = y_i^{k-1} - \langle y_i^{k-1}, v_{k-1} \rangle \, v_{k-1}.$$

Simply put, the point y_i^k is obtained by removing from $(y_i - \bar{y})$ the contributions of the previous directions $v_1, \ldots, v_{k-1}$. In other words, the point y_i^k is the projection of $(y_i - \mu)$ onto the subspace perpendicular to V_{k-1}.

The other way of defining principal component analysis is as the subspaces through the mean that maximize the total variance of the projected data. The total variance for a set of points $y_1, \ldots, y_N$ is defined as

$$\hat{\sigma}^2 = \frac{1}{N} \sum_{i=1}^{N} \| y_i - \bar{y} \|^2.$$

Then the linear subspaces $V_k = \mathrm{span}(\{v_1, \ldots, v_k\})$ are given by the vectors

$$v_k = \arg \max_{\|v\|=1} \sum_{i=1}^{N} \langle y_i^k, v \rangle^2, \tag{2.5}$$

where the y_i^k are defined as before. It can be shown (see [25]) that both definitions of PCA, that is, (2.4) and (2.5), give the same results thanks to the Pythagorean theorem.

The computation of the spanning vectors v_k proceeds as follows. First, the linear average of the data is computed as

$$\bar{y} = \frac{1}{N} \sum_{i=1}^{N} y_i.$$

Next, the sample covariance matrix of the data is computed as

$$S = \frac{1}{N-1} \sum_{i=1}^{N} (y_i - \bar{y})(y_i - \bar{y})^T.$$

This is the unbiased estimate of the covariance matrix, that is, $N - 1$ is used in the denominator instead of N. The covariance matrix is a symmetric positive semidefinite quadratic form, that is, $S = S^T$, and $x^T S x \geq 0$ for any $x \in \mathbb{R}^d$. Therefore, the eigenvalues of S are all real and nonnegative. Let $\lambda_1, \ldots, \lambda_d$ be the eigenvalues of S ordered so that $\lambda_1 \geq \lambda_2 \geq \cdots \geq \lambda_d$, and let $v_1, \ldots, v_d$ be the correspondingly ordered eigenvectors. When repeated eigenvalues occur, there is an ambiguity in the corresponding eigenvectors, that is, there is a hyperplane from which we choose the corresponding eigenvectors. This does not present a problem as any orthonormal set of eigenvectors may be chosen. These directions are the solutions to the defining PCA equations (2.4) and (2.5), and they are called the *principal directions* or *modes of variation*.

Any data point y_i can be decomposed as

$$y_i = \bar{y} + \sum_{k=1}^{d} \alpha_{ik} v_k$$

for real coefficients $\alpha_{ik} = \langle y_i - \bar{y}, v_k \rangle$. The α_{ik} for fixed i are called the *principal components* of y_i. The total variation of the data is given by the sum of the eigenvalues, $\sigma^2 = \sum_{k=1}^{d} \lambda_k$. The dimensionality of the data can be reduced by discarding the principal directions that contribute little to the variation, that is, choosing $m < d$ and projecting the data onto V_m, giving the approximation

$$\tilde{y}_i = \bar{y} + \sum_{k=1}^{m} \alpha_{ik} v_k.$$

One method for choosing the cut-off value m is based on the percentage of total variation that should be preserved.

2.3.2 Principal geodesic analysis

Principal geodesic analysis (PGA) [16,17] generalizes PCA to handle data $y_1, \ldots, y_N$ on a connected complete manifold M. The goal of PGA, analogous to PCA, is to find a sequence of nested geodesic submanifolds that maximize the projected variance of the data. These submanifolds are called the *principal geodesic submanifolds*.

Let $T_{\bar{y}} M$ denote the tangent space of M at the Fréchet mean $\bar{y}$ of the y_i. Let $U \subset T_{\bar{y}} M$ be a neighborhood of 0 such that projection is well-defined for all geodesic submanifolds of $\mathrm{Exp}_{\bar{y}}(U)$. We assume that the data is localized enough to lie within such a neighborhood. The principal geodesic submanifolds are defined by first constructing an orthonormal basis of tangent vectors $v_1, \ldots, v_n \in T_{\bar{y}} M$ that span the tangent space $T_{\bar{y}} M$. These vectors are then used to form a sequence of nested subspaces $V_k = \mathrm{span}(\{v_1, \ldots, v_k\}) \cap U$. The principal geodesic submanifolds are the images of the V_k under the exponential map: $H_k = \mathrm{Exp}_{\bar{y}}(V_k)$. The first principal direction is chosen to maximize the projected variance along the corresponding geodesic:

$$v_1 = \arg \max_{\|v\|=1} \sum_{i=1}^{N} \|\mathrm{Log}_{\bar{y}}(\pi_H(y_i))\|^2, \qquad (2.6)$$

where $\quad H = \mathrm{Exp}_{\bar{y}}(\mathrm{span}(\{v\}) \cap U).$

The remaining principal directions are defined recursively as

$$v_k = \arg \max_{\|v\|=1} \sum_{i=1}^{N} \|\mathrm{Log}_{\bar{y}}(\pi_H(y_i))\|^2, \qquad (2.7)$$

where $\quad H = \mathrm{Exp}_{\bar{y}}(\mathrm{span}(\{v_1, \ldots, v_{k-1}, v\}) \cap U).$

Just as is the case with PCA, we can alternatively define PGA through a least squares fit to the data. In this setting the first principal direction is chosen to minimize the sum-of-squared geodesic distance from the data to the corresponding geodesic:

$$v_1 = \arg \min_{\|v\|=1} \sum_{i=1}^{N} \|\mathrm{Log}_{y_i}(\pi_H(y_i))\|^2, \qquad (2.8)$$

where $\quad H = \mathrm{Exp}_{\bar{y}}(\mathrm{span}(\{v\}) \cap U).$

The remaining principal directions are defined recursively as

$$v_k = \arg \min_{\|v\|=1} \sum_{i=1}^{N} \|\mathrm{Log}_{y_i}(\pi_H(y_i))\|^2, \qquad (2.9)$$

where $\quad H = \mathrm{Exp}_{\bar{y}}(\mathrm{span}(\{v_1, \ldots, v_{k-1}, v\}) \cap U).$

2.3.3 Estimation: tangent approximation and exact PGA

Neither the variance maximization (2.6)–(2.7) nor the residual minimization (2.8)–(2.9) formulation of PGA has a closed-form solution for general manifolds. Therefore Fletcher et al. [17] proposes to approximate PGA in the tangent space to the Fréchet mean of the data. This is done by first mapping the x_i to the tangent space $T_\mu M$ using the Log map. Linear distances in $T_\mu M$ between points close to the origin are similar to the geodesic distances between the corresponding points in M under the Exp map. Therefore, if the data are highly concentrated about the Fréchet mean, then the PGA optimization problem is well approximated by the PCA optimization problem of the Log map transformed points. Fletcher et al. [17] give an explicit expression in the case of the sphere for the approximation error between projections in the tangent space versus on the manifold. This suggests the following tangent space approximation algorithm to PGA.

Algorithm 2.2 Tangent approximation to PGA.

Input: Data $x_1, \ldots, x_N \in M$
Output: Principal directions, $v_k \in T_\mu M$, variances, $\lambda_k \in \mathbb{R}$
$\bar{y}$ = Fréchet mean of $\{y_i\}$ (Algorithm 2.1)
$u_i = \mathrm{Log}_{\bar{y}}(y_i)$
$\mathbf{S} = \frac{1}{N-1} \sum_{i=1}^{N} u_i u_i^T$
$\{v_k, \lambda_k\}$ = eigenvectors/eigenvalues of $\mathbf{S}$.

Later work developed algorithms for exact optimization of the variance maximization formulas (2.6)–(2.7) for PGA. This was first worked out for the particular case of SO(3) by Said et al. [39] and then for general Riemannian manifolds by Sommer et al. [41,42]. This algorithm, often referred to as exact PGA, proceeds by gradient ascent. This requires derivatives of the Riemannian Exp and Log maps, which are given by Jacobi fields. These derivatives are also used in geodesic regression and will be covered in the next section. Chakraborty et al. [7] developed an efficient algorithm for exact PGA on constant curvature manifolds, using closed-form solutions for distances and projections onto geodesic submanifolds. Salehian et al. [44] present an incremental algorithm for computing PGA by updating the parameters with exact newly introduced data point. This has two advantages: (1) it reduces the memory cost over the standard batch mode PGA algorithms, and (2) it allows new data to be easily added later, without recomputing the entire PGA.

2.3.4 Further extensions of PCA to manifolds

Geodesic PCA [20] solves a similar problem to the sum-of-squared residual minimization formulation of PGA (2.8)–(2.9) with the exception that the geodesic principal components are not constrained to pass through the Fréchet mean. In the case of data in Euclidean space the hyperplanes that best fit the data always pass through the mean. However, in the case of data on a manifold with nontrivial curvature, removing the constraint that geodesics pass through the mean can lead to more flexibility in fitting data. For data on a sphere S^d, principal nested spheres (PNS) [22] finds a series of nested subspheres of decreasing dimension that best fit the data. In contrast to PGA, the principal spheres are not constrained to be geodesic spheres (i.e., they can have smaller radius than the original sphere). Also, instead of building up from low dimension to high, PNS iteratively finds nested spheres starting from the full dimension d and removing one dimension at a time. One consequence of this is that the zero-dimensional principal nested sphere is not necessarily the Fréchet mean. Eltzner et al. [13] extend PNS to polyspheres (products of multiple spheres) by developing a procedure for deforming a polysphere into a single sphere where PNS can then be applied. Banerjee et al. [3] present a version of PGA that is robust to outliers, along with an exact algorithm to compute it.

2.4 Regression models

Regression analysis is a fundamental statistical tool for determining how a measured variable is related to one or more potential explanatory variables. The most widely used regression model is linear regression due to its simplicity, ease of interpretation, and ability to model many phenomena. However, if the response variable takes values on a nonlinear manifold, then a linear model is not applicable. Several works have studied regression models on manifolds, where the goal is to fit a curve on a manifold that models the relationship between a scalar parameter and data on the manifold. This is typically done by a least squares fit, similarly to the Fréchet mean definition in (2.2), except that now the optimization is over a certain class of curves on the manifold rather than a point. That is, given manifold data $y_1, \ldots, y_N \in M$ with corresponding real data $x_1, \ldots, x_N \in \mathbb{R}$, the regression problem is to find a curve $\hat{\gamma}(x) \in M$ such that

$$\hat{\gamma} = \arg\min_{\gamma \in \Gamma} \sum_{i=1}^{N} d(\gamma(x_i), y_i)^2, \qquad (2.10)$$

where Γ is a space of curves on M.

In this chapter we focus on nonparametric kernel regression on Riemannian manifolds [9] and geodesic regression [14,15], that is, where Γ is the space of parameterized geodesics on M. Niethammer et al. [34] independently proposed geodesic regression for the case of diffeomorphic transformations of image time series. Hinkle et al. [23] use constant higher-order covariant derivatives to define intrinsic polynomial curves on a Riemannian manifold for regression. Shi et al. [43] proposed a semiparametric model for manifold response data, which also has the ability to handle multiple covariates.

A closely related problem to the regression problem is that of fitting smoothing splines to manifold data. The typical objective function for smoothing splines is a combination of a data-matching term and a regularization term for the spline curve. For example, Su et al. [40] proposed a smoothing spline where the data matching is the same least squares objective as the regression problem (2.10), leading to a smoothing splines optimization of the form

$$\hat{\gamma} = \arg \min_{\gamma \in \Gamma} \sum_{i=1}^{N} d(\gamma(x_i), y_i)^2 + \lambda \mathcal{R}(\gamma), \qquad (2.11)$$

where $\mathcal{R}$ is some regularization functional, and $\lambda > 0$ is a weighting between regularization and data fitting. In this case the search space may be the space of all continuous curve segments, $\Gamma = C([0, 1], M)$. Jupp and Kent [24] proposed solving the smoothing spline problem on a sphere by unrolling onto the tangent space. This unrolling method was later extended to shape spaces by Kume [28]. Smoothing splines on the group of diffeomorphisms has been proposed as growth models by Miller et al. [30] and as second-order splines by Trouvé et al. [46]. A similar paradigm is used by Durrleman et al. [11] to construct spatiotemporal image atlases from longitudinal data. Yet another related problem is the spline *interpolation* problem, where the data-matching term is dropped, and the regularization term is optimized subject to constraints that the curve pass through specific points. The pioneering work of Noakes et al. [33] introduced the concept of a cubic spline on a Riemannian manifold for interpolation. Crouch and Leite [6] investigated further variational problems for these cubic splines and for specific classes of manifolds, such as Lie groups and symmetric spaces. Buss and Fillmore [2] defined interpolating splines on the sphere via weighted Fréchet averaging.

2.4.1 Regression in Euclidean space

2.4.1.1 Multilinear regression

Before formulating geodesic regression on general manifolds, we begin by reviewing multiple linear regression in $\mathbb{R}^d$. Here we are interested in the relationship between a nonrandom *independent* variable $X \in \mathbb{R}$ and a random *dependent* variable Y taking values in $\mathbb{R}^d$. A multiple linear model of this relationship is given by

$$Y = \alpha + X\beta + \epsilon, \qquad (2.12)$$

where $\alpha \in \mathbb{R}^d$ is an unobservable *intercept* parameter, $\beta \in \mathbb{R}^d$ is an unobservable *slope* parameter, and ϵ is an $\mathbb{R}^d$-valued unobservable random variable representing the error. Geometrically, this is

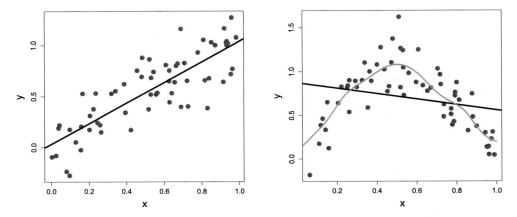

Figure 2.1. Comparison of linear (black) and nonparametric (red (dark gray in print version)) regressions. When the data follows a linear trend (left), a linear regression model is favored due to its ease of interpretation. However, when the data trend is nonlinear (right), nonparametric regression models will fit better.

the equation of a one-dimensional line through $\mathbb{R}^d$ (plus noise), parameterized by the scalar variable X. For the purpose of generalizing to the manifold case, it is useful to think of α as the starting point of the line and β as a velocity vector.

Given realizations of the above model, that is, data $(x_i, y_i) \in \mathbb{R} \times \mathbb{R}^d$ for $i = 1, \dots, N$, the least squares estimates $\hat{\alpha}$ and $\hat{\beta}$ for the intercept and slope are computed by solving the minimization problem

$$(\hat{\alpha}, \hat{\beta}) = \arg \min_{(\alpha, \beta)} \sum_{i=1}^{N} \| y_i - \alpha - x_i \beta \|^2. \qquad (2.13)$$

This equation can be solved analytically, yielding

$$\hat{\beta} = \frac{\frac{1}{N} \sum x_i \, y_i - \bar{x} \, \bar{y}}{\sum x_i^2 - \bar{x}^2},$$

$$\hat{\alpha} = \bar{y} - \bar{x} \, \hat{\beta},$$

where $\bar{x}$ and $\bar{y}$ are the sample means of x_i and y_i, respectively. If the errors in the model are drawn from distributions with zero mean and finite variance, then these estimators are unbiased and consistent. Furthermore, if the errors are homoscedastic (equal variance) and uncorrelated, then the Gauss–Markov theorem states that they will have minimal mean-squared error amongst all unbiased linear estimators.

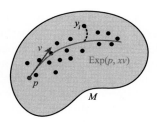

Figure 2.2. Schematic of the geodesic regression model.

2.4.1.2 Univariate kernel regression

Before reviewing the manifold version, we give a quick overview of univariate kernel regression as developed by Nadaraya [32] and Watson [47]. As in the linear regression setting, we are interested in finding a relationship between data $x_1, \ldots, x_N \in \mathbb{R}$, coming from an independent variable X, and data $y_1, \ldots, y_N \in \mathbb{R}$, representing a dependent variable Y. The model of their relationship is given by

$$Y = f(X) + \epsilon,$$

where f is an arbitrary function, and ϵ is a random variable representing the error. Contrary to linear regression, the function f is not assumed to have any particular parametric form.

Instead, the function f is estimated from the data by local weighted averaging:

$$\hat{f}_h(x) = \frac{\sum_{i=1}^N K_h(x - x_i) y_i}{\sum_{i=1}^N K_h(x - x_i)}.$$

In this equation, K is a function that satisfies $\int K(t)\,dt = 1$ and $K_h(t) = \frac{1}{h} K(\frac{t}{h})$ with bandwidth parameter $h > 0$. This is the estimation procedure shown in Fig. 2.1 (red curves (dark gray in print version)).

2.4.2 Regression on Riemannian manifolds

2.4.2.1 Geodesic regression

Let $y_1, \ldots, y_N$ be points on a smooth Riemannian manifold M with associated scalar values $x_1, \ldots, x_N \in \mathbb{R}$. The goal of geodesic regression is to find a geodesic curve γ on M that best models the relationship between x_i and y_i. Just as in linear regression, the speed of the geodesic will be proportional to the independent parameter corresponding to the x_i. Estimation will be set up as a least-squares problem, where we want to minimize the sum-of-squared Riemannian distances between the model and data. A schematic of the geodesic regression model is shown in Fig. 2.2.

Notice that the tangent bundle TM serves as a convenient parameterization of the set of possible geodesics on M. An element $(p, v) \in TM$ provides an intercept p and a slope v, analogous to the α and β parameters in the multiple linear regression model (2.12). In fact, β is a vector in the tangent space $T_\alpha \mathbb{R}^d \cong \mathbb{R}^d$, and thus (α, β) is an element of the tangent bundle $T\mathbb{R}^d$. To this end, it is useful to consider the Exp map as a function of position and velocity, so we will use the notation $\text{Exp}(p, v) = \text{Exp}_p(v)$. Now consider an M-valued random variable Y and a nonrandom variable $X \in \mathbb{R}$. The generalization of the multiple linear model to the manifold setting is the *geodesic model*

$$Y = \text{Exp}(\text{Exp}(p, Xv), \epsilon), \tag{2.14}$$

where ϵ is a random variable taking values in the tangent space at $\text{Exp}(p, Xv)$. Notice that for Euclidean space, the exponential map is simply addition, that is, $\text{Exp}(p, v) = p + v$. Thus, the geodesic model coincides with (2.12) when $M = \mathbb{R}^d$.

Least squares estimation

Consider a realization of the model (2.14): $(x_i, y_i) \in \mathbb{R} \times M$ for $i = 1, \ldots, N$. Given this data, we wish to find estimates of the parameters $(p, v) \in TM$. First, define the sum-of-squared error of the data from the geodesic given by (p, v) as

$$E(p, v) = \frac{1}{2} \sum_{i=1}^{N} d(\text{Exp}(p, x_i v), y_i)^2. \tag{2.15}$$

Following the ordinary least squares minimization problem given by (2.13), we formulate a least squares estimator of the geodesic model as a minimizer of the sum-of-squares energy (2.15), that is,

$$(\hat{p}, \hat{v}) = \arg \min_{(p,v)} E(p, v). \tag{2.16}$$

Again, notice that this problem coincides with the ordinary least squares problem when $M = \mathbb{R}^d$.

Unlike the linear setting, the least squares problem in (2.16) for a general manifold M will typically not yield an analytic solution. Instead, we derive a gradient descent algorithm. Computation of the gradient of (2.15) will require two parts: the derivative of the Riemannian distance function and the derivative of the exponential map. Fixing a point $p \in M$, the gradient of the squared distance function is $\nabla_x d(p, x)^2 = -2\text{Log}_x(p)$ for $x \in V(p)$.

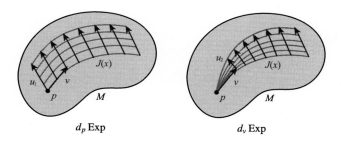

$d_p \operatorname{Exp}$ $d_v \operatorname{Exp}$

Figure 2.3. Jacobi fields as derivatives of the exponential map.

The derivative of the exponential map $\operatorname{Exp}(p, v)$ can be separated into a derivative with respect to the initial point p and a derivative with respect to the initial velocity v. To do this, first consider a variation of geodesics given by $c_1(s, t) = \operatorname{Exp}(\operatorname{Exp}(p, su_1), tv(s))$, where $u_1 \in T_pM$ defines a variation of the initial point along the geodesic $\eta(s) = \operatorname{Exp}(p, su_1)$. Here we have also extended $v \in T_pM$ to a vector field $v(s)$ along η via parallel translation. This variation is illustrated on the left side of Fig. 2.3. Next consider a variation of geodesics $c_2(s, t) = \operatorname{Exp}(p, su_2 + tv)$, where $u_2 \in T_pM$. (Technically, u_2 is a tangent to the tangent space, i.e., an element of $T_v(T_pM)$, but there is a natural isomorphism $T_v(T_pM) \cong T_pM$.) The variation c_2 produces a "fan" of geodesics as seen on the right side of Fig. 2.3.

Now the derivatives of $\operatorname{Exp}(p, v)$ with respect to p and v are given by

$$d_p \operatorname{Exp}(p, v) \cdot u_1 = \frac{d}{ds} c_1(s, t) \Big|_{s=0} = J_1(1),$$

$$d_v \operatorname{Exp}(p, v) \cdot u_2 = \frac{d}{ds} c_2(s, t) \Big|_{s=0} = J_2(1),$$

where $J_i(t)$ are *Jacobi fields* along the geodesic $\gamma(t) = \operatorname{Exp}(p, tv)$. Jacobi fields are solutions to the second-order equation

$$\frac{D^2}{dt^2} J(t) + R(J(t), \gamma'(t)) \, \gamma'(t) = 0, \qquad (2.17)$$

where R is the Riemannian curvature tensor. For more details on the derivation of the Jacobi field equation and the curvature tensor, see, for instance, [8]. The initial conditions for the two Jacobi fields are $J_1(0) = u_1$, $J_1'(0) = 0$ and $J_2(0) = 0$, $J_2'(0) = u_2$, respectively. If we decompose the Jacobi field into a component tangential to γ and a component orthogonal, that is, $J = J^\top + J^\perp$, then the tangential component is linear: $J^\top(t) = u_1^\top + tu_2^\top$. Therefore the only challenge is to solve for the orthogonal component.

Finally, the gradient of the sum-of-squares energy in (2.15) is given by

$$\nabla_p E(p, v) = -\sum_{i=1}^{N} d_p \operatorname{Exp}(p, x_i v)^{\dagger} \operatorname{Log}(\operatorname{Exp}(p, x_i v), y_i),$$

$$\nabla_v E(p, v) = -\sum_{i=1}^{N} x_i \, d_v \operatorname{Exp}(p, x_i v)^{\dagger} \operatorname{Log}(\operatorname{Exp}(p, x_i v), y_i),$$

where we have taken the adjoint of the exponential map derivative, for example, defined by $\langle d_p \operatorname{Exp}(p, v)u, w \rangle = \langle u, d_p \operatorname{Exp}(p, v)^{\dagger} w \rangle$. As we will see in the next section, formulas for Jacobi fields and their respective adjoint operators can often be derived analytically for many useful manifolds.

R^2 statistics and hypothesis testing

In regression analysis the most basic question we would like to answer is whether the relationship between the independent and dependent variables is significant. A common way to test this is to see if the amount of variance explained by the model is high. For geodesic regression, we will measure the amount of explained variance using a generalization of the R^2 statistic, or coefficient of determination, to the manifold setting. To do this, we first define predicted values of y_i and the errors ϵ_i as

$$\hat{y}_i = \operatorname{Exp}(\hat{p}, x_i \hat{v}),$$
$$\hat{\epsilon}_i = \operatorname{Log}(\hat{y}_i, y_i),$$

where $(\hat{p}, \hat{v})$ are the least squares estimates of the geodesic parameters defined before. Note that the $\hat{y}_i$ are points along the estimated geodesic that are the best predictions of the y_i given only the x_i. The $\hat{\epsilon}_i$ are the residuals from the model predictions to the true data.

Now to define the total variance of data $y_1, \dots, y_N \in M$, we use the Fréchet variance, intrinsically defined by

$$\operatorname{var}(y_i) = \min_{y \in M} \frac{1}{N} \sum_{i=1}^{N} d(y, y_i)^2.$$

The unexplained variance is the variance of the residuals, $\operatorname{var}(\hat{\epsilon}_i) = \frac{1}{N} \sum \|\hat{\epsilon}_i\|^2$. From the definition of the residuals it can be seen that the unexplained variance is the mean squared distance of the data to the model, that is, $\operatorname{var}(\hat{\epsilon}_i) = \frac{1}{N} \sum d(\hat{y}_i, y_i)^2$. Using these two variance definitions, the generalization of the R^2 statistic is then given by

$$R^2 = 1 - \frac{\text{unexplained variance}}{\text{total variance}} = 1 - \frac{\text{var}(\hat{\epsilon}_i)}{\text{var}(y_i)}. \qquad (2.18)$$

The Fréchet variance coincides with the standard definition of variance when $M = \mathbb{R}^d$. Therefore it follows that the definition of R^2 in (2.18) coincides with the R^2 for linear regression when $M = \mathbb{R}^d$. Also, because the Fréchet variance is always nonnegative, we see that $R^2 \leq 1$ and that $R^2 = 1$ if and only if the residuals to the model are exactly zero, that is, the model perfectly fits the data. Finally, it is clear that the residual variance is always smaller than the total variance, that is, $\text{var}(\hat{\epsilon}_i) \leq \text{var}(y_i)$. This is because we could always choose $\hat{p}$ to be the Fréchet mean and $v = 0$ to achieve $\text{var}(\hat{\epsilon}_i) = \text{var}(y_i)$. Therefore $R^2 \geq 0$, and it must lie in the interval $[0, 1]$, as is the case for linear models.

We now describe a permutation test for testing the significance of the estimated slope term $\hat{v}$. Notice that if we constrain v to be zero in (2.16), then the resulting least squares estimate $\hat{p}$ of the intercept will be the Fréchet mean of the y_i. The desired hypothesis test is whether the fraction of unexplained variance is significantly decreased by also estimating v. The null hypothesis is $H_0 : R^2 = 0$, which is the case if the unexplained variance in the geodesic model is equal to the total variance. Under the null hypothesis, there is no relationship between the variables X and Y. Therefore the x_i are exchangeable under the null hypothesis, and a permutation test may randomly reorder the x_i data, keeping the y_i fixed. Estimating the geodesic regression parameters for each random permutation of the x_i, we can calculate a sequence of R^2 values $R_1^2, \ldots, R_m^2$, which approximate the sampling distribution of the R^2 statistic under the null hypothesis. Computing the fraction of the R_k^2 that are greater than the R^2 estimated from the unpermuted data gives us a p-value.

2.4.2.2 Kernel regression on manifolds

The regression method of Davis et al. [9] generalizes the Nadaraya–Watson kernel regression method to the case where the dependent variable lives on a Riemannian manifold, that is, $y_i \in M$. Here the model is given by

$$Y = \text{Exp}(f(X), \epsilon),$$

where $f : \mathbb{R} \to M$ defines a curve on M, and $\epsilon \in T_{f(X)}M$ is an error term. As in the univariate case, there are no assumptions on the parametric form of the curve f.

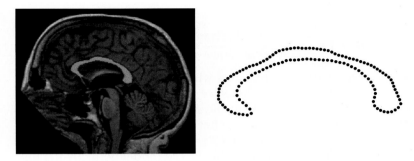

Figure 2.4. Corpus callosum segmentation and boundary point model for one subject.

Motivated by the definition of the Nadaraya–Watson estimator as a weighted averaging, the *manifold kernel regression estimator* is defined using a weighted Fréchet sample mean as

$$\hat{f}_h(x) = \arg \min_{y \in M} \frac{\sum_{i=1}^N K_h(x - x_i)d(y, y_i)^2}{\sum_{i=1}^N K_h(x - x_i)}.$$

Notice that when the manifold under study is a Euclidean vector space equipped with the standard Euclidean norm, this minimization results in the Nadaraya–Watson estimator.

2.4.3 Example of regression on Kendall shape space

We now give examples of both geodesic and nonparametric kernel regression in Kendall shape space (see Chapter 1). The goal of our statistical analysis is to understand the relationship between the age and shape of the corpus callosum. The corpus callosum is the major white matter bundle connecting the two hemispheres of the brain. A midsagittal slice from a magnetic resonance image (MRI) with segmented corpus callosum is shown in Fig. 2.4. The data used is derived from the OASIS brain database (www.oasis-brains.org), and this regression analysis originally appears in [15].

The data consisted of MRI from 32 subjects with ages ranging from 19 to 90 years old. The corpus callosum was segmented in a midsagittal slice using the ITK SNAP program (www.itksnap.org). These boundaries of these segmentations were sampled with 128 points using ShapeWorks (www.sci.utah.edu/software.html). This algorithm generates a sampling of a set of shape boundaries while enforcing correspondences between different point models within the population. An example of a segmented corpus callosum and the resulting boundary point model are shown in Fig. 2.4.

Figure 2.5. Geodesic regression of the corpus callosum. The estimated geodesic is shown as a sequence of shapes from age 19 (blue (dark gray in print version)) to age 90 (red (light gray in print version)).

Each of these preprocessing steps were done without consideration of the subject age, to avoid any bias in the data generation. (See Fig. 2.5.)

The statistical significance of the estimated trend was tested using the permutation test described in paragraph 'R^2 statistics and hypothesis testing' with 10,000 permutations. The p-value for the significance of the slope estimate $\hat{v}$ was $p = 0.009$. The coefficient of determination (for the unpermuted data) was $R^2 = 0.12$. The low R^2 value must be interpreted carefully. It says that age only describes a small fraction of the shape variability in the corpus callosum. This is not surprising: we would expect the intersubject variability in corpus callosum shape to be difficult to fully describe with a single variable (age). However, this does not mean that the age effects are not important. In fact, the low p-value says that the estimated age changes are highly unlikely to have been found by random chance.

Next, we computed a nonparametric kernel regression of the corpus callosum versus age, as described in Section 2.4.2.2. The kernel regression was performed on the same Kendall shape space manifold, and the bandwidth was chosen automatically using the cross-validation procedure described in Section [9]. Next, the resulting corpus callosum shape trend generated by the kernel regression method was compared to the result of the geodesic regression. This was done by again generating shapes from the geodesic model $\hat{\gamma}(x_k)$ at a sequence of ages x_k and overlaying the corresponding generated shapes from the kernel regression model at the same ages. The results are plotted for ages $x_k = 20$, 44, 66, and 90 in Fig. 2.6. Both regression methods give strikingly similar results. The two regression models at other values of ages, not shown, are also close to identical. This indicates that a geodesic curve does capture the relationship between age and corpus callosum shape, and that the additional flexibility offered by the nonparametric regression does not change the estimated trend. However, even though both methods provide a similar estimate of the

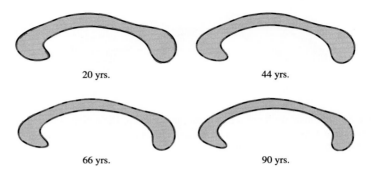

Figure 2.6. Comparison of geodesic regression (solid black) and nonparametric kernel regression (dashed red) of the corpus callosum shape versus age.

trend, the geodesic regression has the advantage that it is simpler to compute and easier to interpret, from the standpoint of the R^2 statistic and hypothesis test demonstrated previously.

2.5 Probabilistic models

2.5.1 Normal densities on manifolds

In this section we review probabilistic formulations for geodesic regression and PGA. Before defining these models, we first consider a basic definition of a manifold-valued normal distribution and give procedures for maximum-likelihood estimation of its parameters. There is no standard definition of a normal distribution on manifolds, mainly because different properties of the multivariate normal distribution in $\mathbb{R}^d$ may be generalized to manifolds by different definitions. Grenander [19] defines a generalization of the normal distribution to Lie groups and homogeneous spaces as a solution to the heat equation. Pennec [37] defines a generalization of the normal distribution based on the maximum intrinsic entropy principle on the manifold. The definition that we use here, introduced in [15] and also used in [23,48], generalizes the connection between least-squares estimation of statistical models and maximum-likelihood estimation under normally distributed errors. The normal distribution used here is equivalent to that of Pennec [37] with an isotropic covariance.

Consider a random variable y taking values on a Riemannian manifold M, defined by the probability density function (pdf)

$$p(y; \mu, \tau) = \frac{1}{C(\mu, \tau)} \exp\left(-\frac{\tau}{2} d(\mu, y)^2\right), \qquad (2.19)$$

$$C(\mu, \tau) = \int_M \exp\left(-\frac{\tau}{2} d(\mu, y)^2\right) dy, \qquad (2.20)$$

where $C(\mu, \tau)$ is a normalizing constant. We term this distribution a *Riemannian normal distribution* and use the notation $y \sim N_M(\mu, \tau^{-1})$ to denote it. The parameter $\mu \in M$ acts as a location parameter on the manifold, and the parameter $\tau \in \mathbb{R}_+$ acts as a dispersion parameter, similar to the precision of a Gaussian. This distribution has the advantages that (a) it is applicable to any Riemannian manifold, (b) it reduces to a multivariate normal distribution (with isotropic covariance) when $M = \mathbb{R}^d$, and (c) much like the Euclidean normal distribution, maximum-likelihood estimation of parameters gives rise to least-squares methods when M is a Riemannian homogeneous space, as shown next.

2.5.1.1 Maximum-likelihood estimation of μ

Returning to the Riemannian normal density in (2.19), the maximum-likelihood estimate of the mean parameter μ is given by

$$\hat{\mu} = \arg\max_{\mu \in M} \sum_{i=1}^N \ln p(y_i; \mu, \tau)$$

$$= \arg\min_{\mu \in M} N \ln C(\mu, \tau) + \frac{\tau}{2} \sum_{i=1}^N d(\mu, y_i)^2.$$

This minimization problem clearly reduces to the least-squares estimate, or Fréchet mean in (2.2), if the normalizing constant $C(\mu, \tau)$ does not depend on the μ parameter. As shown in [15], this occurs when the manifold M is a Riemannian homogeneous space, which means that for any two points $x, y \in M$, there exists an isometry that maps x to y. This is because the integral in (2.20) is invariant under isometries. More precisely, given any two points $\mu, \mu' \in M$, there exists an isometry $\phi : M \to M$ with $\mu' = \phi(\mu)$, and we have

$$C(\mu, \tau) = \int_M \exp\left(-\frac{\tau}{2} d(\mu, y)^2\right) dy$$

$$= \int_M \exp\left(-\frac{\tau}{2} d(\phi(\mu), \phi(y))^2\right) d\phi(y)$$

$$= C(\mu', \tau).$$

Thus in the case of a Riemannian homogeneous space the normalizing constant can be written as

$$C(\tau) = \int_M \exp\left(-\frac{\tau}{2} d(\mu, y)^2\right) dy, \qquad (2.21)$$

and we have the equivalence of the MLE and Fréchet mean, that is, $\hat{\mu} = \bar{y}$.

Two properties of the Riemannian normal distribution are worth emphasizing at this point. First, the requirement that M be a Riemannian homogeneous space is important. Without this, the normalizing constant $C(\mu, \tau)$ may be a function of μ, and if so, the MLE will not coincide with the Fréchet mean. For example, a Riemannian normal distribution on an anisotropic ellipsoid (which is not a homogeneous space) will have a normalizing constant that depends on μ. Second, it is also important that the Riemannian normal density be isotropic, unlike the normal law in [37], which includes a covariance matrix in the tangent space to the mean. Again, a covariance tensor field would need to be a function of the mean point μ, which would cause the normalizing constant to change with μ, unless the covariant derivative of the covariance field was zero everywhere. Unfortunately, such tensor fields are not always possible on general homogeneous spaces. For example, the only symmetric second-order tensor fields with zero covariant derivatives on S^2 are isotropic.

2.5.1.2 Estimation of the dispersion parameter, τ

Maximum-likelihood estimation of the dispersion parameter τ can also be done using gradient ascent. Unlike the case for estimation of the μ parameter, now the normalizing constant is a function of τ, and we must evaluate its derivative. We can rewrite the integral in (2.21) in normal coordinates, which can be thought of as a polar coordinate system in the tangent space $T_\mu M$. The radial coordinate is defined as $r = d(\mu, y)$, and the remaining $n - 1$ coordinates are parameterized by a unit vector v, that is, a point on the unit sphere $S^{n-1} \subset T_\mu M$. Thus we have the change-of-variables $\phi(rv) = \text{Exp}(\mu, rv)$. Now the integral for the normalizing constant becomes

$$C(\tau) = \int_{S^{n-1}} \int_0^{R(v)} \exp\left(-\frac{\tau}{2}r^2\right) |\det(d\phi(rv))|\, dr\, dv, \qquad (2.22)$$

where $R(v)$ is the maximum distance that $\phi(rv)$ is defined. Note that this formula is only valid if M is a complete manifold, which guarantees that normal coordinates are defined everywhere except possibly a set of measure zero on M.

The integral in (2.22) is difficult to compute for general manifolds due to the presence of the determinant of the Jacobian of ϕ. However, for symmetric spaces, this change-of-variables term has a simple form. If M is a symmetric space, then there exists an orthonormal basis $u_1, \ldots, u_n$ with $u_1 = v$ such that

$$|\det(d\phi(rv))| = \prod_{k=2}^{d} f_k(r),\qquad (2.23)$$

where $\kappa_k = K(u_1, u_k)$ denotes the sectional curvature, and f_k is defined as

$$f_k(r) = \begin{cases} \frac{1}{\sqrt{\kappa_k}} \sin(\sqrt{\kappa_k} r) & \text{if } \kappa_k > 0, \\ \frac{1}{\sqrt{-\kappa_k}} \sinh(\sqrt{-\kappa_k} r) & \text{if } \kappa_k < 0, \\ r & \text{if } \kappa_k = 0. \end{cases}$$

Notice that with this expression for the Jacobian determinant there is no longer dependence on v inside the integral in (2.22). Also, if M is simply connected, then $R(v) = R$ does not depend on the direction v, and we can write the normalizing constant as

$$C(\tau) = A_{n-1} \int_0^R \exp\left(-\frac{\tau}{2} r^2\right) \prod_{k=2}^{d} |\kappa_k|^{-1/2} f_k(\sqrt{|\kappa_k|} r) dr,$$

where A_{n-1} is the surface area of the $(n-1)$-hypersphere S^{n-1}. Although this formula works only for simply connected symmetric spaces, other symmetric spaces can be handled by lifting to the universal cover, which is simply connected, or by restricting the definition of the Riemannian normal pdf in (2.19) to have support only up to the injectivity radius $R = \min_v R(v)$.

The derivative of the normalizing constant with respect to τ is

$$C'(\tau) = A_{n-1} \int_0^R \frac{r^2}{2} \exp\left(-\frac{\tau}{2} r^2\right) \prod_{k=2}^{d} |\kappa_k|^{-1/2} f_k(\sqrt{|\kappa_k|} r) dr. \quad (2.24)$$

Both $C(\tau)$ and $C'(\tau)$ involve only a one-dimensional integral, which can be quickly and accurately approximated by numerical integration. Finally, the derivative of the log-likelihood needed for gradient ascent is given by

$$\frac{d}{d\tau} \sum_{i=1}^{N} \ln p(y_i; \mu, \tau) = -N \frac{C'(\tau)}{C(\tau)} - \frac{1}{2} \sum_{i=1}^{N} d(\mu, y_i)^2.$$

2.5.1.3 Sampling from a Riemannian normal distribution

In this section, we describe a Markov Chain Monte Carlo (MCMC) method for sampling from a Riemannian normal distribution with given mean and dispersion parameters (μ, τ). From

(2.22) we see that the Riemannian normal density is proportional to an isotropic Gaussian density in $T_\mu M$ times a change-of-variables term. This suggests using an independence sampler with an isotropic Gaussian as the proposal density.

More specifically, let $y \sim N_M(\mu, \tau^{-1})$, and let $\phi(rv) = \mathrm{Exp}(\mu, rv)$ be normal coordinates in the tangent space $T_\mu M$. Then the density in (r, v) is given by

$$f(r, v) \propto \begin{cases} \exp\left(-\frac{\tau}{2} r^2\right) |\det(d\phi(rv))|, & r \leq R(v), \\ 0 & \text{otherwise.} \end{cases}$$

Notice that the density is zero beyond the cut locus. For the independence sampler, we will not need to compute the normalization constant. We will then use an isotropic (Euclidean) Gaussian in $T_\mu M$ as the proposal density, which in polar coordinates is given by

$$g(r, v) \propto r \exp\left(-\frac{\tau}{2} r^2\right).$$

Algorithm 2.3 Independence sampler for the Riemannian normal distribution.

Input: Parameters μ, τ
Draw initial sample (r, v) from g
for $i = 1$ **to** S **do**
    Sample proposal $(\tilde{r}, \tilde{v})$ from g
    Compute the acceptance probability $\alpha((\tilde{r}, \tilde{v}), (r, v))$ using (2.25)
    Draw a uniform random number $u \in [0, 1]$
    if $\tilde{r} \leq R(\tilde{v})$ **AND** $u \leq \alpha((\tilde{r}, \tilde{v}), (r, v))$ **then**
        Accept: Set $y_i = \mathrm{Exp}(\mu, \tilde{r}\tilde{v})$, and set $(r, v) = (\tilde{r}, \tilde{v})$
    else
        Reject: Set $y_i = \mathrm{Exp}(\mu, rv)$

An iteration of the independence sampler begins with the previous sample (r, v) and generates a proposal sample $(\tilde{r}, \tilde{v})$ from g, which is accepted with probability

$$\alpha((\tilde{r}, \tilde{v}), (r, v)) = \min\left\{1, \frac{f(\tilde{r}, \tilde{v})g(r, v)}{f(r, v)g(\tilde{r}, \tilde{v})}\right\}$$

$$= \min\left\{1, \left|\frac{r \det(d\phi(\tilde{r}\tilde{v}))}{\tilde{r} \det(d\phi(rv))}\right|\right\}. \tag{2.25}$$

So, the acceptance probability reduces to simply a ratio of the Log map change-of-variables factors, which for symmetric spaces can

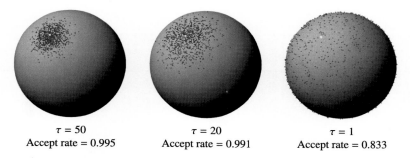

$\tau = 50$ $\tau = 20$ $\tau = 1$
Accept rate = 0.995   Accept rate = 0.991   Accept rate = 0.833

Figure 2.7. Samples from a Riemannian normal density on S^2 for various levels of τ. Samples are in blue (dark gray in print version), and the mean parameter μ is shown in red (light gray in print version).

be computed using (2.23). The final MCMC procedure is given by Algorithm 2.3.

2.5.1.4 Sphere example

We now demonstrate the above procedures for sampling from Riemannian normal densities and ML estimation of parameters on the two-dimensional sphere S^2. Fig. 2.7 shows example samples generated using the independence sampler in Algorithm 2.3 for various levels of τ. Notice that the sampler is efficient (high acceptance rate) for larger values of τ, but less efficient for smaller τ as the distribution approaches a uniform distribution on the sphere. This is because the proposal density well matches the true density, but the sampler rejects points beyond the cut locus, which happen more frequently when τ is small and the distribution is approaching the uniform distribution on the sphere.

Next, to test the ML estimation procedures, we used the independence sampler to repeatedly generate $N = 100$ random points on S^2 from an $N_{S^2}(\mu, \tau)$ density, where $\mu = (0, 0, 1)$ was the north pole, and again we varied $\tau = 1, 20, 50$. Then we computed the MLEs, $\hat{\mu}$, $\hat{\tau}$, using the gradient ascent procedures above. Each experiment was repeated 1000 times, and the results are summarized in Fig. 2.8. For the $\hat{\mu}$ estimates, we plot a kernel density estimate of the points $\mathrm{Log}_\mu \hat{\mu}$. This is a Monte Carlo simulation of the sampling distribution of the $\hat{\mu}$ statistic, mapped into the tangent space of the true mean $T_\mu M$ via the Log map. Similarly, the corresponding empirical sampling distributions of the $\hat{\tau}$ statistics are plotted as kernel density estimates. Although the true sampling distributions are unknown, the plots demonstrate that the MLEs have reasonable behavior, that is, they are distributed about the true parameter values, and their variance decreases as τ increases.

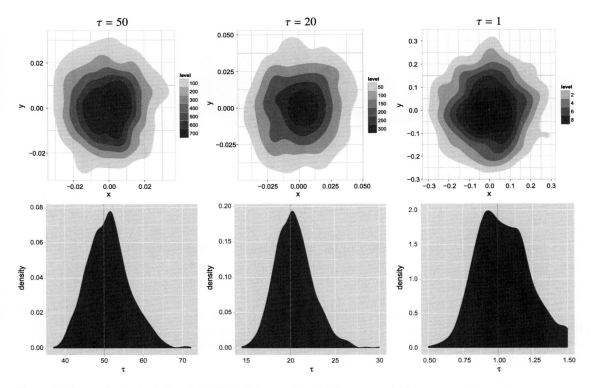

Figure 2.8. Monte Carlo simulation of the MLEs, $\hat{\mu}$ (top row), and $\hat{\tau}$ (bottom row). The true parameter values are marked in red (light gray in print version).

2.5.2 Probabilistic principal geodesic analysis

Principal component analysis (PCA) [26] has been widely used to analyze high-dimensional Euclidean data. Tipping and Bishop [45] proposed probabilistic PCA (PPCA), which is a latent variable model for PCA. A similar formulation was independently proposed by Roweis [38]. The main idea of PPCA is to model an n-dimensional Euclidean random variable y as

$$y = \mu + Bx + \epsilon, \tag{2.26}$$

where μ is the mean of y, x is a q-dimensional latent variable with $x \sim N(0, I)$, B is an $n \times q$ factor matrix that relates x and y, and $\epsilon \sim N(0, \sigma^2 I)$ represents error. We will find it convenient to model the factors as $B = W\Lambda$, where the columns of W are mutually orthogonal, and Λ is a diagonal matrix of scale factors. This removes the rotation ambiguity of the latent factors and makes them analogous to the eigenvectors and eigenvalues of standard PCA (there is still of course an ambiguity of the ordering of the factors). We now generalize this model to random variables on Riemannian manifolds.

2.5.2.1 Probability model

The PPGA model for a random variable y on a smooth Riemannian manifold M is

$$y|x \sim N_M \left(\text{Exp}(\mu, z), \tau^{-1} \right), z = W \Lambda x, \qquad (2.27)$$

where $x \sim N(0, 1)$ are again latent random variables in $\mathbb{R}^q$, μ is a base point on M, W is a matrix with q columns of mutually orthogonal tangent vectors in $T_\mu M$, Λ is a $q \times q$ diagonal matrix of scale factors for the columns of W, and τ is a scale parameter for the noise. In this model a linear combination of $W\Lambda$ and the latent variables x forms a new tangent vector $z \in T_\mu M$. Next, the exponential map shoots the base point μ by z to generate the location parameter of a *Riemannian normal distribution*, from which the data point y is drawn. Note that in Euclidean space the exponential map is an addition operation, $\text{Exp}(\mu, z) = \mu + z$. Thus PPGA coincides with (2.26), the standard PPCA model, when $M = \mathbb{R}^d$.

2.5.2.2 Inference

We develop a maximum likelihood procedure to estimate the parameters $\theta = (\mu, W, \Lambda, \tau)$ of the PPGA model defined in (2.27). Given observed data $y_i \in \{y_1, ..., y_N\}$ on M with associated latent variable $x_i \in \mathbb{R}^q$ and $z_i = W\Lambda x_i$, we formulate an expectation maximization (EM) algorithm. Since the expectation step over the latent variables does not yield a closed-form solution, we develop an HMC method to sample x_i from the posterior $p(x|y; \theta)$, the log of which is given by

$$\log \prod_{i=1}^{N} p(x_i|y_i; \theta) \propto -N \log C - \sum_{i=1}^{N} \frac{\tau}{2} d \left(\text{Exp}(\mu, z_i), y_i \right)^2 - \frac{\|x_i\|^2}{2},$$
$$(2.28)$$

and use this in a Monte Carlo Expectation Maximization (MCEM) scheme to estimate θ. The procedure contains two main steps.

2.5.2.3 E-step: HMC

For each x_i, we draw a sample of size S from the posterior distribution (2.28) using HMC with the current estimated parameters θ^k. Denoting by x_{ij} the jth sample for x_i, the Monte Carlo approximation of the Q function is given by

$$Q(\theta|\theta^k) = E_{x_i|y_i;\theta^k}\left[\prod_{i=1}^{N}\log p(x_i|y_i;\theta^k)\right] \approx \frac{1}{S}\sum_{j=1}^{S}\sum_{i=1}^{N}\log p(x_{ij}|y_i;\theta^k).$$
$$(2.29)$$

Hamiltonian Monte Carlo (HMC) [10] is a powerful gradient-based Markov Chain Monte Carlo sampling method that is applicable to a wide array of continuous probability distributions. It rigorously explores the entire space of a target distribution by utilizing Hamiltonian dynamics as a Markov transition probability. The gradient information of the log probability density is used to efficiently sample from the higher probability regions.

Next, we derive an HMC procedure to draw a random sample from the posterior distribution of the latent variables x. The first step to sample from a distribution $f(x)$ using HMC is to construct a Hamiltonian system $H(x, m) = U(x) + V(m)$, where $U(x) = -\log f(x)$ is a "potential energy", and $V(m) = -\log g(m)$ is a "kinetic energy", which acts as a proposal distribution on an auxiliary momentum variable m. An initial random momentum m is drawn from the density $g(m)$. Starting from the current point x and initial random momentum m, the Hamiltonian system is integrated forward in time to produce a candidate point x^* along with the corresponding forward-integrated momentum m^*. The candidate point x^* is accepted as a new point in the sample with probability

$$P(\text{accept}) = \min(1, \exp(-U(x^*) - V(m^*) + U(x) + V(m)).$$

This acceptance–rejection method is guaranteed to converge to the desired density $f(x)$ under fairly general regularity assumptions on f and g.

In the HMC sampling procedure the potential energy of the Hamiltonian $H(x_i, m) = U(x_i) + V(m)$ is defined as $U(x_i) = -\log p(x_i|y_i;\theta)$, and the kinetic energy $V(m)$ is a typical isotropic Gaussian distribution on a q-dimensional auxiliary momentum variable m. This gives us a Hamiltonian system to integrate: $\frac{dx_i}{dt} = \frac{\partial H}{\partial m} = m$, and $\frac{dm}{dt} = -\frac{\partial H}{\partial x_i} = -\nabla_{x_i}U$. Due to the fact that x_i is a Euclidean variable, we use a standard "leap-frog" numerical integration scheme, which approximately conserves the Hamiltonian and results in high acceptance rates. Now the gradient with respect to each x_i is

$$\nabla_{x_i}U = x_i - \tau\Lambda W^T\{d_{z_i}\text{Exp}(\mu, z_i)^{\dagger}\text{Log}(\text{Exp}(\mu, z_i), y_i)\}. \quad (2.30)$$

M-step: gradient ascent

In this section we derive the maximization step for updating the parameters $\theta = (\mu, W, \Lambda, \tau)$ by maximizing the HMC approximation of the Q function in (2.29). This turns out to be a gradient ascent scheme for all the parameters since there are no closed-form solutions.

Gradient for τ

The gradient term for estimating τ is

$$\nabla_\tau Q = -N \frac{C'(\tau)}{C(\tau)} - \frac{1}{S} \sum_{i=1}^{N} \sum_{j=1}^{S} d(\mathrm{Exp}(\mu, z_{ij}), y_i)^2,$$

where the derivative $C'(\tau)$ is given in (2.24).

Gradient for μ

From (2.28) and (2.29) the gradient term for updating μ is

$$\nabla_\mu Q = \frac{1}{S} \sum_{i=1}^{N} \sum_{j=1}^{S} \tau d_\mu \mathrm{Exp}(\mu, z_{ij})^\dagger \mathrm{Log}\left(\mathrm{Exp}(\mu, z_{ij}), y_i\right).$$

Gradient for Λ

For updating Λ, we take the derivative with respect to each ath diagonal element Λ^a as

$$\frac{\partial Q}{\partial \Lambda^a} = \frac{1}{S} \sum_{i=1}^{N} \sum_{j=1}^{S} \tau (W^a x_{ij}^a)^T \{d_{z_{ij}} \mathrm{Exp}(\mu, z_{ij})^\dagger \mathrm{Log}(\mathrm{Exp}(\mu, z_{ij}), y_i)\},$$

where W^a denotes the ath column of W, and x_{ij}^a is the ath component of x_{ij}.

Gradient for W

The gradient with respect to W is

$$\nabla_W Q = \frac{1}{S} \sum_{i=1}^{N} \sum_{j=1}^{S} \tau d_{z_{ij}} \mathrm{Exp}(\mu, z_{ij})^\dagger \mathrm{Log}(\mathrm{Exp}(\mu, z_{ij}), y_i) x_{ij}^T \Lambda. \quad (2.31)$$

To preserve the mutual orthogonality constraint on the columns of W, we project the gradient in (2.31) onto the tangent space at W, then updating W by shooting the geodesic on the Stiefel manifold in the negative projected gradient direction; see the details in [12].

Algorithm 2.4 Monte Carlo expectation maximization for PPGA.

Input: Data set Y, reduced dimension q.
Initialize μ, W, Λ, σ.
while *gradient is larger than some threshold* **do**
    Sample X according to (2.30)
    Update μ, W, Λ, σ by gradient ascent.

The MCEM algorithm for PPGA is an iterative procedure for finding the subspace spanned by q principal components, shown in Algorithm 2.4. The computation time per iteration depends on the complexity of exponential map, log map, and Jacobi field, which may vary for different manifolds. Note that the cost of the gradient ascent algorithm also linearly depends on the data size, dimensionality, and the number of samples drawn. An advantage of MCEM is that it can run in parallel for each data point. Since the posterior distribution (2.28) is estimated by HMC sampling, to diagnose the convergence of the PPGA MCEM algorithm, we run parallel independent chains to obtain univariate quantities of the full distribution.

2.5.2.4 PPGA of simulated sphere data

Using the generative model for PGA (2.27), we forward simulated a random sample of 100 data points on the unit sphere S^2, with known parameters $\theta = (\mu, W, \Lambda, \tau)$ shown in Table 2.1. Next, we ran the maximum likelihood estimation procedure to test whether we could recover those parameters. We initialized μ from a random uniform point on the sphere. We initialized W as a random Gaussian matrix, to which we then applied the Gram–Schmidt algorithm to ensure the orthonormality of its columns. Fig. 2.9 compares the ground truth principal geodesics and MLE

Table 2.1 Comparison between ground truth parameters for the simulated data and the MLE of PPGA, nonprobabilistic PGA, and standard PCA.

	μ	W	Λ	τ
Ground truth	$(-0.78, 0.48, -0.37)$	$(-0.59, -0.42, 0.68)$	0.40	100
PPGA	$(-0.78, 0.48, -0.40)$	$(-0.59, -0.43, 0.69)$	0.41	102
PGA	$(-0.79, 0.46, -0.41)$	$(-0.59, -0.38, 0.70)$	0.41	N/A
PCA	$(-0.70, 0.41, -0.46)$	$(-0.62, -0.37, 0.69)$	0.38	N/A

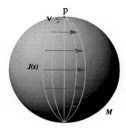 

Figure 2.9. Left: Jacobi fields. Right: the principal geodesic of random generated data on unit sphere. Blue dots (dark gray in print version): random generated sphere data set. Yellow line (light gray in print version): ground truth principal geodesic. Red line (gray in print version): estimated principal geodesic using PPGA.

principal geodesic analysis. A good overlap between the first principal geodesic shows that PPGA recovers the model parameters.

One advantage that the PPGA model has over the least-squares PGA formulation is that the mean point is estimated jointly with the principal geodesics. In the standard PGA algorithm the mean is estimated first (using geodesic least-squares), and then the principal geodesics are estimated. This does not make a difference in the Euclidean case (principal components must pass through the mean), but it does in the nonlinear case. To demonstrate this, we give examples where data can be fit better when jointly estimating mean and PGA than when doing them sequentially. We compared the PPGA model with PGA and standard PCA (in the Euclidean embedding space). The noise variance τ was not valid to be estimated in both PGA and PCA. The estimation error of principal geodesics turned to be larger in PGA compared to PPGA. Furthermore, the standard PCA converges to an incorrect solution due to its inappropriate use of a Euclidean metric on Riemannian data. A comparison of the ground truth parameters and these methods is given in Table 2.1.

References

1. B. Asfari, Riemannian l^p center of mass: existence, uniqueness, and convexity, Proceedings of the American Mathematical Society 139 (2011) 655–673.
2. S.R. Buss, J.P. Fillmore, Spherical averages and applications to spherical splines and interpolation, ACM Transactions on Graphics 20 (2) (2001) 95–126.
3. M. Banerjee, B. Jian, B.C. Vemuri, Robust Fréchet mean and PGA on Riemannian manifolds with applications to neuroimaging, in:

International Conference on Information Processing in Medical Imaging, 2017.

4. R. Bhattacharya, V. Patrangenaru, Large sample theory of intrinsic and extrinsic sample means on manifolds, Annals of Statistics 31 (1) (2003) 1–29.

5. R. Bhattacharya, V. Patrangenaru, Large sample theory of intrinsic and extrinsic sample means on manifolds—II, Annals of Statistics 33 (3) (2005) 1225–1259.

6. P. Crouch, F.S. Leite, The dynamic interpolation problem: on Riemannian manifolds, Lie groups, and symmetric spaces, Journal of Dynamical and Control Systems 1 (2) (1995) 177–202.

7. R. Chakraborty, D. Seo, B.C. Vemuri, An efficient exact-PGA algorithm for constant curvature manifolds, in: Proceedings of the IEEE Conference on Computer Vision and Pattern Recognition, 2016, pp. 3976–3984.

8. M. do Carmo, Riemannian Geometry, Birkhäuser, 1992.

9. B. Davis, P.T. Fletcher, E. Bullitt, S. Joshi, Population shape regression from random design data, in: Proceedings of IEEE International Conference on Computer Vision, 2007.

10. S. Duane, A. Kennedy, B. Pendleton, D. Roweth, Hybrid Monte Carlo, Physics Letters B (1987) 216–222.

11. S. Durrleman, X. Pennec, A. Trouvé, G. Gerig, N. Ayache, Spatiotemporal atlas estimation for developmental delay detection in longitudinal datasets, in: Medical Image Computing and Computer-Assisted Intervention, 2009, pp. 297–304.

12. A. Edelman, T.A. Arias, S.T. Smith, The geometry of algorithms with orthogonality constraints, SIAM Journal on Matrix Analysis and Applications 20 (2) (1998) 303–353.

13. B. Eltzner, S. Jung, S. Huckemann, Dimension reduction on polyspheres with application to skeletal representations, in: International Conference on Networked Geometric Science of Information, 2014, pp. 22–29.

14. P.T. Fletcher, Geodesic regression on Riemannian manifolds, in: MICCAI Workshop on Mathematical Foundations of Computational Anatomy, 2011, pp. 75–86.

15. P.T. Fletcher, Geodesic regression and the theory of least squares on Riemannian manifolds, International Journal of Computer Vision (2012) 1–15.

16. P.T. Fletcher, C. Lu, S. Joshi, Statistics of shape via principal geodesic analysis on Lie groups, in: Proceedings of the IEEE Conference on Computer Vision and Pattern Recognition (CVPR), 2003, pp. 95–101.

17. P.T. Fletcher, C. Lu, S.M. Pizer, S. Joshi, Principal geodesic analysis for the study of nonlinear statistics of shape, IEEE Transactions on Medical Imaging 23 (8) (2004) 995–1005.

18. M. Fréchet, Les éléments aléatoires de nature quelconque dans un espace distancié, Annales de L'Institut Henri Poincaré 10 (3) (1948) 215–310.

19. U. Grenander, Probabilities on Algebraic Structures, John Wiley and Sons, 1963.

20. S. Huckemann, T. Hotz, A. Munk, Intrinsic shape analysis: geodesic PCA for Riemannian manifolds modulo isometric lie group actions, Statistica Sinica (2010) 1–58.

21. H. Hotelling, Analysis of a complex of statistical variables into principal components, Journal of Educational Psychology 24 (417–441) (1933) 498–520.

22. S. Jung, I.L. Dryden, J.S. Marron, Analysis of principal nested spheres, Biometrika 99 (3) (2012) 551–568.

23. S.C. Joshi, J. Hinkle, P.T. Fletcher, Intrinsic polynomials for regression on Riemannian manifolds, Journal of Mathematical Imaging and Vision 50 (1–2) (2014) 32–52.

24. P.E. Jupp, J.T. Kent, Fitting smooth paths to spherical data, Applied Statistics 36 (1) (1987) 34–46.

25. I.T. Jolliffe, Principal Component Analysis, Springer-Verlag, 1986.

26. I.T. Jolliffe, Principal Component Analysis, vol. 487, Springer-Verlag, New York, 1986.

27. H. Karcher, Riemannian center of mass and mollifier smoothing, Communications on Pure and Applied Mathematics 30 (5) (1977) 509–541.

28. A. Kume, I.L. Dryden, H. Le, Shape-space smoothing splines for planar landmark data, Biometrika 94 (3) (2007) 513–528.

29. W.S. Kendall, Probability, convexity, and harmonic maps with small image I: uniqueness and fine existence, Proceedings of the London Mathematical Society 3 (61) (1990) 371–406.

30. M. Miller, Computational anatomy: shape, growth, and atrophy comparison via diffeomorphisms, NeuroImage 23 (2004) S19–S33.

31. M. Moakher, Means and averaging in the group of rotations, SIAM Journal on Matrix Analysis and Applications 24 (1) (2002) 1–16.

32. E.A. Nadaraya, On estimating regression, Theory of Probability and Its Applications 10 (1964) 186–190.

33. L. Noakes, G. Heinzinger, B. Paden, Cubic splines on curved spaces, IMA Journal of Mathematical Control and Information 6 (4) (1989) 465–473.

34. M. Niethammer, Y. Huang, F.-X. Viallard, Geodesic regression for image time-series, in: Proceedings of Medical Image Computing and Computer Assisted Intervention, 2011.

35. K. Pearson, On lines and planes of closest fit to points in space, Philosophical Magazine 2 (1901) 609–629.

36. X. Pennec, Probabilities and statistics on Riemannian manifolds: basic tools for geometric measurements, in: IEEE Workshop on Nonlinear Signal and Image Processing, 1999.

37. X. Pennec, Intrinsic statistics on Riemannian manifolds: basic tools for geometric measurements, Journal of Mathematical Imaging and Vision 25 (1) (2006).

38. S. Roweis, EM algorithms for PCA and SPCA, Advances in Neural Information Processing Systems (1998) 626–632.

39. S. Said, N. Courty, N. Le Bihan, S.J. Sangwine, Exact principal geodesic analysis for data on SO(3), in: 15th European Signal Processing Conference, 2007, pp. 1701–1705.

40. J. Su, I.L. Dryden, E. Klassen, H. Le, A. Srivastava, Fitting smoothing splines to time-indexed, noisy points on nonlinear manifolds, Image and Vision Computing 30 (6) (2012) 428–442.

41. S. Sommer, F. Lauze, S. Hauberg, M. Nielsen, Manifold valued statistics, exact principal geodesic analysis and the effect of linear approximations, in: European Conference on Computer Vision, 2010, pp. 43–56.

42. S. Sommer, F. Lauze, M. Nielsen, Optimization over geodesics for exact principal geodesic analysis, Advances in Computational Mathematics 40 (2) (2014) 283–313.

43. X. Shi, M. Styner, J. Lieberman, J. Ibrahim, W. Lin, H. Zhu, Intrinsic regression models for manifold-valued data, Journal of the American Statistical Association 5762 (2009) 192–199.

44. H. Salehian, D. Vaillancourt, B.C. Vemuri, iPGA: Incremental principal geodesic analysis with applications to movement disorder classification, in: International Conference on Medical Image Computing and Computer-Assisted Intervention, 2014.

45. M.E. Tipping, C.M. Bishop, Probabilistic principal component analysis, Journal of the Royal Statistical Society, Series B, Statistical Methodology 61 (3) (1999) 611–622.

46. A. Trouvé, F.-X. Vialard, A second-order model for time-dependent data interpolation: splines on shape spaces, in: MICCAI STIA Workshop, 2010.

47. G.S. Watson, Smooth regression analysis, Sankhya 26 (1964) 101–116.

48. M. Zhang, P.T. Fletcher, Probabilistic principal geodesic analysis, in: Neural Information Processing Systems (NIPS), 2013.

3

Manifold-valued image processing with SPD matrices

Xavier Pennec

Université Côte d'Azur and Inria, Epione team, Sophia Antipolis, France

3.1 Introduction

Symmetric positive definite (SPD) matrices are geometric data that appear in many applications. In medical imaging, SPD matrices are called tensors when they model the covariance matrix of the Brownian motion of water in Diffusion Tensor Imaging (DTI) [12,42]. They were also used to encode the joint variability at different places in shape analysis [23,24], and they are classically used in computer vision and image analysis to guide the segmentation, grouping, and motion analysis [53,79,14,83]. SPD matrices are also used as local metrics in numerical analysis to drive the size of adaptive meshes to solve PDEs in 3D more efficiently [50]. In echo-Doppler or radar images, circular complex random processes with a null mean are characterized by Teoplitz Hermitian positive definite matrices [56]. In brain–computer interfaces (BCI), the time-correlation of electro-encephalogram (EEG) signals are encoded through positive definite matrices, and the choice of the metric on this space has been shown to drastically impact classification algorithms on these extremely low signal-to-noise ratio data [5].

The space of SPD matrices is a smooth manifold, which is not a vector space with the usual additive matrix structure. Indeed, a classical result in linear algebra states that P is SPD if and only if all its symmetric submatrices (including P itself) have nonnegative determinant [68]. Symmetric submatrices are obtained by removing at most $dim(P) - 1$ rows and the corresponding columns. The space of SPD matrices is thus a subset of symmetric matrices delimited by multiple polynomial constraints on the coefficients. Since all these constraints are homogeneous (invariant under the multiplication by a positive scalar), this defines a convex half-cone in the vector space of symmetric matrices. Thus convex operations like the mean are stable, but many other classical operations on SPD matrices are nonconvex and lead to matrices that are not

Riemannian Geometric Statistics in Medical Image Analysis
https://doi.org/10.1016/B978-0-12-814725-2.00010-8

positive definite. Gradient descent with the classical Frobenius (Euclidean) norm, for instance, amounts to evolve along a line in the vector space of symmetric matrices: one side of this line inevitably hits the boundary of the cone. When performing regularization of DTI images, there is thus almost inevitably a point in the image where the time step is not small enough and where we end-up with negative eigenvalues. A large part of the literature before 2006 was trying to get around these problems using the spectral decomposition of SPD matrices (e.g. [78,17]). However, processing independently the rotation (eigenvectors basis trihedron) and the eigenvalues is creating a continuity problem around equal eigenvalues.

To cope with that problem in the context of Diffusion Tensor Images (DTI), several authors proposed concurrently to consider Riemannian metrics on the space of SPD matrices that are invariant by affine change of the underlying space coordinates. The family of all affine-invariant metrics (up to a global scaling factor) induces the Riemannian distance:

$$\text{dist}^2(P, Q) = \text{Tr}\left(L^2\right) + \beta\,\text{Tr}(L)^2 \quad \text{with} \quad L = \log(P^{-1/2}QP^{-1/2}),$$
(3.1)

where log stands for the matrix logarithm, and $\beta > -1/n$ is a free real parameter. The space of SPD matrices becomes a very regular Hadamard manifold structure (a space without cut-locus globally diffeomorphic to a Euclidean space). This considerably simplifies the computations compared to other noninvariant metrics. With this structure, symmetric matrices with null and infinite eigenvalues are both at an infinite distance of any SPD matrix: the cone of SPD matrices is mapped to a homogeneous space of nonconstant curvature without boundaries. Moreover, there is a unique geodesic joining any two SPD matrices, the mean of a set of SPD matrices exists and is unique, and we can even define globally consistent orthonormal coordinate systems of tangent spaces. Thus the structure obtained has many properties of Euclidean spaces even if it remains a manifold because of the curvature. The drawback with respect to the Euclidean case is the important increase of computational complexity due to the use matrix exponential and logarithms (computed through series or diagonalization of symmetric matrices) in the Riemannian distance/geodesics.

The affine-invariant metric with $\beta = 0$ has been put forward independently for several applications around 2005. [27] used it for the analysis of principal modes of sets of diffusion tensors; [54] analyzed its mathematical properties, which were exploited in [11] for a new anisotropic DTI index; [66] suggested it as the basis to develop the SPD matrix-valued images processing algorithms presented in this chapter; [48] came to the same metric by looking for a natural metric on the space of Gaussian distributions for the segmentation of diffusion tensor images.

In statistics this metric has been introduced in the 1980s to model the geometry of the multivariate normal family [13,71,16]. In this field it is known as the Fisher–Rao metric. This metric is well known in other branches of mathematics [8]. In computer vision the metric was rediscovered to compute with covariance matrices [28]. The Levi-Civita connection of that metric was used in [37] to develop geometric integrators for flows of dynamic systems on the space of symmetric matrices. The geodesic walk along the geodesics of this metric was used for the anisotropic regularization of diffusion tensor images in [18] and [10]. It is noticeable that so many different approaches lead to the same metric on the SPD space.

Although this affine-invariant Riemannian metric is often thought to be unique, a slightly different but still invariant metric was proposed in [46] using a geometric embedding construction. It turns out that both metrics actually share the same affine-invariant connection, so that there is an isometry between the two SPD spaces. The uniqueness of that affine-invariant connection on SPD matrices is well known in differential geometry [57, 39,36,32]. However, the family of all affine-invariant metrics was apparently not described before [63,64].

Other metrics on SPD matrices with different properties can be constructed. By trying to put a Lie group structure on SPD matrices, Vincent Arsigny discovered the log-Euclidean metrics [2,3,1]. These metrics give a vector space structure to the SPD matrix manifold while keeping most of the interesting affine-invariant properties (Section 3.6.1). This drastically simplifies the algorithms and speeds up computations. Other Riemannian or non-Riemannian metrics were also proposed. We briefly present some of them for completeness in Section 3.6.

Chapter organization

In section 3.2, we first describe the matrix exponential and logarithm functions on symmetric matrices and their differentials. Then we turn in section 3.3 to the determination of Riemannian metrics that are invariant with respect to the natural action of the linear group on covariance matrices. We explicitly construct one affine-invariant Riemannian metric on SPD matrices and determine its geodesics and explicit formulas for the Riemannian exp and log maps. Then we turn to the description of all the affine-invariant metrics. We show that there exists a one-parameter family of such metrics (up to a global scaling factor) that are sharing the same Levi-Civita connection. Establishing a globally orthonormal coordinate system for each of these metrics allows us to compute explicitly the sectional, Ricci, and scalar curvatures. They are shown to be nonpositive and bounded from below. Moreover, the expression of the curvatures is identical at all the points of the manifold although it is not constant in all directions. This is a feature of symmetric (and more generally homogeneous) spaces.

Section 3.4 illustrates how the statistical setting of chapter 2 can be implemented on SPD matrices endowed with an affine-invariant metric. Because the space is Hadamard, the Fréchet mean is unique. However, the negative curvature has an important impact on the gradient descent algorithms, and we illustrate cases where the time-step has to be adapted. The discussion of the generalized Gaussian distribution also illustrates how the Ricci curvature modifies the classical inverse relationship between the covariance matrix and the concentration parameter of a Gaussian.

We turn in section 3.5 to the generalization of these statistical tools to more general manifold-valued image processing algorithms. Using weighted Fréchet means, we generalize many different types of interpolation, convolutions, and isotropic and anisotropic filtering algorithms to manifold-valued images.

Because our manifold-valued image processing algorithms only depend on the chosen metric, they can also be used with other families of Riemannian and extrinsic metrics. We detail in section 3.6 some of the metrics on SPD matrices that were proposed in the literature. Certain metrics like the log-Euclidean metrics do not display the full affine-invariance but conserve many of the good properties while providing a Euclidean structure to the space that considerably simplifies the computational framework. Other metrics also give a symmetric space structure but of positive curvature: matrices with zero eigenvalues are then again at a finite distance of SPD matrices. There is indeed no canonical metric on SPD matrices that is suited to all applications: the choice of the metric should be guided by the invariance and computational properties that are important for the application.

Finally, the use of our manifold-valued image processing algorithms is illustrated in section 3.7 with an application to the joint estimation and anisotropic smoothing of diffusion tensor images of the brain and in section 3.8 with the modeling of the variability of the brain anatomy.

3.2 Exponential, logarithm, and square root of SPD matrices

Since we work with matrices in this chapter, we use capital letters like P and Q (instead of p and q or x and y in previous chapters) to denote the points on the manifold of $n \times n$ SPD matrices, and V and W for symmetric matrices (tangent vectors). The number of free parameters of symmetric and SPD matrices (the dimension of the manifold $\mathcal{S}ym_n^+$) is $d = n(n+1)/2$.

We will further extensively use the matrix exponential and logarithm functions. The exponential of a matrix W is defined through the convergent series $\exp(W) = \sum_{k=0}^{+\infty} \frac{W^k}{k!}$. We have drastic simplifications in the symmetric case thanks to the diagonalization $W = UDU^\top$, where U is an orthonormal matrix, and $D = \mathrm{DIAG}(d_i)$ is the diagonal matrix of eigenvalues. Indeed, powers of W can be written in the same basis: $W^k = UD^kU^\top$ and the rotation matrices can be factored out of the series. We are left with the exponential of each eigenvalue on the diagonal:

$$\exp(W) = \sum_{k=0}^{+\infty} \frac{W^k}{k!} = U\,\mathrm{DIAG}(\exp(d_i))\,U^\top. \qquad (3.2)$$

For the inverse of the matrix exponential (the matrix logarithm), we may diagonalize any SPD matrix as $P = U\,\mathrm{DIAG}(d_i)\,U^\top$ with (strictly) positive eigenvalues d_i. Thus the function

$$\log(P) = U\,(\mathrm{DIAG}(\log(d_i)))\,U^\top$$

is always well defined and realizes the inverse of the exponential of symmetric matrices. Moreover, the series defining the usual matrix log converges for small enough eigenvalues ($|d_i - 1| < 1$):

$$\log(P) = U\left(\mathrm{DIAG}\left(\sum_{k=1}^{+\infty} \frac{(-1)^{k+1}}{k}(d_i-1)^k\right)\right)U^\top$$
$$= \sum_{k=1}^{+\infty} \frac{(-1)^{k+1}}{k}(P - \mathrm{Id})^k. \qquad (3.3)$$

Classically, we define the (left) square root of a matrix B as the set $\{B_L^{1/2}\} = \{A \in \mathrm{GL}(n)/AA^\top = B\}$. We could also define the right square root $\{B_R^{1/2}\} = \{A \in \mathrm{GL}(n)/A^\top A = B\}$. For SPD matrices, we define the symmetric square root as

$$P^{1/2} = \{Q \in \mathcal{S}ym_n^+/Q^2 = P\}.$$

The symmetric square root of an SPD matrix is always defined and moreover unique: let $P = UD^2U^\top$ be a diagonalization (with positives values for the d_i's). Then there exists one symmetric positive definite square root $Q = UDU^\top$. To prove that it is unique, let us consider two symmetric positive square roots Q_1 and Q_2 of P. Then their square $Q_1^2 = P$ and $Q_2^2 = P$ obviously commute (because they are equal), and thus they can be diagonalized in the same basis: this means that the diagonal matrices D_1^2 and D_2^2 are equal in this common basis. As the elements of D_1 and D_2 are positive, they are also equal, and $Q_1 = Q_2$.

More generally, we can define any power of an SPD matrix by taking the power of its eigenvalues or using the formula

$$P^\alpha = \exp\left(\alpha (\log P)\right).$$

3.2.1 Differential of the matrix exponential

The matrix exponential and logarithm realize a one-to-one mapping between the space of symmetric matrices to the space of SPD matrices. Moreover, we can show that this mapping is diffeomorphic, since the differential has no singularities. Using the Taylor expansion of the matrix power $(W + \varepsilon V)^k = W^k + \varepsilon \sum_{i=0}^{k-1} W^i V W^{k-i-1} + O(\varepsilon^2)$ for $k \geq 1$, we obtain by identification the directional derivative $\partial_V \exp(W)$ by gathering the first-order terms in ε in the series $\exp(W + \varepsilon V) = \sum_{k=0}^{+\infty} (W + \varepsilon V)^k / k!$:

$$\partial_V \exp(W) = (d \exp(W))(V) = \sum_{k=1}^{+\infty} \frac{1}{k!} \sum_{i=0}^{k-1} W^i V W^{k-i-1}. \qquad (3.4)$$

To simplify the formula, we insert the diagonalization $W = RSR^\top$ in the series to obtain

$$\partial_V \exp(W) = R \left(\partial_{(R^\top V R)} \exp(S) \right) R^\top.$$

Thus we are left with the computation of $\partial_V \exp(S)$ for S diagonal. As $[S^l V S^{k-l-1}]_{ij} = s_i^l v_{ij} s_j^{k-l-1}$, we have

$$[\partial_V \exp(S)]_{ij} = \left\{ \sum_{k=1}^{+\infty} \frac{1}{k!} \sum_{l=0}^{k-1} s_i^l s_j^{k-l-1} \right\} v_{ij} = v_{ij} \frac{\exp(s_i) - \exp(s_j)}{s_i - s_j}. \qquad (3.5)$$

The value $a_{ij} = \frac{\exp(s_i) - \exp(s_j)}{s_i - s_j}$ is numerically unstable for almost equal eigenvalues s_i and s_j. However, we can rewrite this value as

$$a_{ij} = \frac{\exp(s_i) - \exp(s_j)}{s_i - s_j} = \sum_{k=1}^{+\infty} \frac{1}{k!} \frac{s_i^k - s_j^k}{s_i - s_j}$$

$$= \exp(s_j) \left(1 + \frac{(s_i - s_j)}{2} + \frac{(s_i - s_j)^2}{6} + O\left((s_i - s_j)^3\right) \right).$$

The Taylor expansion on the right-hand side gives a numerically stable method to compute a_{ij} for equal eigenvalues. Moreover, since $\exp(s_i) > \exp(s_j)$ whenever $s_i > s_j$, we have $a_{ij} > 0$, so that we can conclude that $d\exp(S)$ is a diagonal linear form that is always invertible: the exponential of a symmetric matrix is a diffeomorphism.

3.2.2 Differential of the matrix logarithm

To compute the differential of the logarithm function, we can simply inverse the differential of the exponential as a linear form: as $\exp(\log(P)) = P$, we have $(d\log(P))(V) = (d\exp(\log(P)))^{-1}V$. Using $D = \exp(S)$, we easily express the inverse for a diagonal matrix: $[(d\exp(S))^{-1}V]_{ij} = v_{ij}/a_{ij}$. Thus we have:

$$[\partial_V \log(D)]_{ij} = v_{ij} \frac{\log(d_i) - \log(d_j)}{d_i - d_j}. \tag{3.6}$$

Like for the exponential, we can expand the value of a_{ij}^{-1} for close eigenvalues:

$$a_{ij}^{-1} = \frac{\log(d_i) - \log(d_j)}{d_i - d_j} = \frac{1}{d_j} \left(1 - \frac{d_i - d_j}{2d_j} + \frac{(d_i - d_j)^2}{3d_j^2} + O\left((d_i - d_j)^3\right) \right).$$

The Taylor expansion of the right-hand side provides a numerically stable formulation for almost equal eigenvalues. Finally, using the identity $\log(P) = R^\top \log(RPR^\top) R$ for any rotation R, we have:

$$\partial_V \log(RDR^\top) = R \left(\partial_{R^\top V R} \log(D) \right) R^\top.$$

Using this formula, we may compute the differential at any point $P = RDR^\top$.

From this expression, we can establish two very useful identities implying the differential of the log:

$$\partial_{\log(P)} \log(P) = P^{-1} \log(P) = \log(P) P^{-1}, \tag{3.7}$$

$$\langle \partial_V \log(P), W \rangle = \langle \partial_W \log(P), V \rangle. \tag{3.8}$$

3.3 Affine-invariant metrics

Let us consider the action $(A, t) \cdot x = Ax + t$ of an element (A, t) of the affine group $\mathrm{Aff}(n) = \mathrm{GL}(n) \ltimes \mathbb{R}^n$ on a point $x \in \mathbb{R}^n$. The symbol $\ltimes$ denotes a semidirect product since the linear part of the transformation interferes with the translation in the composition of two affine transformations: $(A_1, t_1) \circ (A_2, t_2) = (A_1 A_2, A_1 t_2 + t_1)$. Now, if x is a random variable with mean $\bar{x}$ and covariance matrix Σ_{xx}, then $y = Ax + t$ is a random variable with mean $\bar{y} = A\bar{x} + t$ and covariance matrix $\Sigma_{yy} = E[(y - \bar{y})(y - \bar{y})^\top] = A\Sigma_{xx}A^\top$. Thus the action of a linear transformation $A \in \mathrm{GL}(n)$ on covariance matrices $P \in \mathcal{S}ym_n^+$ is

$$A \cdot P = APA^\top \qquad \forall A \in \mathrm{GL}(n) \qquad \text{and} \qquad P \in \mathcal{S}ym_n^+.$$

3.3.1 Affine-invariant distances

Following [60], any invariant distance on $\mathcal{S}ym_n^+$ satisfies $\mathrm{dist}(A \cdot P_1, A \cdot P_2) = \mathrm{dist}(P_1, P_2)$. Choosing $A = P_1^{-1/2}$, we can reduce this to the distance to the identity:

$$\mathrm{dist}(P_1, P_2) = \mathrm{dist}\left(\mathrm{Id}, P_1^{-\frac{1}{2}} P_2 P_1^{-\frac{1}{2}} \right) = N\left(P_1^{-\frac{1}{2}} P_2 P_1^{-\frac{1}{2}} \right).$$

However, this should hold true for all transformations. In particular, the distance to identity N should be invariant by transformations that leaves the identity unchanged, that is, the isotropy group of the identity $\mathcal{H}(\mathrm{Id}) = \mathrm{O}(n) = \{U \in \mathrm{GL}(n) / UU^\top = \mathrm{Id}\}$:

$$\forall U \in \mathrm{O}(n), \qquad N(UPU^\top) = N(P).$$

Using the spectral decomposition $P = UDU^\top$, we can conclude that $N(P)$ has to be a symmetric function of the eigenvalues $d_1 \geq d_2 \geq \cdots > d_n > 0$. Moreover, the symmetry of the invariant distance $\mathrm{dist}(P, \mathrm{Id}) = \mathrm{dist}(\mathrm{Id}, P^{-1})$ implies that $N(P) = N(P^{-1})$.

The sum of the squared logarithms of the eigenvalues is a candidate that satisfies the constraints

$$N(P)^2 = \| \log(P) \|^2 = \sum_{i=1}^{n} (\log(d_i))^2. \tag{3.9}$$

By construction, $N\left(P_1^{-\frac{1}{2}} P_2 P_1^{-\frac{1}{2}} \right)$ fulfills the symmetry and definiteness axioms of the distance. Because $N(P) = 0$ implies that the eigenvalues are $d_i = 1$ (and conversely), the separation axiom is also verified. However, if the triangular inequality $N(P_1) + N(P_2) \geq N(P_1^{-1/2} P_2 P_1^{-1/2})$ can be verified numerically (see e.g. [28]), then a formal proof is quite difficult to establish. Moreover, many other functions N may give rise to other valid distances.

3.3.2 An invariant Riemannian metric

Another way to determine the invariant distance is through a Riemannian metric. For that, we need to define the differential structure of the manifold.

3.3.2.1 Tangent vectors

Tangent vectors to SPD matrices are simply symmetric matrices with no constraint on the eigenvalues: if $\Gamma(t) = P + tW + O(t^2)$ is a curve on the SPD space, then the tangent vector W is obviously symmetric, and there is no other constraint as symmetric and SPD matrices both have the same dimension $d = n(n+1)/2$.

Our group action naturally extends to tangent vectors: if $\Gamma(t) = P + tW + O(t^2)$ is a curve passing at P with tangent vector W, then the curve $A \cdot \Gamma(t) = APA^\top + tAWA^\top + O(t^2)$ passes through $A \cdot P = APA^\top$ with tangent vector $A \cdot W = AWA^\top$. The tangent space $T_P \mathcal{S}ym_n^+$ at the point P is thus identified with the space of symmetric matrices.

3.3.2.2 Riemannian metric

On the tangent space at the identity matrix, we can now choose one of the most simple scalar products: if W_1 and W_2 are tangent vectors (i.e. symmetric matrices, not necessarily definite or positive), then the standard Frobenius scalar product on matrices is $\langle W_1, W_2 \rangle = \mathrm{Tr}(W_1^\top W_2)$. This scalar product is moreover invariant by the isotropy group $O(n)$. Now, if $W_1, W_2 \in T_P \mathcal{S}ym_n^+$ are two tangent vectors at P, then the invariance of the Riemannian metric under the action of $A \in \mathrm{GL}(n)$ means that $\langle W_1, W_2 \rangle_P = \langle A \cdot W_1, A \cdot W_2 \rangle_{A.P}$. Using $A = P^{-1/2}$, we see that we can define the metric at P from the metric at the identity:

$$\langle W_1, W_2 \rangle_P = \left\langle P^{-\frac{1}{2}} W_1 P^{-\frac{1}{2}}, P^{-\frac{1}{2}} W_2 P^{-\frac{1}{2}} \right\rangle_{\mathrm{Id}} = \mathrm{Tr}\left(P^{-1} W_1 P^{-1} W_2 \right).$$

We can easily verify that using any other transformation $A = UP^{-1/2}$ (where U is a free orthonormal matrix) that transports P to the identity does not change the metric since $A \cdot P = APA^\top = UU^\top = \mathrm{Id}$ and $A \cdot W_i = UP^{-1/2} W_i P^{-1/2} U^\top$.

3.3.2.3 A symmetric space structures

The invariant metric construction considers the space of SPD matrices as the quotient $\mathcal{S}ym_n^+ = \mathrm{GL}^+(n)/\mathrm{SO}(n)$ (we take here the connected components of positive determinant to simplify), where $\mathrm{SO}(n)$ is the isotropy group of the identity matrix taken as the origin of $\mathcal{S}ym_n^+$. In this homogeneous space each SPD matrix P is seen as the equivalent class (a coset) of all invertible matrices

$A \in \mathrm{GL}^+(n)$ satisfying $A \, \mathrm{Id} \, A^\top = P$, that is, $A = P^{1/2}V$ for $V \in \mathrm{SO}(n)$. This polar decomposition of the positive linear group into the isotropy group times the SPD manifold can be expressed infinitesimally as the Lie algebra decomposition $\mathfrak{gl}^+(n) = \mathfrak{so}(n) \times \mathfrak{sim}(n)$, where the Lie algebra of the isotropy subgroup $\mathrm{SO}(n)$ is the algebra $\mathfrak{so}(n)$ of skew symmetric matrices (vertical vectors), and $\mathfrak{sim}(n)$ is a complementary space of horizontal vectors that we can choose to be the algebra of symmetric matrices, so that it is $Ad(\mathrm{SO}(n))$-invariant. It is important to realize that many different choices are possible for this complement, but the Ad-invariance and the invariant metric turn the homogeneous space into a naturally reductive homogeneous space for which geodesics are induced by one-parameter subgroups (see below).

In fact, we have in our case an even stronger structure, a symmetric space. Let us consider the mapping $s_P(Q) = P \, Q^{-1} \, P$. We have $s_P^{-1} = s_P$ and $s_P(P + \epsilon W) = P - \epsilon W + O(\epsilon^2)$ for $W \in T_P Sym_n^+$. Thus s_P is a smooth involution of Sym_n^+ that fixes P and acts on the tangent space at P by minus the identity. Moreover, it transforms a tangent vector W at Q into the tangent vector $W' = ds_P|_Q \, W = -P Q^{-1} W Q^{-1} P$ at $Q' = s_P(Q) = P \, Q^{-1} \, P$. Thus we see that our Riemannian metric is in fact invariant under this symmetry:

$$\langle W_1', W_2' \rangle_{Q'} = \mathrm{Tr}\left((Q')^{-1} W_1' (Q')^{-1} W_2' \right) = \mathrm{Tr}\left(Q^{-1} W_1 Q^{-1} W_2 \right)$$
$$= \langle W_1, W_2 \rangle_Q \, .$$

Our symmetry is thus an isometry. These properties establish that the space of SPD matrices with the above metric is a Riemannian symmetric space with more properties than general Riemannian manifolds. For instance, the curvature tensor is covariantly constant.

3.3.2.4 Geodesics

The determination of geodesics usually relies on the computation of the Christoffel symbols in general Riemannian manifolds. However, we may use more powerful tools since we have a naturally reductive homogeneous space. In these spaces geodesics going through a point are generated by the action of the horizontal one-parameter subgroups of the acting Lie group on that point [32,36,39]. In our case the one-parameter subgroups of the linear group are the curves $\exp(tA)$ for $t \in \mathbb{R}$, and the horizontal vectors are the symmetric matrices $A = A^\top \in \mathfrak{sim}(n)$. Thus the geodesic going through Id with tangent vector W need to have the form: $\Gamma_{(\mathrm{Id}, W)}(t) = \exp(tA) \cdot \mathrm{Id} = \exp(tA)\exp(tA)^\top$ with $W = A + A^\top$. Because A is symmetric (horizontal), we find that

$$\Gamma_{(\text{Id},W)}(t) = \exp(tW). \tag{3.10}$$

We obtain the geodesics starting at another point P thanks to the invariance: the geodesic starting at $A \cdot P$ with tangent vector $A \cdot W$ is the transport by the group action of the geodesic starting at P with tangent vector W. Taking $A = P^{-1/2}$ gives $P^{-1/2} \cdot \Gamma_{(P,W)}(t) = \left(\Gamma_{(\text{Id},P^{-1/2}\cdot W)}(t)\right)$ or, in short,

$$\Gamma_{(P,W)}(t) = P^{\frac{1}{2}} \exp\left(t P^{-\frac{1}{2}} W P^{-\frac{1}{2}}\right) P^{\frac{1}{2}}. \tag{3.11}$$

A different expression is appearing in some works. It can be related to this one thanks to the identity $\exp(WP^{-1})P = P\exp(P^{-1}W)$, which can be verified using the series expansion of the matrix exponential.

We now want to compute the distance by integrating the length along geodesics. Let $W = U\text{DIAG}(w_i)U^\top$ be a tangent vector at the identity. The tangent vector at time t to the geodesics $\Gamma_{(\text{Id},W)}(t) = \exp(tW)$ starting from the identity along W is

$$\frac{d\Gamma(t)}{dt} = U\text{DIAG}\left(w_i \exp(tw_i)\right)U^\top = \Gamma(t)^{\frac{1}{2}} W \Gamma(t)^{\frac{1}{2}} = \Gamma(t)^{\frac{1}{2}} \cdot W.$$

This is the transport of the initial tangent vector by the group action. Thus, thanks to our invariant metric, the norm of this vector is constant: $\|\Gamma(t)^{1/2} \cdot W\|^2_{\Gamma(t)^{1/2} \cdot \text{Id}} = \|W\|^2_{\text{Id}}$. This was expected since geodesics are parameterized by arc length. Thus the length of the curve between time 0 and 1 is

$$\mathcal{L} = \int_0^1 \left\|\frac{d\Gamma(t)}{dt}\right\|^2_{\Gamma(t)} dt = \|W\|^2_{\text{Id}}.$$

Solving for $\Gamma_{(\text{Id},W)}(1) = P$, we obtain the distance to identity $N(P) = \text{dist}^2(P, \text{Id}) = \|\log(P)\|^2_{\text{Id}} = \sum_i (\log d_i)^2$ of Eq. (3.9). To obtain the distance from another point, we use the invariance properties of our metric, as in Section 3.3.1:

$$\text{dist}(P, Q) = \text{dist}\left(\text{Id}, P^{-\frac{1}{2}} Q P^{-\frac{1}{2}}\right) = \left\|\log\left(P^{-1/2} Q P^{-1/2}\right)\right\|^2_{\text{Id}}.$$

With the geodesic equation and the distance formula, we clearly see that SPD matrices with null eigenvalues are the limits at infinity of geodesics with positive eigenvalues everywhere. The other side of this geodesic has the corresponding eigenvalues going to infinity. Symmetric matrices with infinite and null eigenvalues are thus as far from any SPD matrix that they could be, at infinity. This contrasts with the flat Euclidean metric where zero eigenvalues PSD matrices are at finite distance: the cone of SPD matrices is neither geodesically complete nor metrically complete with the Euclidean metric. From a computational point of view, the geodesic completeness of the affine-invariant structure ensures that any finite geodesic walking scheme will remain in the space of SPD matrices, contrarily to the Euclidean case.

3.3.2.5 Riemannian exponential and log maps

As in all geodesically complete Riemannian manifolds, geodesics map the tangent space at P to a neighborhood of P in the manifold: $\Gamma_{(P,W)}(1) = \text{Exp}_P(W)$ associates with each tangent vector $W \in T_P Sym_n^+$ a point of the manifold. This mapping is a local diffeomorphism called the exponential map, because it corresponds to the usual exponential in some matrix groups. This is exactly our case for the exponential map around the identity:

$$\text{Exp}_{\text{Id}}(U D U^\top) = \exp(U D U^\top) = U \text{DIAG}\left(\exp(d_i)\right) U^\top.$$

However, the Riemannian exponential map associated with our invariant metric has a more complex expression at other SPD matrices:

$$\text{Exp}_P(W) = P^{\frac{1}{2}} \exp\left(P^{-\frac{1}{2}} W P^{-\frac{1}{2}}\right) P^{\frac{1}{2}}. \tag{3.12}$$

In our case this diffeomorphism is global, and we can uniquely define the inverse mapping everywhere:

$$\overrightarrow{PQ} = \text{Log}_P(Q) = P^{\frac{1}{2}} \log\left(P^{-\frac{1}{2}} Q P^{-\frac{1}{2}}\right) P^{\frac{1}{2}}. \tag{3.13}$$

Thus Exp_P gives us a collection of one-to-one complete charts of the manifold centered at any point P.

3.3.3 The one-parameter family of affine-invariant metrics

We can question the uniqueness of the previous affine-invariant Riemannian metric. Indeed, the previous construction uses one particular scalar product at the identity (the Frobenius one), but other scalar products could also work. It was shown in [63,64] that there is in fact a one-parameter family of such affine-invariant Riemannian metrics on SPD matrices that all share the same connection. This is the affine-invariant connection on homogeneous spaces of [57], well known in symmetric spaces [39, 36,32].

3.3.3.1 GL(n)-*invariant metrics*

A GL(n)-invariant scalar product has to satisfy $\langle V, W \rangle_P = \langle AVA^\top, AWA^\top \rangle_{APA^\top}$. In particular, this should be true for the isotropy group of the identity (the linear transformations that leave the identity matrix unchanged, the rotation matrices). All the rotationally invariant scalar products on symmetric matrices are given (up to a constant global multiplicative factor) by

$$\langle V, W \rangle_{\mathrm{Id}} = \mathrm{Tr}(VW) + \beta \mathrm{Tr}(V)\mathrm{Tr}(W) \qquad \text{with } \beta > -\frac{1}{n},$$

where n is the dimension of the space (see e.g. [63,64]). The sketch of the proof is the following: these scalar products are derived from rotationally invariant norms $\|W\|^2$, which are quadratic forms on (symmetric) matrices. By isotropy such forms can only depend on the matrix invariants $\mathrm{Tr}(W)$, $\mathrm{Tr}(W^2)$, $\mathrm{Tr}(W^3)$, and so on. However, as the form is quadratic in W, we are left only with $\mathrm{Tr}(W)^2$ and $\mathrm{Tr}(W^2)$ that can be weighted by α and β. We easily verify that $\beta > -\alpha/n$ is a necessary and sufficient condition to ensure positive definiteness. This metric at the identity can then be transported at any point by the group action using the (symmetric or any other) square root $P^{1/2}$ considered as a group element:

$$
\begin{aligned}
\langle V, W \rangle_P &= \left\langle P^{-1/2}VP^{-1/2}, P^{-1/2}WP^{-1/2} \right\rangle_{\mathrm{Id}} \\
&= \alpha \mathrm{Tr}\left(VP^{-1}WP^{-1}\right) + \beta \mathrm{Tr}\left(VP^{-1}\right)\mathrm{Tr}\left(WP^{-1}\right)
\end{aligned}
$$

Theorem 3.1 (Family of affine-invariant metrics on SPD matrices [63,64]). *All the metrics on the space $\mathcal{S}ym_n^+$ of SPD matrices that are invariant under the* GL(n) *action* $A \cdot P = APA^\top$ *are given by the one-parameter family (up to a global scaling factor):*

$$\langle V, W \rangle_P = \mathit{Tr}\left(VP^{-1}WP^{-1}\right) + \beta \mathit{Tr}\left(VP^{-1}\right)\mathit{Tr}\left(WP^{-1}\right)$$

$$\mathit{with}\ \beta > -\frac{1}{n}. \tag{3.14}$$

For $\beta = 0$, we retrieve the affine-invariant metric that was proposed in [71,28,8,27,48,66]. Up to our knowledge, the only case of a different invariant metric was proposed by [46] with $\beta = -1/(n+1)$. This metric was obtained by embedding the space of SPD matrices of dimension n into the space of $n + 1$ square matrices using homogeneous coordinates and by quotienting out $(n + 1)$-dimensional rotations. This type of embedding is interesting as it allows us to represent also the mean of Gaussian distributions in addition to its covariance matrix. The embedding can be done in spaces of square matrices of dimension $n + k$ ($k \geq 1$), in which case we would obtain the invariant metric with $\beta = -1/(n + k)$. It is interesting that the metric proposed by [46] with $-1/\beta = n + 1$ is the first authorized integer to obtain a proper metric.

Although many people favor the value $\beta = 0$, there is no invariance reason to do so. Indeed, the general linear group $\mathrm{GL}(n)$ can be seen as the direct product $\mathrm{GL}(n) = \mathrm{SL}(n) \otimes \mathbb{R}^*$, where $\mathrm{SL}(n)$ is the unimodular group (unit determinant matrices), and $\mathbb{R}^*$ is the multiplicative group of real numbers. Likewise, SPD matrices can be decomposed into unimodular SPD matrices $\mathcal{U}\mathcal{S}ym_n^+ = \{P \in \mathcal{S}ym_n^+, \det(P) = 1\}$ and their determinant in $\mathbb{R}_*^+$: $\mathcal{S}ym_n^+ = \mathcal{U}\mathcal{S}ym_n^+ \otimes \mathbb{R}_*^+$. The split decomposes an element of the tangent space at identity $W \in T_{\mathrm{Id}}\mathcal{S}ym_n^+$ into the traceless part $W_0 = W - \mathrm{Tr}(W)/n \, \mathrm{Id}$ and the trace part $\mathrm{Tr}(W) \in \mathbb{R}$. Since the group action splits into two independent group actions, we can choose an invariant metric on each part and recombine them afterward. For the unimodular part $\mathcal{U}\mathcal{S}ym_n^+$, the $\mathrm{SL}(n)$-invariant metric at $P \in \mathcal{U}\mathcal{S}ym_n^+$ is uniquely defined by $< V_0, W_0 >_P = \mathrm{Tr}(V_0 P^{-1} W_0 P^{-1})$ (up to a scale factor), since the trace part of each tangent vector vanishes. Likewise, the multiplicative-invariant metric on the scale is unique (up to a scale factor). Now, when recombining both parts, we can independently scale the two parts with the direct product, which exactly describes all the $\mathrm{GL}(n)$-invariant metrics on SPD matrices.

In the limit case $\beta = -1/n$ the bilinear form becomes degenerate in the direction of the trace of the matrix at the identity: $\|V - \mathrm{Tr}(V)\,\mathrm{Id}\|_{\mathrm{Id}} = \|V\|_{\mathrm{Id}}$. This direction in the tangent space corresponds to the scalar multiplication of SPD matrices: the SPD matrix $s\,P$ (for any $s > 0$) is at null distance of the SPD matrix P with this metric. Thus this is still defining a metric on the space of unimodular SPD matrices, but not on the full SPD matrix space. For $\beta < -1/n$, the bilinear form has a negative eigenvalue in the trace direction and defines a semi-Riemannian metric.

3.3.3.2 Different metrics for a unique affine connection

The Koszul formula below is the key step to establish the uniqueness of the Levi-Civita connection of a Riemannian metric [15, p. 55]:

$$2 \langle \nabla_V W, U \rangle = \partial_V \langle W, U \rangle + \partial_W \langle V, U \rangle - \partial_U \langle V, W \rangle$$
$$+ \langle [V, W], U \rangle - \langle [V, U], W \rangle - \langle [W, U], V \rangle.$$

In our case, expanding the terms in the Koszul formula by chain rule and using $\partial_X \Sigma^{-1} = -\Sigma^{-1}(\partial_X \Sigma)\,\Sigma^{-1}$, we obtain that all the affine-invariant metrics have the same Levi-Civita connection:

$$\nabla_V W = \partial_V W - \frac{1}{2}(V P^{-1} W + W P^{-1} V). \qquad (3.15)$$

This formula is in agreement with the connection computed for $\beta = 0$ by [71] (note that $\partial_V W$ is omitted in this work).

Since all the invariant metrics have the same Levi-Civita connection, they share the same geodesics and the Riemannian exp and log maps at each point:

$$\begin{aligned}
\mathrm{Exp}_P(W) &= P^{1/2} \exp\left(P^{-1/2} W P^{-1/2}\right) P^{1/2}, \\
\overrightarrow{PQ} = \mathrm{Log}_P(Q) &= P^{1/2} \log\left(P^{-1/2} Q P^{-1/2}\right) P^{1/2}.
\end{aligned}$$

However, we should be careful that the orthonormal bases are different for each metric, which means that distances along the geodesics are different. The Riemannian distance is obtained as before by integration or more easily by the norm of the initial tangent vector of the geodesic joining the two points:

$$\begin{aligned}
\mathrm{dist}^2(P, Q) = \|\mathrm{Log}_P(Q)\|_P^2 &= \left\| P^{-1/2} \mathrm{Log}_P(Q) P^{-1/2} \right\|_{\mathrm{Id}}^2 \\
&= \mathrm{Tr}\left(\log(Q P^{-1})^2\right) + \beta \mathrm{Tr}\left(\log(Q P^{-1})\right)^2.
\end{aligned}$$

3.3.3.3 Orthonormal coordinate systems

For many computations, it is convenient to use a minimal representation (e.g. six parameters for 3×3 SPD matrices) in an orthonormal basis. In classical Euclidean matrix spaces this can be realized through the classical "Vec" operator that maps the element $a_{i,j}$ of an $n \times n$ matrix A to the $(in+j)$th element $\mathrm{Vec}(A)_{in+j}$ of an n^2-dimensional vector $\mathrm{Vec}(A)$. Since we are working with symmetric matrices, we have only $d = n(n+1)/2$ independent coefficients, say the upper triangular part of the symmetric matrix $W \in T_P \mathcal{S}ym_n^+$. This corresponds to taking the basis vectors $F_{ii} = e_i e_i^{\top}$ and $F_{ij} = e_i e_j^{\top} + e_j e_i^{\top}$ $(1 \le i < j \le n)$ for the space of symmetric matrices, where the e_i are the standard basis vectors of $\mathbb{R}^n$. However, this basis is not orthonormal at the identity: a direct computation of the Gram matrix

$$g_{ij,kl} = \langle F_{ij}, F_{kl} \rangle_{\mathrm{Id}} = \mathrm{Tr}(F_{ij} F_{kl}) + \beta \mathrm{Tr}(F_{ij})(F_{kl})$$

shows that the nonzero terms are $g_{ii,ii} = \|F_{ii}\|_{\mathrm{Id}}^2 = 1 + \beta$, $g_{ii,jj} = \beta$ for $j \neq i$, and $g_{ij,ij} = \|F_{ij}\|_{\mathrm{Id}}^2 = 2$ for $i < j$.

A field of orthonormal bases for $\beta = 0$

The previous nonorthonormal basis can be easily corrected for $\beta = 0$ by normalizing the basis vectors for the off-diagonal coefficient: an orthonormal basis of $T_{\mathrm{Id}}\mathcal{S}ym_n^+$ for the affine-invariant metric with $\beta = 0$ is given by the vectors

$$
E_{ij}^0 = \left\{ \begin{array}{ll} e_i e_i^\top & (1 \leq i = j \leq n), \\ (e_i e_j^\top + e_j e_i^\top)/\sqrt{2} & (1 \leq i < j \leq n). \end{array} \right.
$$

The vector of coordinates in this basis is

$$
\mathrm{Vec}_{\mathrm{Id}}^0(W) = \left(w_{1,1}, \ldots, w_{n,n}, \sqrt{2}\, w_{1,2}, \ldots, \sqrt{2}\, w_{(n-1)n} \right)^\top.
$$

This realizes an explicit isomorphism between $T_{\mathrm{Id}}\mathcal{S}ym_n^+$ endowed with the Frobenius metric and $\mathbb{R}^d$ with the L_2 metric.

It is important to notice that the above basis is orthonormal only at the identity and not at other places due to the curvature of the Riemannian manifold: a field of orthonormal bases usually depends on the base-point P of the tangent space $T_P\mathcal{S}ym_n^+$. Such a frame-field can be obtained by the group action since we are dealing with a naturally reductive homogeneous space: $E_{ij}^0|_P = P^{\frac{1}{2}} E_{ij}^0 P^{\frac{1}{2}}$ with $1 \leq i \leq j \leq n$. Because there are no closed geodesics, $E_{ij}^0|_P$ is a smooth vector field over $\mathcal{S}ym_n^+$, and the set of vectors fields $\{E_{ij}^0|_P\}_{1 \leq i \leq j \leq n}$ constitutes a smooth global frame-field. Moreover, the vector of coordinates $\mathrm{Vec}_P^0(W) = \mathrm{Vec}_{\mathrm{Id}}^0(P^{-1/2} \cdot W) = \mathrm{Vec}_{\mathrm{Id}}^0(P^{-1/2} W P^{-1/2})$ in the frame at point P also realizes an explicit isomorphism between $T_P\mathcal{S}ym_n^+$ with the metric $\langle U, V \rangle_P^0 = \mathrm{Tr}(U P^{-1} V P^{-1})$ and $\mathbb{R}^d$ with the canonical L_2 metric.

A field of orthonormal bases for $\beta \neq 0$

To obtain an orthonormal basis for the affine-invariant metric with $\beta \neq 0$, we can build an isomorphism of Riemannian manifolds by modifying the trace part. First, we observe that $A_\alpha(V) = V - \alpha \mathrm{Tr}(V) \mathrm{Id}$ is a linear map of the space of symmetric matrices identified to $T_{\mathrm{Id}}\mathcal{S}ym_n^+$. This map leaves the off-diagonal coefficients unchanged and transforms the diagonal basis vectors according to

$$
E_{ii}^\beta = A_\alpha(E_{ii}^0) = E_{ii}^0 - \alpha \sum_{j=1}^n E_{jj}^0.
$$

Thus when restricted to the basis $(E_{11}^0, \ldots, E_{nn}^0)$, this mapping can be written in matrix form $A_\alpha = \mathrm{Id}_n - \alpha \mathbb{1}_n \mathbb{1}_n^\top$ with $\mathbb{1}_n^\top = (1, \ldots, 1)$

(we should be careful that this matrix just operates on the diagonal of symmetric matrices and not on the standard Euclidean space $\mathbb{R}^n$). Its determinant is $\det(A_\alpha) = \det(\operatorname{Id}_n - \alpha \mathbb{1}_n \mathbb{1}_n^\top) = 1 - \alpha n$, so that the linear map has positive determinant if $\alpha < 1/n$. Thus we can invert it by Sherman–Morrison formula to get $A_\alpha^{-1} = \operatorname{Id} + \alpha \mathbb{1}_n \mathbb{1}_n^\top / (1 - \alpha n)$.

Now we can look for the value of α such that the mapping A_α transforms the affine-invariant metric $\langle \cdot, \cdot \rangle_P$ of Eq. (3.14) with $\beta \neq 0$ to the previous affine invariant metric with $\beta = 0$. This equation reads $\langle A_\alpha(V), A_\alpha(W) \rangle_P = \langle A_0(V), A_0(W) \rangle_P$, or

$$\operatorname{Tr}(A_\alpha(V) P^{-1} A_\alpha(W) P^{-1}) + \beta \operatorname{Tr}(A_\alpha(V) P^{-1}) \operatorname{Tr}(A_\alpha(W) P^{-1})$$
$$= \operatorname{Tr}(V P^{-1} W P^{-1}).$$

Thanks to the invariance, this is verified for all P if this holds for $P = \operatorname{Id}$. Plugging $A_\alpha(V) = V - \alpha \operatorname{Tr}(V) \operatorname{Id}$ into the above equation with $P = \operatorname{Id}$ leads to

$$\operatorname{Tr}((V - \alpha \operatorname{Tr}(V) \operatorname{Id})(W - \alpha \operatorname{Tr}(W) \operatorname{Id})) + \beta (1 - n\alpha)^2 \operatorname{Tr}(V) \operatorname{Tr}(W)$$
$$= \operatorname{Tr}(VW).$$

Thus we have to solve $n\alpha^2 - 2\alpha + \beta(1 - n\alpha)^2 = 0$. This leads to the second-order equation $n\alpha^2 - 2\alpha + \beta/(1 + n\beta) = 0$. Because $\beta > -1/n$, it has two solutions, and the one that gives a positive determinant for the linear mapping A_α is $\alpha = \frac{1}{n}\left(1 - 1/\sqrt{1 + n\beta}\right)$. We can now verify by direct computation of the Gram matrix that the vectors

$$E_{ij} = \begin{cases} e_i e_i^\top - \alpha \operatorname{Id} & (1 \leq i = j \leq n), \\ (e_i e_j^\top + e_j e_i^\top)/\sqrt{2} & (1 \leq i < j \leq n), \end{cases}$$

constitute an orthonormal basis of $T_{\operatorname{Id}} Sym_n^+$ with the affine-invariant metric with any value of $\beta > -1/n$. By invariance the vectors $\{E_{ij}|_P = P^{1/2} E_{ij} P^{1/2}\}_{1 \leq i \leq j \leq n}$ form an orthonormal basis of $T_P Sym_n^+$ for the affine-invariant metric.

To obtain a mapping $\operatorname{Vec}_P(W)$ that realizes an explicit isomorphism between $T_P Sym_n^+$ with the general affine-invariant metric and $\mathbb{R}^d$ with the canonical L_2 metric, we have first to transport W to the tangent space at identity using the action of $P^{-1/2}$ and then use the inverse mapping A_α^{-1} on the diagonal coefficients before using the previous mapping $\operatorname{Vec}_{\operatorname{Id}}^0$:

$$\operatorname{Vec}_P(W) = \operatorname{Vec}_{\operatorname{Id}}(P^{-\frac{1}{2}} W P^{-\frac{1}{2}}) = \operatorname{Vec}_{\operatorname{Id}}^0(A_\alpha^{-1}(P^{-\frac{1}{2}} W P^{-\frac{1}{2}})).$$

Since $A_\alpha^{-1}(V) = V + \alpha \operatorname{Tr}(V) \operatorname{Id}/(1 - \alpha n) = V + \frac{1}{n}\left(\sqrt{1 + \beta n} - 1\right) \times \operatorname{Tr}(V) \operatorname{Id}$, we get the following theorem.

Theorem 3.2 (Orthonormal field for the affine invariant metric).
The $d = n(n-1)/2$ vectors

$$
E_{ij}|_P = \begin{cases} P^{\frac{1}{2}} e_i e_i^\top P^{\frac{1}{2}} - \frac{1}{n}\left(1 - \frac{1}{\sqrt{1+n\beta}}\right) P & (1 \le i = j \le n), \\ P^{\frac{1}{2}}(e_i e_j^\top + e_j e_i^\top) P^{\frac{1}{2}}/\sqrt{2} & (1 \le i < j \le n), \end{cases}
$$

*form an orthonormal basis of $T_P Sym_n^+$ with the affine-invariant
metric for any value of $\beta > -1/n$. Moreover, the mapping $\mathrm{Vec}_P(W) =$
$\mathrm{Vec}_{\mathrm{Id}}(P^{-\frac{1}{2}} W P^{-\frac{1}{2}})$ with*

$$
\mathrm{Vec}_{\mathrm{Id}}(W) = \left(w_{1,1} + \delta, \dots w_{n,n} + \delta, \sqrt{2} w_{1,2}, \dots \sqrt{2} w_{(n-1),n}\right)^\top
$$
$$
and \quad \delta = \frac{1}{n}\left(\sqrt{1+\beta n} - 1\right) Tr(W)
$$

*realizes an explicit isomorphism between $T_P Sym_n^+$ with the general
affine-invariant metric and $\mathbb{R}^d$ with the canonical L_2 metric.*

3.3.4 Curvature of affine-invariant metrics

Thanks to the explicit expression of the connection, we can
compute the Riemannian curvature tensor $R(V, W)U = \nabla_V \nabla_W U -
\nabla_W \nabla_V U - \nabla_{[V,W]} U$. We find

$$
R(V, W)U = \frac{1}{4}\left(W P^{-1} V P^{-1} U + U P^{-1} V P^{-1} W - V P^{-1} W P^{-1} U \right.
$$
$$
\left. - U P^{-1} W P^{-1} V\right).
$$

Equivalently, the $(0, 4)$-Riemannian curvature tensor is given by

$$
\begin{aligned}
R(U, V, W, Z) &= \langle R(U, V)Z, W \rangle \\
&= \frac{1}{2}\mathrm{Tr}\left(U P^{-1} V P^{-1} W P^{-1} Z P^{-1} - U P^{-1} V P^{-1} Z P^{-1} W P^{-1}\right).
\end{aligned}
$$

The conventions used here are those of section 1.4.4 of chapter 1.
Notice that there is a factor -2 with respect to the formula of [71],
which is due to a global scaling of $1/2$ of their Riemannian metric
with respect to ours when $\beta = 0$ and an opposite convention for
the $(0, 4)$ Riemannian tensor.

3.3.4.1 Sectional curvature

From this tensor we get the sectional curvature $\kappa(U, V)|_P$ in the
subspaces spanned by the vector fields U and V at P (see Eq. (1.12)

in chapter 1). We recall that this measures the Gauss curvature of the 2D geodesic surface generated by linear combinations of the two vectors. This is the function

$$\kappa(U, V) = \frac{\langle R(U, V)V, U \rangle}{\langle U, U \rangle \langle V, V \rangle - \langle U, V \rangle^2} = \frac{R(U, V, U, V)}{\langle U, U \rangle \langle V, V \rangle - \langle U, V \rangle^2}.$$

This sectional curvature can be computed easily in our previous orthonormal basis $E_{ij}|_P$. We find that the only nonzero terms are independent of P:

$$\kappa(E_{ii}, E_{ij}) = \kappa(E_{ii}|_P, E_{ij}|_P) = \kappa(E_{ij}|_P, E_{jj}|_P) = -\frac{1}{4} \quad (j \neq i),$$

$$\kappa(E_{ij}, E_{ik}) = \kappa(E_{ij}|_P, E_{ik}|_P) = \kappa(E_{ij}|_P, E_{kj}|_P) = -\frac{1}{8} \quad (i \neq j \neq k \neq i).$$

Other 2-subspaces are obtained by rotating the vectors $U|_P$ and $V|_P$ with respect to our orthonormal basis vectors. The sectional curvature is thus in between $\kappa_{\min} = -1/4$ and $\kappa_{\max} = 0$. In consequence, the manifold of SPD matrices with any affine-invariant metric has bounded nonpositive curvature and is a Hadamard manifold.

Thanks to our well-chosen orthonormal basis, it is immediately clear that the sectional curvature is "the same" at every point of the manifold. This is *not* a constant curvature since it varies depending on the chosen 2-subspace within the tangent space, but it is comparable at every point up to a rotation. This is a feature of homogeneous manifolds: there exists a way to compare the geometry at every point thanks to the group action. The fact that the sectional curvature does not depend on β was expected since all the affine-invariant Riemannian spaces are isomorphic to each other.

To compare our results to those of [71] for $\beta = 0$, we have to compute the curvature in the planes spanned by two vectors of the basis $\{F_{ij}\}$. We recall that this basis is orthogonal but not orthonormal at Id, and not orthogonal at other values of P. In our case we find $\kappa(F_{ii}, F_{ij})|_P = -1/4$. Because of the nonorthogonality of this basis at $P \neq$ Id, we also get the extra nonvanishing term $\kappa(F_{ii}, F_{ij})|_P = -\frac{1}{2}\bar{\rho}_{ij}^2/(1 + \bar{\rho}_{ij}^2)$, where $\bar{\rho}_{ij}^2 = (e_i^\top P^{-1} e_j)^2/(e_i^\top P^{-1} e_i e_j^\top P^{-1} e_j)$ is the ij partial correlation coefficient of P. These results are consistent with those of [71], up to a factor 2 due the global scaling of the metric. Surprisingly, the nonvanishing term $\kappa(E_{ij}, E_{ik}) = -1/8$ seems to be forgotten in their work.

3.3.4.2 Ricci curvature

The Ricci curvature is the trace of the linear operator $U \to R(U, V)Z$. In coordinates this writes $\text{Ric}_{ab} = R^c_{acb} = g^{dc}R_{dacb} = \sum_c R(e_c, e_a, e_c, e_b)$, where the right-hand side is only valid in an orthonormal basis $\{e_c\}$. Because this is a bilinear form, it is entirely described by the quadratic form $\text{Ric}(V)|_P = \text{Ric}(V, V)|_P$ for all the unit vectors in the tangent space at P; $\text{Ric}(V)$ is thus is the average (up to a scale factor n) of the sectional curvatures $\kappa(V, W)$ of 2-planes of the tangent space containing the vector V, assuming that W follows a uniform distribution on the unit sphere in the tangent space. The scalar curvature is the metric trace of the Ricci curvature matrix: $R = \text{Tr}_g(\text{Ric}) = g^{ab}R_{ab}$. The scalar curvature describes how the volume of geodesic ball in a manifold deviates from the volume of standard Euclidean ball with the same radius.

In dimensions 2 and 3 the Ricci curvature determines the Riemannian curvature tensor, like the sectional curvature. In dimension greater than 3 the sectional curvature continues to determine the full curvature tensor but the Ricci curvature generally contains less information. However, it encodes important information about the diffusion on the manifold (using the Laplace–Beltrami operator) since $\text{Ric}(V)|_P$ encodes how the volume of an infinitesimal neighborhood of a point evolves when it is transported along the geodesic starting at P in the direction V. In a normal coordinate system at P we have indeed the Taylor expansion or the Riemannian measure:

$$ d\mathcal{M}\left(\text{Exp}_P(V)\right) = \left(1 - \tfrac{1}{6}\text{Ric}(V)|_P + O(\|V\|^3_P)\right) dV. $$

A related formulation is developed in the excellent paper of Yann Ollivier *a visual introduction to curvature* [59]: if C is a small neighborhood of P, then the volume of the neighborhood $C_V = \{\exp_Q(\Pi^Q_P V), Q \in C\}$ transported along the geodesics in the direction V evolves at second order in V with the multiplicative factor $(1 - \tfrac{1}{6}\text{Ric}(V)|_P)$. Thus a negative Ricci curvature indicates a volume expansion of the neighborhood, whereas a positive curvature indicates a volume contraction in the direction V.

Coming back to SPD matrices with the affine-invariant metric, we want to compute the Ricci curvature in our orthonormal basis $\{E_{ij}|_P\}$ at any point P. Using $E_{ij}|_P = P^{1/2}E_{ij}P^{1/2}$ and the above expression of the $(0, 4)$ Riemannian tensor, we get that

$$ R(E_{ab}|_P, E_{ij}|_P, E_{ab}|_P, E_{kl}|_P) = \frac{1}{2}\text{Tr}\left(E_{ab}E_{ij}E_{ab}E_{kl} - E_{ab}E_{ij}E_{kl}E_{ab}\right). $$

Thus we see that the Ricci curvature matrix at any point is the same as at identity *in our specific coordinate system*:

$$\text{Ric}(E_{ij}, E_{kl}) = \sum_{1 \leq a \leq b \leq n} R(E_{ab}, E_{ij}, E_{ab}, E_{kl})$$

$$= \frac{1}{2} \sum_{1 \leq a \leq b \leq n} \text{Tr}\left(E_{ab} E_{ij} E_{ab} E_{kl} - E_{ab} E_{ij} E_{kl} E_{ab}\right).$$

Lengthy computations verified by computer show that only the following terms do not vanish: $\text{Ric}(E_{ii}, E_{ii}) = -\frac{n-1}{4}$, $\text{Ric}(E_{ij}, E_{ij}) = -\frac{n}{4}$ for $i \neq j$, and $\text{Ric}(E_{ii}, E_{jj}) = \frac{1}{4}$. Ordering the n diagonal basis vectors E_{ii} before the $n(n-1)/2$ off-diagonal basis vectors E_{ij} ($i < j$), we obtain the following diagonal by block Ricci curvature matrix:

$$\text{Ric} = -\frac{n}{4} \begin{bmatrix} \text{Id}_n - \frac{1}{n} \mathbb{1}_n \mathbb{1}_n^\top & 0 \\ 0 & \text{Id}_{n(n-1)/2} \end{bmatrix}.$$

We easily see that this matrix has one eigenvector $(\mathbb{1}_n^\top, 0_{n(n-1)/2})^\top$ with eigenvalue 0 and $d - 1$ orthogonal eigenvectors associated with the multiple eigenvalue $-n/4$. The null eigenvalue along the trace part in the tangent space of SPD matrices at identity (which corresponds to a scalar multiplication of SPD matrices when it is exponentiated) means that the volume of a neighborhood remains constant when we shoot in the direction of SPD matrix rescaling. In all other directions the Ricci curvature is negative, which indicates that a neighborhood is volume increasing.

Theorem 3.3 (Curvature of affine-invariant metrics). *The space $\mathcal{S}ym_n^+$ of SPD matrices of dimension $n \geq 2$ endowed with the affine invariant metric*

$$\langle V, W \rangle_P = Tr\left(V P^{-1} W P^{-1}\right) + \beta Tr\left(V P^{-1}\right) Tr\left(W P^{-1}\right)$$

with $\beta > -\frac{1}{n}$ has the Riemannian curvature tensor

$$R(U, V, W, Z)$$
$$= \langle R(U, V)Z, W \rangle$$
$$= \frac{1}{2} Tr\left(U P^{-1} V P^{-1} W P^{-1} Z P^{-1} - U P^{-1} V P^{-1} Z P^{-1} W P^{-1}\right).$$

$$(3.16)$$

The sectional curvature is

$$\kappa(E_{ij}, E_{ik}) = \kappa(E_{ij}, E_{ki}) = \begin{cases} -\frac{1}{8} & \text{if } i \neq j \neq k \neq i, \\ -\frac{1}{4} & \text{if } j = i \neq k \text{ or } k = i \neq j, \\ 0 & \text{otherwise.} \end{cases}$$

(3.17)

The Ricci curvature matrix is block-diagonal:

$$\text{Ric} = -\frac{n}{4} \begin{bmatrix} \text{Id}_n - \frac{1}{n}\mathbb{1}_n\mathbb{1}_n^\top & 0 \\ 0 & \text{Id}_{n(n-1)/2} \end{bmatrix}.$$

(3.18)

It has one vanishing eigenvalue along the trace-part and $(d-1)$ orthogonal eigenvectors associated with the multiple eigenvalue $-n/4$. Finally, the scalar curvature is

$$R = -\frac{n(n-1)(n+2)}{8}.$$

(3.19)

The sectional, Ricci, and scalar curvatures are nonpositive.

3.4 Basic statistical operations on SPD matrices

Now that we have the atomic Exp and Log maps for SPD matrices and that we have reviewed the main geometrical properties of the affine-invariant structure on SPD matrices, let us turn to statistical inference methods in this space. As the manifold has a nonpositive curvature and there is no cut locus (the injection radius is infinite), the statistical properties detailed in previous chapters hold in their most general form.

3.4.1 Computing the mean and the covariance matrix

Let $P_1, \ldots, P_m$ be a set of measurements of SPD matrices. It can be seen as a distribution using a mixture of delta Diracs at the sample points, $\mu = \frac{1}{m}\sum_{i=1}^{n}\delta_{P_i}$. We recall from Chapter 2 that the empirical Fréchet mean is the set of SPD matrices minimizing the sum of squared distances $\text{Var}(P) = \frac{1}{m}\sum_{i=1}^{m}\text{dist}^2(P, P_i)$. Since the manifold has no cut-locus, the variance is everywhere smooth.

The first-order moment of the sample distribution is the contravariant vector field defined all over the SPD matrix manifold by

$$\mathfrak{M}_1(P) = \int_{\mathcal{M}} \overrightarrow{PQ}\, \mu(dQ) = \frac{1}{m}\sum_{i=1}^{m} \overrightarrow{PP_i}$$

$$= \frac{1}{m} \sum_{i=1}^{m} P^{\frac{1}{2}} \log \left(P^{-\frac{1}{2}} P_i P^{-\frac{1}{2}} \right) P^{\frac{1}{2}}. \qquad (3.20)$$

Note that this expression cannot be further simplified in general when the data P_i and the matrix P do not commute. The gradient of the variance is related very simply to this first-order moment by $\nabla \mathrm{Var}(P) = -2\,\mathfrak{M}_1(P)$, and the critical points of the variance (exponential barycenters) are the zeros of this field. Because SPD matrices have a nonpositive curvature and an infinite injection radius with an affine invariant metric, there is one and only one global minimum, that is, the Fréchet mean $\bar{P}$ is unique [38].

Algorithm 3.1 Intrinsic gradient descent to compute the mean SPD matrix.

Initialize

    Set current estimate of the mean with one of the data points, e.g., $\bar{P}_0 = P_1$.

    Set error $\epsilon_0 = \|\mathfrak{M}_1(\bar{P}_0)\|_{\bar{P}_0}$, step-size $\tau = 1/2$, and time $t = 0$.

Iterate

    $t = t + 1$.

    $\bar{P}_t = \mathrm{Exp}_{\bar{P}_{t-1}} \left(2\tau\, \mathfrak{M}_1(\bar{P}_{t-1}) \right)$.

    $\epsilon_t = \|\mathfrak{M}_1(\bar{P}_t)\|_{\bar{P}_t}$.

    if $\epsilon_t > \epsilon_{t-1}$ then $\tau = \tau/2$ and $\bar{P}_t = \bar{P}_{t-1}$.

Until $\epsilon_t < \epsilon$.

To compute this mean, we can use the gradient descent algorithm on the space of SPD matrices described in Algorithm 3.1. The idea is to follow the flow of the gradient of the variance for a certain time step τ:

$$\bar{P}_{t+1} = \mathrm{Exp}_{\bar{P}_t} \left(-\tau\, \nabla \mathrm{Var}(\bar{P}_t) \right) = \mathrm{Exp}_{\bar{P}_t} \left(2\tau\, \mathfrak{M}_1(\bar{P}_t) \right). \qquad (3.21)$$

With the time-step $\tau = 1/2$, this iterative algorithm corresponds to the classical Gauss–Newton gradient descent algorithm on manifolds, which was shown to be globally convergent when the data are sufficiently concentrated in Riemannian symmetric spaces and compact Lie groups [43,49]. In practice the Gauss–Newton algorithm converges very quickly when the data points are sufficiently close to each other.

However, the algorithm may diverge when the SPD matrices are too far away from each other, as noted in [27]. Sufficient conditions on the time-step τ for the convergence of the algorithm were established in [9] based on the condition numbers (ratio of minimal and maximal eigenvalues) of $\bar{P}_t^{-1/2} P_i \bar{P}_t^{-1/2}$. When the matrices $P_1, \ldots, P_n$ commute, the choice of $\tau = 1/2$ is in fact optimal and leads to a super-linear (quadratic) convergence. When these matrices are close to each other, a fast convergence is still expected, although it is not quadratic any more. However, when the matrices are far away from each other, [9] showed that the Gauss–Newton algorithm may diverge even if the matrices almost commute. For example, computing the mean of the three SPD matrices $\left(\begin{smallmatrix} 1 & 0 \\ 0 & 1 \end{smallmatrix}\right)$, $\left(\begin{smallmatrix} 2 & 1 \\ 1 & 2 \end{smallmatrix}\right)$, and $\left(\begin{smallmatrix} x & 1 \\ 1 & 2 \end{smallmatrix}\right)$ converges for $x = 1000$ but diverges for $x = 10000$. Thus it is generally necessary to use an adaptive time-step τ in the Riemannian gradient descent. One of the simplest adaptive algorithm is to start with $\tau = 1/2$ and decrease it instead of updating $\bar{P}_{t+1}$ when the variance increases during the optimization [27], as described in Algorithm 3.1.

The divergence of the Gauss–Newton scheme with a fixed time-step is due to the curvature of the manifold. This can be illustrated in constant curvature spaces, where we can explicitly compute the eigenvalues of the Hessian of the square Riemannian distance (see e.g. [65]). On the sphere (positive curvature), the eigenvalues are lower than 2 and can become negative when data leave the Kendall/Karcher conditions of uniqueness. Because the inverse of the Hessian is used to modulate the gradient in Newton methods, $\tau = 1/2$ is a conservative bound, which guaranties the convergence, with potentially a suboptimal rate. On the contrary, the Hessian has eigenvalues larger than 2 in the hyperbolic space (negative curvature), so that a time-step of $\tau = 1/2$ can be too large. Computing explicit tight bounds on the spectrum of the Hessian of the variance is possible in connected locally symmetric spaces [31], and this enables the use of Newton methods with a quadratic convergence rate.

The covariance, or second-order moment of the sample distribution, is the 2-contravariant field defined all over the SPD matrix manifold by the tensor product

$$\mathfrak{M}_2(P) = \int_{\mathcal{M}} \overrightarrow{PQ} \otimes \overrightarrow{PQ} \, \mu(dQ) = \frac{1}{m} \sum_{i=1}^{m} \overrightarrow{PP_i} \otimes \overrightarrow{PP_i}.$$

The covariance matrix is the value of this field at the Fréchet mean $\bar{P}$. This tensor can be expressed as a matrix in our orthonormal basis using the *Vec* mapping:

$$\Sigma = \frac{1}{m} \sum_{i=1}^{m} \mathrm{Vec}_{\bar{P}} \left(\overrightarrow{\bar{P}P_i} \right) \mathrm{Vec}_{\bar{P}} \left(\overrightarrow{\bar{P}P_i} \right)^{\top}.$$

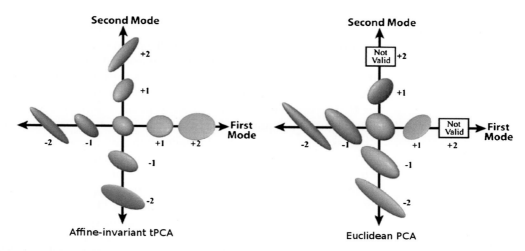

Figure 3.1. The first two modes of variation of the simulated data: (left) using the affine-invariant tPCA, and (right) using linear PCA. Units are in standard deviations. The boxes labeled "Not Valid" indicate that the tensor was not positive-definite, i.e., it had negative eigenvalues. Reprinted by permission from Elsevier, Signal Processing, Riemannian geometry for the statistical analysis of diffusion tensor data. P. Thomas Fletcher and Sarang Joshi, February 2007.

3.4.2 Tangent PCA and PGA of SPD matrices

Assume that we have computed the sample Fréchet mean $\bar{P}$ and the sample covariance matrix Σ of a set of SPD matrices. We may want to identify subspaces of low dimensions that best approximate our SPD data. In Euclidean spaces this is usually done using Principal Component Analysis (PCA). As explained in Chapter 2, we have several choices in a manifold. We can first maximize the explained variance, which corresponds to choosing the subspace generated by the eigenvectors of the largest eigenvalues of the covariance matrix. This is called tangent PCA (tPCA). We can also minimize the unexplained variance, which is measured by the sum of square of residues, which are the tangent vectors pointing from each data point to the closest point on the geodesic subspace generated by k modes at the mean (Principal Geodesic Analysis, PGA).

Fig. 3.1, adapted from [27], presents an example of the difference between PCA on SPD matrices with the Euclidean metric and tPCA with one of the affine-invariant metrics. One of the main differences is that any matrix generated by the principal geodesic subspace remains positive definite, contrarily to the Euclidean PCA.

3.4.3 Gaussian distributions on SPD matrices

Several definitions have been proposed to extend the notion of Gaussian distribution to Riemannian manifolds. The natural definition from the stochastic point of view is the heat kernel $p_t(x, y)$, which is the transition density of the Brownian motion (see Chapter 4). The heat kernel is the smallest positive fundamental solution to the heat equation $\frac{\partial f}{\partial t} - \Delta f = 0$, where $\Delta f = \text{Tr}_g(\text{Hess } f) = g^{ij}(\text{Hess } f)_{ij} = \nabla^i \nabla_i f$ is the Laplace–Beltrami operator. However, the heat kernel has a nonlinear dependency in time, which makes it difficult to use in statistics as a classical Gaussian distribution.

To obtain more tractable formulas, the wrapped Gaussian distribution was proposed in several domains [34,52]. The idea is to take a Gaussian distribution in the tangent space at the mean value and to consider the push-forward distribution on the manifold that wraps the distribution along the closed geodesics. The proper renormalization of this push-forward distribution is an issue since the renormalization constant includes infinite series along these closed geodesics. The wrapped Gaussian distribution naturally corresponds to the infinitesimal heat kernel for small time steps and tends toward the Dirac mass distribution if the variance goes to zero. In the compact case it also tends toward the Riemannian uniform distribution for a large variance. [58] considered an extension of this definition with noncentered Gaussian distributions on the tangent spaces of the manifold in order to tackle the asymptotic properties of estimators. In this case the mean value is generally not anymore simply linked to the Gaussian parameters.

A third approach, detailed further, considers the probability density function (pdf) that minimizes the information (or equivalently maximizes the entropy) knowing the mean and the covariance matrix. This approach was taken for example in [73] for dynamical Lie groups and in [61,62] for Riemannian manifolds. This leads to another family of exponential distributions that are cut at the tangential cut-locus. Obviously, wrapped and cut Gaussians in tangent spaces are the same in Hadamard spaces since the cut-locus is at infinity in all directions.

To define the entropy, we consider a probability $\mu = \rho \, d\mathcal{M}$ that is absolutely continuous with respect to the Riemannian measure so that it has a pdf ρ that is an integrable nonnegative function on $\mathcal{M}$. With the affine-invariant metric, the Riemannian measure on the space of SPD matrices can be expressed as

$$d\mathcal{M}(P) = 2^{n(n-1)/4}\sqrt{(1 + \beta n)} \, \det(P)^{-1} \, dP \propto \det(P)^{-1} \, dP$$

with respect to the standard Lebesgue measure on the upper triangular coefficients of the SPD matrix P. This expression is obtained by expressing the formula of the Riemannian measure $d\mathcal{M}(P) = \sqrt{\det(g|_P)}\, dP$ (see Chapter 1, Section 1.4.3) in the chart of upper triangular coefficients F_{ij} of Section 3.3.3.3. The change of coordinates from the orthonormal basis $E_{ij}|_P$ to the basis $E_{ij}|_{\text{Id}}$ at identity is responsible for the term $\det(P)^{-1}$. The mapping $A_\alpha^{-1} = \text{Id} + \alpha \mathbb{1}_n \mathbb{1}_n^\top / (1 - \alpha n)$ transforming to the basis $E_{ij}^0|_{\text{Id}}$ has the determinant $\det(A_\alpha^{-1}) = 1/(1 - \alpha n) = \sqrt{(1 + \beta n)}$. Finally, the rescaling of the $n(n - 1)/2$ off diagonal terms by $\sqrt{2}$ to obtain the L_2 metric accounts for the factor $2^{n(n-1)/4}$. Changing for the Lebesgue measure on the full matrix coefficients only changes this last constant multiplicative factor. Then the entropy of an absolutely continuous distribution $\mu = \rho\, d\mathcal{M}$ is

$$H(\mu) = -\int_{\mathcal{M}} \log(\rho(P))\rho(P)d\mathcal{M}(P) = -\int_{Sym_n^+} \log(\rho(P)) \frac{\rho(P)}{\det(P)} dP.$$

Its negative is called the information or negentropy. We can verify that the pdf maximizing the entropy in a compact set is the uniform distribution over that set with respect to the Riemannian measure. Maximizing the entropy is thus consistent with the Riemannian framework.

Applying the maximum entropy principle to characterize Gaussian distributions, we can look for the pdf maximizing the entropy with a fixed mean and covariance matrix. The constraints are thus:

- the normalization $\int_{\mathcal{M}} \rho(Q)\, d\mathcal{M}(Q) = 1$,
- the prescribed mean value $\int_{\mathcal{M}} \overrightarrow{PQ}\, \rho(Q)\, d\mathcal{M}(Q) = 0$, and
- the prescribed covariance $\int_{\mathcal{M}} \overrightarrow{PQ} \otimes \overrightarrow{PQ}\, \rho(Q)\, d\mathcal{M}(Q) = \Sigma$.

These constraints can be expressed in a normal coordinate system at the mean, and using the convexity of the real function $-x \log(x)$, we can show that the maximum entropy is attained by the distributions of density $\rho(v) = k\, \exp\left(-\langle\beta, v\rangle_x - \frac{1}{2}\Gamma(v, v)\right)$, where v is a tangent vector at the mean, provided that there exist a constant k, a vector β, and a bilinear form Γ on the tangent space at the mean such that our constraints are fulfilled. Moreover, when the tangential cut-locus at the mean is symmetric, we find that $\beta = 0$ satisfies the prescribed mean.

Theorem 3.4 (Normal density on a Riemannian manifold [62]). *In a complete Riemannian manifold with a symmetric tangential cut-locus at P, the density maximizing the entropy with a prescribed mean P and covariance Σ has the form of a Gaussian in the tan-*

gent space at P truncated at the cut-locus:

$$G(Q) = k \, \exp\left(-\frac{1}{2}\overrightarrow{PQ}^\top \, \Gamma \, \overrightarrow{PQ}\right).$$

The exponential of the squared distance $G(Q) = \exp\left(-\frac{\tau}{2}\mathrm{dist}^2(P, Q)\right)$ used in Chapter 2 is a particular case obtained with an isotropic concentration matrix $\Gamma = \tau \mathrm{Id}$.

Let $r = i(\mathcal{M}, P)$ be the injectivity radius at the mean point (by convention $r = +\infty$ if there is no cut-locus). Assuming a finite variance for any concentration matrix Γ, we have the following approximations of the normalization constant and concentration matrix for a covariance matrix Σ of small variance $\sigma^2 = \mathrm{Tr}(\Sigma)$:

$$k = \frac{1 + O(\sigma^3) + \epsilon\left(\frac{\sigma}{r}\right)}{\sqrt{(2\pi)^n \, \det(\Sigma)}} \qquad \textit{and} \qquad \Gamma = \Sigma^{-1} - \frac{1}{3}\mathrm{Ric} + O(\sigma) + \epsilon\left(\frac{\sigma}{r}\right).$$

Here $\epsilon(x)$ is a function that is a $O(x^k)$ for any positive k, with the convention that $\epsilon\left(\frac{\sigma}{+\infty}\right) = \epsilon(0) = 0$.

In Riemannian symmetric spaces the tangential cut-locus is symmetric at all points. Indeed, the geodesic symmetry with respect to a point P reads $\overrightarrow{PQ} \to -\overrightarrow{PQ}$ in the log-map at P. Since this is an isometry, the distance to the tangential cut-locus is the same in opposite directions. In the case of our SPD matrices space this distance is moreover infinite, and the conditions involving the injection radius can be waved since we are in a Hadamard manifold. Thus we obtain a generalization of the Gaussian distribution on the space of SPD matrices, which is a standard Gaussian in the tangent space at the mean:

$$G_{(\bar{P},\Gamma)}(Q) = k \, \exp\left(-\frac{1}{2}\overrightarrow{PQ}^\top \, \Gamma \, \overrightarrow{PQ}\right).$$

However, contrarily to the Euclidean case where the concentration matrix Γ is simply the precision matrix Σ^{-1}, there is a correction term for the curvature due to the change of the volume of infinitesimal geodesic balls with respect to Euclidean spaces. It is thus natural to see the Ricci curvature appearing as a correction term. To understand better what this means, let us consider a Gaussian distribution at $\bar{P} = \mathrm{Id}$ (by invariance we are not loosing any generality) with covariance matrix Σ and concentration matrix Γ that are jointly diagonal with the Ricci curvature matrix. According to Theorem 3.3, the Ricci curvature matrix is block-diagonal in the basis $\{E_{ij}\}$. Let Γ_{ij} and Σ_{ij} be the coefficients of the diagonal concentration / covariance matrices. Theorem 3.4 states that $\Gamma_{ij} = \Sigma_{ij}^{-1} - \frac{1}{3}\text{Ric}(E_{ij}) + O(\sigma)$. Thus we see that that the Ricci curvature acts as the inverse of a typical length separating two different behaviors: when the variance is small ($\Sigma_{ij} \ll \text{Ric}(E_{ij})^{-1}$), the curvature correction term can be neglected, and the usual Gaussian in the tangent space is a good model. This is also the regime where tangent PCA (tPCA) will work without having to worry about curvature. On the contrary, if the variance is large with respect to the curvature ($\Sigma_{ij} \gg \text{Ric}(E_{ij})^{-1}$), then the curvature has to be taken into account and tPCA, and principal geodesic analysis (PGA) will give different results.

3.5 Manifold-valued image processing

We turn in this section to a generalization of image processing algorithms like interpolation and diffusion to manifold-valued images. We show that most interpolation and filtering methods can be reformulated using weighted Fréchet means. The linear and nonlinear diffusion schemes can be adapted to manifolds through PDEs, provided that we take into account the variations of the metric. For details, we refer the reader to [66]. More elaborate methods were developed since then using total variation [80, 35] or second-order [6] regularization, as well as nonlocal mean denoising of manifold-valued images [47].

In this section $P(x)$ is an $n \times n$ SPD matrix-valued image with Euclidean coordinates $x \in \mathbb{R}^m$. Because we are in a Hadamard space, where there exists a global coordinate system (e.g. $E_{ij}(P(x))$), this SPD image can be represented as a d-dimensional vector image with $d = n(n + 1)/2$. This would not be possible for an image of orientations belonging to a sphere, for instance. However, we will see further that processing manifold-valued images is in both cases different from processing vector images. In practice the image coordinates are sampled at the points x_k of a grid where $k = \{k_1, \ldots, k_m\}$ is the index of the signal element ($m = 1$), the pixel ($m = 2$), or the voxel ($m = 3$). The SPD matrix-valued image is thus encoded by the m-dimensional array of values $P_k = P(x_k)$ at the voxels x_k.

3.5.1 Interpolation

One of the important operations in geometric data processing is to interpolate values between known measurements. Beyond the nearest neighbor interpolation, which is not continuous, one of the simplest interpolation for 1D signal processing is linear interpolation. In 2D and 3D image processing this generalizes to bilinear and trilinear interpolation, which are particularly popular due to their very low computational complexity. Higher-order methods include quadratic, cubic, and higher-order spline interpolation [74,51].

Assuming that we have signal values f_k sampled on a regular lattice with integer coordinates $x_k \in \mathbb{Z}^m$. It is usual to interpolate the value at a noninteger coordinates x using a linear combination of the signal value $f(x) = \sum_k w(x - x_k) f_k$ weighted by a kernel w normalized with $w(0) = 1$ and $w(k) = 0$ at other integer values so that the interpolated signal $f(x_k) = f_k$ is equal to the sampled measure at the lattice points. A typical example of an interpolation kernel with infinite support is the sinus cardinal. Classical finite support kernels are the nearest-neighbor, linear (or trilinear in 3D), and piecewise polynomial kernels realizing spline interpolations [74,51].

When the weights are summing up to one, this can be seen as a weighted Fréchet mean. Thus interpolation of manifold-valued images can be formulated as an optimization problem: the interpolated value is then defined as

$$P(x) = \arg \min_{Q \in \mathcal{M}} \left(\sum_k w(x - x_k) \operatorname{dist}^2(P_k, Q) \right).$$

The cost to pay is that the value has to be determined by gradient descent, for instance, using the extension of Algorithm 3.1 with weights. Linear interpolation between two points $P(0) = P$ and $P(1) = Q$ can be written explicitly since it is a simple geodesic walking scheme: $P(t) = \operatorname{Exp}_P(t \overrightarrow{PQ}) = \operatorname{Exp}_Q((1-t)\overrightarrow{QP})$.

For our SPD matrices example, this gives the following interpolation with the standard Euclidean and affine-invariant metrics:

$$
\begin{aligned}
P_{Eucl}(t) &= (1-t)P + tQ, \\
P_{Aff}(t) &= P^{1/2} \exp\left(t \log \left(P^{-1/2} Q P^{-1/2} \right) \right) P^{1/2}.
\end{aligned}
$$

For a Euclidean metric, the trace is linearly interpolated. With an affine invariant metric, the trace is not linear anymore, but the determinant is geometrically interpolated, and its logarithm is linearly interpolated [3]. This is illustrated in Fig. 3.2 for the linear interpolation and in Fig. 3.3 for the bilinear interpolation with the Euclidean and affine-invariant metric.

3.5.2 Gaussian and Kernel-based filtering

Considering weighted means allows us to generalize many other image processing operations. A kernel convolution, for in-

Figure 3.2. Linear interpolation of SPD matrices. *Left:* linear interpolation on coefficients. *Right:* affine-invariant interpolation. We can notice the characteristic swelling effect observed in the Euclidean case, which is not present in the Riemannian framework. Reprinted by permission from Society for Industrial and Applied Mathematics: SIAM J. Matrix Anal. Appl., 29(1), 328–347, Geometric Means in a Novel Vector Space Structure on Symmetric Positive–Definite Matrices by Vincent Arsigny, Pierre Fillard, Xavier Pennec, and Nicholas Ayache, 2007.

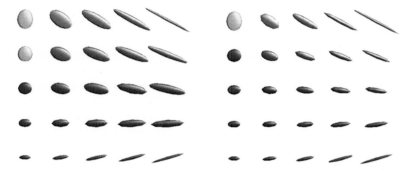

Figure 3.3. Bilinear interpolation of SPD matrices. *Left:* linear interpolation on coefficients. *Right:* affine-invariant interpolation. We can notice once again the characteristic swelling effect observed in the Euclidean case, which is not present in the Riemannian framework. Reprinted by permission from Society for Industrial and Applied Mathematics: SIAM J. Matrix Anal. Appl., 29(1), 328–347, Geometric Means in a Novel Vector Space Structure on Symmetric Positive–Definite Matrices by Vincent Arsigny, Pierre Fillard, Xavier Pennec, and Nicholas Ayache, 2007.

stance, can be viewed as the average value of the signal at neighboring points weighted by the respective kernel value. For a translation invariant kernel $k(x, y) = k(y - x)$ in a Euclidean space, the convolution $\hat{f}(x) = \int_{\mathbb{R}^n} k(u) f(x + u) \, du$ is indeed the minimizer of the criterion $C(\hat{f}) = \int_{\mathbb{R}^n} k(u) \, \mathrm{dist}^2 (f(x + u), \, \hat{f}(x)) \, du$. Here the kernel may be a discrete measure, for instance, when sample points are localized at discrete nodes of grid.

This variational formulation is still valid in Riemannian manifolds. However, in general, the minimum may neither exist nor be unique. For Hadamard spaces (thus for SPD matrices with an affine-invariant metric), the existence and uniqueness are ensured for a nonnegative kernel. In general, there is no closed form for the minimizer of this cost function. Thus we need to rely on an iterative gradient descent algorithm. Assuming that the kernel is normalized ($\int_{\mathbb{R}^n} k(u)\,du = 1$), we can use

$$\hat{P}_{t+1}(x) = \mathrm{Exp}_{P_t}\left(\tau \int_{\mathbb{R}^n} k(u)\,\mathrm{Log}_{\hat{P}_t(x)}(P(x+u))\,du\right), \qquad (3.22)$$

where the time-step τ is updated like in Algorithm 3.1. Fig. 3.4 illustrates the Gaussian filtering of an SPD image (here a diffusion tensor image) with the flat and affine-invariant metrics. We can visualize the blurring that occurs on the corpus callosum fiber tracts using the flat metric.

3.5.3 Harmonic regularization

To filter an image, we can also want to minimize the norm of the derivative of the field in the direction u. The directional derivative $\partial_u P(x)$ is a tangent vector of $T_{P(x)}\mathcal{M}$, which can be evaluated using finite differences: $\partial_u P(x) \simeq \mathrm{Log}_{P(x)}(P(x+u)) + O(\|u\|^2)$. The norm of this vector has to be measured with the Riemannian metric at the foot-point, $\|\partial_u P(x)\|_{P(x)}$. However, penalizing the derivative only in one direction of the space is not sufficient. The spatial differential of the field $P(x)$ is the linear form that maps to any spatial direction u the directional derivative $dP(x)\,u = \partial_u P(x)$. It can be expressed as a matrix with column coefficients related to the spatial basis (say e_i) and row coefficients related to a basis of the $T_{P(x)}\mathcal{S}ym_n^+$ (e.g. $E_{jk}(P(x))$). The dual of that $d \times m$ matrix with respect to the spatial metric (this is the transpose of the matrix in an orthonormal coordinate system) has columns that gives the direction of the spatial domain in which each component of the SPD matrix field evolves the fastest: we denote this gradient by $\nabla_x P(x) = dP(x)^\top$ to differentiate it from the connection ∇.

As there are more directional derivatives in classical 6, 18, or 26 neighborhoods (in 3D) than the three needed to compute the full gradient matrix, the gradient may be approximated by minimizing the least square error:

$$\nabla_x P(x) = \arg\min_{A \in M_{m \times d}} \sum_i \|A^\top u_i - \mathrm{Log}_{P(x)}(P(x+u_i))\|_{P(x)}^2,$$

where A is a matrix with 3 rows and 6 columns in the case of a 3D image of 3D SPD matrices. The simplest regularization criterion based on the spatial gradient is the harmonic energy

$$Reg(P) = \frac{1}{2}\int_\Omega \|\nabla_x P(x)\|_{P(x)}^2\,dx = \frac{1}{2}\sum_{i=1}^m \int_\Omega \|\partial_{x_i} P(x)\|_{P(x)}^2\,dx.$$

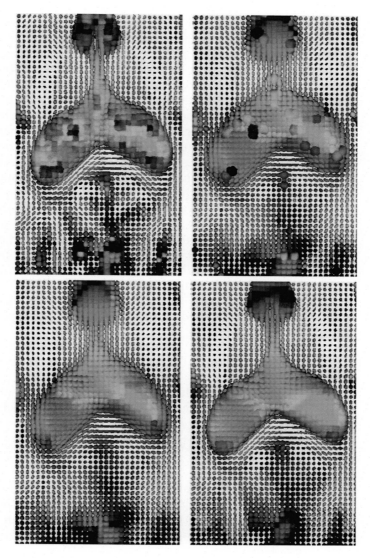

Figure 3.4. Results of Euclidean Gaussian, Riemannian Gaussian, and Riemannian anisotropic filtering on a 3D DTI of the brain (Closeup on one slide around the splenium of the corpus callosum). The color codes for the direction of the principal eigenvector (red (mid gray in print version): left–right, green (light gray in print version): posterior–anterior, blue (dark gray in print version): inferior–superior). *Top left:* Original image. *Top right:* Gaussian filtering using the flat metric (5×5 window, $\sigma = 2.0$). This metric gives too much weight to SPD matrices with large eigenvalues, thus leading to clear outliers in the ventricles or in the middle of the splenium tract. *Bottom left:* Gaussian filtering using the Riemannian metric (5×5 window, $\sigma = 2.0$). Outliers disappeared, but the discontinuities are not well preserved, for instance, in the ventricles at the level of the cortico-spinal tracts (upper-middle part of the images). *Bottom right:* Anisotropic filtering in the Riemannian framework (time step 0.01, 50 iterations). The ventricles boundary is very well conserved with an anisotropic filter and both isotropic (ventricles), and anisotropic (splenium) regions are regularized. Note that the U-shaped tracts at the boundary of the grey/white matter (lower left and right corners of each image) are preserved with an anisotropic filter and not with a Gaussian filter. Reprinted by permission from Springer Nature, International Journal of Computer Vision, 66(1), 41–66: A Riemannian Framework for Tensor Computing by X. Pennec, P. Fillard and N. Ayache, January 2006.

The expression on the right assumes an orthonormal coordinate system $\partial_{x_1}, \ldots, \partial_{x_m}$ of the image domain. The Euler–Lagrange equation $\nabla_P Reg(P)(x) = -\Delta P(x)$ of this harmonic regularization criterion with Neumann boundary conditions involves the Laplace–Beltrami operator $\Delta P(x)$ on the manifold. In addition to summing the flat Euclidean second-order directional derivatives $\partial_{x_i}^2 P(x)$ in a locally orthogonal system, this operator has an additional term encoding the curvature of the manifold that distorts the orthonormality of this coordinate system from one point to another in the neighborhood. However, we need not compute the full Riemannian curvature operator to compute the Laplace–Beltrami operator. Indeed, we only need to access to the second-order derivative along geodesics starting with orthonormal vectors at a point. Because the Christoffel symbols and their radial derivatives (along the geodesics starting from the foot-point P) vanish in a normal coordinate system at P, computing the standard Laplacian *in this specific coordinate system* actually already includes the correction for the curvature.

This gives rise to the following very general and efficient scheme for the second-order derivative in the spatial direction u [66]:

$$\Delta_u P = \mathrm{Log}_{P(x)}(P(x + u)) + \mathrm{Log}_{P(x)}(P(x - u)) + O(\|u\|^4).$$

Averaging over all the spatial directions in a spatial neighborhood $\mathcal{V}$ finally gives a robust and efficient estimation scheme

$$\Delta P(x) \propto \sum_{u \in \mathcal{V}} \frac{1}{\|u\|^2} \mathrm{Log}_{P(x)}(P(x + u)). \tag{3.23}$$

The optimization of the harmonic energy can be performed as previously using a first-order gradient descent technique $P^{t+1}(x) = \mathrm{Exp}_{P^t(x)}\left(-\tau \, \Delta P^t(x)\right)$ that iteratively shoots for an adaptive time-step τ in the (opposite) direction of the regularization criterion gradient.

3.5.4 Anisotropic diffusion

To filter in homogeneous regions and to keep edges sharp, we can modulate the regularization depending on the direction u. A large body of work has been focusing on the inhomogeneous and anisotropic filtering of classical grey-valued images (see e.g. [81,82]). A comparatively much smaller part of this early literature has been devoted to anisotropic diffusion on very specific manifold-valued images, like circular data [77]. The case of SPD-valued images illustrated further was investigated in [66] and generalizes easily to generic Riemannian-valued images.

A first method constists in smoothing the image in the direction u if the directional derivative $\partial_u P(x)$ is small and penalizing the smoothing whenever we cross an edge as measured by a large directional derivative [67,33]. This can be realized directly in the discrete implementation of the Laplacian by weighting the directional contribution $\Delta_u P = \mathrm{Log}_{P(x)}(P(x+u))/\|u\|$ to the Laplacian with a decreasing function of the norm $\|\partial_u P\|_P$. Thus a natural generalization of the weighted Laplacian to manifold-valued images is $\Delta_u^\phi P = \sum_u \phi(\|\partial_u P\|_P)\Delta_u P$, for instance, with $\phi(x) = \exp\left(-x^2/\kappa^2\right)$ [66].

One of the key problems of the anisotropically weighted Laplacian is that its evolution equation is not guarantied to converge, even with Euclidean images, since the anisotropic regularization "forces" may not derive from a well-posed energy. An alternative is to construct a variational formulation with a weighted regularization criterion that penalizes the spatial variations of the field in the homogeneous areas. It is classical to take, for instance, a robust M-estimator of the Riemannian norm, $Reg_\phi(P) = \frac{1}{2}\int_\Omega \phi\left(\|\nabla_x P(x)\|_{P(x)}\right) dx$. By choosing an adequate ϕ-function (e.g. $\phi(s) = 2\sqrt{1+s^2/\kappa^2} - 2$) we can give to the regularization an isotropic or an anisotropic behavior [4]. The main difference with a classical Euclidean calculation is the use of the Laplace–Beltrami operator and the Riemannian norm [22]. Using $\Psi(x) = \phi'(x)/x$, we get the following gradient:

$$\nabla_P Reg_\phi(P) = -\Psi(\|\nabla_x P\|_P)\,\Delta P - \sum_{i=1}^d \partial_{x_i}\Psi(\|\nabla_x P\|_P)\,\partial_{x_i}P.$$

Thus the evolution equation is $\partial_t P = -\nabla_P Reg_\phi(P)$. An illustration of the anisotropic diffusion of an SPD image (here a diffusion tensor image) is given in Fig. 3.4. We can notice that some important U-shaped tracts at the boundary of the grey/white matter are preserved with our Riemannian anisotropic filter and not with a Gaussian filter.

3.5.5 Inpainting and extrapolation of sparse SPD fields

The harmonic or anisotropic diffusion schemes developed previously reduce not only the noise on the image but also the information that it contains. Indeed, an infinite diffusion time leads to a completely homogeneous field. Thus it is interesting to consider adding a data attachment term (a data likelihood) in addition to the regularization, which then constitutes a spatial prior. An independent Gaussian noise is usually assumed at each observed point of the image so that the maximum likelihood corresponds to a least-square criterion. This is still the case up to the first order with our definition of the Gaussian on manifolds of Section 3.4.3 when the variance is small enough. However, correction terms should be considered for covariances that are larger than the Ricci curvature (see also Chapter 2 on regression on manifolds).

When we have a dense data field $Q(x)$ as previously, the natural similarity criterion is the classical sum of square differences $\mathrm{Sim}(P) = \int_{\Omega} \mathrm{dist}^2\,(P(x), Q(x))\,dx$, expressed with the Riemannian distance. This criterion adds a geodesic spring (whose strength depends on the weighting of each criterion) $\nabla_P \mathrm{dist}^2(P, Q) = -2\overrightarrow{PQ}$ to the gradient of the regularization, which prevents from getting too much away from the data.

For sparse delta-Dirac measurements Q_i at points x_i, we need to restrict the integral in the above similarity criterion to the points where we have measurements. Unfortunately, these mass distributions induce singularities in the gradients. One solution is to regularize the data attachment term with Gaussian convolutions,

$$\mathrm{Sim}(P(x)) = \int_{\Omega} \sum_{i=1}^{n} G_{\sigma}\,(x - x_i)\,\mathrm{dist}^2\,(P(x), Q_i)\,dx.$$

This leads to the regularized derivative [66]

$$\nabla_P \mathrm{Sim}(x) = -2 \sum_{i=1}^{n} G_{\sigma}\,(x - x_i)\,\overrightarrow{P(x)P_i}.$$

An example of extrapolation (inpainting) of a whole image from four SPD matrix measurements is illustrated in Fig. 3.5.

3.6 Other metrics on SPD matrices

Affine-invariant and Euclidean metrics are two families of metrics that endow the space of SPD matrices with very different properties. There are in fact quite a few other families of metrics that are interesting to know.

3.6.1 Log-Euclidean metrics

In 2006 soon after the affine-invariant metrics were proposed, [2,3] realized that the matrix exponential was a global diffeomorphism from the space of symmetric matrices to the space of SPD

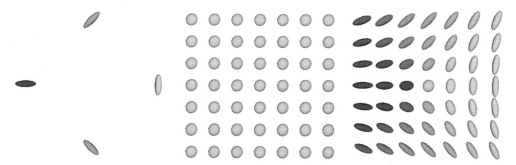

Figure 3.5. Extrapolation of SPD matrix values from four measurements using harmonic diffusion. *Left:* The four initial SPD matrix values. *Middle:* result of the diffusion without the data attachment term. The field of SPD matrix converges to a uniform image with the Fréchet mean value of the four SPD matrices. *Right:* result of the diffusion with a strong data attachment term. The diffusion smoothly extrapolates outside the measurements with a very small smoothing toward the mean at each of the original measurements. Notice that the center point is a multiple of the identity matrix, around which it is not possible to consistently orient the principal eigenvector.

matrices (a proof of that fact is given in Section 3.2 of this chapter), a fact which is mathematically well known in Hadamard manifolds. However, it was apparently not used previously to transfer the vector space structure of symmetric matrices to SPD matrices. In particular, it is possible to endow SPD matrices with a commutative Lie group structure where the composition is defined by $P_1 \diamond P_2 = \exp(\log(P_1) + \log(P_2))$ (the log-product). With the logarithmic scalar multiplication $\lambda . P = \exp(\lambda \log(P)) = P^\lambda$ in addition, this endows the SPD space with a vector space structure. To finish, any Euclidean metric on symmetric matrices is also transformed into a biinvariant Riemannian metric on SPD matrices thanks to the differential of the matrix logarithm:

$$\langle V, W \rangle_P^{LE} = \langle d \log(P)(V), d \log(P)(W) \rangle_{Eucl}$$
$$= \langle \partial_V \log(P), \partial_W \log(P) \rangle_{Eucl}.$$

We recall that the differential of the matrix logarithm was explicitly determined in Section 3.2.2. It is well defined and invertible everywhere on the space of SPD matrices.

Using the fact that Euclidean geodesics are straight lines in the space of symmetric matrices, the expression of the Exp, Log, and distance maps metric are easily determined for the log-Euclidean metric:

$$\text{Exp}_P^{LE}(W) = \exp(\log(P) + \partial_W \log(P)),$$
$$\text{Log}_P^{LE}(Q) = d \exp(\log(P))(\log(Q) - \log(P))$$
$$= \partial_{\log(Q) - \log(P)} \exp(\log(P)),$$

$$\text{dist}_{LE}^2(P_1, P_2) \;\; = \;\; \|\log(P_1) - \log(P_2)\|_{Eucl}^2 \,.$$

Because the differential of the matrix log at the identity is the identity, we can see that log-Euclidean geodesics through the identity are the same as the affine-invariant geodesics. However, this is not true at other points of the SPD manifold [3].

By construction, log-Euclidean metrics are invariant by inversion and by a change of scale of the space. If we choose in addition a Euclidean scalar product that is invariant by rotation (we already know that they are all of the form $\|W\|_{Eucl}^2 = \text{Tr}(W^2) + \beta\text{Tr}(W)^2$ with $\beta > -1/n$), we conclude that all the similarity-invariant log-Euclidean Riemannian distances are:

$$
\begin{aligned}
\text{dist}_{LE}^2(P, Q) \;\; &= \;\; \|\log(P) - \log(Q)\|_{Eucl}^2 \\
&= \;\; \text{Tr}\left((\log(P) - \log(Q))^2\right) + \beta\text{Tr}\left(\log(P) - \log(Q)\right)^2 \,.
\end{aligned}
$$

The relative complexity of the exp/log formulas with respect to the affine-invariant case is due to the use of matrix exponential and logarithm differentials. However, log-Euclidean exp and log are nothing else than the transport of the addition and subtraction through the exponential of symmetric matrices. In practice the log-Euclidean framework consists in taking the logarithm of the SPD matrices, computing like usual in the Euclidean space of symmetric matrices, and coming back at the end to the SPD matrix space using the exponential [2,1]. The vector space structure gives a closed-form expression to many of the operations that were defined in this chapter through optimization. For instance, the log-Euclidean mean is simply [1]

$$\bar{P}_{LE} = \exp\left(\frac{1}{n}\sum_{i}^{n}\log(P_i)\right),$$

whereas the affine-invariant mean has to be obtained through the iterative Algorithm 3.1 of Section 3.4.1.

This shows that we can have very different flat structures on the space of SPD matrices. In fact, the log-Euclidean structure is much closer to the affine-invariant structure than to the Euclidean structure: log-Euclidean geodesics are complete (never leaving the space) and are identical to the affine-invariant geodesics at the identity, contrarily to Euclidean geodesics. The log-Euclidean and affine-invariant means are identical if the mean commutes with all the data. When they are not equal, we can show that (close enough to the identity) the log-Euclidean mean is slightly more anisotropic [3]. A careful comparison of both metrics in practical applications [1,2] showed that there were very few differences on the results (of the order of 1%) on real diffusion tensor images (see the next section), with a gain of computation time from 4 to 10 folds for the log-Euclidean. The difference is in fact due to the curvature induced by the affine-invariant metric (the log-Euclidean structure is flat since it is a vector space): when the distance of the data to the identity is less than the typical Ricci curvature, we can conclude that the log-Euclidean framework is a good first-order approximation of the affine-invariant computations. When there is another reference point $\bar{Q}$ that is more central than the identity matrix Id for the data, we can also use the log-Euclidean structure induced by $\bar{Q}^{1/2}\log\left(\bar{Q}^{-1/2}P\bar{Q}^{-1/2}\right)\bar{Q}^{1/2}$ instead of $\log(P)$.

For other types of applications where the variability or the anisotropy of the SPD matrices is higher than the affine-invariant Ricci curvature, affine-invariant and log-Euclidean results might change a lot. This is, for instance, the case in adaptive re-meshing [50]. However, initializing the iterative optimizations of affine-invariant algorithms with the log-Euclidean result drastically speeds up the convergence.

3.6.2 Cholesky metrics

Other families of metrics were also proposed to work with SPD matrices. For instance, [86] proposed to parameterize tensors by their Cholesky decomposition $P = LL^\top$ where L is upper triangular with positive diagonal entries. Taking the standard flat Euclidean metric on the (positive) upper diagonal matrices leads to straight line geodesics in that space: $L_t = L + t\dot{L}$ is the geodesic starting at L with (upper-triangular) tangent vector $\dot{L}$. It can be transported to a Cholesky geodesic in SPD matrix space using the product $P_t = L_t L_t^\top = P + t(\dot{L}L^\top + L\dot{L}^\top) + t^2\dot{L}\dot{L}^\top$. We see that the matrix product $L \to LL^\top$ plays here the role that was taken by the matrix exponential in the log-Euclidean framework. This mapping is a diffeomorphism between positive definite upper triangular and SPD matrices. However, contrarily to the log-Euclidean case, symmetric matrices with null eigenvalues are at a finite distance of any SPD matrix with the Cholesky metric, like for the Euclidean case.

3.6.3 Square root and Procrustes metrics

Since $P = (LR)(LR)^\top$ is also a valid decomposition of P for any rotation R, other definitions of square roots of SPD matrices can be used. For instance, the symmetric square root $P^{1/2} = (P^{1/2})^\top$ leads to a well-defined metric on tensors, which has similar properties to the Cholesky metric, yet having different geodesics. The fact that the rotation R can be freely chosen to compute the square root led [19] to the proposal of a distance measuring the shortest extrinsic distance between all the square roots $L_1 R_1$ of P_1 and $L_2 R_2$ of P_2. The minimal extrinsic distance is realized by the Procrustes match of the square roots:

$$\text{dist}(P_1, P_2) = \min_{R \in O(n)} \| L_2 - L_1 R \|_{Eucl},$$

and the optimal rotation $\hat{R} = U V^\top$ is obtained thanks to the singular value decomposition of $L_2^\top L_1 = U S V^\top$. This distance is in fact the standard Kendall structure on the reflection size-and-shape space of $n + 1$ points in dimension n [19,20,72], the geometry of which is well known. For instance, the minimal geodesic joining P_1 to P_2 is given by

$$P(t) = \left((1 - t)L_1 + t L_2 \hat{R} \right) \left((1 - t)L_1 + t L_2 \hat{R} \right)^\top.$$

From the equation of the geodesics, we can derive the Riemannian exp and log map and proceed with the general computing framework. However, we must be careful that this space is not complete and has singularities when the matrix P has rank $n - 2$, that is, when two eigenvalues are going to zero [44]. The curvature of this space is positive, which makes an important difference with the affine-invariant/log-Euclidean setting.

3.6.4 Extrinsic "distances"

The symmetrized Kullbac–Leibler divergence (J-divergence) was proposed as a "distance" on the SPD matrix space in [85] (it is specified in the paper that triangular inequality might not be verified):

$$\text{dist}_J^2(P_1, P_2) = \text{Tr}\left(P_1 P_2^{-1} + P_2 P_1^{-1} \right) - 2n.$$

This J-distance has interesting properties: it is affine invariant, and the Fréchet mean value of a set of tensors P_i has a closed-form solution:

$$\bar{P} = B^{-1/2} \left(B^{1/2} A B^{1/2} \right)^{1/2} B^{-1/2}$$

with $A = \sum_i P_i$ and $B = \sum_i P_i^{-1}$. However, this is not a Riemannian distance as a Taylor expansion

$$\text{dist}_J^2(P, P + \epsilon V) = \frac{\epsilon^2}{2} \text{Tr}(P^{-1} V P^{-1} V) + O(\epsilon^3)$$

shows that the underlying infinitesimal dot product is the usual affine-invariant metric $\langle V, W \rangle_P = \frac{1}{2}\mathrm{Tr}(P^{-1}VP^{-1}W)$. In fact, this divergence is probably an extrinsic distance (whose triangular inequality remains to be shown), and it would be quite interesting to determine the underlying embedding. In any case the algorithms based on this symmetric divergence should have results close to the affine-invariant ones when the data are sufficiently concentrated, provided that these algorithms can accommodate an extrinsic distance without direct correspondence to geodesics.

3.6.5 Power-Euclidean metrics

In between a Euclidean metric and its log-Euclidean counterpart we can design a family of Riemannian metrics based on power of the SPD matrices [21]. The basic idea is to take the Euclidean distance after the power transformation $\frac{1}{\alpha}P^\alpha$ for $\alpha \neq 0$, so that the distance is

$$\mathrm{dist}_\alpha^2(P, Q) = \frac{1}{\alpha}\|P^\alpha - Q^\alpha\|_{Eucl}^2.$$

The mapping $\exp(\alpha(\log P))/\alpha$ has a smooth invertible differential $d\exp|_{\alpha(\log P)}d\log|_P$, which realizes an isometry between Sym_n^+ and a subset of symmetric matrices with a Euclidean metric. SPD matrices with power-Euclidean metrics are thus flat spaces.

We recall from Section 3.2 that the power α of an SPD matrix is obtained by taking the power of the eigenvalues in the eigen-decomposition $P = U\,\mathrm{DIAG}(d_i)\,U^\top$ using the formula $P^\alpha = U\,\mathrm{DIAG}(d_i^\alpha)\,U^\top = \exp(\alpha(\log P))$. Since $\lim_{\alpha\to 0}(x^\alpha - 1)/\alpha = \log(x)$, we see that the family tends to the log-Euclidean metric for $\alpha = 0$ and comprises the Euclidean metric for $\alpha = 1$ and the Euclidean metric on the precision matrix for $\alpha = -1$. If $\alpha \leq 0$, then the symmetric matrices must be positive definite or have infinite eigenvalues, but if $\alpha > 0$, then we can also compare symmetric positive semi-definite (PSD) matrices.

The question of how to choose the value of α in practice for a specific dataset was investigated in [21] using statistical inference to find the optimal value for which the data are as Gaussian as possible after transformation, similarly to a Box–Cox transformation. Preliminary tests on canine diffusion tensor image data suggested that an intermediate value between Euclidean and log-Euclidean $\alpha = 1/2$ (a square-root metric) could lead to a good description of the data in this specific case.

3.6.6 Which metric for which problem?

The zoo of intrinsic Riemannian and extrinsic metrics that we just described raises the problem of the choice of the metric, which has to be data dependent. We can think of optimizing the best suited metric, as described in [21] for the power-Euclidean metrics. Taking into account all the metrics mentioned would require finding a larger parametric family comprising all of them. This is an interesting challenge. A simpler method is to list the main properties of these metrics to identify which of them make sense for the data under investigation.

The space of SPD matrices endowed with affine-invariant and log-Euclidean metrics is geodesically and metrically complete. This is a desirable feature when we want to have matrices with null eigenvalues at an infinite distance of any SPD matrix and cannot be reached in finite time in practice. This is an important feature for gradient descent algorithms. In both the Hadamard and flat log-Euclidean cases the mean always exists and is unique, which simplifies many algorithms. For diffusion tensor data, the negative curvature of the affine-invariant metric seems to be small enough, so that algorithms can be made much more efficient using the flat log-Euclidean metric.

For many other flat or positively curved metrics (e.g. power-Euclidean of Cholesky), the space of SPD matrices is open and has a boundary including some rank-deficient matrices that can be reached in finite time. This means that positive semidefinite (PSD) matrices should make sense for the investigated data and that most of the algorithms developed so far need to be adapted to manifold with boundaries. Moreover, the potential multiplicity of the mean value in positively curved (or in flat but nonconvex) manifolds raises other algorithmic challenges.

An example of PSD matrix data is found in computer vision with the structure tensor of an image [40]. This is the Gaussian convolution of the gradient of the image tensored by itself $S_\sigma = G_\sigma \star (\nabla I \nabla I^\top)$. The structure tensor field reveals structural information like edges and corners, which are used to guide the anisotropic smoothing of the original image. High values of σ favor smooth structure tensor fields, whereas smaller values can help extracting low level features in images but produces a lot of noise on the field. Smoothing anisotropically this tensor field may help regularizing homogeneous regions while preserving edges. Here filtering the coefficients only (using the Euclidean metric) produces negative eigenvalues, whereas filtering with the affine-invariant or log-Euclidean metrics forbids being close to null eigenvalues and gives the same importance to small differences in small tensors as to large differences in large ones [22].

Figure 3.6. Geodesic shooting with several metrics from the SPD matrix $P = \text{DIAG}(4, 1)$ with the tangent vector $\dot{P} = -4P$. *Left:* Along the Euclidean geodesic, the geodesic is $P_t = (1 - 4t)P$, so that both eigenvalues vanish at $t = 1/4$, and the geodesic cannot be continued after in Sym_n^+. We can see the linear height decrease. *Middle:* The Cholesky decomposition of P gives the diagonal (thus upper diagonal) matrix $L = \sqrt{P} = \text{DIAG}(2, 1)$ and the tangent vector $\dot{L} = -2L$. The Cholesky geodesic is thus $P_t = (L + t\dot{L})^2 = (1 - 2t)^2 P$. Both eigenvalues vanish at $t = 1/2$ and regrow symmetrically on the other side. Notice the quadratic height evolution. *Right:* along the log-Euclidean geodesic, matrices are always SPD. The height decrease is exponential.

This means that the anisotropic diffusion enhances these small details as much as the large scale ones. In fact, we should realize that structure tensors with one vanishing eigenvalue in 2D (or two vanishing eigenvalues in 3D) represents a perfect infinite edge in the image. This type of PSD matrices should thus be naturally reachable (i.e. at a finite distance), whereas negative eigenvalues should be forbidden. In this case metrics with flat or positive curvature like Cholesky or Procrustes could be better suited.

To understand the behavior of each type of metric, Fig. 3.6 illustrates the geodesic shooting from an SPD matrix with the same tangent vector with the Euclidean, log-Euclidean metric (affine-invariant is very similar), and Cholesky metrics. The Euclidean geodesic quickly reaches the boundary of the space (a matrix with zero eigenvalues), after which it is not defined anymore. The log-Euclidean geodesic reaches null eigenvalues asymptotically at infinity, whereas the Cholesky geodesic reaches the null eigenvalue in finite time but bounce back and becomes positive anew after that point. There is thus no universal metric for SPD matrices but many different families of metrics sharing similar or distinct characteristics that we have to investigate to choose the most adapted to the application needs.

3.7 Applications in diffusion tensor imaging (DTI)

Diffusion Tensor Imaging (DTI) is a Magnetic Resonance Imaging (MRI) modality, which was developed to measure in vivo oriented structures within tissues thanks to the directional measure of the water diffusion. The measure of intravoxel incoherent motions within each voxel was proposed as early as 1986 [41]. Specific gradient pulses produce a spin-echo attenuation, which can be related to the diffusion in the gradient direction. Thus we can estimate an Apparent Diffusion Coefficient (ADC) from a reference B_0 image (without gradient) and a few Diffusion Weighted Images (DWI) with gradients in different directions. In 1993 the single isotropic model of diffusion evolved into a matrix field that is allowing the measure of the anisotropic behavior of diffusion [12], in particular, within the white matter. The diffusion matrix is symmetric and can be interpreted as the covariance matrix of the Brownian motion of water in the tissues. This symmetric matrix image model was named Diffusion Tensor Imaging (DTI), and symmetric positive definite matrices are now classically referred to as tensors in medical image analysis. The Stejskal–Tanner equation relates the diffusion tensor D to noise-free DWI B_i acquired with the encoding gradient g_i and diffusion factor b:

$$B_i = B_0 \exp(-b g_i^\top D g_i). \tag{3.24}$$

Taking the logarithm of this equation leads to a very simple linear system, which can be solved in the least-square sense using algebraic methods (see e.g. [84]).

In an ideal fibrous tissue the principal eigenvector of the diffusion tensor is aligned with the fiber orientation. This gives an information about the direction of the neural tracts at each point of the image, whose global shape can be reconstructed into fiber bundles using tractography. Thus diffusion imaging provides in vivo imaging of the white mater architecture of nervous fibers (axons) and allows us to get an insight on the brain's information highways! Fiber tracking is providing a massive amount of detailed information about the macroscopic structures of the brain and is used in many neuroscience studies, even if the validity of the anatomical interpretation of tractographies at the microscopic level remains under discussion. Higher-order models of diffusion are nowadays developed (Diffusion Spectrum Imaging (DSI), High Angular Resolution Diffusion Imaging (HARDI), Q-ball, etc. [76]) both to increase the orientation accuracy and to determine the different compartments at the microstructure level within each voxel. In all cases good images require a good scanner quality (in particular very high and fast gradients) and a relatively long acquisition time.

On the other side of the application spectrum, DTI is finding clinical applications in brain tumors, spinal chord pathologies, epilepsy, diffuse axonal injury, multiple Sclerosis, Alzheimer Disease, and ischemic stroke [45]. Here DTI as a quantitative tool for medical diagnosis is hampered by the lower scanners quality in clinical environments and by the limited time for a clinical MRI acquisition. This results in images with a quite low signal-to-noise ratio (SNR) and a limited number of encoding gradients. Because the estimation of the tensor field from DWIs is quite noise sensitive, fiber tracking is often difficult with clinical DTI.

Simple methods estimate the tensor image with the above linear method and then spatially regularize the tensor field. From the signal processing point of view, this amounts to assume a log-Gaussian noise on the images, while it is rather Rician in MRI as we take the amplitude of a complex Gaussian signal in the k-space [69]. The Gaussian or log-Gaussian noise assumption is valid only for high SNR images, and it biases the estimation for low SNR clinical DTI. Rician noise removal on DWI images has been investigated [7]. However, smoothing independently, each DWI before estimating the tensor may blur the transitions between distinct fiber tracts, which delimit anatomical and functional brain regions since the transitions may not be seen correctly in all gradient directions.

Instead of separating the tensor estimation from the DWI and the DTI regularization, a statistically more interesting model is to consider the spatial regularization as a prior distribution in a Bayesian tensor estimation with a Rician DWI likelihood [25, 26]. For instance, a maximum a posteriori (MAP) algorithm jointly (rather than sequentially) performs the estimation and the regularization of the tensor field. Such an optimization is very easily developed in the log-Euclidean framework. We could also formulate it with an affine-invariant metric, but calculations are slightly more complex. Let us consider a Gaussian DWI noise model to start. The tensor image $D(x) = \exp(W(x))$ is parameterized by an unconstrained symmetric matrix $W(x)$. In the following we skip the position x in the image when not necessary. The log-likelihood for a Gaussian noise is $\text{Sim}_{Gauss}(W) = \sum_i (\hat{B}_i - B_i(W))^2$, where $\hat{B}_i$ is the DWI observed with the gradient direction g_i, and $B_i(W) = B_0 \exp(-b g_i^\top \exp(W) g_i)$ is the value modeled from the tensor parameter W using the Stejskal–Tanner equation. The derivative of this criterion with respect to W is

$$\nabla_W \text{Sim}_{Gauss}(W) = 2b \sum_i \left(\hat{B}_i - B_i(W) \right) \partial_W B_i(W)$$

with $\partial_W B_i(W) = B_i(W) \partial_{g_i g_i^\top} \exp(W)$.

The partial derivative of the matrix exponential was computed in Eq. (3.4).

To take into account the native Gaussian noise in the k-space, [86] developed an estimation criterion on the complex DWI signal with a computationally grounded optimization framework based on the Cholesky decomposition. In clinical images the phase is often discarded to conserve only the amplitude. For a Rician noise of variance σ^2 on the data, the probability density of the measured signal $\hat{B}$ knowing the expected signal B is in that case [70]

$$\rho\left(\hat{B}|B\right) = \frac{\hat{B}}{\sigma^2}\exp\left(-\frac{\hat{B}^2 + B^2}{2\sigma^2}\right)I_0\left(\frac{B\hat{B}}{\sigma^2}\right), \qquad (3.25)$$

where I_0 is the modified 0-order Bessel function of the first kind. The Rician noise induces a signal-dependent bias of the order of $\sigma^2/2B$ on the DWI signal [70]. As a consequence, tensors are underestimated with the least-squares estimation because the signal is systematically overestimated.

Under a Rician noise, the log-likelihood of DWI images with independent voxels then is $\mathrm{Sim}_{Rice}(W) = -\sum_i \log\left(\rho\left(\hat{B}_i|B_i(W)\right)\right)$. The derivative of this criterion with respect to the tensor parameter W is quite simple [25,26]:

$$\nabla_W\mathrm{Sim}_{Rice}(W) = -\frac{2b}{\sigma^2}\sum\left(B_i(W) - \alpha\left(\frac{\hat{B}_iB_i(W)}{\sigma^2}\right)\hat{B}_i\right)\partial_W B_i(W)$$

$$\text{with}\quad \alpha(x) = \frac{I_0'(x)}{I_0(x)}.$$

It is very similar to the previous Gaussian case up to a correction factor α that depends on the signal and the noise variance. The variance of the noise is usually estimated on the background of the image where there is no signal.

The Markovian prior $p(P(x+dx)|P(x)) \propto \exp\left(-\frac{1}{\lambda}\|\partial_{dx}P(x)\|_{P(x)}\right)$ is the discrete version of the harmonic energy of Section 3.5.3 for the spatial regularity. For preserving discontinuities, we may use a redescending M-estimator such as $\phi(s) = 2\sqrt{1 + s^2/\kappa^2} - 2$ [26]. The ϕ-function helps preserving the edges of the tensor field while promoting the smoothing of homogeneous regions. The prior becomes $\mathrm{Reg}(W) = \int_\Omega \phi(\|\nabla W\|)$. To adapt the previous maximum-likelihood (ML) gradient descent into a maximum a posteriori (MAP) estimation, we simply need to add the derivative of this prior to the ML criterion gradient:

$$\nabla_W\mathrm{Reg}(W) = -\psi(\|\nabla W\|)\Delta W - \sum_i \partial_i(\psi(\|\nabla W\|))\,\partial_i W,$$

$$\text{where}\quad \psi(s) = \phi\prime(s)/s.$$

The directional derivatives, gradient, and Laplacian can be estimated with finite differences like for scalar images (see [25,26] for details).

Experiments on synthetic data with a Rician noise showed that the MAP technique was correctly avoiding the negative eigenvalues, which inevitably appear in the standard linear estimation technique. The results of the ML (without regularization) and the MAP (with regularization) estimation methods with a log-Euclidean parameterization of the tensor image showed that the volume of the tensors was underestimated by 20% when we assume a log-Gaussian noise. Assuming a Gaussian noise model leads to an even higher underestimation of 30%. The estimation of the volume was within 5% with the Rician ML and MAP methods [26].

Results on two clinical acquisitions are presented in Fig. 3.7 and Fig. 3.8. A first dataset is a brain image with a very low SNR (Fig. 3.7), and a second dataset is an experimental acquisition of a tumor in the spinal chord (Fig. 3.8), both with seven gradient directions [29]. This last type of acquisition is sometimes difficult to perform because the position is uncomfortable due to the tumor and the coil cannot be perfectly adapted to the body as it is for the head. Consequently, spinal chord images are noisier than brain ones.

As for synthetic data, the negative tensor eigenvalues of the standard method disappear with the ML or MAP estimation. Several biomarkers such as the fractional anisotropy (FA) and the volume of the diffusion tensors in the ventricles/corpus callosum were used to assess the influence of the noise model used. Results using the Rician ML estimation showed an increase of the tensor volume and the ADC of about 10% in isotropic brain regions, 1 to 2% in anisotropic brain regions, and about 30% in the spinal chord, without modifying the FA [26]. These values are in line with the expected correction of the shrinking effect due to the log-Gaussian noise model.

In MAP methods where spatial regularization is added, Gaussian and log-Gaussian Rician noise models exhibited a more severe decrease of the FA than the Rician noise model. Moreover, the effect is much stronger in homogeneous regions (15% FA decrease in the ventricles with Rician vs 30% with log-Gaussian) than in anisotropic regions (3% FA decrease in the corpus callosum with Rician vs 11% with log-Gaussian). Thus the reproducibility of the biomarkers measurements is higher with the MAP Rician tensor reconstruction. The tractography results with the MAP Rician estimation showed more numerous, longer, smoother, and less dispersed fibers. In fact, tracts that were previously stopped because of the noise seem to be fully reconstructed. The radiologists found these results anatomically more meaningful.

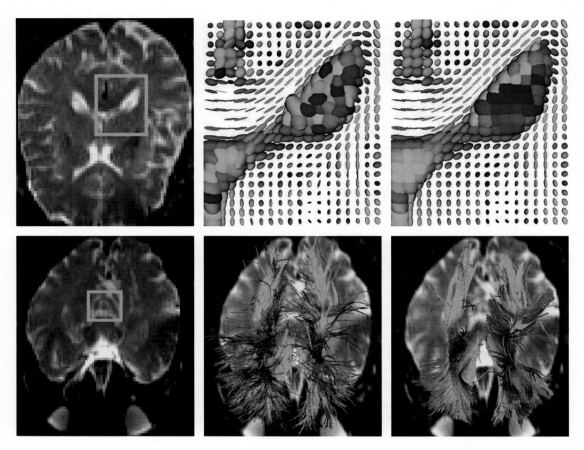

Figure 3.7. Tensor field estimation of a brain (top row) and improvement of the fiber tracking (bottom row). *Top left:* A slice of the B_0 image. *Top middle:* The classic log-Gaussian estimation on the ROI. The color codes for the principal direction of tensors: *red (mid gray in print version):* left–right, *green (light gray in print version):* anterior–posterior, *blue (dark gray in print version):* inferior–superior. Missing tensors in the splenium region are nonpositive. *Top right:* The MAP estimation of the same region. *Bottom left:* ROI where the tracking is initiated. *Bottom middle:* The cortico-spinal tract reconstructed after a classic estimation. *Bottom right:* Same tract reconstructed after the MAP estimation. Reprinted by permission from Springer, Berlin, Heidelberg: Pennec X. (2009) Statistical Computing on Manifolds: From Riemannian Geometry to Computational Anatomy. In: Nielsen F. (ed.) Emerging Trends in Visual Computing. ETVC 2008. Lecture Notes in Computer Science, vol. 5416.

3.8 Learning brain variability from Sulcal lines

Modeling the statistical variability of the brain shape in a population from 3D images is a second interesting application of SPD-matrix-valued image processing [23,24]. In Chapters 4 and 5 the

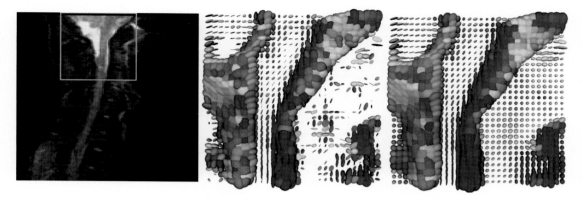

Figure 3.8. Tensor field estimation of the spinal chord. *Left:* A slice of the B_0 image with the ROI squared in green. *Middle:* Classic *log-Gaussian ML* tensor estimation. There are many missing (nonpositive) tensors around and in the spinal cord. *Right: Rician MAP* tensor estimation: tensors are all positive, and the field is much more regular while preserving discontinuities. Original DWI are courtesy of D. Ducreux, MD. Reprinted by permission from Springer, Berlin, Heidelberg: Pennec X. (2009) Statistical Computing on Manifolds: From Riemannian Geometry to Computational Anatomy. In: Nielsen F. (ed.) Emerging Trends in Visual Computing. ETVC 2008. Lecture Notes in Computer Science, vol. 5416.

interindividual shape variability will be modeled by a diffeomorphic deformation from a template to all the subject images. In this section we assume a simpler setting, where we identify the corresponding anatomical features (points or more generally lines or surfaces) among the anatomy of individuals (structural homologies). The statistical analysis is then performed on the displacement field between the template and the individuals. The covariance matrix of each point of the template independently could be seen as a first-order estimation of the spatial Riemannian metric that we should use for intersubject registration. Because structural variations are larger along certain directions [75], we cannot simplify this SPD matrix field into a simpler scalar variance function. Since the structural homologies can only be sparsely estimated, we actually have to extrapolate an SPD matrix field from sparse measurements, similarly to Section 3.5.5.

Sulcal lines are low-dimensional structures easily identified by neuroscientists that consistently appear in the normal brain anatomy. The main sulcal lines are used to subdivide the cortex into major lobes and gyri [55]. In [23,24], 72 sulcal curves that consistently appear in all subjects were selected. The curves were manually delineated in 98 subjects by expert neuroanatomists according to a precise protocol with formal rules governing the handling of branching patterns, breaks in sulci, and doubling of specific sulci (see above references for details). The inter- and in-

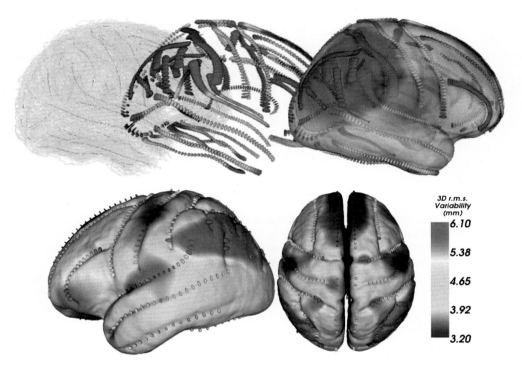

Figure 3.9. *Top:* From sulcal lines to the brain variability. Left: sulcal lines of 80 subjects in green (light gray in print version) with the mean sulcal lines in red (mid gray in print version). Middle: variability measured along the mean sulcal lines (covariance matrix at one sigma). Right: the color encodes the amount of variability everywhere on the cortex after the extrapolation of the covariance onto the whole 3D space. *Bottom:* The 366 SPD matrices selected along each sulcal lines, and the trace of the extrapolated covariance matrix. Lateral view from the left (on the left) and from above (right). Images courtesy of P. Fillard.

trarater error (reliability) is less than 2 mm (in r.m.s.) everywhere, and in most regions less than 1 mm, far less than the intersubject anatomical variance. To determine the point correspondences between different instances of each sulcal line, a classical method is to alternate the computation of the closest point from the mean curve to each instance and the reestimation of the mean curve from the updated correspondences (this is the max–max algorithm of Chapter 9). A constraint imposing monotonic matches along the curves was added with dynamic programming, and a global affine transformation per subject was also removed. This matching obviously underestimates the variability in the tangent direction to the sulcal lines except maybe at the endpoints that can be considered as landmarks. The mean sulcal lines are illustrated in Fig. 3.9.

The correspondences from the mean sulcal lines to all subjects are then summarized in a covariance matrix along each sulcal line that encodes the pointwise variability up to second order (since the mean is zero by construction of the mean sulcal lines). These covariance matrices are highly correlated along each line. To retain only the informative ones, the subset of SPD matrices optimizing a prescribed maximal distance (0.2 in the affine-invariant metric sense) between interpolated and measured tensors along the line is computed. The selection of 366 covariance matrices was found to be sufficient to encode the variability of the 72 sulci with a low RMS error. The resulting sparse field of SPD matrices was then extrapolated to the whole space using the framework described in Section 3.5.5 (see Fig. 3.9).

The obtained dense map of covariance matrices was qualitatively agreeing with the previously reported brain variability results [24]: areas that are highly specialized and lateralized, such as the planum parietale and the temporo-parietal areas, exhibit the largest variability. Phylogenetically older areas (e.g. orbitofrontal cortex) and primary cortices that myelinate earliest during development (e.g. primary somatosensory and auditory cortex) display the minimum of variability.

However, the 3D covariance matrix field contains more information than a scalar evaluation of the variability: it also contains directions that could be used to better guide the registration for instance. Even more interestingly, it is possible to study with this approach the covariability of different areas of the brain: instead of constructing the covariance matrix of the intersubject displacements at each point, we may construct the joint variance–covariance matrix of the intersubject displacements at two points x and y of the space. For prescribe initial points x, this amount to extrapolate an image of 6×6 covariance matrices (the point y being the spatial coordinate of the image). The total covariance matrix $\Lambda(x, y) = \begin{bmatrix} \Sigma_{xx} & \Sigma_{xy} \\ \Sigma_{xy}^{\top} & \Sigma_{yy} \end{bmatrix}$ can be analyzed using Canonical Correlation Analysis (CCA): the correlation matrix $\Gamma(x, y) = \Sigma_{xx}^{-1/2} \Sigma_{xy} \Sigma_{yy}^{-1/2}$ is decomposed using SVD to find the correlation coefficients between the x and y variables. A chi-square test allows us to state if the correlation matrix is significantly different from zero (i.e. if there exists at least an axis in which there is some correlation), in which case we may report the maximal correlation coefficient and the related axes in which this correlation happens at both points. In this process the components that are tangential to the sulcal lines may be questioned since they are known to be notably underestimated (this is called the aperture problem). They can be removed completely from the test at this stage

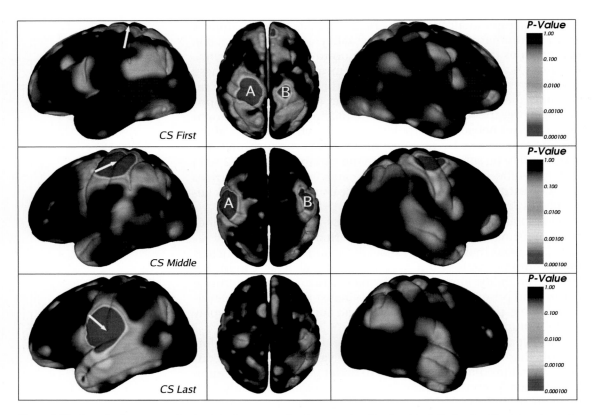

Figure 3.10. Correlation maps between the central sulcus and other brain regions. A white arrow in each row indicates a reference landmark; correlations with the reference landmark are plotted. Correlations for three reference landmarks on the CS are shown: the first (top row), the middle (second row), and the last, i.e., most inferior, position (third row) on the sulcal trace. Corresponding regions in the opposite hemisphere are highly correlated for the top and middle points (marked A and B). The lower end of the sulcus, however, exhibits low correlation with its symmetric contralateral counterpart. It is interesting to notice an unexpected long-range correlation between the variability of the top point of the left CS and a point of the right frontal lobe.

to avoid biases. Since this test should be corrected for multiple comparisons, it is also important to limit the number of candidate pairs of points that are tested.

In [30] three reference positions (beginning, middle, and end point) were selected along two important sulci, the Central Sulcus (CS) and the Inferior Temporal Sulcus (ITS). These sulci lie in different lobes, develop at different times during gyrogenesis (CS developing earlier), and are distant in terms of fiber and functional connectivity: we expect a priori a very low correlation between them. Thus they are good candidates for assessing inter-structure correlation. The correlation maps over the brain surface

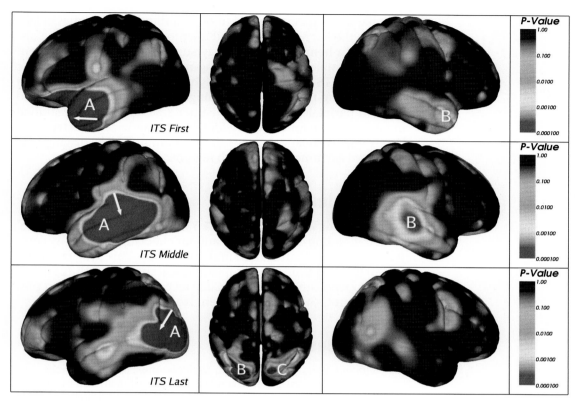

Figure 3.11. Correlation maps between the inferior temporal sulcus (ITS) and other brain regions.
A white arrow in each row indicates a reference landmark; correlations with the reference landmark are plotted.
Correlations for three reference landmarks on the ITS are shown: the first (top row), the middle (second row), and the
last, i.e., most inferior, position (third row) on the sulcal trace. The first and middle positions are symmetrically
correlated (marks A and B). The last position (third row) correlates less with its opposite hemisphere counterpart than
with the intraparietal sulci (marked B and C). This could be expected because the intersubject variability is very low
and reaching the interrater reliability. [Figure reproduced from [30].]

are displayed in Fig. 3.10 and Fig. 3.11 colored by their p-value.
The threshold for statistical significance of the CCA was set to
0.0001 to correct for multiple comparisons. A large area around
the reference points shows high p-values: points that are anatomically close to the reference are likely to have a correlated distribution among individuals. More interestingly, corresponding brain
regions in each hemisphere are highly correlated, except for regions including Wernicke's and Broca's areas, which are known to
be functionally specialized in one hemisphere.

The posterior tip of the ITS is also very loosely correlated to
its opposite hemisphere counterpart. As this structure is highly

variable and is specialized for understanding the semantics of language in the left hemisphere and the prosodic aspects of language in the right hemisphere, this may suggest partially independent developmental programs. The long-range correlation between the back of the ITS and the left and right intraparietal sulci is in itself an interesting neuroscience finding: the planum temporale and planum parietale are the two distinct areas most widely studied in neuroscience for their very high hemispheric asymmetry. Such long-range correlations may reflect common factors driving programmed asymmetries for both regions.

Acknowledgments

The author would like to thank Yann Thanwerdas for the careful proofreading of the chapter and for checking the lengthy computations of the connection and curvatures. This project has received funding from the European Research Council (ERC) under the European Unions Horizon 2020 research and innovation program (grant G-Statistics agreement No 786854).

References

1. Vincent Arsigny, Pierre Fillard, Xavier Pennec, Nicholas Ayache, Fast and simple calculus on tensors in the log-Euclidean framework, in: J. Duncan, G. Gerig (Eds.), Proceedings of the 8th Int. Conf. on Medical Image Computing and Computer-Assisted Intervention – MICCAI 2005, Part I, Palm Springs, CA, USA, October 26–29, 2005, in: LNCS, vol. 3749, Springer, 2005, pp. 115–122, PMID: 16685836.
2. Vincent Arsigny, Pierre Fillard, Xavier Pennec, Nicholas Ayache, Log-Euclidean metrics for fast and simple calculus on diffusion tensors, Magnetic Resonance in Medicine 56 (2) (August 2006) 411–421, PMID: 16788917.
3. Vincent Arsigny, Pierre Fillard, Xavier Pennec, Nicholas Ayache, Geometric means in a novel vector space structure on symmetric positive-definite matrices, SIAM Journal on Matrix Analysis and Applications 29 (1) (2007) 328–347.
4. Gilles Aubert, Pierre Kornprobst, Mathematical Problems in Image Processing – Partial Differential Equations and the Calculus of Variations, Applied Mathematical Sciences, vol. 147, Springer, 2001.
5. Alexandre Barachant, Stéphane Bonnet, Marco Congedo, Christian Jutten, Multiclass brain–computer interface classification by Riemannian geometry, IEEE Transactions on Biomedical Engineering 59 (4) (April 2012) 920–928.
6. Miroslav Bačák, Ronny Bergmann, Gabriele Steidl, Andreas Weinmann, A second order nonsmooth variational model for restoring manifold-valued images, SIAM Journal on Scientific Computing 38 (1) (January 2016) A567–A597.

7. Saurav Basu, Thomas Fletcher, Ross Whitaker, Rician noise removal in diffusion tensor MRI, in: Rasmus Larsen, Mads Nielsen, Jon Sporring (Eds.), Medical Image Computing and Computer-Assisted Intervention – MICCAI 2006, Springer, Berlin, Heidelberg, 2006, pp. 117–125.

8. Rajendra Bhatia, On the exponential metric increasing property, Linear Algebra and Its Applications 375 (2003) 211–220.

9. Dario A. Bini, Bruno Iannazzo, Computing the Karcher mean of symmetric positive definite matrices, Linear Algebra and Its Applications 438 (4) (February 2013) 1700–1710.

10. Joris Bierkens, Geometric Methods in Diffusion Tensor Regularization, Master's thesis, Technishe Universiteit Eindhoven, Dept. of Math and Comp. Sci., 2004.

11. Philip Batchelor, Maher Moakher, David Atkinson, Fernando Calamante, Alan Connelly, A rigorous framework for diffusion tensor calculus, Magnetic Resonance in Medicine 53 (2005) 221–225.

12. Peter J. Basser, James Mattiello, Denis Le Bihan, MR diffusion tensor spectroscopy and imaging, Biophysical Journal 66 (1994) 259–267.

13. Jacob Burbea, C. Radhakrishna Rao, Entropy differential metric, distance and divergence measures in probability spaces: a unified approach, Journal of Multivariate Analysis 12 (1982) 575–596.

14. Thomas Brox, Johachim Weickert, Bernhard Burgeth, Pavel Mrázek, Nonlinear structure tensors, Image and Vision Computing 24 (1) (2006) 41–55.

15. Manfredo P. do Carmo, Riemannian Geometry. Mathematics. Theory & Applications, Birkhäuser, Boston, 1992.

16. Miquel Calvo, Josep M. Oller, An explicit solution of information geodesic equations for the multivariate normal model, Statistics and Decisions 9 (1991) 119–138.

17. Christophe Chefd'hotel, David Tschumperlé, Rachid Deriche, Olivier Faugeras, Constrained flows of matrix-valued functions: application to diffusion tensor regularization, in: A. Heyden, G. Sparr, M. Nielsen, P. Johansen (Eds.), Proc. of ECCV 2002, in: LNCS, vol. 2350, Springer Verlag, 2002, pp. 251–265.

18. Christophe Chefd'hotel, David Tschumperlé, Rachid Deriche, Olivier Faugeras, Regularizing flows for constrained matrix-valued images, Journal of Mathematical Imaging and Vision 20 (1–2) (January–March 2004) 147–162.

19. Ian L. Dryden, Alexey Koloydenko, Diwei Zhou, Non-Euclidean statistics for covariance matrices, with applications to diffusion tensor imaging, Annals of Applied Statistics 3 (3) (September 2009) 1102–1123.

20. Ian L. Dryden, Kanti V. Mardia, Statistical Shape Analysis, John Wiley, Chichester, 1998.

21. Ian L. Dryden, Xavier Pennec, Jean-Marc Peyrat, Power Euclidean metrics for covariance matrices with application to diffusion tensor imaging, arXiv:1009.3045 [stat], September 2010.

22. Pierre Fillard, Vincent Arsigny, Nicholas Ayache, Xavier Pennec, A Riemannian framework for the processing of tensor-valued images, in: Ole Fogh Olsen, Luc Florak, Arjan Kuijper (Eds.), Deep Structure, Singularities, and Computer Vision (DSSCV), in: LNCS, Springer, June 2005, pp. 112–123.

23. Pierre Fillard, Vincent Arsigny, Xavier Pennec, Paul M. Thompson, Nicholas Ayache, Extrapolation of sparse tensor fields: application to the modeling of brain variability, in: Gary Christensen, Milan Sonka (Eds.), Proc. of Information Processing in Medical Imaging 2005 (IPMI'05), Glenwood Springs, Colorado, USA, in: LNCS, vol. 3565, Springer, July 2005, pp. 27–38, PMID: 17354682.

24. Pierre Fillard, Vincent Arsigny, Xavier Pennec, Kiralee M. Hayashi, Paul M. Thompson, Nicholas Ayache, Measuring brain variability by extrapolating sparse tensor fields measured on sulcal lines, NeuroImage 34 (2) (January 2007) 639–650, also as INRIA Research Report 5887, April 2006, PMID: 17113311.

25. Pierre Fillard, Vincent Arsigny, Xavier Pennec, Nicholas Ayache, Clinical DT-MRI estimation, smoothing and fiber tracking with log-Euclidean metrics, in: Proceedings of the IEEE International Symposium on Biomedical Imaging (ISBI 2006), Crystal Gateway Marriott, Arlington, Virginia, USA, April 2006, pp. 786–789.

26. Pierre Fillard, Vincent Arsigny, Xavier Pennec, Nicholas Ayache, Clinical DT-MRI estimation, smoothing and fiber tracking with log-Euclidean metrics, IEEE Transactions on Medical Imaging 26 (11) (November 2007) 1472–1482, PMID: 18041263.

27. P. Thomas Fletcher, Sarang Joshi, Riemannian geometry for the statistical analysis of diffusion tensor data, Signal Processing 87 (2) (February 2007) 250–262.

28. Wolfgang Förstner, Boudewijn Moonen, A metric for covariance matrices, in: F. Krumm, V.S. Schwarze (Eds.), Qua Vadis Geodesia...? Festschrift for Erik W. Grafarend on the Occasion of His 60th Birthday, Stuttgart University, 1999, pp. 113–128, number 1999.6 in Tech. Report of the Dpt of Geodesy and Geoinformatics.

29. David Facon, Augustin Ozanne, Pierre Fillard, Jean-François Lepeintre, Caroline Tournoux-Facon, Denis Ducreux, MR diffusion tensor imaging and fiber tracking in spinal cord compression, American Journal of Neuroradiology 26 (2005) 1587–1594.

30. Pierre Fillard, Xavier Pennec, Paul Thompson, Nicholas Ayache, Evaluating brain anatomical correlations via canonical correlation analysis of sulcal lines, in: MICCAI'07 Workshop on Statistical Registration: Pair-Wise and Group-Wise Alignment and Atlas Formation, Brisbane, Australia, 2007, https://hal.inria.fr/inria-00616033.

31. Ricardo Ferreira, Joao Xavier, Joao P. Costeira, Victor Barroso Newton, Algorithms for Riemannian distance related problems on connected locally symmetric manifolds, IEEE Journal of Selected Topics in Signal Processing 7 (4) (August 2013) 634–645.

32. R.V. Gamkrelidze (Ed.), Geometry I, in: Encyclopaedia of Mathematical Sciences, vol. 28, Springer Verlag, 1991.

33. Guido Gerig, Ron Kikinis, Olaf Kübler, Ferenc A. Jolesz, Nonlinear anisotropic filtering of MRI data, IEEE Transactions on Medical Imaging 11 (2) (June 1992) 221–232.
34. Ulf Grenander, Probabilities on Algebraic Structures, Whiley, 1963.
35. Philipp Grohs, Markus Sprecher, Total variation regularization on Riemannian manifolds by iteratively reweighted minimization, Information and Inference 5 (4) (December 2016) 353–378.
36. Sigurdur Helgason, Differential Geometry, Lie Groups, and Symmetric Spaces, Academic Press, 1978.
37. Uwe Helmke, John B. Moore, Optimization and Dynamical Systems, Communication and Control Engineering Series, Springer, 1994.
38. Wilfrid S. Kendall, Probability, convexity, and harmonic maps with small image I: uniqueness and fine existence, Proceedings of the London Mathematical Society 61 (2) (1990) 371–406.
39. Shoshichi Kobayashi, Katsumi Nomizu, Foundations of Differential Geometry, vol. II, Interscience Tracts in Pure and Applied Mathematics, vol. 15, John Whiley & Sons, 1969.
40. Hans Knutsson, Carl-Fredrik Westin, Mats Andersson, Representing local structure using tensors, in: Anders Heyden, Fredrik Kahl (Eds.), Image Analysis, Springer, Berlin, Heidelberg, 2011, pp. 545–556, Berlin Heidelberg.
41. Denis Le Bihan, Eric Breton, D. Lallemand, P. Grenier, E. Cabanis, M. Laval-Jeantet, MR imaging of intravoxel incoherent motions: application to diffusion and perfusion in neurologic disorders, Radiology 161 (2) (November 1986) 401–407.
42. Denis Le Bihan, Jean-François Mangin, Cyril Poupon, C.A. Clark, S. Pappata, N. Molko, H. Chabriat, Diffusion tensor imaging: concepts and applications, Journal of Magnetic Resonance Imaging 13 (4) (2001) 534–546.
43. Huiling Le, Locating Fréchet means with application to shape spaces, Advances in Applied Probability 33 (2) (2001) 324–338.
44. Huiling Le, David G. Kendall, The Riemannian structure of Euclidean shape space: a novel environment for statistics, Annals of Statistics 21 (1993) 1225–1271.
45. Alexander Lerner, Monique A. Mogensen, Paul E. Kim, Mark S. Shiroishi, Darryl H. Hwang, Meng Law, Clinical applications of diffusion tensor imaging, World Neurosurgery 82 (1–2) (July 2014) 96–109.
46. Miroslav Lovrić, Maung Min-Oo, Multivariate normal distributions parametrized as a Riemannian symmetric space, Journal of Multivariate Analysis 74 (1) (2000) 36–48.
47. Friederike Laus, Mila Nikolova, Johannes Persch, Gabriele Steidl, A nonlocal denoising algorithm for manifold-valued images using second order statistics, SIAM Journal on Imaging Sciences 10 (1) (January 2017) 416–448.
48. Christophe Lenglet, Michael Rousson, Rachid Deriche, Olivier Faugeras, Statistics on the manifold of multivariate normal distributions: theory and application to diffusion tensor MRI processing, Journal of Mathematical Imaging and Vision 25 (3) (October 2006) 423–444.

49. Jonathan H. Manton, A globally convergent numerical algorithm for computing the centre of mass on compact Lie groups, in: Proc. of ICARCV 2004 8th Control, Automation Robotics and Vision Conference, vol. 3, IEEE, 2004, pp. 2211–2216.

50. Houman Borouchaki, Paul-Louis George, Bijan Mohammadi, Delaunay mesh generation governed by metric specifications. Part II: applications, Finite Elements in Analysis and Design (1997) 85–109.

51. Eric Meijering, A chronology of interpolation: from ancient astronomy to modern signal and image processing, Proceedings of the IEEE 90 (3) (March 2002) 319–342.

52. Kanti V. Mardia, Peter E. Jupp, Directional Statistics, Whiley, Chichester, 2000.

53. Gérard Medioni, Mi-Suen Lee, Chi-Keung Tang, A Computational Framework for Segmentation and Grouping, Elsevier, 2000.

54. Maher Moakher, A differential geometric approach to the geometric mean of symmetric positive-definite matrices, SIAM Journal on Matrix Analysis and Applications 26 (3) (2005) 735–747.

55. Jean-François Mangin, Denis Rivière, Arnaud Cachia, Edouard Duchesnay, Yves Cointepas, Dimitri Papadopoulos-Orfanos, Paola Scifo, T. Ochiai, Francis Brunelle, Jean Régis, A framework to study the cortical folding patterns, NeuroImage 23 (Supplement 1) (2004) S129–S138.

56. Bill Moran, Sofia Suvorova, Stephen Howard, Sensor management for radar: a tutorial, in: Advances in Sensing with Security Applications, 17–30 July 2005, Il Ciocco, Italy, NATO Advanced Study Institute, July 2005.

57. Katsumi Nomizu, Invariant affine connections on homogeneous spaces, American Journal of Mathematics 76 (1954) 33–65.

58. Josep M. Oller, José Manuel Corcuera, Intrinsic analysis of statistical estimation, Annals of Statistics 23 (5) (1995) 1562–1581.

59. Yann Ollivier, A visual introduction to Riemannian curvatures and some discrete generalizations, in: Alina Stancu, Galia Dafni, Robert McCann (Eds.), Analysis and Geometry of Metric Measure Spaces: Lecture Notes of the 50th Séminaire de Mathématiques Supérieures (SMS), Montréal, 2011, AMS, 2013, pp. 197–219.

60. Xavier Pennec, Nicholas Ayache, Uniform distribution, distance and expectation problems for geometric features processing, Journal of Mathematical Imaging and Vision 9 (1) (July 1998) 49–67, a preliminary version appeared as INRIA Research Report 2820, March 1996.

61. Xavier Pennec, L'incertitude dans les Problèmes de Reconnaissance et de Recalage – Applications en Imagerie Médicale et Biologie Moléculaire, Thèse de sciences (phd thesis), Ecole Polytechnique, Palaiseau (France), December 1996.

62. Xavier Pennec, Intrinsic statistics on Riemannian manifolds: basic tools for geometric measurements, Journal of Mathematical Imaging and Vision 25 (1) (2006) 127–154, a preliminary appeared as INRIA RR-5093, January 2004.

63. Xavier Pennec, Statistical Computing on Manifolds for Computational Anatomy, Habilitation à diriger des recherches, Université Nice Sophia-Antipolis, December 2006.
64. Xavier Pennec, Statistical computing on manifolds: from Riemannian geometry to computational anatomy, in: Frank Nielsen (Ed.), Emerging Trends in Visual Computing, in: LNCS, vol. 5416, Springer, 2008, pp. 347–386.
65. Xavier Pennec, Barycentric subspace analysis on manifolds, Annals of Statistics 46 (6A) (2018) 2711–2746.
66. Xavier Pennec, Pierre Fillard, Nicholas Ayache, A Riemannian framework for tensor computing, International Journal of Computer Vision 66 (1) (January 2006) 41–66, a preliminary version appeared as INRIA Research Report 5255, July 2004.
67. Pietro Perona, Jitendra Malik, Scale-space and edge detection using anisotropic diffusion, IEEE Transactions on Pattern Analysis and Machine Intelligence 12 (7) (1990) 629–639.
68. Calyampudi Radhakrishna Rao (Ed.), Linear Statistical Inference and its Applications, John Wiley and Sons, 1965.
69. Jan Sijbers, Arnold J. den Dekker, Maximum likelihood estimation of signal amplitude and noise variance from MR data, Magnetic Resonance in Medicine 51 (3) (March 2004) 586–594.
70. Jan Sijbers, Arnold J. den Dekker, Paul Scheunders, Dirk Van Dyck, Maximum likelihood estimation of Rician distribution parameters, TMI 17 (3) (June 1998).
71. Lene Theil Skovgaard, A Riemannian geometry of the multivariate normal model, Scandinavian Journal of Statistics 11 (1984) 211–223.
72. Christopher G. Small, The Statistical Theory of Shapes, Springer Series in Statistics, Springer, 1996.
73. Jean-Marie Souriau, Structure des systèmes Dynamiques, Dunod, 1970.
74. Philippe Thévenaz, Thierry Blu, Michael Unser, Interpolation revisited, IEEE Transactions on Medical Imaging 19 (7) (July 2000) 739–758.
75. Paul M. Thompson, Michael S. Mega, Roger P. Woods, Chris I. Zoumalan, Chris J. Lindshield, Rebecca E. Blanton, Jacob Moussai, Colin J. Holmes, Jeffrey L. Cummings, Arthur W. Toga, Cortical change in Alzheimer's disease detected with a disease-specific population-based brain atlas, Cerebral Cortex 11 (1) (January 2001) 1–16.
76. David S. Tuch, Timothy G. Reese, Mette R. Wiegell, Nikos Makris, John W. Belliveau, Van J. Wedeen, High angular resolution diffusion imaging reveals intravoxel white matter fiber heterogeneity, Magnetic Resonance in Medicine 48 (4) (October 2002) 577–582.
77. Bei Tang, Guillermo Sapiro, Vicent Caselles, Diffusion of general data on non-flat manifolds via harmonic maps theory: the direction diffusion case, International Journal of Computer Vision 36 (2) (2000) 149–161.
78. David Tschumperlé, PDE-Based Regularization of Multivalued Images and Applications, PhD thesis, University of Nice-Sophia Antipolis, dec 2002.

79. Johachim Weickert, Thomas Brox, Diffusion and regularization of vector- and matrix-valued images, in: M.Z. Nashed, O. Scherzer (Eds.), Inverse Problems, Image Analysis, and Medical Imaging, in: Contemporary Mathematics, vol. 313, AMS, Providence, 2002, pp. 251–268.

80. Andreas Weinmann, Laurent Demaret, Martin Storath, Total variation regularization for manifold-valued data, SIAM Journal on Imaging Sciences 7 (4) (January 2014) 2226–2257.

81. Joachim Weickert, A review of nonlinear diffusion filtering, in: Gerhard Goos, Juris Hartmanis, Jan Leeuwen, Bart Haar Romeny, Luc Florack, Jan Koenderink, Max Viergever (Eds.), Scale-Space Theory in Computer Vision, vol. 1252, Springer Berlin Heidelberg, Berlin, Heidelberg, 1997, pp. 1–28.

82. Joachim Weickert, Anisotropic Diffusion in Image Processing, ECMI Series, Teubner-Verlag, Stuttgart, Germany, 1998.

83. Joachim Weickert, Hans Hagen (Eds.), Visualization and Processing of Tensor Fields. Mathematics and Visualization, Springer, 2006.

84. Carl-Frederic Westin, Stephan E. Maier, Hatsuho Mamata, Arya Nabavi, Ferenc A. Jolesz, Ron Kikinis, Processing and visualization for diffusion tensor MRI, Medical Image Analysis 6 (2) (June 2002) 93–108.

85. Zhizhou Wang, Baba C. Vemuri, DTI segmentation using an information theoretic tensor dissimilarity measure, IEEE Transactions on Medical Imaging 24 (10) (October 2005) 1267–1277.

86. Zhizhou Wang, Baba C. Vemuri, Yunmei Chen, Thomas H. Mareci, A constrained variational principle for direct estimation and smoothing of the diffusion tensor field from complex DWI, IEEE Transactions on Medical Imaging 23 (8) (2004).

Riemannian geometry on shapes and diffeomorphisms

Statistics via actions of the diffeomorphism group

Stephen Marsland[a], Stefan Sommer[b]

[a]*Victoria University of Wellington, School of Mathematics and Statistics, Wellington, New Zealand.* [b]*University of Copenhagen, Department of Computer Science, Copenhagen, Denmark*

4.1 Introduction

This chapter provides an introduction to the analysis of shapes based on geometric concepts. Shapes – for example sets of landmark points, curves, and surfaces – constitute a broad class of objects. However, it is possible to unite them in a common mathematical framework induced from the action of elements of the group of diffeomorphisms on the domain in which the shapes reside. Diffeomorphisms are smooth invertible mappings that deform or "warp" the underlying domain, and shapes are carried along by this deformation.

The set of diffeomorphisms has many desirable mathematical properties. In particular, it is a group and also a differentiable manifold, and hence an infinite-dimensional analogue of a Lie group. The manifold can be endowed with a Riemannian metric, enabling distances between shapes to be defined. This in turn enables statistical analysis of sets of shapes, albeit in a Riemannian manifold rather than in a Euclidean space.

This idea of encoding shape variation by the action of diffeomorphisms is very general, and it allows broad classes of objects to be treated with one formal construction. As well as shapes, images and generalizations of images such as tensor fields, can be transformed by diffeomorphisms acting on their underlying domain. The Large Deformation Diffeomorphic Metric Mapping (LDDMM) framework uses this approach to provide a way to interpret and compute diffeomorphic transformations between shapes. We will describe the geometric ideas underlying this framework and show how to construct diffeomorphisms to match

Riemannian Geometric Statistics in Medical Image Analysis
https://doi.org/10.1016/B978-0-12-814725-2.00011-X

pairs of shapes. Following this, we will describe ways in which this construction allows statistical analysis of sets of shapes. The chapter concludes with an overview of some relevant literature on the LDDMM framework and shape analysis.

4.2 Shapes and actions

We distinguish between two key concepts: the shapes themselves and the actions of a set of deformations on the space on which the shapes are defined. Consider a curve such as that displayed in Fig. 4.1 and imagine it drawn on a rubber sheet. By stretching and bending the sheet it is possible to make the curve drawn on the sheet look more and more like another curve. If the curves have the same topology, by which we mean informally that we do not have to introduce holes or folds into the sheet, we can find a way to continuously deform the sheet so that the two curves match to arbitrary accuracy. The stretching and bending can be represented mathematically by a diffeomorphism acting on the domain of the rubber sheet.

Over the past 20 years a mathematical framework has been developed that enables us to compute and analyze the deformations that transform one shape to another and to compute a distance measure that identifies how far apart pairs of shapes are. The LDDMM framework applies to any space of shapes on which we can define an action of diffeomorphisms. We start by describing two common and relatively simple cases: curves and landmarks; in Section 4.5 we provide more details of these cases and additional examples of shape spaces. The LDDMM framework allows us to treat all these cases with one common theory.

To describe the action of a diffeomorphism on curves precisely, we define a closed curve as a map $\gamma : \mathbb{S}^1 \to \Omega$ from the unit circle $\mathbb{S}^1$ to an ambient space Ω, often $\mathbb{R}^2$ or $\mathbb{R}^3$. The action of a diffeomorphism (here denoted by a ".") is $\phi : \Omega \to \Omega$ on γ, defined by $\phi.\gamma = \phi \circ \gamma$. This means that the curve follows the deformation encoded in ϕ as it warps the underlying space. An example of an action of a diffeomorphism is illustrated in Fig. 4.1, where the deformation encoded in ϕ is illustrated by the deformation of an initially regular grid on Ω.

Another important example of a shape space is the space of landmarks, ordered configurations of a fixed number N of distinct points $q = (x_1, \ldots, x_N)$ with each $x_i \in \Omega$. The action of diffeomorphisms on landmark configurations is again composition with ϕ, by applying ϕ to each landmark x_i in q: $\phi.q = (\phi(x_1), \ldots, \phi(x_N))$. The action applied to a landmark representation of the curve shape is illustrated in the second row of Fig. 4.1. Note that the landmarks represent the curve as a set of discrete points. These points could be regularly spaced along the curve or defined by a human as points of special interest: we do not distinguish between these cases. The curve itself can be considered as the shape arising when the number of landmarks goes to infinity.

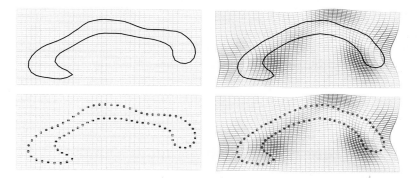

Figure 4.1. The top row shows a curve γ representing the shape of the corpus callosum (a region of the brain involved in the communication between the left and right hemispheres) together with the action of a diffeomorphism ϕ that transforms γ by the action $\phi . \gamma = \phi \circ \gamma$. The initially regular grid (*left*) is transformed by ϕ, resulting in the deformed grid underlying the deformed curve (*right*). On the bottom row a configuration of landmarks $q = (x_1, \ldots, x_N)$ representing the same corpus callosum shape is shown on the left. The landmark configuration is moved by the diffeomorphism action $\phi . q = (\phi(x_1), \ldots, \phi(x_N))$, and the result is shown on the right. The deformed grids are colored by the log-trace of the Cauchy–Green strain tensor.

The set of all possible shapes is called a *shape space*, a term that has been used in the statistics literature since the 1970s. Starting with the landmark spaces of Kendall, shapes are often considered as objects modulo the translation, rotation, and scaling of their domain: two point configurations in $\mathbb{R}^2$ are considered equal if they differ only by the action of the similarity group; in other words, only nonlinear effects define shape change. We can consider the original data to be lying in a "preshape space" and then transform one of the sets of datapoints to align them by translating, rotating, and scaling them to match the other set as closely as possible. The space in which these transformed shapes live is the shape space. The removal of the linear transformations of the points is known as quotienting out the action of the similarity group. In the LDDMM literature it is most common to prealign a set of shapes by rotating and translating each shape to align with the others and then continue with the shape analysis without quotienting out the action of the rotation and scaling group.

Although prealignment is not equivalent to mapping from the pre-shape space to the quotient, it provides much the same effect for practical purposes.

For many shape objects, such as curves and surfaces, the parameterization of the shape does not provide useful information and must be removed. Consider a closed curve γ in $\mathbb{R}^2$. The right action on γ of any diffeomorphism of the circle $\mathbb{S}^1$ changes the parameterization of γ without changing its image $\gamma(\mathbb{S}^1)$. Therefore the shape that γ represents does not change, meaning that the representation is not unique. To remove this nonuniqueness, the group $\mathrm{Diff}(\mathbb{S}^1)$ can be quotiented out. We will describe particular shape spaces and removal of parameterization in more detail in Section 4.5.

4.3 The diffeomorphism group in shape analysis

We consider shapes as subsets of a domain Ω. More generally, we include functions on Ω (such as images) in the concept of shapes because LDDMM allows us to handle all types of objects on which we can define an action of diffeomorphisms. Typically, we let $\Omega \subseteq \mathbb{R}^k$ for $k = 2, 3$. To avoid boundary effects, we can work with $\Omega = \mathbb{R}^k$. There can be computational reasons for working with more complicated representations of shapes, such as Fourier representations; in these cases it can be useful to consider $\Omega = \mathbb{T}^k$, but we will not consider that further here.

We can deform Ω by *warping* it by applying a map from Ω to itself that deforms its geometry. There are many choices for sets of deformations that can be used as warps, and different applications will have different requirements. Here we will consider a reasonably general case where the deformations are required to be smooth, that is, differentiable to some order r, and bijective, with the inverse also being smooth. This describes the set of *diffeomorphisms* from Ω to itself. We will denote elements of the set $\mathrm{Diff}(\Omega)$ of diffeomorphisms of Ω by ϕ, ψ.

The set of diffeomorphisms is an infinite-dimensional manifold. The diffeomorphisms are also a group under composition, since (i) composing two diffeomorphisms provides another diffeomorphism, (ii) they are invertible by definition, and (iii) the identity map Id, which leaves every point exactly where it is, is clearly a diffeomorphism: it is equal to the group identity, that is, $\phi \circ \phi^{-1} = \mathrm{Id} = e$. The diffeomorphism group has subgroups of both infinite and finite dimensionality.

4.3.1 Fréchet–Lie groups

A finite-dimensional group that is also a smooth differentiable manifold is a Lie group; these were introduced in Chapter 1. Unfortunately, not everything that works in finite dimensions continues to be true in the infinite-dimensional case. For example, in finite dimensions, we can identify local neighborhoods with open subsets of $\mathbb{R}^n$ using charts. In infinite dimensions we must make the identification with an infinite-dimensional modeling space C. It is then necessary to see what requirements we have for this space. If we wish to construct derivatives, then we require that C is a topological vector space. However, since we wish to perform statistical analysis, this is too weak: we need to compute distances on the manifold, and so we will require at least a metric on C. A space that allows this is a Fréchet space. (Fréchet spaces having a translation-invariant metric are locally convex and complete with respect to the metric.) When C is a Fréchet space, then the corresponding manifold becomes a Fréchet manifold.

Note that the requirement for a metric is less strong than the requirement for a norm (spaces with norms are known as Banach spaces), which is less strong than the requirement for an inner product (which produces a Hilbert space). The lack of norms and inner products is quite restrictive, and it is worth asking whether or not it is possible to work in at least a Banach space. However, even in finite dimensions, the space of smooth mappings from $\mathbb{R}^n$ into $\mathbb{R}$ is a Fréchet space, which suggests that we will not be able to produce anything stronger than that in the infinite-dimensional case. This intuition is correct: if we allow C to be a Banach space, then the group actions stop being differentiable, and so the group is not a Lie group. We are thus constrained to accept a manifold where the modeling space has a metric, but not a norm. This is, however, sufficient to describe directional derivatives, and also differential forms, which will get us a long way in our construction.

If Ω is a compact Riemannian manifold, then $\text{Diff}(\Omega)$ is a Fréchet–Lie group that is modeled on the space $V(\Omega)$ of smooth vector fields on Ω. In Chapter 1 we saw that a Riemannian metric assigns an inner product to every pair of tangent vectors $u, v \in T_x \mathcal{M}$ at a point $x \in \mathcal{M}$ for some manifold $\mathcal{M}$. We will construct a right-invariant metric on $\text{Diff}(\Omega)$. Right-invariance implies that $d(g, h) = d(g \circ \phi, h \circ \phi)$, $g, h, \phi \in \text{Diff}(\Omega)$, that is, the distance between two points on the manifold stays the same if both points are acted on from the right by the same group element.

A right-invariant metric on $\text{Diff}(\Omega)$ can be constructed in the following way. Consider the Lie algebra $\mathfrak{g}$ of $G = \text{Diff}(\Omega)$, the tangent space at the identity element $T_{\mathrm{Id}}\mathrm{Diff}(\Omega)$. This tangent space, and hence the Lie algebra, can be identified with the space of smooth vector fields $V(\Omega)$ on Ω. We can use the differential of right multiplication to transport any vector in a tangent space $T_{\phi}\mathrm{Diff}(\Omega)$ at a point $\phi \in \mathrm{Diff}(\Omega)$ to the Lie algebra. We now define an inner product on $V(\Omega)$ and extend this to the entire group by transporting tangent vectors to the Lie algebra using right multiplication. More formally, consider the action of right multiplication by a group element ϕ: $R_{\phi} : \mathrm{Diff}(\Omega) \to \mathrm{Diff}(\Omega) : R_{\phi}\psi = \psi \circ \phi$, where $\circ$ is the group operation. Let $(R_{\phi})_*$ denote the pushforward map, its derivative with respect to ψ. Now, for a pair of tangent vectors $u, v \in T_{\phi}\mathrm{Diff}(\Omega)$, there are unique vectors $h, k \in T_{\mathrm{Id}}\mathrm{Diff}(\Omega)$ such that $(R_{\phi})_* h = u$ and $(R_{\phi})_* k = v$. We now define the inner product at $T_{\phi}\mathrm{Diff}(\Omega)$ by $\langle u, v\rangle_{\phi} := \langle h, k\rangle_{\mathrm{Id}}$, where the subscript denotes the base point. This gives us a right-invariant metric.

4.3.2 Geodesic flows

Invariance of the metric to left- or right-translation has the additional benefit that the geodesic equation, the differential equation describing geodesics, can be reduced from dynamics on the group to dynamics in the Lie algebra. This is a form of what is known as Euler–Poincaré reduction. The Lie algebra flow can be reconstructed to retrieve the group variable. We will use this in Section 4.5.1. The equations also have links to Hamiltonian mechanics, which are explored in the research field known as geometric mechanics.

As we saw in Chapter 1, geodesics are smooth curves $\phi :$ $[a, b] \to \mathcal{M}$ (here, $\mathcal{M}$ is $\mathrm{Diff}(\Omega)$ or a subgroup of $\mathrm{Diff}(\Omega)$), that have minimum length

$$\mathcal{L}(\phi) = \int_a^b \langle \dot{\phi}(t), \dot{\phi}(t)\rangle_{\phi(t)}^{\frac{1}{2}} \, dt \qquad (4.1)$$

with regard to the metric $\langle \cdot, \cdot\rangle_{\phi(t)}$, where $\dot{\phi}$ denotes differentiation with respect to time. It is generally more convenient to work with the energy

$$\mathcal{E}(\phi) = \frac{1}{2}\int_a^b \langle \dot{\phi}(t), \dot{\phi}(t)\rangle_{\phi(t)} \, dt = \frac{1}{2}\int_a^b \|\dot{\phi}(t)\|_{\phi(t)}^2 dt \qquad (4.2)$$

rather than with the length: the energy can be easier to handle numerically, and it removes the potential for reparameterizations of the curve that do not affect its length, since it has the additional property that the speed remains constant in time.

In 1966, Vladimir Arnold demonstrated the remarkable fact that some equations describing physical systems arise as geodesic flows on a Lie group with respect to a one-sided invariant metric. Arnold gave two examples: the motion of a rigid body with a fixed point, which arises from the Lie group of rotations SO(3) with a left-invariant metric, and the Euler equations that describe the motion of an incompressible fluid, which arise from the group of volume-preserving diffeomorphisms together with a right-invariant L^2-metric. Since then, many other equations of mathematical physics have been shown to be geodesic equations of an invariant metric on a Lie group. The example of the full diffeomorphism group is no exception: the particular Euler equations in this case are sometimes called the Euler–Poincaré equations on the diffeomorphism group, or just EPDiff.

Arnold's result largely arises from the simplification of the geodesic equation that a left- or right-invariant metric provides. In what follows, we will use right-invariance, but the same computations (up to some changes of sign) are true for a left-invariant metric.

We apply the pushforward map $(R_\phi)_*$ of the right-translation R_ϕ to the velocity $\dot{\phi}(t)$ of $\phi(t)$ to compute the time-dependent Lie algebra vector $v(t) = (R_{\phi(t)^{-1}})_* \dot{\phi}(t)$. The right-invariance of the Riemannian metric implies that the energy (4.2) can be specified as a function of $v(t)$ instead of $\dot{\phi}(t)$. For this, we define the map $l : \mathfrak{g} \to \mathbb{R}$ by $l(v) := \|v\|^2$, and we apply l to the right-translated velocity $v(t)$ to write the energy as $\mathcal{E}(\phi) = \frac{1}{2} \int_a^b l(v(t)) dt$.

Following the approach of Euler–Poincaré reduction, we now use the calculus of variations to find a particular form of the EPDiff equations. Note that there are analytic complexities hidden in the formulation (particularly in the infinite-dimensional case that is our main consideration) that we will ignore. The fact that $\phi(t)$ is optimal with respect to the energy implies the variational principle

$$\delta \mathcal{E}(\phi) = \delta \frac{1}{2} \int_a^b l(v(t)) dt = 0$$

for variations of the curve $\delta\phi(t)$ that vanish at the endpoints $\phi(a)$ and $\phi(b)$.

Let $w(t) := (R_{\phi(t)^{-1}})_* \delta\phi(t)$ be the right-translates of this variation for each t. The corresponding variation $\delta v(t)$ of $v(t)$ is related to $w(t)$ by $\delta v(t) - \dot{w}(t) = [v, w] = -\text{ad}_v w$ using the adjoint operator ad defined in Chapter 1. In short, the bracket encodes the lack of commutativity between δ variations and variation in time d/dt. Let $\frac{\delta l}{\delta v}$ denote the derivative of l with respect to v, and

$\left(\frac{\delta l}{\delta v}\big|\delta v\right) := \delta l(v)$ the pairing of this with a variation of v. We then obtain

$$\delta \int_a^b l(v(t))dt = \int_a^b \left(\frac{\delta l}{\delta v}\big|\delta v(t)\right)dt = \int_a^b \left(\frac{\delta l}{\delta v}\big|\dot{w}(t) - \mathrm{ad}_v w\right)dt$$

$$= \int_a^b \left(\frac{\delta l}{\delta v}\big|\dot{w}(t)\right)dt - \int_a^b \left(\frac{\delta l}{\delta v}\big|\mathrm{ad}_v w\right)dt$$

$$= -\int_a^b \left(\frac{d}{dt}\frac{\delta l}{\delta v} + \mathrm{ad}_v^* \frac{\delta l}{\delta v}\big|w\right)dt\,.$$

In the last equality we used integration by parts and the fact that $w(t)$ vanishes at the endpoints for the first term, and the relation $\left(\mathrm{ad}_v^* \frac{\delta l}{\delta v}\big|w\right) = \left(\frac{\delta l}{\delta v}\big|\mathrm{ad}_v w\right)$ between the adjoint ad_v and its dual ad_v^* for the second term. Since $\delta \mathcal{E}(\phi)$ vanishes for all such variations, we conclude that

$$\frac{d}{dt}\frac{\delta l}{\delta v} + \mathrm{ad}_v^* \frac{\delta l}{\delta v} = 0\,. \tag{4.3}$$

These equations are known as the Euler–Poincaré equations for general Lie groups and as the EPDiff equations in the case $G = \mathrm{Diff}(\Omega)$.

The derivative $\frac{\delta l}{\delta v} \in \mathfrak{g}^*$ is called the momentum m associated with v. This link between velocity and momentum is the inertia or momentum operator, often written as $L : \mathfrak{g} \to \mathfrak{g}^*$. The operator acts on elements of the Lie algebra $\mathfrak{g}$ and produces elements of its dual. It is connected to the metric via the map l and satisfies $\langle u, v \rangle = Lv(u)$ for all $u, v \in \mathfrak{g}$. We will consider the definition of the metric and L further in Section 4.4.3. Note that the velocity $v(t)$ is time-dependent, and hence so is the momentum $m(t) = Lv(t)$, although this time-dependence is sometimes left implicit in the notation.

The EPDiff equation (4.3) describes the evolution of the momentum $m(t)$ and thereby the velocity $v(t)$. The actual diffeomorphism curve $\phi(t)$ can be obtained by a reconstruction equation, as we will discuss in Section 4.4.2 (see Eq. (4.8)).

The EPDiff equations can also be written in other forms. One that can help in their interpretation can be found by recalling that the velocity $v(t) \in \mathfrak{g}$ is a vector field on Ω for each t. In the present case, where $\Omega \subseteq \mathbb{R}^k$, the momentum can be written as a one-form vector field on Ω, that is, for vector fields w on Ω, $m(w) = \int_\Omega m(x)(w(x))dx$ with $m(x) \in (\mathbb{R}^k)^*$ for each $x \in \Omega$. The EPDiff equations can then be expressed in Euclidean coordinates as

$$\frac{\partial m}{\partial t} + v \cdot \nabla m + \nabla v^T \cdot m + m\nabla \cdot v = 0, \quad m = Lv\,. \tag{4.4}$$

In the first equation the terms correspond to the rate of change of momentum with respect to time, followed by terms for convection, stretching, and expansion. The link between the velocity and momentum in the second equation is based on the inertia operator $L : \mathfrak{g} \to \mathfrak{g}^*$. Note that the Euler equations, including the EPDiff equations, conserve momentum and energy, which is a consequence of Noether's theorem.

In this section, we have introduced the actions of the diffeomorphism group, the difficulties of working in an infinite-dimensional manifold, and the benefits of the right-invariance of the metric. We will now move on to consider how elements of the diffeomorphism group act on Ω, how we can construct a geodesic that transforms one shape to another, and how metrics on the diffeomorphism group can be transferred to the shape space.

4.4 Riemannian metrics on shape spaces

The action of an element $\phi \in \text{Diff}(\Omega)$ transforms one shape to another. One natural question is whether or not we can reach all shapes in this way. In other words, given any two shapes q_s, q_t, can we find a deformation $\phi \in \text{Diff}(\Omega)$ such that $\phi . q_s = q_t$. The subscripts on q_s and q_t refer to the *source* and *target*, respectively (i.e., the subscript t is not time). The action of a group is called transitive if we can always find such a deformation between any pair of shapes. It is related to the concept of an orbit: the set of elements that is generated by applying the elements of a group, in this case $\text{Diff}(\Omega)$, to a fixed base element is often called a template. Denoting the orbit $\text{Diff}(\Omega).q_s$ where q_s is the template, this gives $\text{Diff}(\Omega).q_s = \{\phi . q_s \mid \phi \in \text{Diff}(\Omega)\}$. There is precisely one orbit in the case that a group action is transitive, since it is possible to reach every other element of the set using group elements.

There are examples of shape spaces on which $\text{Diff}(\Omega)$ does not act transitively. For example, curves that self-intersect cannot be matched diffeomorphically to those that do not, and images very rarely have precisely the same set of pixel intensities, and thus there is no diffeomorphism that takes one image precisely onto another by warping the underlying domain. In these cases we will define the shape space $\mathcal{S}$ to be all elements that are reachable from the source q_s: $\mathcal{S} = \text{Diff}(\Omega).q_s$. This is sometimes known as an orbit space, and it enables us to consider a shape space that by construction is transitive. We will refer to shape spaces with the symbol $\mathcal{S}$ and assume that, where necessary, we have a transitive action.

The reason why transitivity is important is that it enables us to use the diffeomorphism group as the space in which to perform

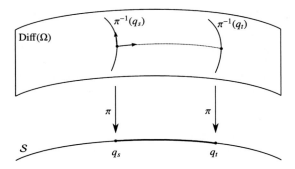

Figure 4.2. The action of the diffeomorphism group on the shape space $\mathcal{S}$ defines the mapping $\pi(\phi) = \phi.q$. The fiber $\pi^{-1}(q)$ is a subgroup of $\mathrm{Diff}(\Omega)$ with a vertical component corresponding to variations in ϕ keeping q fixed and a horizontal component that is orthogonal with respect to the invariant metric on the diffeomorphism group. A curve between two shapes q_s and q_t in $\mathcal{S}$ (*thick line*) can be lifted to horizontal curves between the fibers above q_s and q_t (*dashed line*). Horizontal curves are tangential to horizontal tangent vectors and minimizing with respect to the Riemannian metric on $\mathrm{Diff}(\Omega)$. Letting the metric on $\mathrm{Diff}(\Omega)$ descend to $\mathcal{S}$ makes π a Riemannian submersion, i.e., π_* preserves the metric on horizontal vectors. The invariance of the metric allows this construction.

analysis, rather than $\mathcal{S}$. Although it might seem odd that it is easier to work in an infinite-dimensional space rather than directly on the shape space, which is likely to be of lower dimensionality, shape spaces tend to be very nonlinear. The group structure of $\mathrm{Diff}(\Omega)$ means that we can compute distances between elements of $\mathcal{S}$ by measuring the length of the geodesic between them in $\mathrm{Diff}(\Omega)$. This length can be conveniently defined be specifying a right-invariant metric, and the EPDiff equations allows us to compute geodesics. With a right-invariant metric on $\mathrm{Diff}(\Omega)$, the metric structure descends to a Riemannian metric on $\mathcal{S}$ in certain cases.

Consider a particular choice of initial shape $q_s \in \mathcal{S}$. If the group action is transitive, then the choice of q_s is arbitrary, and there exists $\phi \in \mathrm{Diff}(\Omega)$ such that $\phi.q_s = q_t$ for any target shape $q_t \in \mathcal{S}$. Equally, a curve $s(t)$ in $\mathcal{S}$ has a corresponding curve $\phi(t) \in \mathrm{Diff}(\Omega)$ satisfying $s(t) = \phi(t).q_s$. Note that neither ϕ nor the curve $\phi(t)$ will be unique.

4.4.1 Shapes and descending metrics

Given a shape $q \in \mathcal{S}$ with corresponding tangent space $T_q\mathcal{S}$, we wish to find a way to lift curves in $\mathcal{S}$ to curves in $\mathrm{Diff}(\Omega)$ in order to take advantage of the metric on $\mathrm{Diff}(\Omega)$. Define the mapping π : $\mathrm{Diff}(\Omega) \to \mathcal{S}$ by $\pi(\phi) = \phi.q$. Now, given two tangent vectors $u, v \in$

$T_q\mathcal{S}$, we can find tangent vectors $h, k \in T_\phi\mathrm{Diff}(\Omega)$ such that $\pi_*(h) = u$ and $\pi_*(k) = v$, where ϕ is a point in $\mathrm{Diff}(\Omega)$ that corresponds to q in the sense that $\pi(\phi) = q$; these tangent vectors may again not be unique. We would like to define a Riemannian metric on $\mathcal{S}$ by setting

$$\langle u, v \rangle_q := \langle h, k \rangle_\phi, \tag{4.5}$$

where the subscripts signify the base point to make it clear which space we are working in.

However, because of the nonuniqueness of h and k, we will have to do more work to ensure that the construction is well-defined. To start with, consider the preimage $\pi^{-1}(q)$ of q. This is called a *fiber* over the point q, see Fig. 4.2. We can consider moving on the base space by changing q, and also moving along a fiber, so that q stays fixed. This intuition suggests a way to decompose $T_\phi\mathrm{Diff}(\Omega)$ into two orthogonal components, which are known as the vertical and horizontal subspaces of $T_\phi\mathrm{Diff}(\Omega)$. The vertical subspace (moving along the fiber) is simply those tangent vectors at ϕ for which π_* vanishes: $V_\phi\mathrm{Diff}(\Omega) = \ker \pi_*|_{T_\phi\mathrm{Diff}}$. The horizontal subspace is then $H_\phi\mathrm{Diff}(\Omega) = \{ h \in T_\phi\mathrm{Diff}(\Omega) \mid \langle h, k \rangle_\phi = 0 \, \forall k \in V_\phi\mathrm{Diff}(\Omega) \}$. For a given ϕ, there is a one-to-one correspondence between $H_\phi\mathrm{Diff}(\Omega)$ and $T_q\mathcal{S}$, and so $\pi_*|_{H_\phi\mathrm{Diff}}$ is injective and in fact an isometry under the metric (4.5). We can thus make the choice of h and k in (4.5) explicit by exchanging the definition of the metric with

$$\langle u, v \rangle_q := \langle \pi_*^{-1}|_{H_\phi\mathrm{Diff}}(h), \pi_*^{-1}|_{H_\phi\mathrm{Diff}}(k) \rangle_\phi. \tag{4.6}$$

Equivalently, we could define the following norm on $T_q\mathcal{S}$:

$$\|u\|_q^2 = \inf\{ \|h\|_\phi^2 \mid \pi_*(h) = u, h \in T_\phi\mathrm{Diff}(\Omega) \}. \tag{4.7}$$

We now need to check how this metric behaves when the tangent vectors are based at different points on the same fiber. Suppose that $\phi, \psi \in \mathrm{Diff}(\Omega)$ are both in the fiber $\pi^{-1}(q)$. Let $h \in H_\phi\mathrm{Diff}(\Omega)$ attain the infimum in (4.7). Then $(R_{\phi^{-1}\circ\psi})_* h$ is in $H_\psi\mathrm{Diff}(\Omega)$ and therefore attains the infimum $\inf\{ \|k\|_\psi^2 \mid \pi_*(k) = u, k \in T_\psi\mathrm{Diff}(\Omega) \}$. By right-invariance $\left\| (R_{\phi^{-1}\circ\psi})_* h \right\| = \|h\|$. Therefore $\|u\|_q^2$ is independent of which point in the fiber $\pi^{-1}(q)$ is used in the definition of the metric.

This analysis is also useful for examples other than shapes. We have already mentioned fluid dynamics and the fact that Arnold's work was originally concerned with the Euler equations of a perfect fluid, using the group of volume-preserving diffeomorphisms;

another example is optimal mass transport on densities with the full diffeomorphism group. We provide a reference for this at the end of the chapter.

4.4.2 Constructing diffeomorphisms

We are now ready to consider how to construct diffeomorphisms that transfer one shape to another. Consider a pair of shapes, the source q_s and target q_t, both in some shape space $\mathcal{S}$. The aim of matching is to construct a diffeomorphism ϕ such that $\phi . q_s = q_t$. If $\mathrm{Diff}(\Omega)$ acts transitively on the shape space, then we know that such a matching exists. As we have already mentioned, there are cases where there is no diffeomorphism between the two objects, for example when considering images, where there is very rarely a perfect mapping between the set of pixel values of one image and the pixel values of another. In this case we will only find an approximate match between the pair of shapes; this is referred to as an *inexact* matching and will be considered further in Section 4.5.2.

The size of the diffeomorphism group means that there will be a family of solutions that all map the two shapes onto each other (whether exactly or inexactly). However, the mathematical machinery we have just sketched gives us an understanding of which one we want to find: a diffeomorphism generated by a minimal geodesic curve in the diffeomorphism group with respect to our chosen metric (although note that even such curves may not be unique).

Finding a geodesic that matches two shapes can therefore be phrased as an optimization problem. We have seen in Eq. (4.3) that the EPDiff equation can be written as equations in two sets of variables, position and momentum, and so the matching problem can be thought of as finding initial momenta or initial velocities that transform the initial positions into the final positions; we will see an explicit formulation of this in Section 4.5.1. The initial and final positions are given in the specification of q_s and q_t, and so the optimization is over the momentum variable. Before that, though, we need to generate a flow of diffeomorphisms that transfers q_s to q_t. The key ingredient is a flow equation. As the composition of diffeomorphisms generates more diffeomorphisms, we can use this flow equation to move between the two shapes. As we start at q_s, the initial diffeomorphism is the identity element Id, which does not change it.

We now need to introduce two things: a set of vector fields V that describe how the curve moves (V being a subset of $V(\Omega)$), and an (artificial) time variable that we use to parameterize a curve that starts at Id at time $t = 0$ and follows the flow described by a t-dependent family of vector fields $v(t) \in V$:

$$\frac{d}{dt}\phi(x, t) = v(\phi(x, t), t), \quad x \in \Omega. \tag{4.8}$$

We can also write this in short form as $\frac{d}{dt}\phi(t) = v(t) \circ \phi(t)$, $\phi(0) =$ Id. Solving this flow equation provides a time-dependent family $\phi(t)$ in $\mathrm{Diff}(\Omega)$. The smoothness of the diffeomorphisms constructed in this way depends on the smoothness of v. For example, if $v(t)$ are $C^\infty(\Omega, \mathbb{R}^k)$ for each t, then the solution $\phi(t)$ will satisfy $\phi(t), \phi(t)^{-1} \in C^\infty(\Omega, \Omega)$ for each t. We write $\phi^v(t)$ for solutions to (4.8) for a given family of vector fields $v(t)$. In the language of fluid dynamics, $\frac{d}{dt}\phi^v(t)$ is a Lagrangian vector field, whereas $v(t)$ is an Eulerian field. In other words, $\frac{d}{dt}\phi^v(t)$ follows a particular point in the flow, whereas $v(t)$ describes the velocity seen at fixed points in Ω.

Since each $\phi(t)$ generated by (4.8) acts on elements of $\mathcal{S}$, we have the corresponding flows or curves of shapes $\phi(t).q_s$, $q_s \in \mathcal{S}$. We can now take two interrelated views of distances and geodesics on $\mathcal{S}$ and $\mathrm{Diff}(\Omega)$: distances realized via geodesics on $\mathcal{S}$ and geodesics on $\mathrm{Diff}(\Omega)$ realizing minimal distances on $\mathcal{S}$ corresponding to exact matching of shapes. This combination of spaces and geodesics, together with the role geodesics play in matching shapes, is the basis of LDDMM.

Geodesics on $\mathcal{S}$ can be realized from the action of geodesics $\phi(t)$ on $\mathrm{Diff}(\Omega)$ through the action $\phi(t).q_s$, and we can therefore search for geodesics on the shape space by searching for geodesics on $\mathrm{Diff}(\Omega)$. With the notation from Chapter 1, such geodesics arise from the exponential mapping $\mathrm{Exp}_{\mathrm{Id}} v$, $v \in T_{\mathrm{Id}}\mathrm{Diff}(\Omega)$, and the geodesics arise as solutions to the EPDiff equations (4.3). Because vector fields in V belong to $T_{\mathrm{Id}}\mathrm{Diff}(\Omega)$ and geodesics are determined by their initial velocity, we can in turn parameterize geodesics on $\mathrm{Diff}(\Omega)$ and geodesics on $\mathcal{S}$ by elements of V. Note that this removes the time parameter in $v(t)$ that we used before. Looking only at the endpoints, we can thus parameterize elements of $\mathcal{S}$ by elements of V, although not necessarily uniquely. This representation of $q_t \in \mathcal{S}$ as $q_t = (\mathrm{Exp}_{\mathrm{Id}} v_t).q_s$ by the initial velocity v_t in the linear vector space V of a geodesic in $\mathrm{Diff}(\Omega)$ allows us to apply linear statistics to elements of the nonlinear shape space $\mathcal{S}$, as we will see in Section 4.6. Note that there is no guarantee that the geodesics exist in all cases; we will consider this later in the chapter.

It simply remains to find a way to define a space of vector fields V and ensure that it is indeed a Hilbert space and so provides a norm and inner product, as well as the desired smoothness of the diffeomorphisms.

4.4.3 Reproducing kernel Hilbert spaces

Recall that the space of vector fields $V(\Omega)$ can be informally identified with the Lie algebra. We have seen how to construct right-invariant metrics from an inner product on the Lie algebra, but we still need a way to construct this inner product and to be explicit about the regularity we wish to enforce on the vector fields. One method of doing this is to use the notion of reproducing kernels with the resulting subspace of vector fields being a *reproducing kernel Hilbert space* (RKHS). We use the kernel to define an inner product on a subspace V of $V(\Omega)$, and we subsequently extend the subspace to get a complete Hilbert space.

The method enables us to specify the space $V \subset V(\Omega)$ and at the same time equip it with an inner product. Vector fields in V will have more regularity than arbitrary elements of $V(\Omega)$, and flows generated using Eq. (4.8) inherit this regularity. The construction of V thus specifies which time-dependent vector fields $v(t)$ are available for parameterizing flows of diffeomorphisms $\phi(t)^v$ and hence the subgroup of $\text{Diff}(\Omega)$ for which we can generate diffeomorphisms. By increasing the smoothness of the vector fields in V we get a corresponding increase in the smoothness of the solution $\phi(t)^v$.

In Section 4.3.2 we defined the momentum as $m = Lv$ using the operator L. Although the momentum can be singular, we need smooth vector fields to construct diffeomorphisms. We can use a kernel arising from the operator L to perform this smoothing for us. To identify the kernel, we consider the momentum operator $L : V \to V^*$ as a mapping of vector fields into their dual space, the space of continuous linear maps from V to $\mathbb{R}$. L can be a differential operator, and we can then find the kernel K as the Green's function $K = L^{-1} : V^* \to V$ of L. The kernel here takes covectors (i.e., elements of V^*) to vectors, elements of V, intuitively by smoothing them. An inner product and norm on V can be defined from L by setting $\langle v, v \rangle_V := Lv(v)$. The kernel is likewise linked to the inner product by $\langle Kf, v \rangle_V = f(v)$ for $f \in V^*$.

The kernel K can be regarded a symmetric function of two variables $K : \Omega \times \Omega \to \mathbb{R}^{k \times k}$ that satisfies the positivity constraint

$$\sum_{i,j=1}^{n} a_i^T K(x_i, x_j) a_j \geq 0 \quad \forall a_i \in \mathbb{R}^k, \ x_i \in \Omega, \ n \in \mathbb{N}. \tag{4.9}$$

The kernel K must be at least C^1 in both of its arguments. For fixed $x \in \Omega$ and $a \in \mathbb{R}^k$, the function $K(\cdot, x)a$ is a vector field on Ω. We can use this to build an intermediary space $\tilde{V}$ consisting of finite linear combinations of such vector fields:

$$\tilde{V} = \left\{ \sum_{i=1}^{n} K(\cdot, x_i)a_i \mid a_i \in \mathbb{R}^k, \ x_i \in \Omega, n \in \mathbb{N} \right\}. \qquad (4.10)$$

From the symmetry and positive-definiteness of K we get an inner product on V using the kernel by setting

$$\langle K(\cdot, x)a, K(\cdot, y)b \rangle_V := a^T K(x, y)b \qquad (4.11)$$

and extending this to the finite sums in (4.10) by linearity. We now let V be the completion of $\tilde{V}$. By continuity the inner product on $\tilde{V}$ extends to an inner product on V. Now V is a Hilbert space with inner product $\langle \cdot, \cdot \rangle_V$ and norm $\|v\|_V^2 = \langle v, v \rangle_V$, and vector fields in V will inherit the smoothness of the kernel K. The inner product defined in this way will coincide with the inner product defined in terms of L.

It can be shown that the completion V is embedded in $L^2(\Omega, \mathbb{R}^k)$. By the standard identification between L^2-spaces and their duals, vector fields $w \in L^2(\Omega, \mathbb{R}^k)$ determine covectors $v \mapsto \int_\Omega w(x)^T v(x) dx$ on $L^2(\Omega, \mathbb{R}^k)$. Such covectors are in turn also elements of V^*. Optimal flows $v(t)$ of (4.8) matching sufficiently smooth images will have momentum fields $w(t) = Lv(t)$ where, for each t, $w(t)$ is of this form with a vector field whose smoothness depends on both the momentum operator L and the images; shapes such as landmarks and curves will have singular momentum fields Lv that are not represented by vector fields in this way.

Kernels are often scalar in the sense that they appear as a scalar function times the identity matrix $K(x, y) = k(x, y)I_k$. In this case the identity matrix is often omitted from the notation, and the function $k : \Omega \times \Omega \to \mathbb{R}$ is described as a kernel. The inner product (4.11) will then be of the form

$$\langle K(\cdot, x)a, K(\cdot, y)b \rangle_V = k(x, y)a^T b,$$

which uses the standard $\mathbb{R}^k$ inner product between the vectors a and b.

There are a variety of kernels that can be used for shape matching, two of which are particularly common. Both have parameters, which we will mention briefly. Arguably the most commonly used kernel is the Gaussian kernel $k(x, y) = \beta e^{-\|x-y\|^2/(2\sigma^2)}$ with parameters $\beta, \sigma > 0$. The parameters control the amplitude and width of the kernel. The width is linked to the length-scale of the deformation: how far away from a point the effects of it moving can be felt by other points. Setting the width very small means that points will move almost in isolation, whereas making it very large means that one point of the domain moving will affect all the others. In this sense the kernel is related to covariance operators in statistics. The Gaussian kernel is infinitely differentiable, and elements of V will therefore be $C^\infty(\Omega, \mathbb{R}^k)$.

Another common kernel is based more explicitly on the Green's function of a differential operator, specifically, $Lv = \beta^{-1}(I - \sigma \nabla^2)^\alpha v$. The parameters here are the order parameter α, the amplitude β, and the length-scale σ. The order corresponds to the Sobolev order of the induced norm. For $\alpha = 1$, the corresponding scalar kernel is the exponential kernel $k(x, y) = \beta e^{-\frac{\|x-y\|}{\sigma}}$; see also Section 4.7. Note that this kernel is continuous, but not C^1.

Both of these kernels have infinite support, which has both theoretical and computational disadvantages. For practical computations, they can be truncated so that they do not affect elements far from their center point. It is also possible to use kernels that have compact support directly, for example, Wendland kernels.

Kernels can be combined either linearly as $\beta_1 K_1 + \beta_2 K_2$ (with weights β_1, β_2) or through convolution as $K_1 * K_2$. This enables multiple length scales to be taken into account simultaneously.

4.5 Shape spaces

The previous sections have given an overview of the general methods of diffeomorphic shape transformation. However, although the overarching ideas are the same for many different examples of shapes, the exact details vary. In this section we describe the most common examples of shape spaces. The tight connection between diffeomorphisms and shapes gives a general definition of shapes as objects on which $\mathrm{Diff}(\Omega)$ acts. Note that the action for the first examples of shapes is simply by letting the shape be directly deformed with $\phi \in \mathrm{Diff}(\Omega)$, whereas the later examples include more general definitions of shapes and have less immediate actions.

Landmarks We saw the action $\phi.q = (\phi(x_1), \dots, \phi(x_N))$ of a diffeomorphism on a landmark configuration $q = (x_1, \dots, x_N)$ at the start of the chapter. The space of landmarks is finite dimensional and so rather simpler than the other cases that we will consider. This has computational benefits, but landmarks are also an example that is of practical importance: it is common in many applications to be given a set of distinct points that describe particular features of the outline of the shape of an object, for example, produced by human annotation of images.

Diffeomorphisms act on landmarks on the left: $(\psi \circ \phi).x = \psi.(\phi.x)$. In Section 4.5.1 we will work out this case more fully and build on it in Section 4.6.4.

Curves To define a space of closed loops in the plane, consider starting from the unit circle $\mathbb{S}^1$ and apply functions $\gamma : \mathbb{S}^1 \to \Omega = \mathbb{R}^2$ to map the circle to $\mathbb{R}^2$. If these functions γ are smooth, are without self-intersections, and have a nowhere-vanishing derivative, then the shape space is the set of embeddings of $\mathbb{S}^1$ into $\mathbb{R}^2$. The same curve, regarded as a subset of Ω, can in this representation be described by many different functions $\gamma : \mathbb{S}^1 \to \Omega = \mathbb{R}^2$, and we would like curves that differ only by their parameterization to be the same. This means that the shape space we actually want (sometimes known as Mumford's shape space) is $\mathrm{Emb}(\mathbb{S}^1, \mathbb{R}^2)/\mathrm{Diff}(\mathbb{S}^1)$, which quotients out the action of diffeomorphisms of the circle and thereby removes differences in parameterizations. This shape space has removed the right action of the diffeomorphism group, which corresponds to reparameterization. The left action, which as in the landmark case is by composition $\phi.\gamma = \phi \circ \gamma$, descends naturally to the quotient shape space $\mathrm{Emb}(\mathbb{S}^1, \Omega)/\mathrm{Diff}(\mathbb{S}^1)$ by $g.[\gamma] = [g.\gamma]$, where $[\cdot]$ denotes the shape after quotienting.

Surfaces The space of embedded curves extends naturally to the set of embedded surfaces. We parameterize such surfaces by maps $\gamma : \mathbb{S}^2 \to \mathbb{R}^3$, which must be injective to avoid self-intersections. In addition, we require γ_* to have rank equal to the dimension of its domain at all points, giving the set of embedded surfaces:

$$\mathrm{Emb}(\mathbb{S}^2, \mathbb{R}^3)$$
$$= \{\gamma \in C^\infty(\mathbb{S}^2, \mathbb{R}^3) \,|\, \gamma \text{ injective, rank}\, \gamma_*(s) = 2 \,\forall s \in \mathbb{S}^2\} .$$
$$(4.12)$$

We use here that the derivative γ_* is a linear map between the tangent spaces at s and $\gamma(s)$, that is, a map $\gamma_* : T_s\mathbb{S}^2 \to T_{\gamma(s)}\mathbb{R}^3$, to define its rank. The action of the diffeomorphism group on $\mathrm{Emb}(\mathbb{S}^2, \mathbb{R}^3)$ and $\mathrm{Emb}(\mathbb{S}^2, \mathbb{R}^3)/\mathrm{Diff}(\mathbb{S}^2)$ is again by composition.

Images We consider images I as maps from $\mathbb{R}^k$ ($k = 2, 3$) to the real numbers, that is, $I : \mathbb{R}^k \to \mathbb{R}$. This provides only one value for pixel intensity of each pixel. To define color images, we need to consider, for example, $\mathbb{R}^3$ (red, green, and blue) instead of $\mathbb{R}$.

The action by $\phi \in \text{Diff}(\mathbb{R}^k)$ is by composition with the inverse of ϕ: $\phi . I = I \circ \phi^{-1}$. Consider a pixel at $x \in I$. The transformation ϕ maps this pixel to $y = \phi(x)$, which does not change the pixel intensity, and hence $(\phi . I)(y) = I(x)$. Setting $x = \phi^{-1}(y)$ enables the intensities of all transformed pixels to be computed. The use of the inverse of ϕ in the action implies that we again obtain a left action: $(\phi \circ \psi).I = I \circ (\phi \circ \psi)^{-1} = (I \circ \psi^{-1}) \circ \phi^{-1} = \phi . (\psi . I)$.

Tensor fields We very briefly describe a generalization of images, tensor fields. In the same way that an image assigns an intensity (or set of color intensities) to a set of pixels, so a tensor field assigns a tensor to each pixel, usually described as maps $\mathcal{T}_l^n(\Omega, \mathbb{R}^k)$ that to each $x \in X$ give tensors $T_l^n(x)$: $(\mathbb{R}^{k*})^l \times (\mathbb{R}^k)^n \to \mathbb{R}$. In coordinates such tensors have l upper indices and n lower indices, which specify the contravariant and covariant parts of the tensor, respectively. A natural generalization of the image action above is then

$$\phi . T(x)(w^1, \ldots, w^l, v_1, \ldots, v_n)$$
$$= T(\phi^{-1}(x))(\phi^* w^1, \ldots, \phi^* w^l, \phi^* v_1, \ldots, \phi^* v_n) \quad (4.13)$$

for $T \in \mathcal{T}_l^n(\Omega, \mathbb{R}^k)$, $\phi \in \text{Diff}(\Omega)$, where we specified the value of the tensor $\phi . T(x)$ by evaluating it on covectors $w^1, \ldots, w^l$ and vectors $v_1, \ldots, v_n$. This definition uses the pullback action by ϕ on vectors and covectors. For a vector $v \in T_{\phi(x)}\Omega$, the pullback $\phi^* v$ is the vector $(D\phi^{-1})v$ in $T_x\Omega$, where $D\phi^{-1}$ is the differential of ϕ^{-1}. There is an equivalent push-forward action ϕ_* that moves vectors from $T_x\Omega$ to $T_{\phi(x)}\Omega$ by multiplying by the differential $D\phi$. For covectors $w \in T^*_{\phi(x)}\Omega$, the pullback is given by evaluation on vectors $v \in T_x\Omega$ as $\phi^* w(v) = w(\phi_* v)$, that is, by pushing v forward and evaluating w.

One example of the use of tensor fields is in diffusion imaging. As described in Chapter 3, diffusion weighed magnetic resonance imaging measures the diffusion of water in biological tissue such as the human brain. The acquired signal can be summarized in a tensor field known as a diffusion tensor image (DTI). The action shown in (4.13) is only one example of a tensor action, and in some applications other actions can be preferred, such as one that only rotates the diffusion tensors.

For points, curves, and surfaces, we saw that the natural action of $\text{Diff}(\Omega)$ arises by composition. For images, the action is by composition on the right with the inverse of ϕ. For tensors, the derivative of the diffeomorphism needs to be accounted for as well. The former cases can be considered as push-forward actions, because, regarding the shapes as maps from the index set $\{1, \ldots, N\}$, $\mathbb{S}^1$ or $\mathbb{S}^2$, the shape is changed from being a map to the domain of $\phi \in \mathrm{Diff}(\Omega)$ to a map to the image of ϕ. This notion would be somewhat clearer if, instead of ϕ, we considered the push-forward $\phi_* s = \phi \circ s$ of a map $\phi : \Omega_1 \to \Omega_2$ between two different manifolds Ω_1 and Ω_2 instead of the present case, where the domain and image of ϕ are both the same manifold Ω. In the same way the image action is by pullback, since the image regarded as a function on the image of ϕ is transferred to a function on the domain of ϕ by composition with the inverse of ϕ. Again, considering a map $\phi : \Omega_1 \to \Omega_2$, the pullback $\phi^* I$ of the image $I : \Omega_2 \to \mathbb{R}$ would give an image $\phi^* I : \Omega_1 \to \mathbb{R}$, justifying the notion of pullback. For tensor fields, these operations apply not only to the space variable $x \in \Omega$, but also to the tensors themselves through the differential of ϕ, as we saw before.

We now focus two of the most commonly used examples of these shapes and provide more details of the geodesic equations.

4.5.1 Landmarks

In the landmark space, shapes are described by ordered sets $q = (x_1, \ldots, x_N)$ of landmarks x_i in $\mathbb{R}^k$. Given two landmark configurations q_s and q_t, we wish to find a diffeomorphism ϕ that aligns the two pairs. The diffeomorphism group acts transitively on the landmark space, so with the LDDMM approach, we ask for a ϕ arising as the endpoint of a minimizing geodesic on $\mathrm{Diff}(\Omega)$ such that $\phi.q_s = q_t$. This geodesic $\phi(t)$ on $\mathrm{Diff}(\Omega)$ will correspond to a geodesic $q(t) = \phi(t).q_s = (\phi(t)(x_{s,1}), \ldots, \phi(t)(x_{s,N}))$ on the landmark space. While $\phi(t)$ will be a solution to the EPDiff equations, we can conveniently find $q(t)$ as a solution to a Hamiltonian system.

For this, we use that in the landmark case the momentum $m(t)$ for optimal $\phi(t)$ will be concentrated on a set of Dirac delta functions positioned at the set of particle position so that $m(t) = \sum_{i=1}^{N} p_i(t)\delta_{x_i(t)}$. When the momentum is on this form, $v(t) = Km(t)$ is horizontal, as discussed in Section 4.4.1. The quantities $p_i(t) \in \mathbb{R}^k$ can be interpreted as the momenta of each landmark q_i at time t. We then define the Hamiltonian

$$H(q, p) = \frac{1}{2} \sum_{i,j=1}^{N} p_i^T K(x_i, x_j) p_j, \qquad (4.14)$$

where $K(\cdot,\cdot)$ is the kernel as discussed in Section 4.4.3, and x_i are the landmarks in q. Hamilton's equations of motion are now

$$\dot{x}_i = \nabla_p H = \sum_{j=1}^{N} K(x_i, x_j) p_j,$$

$$\dot{p}_i = -\nabla_q H = -\sum_{j=1}^{N} p_j^T D_1 K(x_i, x_j)^T p_i, \tag{4.15}$$

where $D_1 K$ denotes the kernel differentiated with respect to its first argument. In two dimensions ($k = 2$) these equations have four first integrals (conserved quantities): the Hamilton, the linear momentum, and the two dimensions of the angular momentum. This can be used to build effective numerical integrators to solve the equations computationally.

4.5.2 Images

Images provide a rather different case for diffeomorphic matching. We consider images on a subset of $\mathbb{R}^2$ or $\mathbb{R}^3$ that are sampled on a regular grid of pixels, with an intensity value being assigned to every pixel. This can be a single number, which corresponds to greyscale images, or an element of $\mathbb{R}^3$ corresponding to three color channels. As the diffeomorphism acts on the spatial domain of the images, not the intensity values, there is no difference between these two cases for our purposes.

However, it is extremely unlikely that the images have exactly the same distribution of pixel intensities, so that there is no diffeomorphism that takes one of the images precisely onto the other. This means that the action of the diffeomorphism group is not transitive. The solution to the lack of a diffeomorphism that matches precisely is to relate images by inexact matching. Instead of simply minimizing some norm of the difference between the deformed version of the source image $\phi.q_s$ and the template image q_t, we add a regularization term $\text{Reg}(\phi)$ that penalizes some property of the diffeomorphism ϕ:

$$\min_{\phi \in \text{Diff}} \mathcal{E}_{q_s, q_t}(\phi) = \lambda \text{Reg}(\phi) + \|\phi.q_s - q_t\|^2. \tag{4.16}$$

Here λ is a parameter that weights the importance placed on the regularizer $\text{Reg}(\phi)$; its effect will be discussed shortly. Typical choices of norm $\|\cdot\|$ on the image difference $\phi.q_s - q_t$ include the sum-of-squares distance or mutual information; for the present, we only require that the function we are minimizing is a differentiable function. However, the regularizer changes the nature of the problem: potentially, a regularization term could prevent the deformation being a diffeomorphism. This can be avoided if the form of Reg() comes from a flow in Diff(Ω). Then the energy of the flow or a similar function makes an appropriate regularizer.

Recall from Section 4.4.2 that we have a vector space V of vector fields on Ω, so that each $v \in V$ is a map $\Omega \to \mathbb{R}^k$. If we use the RKHS formulation from Section 4.4.3, then we have a norm $\|\cdot\|_V$ and inner product $\langle \cdot, \cdot \rangle_V$, and we can construct flows of elements of V, as we did previously by using the flow equation (4.8).

The same construction gives a direct way to define the regularization term Reg() in (4.16): we generate elements of Diff(Ω) by flows with $v(t) \in V$ and measure the integral of the norm of $v(t)$ as t runs from 0 to 1, that is, $\text{Reg}(v(t)) = \int_0^1 \|v(t)\|_V^2 \, dt$. Intuitively, $v(t)$ models the infinitesimal displacements that, in combination, move from the identity element Id toward the endpoint diffeomorphism $\phi(1)$. Since the regularization term Reg(ϕ) is explicitly a function of ϕ in (4.16), and because multiple flows $v(t)$ can lead to the same endpoint ϕ, we modify Reg() to measure the minimum energy of flows $v(t)$ with the same solution:

$$\text{Reg}(\phi) = \inf_{v(t), \phi^v(1)=\phi} \int_0^1 \|v(t)\|_V^2 \, dt \ . \tag{4.17}$$

Notice that the infimum is taken over all flows reaching ϕ at time $t = 1$, and the regularization is the infimum of the energies of such flows. Since the energy corresponds to the energy (4.2) that is minimized by geodesics, optimal flows for (4.17) will be geodesics in the diffeomorphism group. In particular, they will be solutions to the EPDiff equations. This formulation of the matching procedure served as the inspiration for using Riemannian geometries on Diff(Ω) in image matching and on orbit shape spaces Diff(Ω).q_s for shapes q_s.

The weight λ on the regularization term has an important role. Even if there is an exact match, then as λ increases in value, so the optimal match found will tend away from that exact mapping, preferring a shorter curve that performs only inexact matching. Only when $\lambda = 0$ is an exact match guaranteed, supposing that it exists. Regardless, if $\phi(t)$ is an optimal curve for Reg() in the energy (4.16), then $\phi(t)$ must necessarily be minimal among the curves reaching ϕ. In particular, it will be a geodesic from Id to ϕ. We can therefore often treat the exact and inexact problems similarly as a search for geodesics in Diff(Ω).

Finding a matching between a pair of images now uses (4.16) and (4.17), and optimal diffeomorphism flows $\phi(t)$ and image flows $\phi(t).q_s$ will be geodesics on Diff(Ω) and $\mathcal{S} = \text{Diff}(\Omega).q_s$, respectively. Using the L^2-norm for the image difference $\|\phi.q_s - q_t\|_2$,

Figure 4.3. Image geodesic between source image q_s (*leftmost*) and target q_t (*rightmost*). The matching is inexact, causing the gradual deformation of q_s (*left to right*) to only approximate q_t at the endpoint of the geodesic (second image from right).

the Euler–Lagrange equations for the extremal curves $\phi^v(t)$ of the matching functional (4.16) can be explicitly stated as the vector field $v(t)$ satisfying

$$2v(t) - K\left(2\lambda \,|D\phi^v(t,1)^{-1}|\,\nabla\phi^v(0,t).q_s\left[\phi^v(0,t).q_s - \phi^v(1,t).q_t\right]\right)$$
$$= 0. \tag{4.18}$$

Here we denote by $\phi(p,r)$ a solution of (4.8) integrated from time $t = p$ to $t = r$. In particular, $\phi(1,t)$ is the solution obtained when flowing backward in time from time 1 to t, $D\phi$ denotes the spatial derivative matrix $\left(\frac{d}{dx_j}\phi(x^i)\right)^i_j$ of ϕ, $|D\phi|$ is the determinant of $D\phi$, and K is an RKHS kernel on V. The left-hand side of the equation appears as the derivative $D_{v(t)}E$ of the energy

$$\mathcal{E}(v(t)) = \lambda \int_0^1 \|v(t)\|_V^2 dt + \|\phi^v.q_s - q_t\|^2, \tag{4.19}$$

that is, the energy (4.16) written as a function of v instead of $\phi^v(1)$.

Eq. (4.18) is the basis for gradient descent-based optimization algorithms that find optimal curves by iteratively updating a current value of $v(t)$ by subtracting a constant times $D_{v(t)}\mathcal{E}$. Note that the $t = 1$ value $\phi^v(1)$ of $\phi^v(t)$ appears in the expression for $v(t)$, and algorithms therefore need to integrate forward in time to compute the time t update. In practice such algorithms sweep t back and forth between 0 and 1 and update $v(t)$ using $D_{v(t)}\mathcal{E}$.

4.6 Statistics in LDDMM

This chapter has so far been concerned with describing mappings between shapes that correspond to geodesic flows on $\mathrm{Diff}(\Omega)$. This has enabled us to define these mappings as elements of a Riemannian manifold, meaning that we have a metric distance between pairs of related shapes or images. The principal reason why this is important is to enable families of them to be statistically analyzed, which is useful in a variety of applications. For example, in medical imaging, a statistical analysis of sets of images of some region of the human body might be able to assist in diagnosis by clustering together images that need very little transformation to map one to another, or in evolutionary biology it might enable related organisms to be identified. Both examples assume that form follows function, that is, the structure of a biological object, and hence its appearance, is based on what it does.

In general, shape spaces are not flat spaces; they can be Riemannian manifolds or orbifolds, meaning that standard Euclidean statistics are not sufficient. However, for the particular case of LDDMM, things get simpler, since we can consider statistics of velocities in the linear space V. This is effectively a tangent space linearization, albeit to the Lie algebra $\mathfrak{g} \simeq V$ instead of to the tangent space of a mean in Ω. In this section we describe the basic constructs of statistics in LDDMM, template estimation, and the random orbit model with the Lie algebra representation. We then introduce a stochastic version of landmark matching.

4.6.1 Random orbit model

Let μ_{Diff} be a probability distribution on $\mathrm{Diff}(\Omega)$, and let $\pi :$ $\mathrm{Diff}(\Omega) \to \mathcal{S}$ (recall that $\mathcal{S}$ is a shape space) be the map $\phi \mapsto \phi.q$ for some template shape q. The push-forward distribution $\pi_* \mu$ is then a distribution on $\mathcal{S}$, which we call a random orbit. The main reason for choosing this view is that distributions on $\mathrm{Diff}(\Omega)$ are easier to construct due to the Lie group structure. In particular, we can define a distribution μ_V in V and use the exponential map $\mathrm{Exp}_{\mathrm{Id}}$ to generate μ_{Diff}, that is, $\mu_{\mathrm{Diff}} = (\mathrm{Exp}_{\mathrm{Id}})_* \mu_V$, as in Section 4.4.2. Since V is a linear space, we have a rich set of distributions to choose from. This model amounts to adding noise to the initial velocity vector fields for geodesics.

One example of such a distribution comes from restricting the possible flow fields to a finite-dimensional subspace V^k of V and defining a Gaussian normal distribution $N(0, \Sigma)$ in V^k. We will see this case appearing further when discussing template estimation and Fréchet means. The subspace V^k can be chosen using the data as a best-fitting subspace, or it can come from the geometry of the data space. For the latter approach, consider the case of Ω being the landmark shape space. As described in Section 4.4.1, vector fields lift from $\mathcal{S}$ to horizontal vector fields on $\mathrm{Diff}(\Omega)$ and, via right-invariance, horizontal vector fields in V. Because $\mathcal{S}$ is of finite dimension kN (N landmarks in $\mathbb{R}^k$), the span of the lifted horizontal vector fields are likewise of dimension kN. This subspace is a natural candidate for V^k. It is in a certain sense optimal, because any variation orthogonal to V^k will have no effect on $\mathcal{S}$ and therefore cannot be observed when the data is landmarks alone. This observation has been used effectively to model variation even for objects such as images, where the horizontal space is not finite dimensional, by choosing a set of representative landmark locations and using the finite-dimensional horizontal span of those to give a plausible candidate for V^k.

Note that when doing statistics in V via the initial velocity or momentum field representation, the choice of inner product becomes important. The most direct choice is to use the inner product $\langle \cdot, \cdot \rangle_V$ from the RKHS structure and the kernel K. However, we can also shift from velocity fields in V to momentum fields in V^*. In this case we have the cometric on V^* induced from the metric on V. Alternatively, we could also choose to use, for example, the L^2-metric.

4.6.2 Template estimation

The template q used in the random orbit model of $\mathcal{S}$ will not in general be known a priori, and an important challenge is estimating it from data. We consider here two cases: the transitive case, where template estimation is equivalent to finding the sample Fréchet mean (see Chapter 2), and the nontransitive case, where, for example, image information from the observations is transported via the estimated diffeomorphisms to the template. In both cases we assume that we have N different sample shapes q^i $(i = 1, \dots, N)$.

We can formulate a general template energy as the sum of the match energy (4.16) over all N shapes q^i, that is, we set:

$$\mathcal{E}_{\text{template}}(q) = \sum_{i=1}^{N} \min_{\phi} \mathcal{E}_{q,q^i}(\phi) . \tag{4.20}$$

The template estimation problem can then be formulated as finding $\bar{q} = \min_q \mathcal{E}_{\text{template}}(q)$.

For landmarks and other transitive shape spaces, we can sum the exact matching energy (setting $\lambda = 0$):

$$\mathcal{E}_{\text{template}}(q) = \sum_{i=1}^{N} d_{\mathcal{S}}(q, q^i)^2 . \tag{4.21}$$

Here $d_{\mathcal{S}}$ is the geodesic distance of the deformation from q to each shape q^i.

A minimizer of this is exactly a sample Fréchet mean estimator. The function formally corresponds to the negative log-likelihood of a normal distribution on V because $d_{\mathcal{S}}(q, q^i)^2 = \left\| v^i \right\|_V^2$, where

v^i encodes an optimal initial velocity that takes q to each q^i. If all the v^i are included in a finite-dimensional subspace V^k, then we can make this concrete by considering the density $p(v) = (2\pi k)^{-\frac{1}{2}} e^{-\frac{\|v\|^2}{2}}$ of a normal distribution $N(0, \mathrm{Id}_{V^k})$ on V^k. The negative log-likelihood, $-\log p(v^i)$, is then equal to $d_{\mathcal{S}}(q, q^i)^2$ up to an additive constant. The relation is only formal if we let $k \to \infty$ and thus increase the dimensionality to approach the infinite-dimensional space V, because the constant $\log(2\pi k)^{-\frac{1}{2}}$ in the log-density becomes infinite.

For inexact matching ($\lambda > 0$), we use this intuition to interpret (4.20) as an estimator that is close to the Fréchet mean, but for the generative model, $q^i = \mathrm{Exp}_{\mathrm{Id}} v^i . q + \epsilon$ where ϵ is independent and identically distributed (i.i.d.) noise in $\mathbb{R}^{kN}$. This can be interpreted as a trade-off between shape variation as measured with the metric on the shape space $\mathcal{S}$ and measurement variation, which can be assumed i.i.d. in the measurement space. The most common case is for image template estimation, with q being the template image that needs to be identified. Since the diffeomorphism group only encodes deformation variation in the images, we cannot expect $\phi . q$ to match the observed images q^i. However, we can still pose the estimation problem (4.20) and search for a q that minimizes a version of (4.21). This can be achieved by using the estimated ϕ for each q^i to map the images back to the template space, that is, consider the images $\phi^{-1}.q^i$. The current template guess q can then be updated by the pointwise mean of the transformed images and by iterating the following steps:

$$\phi^i = \min_\phi \mathcal{E}_{q,q^i}(\phi),$$
$$q = \tfrac{1}{N} \sum_{i=1}^{N} (\phi^i)^{-1}.q^i.$$

This algorithm can be formally interpreted as a maximum-likelihood estimation of q with L^2-noise on the images. The template estimation problem for images can be given a rigorous probabilistic interpretation in a maximum-likelihood or Bayesian setting with estimation algorithms that are in essence close to the previous steps.

4.6.3 Estimation in a general setting

In the previous cases we implicitly assumed that the metric, as encoded in the RKHS structure on V, is known a priori. This metric can be estimated either with Bayesian approaches or by full estimation of the kernel. However, rather than estimating the full kernel nonparametrically, a limited set of parameters for the kernel can be estimated. This can even be pursued with more general probability models than treated before, for example, by constructing Brownian motion or similar processes on $\mathrm{Diff}(\Omega)$ and $\mathcal{S}$ and by estimating parameters based on those.

4.6.4 Stochastics

When we considered landmarks in Section 4.5.1, we produced a Hamiltonian formulation of shape deformation (4.15). This enabled us to construct a flow between the initial positions of the landmarks and their final positions at time $t = 1$, parameterized by the momenta. In addition to uncertainty in the initial and final positions of the landmarks, there may be stochastic effects that perturb the shape evolution on the entire time interval $[0, 1]$. To allow incorporation of such time-continuous random effects, the set of ODEs for the geodesics evolution of landmarks can be transferred to a set of SDEs (stochastic differential equations). The noise takes the form of a Brownian motion or a Wiener process, a process with independent Gaussian zero-mean increments that is added to the flow. The Hamiltonian phase-space formulation makes it easy to introduce noise that is coupled to either the position variables, the momentum variables, or a combination of the two.

There are different possible choices of where and how the noise should be added, which depends upon the particular aim of the analysis. One option is to add a noise term into the update of the momentum: $dp = -\nabla_q H dt + \sigma dB(t)$, where $dB(t)$ is the Brownian motion, and σ is its variance. Alternatively, it can be useful to consider that the system of ODEs is embedded into a heat bath that dissipates heat from the system, which leads to the Langevin formulation. The only change is that the momentum update equation includes a dissipation term with parameter λ: $dp = [-\lambda \nabla_p H - \nabla_q H]dt + \sigma dB(t)$. It has the benefit that the start- and end-points are treated equally (so that there be noise in both), and the flow is time-reversible. An alternative way to introduce noise is to add it into the time-dependent vector fields that arise from the LDDMM formulation, which leads to a stochastic form of EPDiff. A family of fields $\sigma_1, \ldots, \sigma_J$ is defined on the landmark domain Ω, and noise is multiplied on these fields:

$$dx_i = \frac{\partial H}{\partial p_i} dt + \sum_{l=1}^{J} \sigma_l(x_i) \circ dB_l(t),$$

$$dp_i = -\frac{\partial H}{\partial x_i} dt - \sum_{l=1}^{J} \frac{\partial}{\partial x_i} \left(p_i \cdot \sigma_l(x_i) \right) \circ dB_l(t).$$

(4.22)

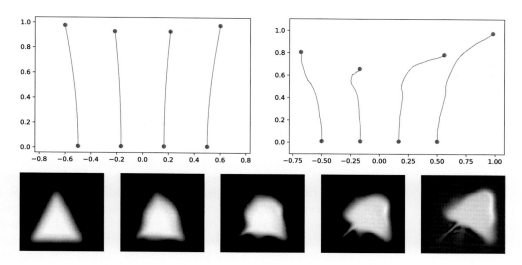

Figure 4.4. *(Top row) (left)* Geodesic evolution with 4 landmarks; *(right)* landmark geodesic perturbed by Langevin noise. *(Bottom row)* Stochastic image trajectory with the stochastic EPDiff model corresponding to a noisy version of the deterministic geodesic in Fig. 4.3.

Methods for parameter estimation for these processes can be based on Brownian bridge simulation, as described in Chapter 10, and see Fig. 4.4 for examples.

4.7 Outer and inner shape metrics

The LDDMM metrics on shapes are derived from the action of diffeomorphisms on the entire domain Ω. These are known as *outer metrics*, and variations of such deformations sense the entire domain, so that the movement of one landmark in a configuration has an effect on the other landmarks in the configuration, as encoded by the kernel. This means that points between landmarks will move, since they are influenced by other parts of the object, and also that a closed curve will resist being shrunk, because the diffeomorphism metrics generally sense compression of the domain in the interior part of the domain that is bounded by the curve. It is possible to define metrics based only on the shapes and their geometry, without referring to deformations of the domain in which the shapes reside. These are known as *inner metrics*.

We will focus on shapes $\gamma(\mathbb{S}^1)$ represented by closed curves $\gamma \in \text{Emb}(\mathbb{S}^1, \mathbb{R}^2)$. This means that the constructions will generally be invariant to the representation encoded in γ. The most basic of such invariant constructions are the arclength derivative $D_s = \|\partial_\theta \gamma\|^{-1} \partial_\theta$ and the volume form $ds = \|\partial_\theta \gamma\| \, d\theta$. The most direct example of an inner metric on shape-tangent spaces is the L^2-metric, which on $\mathrm{Emb}(\mathbb{S}^1, \mathbb{R}^2)$ takes the form

$$g(v, w) = \int_{\mathbb{S}^1} \langle v(\theta), w(\theta) \rangle \, ds \,, \tag{4.23}$$

where the integration is with respect to the arclength volume, and the $\mathbb{R}^2$ inner product is used pointwise for the tangent vectors $v, w \in T_\gamma \mathrm{Emb}(\mathbb{S}^1, \mathbb{R}^2)$ evaluated at each $\theta \in \mathbb{S}^1$. The tangent vectors v, w of the curve can be seen as arclength-parameterized vectors in $\mathbb{R}^2$ or as vector fields in $\mathbb{S}^1$, in which case the inner product is the pullback metric from the embedding of the shape in $\mathbb{R}^2$. This is very simple to define, but it has an extremely surprising problem: the geodesic distance vanishes in the shape space $\mathrm{Emb}(\mathbb{S}^1, \mathbb{R}^2)/\mathrm{Diff}(\mathbb{S}^1)$, that is, geodesics of arbitrary small length can be found between any pair of curves, and so it is degenerate. Intuitively, the reason why this happens is that the metric is blind to "spikes" that shoot up to join the two curves, and, given enough of these spikes, the two curves are indistinguishable. Such geodesics will have large variation in their derivatives, but the pointwise metric does not sense this. The same situation arises on $\mathrm{Emb}(\mathbb{S}^1, \mathbb{R}^2)$. This is a purely infinite-dimensional phenomenon; in finite dimensions, Riemannian metrics always induce nondegenerate geodesic distances.

To have positive geodesic distances, stronger metrics that prevent this strange behavior are needed. This can be achieved by including higher-order derivatives in the metric. Let L_γ be a map $T_\gamma \mathrm{Emb}(\mathbb{S}^1, \mathbb{R}^2) \to T_\gamma \mathrm{Emb}(\mathbb{S}^1, \mathbb{R}^2)$ and use this to generalize (4.23) to

$$g(v, w) = \int_{\mathbb{S}^1} \langle L_\gamma v(\theta), w(\theta) \rangle \, ds \,. \tag{4.24}$$

To give an inner product, L_γ must be linear and symmetric, and we furthermore assume that $g(v, w)$ is positive-definite. In the case of L_γ being a pseudo-differential operator, the resulting metrics are of Sobolev type. If the operator L_γ is equivariant to reparameterizations of $\mathbb{S}^1$ (i.e., $L_{\gamma \circ \phi} h \circ \phi = (L_\gamma h) \circ \phi$), then the inner product descends to the shape space $\mathrm{Emb}(\mathbb{S}^1, \mathbb{R}^2)/\mathrm{Diff}(\mathbb{S}^1)$.

Examples of Sobolev inner metrics are the H^1 metric with $L_\gamma = I_n - D_s^2$ (where I_n is the $n \times n$ identify matrix), which we already saw in Section 4.4.3, and the $\dot{H}^1$-metric with $L_\gamma = D_s^2$. The latter metric omits the L^2-part of the metric, which means that it is only positive on $\mathrm{Emb}(\mathbb{S}^1, \mathbb{R}^k)$ modulo translations of $\mathbb{R}^k$. There are also a set of metrics known as the elastic metrics, which will be described in further detail in Chapter 11. They can be written as

$$g^{a,b}(h,k) = \int_{\mathbb{S}^1} a^2 |(D_s h)^\perp| \, |(D_s k)^\perp| + b^2 |(D_s h)^\top| \, |(D_s k)^\top| ds, \quad (4.25)$$

where $D_s = \frac{1}{|c'|} \partial_\theta$ is the arclength derivative, $ds = |c'| d\theta$ is the arclength parameter for integration, $|(D_s h)^\top| = \langle D_s h(\theta), v(\theta) \rangle$ is the tangential component of $D_s h$ (where $v = D_s c$ is the unit length tangent vector), and $|(D_s h)^\perp| = D_s h - (D_s h)^\top v$, the normal component. These tangential and normal components correspond to the bending and stretching of the curve.

Beyond first order, the family of metrics of the form

$$g^{a_i}(v, w) = \int_{\mathbb{S}^1} a_0 \langle v(\theta), w(\theta) \rangle + a_0 \langle D_s v(\theta), D_s w(\theta) \rangle + \cdots$$
$$+ a_n \langle D_s^n v(\theta), D_s^n w(\theta) \rangle ds \quad (4.26)$$

are the Sobolev metrics (for nth order) with constant coefficients.

4.7.1 Sobolev geodesics

In contrast to the L^2-metric (4.23), higher-order Sobolev metrics are nondegenerate on the shape space $\mathrm{Emb}(\mathbb{S}^1, \mathbb{R}^k)/\mathrm{Diff}(\mathbb{S}^1)$ in the sense that the geodesic distance between nonequal curves is nonvanishing. In addition, their geodesic equation is locally well-posed (and for second-order metrics, even globally well-posed).

For the constant coefficient Sobolev metrics (4.26), the geodesic equation is a PDE that, in the second-order case, takes the explicit form

$$\partial_t p = -\frac{a_0}{2} \|\partial_\theta \gamma\| \, D_s \left(\langle \partial_t \gamma, \partial_t \gamma \rangle \, D_s \gamma \right)$$
$$+ \frac{a_1}{2} \|\partial_\theta \gamma\| \, D_s \left(\langle D_s \partial_t \gamma, D_s \partial_t \gamma \rangle \, D_s \gamma \right)$$
$$- \frac{a_2}{2} \|\partial_\theta \gamma\| \, D_s \left(\langle D_s^3 \partial_t \gamma, D_s \partial_t \gamma \rangle \, D_s \gamma \right)$$
$$+ \frac{a_2}{2} \|\partial_\theta \gamma\| \, D_s \left(\langle D_s^2 \partial_t \gamma, D_s^2 \partial_t \gamma \rangle \, D_s \gamma \right), \quad (4.27)$$

where the momentum $p = \|\partial_\theta \gamma\| (a_0 \partial_t \gamma - a_1 D_s^2 \partial_t \gamma + a_2 D_s^4 \partial_t \gamma)$. Fig. 4.5 shows a second-order Sobolev metric between two curves.[1]

---

[1] Computed using h2metrics https://github.com/h2metrics/.

Figure 4.5. Geodesic between two corpus callosum shapes with a second-order Sobolev metric.

4.8 Further reading

We here provide some references to enable the interested reader to follow up on particular areas. A very large literature has grown up on shape analysis over the last 20 years; our aim is not to summarize it, but to provide some references to other introductory or particularly important works. For the same reason, we emphasize expository material over research publications.

A general introduction to shape and diffeomorphisms can be found in [33], particularly with respect to LDDMM; survey articles summarizing LDDMM include [22] and [23]. A description of non-diffeomorphic methods of image registration and suitable algorithms for image transformation, can be found in [19]. A more general survey of signal processing, which includes diffeomorphic shape matching as one of the main examples, is [16]. There is an introduction to pattern theory, of which computational anatomy is a part, in [8]. The book that is generally credited with the idea of transforming objects by deforming an underlying grid on which they lie is D'Arcy Thompson's 1917 masterpiece "On Growth and Form", the second edition is [29]; see particularly chapter XVII.

The Arnold formulation of Euler equations as geodesics on groups is described in [3]; another useful reference is [14]. This latter reference also gives various examples of other applications, including optimal mass transport, in the appendices. The derivation of the EPDiff equation as presented in this chapter follows [20] and [9].

Some introductions to the underlying mathematics, particularly from the viewpoint of geometric mechanics, include [20,2] and [9], as well as [27]. More careful considerations of the analytical difficulties are considered in [7] and also [12]; see also [13]. A helpful reference is [24]. Another view of shape and geometry that is more linked to computer vision can be found in [6].

Introductions to reproducing kernel Hilbert spaces can be found in [32,25]; they are also treated in [33].

A description of the Hamiltonian formulation of EPDiff based on the particle ansatz and the links to the various metrics can be found in [17]. The three approaches to stochastic landmark development that were described can be found in [30,21,1]. Template estimation is treated in [10] and in the Bayesian case in [34]. For metric estimation, see [31], and from a stochastic viewpoint, see [26].

For an overview of the metrics on shape spaces, see [18,4] and references therein.

The statistical analysis of shape and the original concept of shape spaces are surveyed in [15] and [5]; see also [28]. LDDMM-based image template estimation was introduced in [10].

The figures were produced using the landmark code in Theano geometry https://bitbucket.org/stefansommer/theanogeometry [11] and h2metrics https://github.com/h2metrics/h2metrics.

References

1. Alexis Arnaudon, Darryl D. Holm, Stefan Sommer, A geometric framework for stochastic shape analysis, Foundations of Computational Mathematics (July 2018).
2. Ralph Abraham, Jerry Marsden, Tudor Ratiu, Manifolds, Tensor Analysis and Applications, Springer, 2004.
3. V.I. Arnold, Mathematical Methods of Classical Mechanics, 2nd edition, Springer, New York, 1989.
4. Martin Bauer, Martins Bruveris, Peter W. Michor, Overview of the geometries of shape spaces and diffeomorphism groups, Journal of Mathematical Imaging and Vision 50 (1–2) (September 2014) 60–97.
5. Ian Dryden, Kanti Mardia, Statistical Shape Analysis, John Wiley & Sons, New Jersey, 1998.
6. M.C. Delfour, J-P. Zolésio, Shapes and Geometries: Metrics, Analysis, Differential Calculus, and Optimization, SIAM, 2001.
7. David Ebin, Jerrold Marsden, Groups of diffeomorphisms and the motion of an incompressible fluid, Annals of Mathematics 92 (1970) 102–163.
8. Ulf Grenander, Michael I. Miller, Pattern Theory: From Representation to Inference, Oxford University Press, Oxford, 2007.
9. Darryl D. Holm, Tanya Schmah, Cristina Stoica, Geometric Mechanics and Symmetry: From Finite to Infinite Dimensions, Oxford University Press, Oxford, 2009.
10. S. Joshi, Brad Davis, B. Matthieu Jomier, B. Guido Gerig, Unbiased diffeomorphic atlas construction for computational anatomy, NeuroImage 23 (2004) 151–160.
11. Line Kühnel, Alexis Arnaudon, Stefan Sommer, Differential geometry and stochastic dynamics with deep learning numerics, Applied Mathematics and Computation 356 (1 September 2019) 411–437.

12. Boris Khesin, J. Lenells, Gerard Misiolek, Stephen C. Preston, Geometry of diffeomorphism groups, complete integrability and geometric statistics, Geometric and Functional Analysis 23 (2013) 334–366.
13. Andreas Kriegl, Peter Michor, The Convenient Setting of Global Analysis, American Mathematical Society, 1997.
14. Boris Khesin, Robert Wendt, The Geometry of Infinite Dimensional Groups, Springer, Berlin, 2009.
15. Huiling Le, David G. Kendall, The Riemannian structure of Euclidean shape spaces: a novel environment for statistics, The Annals of Statistics 21 (3) (1993) 1225–1271.
16. David Mumford, Agnés Desolneux, Pattern Theory: The Stochastic Analysis of Real-World Signals, AK Peters, Massachusetts, 2010.
17. Robert I. McLachlan, Stephen Marsland, N-particle dynamics of the Euler equations for planar diffeomorphisms, Dynamical Systems 22 (3) (2007) 269–290.
18. Peter Michor, David Mumford, An overview of the Riemannian metrics on spaces of curves using the Hamiltonian approach, Applications of Computational Harmonic Analysis 23 (1) (2007) 74–113.
19. Jan Modersitzki, Numerical Methods for Image Registration, Oxford University Press, Oxford, 2003.
20. Jerrold Marsden, Tudor Ratiu, Introduction to Mechanics and Symmetry, 2nd edition, Springer, Berlin, 1999.
21. S. Marsland, T. Shardlow, Langevin equations for landmark image registration with uncertainty, SIAM Journal on Imaging Sciences 10 (2) (January 2017) 782–807.
22. Michael I. Miller, Alain Trouvé, Laurent Younes, On the metrics and Euler–Lagrange equations of computational anatomy, Annual Review of Biomedical Engineering 4 (1) (2002) 375–405.
23. Michael I. Miller, Alain Trouvé, Laurent Younes, Hamiltonian systems and optimal control in computational anatomy: 100 years since D'Arcy Thompson, Annual Review of Biomedical Engineering 17 (1) (2015) 447–509.
24. Karl-Hermann Neeb, Nancy lectures on infinite-dimensional Lie groups, 2002.
25. Jeff M. Phillips, Suresh Venkatasubramanian, A gentle introduction to the kernel distance, arXiv:1103.1625, 2011.
26. Stefan Sommer, Alexis Arnaudon, Line Kuhnel, Sarang Joshi, Bridge simulation and metric estimation on landmark manifolds, in: Graphs in Biomedical Image Analysis, Computational Anatomy and Imaging Genetics, in: Lecture Notes in Computer Science, Springer, September 2017, pp. 79–91.
27. Rudolf Schmid, Infinite dimensional Lie groups with applications to mathematical physics, Journal of Geometry and Symmetry in Physics 1 (2004) 54–120.
28. Anuj Srivastava, Eric Klassen, Functional and Shape Data Analysis, Springer, 2016.
29. D'Arcy W. Thompson, On Growth and Form, 2nd edition, Cambridge University Press, Cambridge, 1942.

30. Alain Trouve, François-Xavier Vialard, Shape splines and stochastic shape evolutions: a second order point of view, Quarterly of Applied Mathematics 70 (2) (2012) 219–251.
31. François-Xavier Vialard, Laurent Risser, Spatially-varying metric learning for diffeomorphic image registration: a variational framework, in: MICCAI, Springer, 2014, pp. 227–234.
32. Grace Wahba, Spline Models for Observational Data, SIAM, 1990.
33. Laurent Younes, Shapes and Diffeomorphisms, Springer, 2010.
34. Miaomiao Zhang, Nikhil Singh, P. Thomas Fletcher, Bayesian estimation of regularization and atlas building in diffeomorphic image registration, in: Information Processing for Medical Imaging (IPMI), in: Lecture Notes in Computer Science, Springer, 2013, pp. 37–48.

5

Beyond Riemannian geometry
The affine connection setting for transformation groups

Xavier Pennec, Marco Lorenzi
Université Côte d'Azur and Inria, Epione team, Sophia Antipolis, France

5.1 Introduction

In computational anatomy, we need to perform statistics on shapes and transformations and to transport these statistics from one point to another (e.g. from a subject to a template or to another subject). In this chapter we consider the points of view of abstract transformations, independently of their action on objects. To perform statistics on such transformation groups, the methodology developed in the previous chapters consists in endowing the Lie group with a left- (or right-)invariant metric, which turns the transformation group into a Riemannian manifold. Then we can use the tools developed in Chapter 2 such as the Fréchet mean, tangent PCA, or PGA.

On a Lie group this Riemannian approach is consistent with the group operations if a biinvariant metric exists, which is, for example, the case for compact groups such as rotations. In this case, the biinvariant Fréchet mean has many desirable invariance properties: it is invariant with respect to left- and right-multiplication, as well as to inversion. However, a left-invariant metric on a Lie group is generally not right-invariant (and conversely). Since the inverse operation exchanges a left-invariant metric for a right-invariant one, such metrics are generally not inverse consistent either. In this case the Fréchet mean based on a left-invariant distance is consistent neither with right translations nor with inversions. A simple example of this behavior is given in Section 5.5.2.4 with 2D rigid-body transformations.

In parallel to Riemannian methods based on left- or right-invariant metrics, numerous methods in Lie groups are based on the group properties and in particular on one-parameter subgroups, realized by the matrix exponential in matrix Lie groups. There exist particularly efficient algorithms to compute the matrix exponential like the scaling and squaring procedure [35] or for

Riemannian Geometric Statistics in Medical Image Analysis
https://doi.org/10.1016/B978-0-12-814725-2.00012-1

integrating differential equations on Lie groups in geometric numerical integration theory [32,37]. In medical image registration, parameterizing diffeomorphism with the flow of Stationary Velocity Fields (SVFs) was proposed in [8] and very quickly adopted by many other authors. The group structure was also used to obtain efficient polyaffine transformations in [9]. Last but not least, [7,69] showed that the biinvariant mean could be defined on Lie groups when the square root (thus the log) of the transformations exists.

The goal of this chapter is explaining the mathematical roots of these algorithms, which are in fact based on an affine connection structure instead of a Riemannian one. The connection defines the parallel transport and thus the notion of geodesics that extends straight lines: the tangent vector to an autoparallel curve stays parallel to itself all along the curve. In finite dimension these geodesics define exponential and log maps locally, so we may generalize some of the statistical tools developed in Chapter 2 to affine connection spaces. As there is no distance, the Fréchet/Karcher means have to be replaced by the weaker notion of exponential barycenters (which are the critical points of the variance in Riemannian manifolds). Higher-order moments and the Mahalanobis distance can be defined (locally) without trouble. However, tangent PCA is not easy to generalize as there is no reference metric to diagonalize the covariance matrix.

In the case of Lie groups we describe in Section 5.3 the natural family of connections proposed by Cartan and Schouten in 1926, which are left- and right-invariant, and for which one-parameter subgroups (the flow of left-invariant vector fields) are the geodesics going through the identity. Among these, there is a unique symmetric (torsion free) connection, called the canonical symmetric Cartan–Schouten (CCS) connection. We show in Section 5.4 that when there exists a biinvariant metric on the Lie group (i.e. when the group is the direct product of Abelian and compact groups), the CCS connection is the Levi-Civita connection of that metric. However, the CCS connection still exists even when there is no biinvariant metric. This is also the unique affine connection induced by the canonical symmetric space structure of the Lie groups with the symmetry $s_g(h) = gh^{-1}g$.

Based on the biinvariance properties of the CCS connection, we turn in Section 5.5 to biinvariant group means defined as exponential barycenters. These means exist locally and are unique for sufficiently concentrated data. In a number of Lie groups that do not support any biinvariant metric, for instance, nilpotent or some specific solvable groups, we show that there is even global uniqueness. Thus, the group mean appears to be a very general and natural notion on Lie groups. However, the absence of a metric significantly complexifies the analysis to identify whenever data are sufficiently concentrated or not, contrarily to Riemannian manifolds, where we now have fairly tight conditions on the support of the distribution to ensure the existence and uniqueness of the Riemannian Fréchet mean. The particular case of rigid-body transformations shows that fairly similar conditions could be derived for the biinvariant group mean. The question of how this result extends to other Lie groups remains open.

Section 5.6 investigates the application of the CCS affine connection setting to Lie groups of diffeomorphisms, which justifies the use of deformations parameterized by the flow of stationary velocity fields (SVFs) in medical image registration. Although a number of theoretical difficulties remains when moving to infinite dimensions, very efficient algorithms are available, like the scaling and squaring to compute the group exponential and its (log)-Jacobian, the composition using the Baker–Campbell–Hausdorff formula, and so on. This allows the straightforward extension of the classical "demons" image registration algorithm to encode diffeomorphic transformations parameterized by SVFs. A special feature of the log-demons registration framework is to enforce almost seamlessly the inverse consistency of the registration.

The log-demons algorithm can be used to accurately evaluate the anatomical changes over time for different subjects from time sequences of medical images. However, the resulting deformation trajectories are expressed in each subject's own geometry. Thus it is necessary to transport the intrasubject deformation information to a common reference frame to evaluate the differences between clinical groups in this type of longitudinal study. Instead of transporting a scalar summary of the deformation trajectory (usually the (log)-Jacobian determinant), we can transport the parameters of the full deformation thanks to the parallel transport. We detail in Section 5.7 two discrete parallel transport methods based on the computation of the geodesics, the Schild's ladder and a more symmetric variant called the pole ladder, specialized for the parallel transport along geodesics. Most parallel transport methods are shown to be first-order approximations. It is noticeable that the pole ladder is actually a third-order scheme, which becomes exact in symmetric spaces. We illustrate the computational advantages and demonstrate the numerical accuracy of this method by providing an application to the modeling of the longitudinal atrophy progression in Alzheimer's disease (AD). The quality of the resulting average models of normal and disease deformation trajectories suggests that an important gain in sensitivity could be expected in groupwise comparisons. For example, a statistically significant association between the brain shape evolution and the $A\beta_{1-42}$ biomarker among normal subjects of the ADNI study was identified in [52]. Moreover, this framework is among the leading methods benchmarked in [20] for the quantification of longitudinal hippocampal and ventricular atrophy, showing favorable results compared to state-of-the-art approaches based on image segmentation.

5.2 Affine connection spaces

Geodesics, exponential and log maps are among the most fundamental tools to work on differential manifolds, as we have seen in the previous chapters. However, when our manifold is given an additional structure, which is the case, for instance, for Lie groups, a compatible Riemannian metric does not always exist. We investigate in this section how we can define the notion of geodesics in non-Riemannian spaces. The main idea is to rely on the notion of curve with vanishing acceleration or, equivalently, of curves whose tangent vectors remain parallel to themselves (autoparallel curves). To compare vectors living in different tangent spaces (even at points that are infinitesimally close), we need to provide a notion of parallel transport from one tangent space to the other. Likewise, computing accelerations requires the notion of infinitesimal parallel transport, which is called a connection.

We consider a smooth differential manifold $\mathcal{M}$. We denote by $T_p\mathcal{M}$ the tangent space at $p \in \mathcal{M}$ and by $T\mathcal{M}$ the tangent bundle. A section of that bundle $X : \mathcal{M} \mapsto T\mathcal{M}$ is a smooth vector field whose value at p is denoted $X|_p$. The set of vector fields, denoted $\Gamma(\mathcal{M})$, can be identified with derivations. Recall that a derivation δ is a linear map from $\Gamma(\mathcal{M})$ to itself that satisfies the Leibniz's law: $\delta(fX) = (df)X + f(\delta X)$ for any $f \in C^\infty(\mathcal{M})$ and $X \in \Gamma(\mathcal{M})$. In a local coordinate system a derivation writes as $X\phi|_p = \partial_X\phi|_p = \frac{d}{dt}\left(\phi(p + tX|_p)\right)$. In this chapter we prefer the notation $\partial_X\phi$ to the notation $X\phi$. Composing two derivations is in general not a derivation because a term with second-order derivative appears when we write it in a local coordinate system. However, this second-order term can be canceled by subtracting the symmetric composition, so that the bracket $[X, Y](\phi) = \partial_X\partial_Y\phi - \partial_Y\partial_X\phi$ of two vector fields is itself a vector field. Endowed with this bracket, the set of vector fields $\Gamma(\mathcal{M})$ is the algebra of derivations of smooth functions $\phi \in C^\infty(\mathcal{M})$.

5.2.1 Affine connection as an infinitesimal parallel transport

To compare vectors in the tangent space at one point of the manifold with vectors that are tangent at a different point, we need to define a mapping between these two tangent spaces; this is the notion of parallel transport. As there is generally no way to define globally a linear operator $\Pi_p^q : T_p\mathcal{M} \to T_q\mathcal{M}$ that is consistent with the composition (i.e. $\Pi_p^q \circ \Pi_r^p = \Pi_r^q$), the path connecting the two points p and q has to be specified.

Definition 5.1 (Parallel transport along a curve). *Let γ be a curve in $\mathcal{M}$ joining $\gamma(s)$ to $\gamma(t)$. A parallel transport assigns to each curve a collection of mappings $\Pi(\gamma)_s^t : T_{\gamma(s)}\mathcal{M} \to T_{\gamma(t)}\mathcal{M}$ such that:*
- *$\Pi(\gamma)_s^s = \mathrm{Id}$, the identity transformation of $T_{\gamma(s)}\mathcal{M}$.*
- *$\Pi(\gamma)_u^t \circ \Pi(\gamma)_s^u = \Pi(\gamma)_s^t$ (consistency along the curve).*
- *The dependence of Π on γ, s, and t is smooth.*

The notion of (affine) connection, also called the covariant derivative, is the infinitesimal version of the parallel transport for the tangent bundle. Let $X|_p = \dot{\gamma}(0)$ be the tangent vector at the initial point p of the curve γ, and let Y be a vector field. Then $\nabla_X Y = \frac{d}{dt}\Pi(\gamma)_t^0 Y|_{\gamma(t)}\big|_{t=0}$ defines a bilinear map, which is independent of the curve γ and only depends on the vector fields X and Y.

Definition 5.2 (Affine connection). *An affine connection (or covariant derivative) on the manifold $\mathcal{M}$ is a bilinear map $(X, Y) \in \Gamma(\mathcal{M}) \times \Gamma(\mathcal{M}) \mapsto \nabla_X Y \in \Gamma(\mathcal{M})$ such that for all smooth functions $\phi \in C^\infty(\mathcal{M})$:*
- *$\nabla_{\phi X} Y = \phi \nabla_X Y$, that is, ∇ is smooth and linear in the first variable;*
- *$\nabla_X(\phi Y) = \partial_X \phi Y + \phi \nabla_X Y$, that is, ∇ satisfies the Leibniz rule in the second variable.*

In a local chart the vector fields ∂_i constitute a basis of $\Gamma(\mathcal{M})$: a vector field $X = x^i \partial_i$ has coordinates $x^i \in C^\infty(\mathcal{M})$ (using Einstein summation convention). Similarly, let $Y = y^i \partial_i$. Using the two rules, we can write the connection

$$\nabla_X Y = x^i \nabla_{\partial_i}(y^j \partial_j) = x^i y^j \nabla_{\partial_i}\partial_j + x^i \partial_i y^j \partial_j = x^i y^j \nabla_{\partial_i}\partial_j + \partial_X Y.$$

This means that the connection is completely determined by its coordinates on the basis vector fields $\nabla_{\partial_i}\partial_j = \Gamma_{ij}^k \partial_k$. The n^3 coordinates Γ_{ij}^k of the connection are called the Christoffel symbols. They encode how the transport from one tangent space to neighboring ones modifies the standard derivative of a vector field in a chart: $\nabla_X Y = \partial_X Y + x^i y^j \Gamma_{ij}^k \partial_k$.

Definition 5.3 (Covariant derivative along a curve). *Let $\gamma(t)$ be a curve on $\mathcal{M}$, and let $Y = Y(\gamma(t))$ be a vector field along the curve. The covariant derivative of Y along $\gamma(t)$ is*

$$\frac{\nabla Y}{dt} = \nabla_{\dot{\gamma}} Y = \partial_{\dot{\gamma}} Y + Y^i \dot{\gamma}^j \Gamma_{ij}^k(\gamma) \partial_k.$$

A vector field is covariantly constant along the curve γ if $\nabla Y/dt = \nabla_{\dot{\gamma}} Y = 0$. This defines the parallel transport according to the connection: specifying the value of the field at one point $Y(\gamma(0)) = u$ determines the value $Y(\gamma(t)) = \Pi(\gamma)_0^t u$ of a covariantly constant field at all the other points of the curve.

The connection we defined so far is differentiating vector fields. It can be uniquely extended to covectors and more general tensor fields by requiring the resulting operation to be compatible with tensor contraction and the product rule $\nabla_X(Y \otimes Z) = (\nabla_X Y) \otimes Z + Y \otimes (\nabla_X Z)$.

5.2.2 Geodesics

Looking for curves whose tangent vectors are covariantly constant provides a definition of geodesics in affine connection spaces that generalizes straight lines; these are the curves that remain parallel to themselves (autoparallel curves).

Definition 5.4 (Affine geodesics). $\gamma(t)$ *is a geodesic if its tangent vector $\dot{\gamma}(t)$ remains parallel to itself, that is, if the covariant derivative $\nabla_{\dot{\gamma}} \dot{\gamma} = 0$ of γ is zero. In a local coordinate system the equation of the geodesics is thus $\ddot{\gamma}^k + \Gamma_{ij}^k \dot{\gamma}^i \dot{\gamma}^j = 0$.*

We retrieve here the standard equation of the geodesics in Riemannian geometry without having to rely on any particular metric. However, it is remarkable that we still conserve many properties of the Riemannian exponential map in affine connection spaces: as geodesics are locally defined by a second-order ordinary differential equation, the geodesic $\gamma_{(p,v)}(t)$ starting at any point p with any tangent vector v is defined for a sufficiently small time, which means that we can define the affine exponential map $\exp_p(v) = \gamma_{(p,v)}(1)$ for a sufficiently small neighborhood. Moreover, the *strong Whitehead theorem* still holds.

Theorem 5.1 (Strong form of Whitehead theorem). *Each point of an affine connection space has a* normal convex neighborhood *(NCN) in the sense that for any couple of points (p, q) in this neighborhood, there exists a unique geodesic $\gamma(t)$ joining them that is entirely contained in this neighborhood. Moreover, the geodesic $\gamma(t)$ depends smoothly on the points p and q.*

The proof of this theorem essentially involves the nonsingularity of the differential of the map $\Phi(p, v) = (p, \exp_p(v))$ and the inverse function theorem, with the use of an auxiliary Euclidean metric on the tangent spaces around the point of interest. We refer to [71, Proposition 1.3, p. 13] for a detailed proof.

As geodesics control many properties of the space, it is interesting to know which affine connections lead to the same geodesics. Intuitively, a geodesic for a connection ∇ will remain a geodesic for another connection $\bar{\nabla}$ if the parallel transport of the tangent vector *in the direction of this tangent vector* is the same, that is, if $\nabla_X X = \bar{\nabla}_X X$ for any vector field X. However, the parallel transport of other vectors of a frame can change: this can be measured by torsion. The curvature is a second-order measure of how the parallel transport differ along different paths.

Definition 5.5 (Torsion and curvature tensors of an affine connection). *The torsion of an affine connection is*

$$T(X, Y) = \nabla_X Y - \nabla_Y X - [X, Y] = -T(Y, X).$$

This tensor measures how the skew-symmetric part differs from the Lie derivative $\mathcal{L}_X Y = [X, Y]$. The connection is called torsion-free (or symmetric) if the torsion vanishes. The curvature tensor is defined by

$$R(X, Y)Z = \nabla_X \nabla_Y Z - \nabla_Y \nabla_X Z - \nabla_{[X,Y]}Z.$$

It measures how the infinitesimal parallel transport differs along the sides of a geodesic parallelogram.

We can show that two connections have the same geodesics if they have the same symmetric part $(\nabla_X Y + \nabla_Y X)/2$, that is, if they only differ by torsion. Thus, at least for the geodesics, we can restrict our attention to the torsion-free connections. Conversely, any procedure involving only geodesics (such as the Schild's or the pole ladders developed later in this chapter) is insensitive to the torsion of a connection.

5.2.3 Levi-Civita connection of a Riemannian metric

Now that we have developed the theory of affine connection spaces, it is time to see how it relates to Riemannian geometry. Let $g_{ij} = \langle \partial_i, \partial_j \rangle$ be a smooth positive definite bilinear symmetric form on $T\mathcal{M}$. With this metric, we can define geodesics that are (locally) length minimizing. Is there a specific connection for which the two notions of geodesics are the same? The answer is yes; the two constructions do agree thanks to the fundamental theorem of Riemannian geometry.

Theorem 5.2 (Levi-Civita connection of a Riemannian manifold). *On any Riemannian manifold, there exists a unique torsion-free connection that is compatible with the metric as a derivation, called the* Levi-Civita connection. *It satisfies:*

- $T(X, Y) = \nabla_X Y - \nabla_Y X - [X, Y] = 0$ *(symmetry)*,
- $\partial_X \langle Y, Z \rangle = \langle \nabla_X Y, Z \rangle + \langle Y, \nabla_X Z \rangle$ *(compatibility with the metric)*.

The proof is constructive. First, we expand $\partial_X \langle Y, Z \rangle + \partial_Y \langle X, Z \rangle - \partial_Z \langle X, Y \rangle$ using the metric compatibility condition. Then we use the zero torsion formula to replace $\nabla_Y X$ by $\nabla_X Y + [Y, X]$ and similarly for $\nabla_Z Y$ and $\nabla_Z X$. We obtain the Khozul formula, which uniquely defines the scalar product of the connection with any vector field (thus the connection):

$$2 \langle \nabla_X Y, Z \rangle = \partial_X \langle Y, Z \rangle + \partial_Y \langle X, Z \rangle - \partial_Z \langle X, Y \rangle + \langle [X, Y], Z \rangle$$
$$- \langle [X, Z], Y \rangle - \langle [Y, Z], X \rangle .$$

Written in a local coordinate system, we have $\langle \nabla_{\partial_i} \partial_j, \partial_k \rangle = g_{mk} \Gamma_{ij}^m$. Let $[g^{ij}] = [g_{ij}]^{-1}$ be the inverse of the metric matrix. Then the extension of the right part of the Khozul formula shows that the Christoffel symbols of the Levi-Civita connection are

$$\Gamma_{jk}^i = \frac{1}{2} g^{im} \left(\partial_k g_{mj} + \partial_j g_{mk} - \partial_m g_{jk} \right) . \tag{5.1}$$

5.2.4 Statistics on affine connection spaces

In a connected manifold of dimension d that is orientable and countable at infinity (we even need not the affine structure) the bundle of smooth d-forms $\Omega^d(\mathcal{M}) = \Lambda^d T^* \mathcal{M}$ is trivial, so that there exist sections that never vanish (volume forms). Focusing on nonnegative forms that sum-up to 1, we get the space of probabilities $\text{Prob}(M) = \{ \mu \in \Omega^d(\mathcal{M}) \mid \int_M \mu = 1, \ \mu \geq 0 \}$. With this definition, the space of probabilities is not a manifold but a stratified space because we hit a boundary at each point where $\mu(dx) = 0$. Imposing $\mu > 0$ gives the smooth manifold of never vanishing probabilities that can be endowed with the canonical Fisher–Rao metric, which is the unique metric invariant under the action of diffeomorphisms (reparameterizations of $\mathcal{M}$) for compact manifolds [12]. However, we do not need this metric structure here, so it is more interesting to consider the space $\text{Prob}(M)$ comprising both smooth probabilities and sample distributions like $\mu = \frac{1}{n} \sum_{i=1}^n \delta_{x_i}$.

As for Riemannian manifolds, we cannot define the mean value in an affine connection space with an expectation, unless the space is linear. Since we do not have a distance, we cannot use the minimization of the expected square distance either (the Fréchet mean). However, we may rely on one of their properties, the implicit localization of the mean as a barycenter in exponential coordinates. The weaker affine structure makes it challenging to determine the existence and uniqueness conditions of this more general definition. However, this can be worked out locally. We can also define higher-order moments and some simple statistical tools like the Mahalanobis distance. Other notions like principal component analysis cannot be consistently defined without an additional structure. In the generalization of statistics from Riemannian manifolds to affine connection spaces that we investigate in this section, an important issue is to distinguish the affine notions (relying on geodesics) from the Riemannian ones (relying on the distance).

Mean values with exponential barycenters

Let us start by recalling the classical definition of a mean in the Euclidean space $\mathbb{R}^d$: the mean (or *barycenter*) of a probability μ (or a set of points $\mu = \frac{1}{n} \sum_{i=1}^n \delta_{p_i}$) is the unique point p that satisfies the barycentric equation $\int_{\mathbb{R}^d} (p - q)\, \mu(dq) = 0$. At the mean, the sum of the weighted displacements to each of the sample points is null, that is, the mean is at the center of the data. Notice that this definition is affine because it does not require the dot product.

In a manifold with Riemannian metric $\|\cdot\|_p$ the Fréchet mean of a probability μ is the set of minima of the variance $\sigma^2(p) = \int_{\mathcal{M}} \text{dist}(p, q)^2\, \mu(dq) = \int_{\mathcal{M}} \|\text{Log}_p(q)\|_p^2\, \mu(dq)$. When the cut locus has null measure $\mu(Cut(p)) = 0$, the variance is differentiable, and its gradient is $\nabla \sigma^2(p) = -2 \int_{\mathcal{M}} \text{Log}_p(q)\, \mu(dq) = -2\mathfrak{M}_1(\mu)$. The local minima being critical points, they satisfy the barycentric equation $\int_{\mathcal{M}} \text{Log}_p(q)\, \mu(dq) = 0$ when they belong to the punctured manifold $\mathcal{M}_\mu^* = \{p \in \mathcal{M} \mid \mu(Cut(p)) = 0\}$. This critical condition equation can also be taken as the definition of the mean, which leads to the notion of exponential barycenter proposed in [16,23, 3,4,21].

In an affine connection space the notion of exponential barycenter still makes sense as soon as we can compute the affine logarithm. The Whitehead Theorem 5.1 tells us that there exists a normal convex neighborhood U at each point of the manifold. For sufficiently concentrated probabilities $\mu \in \text{Prob}(U)$ with support in such a neighborhood U, computing the first moment field $\mathfrak{M}_1(\mu) = \int_{\mathcal{M}} \log_p(q)\, \mu(dq)$ makes sense for $p \in U$.

Definition 5.6 (Exponential barycenter in an affine connection space). *For sufficiently concentrated probabilities $\mu \in \text{Prob}(U)$ whose support is included in a normal convex neighborhood U,* *exponential barycenters (of that neighborhood) are the points implicitly defined by*

$$\mathfrak{M}_1(\mu)|_p = \int_{\mathcal{M}} \log_p(q)\, \mu(dq) = 0. \tag{5.2}$$

This definition is close to the Riemannian center of mass (or more specifically, the Riemannian average) of [31] but uses the logarithm of the affine connection instead of the Riemannian logarithm. Notice however that there is an implicit dependency of the convex neighborhood considered in that definition. In the absence of an auxiliary metric there is no evident way to specify a natural convex neighborhood which might be maximal.

Theorem 5.3 (Existence of exponential barycenters). *Distributions with compact support in a normal convex neighborhood U of an affine manifold (M, ∇) have at least one exponential barycenter. Moreover, exponential barycenters are stable by affine diffeomorphisms (connection-preserving maps, which thus preserve the geodesics and the normal convex neighborhoods).*

Proof. The skecth of the proof of [69] is the following. First, the normal neighborhood U being star-shaped, it is homeomorphic to a sphere. Second, because U is convex, the convex combination of vectors of $\log_p(q) \in \log_p(U)$ remains in $\log_p(U)$, so that geodesic shooting along $\mathfrak{M}_1(\mu)$ remains in the normal convex neighborhood: $\exp_p(\mathfrak{M}_1(\mu)) \in U$. By Brouwer's fixed-point theorem there is thus a fixed point within U satisfying $\exp_p(\mathfrak{M}_1(\mu)) = p$ or, equivalently, $\mathfrak{M}_1(\mu) = \int_{\mathcal{M}} \log_p(q)\, \mu(dq) = 0$. A slightly different proof of existence using the index of the vector field $\mathfrak{M}_1(\mu)$ is due to [16]. See also this reference for the stability under affine maps. $\quad\square$

Remark 5.1. For distributions whose supports are too large, exponential barycenters may not exist. One reason is that the affine logarithm might fail to exist, even for geodesically complete affine connection manifolds. The classical example is the group of unimodular real matrices of dimension two $SL(2, \mathbb{R}) = \{A \in GL(2, \mathbb{R}) \mid \det(A) = 1\}$ endowed with the canonical symmetric connection (see the next section), for which we can show that a matrix $A \in SL(2, \mathbb{R})$ has the form $\exp(X)$ iff $A = -\,\mathrm{Id}_2$ or $\mathrm{Tr}(A) > -2$. Thus matrices with $\mathrm{Tr}(A) < -2$ cannot be reached by any geodesic starting from identity. As a consequence, distributions on $SL(2, \mathbb{R})$ with some mass in this domain and at the identity do not fit in a normal convex neighborhood. Such a distribution has no exponential barycenter. We should relate this failure of existence of the mean to a classical phenomenon observed in Euclidean spaces with heavy-tailed distributions, where the first moment is unbounded. It is currently not known if bounding the first moments (with respect to an auxiliary norm) is a sufficient condition for the existence of exponential barycenters in affine connection spaces.

Uniqueness conditions of the exponential barycenter are harder to determine. There exist convex manifolds (affine connection spaces restrained to a convex neighborhood) that do not have a unique exponential barycenter. This is the case of the propeller manifold of [39], where a sample probability of three points with four exponential barycenters is explicitly constructed. Under additional assumptions, controlling the covariant derivative of the logarithm inherited from Riemannian manifolds [16] could show the uniqueness of the exponential barycenter. Generalizing these curvature-based conditions to general affine connection spaces remains to be done.

A different approach relying on a stronger notion of convexity was proposed by Arnaudon and Li [2].

Definition 5.7 (p-convexity). *Let* $(\mathcal{M}, \nabla)$ *be an affine manifold. A separating function on* $\mathcal{M}$ *is a convex function* $\phi : \mathcal{M} \times \mathcal{M} \to \mathbb{R}^+$ *vanishing exactly on the diagonal of the product manifold (considered as an affine manifold with the direct product connection). Here convex means that the restriction of* $\phi(\gamma(t))$ *to any geodesic* $\gamma(t)$ *is a convex function from* $\mathbb{R}$ *to* $\mathbb{R}^+$. *A manifold that carries a smooth separating function* ϕ *such that*

$$c \, d(p, q)^p \leq \phi(p, q) \leq C \, d(p, q)^p$$

for some constants $0 < c < C$, *some positive integer* p, *and some Riemannian distance function* d *is called a manifold with* p-*convex geometry.*

A separating function generalizes the separating property of a distance $(\phi(p, q) = 0 \Leftrightarrow p = q)$ and the ever increasing value when q gets away from p along geodesics but does not respect the triangular inequality. The Whitehead theorem tells us in essence that any point in an affine connection space has a convex neighborhood with 2-convex geometry. In Riemannian manifolds sufficiently small geodesic balls have 2-convex geometry. The p-convexity (for $p \geq 2$) is sufficient to ensure the uniqueness, but there are examples of manifolds where we can prove the uniqueness although they do not have p-convex geometry for any p. This is the case of open hemispheres endowed with the classical Euclidean embedding metric even if each geodesic ball strictly smaller than an open hemisphere has p-convex geometry for some p depending on the radius [38]. This motivates the following extension.

Theorem 5.4 (Uniqueness of the exponential barycenter in CSLCG Manifolds [2]). *A convex affine manifold (M, ∇) is said to be CSLCG (convex, with semilocal convex geometry) if there exists an increasing sequence $(U_n)_{n \geq 1}$ of relatively compact open convex subsets of $\mathcal{M}$ such that $\mathcal{M} = \cup_{n \geq 1} U_n$ and for every U_n ($n \geq 1$), U_n has p-convex geometry for some $p \in 2\mathbb{N}$ depending on n. On a CSLCG manifold, every probability measure with compact support has a unique exponential barycenter.*

Covariance matrix and higher-order moments

The mean is an important statistic that indicates the location of the distribution in the group, but higher-order moments are also needed to characterize the dispersion of the population around this central value. Exponential barycenters are previously defined for sufficiently concentrated probabilities $\mu \in \text{Prob}(U)$ with support in a normal convex neighborhood U, so that computing the first moment field $\mathfrak{M}_1(\mu) = \int_{\mathcal{M}} \log_p(q)\,\mu(dq)$ makes sense for $p \in U$. In this neighborhood, computing higher-order moments also makes sense.

Definition 5.8 (Moments of a probability distribution in an affine connection space). *For sufficiently concentrated probabilities $\mu \in \text{Prob}(U)$ whose support is included in a normal convex neighborhood U, the kth-order moment is the k-contravariant tensor*

$$\mathfrak{M}_k(\mu)|_p = \int_{\mathcal{M}} \underbrace{\log_p(q) \otimes \log_p(q) \ldots \otimes \log_p(q)}_{k \ times}\,\mu(dq). \tag{5.3}$$

In particular, the covariance field is the 2-contravariant tensor with the following coordinates in any basis of the tangent space $T_p\mathcal{M}$:

$$\Sigma|_p^{ij} = \int_{\mathcal{M}} [\log_p(q)]^i [\log_p(q)]^j\,\mu(dq),$$

and its value $\Sigma = \Sigma|_{\bar{p}}$ at the exponential barycenter $\bar{p}$ solution of $\mathfrak{M}_1(\mu)|_{\bar{p}} = 0$ (assuming that it is unique) is called the covariance of μ.

We should be careful that the covariance defined here is a rank $(2, 0)$ (2-contravariant) tensor which is not equivalent to the usual covariance matrix seen as a bilinear form (a 2-covariant or rank $(0, 2)$ tensor belonging to $T_{\bar{p}}^*\mathcal{M} \otimes T_{\bar{p}}^*\mathcal{M}$), unless we have an auxiliary metric to lower the indices. In particular, the usual interpretation of the coordinates of the covariance matrix using the scalar products of data with the basis vectors $\Sigma_{ij} = \int_{\mathcal{M}} <\log_p(q), e_i> <\log_p(q), e_j>\,\mu(dq)$ is valid only if we have a local metric $<\cdot, \cdot>$

that also defines the orthonormality of the basis vectors e_i. Likewise, diagonalizing Σ to extract the main modes of variability only makes sense with respect to a local metric: changing the metric of $T_{\bar{p}}\mathcal{M}$ will not only change the eigenvectors and the eigenvalues but also potentially the order of the eigenvalues. This means that Principle Component Analysis (PCA) cannot be generalized to the affine connection space setting without an additional structure. This is the reason why PCA is sometimes called Proper Orthogonal Decomposition (POD) in certain domains.

Mahalanobis distance

Despite the absence of a canonical reference metric, some interesting tools can be defined from the 2-contravariant tensor in an intrinsic way without having to rely on an auxiliary metric. One of them is the Mahalanobis distance of a point q to a given distribution (in the normal convex neighborhood specified before):

$$d_{\mu}^2(q) = d_{(\bar{p}, \Sigma)}^2(q) = [\log_{\bar{p}}(q)]^i \, \Sigma_{ij}^{-1} [\log_{\bar{p}}(q)]^j. \qquad (5.4)$$

In this formula, $\bar{p}$ is the exponential barycenter of μ, and Σ_{ij}^{-1} are the coefficients of the inverse of the covariance $\Sigma|_{\bar{p}}^{ij}$ in a given basis. We verify that this definition does not depend on the basis chosen for $T_{\bar{p}}\mathcal{M}$. Furthermore, the Mahalanobis distance is invariant under affine diffeomorphisms of the manifold. Indeed, if ϕ is an affine diffeomorphism preserving the connection, then $U' = \phi(U)$ is a normal convex neighborhood that contains the support of the push-forward probability distribution $\mu' = \phi_* \mu$, and the differential $d\phi$ acts as a linear map on the tangent spaces: $\log_{\bar{\phi}(p)}(\phi(q)) = d\phi \log_{\bar{p}}(q)$. This shows that the exponential barycenter (assumed to be unique) is equivariant, $\bar{p}' = \overline{\phi(p)} = \phi(\bar{p})$, and that the covariance is transformed according to $\Sigma' = d\phi \, \Sigma \, d\phi^\top$ in the transformed coordinate system $e_i' = d\phi \, e_i$. Because of the inversion of the matrix Σ' in the Mahalanobis distance, we get the invariance property $d_{(\bar{p}', \Sigma')}^2(q') = d_{(\bar{p}, \Sigma)}^2(q)$ or, more evidently, $d_{\phi_* \mu}^2(\phi(q)) = d_{\mu}^2(q)$.

Open problems for generalizing other statistical tool

This simple extension of the Mahalanobis distance suggests that it might be possible to extend much more statistical definitions and tools on affine connection spaces in a consistent way. One of the key problems is that everything we did so far is limited to small enough normal convex neighborhoods. To tackle distributions of larger nonconvex support, we probably need an additional structure to specify a unique choice of a maximal domain for the log function, as this is done in the Riemannian case by the shortest distance criterion. A second difficulty relies in the absence of a natural reference measure on an affine connection space. This means that probability density functions have to be defined with respect to a given volume form and would be different with the choice of another one. Thus the notions of uniform distribution and entropy of a distribution need to be related to the chosen reference measure. This may considerably complexify the maximum entropy principle used in [66] and Chapter 3 to define the Gaussian distributions (Section 3.4.3). However, certain specific geometric structures like Lie groups may provide additional tools to solve some of these problems, as we will see in the next sections.

5.3 Canonical connections on Lie groups

Let us come back now to Lie groups. We first recall a series of properties of Lie groups in Section 5.3.1 before turning to the search for affine connections that are compatible with the Lie group operations in Section 5.3.2.

5.3.1 The lie group setting

Recall from Chapter 1 that a Lie group G is a smooth manifold provided with an identity element e, a smooth composition rule $(g, h) \in G \times G \mapsto gh \in G$, and a smooth inversion rule Inv: $f \mapsto f^{-1}$, which are both compatible with the manifold structure. The composition operation defines two canonical automorphisms of G called the left and the right translations, $L_g : f \mapsto gf$ and $R_g : f \mapsto fg$. The differential dL_g of the left translations maps the tangent space $T_h G$ to the tangent space $T_{gh} G$. In particular, dL_g maps any vector $x \in T_e G$ to the vector $dL_g x \in T_g G$, giving rise to the vector field $\tilde{x}|_g = dL_g x$. We verify that this vector field is left-invariant: $\tilde{x} \circ L_g = dL_g \tilde{x}$. Conversely, every left-invariant vector field is determined by its value at identity. Moreover, the bracket of two left-invariant vector fields $\tilde{x} = dL x$ and $\tilde{y} = dL y$ is also left-invariant and determined by the vector $[x, y] = [\tilde{x}, \tilde{y}]|_e \in T_e G$. Thus left-invariant vector fields constitute a subalgebra of the algebra of vector fields $\Gamma(G)$ on the group. This is a fundamental algebra for Lie groups, which is called the *Lie algebra* $\mathfrak{g}$. As we have seen, the Lie algebra can be identified with the tangent vector space at identity, endowed with the bracket defined before. Thus the Lie algebra has the same dimension as the group. Because any basis of the tangent space at identity is smoothly transported by left translation into a basis of the tangent space at any point, we can decompose any smooth vector field on the basis of left-invariant ones with coefficients that are smooth functions on the manifold. This means that the algebra of vector fields $\Gamma(G)$ is a finite-dimensional module of dimension $dim(G)$ over the ring $C^\infty(G)$ of smooth functions over the group.

By symmetry we can also define the subalgebra of right-invariant vector fields $\bar{X}|_g = dR_g X$ and identify it with the tangent vector space at identity. However, we should be careful that the right-bracket defined on the tangent space at identity is the opposite of the left bracket. This can be explained by the fact that left and right Lie algebras are related by the inversion map $\text{Inv}: f \mapsto f^{-1}$ of the group, which exchanges left and right compositions, and whose differential at identity is $-\text{Id}_{T_e G}$. As the algebra of right-invariant vector fields is usually used for diffeomorphisms instead of the traditional left-invariant ones for finite-dimensional Lie groups, this explains why there is sometimes a minus sign in the bracket (see Section 5.6.2.4 and comments in [82,15]).

Adjoint group

A third important automorphism of G is the conjugation $C_g: f \mapsto gfg^{-1}$. Differentiating the conjugation with respect to f gives an automorphism of the Lie algebra called the *adjoint action*: an element g of G acts on an element x of $\mathfrak{g}$ by

$$\text{Ad}(g)x = dL_g|_{g^{-1}} dR_{g^{-1}}|_e x = dR_{g^{-1}}|_g dL_g|_e x.$$

In the matrix case we have the classical formula $\text{Ad}(B)M = BMB^{-1}$.

Thus we can map each element of the group to a *linear operator* that acts on the Lie algebra. The mapping $\text{Ad}: G \to \text{GL}(\mathfrak{g})$ is moreover a Lie group homomorphism from G to $\text{GL}(\mathfrak{g})$ since it is smooth and compatible with the group structure: $\text{Ad}(e) = \text{Id}$, $\text{Ad}(g^{-1}) = \text{Ad}(g)^{-1} \ \forall g \in G$, and $\text{Ad}(gh) = \text{Ad}(g)\text{Ad}(h) \ \forall g, h \in G$. Thus G can be "represented" by the adjoint operators acting on $\mathfrak{g}$ in the sense of the representation theory (see [45] for a complete treatment). The subgroup $\text{Ad}(G)$ of the general linear group $\text{GL}(\mathfrak{g})$ is called the *adjoint group*. The properties of this representation and the existence of biinvariant metrics on the group G are intricated.

Taking the derivative of the adjoint map at the identity gives a representation of its Lie algebra: let $g(t)$ be a curve passing through the identity $g(0) = e$ with tangent vector $x \in \mathfrak{g}$. Then, for any $y \in \mathfrak{g}$, $d\text{Ad}(g)y/dt = \text{ad}x(y) = [x, y]$. Thus, $\text{ad}x$ is a linear operator on the Lie algebra $\mathfrak{g}$.

Matrix lie group exponential and logarithm

In the matrix case, the exponential $\exp(M)$ of a square matrix M is given by $\exp(M) = \sum_{k=0}^{\infty} M^k/k!$. Conversely, let $A \in \mathrm{GL}(d)$ be an invertible square matrix. If there exists a matrix $M \in M(d)$ such that $A = \exp(M)$, then M is said to be a logarithm of A. In general, the logarithm of a real invertible matrix may not exist, and it may not be unique if it does. The lack of existence is an unavoidable phenomenon in certain connected Lie groups: we generally need *two* exponentials to reach every element [83]. When a real invertible matrix has no (complex) eigenvalue on the (closed) half-line of negative real numbers, then it has a unique real logarithm whose (complex) eigenvalues have an imaginary part in $(-\pi, \pi)$ [40,27]. In this case this particular logarithm is well-defined and called the *principal logarithm*. We will write $\log(M)$ for the principal logarithm of a matrix M whenever it is defined.

Thanks to their remarkable algebraic properties and essentially to their link with one-parameter subgroups, matrix exponential and logarithms can be quite efficiently numerically computed, for instance, with the popular "Scaling and Squaring Method" [35] and "Inverse Scaling and Squaring Method" [36].

One-parameter subgroups and group exponential

For general Lie groups, the flow $\gamma_x(t)$ of a left-invariant vector field $\tilde{x} = dL\,x$ starting from e with tangent vector x exists for all times. Its tangent vector is $\dot{\gamma}_x(t) = dL_{\gamma_x(t)}x$ by the definition of a flow. Now fix $s \in \mathbb{R}$ and observe that the two curves $\gamma_x(s + t)$ and $\gamma_x(s)\gamma_x(t)$ are going through point $\gamma_x(s)$ with the same tangent vector. By the uniqueness of the flow they are the same, and γ_x is a one-parameter subgroup, that is, a group morphism from $(\mathbb{R}, 0, +)$ to $(G, e, .)$: $\gamma_x(s + t) = \gamma_x(s)\,\gamma_x(t) = \gamma_x(t + s) = \gamma_x(t)\,\gamma_x(s)$.

Definition 5.9 (Group exponential). *Let G be a Lie group, and let x be an element of the Lie algebra $\mathfrak{g}$. The group exponential of x, denoted $\exp(x)$, is given by the value at time 1 of the unique function $\gamma_x(t)$ defined by the ordinary differential equation (ODE) $\dot{\gamma}_x(t) = dL_{\gamma_x(t)}x$ with initial condition $\gamma_x(0) = e$.*

We should be very careful that the group exponential is defined from the group properties only and does not require any Riemannian metric. It is thus generally different from the Riemannian exponential map associated with a Riemannian metric on the Lie group. However, both exponential maps share properties: in finite dimension the group exponential is diffeomorphic locally around 0.

Theorem 5.5 (Group logarithm). *In finite dimension the group exponential is a diffeomorphism from an open neighborhood of 0 in* g *to an open neighborhood of e in G, and its differential map at* 0 *is the identity. This implies that we can define without ambiguity an inverse map, called* the group logarithm map *in an open neighborhood of e: for every g in this open neighborhood, there exists a unique x in the open neighborhood of* 0 *in* g *such that g* = exp(*x*).

Indeed, the exponential is a smooth mapping, and its differential map is invertible at *e*. Thus, the inverse function theorem guarantees that it is a diffeomorphism from some open neighborhood of 0 to an open neighborhood of exp(0) = *e* [71, Proposition 1.3, p. 13]. We write *x* = log(*g*) for this logarithm, which is the (abstract) equivalent of the (matrix) *principal* logarithm. Notice that we use lower case exp and log to clearly distinguish the group exponential and logarithm from their Riemannian counterparts Exp and Log. The absence of an inverse function theorem in infinite-dimensional Fréchet manifolds prevents the straightforward extension of this property to general groups of diffeomorphisms [41].

Baker–Campbel–Hausdorff (BCH) formula

A number of interesting formulas involving the group exponential map can be obtained in a finite-dimensional Lie group (or more generally in a BCH–Lie group) as particular cases of the BCH formula. This formula is an infinite series of commutators that allows us to write the composition of two group exponentials as a single exponential: exp(*x*) exp(*y*) = exp(*BCH*(*x*, *y*)). Intuitively, this formula shows how much log(exp(*x*) exp(*y*)) deviates from *x* + *y* due to the noncommutativity of the multiplication in *G*. Remarkably, this deviation can be expressed only in terms of Lie brackets between *x* and *y* [30, Chap. VI].

Theorem 5.6 (Series form of the BCH formula). *Let x, y be in* g. *If they are small enough, then the logarithm of the product* exp(*x*) exp(*y*) *is well-defined, and we have the following development:*

$$BCH(x, y) = \log(\exp(x) \, \exp(y))$$

$$= x + y + \frac{1}{2}([x, y]) + \frac{1}{12}([x, [x, y]] + [y, [y, x]]) \quad (5.5)$$

$$+ \frac{1}{24}([[x, [x, y]], y]) + O((\|x\| + \|y\|)^5).$$

A fundamental property of this function is the following: it is not only C^∞ but also *analytic* around 0, which means that

$BCH(x, y)$ (near 0) is the sum of an absolutely converging multivariate infinite series (here the usual multiplication is replaced by the Lie bracket). This implies in particular that all the (partial) derivatives of this function are also analytic. The BCH formula is probably the most important formula from a practical point of view: it is the cornerstone approximation used to efficiently update the transformation parameters in SVF-based registration algorithms of Section 5.6.2.

5.3.2 Cartan–Schouten (CCS) connections

For each tangent vector $x \in \mathfrak{g} \simeq T_e G$, the one-parameter subgroup $\gamma_x(t)$ is a curve that starts from identity with this tangent vector. To see if these curves could be seen as geodesics, we now investigate natural connections on Lie groups. We start with left-invariant connections satisfying $\nabla_{dL_g X} dL_g Y = dL_g \nabla_X Y$ for any vector fields X and Y and any group element $g \in G$. As the connection is completely determined by its action on the subalgebra of left-invariant vector fields, we can restrict it to the Lie algebra. Let $\tilde{x} = dL\,x$ and $\tilde{y} = dL\,y$ be two left-invariant vector fields. Stating that the covariant derivative of $\tilde{y}$ along $\tilde{x}$ is left-invariant amounts to say that the field $\nabla_{\tilde{x}} \tilde{y} = dL(\nabla_{\tilde{x}} \tilde{y}|_e)$ is determined by its value at identity $\alpha(x, y) = \nabla_{\tilde{x}} \tilde{y}|_e \in \mathfrak{g}$. Conversely, each bilinear operator of the Lie algebra $\alpha : \mathfrak{g} \times \mathfrak{g} \to \mathfrak{g}$ uniquely defines the connection at the identity and thus on all left-invariant vector fields: $\nabla_{\tilde{x}}^{\alpha} \tilde{y} = \tilde{\alpha}(x, y)$. The connection is then uniquely extended to all vector fields using the linearity in the first variable and the Leibniz rule.

Definition 5.10 (Cartan–Schouten and biinvariant connections). *Among the left-invariant connections, the* Cartan–Schouten *connections are the ones for which geodesics going through identity are one-parameter subgroups. Biinvariant connections are both left- and right-invariant.*

The definition of Cartan–Schouten connection used here is due to [71, Def. 6.2, p. 71]. It generalizes the three classical +, −, and 0 Cartan–Schouten connections [19] detailed further in Theorem 5.8.

Theorem 5.7. *Cartan–Schouten connections are uniquely determined by the property $\alpha(x, x) = 0$ for all $x \in \mathfrak{g}$. Biinvariant connections are characterized by the condition*

$$\alpha([z, x], y) + \alpha(x, [z, y]) = [z, \alpha(x, y)] \quad \forall x, y, z \in \mathfrak{g}. \tag{5.6}$$

The one-dimensional family of connections generated by $\alpha(x, y) = \lambda[x, y]$ satisfies these two conditions. Moreover, there is a unique *symmetric biinvariant Cartan–Schouten connection called the* Canonical Cartan–Schouten (CCS) *connection of the Lie group (also called mean or 0-connection) defined by* $\alpha(x,y) = \frac{1}{2}[x,y]$ *for all* $x, y \in \mathfrak{g}$*, that is,* $\nabla_{\tilde{x}}\tilde{y} = \frac{1}{2}[\tilde{x},\tilde{y}]$ *for two left-invariant vector fields.*

Indeed, let us consider the one-parameter subgroup $\gamma_x(t)$ starting from e with initial tangent vector $x \in \mathfrak{g}$. As this is the integral curve of the left-invariant vector field $\tilde{x} = dL\,x$, its tangent vector is $\dot{\gamma}_x(t) = dL_{\gamma_x(t)}x = \tilde{x}|_{\gamma_x(t)}$. The curve is a geodesic if and only if it is autoparallel, that is, if $\nabla_{\dot{\gamma}_x}\dot{\gamma}_x = \nabla_{\tilde{x}}\tilde{x} = \tilde{\alpha}(x,x) = 0$. Thus the one-parameter subgroup $\gamma_x(t)$ is a geodesic if and only if $\alpha(x,x)=0$.

This condition implies that the operator α is skew-symmetric. However, although any skew-symmetric operator gives rise to a left-invariant connection, this connection is not always right-invariant. The connection is right-invariant if $\nabla_{dR_g X} dR_g Y = dR_g \nabla_X Y$ for any vector fields X and Y and any group element g. As we have $(dR_g\tilde{x}) = \widetilde{\mathrm{Ad}(g^{-1})x}$ for any left-invariant vector field $\tilde{x} = dL\,x$, the right-invariance is equivalent to the Ad-invariance of the operator α:

$$\alpha\left(\mathrm{Ad}(g^{-1})x, \mathrm{Ad}(g^{-1})y\right) = \mathrm{Ad}(g^{-1})\,\alpha(x,y)$$

for any two vectors $x, y \in \mathfrak{g}$ and $g \in G$. We can focus on the infinitesimal version of this condition by taking the derivative at $t = 0$ with $g^{-1} = \exp(tz)$. Since $\frac{d}{dt}\mathrm{Ad}(\exp(tz))x = [z,x]$, we obtain the requested characterization of biinvariant connections: $\alpha([z,x],y) + \alpha(x,[z,y]) = [z,\alpha(x,y)]$.

The well-known one-dimensional family of connections generated by $\alpha(x,y) = \lambda[x,y]$ obviously satisfies this condition (in addition to $\alpha(x,x)=0$). It was shown by Laquer [79] that this family basically describes all the biinvariant connections on compact simple Lie groups (the exact result is that the space of biinvariant affine connections on G is one-dimensional) *except* for SU(d) when $d > 3$, where there is a two-dimensional family of biinvariant affine connections.

Torsion and curvature of Cartan–Schouten connections

The torsion of a connection can be expressed in the basis of left-invariant vector fields: $T(\tilde{x},\tilde{y}) = \nabla_{\tilde{x}}\tilde{y} - \nabla_{\tilde{y}}\tilde{x} - [\tilde{x},\tilde{y}] = \tilde{\alpha}(x,y) - \tilde{\alpha}(y,x) - \widetilde{[x,y]}$. This is itself a left-invariant vector field characterized by its value at identity $T(x,y) = \alpha(x,y) - \alpha(y,x) - [x,y]$. Thus the torsion of a Cartan connection is $T(x,y) = 2\alpha(x,y) - [x,y]$. In conclusion, there is a unique torsion-free Cartan connection, called the symmetric Cartan–Schouten connection, which is characterized by $\alpha(x,y) = \frac{1}{2}[x,y]$, that is, $\nabla_{\tilde{x}}\tilde{y} = \frac{1}{2}[\tilde{x},\tilde{y}]$.

The curvature can also be expressed in the basis of left-invariant vector fields: $R(\tilde{x}, \tilde{y})\tilde{z} = \nabla_{\tilde{x}}\nabla_{\tilde{y}}\tilde{z} - \nabla_{\tilde{y}}\nabla_{\tilde{x}}\tilde{z} - \nabla_{[\tilde{x},\tilde{y}]}\tilde{z}$. It is once again left-invariant and characterized by its value in the Lie algebra:

$$R(x, y)z = \alpha(x, \alpha(y, z)) - \alpha(y, \alpha(x, z)) - \alpha([x, y], z).$$

For connections of the form $\alpha(x, y) = \lambda[x, y]$, the curvature becomes

$$R(x, y)z = \lambda^2[x, [y, z]] + \lambda^2[y, [z, x]] + \lambda[z, [x, y]] = \lambda(\lambda - 1)[[x, y], z],$$

where the last equality is obtained thanks to the Jacobi identity of the Lie bracket. For $\lambda = 0$ and $\lambda = 1$, the curvature is obviously null. These two flat connections are called the left and right (or + and −) Cartan–Schouten connections. For the CCS connection (often called mean or 0-connection), the curvature is $R(x, y)z = -\frac{1}{4}[[x, y], z]$, which is generally nonzero.

Theorem 5.8 (Properties of Cartan–Schouten connections). *Among the biinvariant Cartan–Schouten connections on a Lie group, there is a natural one-parameter family of the form $\alpha(x, y) = \lambda[x, y]$ that comprises three canonical connections called the 0, +, − (or mean, left, right) connections:*
- *The − connection is the unique connection for which all the left-invariant vector fields are covariantly constant along any vector field, inducing a global parallelism.*
- *The + connection is the only connection for which all the right-invariant vector fields are covariantly constant along any vector field, inducing also a global parallelism.*
- *The CCS or 0-connection is the unique torsion-free Cartan–Schouten connection. Its curvature tensor is generally nonzero, but it is covariantly constant. It is thus a locally symmetric space, and the symmetry $s_g(h) = gh^{-1}g$ turns it into a globally affine symmetric space.*

These three connections have the same geodesics (left or right translations of one-parameter subgroups) because they share the same symmetric part $\nabla_X Y + \nabla_Y X = \partial_X Y + \partial_Y X$. Their curvature and torsion are summarized in Table 5.1.

When we only focus on geodesics, we can thus restrict to the symmetric CCS connection. However, we should be careful that the parallel transport differ for the three connections as we will further see.

Table 5.1 Torsion and curvature of the classical one-parameter family of Cartan–Schouten connections.

Connection		$T(\tilde{x}, \tilde{y})$	$R(\tilde{x}, \tilde{y})\tilde{z}$
$\nabla_{\tilde{x}}^{\lambda}\tilde{y} = \lambda[\tilde{x}, \tilde{y}]$	λ	$(2\lambda - 1)[\tilde{x}, \tilde{y}]$	$\lambda(\lambda - 1)[[\tilde{x}, \tilde{y}], \tilde{z}]$
$\nabla_{\tilde{x}}^{-}\tilde{y} = 0$	$0\,(-)$	$-[\tilde{x}, \tilde{y}]$	0
$\nabla_{\tilde{x}}^{s}\tilde{y} = \frac{1}{2}[\tilde{x}, \tilde{y}]$	$\frac{1}{2}\,(0)$	0	$-\frac{1}{4}[[\tilde{x}, \tilde{y}], \tilde{z}]$
$\nabla_{\tilde{x}}^{+}\tilde{y} = [\tilde{x}, \tilde{y}]$	$1\,(+)$	$+[\tilde{x}, \tilde{y}]$	0

5.3.3 Group geodesics, parallel transport

We call group geodesics the geodesics of the canonical Cartan–Schouten connection. We already know that the geodesics going through identity are the one-parameter subgroups (by the definition of the Cartan–Schouten connections). The canonical Cartan connection being left-invariant, the curve $\gamma(t) = g\exp(tx)$ is also a geodesic. We have indeed $\dot{\gamma} = dL_g\dot{\gamma}_x$ and $\nabla_{\dot{\gamma}}\dot{\gamma} = dL_g\nabla_{\dot{\gamma}_x}\dot{\gamma}_x = 0$. As $\gamma(0) = dL_g x$, we finally obtain the following:

Theorem 5.9 (Group exponential). *The group geodesic starting at g with tangent vector $v \in T_g G$ is $\gamma_{(g,v)}(t) = g\exp(t\,dL_{g^{-1}}v)$. Thus the (group) exponential map at point g is*

$$\exp_g(v) = \gamma_{g,v}(1) = g\exp(dL_{g^{-1}}v).$$

As noted in Theorem 5.1, for each point g of G, there exists a normal convex neighborhood (NCN) in the sense that for any couple of points (p, q) in this neighborhood, there exists a unique geodesic of the form $\exp_p(tv)$ joining them that lies completely in this neighborhood. Furthermore, an NCN $\mathcal{V}_e$ of the identity is transported by left-invariance into an NCN $g\mathcal{V}_e$ of any point $g \in G$.

Of course, we could have defined the geodesics using the right translations to obtain curves of the form $\exp(t\,dR_{g^{-1}}v)\,g$. In fact, those two types of group geodesic are the same and are related by the adjoint operator, as shown further. However, we should be careful that the left and right transport of the NCN at the identity lead to different NCNs of a point g: $g\mathcal{V} \neq \mathcal{V}g$.

Theorem 5.10. *Let x be in $\mathfrak{g}$ and g in G. Then we have:*

$$g\exp(x) = \exp(Ad(g)x)\,g.$$

For all g in G, there exists an open neighborhood $\mathcal{W}_g$ of $e \in G$ (namely, $\mathcal{W}_g = \mathcal{V}_e \cap g\mathcal{V}_e g^{-1}$, where $\mathcal{V}_e$ is any NCN of e) such that for *all $m \in \mathcal{W}_g$, the quantities $\log(m)$ and $\log(g\,m\,g^{-1})$ are well-defined and are linked by the following relationship:*

$$\log(g\,m\,g^{-1}) = Ad(g)\log(m).$$

Notice that in general the NCN $\mathcal{W}_g$ depends on g unless we can find an NCN $\mathcal{V}_e$ that is stable by conjugation. These equations are simply a generalization to (abstract) Lie groups of the well-known matrix properties: $G\exp(V)\,G^{-1} = \exp(GVG^{-1})$ and $G\log(V)\,G^{-1} = \log(GVG^{-1})$.

Corollary 5.1 (Group exponential and log map at any point). *For all g in G, there exists an open neighborhood $\mathcal{V}_g$ of g such that the local exponential and logarithmic maps of the CCS connection are well-defined and the inverse of each other. Moreover, their left and right expressions are:*

$$\exp_g(v) = g\exp(dL_{g^{-1}}v) = \exp(dR_{g^{-1}}v)\,g \quad \textit{for} \quad v \in T_gG;$$

$$\log_g(x) = dL_g\log(g^{-1}x) = dR_g\log(xg^{-1}) \quad \textit{for} \quad x \in \mathcal{V}_g.$$

Parallel transport along geodesics

To obtain the parallel transport, we have to integrate the infinitesimal parallel transport given by the connection along the path. Because left and right translations commute, the parallel transport for the λ-Cartan connection of $y \in \mathfrak{g}$ to $T_{\exp(x)}G$ along the one-parameter subgroup $\exp(tx)$ is

$$\Pi_e^{\exp(x)}y = dL_{\exp((1-\lambda)x)}dR_{\exp(\lambda x)}y.$$

We can verify that this formula is consistent with the infinitesimal version (the λ-Cartan connection): $\frac{d}{dt}\Pi(\exp(tx))_t^0\tilde{y} = \lambda[\tilde{x}, \tilde{y}]$. In particular, we observe that the parallel transport of the left (resp., right) Cartan–Schouten connection ($\lambda = 0$, resp., $\lambda = 1$) is the left (resp., right) translation. Both are independent of the path: the Lie group endowed with these connections is a space with absolute parallelism (but with torsion). This was expected since the curvature of these two connections vanishes.

For the canonical symmetric Cartan–Schouten connection ($\lambda = 1/2$), the parallel transport is a geometric average where we transport on the left for half of the path and on the right for the other half: $\Pi_e^{\exp(x)}y = dL_{\exp(x/2)}dR_{\exp(x/2)}y$. Parallel translation along other geodesics is obtained by left (or right) translation or this formula.

5.4 Left, right, and biinvariant Riemannian metrics on a Lie group

In the case of Lie groups- there are two natural families of left- (resp., right)-invariant Riemannian metrics that are determined by an inner product at the tangent space of the identity and prolonged everywhere by left (resp., right) translation: $< v, w >^L_g = < dL_{g^{-1}}v, dL_{g^{-1}}w >_e$. Conversely, a Riemannian metric is left-invariant if all left translations are isometries. Right-invariant metrics are defined similarly. It is interesting to understand if and when their geodesics coincide with the group geodesics, and if not, then how much they differ.

5.4.1 Levi-Civita connections of left-invariant metrics

Let us define the operator ad* as the metric adjoint of the adjoint operator ad: this is the unique bilinear operator satisfying for all vector fields $X, Y, Z \in \Gamma(G)$:

$$\langle \mathrm{ad}^*(Y, X), Z \rangle = \langle [X, Z], Y \rangle .$$

This allows us to rewrite the Khozul formula for the Levi-Civita connection as

$$2 \langle \nabla_X Y, Z \rangle = \langle [X, Y] - \mathrm{ad}^*(X, Y) - \mathrm{ad}^*(Y, X), Z \rangle$$
$$+ \partial_X \langle Y, Z \rangle + \partial_Y \langle X, Z \rangle - \partial_Z \langle X, Y \rangle .$$

Without loss of generality, we restrict to left-invariant vector fields because they constitute a basis of all vector fields (with functional coefficients). Since the dot product is covariantly constant for left-invariant metrics, we are left with

$$\nabla_{\tilde{x}} \tilde{y} = \frac{1}{2} \left([\tilde{x}, \tilde{y}] - \mathrm{ad}^*(\tilde{x}, \tilde{y}) - \mathrm{ad}^*(\tilde{y}, \tilde{x}) \right) . \tag{5.7}$$

Denoting by $\mathrm{ad}^*(x, y) = \mathrm{ad}^*(\tilde{x}, \tilde{y})|_e$ the restriction of the ad* operator to the Lie algebra, we end up with the following bilinear form characterizing the Levi-Civita connection of a left-invariant metric in the Lie algebra:

$$\alpha^L(x, y) = \frac{1}{2} \left([x, y] - \mathrm{ad}^*(x, y) - \mathrm{ad}^*(y, x) \right) .$$

Let γ_t be a curve, and let $x^L_t = dL_{\gamma_t^{-1}} \dot{\gamma}_t$ be the *left angular speed vectors* (i.e. the left translation of the tangent vector to the Lie algebra). Then the curve γ_t is a geodesic of the left-invariant metric if

$$\dot{x}_t^L = \alpha^L(x_t^L, x_t^L) = -\text{ad}^*(x_t^L, x_t^L). \tag{5.8}$$

This remarkably simple quadratic equation in the Lie algebra is called the Euler–Poincaré equation. A very clear derivation is given in [44].

Since the CCS connection is determined by $\alpha(x, y) = \frac{1}{2}[x, y]$, the geodesic of the left-invariant metric γ_t is also a geodesic of the canonical Cartan connection if $x_t^L = x$ is constant. Thus we see that the geodesic of a left-invariant Riemannian metric going through identity with tangent vector x is a one-parameter subgroup if and only if $\text{ad}^*(x, x) = 0$. Such vectors are called normal elements of the Lie algebra. For other elements, the symmetric part of ad^* encodes the acceleration of one-parameter subgroups with respect to the left-invariant geodesics starting with the same tangent vector.

5.4.2 Canonical connection of bi-invariant metrics

Riemannian metrics which are simultaneously left- and right-invariant are called *biinvariant*. For these special metrics, we have the very interesting result.

Theorem 5.11. *A left-invariant metric on a Lie group is biinvariant if and only if for all $g \in G$, the adjoint operator $Ad(g)$ is an isometry of the Lie algebra $\mathfrak{g}$,*

$$\langle Ad(g)y, Ad(g)z \rangle = \langle y, z \rangle ,$$

or, equivalently, if and only if for all elements $x, y, z \in \mathfrak{g}$,

$$\langle [x, y], z \rangle + \langle y, [x, z] \rangle = 0 \quad or \quad ad^*(x, y) = -ad^*(y, x). \tag{5.9}$$

Thus the Levi-Civita connection of a biinvariant metric is necessarily the canonical symmetric Cartan–Schouten connection characterized by $\alpha(x, y) = \frac{1}{2}[x, y]$ on the Lie algebra. Moreover, a biinvariant metric is also invariant w.r.t. inversion. Group geodesics of G (including one-parameter subgroups) are the geodesics of such metrics.

Eq. (5.9) is the infinitesimal version of the invariance of the dot product by the adjoint group. It in fact specifies that the metric dual of the adjoint ad^* is skew-symmetric, that is, the Levi-Civita connection of the metric considered is the canonical symmetric Cartan–Schouten connection of the Lie group.

The proof is given in [77, Chap. V] and [71, Chap. 25]. In short, any element close to identity can be written $g = \exp(tx)$, for which we have $d\mathrm{Ad}(g)y/dt = [x, y]$. Thus differentiating $\langle \mathrm{Ad}(g)y, \mathrm{Ad}(g)z \rangle = \langle y, z \rangle$ gives the left part of Eq. (5.9). Since this should be verified for all $x \in \mathfrak{g}$, we obtain the skew symmetry of the ad^* operator. Thus the mean Cartan–Schouten connection is the Levi-Civita connection of any biinvariant metric: the affine framework corresponds to the Riemannian framework when this last one is fully consistent with the group operations.

An interesting consequence is that any Lie group with a biinvariant metric has a nonnegative sectional curvature. Indeed, the sectional curvature in the two-plane span(x, y) for $x, y \in \mathfrak{g}$ can be computed using left-invariant vector fields:

$$k(x, y) = \frac{\langle R(x, y)y, x \rangle}{\|x\|^2 \|y\|^2 - \langle x, y \rangle^2} = \frac{1}{4} \frac{\|[x, y]\|^2}{\|x\|^2 \|y\|^2 - \langle x, y \rangle^2}, \qquad (5.10)$$

where we used the expression $R(x, y)z = -\frac{1}{4}[[x, y], z]$ of the Riemannian curvature and Eq. (5.9) to move one bracket from left to right in the inner product. Thus taking two orthonormal vectors of the Lie algebra, the section curvature reduces to $k(x, y) = \frac{1}{4}\|[x, y]\|^2$, which is nonnegative.

Compactness, commutativity, and existence of biinvariant metrics

The next question is to understand under which conditions such a biinvariant metric exists. From Theorem 5.11 we see that if a biinvariant metric exists for the Lie group, then $\mathrm{Ad}(g)$ is an isometry of $\mathfrak{g}$ and can thus be looked upon as an element of the orthogonal group $O(d)$ where $d = \dim(G)$. As $O(d)$ is a *compact* group, the adjoint group $\mathrm{Ad}(G) = \{\mathrm{Ad}(g)/g \in G\}$ is necessarily *included in a compact set*, a situation called *relative compactness*. This notion actually provides a sharp criterion, since the theory of differential forms and their integration can be used to explicitly construct a biinvariant metric on relatively compact subgroups [77, Theorem V.5.3.].

Theorem 5.12. *The Lie group G admits a biinvariant metric if and only if its adjoint group Ad(G) is relatively compact.*

In the case of *compact* Lie groups, the adjoint group is also compact, and Theorem 5.12 implies that biinvariant metrics exist. This is the case of *rotations*, for which biinvariant Fréchet means have been extensively studied and used in practical applications, for instance, in [64,65,60]. In the case of commutative Lie groups left and right translations are identical, and any left-invariant metric is trivially biinvariant. Direct products of compact Abelian groups obviously admit biinvariant metrics, but Theorem 5.12

shows that in the general case a noncompact and noncommutative Lie group that is not the direct product of such groups may fail to admit a biinvariant metric.

Biinvariant pseudo-Riemannian metrics (quadratic Lie groups)

The class of Lie groups that admits biinvariant metrics is quite small and does not even include rigid-body transformations in 2D or 3D. Looking for a biinvariant Riemannian framework for larger groups is thus hopeless. One possibility is to relax the positivity of the Riemannian metric to focus on biinvariant *pseudo-Riemannian* metrics only, for which the bilinear forms on the tangent space of the manifold are definite but may not be positive (eigenvalues are just nonzero). Based on the classification of quadratic Lie algebras of [55,56], Miolane [58] developed an algorithm to compute all the biinvariant pseudometrics on a given Lie group (if they exist). This algorithm was applied to simple Lie groups that have a locally unique biinvariant mean (scaling and translations, the Heisenberg group, upper triangular matrices, and Euclidean motions). It showed that most of them possess no biinvariant pseudometric. The special Euclidean motion group in 3D is a notable exception. Thus the generalization of the statistical theory to pseudo-Riemannian metrics may not be so interesting in practice.

5.4.3 Example with rigid-body transformations

In medical imaging the simplest possible registration procedure between two images uses rigid-body transformations, characterized by a rotation matrix and a translation vector. Since there exist biinvariant metrics on rotations and on translations, we could hope for the existence of biinvariant metrics. We further show that this is not the case.

The Lie group of rigid-body transformations in the d-dimensional Euclidean space, written here SE(d), is the semidirect product of (SO(d), $\times$) (rotations) and ($\mathbb{R}^d$, $+$) (translations). An element of SE(d) is uniquely represented by a couple $(R, t) \in$ SO(d) $\ltimes \mathbb{R}^d$ with the action on a point x of $\mathbb{R}^d$ defined by $(R, t).x = Rx + t$. Then the multiplication is $(R', t')(R, t) = (R'R, R't + t')$, the neutral element is (Id, 0), and the inverse is $(R^\top, -R^\top t)$. The fact that the product between rotations and translations is semidirect and not direct (there is a coupling between rotation and translation in the composition) is at the heart of the nonexistence of a biinvariant metric on the product group.

We obtain a faithful representation of SE(d), and its Lie algebra using homogeneous coordinates: $(R, t) \simeq \left(\begin{smallmatrix} R & t \\ 0 & 1 \end{smallmatrix}\right)$ and $(\Omega, v) \simeq \left(\begin{smallmatrix} \Omega & v \\ 0 & 0 \end{smallmatrix}\right)$, where Ω is any skew $d \times d$ matrix, and v is any vector of $\mathbb{R}^d$. In the homogeneous representation the Lie bracket $[\cdot, \cdot]$ is simply the matrix commutator, which gives the following Lie bracket for the Lie algebra $\mathfrak{se}(n) = \mathfrak{so}(d) \ltimes \mathbb{R}^d$: $[(\Omega, v), (\Omega', v')] = (\Omega\Omega' - \Omega'\Omega, \Omega v' - \Omega' v)$.

Proposition 5.1. *The action of the adjoint operator Ad of the group of rigid-body transformations* SE(d) *at the point* (R, t) *on an infinitesimal displacement* $(\Omega, v) \in \mathfrak{se}(d)$ *is given by*

$$Ad(R, t)(\Omega, v) = (R\Omega R^\top, -R\Omega R^\top t + Rv).$$

As it is unbounded, no biinvariant Riemannian metric exists on the space of rigid-body transformations for $d > 1$.

Such a result was already known for SE(3) [85]. It is established here for all dimensions. A very interesting result of [58] is that there is no biinvariant pseudo-Riemannian metric on SE(d), except for $d = 3$.

5.5 Statistics on Lie groups as symmetric spaces

Although biinvariant metrics may fail to exist, any Lie group has a symmetric canonical Cartan–Schouten connection for which group means can be defined implicitly as exponential barycenters, at least locally. As will be shown further, this definition has all the desirable biinvariance properties, even when biinvariant metrics do not exist. Moreover, we can show the existence and uniqueness of the group mean even globally in a number of cases. Group means were investigated for compact and nilpotent Lie groups in [16, Chapter 8] as side results in the study of almost flat metrics. In the medical image analysis domain, group means were originally proposed in [7] under the name "biinvariant means" and fully developed as exponential barycenters of the CCS connection in [69].

5.5.1 Biinvariant means with exponential barycenters of the CCS connection

Every Lie group is orientable and has a Haar volume form. When the group is unimodular (e.g. in SE(d)), the Haar measure is biinvariant and provides a canonical reference measure to define intrinsic probability density functions on the group. However, left and right Haar measures differ by a function (the determinant of the adjoint) in nonunimodular groups such as GL(d), so that this property cannot be used in general. In any case we can consider probability measures on the group $\mu \in Prob(G)$ that include sample distributions $\mu = \frac{1}{n} \sum_{i=1}^{n} \delta_{g_i}$ of n transformations g_i in the group G. The left and right translations and inversion being smooth and one-to-one, there is no problem to consider their push-forward action on measures, which write in the case of the above sample distribution as $dL_h\mu = \sum_{i=1}^{n} \delta_{hg_i}$, $dR_h\mu = \sum_{i=1}^{n} \delta_{g_i h}$, and $d\mathrm{Inv}\mu = \sum_{i=1}^{n} \delta_{g_i^{-1}}$.

Definition 5.11 (Groups means). *Let $\mu \in Prob(G)$ be a probability distribution on G with compact support $Supp(\mu)$ belonging to an open set $\mathcal{V}$ diffeomorphic to a sphere such that $\log(g^{-1}h)$ and $\log(hg^{-1}) = Ad(g)\log(g^{-1}h)$ exist for any point $g \in \mathcal{V}$ and $h \in Supp(\mu)$. The points $\bar{g} \in \mathcal{V}$ solutions of the following group barycentric equation (if there are some) are called group means:*

$$\int_G \log(\bar{g}^{-1}h)\,\mu(dh) = 0. \tag{5.11}$$

This definition translates the exponential barycenters in the language of Lie groups. However, the definition is a bit more general since we do not require $\mathcal{V}$ to be a convex normal neighborhood. Therefore we cannot conclude about the existence in general, but we know that it is ensured for a sufficiently concentrated distribution. This definition is close to the Riemannian center of mass (or more specifically the Riemannian average) of [31] but uses the group logarithm instead of the Riemannian logarithm. Notice that the group geodesics cannot be seen as Riemannian geodesics when the CCS connection is nonmetric, so that the group means are different (in general) from the Fréchet or Karcher mean of some Riemannian metric.

The consistency constraint under the adjoint action on this neighborhood was also added to obtain the following equivariance theorem, which is stated with empirical means (sample distributions) for simplicity.

Theorem 5.13 (Equivariance of group means). *Group means, when they exist, are left-, right-, and inverse-equivariant: if $\bar{g}$ is a mean of n points $\{g_i\}$ of the group and $h \in G$ is any group element, then $h\bar{g}$ is a mean of the points hg_i, $\bar{g}h$ is a mean of the points $\{g_i h\}$, and $\bar{g}^{-1}$ is a mean of $\{g_i^{-1}\}$.*

Proof. We start with the left-equivariance. If $\bar{g}$ is a mean of the points $\{x_i\}$ and $h \in G$ is any group element, then $\log((h\bar{g})^{-1}hg_i) = \log(g^{-1}g_i)$ exists for all points hg_i. Thus the point $h\bar{g} \in h\mathcal{V}$ is a solution of the barycentric equation $\sum_i \log((h\bar{g})^{-1}hg_i) = 0$, which proves the left-equivariance. For the right-invariance, we have to apply Theorem 5.10: $\mathrm{Ad}(\bar{g})\left(\sum_i \log(\bar{g}^{-1} g_i)\right) = \sum_i \log(g_i \bar{g}^{-1})$. Since $\mathrm{Ad}(\bar{g})$ is invertible, the usual barycentric equation, which is left-invariant, is equivalent to a right-invariant barycentric equation, and $\bar{g}h$ is a mean of the points $\{g_i h\}$. The equivariance with respect to inversion is obtained with $\sum_i \log(g_i^{-1} \bar{g}) = -\sum_i \log(\bar{g}^{-1} g_i)$. □

Theorem 5.14 (Local uniqueness and convergence to the group mean). *If the transformations $\{g_i\}$ belong to a sufficiently small normal convex neighborhood $\mathcal{V}$ of some point $g \in G$, then there exists a unique solution of Eq. (5.11) in $\mathcal{V}$. Moreover, the following iterated fixed point strategy converges at least at a linear rate to this unique solution:*

1. *Initialize $\bar{g}_0$, for example, with $\bar{g}_0 := g_1$.*
2. *Iteratively update the estimate of the mean:*

$$\bar{g}_{t+1} := \bar{g}_t \exp\left(\frac{1}{n}\sum_{i=1}^{n} \log(\bar{g}_t^{-1} g_i)\right). \qquad (5.12)$$

Until convergence: $\| \log(\bar{g}_t^{-1} \bar{g}_{t+1})\| < \epsilon \sqrt{\frac{1}{n}\sum_{i=1}^{n} \left\| \log(\bar{g}_t^{-1} g_i)\right\|^2}.$

The proof is detailed in [69]. The uniqueness of the mean and the convergence rate are linked to the contraction properties of the above iteration. The proof relies on an auxiliary metric $\| \cdot \|$ on $\mathfrak{g}$ such that for all x, y sufficiently small, we have $\|[x, y]\| \le \|x\| \|y\|$. The left-invariant function $\phi(g, h) = \| \log(g^{-1} h)\|^2$ can then be used as a surrogate of a distance in this neighborhood. This function is sometimes called the group distance. However, this is an improper name since the triangular inequality is generally not respected. Notice that this is not a left-invariant Riemannian metric either because we use the group logarithm and not the left-invariant Riemannian log.

As in the case of the Fréchet mean, there is a closed form for the group mean of two points since this point is on the geodesic joining them.

Proposition 5.2. *Let h be in a normal convex neighborhood of $g \in G$. Then the group mean of g and h (with weights $1 - \alpha$ and $\alpha > 0$) is given by*

$$\bar{g}_\alpha = g \exp\left(\alpha \log(g^{-1} h)\right) = g(g^{-1} h)^\alpha. \qquad (5.13)$$

This explicit formula is quite exceptional. In general, there is no closed form for the group mean of more than two points. However, there are some specific groups where a closed form exists for the biinvariant mean in all cases as we will detail in the next section.

5.5.2 Existence and uniqueness results in specific matrix groups

First, it is worth noticing that compact Lie groups carry a biinvariant metric for which we can use the Riemannian result. Using a normalized metric in $\mathfrak{g}$ such that $\|\mathrm{ad}x\| \leq \|x\|$, [16] established the convexity of geodesic balls of radius $\rho < \pi/2$, so that the group mean is unique for distributions with support in a geodesic ball of radius strictly less than $\pi/4$. [16] also considered simply connected nilpotent Lie groups endowed with the canonical symmetric Cartan–Schouten connection. Despite the fact that these groups generally cannot carry biinvariant metrics (their Killing form is zero), they proved that any distribution with compact support has a unique group mean. We summarize their results in the following theorem without demonstration.

Theorem 5.15 (Uniqueness of group means in compact Lie groups [16]). *A compact connected Lie group can be endowed with a biinvariant metric normalized so that $\|ad x\| \leq \|x\|$, which is compatible with the canonical symmetric Cartan–Schouten connection. With these conventions, any probability distribution with support in a regular geodesic ball of radius strictly less than $\pi/4$ has a unique group mean.*

Theorem 5.16 (Uniqueness of group means in nilpotent Lie groups [16]). *A probability with compact support in a simply connected nilpotent Lie group endowed with the canonical symmetric Cartan–Schouten connection has a unique group mean.*

The Heisenberg group in the next subsection is a good example of a simply connected nilpotent Lie group that has no biinvariant metric but a unique group mean. Then we turn to the more general class of solvable Lie groups, which was not addressed by Buser and Karcher. With scaling translations $\mathrm{ST}(d)$ and the upper triangular matrices with scalar diagonal $\mathrm{UT}(d)$, we give two examples of nonnilpotent groups with no biinvariant metric that have unique group means as well. Moreover, the computation of the group mean can be done in finite time using an iterative scheme solving each coordinate at a time. We conjecture that this could be a feature of solvable groups. Last but not least, we look at rigid-body transformations and some properties of $\mathrm{GL}(d)$. These examples are summarized further; we refer the reader to [69] for more detail.

5.5.2.1 The Heisenberg group

This is the group of 3D upper triangular matrices of the form $\begin{bmatrix} 1 & x & z \\ 0 & 1 & y \\ 0 & 0 & 1 \end{bmatrix}$. Parameterizing each element by the triplet (x, y, z), the group composition is $(x_1, y_1, z_1)(x_2, y_2, z_2) = (x_1 + x_2, y_1 + y_2, z_1 + z_2 + x_1 y_2)$. The Heisenberg group is thus a semidirect product of $(\mathbb{R}^2, +)$ and $(\mathbb{R}, +)$, which is not commutative. The inversion is $(x, y, z)^{-1} = (-x, -y, -z + xy)$ with neutral element $(0, 0, 0)$.

The entire Heisenberg group is a normal convex neighborhood, and we have:

$$\exp(u, v, w) = (u, v, w + \tfrac{1}{2}uv),$$
$$\log(x, y, z) = (x, y, z - \tfrac{1}{2}xy).$$

Proposition 5.3. *The action of the adjoint operator Ad of the Heisenberg group at a point (x, y, z) on an infinitesimal displacement (u, v, w) is given by*

$$Ad(x, y, z)(u, v, w) = (u, v, -yu + xv + w).$$

Because it is unbounded, no biinvariant metric exists. However, the group mean $(\bar{x}, \bar{y}, \bar{z})$ of a set of points $\{(x_i, y_i, z_i)\}_{1 \le i \le n}$ in the Heisenberg group is unique and given explicitly by

$$(\bar{x}, \bar{y}, \bar{z}) = \tfrac{1}{n}\left(\sum_i x_i, \sum_i y_i, \sum_i z_i + \tfrac{1}{2}\left((\sum_i x_i) \cdot (\sum_i y_i) - \sum_i x_i y_i\right)\right).$$

5.5.2.2 Scaling and translations $\mathrm{ST}(d)$

The group of scaling and translations in dimension d is one of the simple cases of noncompact, noncommutative, nonnilpotent but solvable Lie groups that does not possess any biinvariant Riemannian metric. An element of $\mathrm{ST}(d)$ can be uniquely represented by a scaling factor $\lambda \in \mathbb{R}_+^*$ and a translation $t \in \mathbb{R}^d$. The action of an element $(\lambda, t) \in \mathbb{R}_+^* \ltimes \mathbb{R}^d$ on a vector $x \in \mathbb{R}^d$ is $(\lambda, t)x = \lambda x + t$. Accordingly, the composition in $\mathrm{ST}(d)$ is $(\lambda', t')(\lambda, t) = (\lambda'\lambda, \lambda't + t')$, and inversion is $(\lambda, t)^{-1} = (1/\lambda, -t/\lambda)$. A faithful matrix representation of $\mathrm{ST}(d)$ is the subgroup of triangular matrices of the form $\left(\begin{smallmatrix} \lambda & \mathrm{Id}_d\, t \\ 0 & 1 \end{smallmatrix}\right)$. The elements of the Lie algebra are of the form (α, v), where $\alpha \in \mathbb{R}$ and $v \in \mathbb{R}^d$. Using e^α and $\ln(\lambda)$ to denote the scalar exponential and logarithm functions, the group exponential and logarithm can be written

$$\exp(\alpha, v) = \left(e^\alpha, (e^\alpha - 1)/\alpha\, v\right),$$
$$\log(\lambda, t) = \left(\ln(\lambda), \ln(\lambda)/(1 - \lambda)\, t\right).$$

Once again, the entire space $\mathrm{ST}(d)$ is a normal convex neighborhood: any two points can be joined by a unique group geodesic.

The adjoint action on the Lie algebra can be computed in the matrix representation:

$$\mathrm{Ad}((\lambda, t))(\alpha, v) = \begin{pmatrix} \lambda \ \mathrm{Id}_d & t \\ 0 & 1 \end{pmatrix} \begin{pmatrix} \alpha \ \mathrm{Id}_d & v \\ 0 & 0 \end{pmatrix} \begin{pmatrix} \frac{1}{\lambda} \ \mathrm{Id}_d & -\frac{t}{\lambda} \\ 0 & 1 \end{pmatrix}.$$

Proposition 5.4. *The action of the adjoint operator Ad of the* $\mathrm{ST}(d)$ *group at a point* (λ, t) *on an infinitesimal displacement* (α, v) *is given by*

$$Ad((\lambda, t))(\alpha, v) = (\alpha, \ \lambda v - \alpha t).$$

Because the translation t and the scale λ in $\lambda v - \alpha t$ are unbounded, no biinvariant metric exists on $\mathrm{ST}(d)$, *although it is the semidirect product of two commutative groups. Nevertheless, the group mean* $(\bar{\lambda}, \bar{t})$ *of a set of points* $\{(\lambda_i, t_i)\}_{1 \le i \le n}$ *in the* $\mathrm{ST}(d)$ *group is unique and given explicitly by*

$$\bar{\lambda} = \exp\left(\tfrac{1}{n} \textstyle\sum_i \ln(\lambda_i)\right), \quad \bar{t} = \frac{\sum_i \alpha_i t_i}{\sum_i \alpha_i}, \quad \text{with} \quad \alpha_i = \frac{\ln\left(\lambda_i / \bar{\lambda}\right)}{\lambda_i / \bar{\lambda} - 1}.$$

$$(5.14)$$

5.5.2.3 Scaled upper unitriangular matrix group

We consider the group $\mathrm{UT}(d)$ of $d \times d$ upper triangular matrices with scaled unit diagonal. Such matrices have the form $M = \lambda \ \mathrm{Id} + N$, where λ is a positive scalar, Id the identity matrix, and N an upper triangular nilpotent matrix ($N^d = 0$) with only zeros in its diagonal. This group generalizes the Heisenberg group, which is the subgroup of matrices of $\mathrm{UT}(3)$ with $\lambda = 1$. The group composition is $M'M = (\lambda' \lambda) \ \mathrm{Id} + (\lambda' N + \lambda N' + N'N)$. The nilpotency of N allows us to write the inversion in closed form:

$$M^{-1} = (\lambda \ \mathrm{Id} + N)^{-1} = \lambda^{-1} \left(\mathrm{Id} + \tfrac{N}{\lambda}\right)^{-1} = \lambda^{-1} \sum_{k=0}^{n-1} (-1)^k \tfrac{N^k}{\lambda^k}.$$

The group exponential and logarithm are

$$\exp(X) = \exp(\mu \ \mathrm{Id} + Y) = \exp(\mu \ \mathrm{Id}) \exp(Y) = e^{\mu} \sum_{k=0}^{n-1} \tfrac{(Y)^k}{k!},$$

$$\log(M) = \log\left((\lambda \ Id)\left(\mathrm{Id} + \tfrac{1}{\lambda} N\right)\right) = \ln(\lambda) \ \mathrm{Id} + \sum_{k=1}^{n-1} \tfrac{(-1)^{k+1}}{k} \tfrac{N^k}{\lambda^k}.$$

Using these closed forms, we can derive the following equation:

$$\log(M'M) = \ln(\lambda'\lambda) \ \mathrm{Id} + \sum_{k=1}^{n-1} \frac{(-1)^{k+1}}{k} \left(\frac{1}{\lambda} N + \frac{1}{\lambda'} N' + \frac{1}{\lambda'\lambda} NN'\right)^k,$$

which in turn allows us to simplify the equation $\sum_i \log(\bar{M}^{-1} M_i) = 0$ satisfied by the group mean $\bar{M} = \bar{\lambda} \ \mathrm{Id} + \bar{N}$ in $\mathrm{UT}(d)$. Using $\sum_i \log(\bar{M}^{-1} M_i) = -\sum_i \log(M_i^{-1} \bar{M})$, we have

$$\sum_i \left(\ln(\bar{\lambda}\lambda_i^{-1}) \ \mathrm{Id} \right)$$

$$+ \sum_i \sum_{k=1}^{n-1} \frac{(-1)^{k+1}}{k} \left(\frac{1}{\lambda_i^{-1}} N_i^{-1} + \frac{1}{\bar{\lambda}} \bar{N} + \frac{1}{\bar{\lambda}\lambda_i^{-1}} N_i^{-1} \bar{N} \right)^k = 0,$$

$$(5.15)$$

where N_i^{-1} is the nilpotent part of M_i^{-1}. To solve this equation, we see that $\bar{\lambda}$ is the geometric mean of the λ_i and that the coefficient of $\bar{N}$ can be recursively computed, starting from coefficients above the diagonal. The key idea is that the kth power of a nilpotent matrix N has nonzero coefficients only in its kth upper diagonal. Thus we only need to consider the terms $N_i^{-1}/\lambda_i^{-1} + \bar{N}/\bar{\lambda} = 0$ to compute the coefficients of $\bar{M}$ above the diagonal. These coefficients are uniquely defined as a weighted arithmetic mean of the coefficients above the diagonal in the data. Thanks to this result, we can compute the above secondary diagonal elements, which will be a weighted arithmetic mean of the corresponding coefficients in the data with a quadratic correction involving the previous coefficients. We can continue this way until all the coefficients of the mean have been effectively computed.

Proposition 5.5. *The adjoint group of the group* $\mathrm{UT}(d)$ *of* $d \times d$ *upper triangular with scaled unit diagonal includes in particular the adjoint group of the subgroup of scaling and translations* $\mathrm{ST}(d)$. *Thus it is unbounded, and there exists no biinvariant metric. Nevertheless, the group mean* $(\bar{\lambda} \ \mathrm{Id} + \bar{N})$ *of a set of points* $\{(\lambda_i \ \mathrm{Id} + N_i)\}_{1 \leq i \leq n}$ *in the* $\mathrm{UT}(d)$ *group is unique and can be computed by a sequence of d geometric means on the diagonal followed by $d-1, d-2, \ldots, 1$ arithmetic means (with a polynomial of degree $1, 2, \ldots, d-1$ correction based on the already computed coefficients) for the coefficient of each parallel above the diagonal.*

5.5.2.4 General rigid-body transformations

We have seen in Section 5.4.3 that no biinvariant metric exists in the rigid-body case. We may now ask the question: is there a simple criterion for the existence/uniqueness of the biinvariant group mean of rigid-body transformations? We use in this section the notations previously introduced in Section 5.4.3. Recall that $(R, t) \in \mathrm{SE}(d) = \mathrm{SO}(d) \ltimes \mathbb{R}^d$ can be faithfully represented by the homogeneous matrix embedding $\left(\begin{smallmatrix} R & t \\ 0 & 1 \end{smallmatrix} \right)$, and the Lie algebra by matrices $(\Omega, v) \simeq \left(\begin{smallmatrix} \Omega & v \\ 0 & 0 \end{smallmatrix} \right)$, where Ω is a skew $d \times d$ matrix, and v is a vector of $\mathbb{R}^d$. The group exponential can be computed using directly the matrix representation or by identifying the one-parameter subgroups of SE(d):

$$\exp(\Omega, v) = (\exp(\Omega), \, M(\Omega) \, v)$$

$$\text{with} \quad M(\Omega) = \sum_{k=0}^{\infty} \frac{\Omega^k}{(k+1)!} = \exp(\Omega) \int_0^1 \exp(-t\Omega) dt.$$

To compute explicitly the value of the matrix $M(\Omega)$, we use the fact that any skew-symmetric matrix can be diagonalized in the block diagonal form $U \Omega U^\top = \mathrm{diag}\left(\{\theta_j J\}, \, 0\right)$, where U is an orthonormal matrix, θ_i are the 2D rotation angles, and $J = \begin{pmatrix} 0 & -1 \\ 1 & 0 \end{pmatrix}$ is a normalized 2D skew-symmetric matrix (see Chapter 1 Section 1.7.3 on rotations). In this coordinate system we have already computed in Chapter 1 that $\exp(\theta_j J)$ is a 2D rotation matrix of angle θ_j. A few extra steps yield

$$M(\theta_j \, J) = \frac{\sin \theta_j}{\theta_j} \, \mathrm{Id}_2 + \frac{\cos \theta_j - 1}{\theta_j} J = \frac{1}{\theta_j} \begin{pmatrix} \sin \theta_j & \cos \theta_j - 1 \\ -\cos \theta_j + 1 & \sin \theta_j \end{pmatrix}.$$

The determinant of this matrix is $\det(M(\theta_j \, J)) = 2(1 - \cos \theta_j)/\theta_j^2 > 0$ for $0 < |\theta_j| < 2\pi$, so that $M(\Omega)$ is invertible in this domain. A direct computation shows that the inverse of $M(\theta_j \, J)$ can be written as

$$M(\theta_j \, J)^{-1} = \frac{\theta_j \sin \theta_j}{2(1 - \cos \theta_j)} \, \mathrm{Id}_2 + \frac{\theta_j}{2} J = \begin{pmatrix} \frac{\theta_j \sin \theta_j}{2(1 - \cos \theta_j)} & \frac{\theta_j}{2} \\ -\frac{\theta_j}{2} & \frac{\theta_j \sin \theta_j}{2(1 - \cos \theta_j)} \end{pmatrix}.$$

Proposition 5.6. *The principal logarithm of a rigid-body transformation (R, t) is well-defined if and only if the logarithm of its rotation part R is well-defined, that is, if the angles of the 2D rotations of its decomposition are strictly less than π in absolute value. In that case $M(\Omega)$ is invertible, and we get the group logarithm on SE(d):*

$$\log(R, t) = (\Omega, v) \quad \text{with} \quad \Omega = \log(R), \quad v = M(\Omega)^{-1} t$$

$$\text{or} \quad \begin{pmatrix} \Omega & v \\ 0 & 0 \end{pmatrix} = \log \begin{pmatrix} R & t \\ 0 & 1 \end{pmatrix}.$$

The proof relies on the block upper-triangular structure of the homogeneous matrix representing the transformation (R, t): the eigenvalues of such a matrix depend only on the blocks in its diagonal, that is, only on R and 1, and not on t.

This theorem highlight the fact that the difficult part is the rotation group. Because the symmetric Cartan–Schouten connection on rotations is the Levi-Civita connection of the biinvariant metric developed in Chapter 1 (Section 1.3.4), we know by the Karcher theorem (Chapter 2, Theorem 2.2) that the mean rotation is unique if the support of the rotation distribution is contained in a geodesic ball of radius $r < r^* = \pi/2$. Remarkably, this is sufficient to guarantee the existence and uniqueness of the biinvariant mean of rigid-body transformations.

Proposition 5.7. *Let $\{R_i, t_i\}$ be a set of rigid-body transformations with rotations within a geodesic ball $\mathcal{B}_r$ of radius $r < \frac{\pi}{2}$. Then the biinvariant Riemannian mean $\bar{R}$ of their rotation parts is unique in this geodesic ball, and there exists a unique group mean $(\bar{R}, \bar{t})$ on* SE(d) *with $\bar{R} \in \mathcal{B}_r$.*

Proof. We are looking for the solutions $(\bar{R}, \bar{t})$ of the group barycentric equation

$$\sum_i \log((\bar{R}, \bar{t})^{-1}(R_i, t_i)) = \sum_i \log\left(\bar{R}^{-1}R_i, \ \bar{R}^{-1}(t_i - \bar{t})\right).$$

Denoting $\Omega_i = \log(\bar{R}^{-1}R_i)$, this boils down to $\sum_i \Omega_i = 0$ for the rotation part, which is uniquely satisfied by the biinvariant rotation mean $\bar{R}$ in the geodesic ball $\mathcal{B}_r$ by assumption. For the translation part, we get $\sum_i M(\Omega_i)^{-1}\bar{R}^{-1}(t_i - \bar{t}) = 0$. Thus, if $M = \sum_i M(\Omega_i)^{-1}$ is invertible, then this equation has a unique solution

$$\bar{t} = \bar{R}\left(M^{-1}\right)^{-1}\sum_i M(\Omega_i)^{-1}\bar{R}^{-1}t_i.$$

To show that this is the case under our assumptions, we note that $M(\Omega)^{-1} = S + \Omega/2$, where S is a symmetric matrix with positive eigenvalues $\frac{\theta_j \sin\theta_j}{2(1-\cos\theta_j)} > 0$ whenever the 2D rotation angles satisfy $|\theta_j| < \pi$. This is a consequence of the block diagonalization $UM(\Omega)^{-1}U^\top = \text{diag}\left(\{M(\theta_j J)^{-1}\}, 1\right)$ with $M(\theta_j J)^{-1} = \frac{\theta_j \sin\theta_j}{2(1-\cos\theta_j)}\text{Id}_2 + \frac{\theta_j}{2}J$. Thus the sum $M = \sum_i M(\Omega_i)^{-1} = \tilde{S} + \tilde{A}$ of the matrices of this type can also be written as the sum of a positive definite symmetric matrix $\tilde{S} = \sum_i S_i$ (a convex combination of SPD matrices is an SPD matrix) and a skew-symmetric matrix $\tilde{A} = \sum_i \Omega_i/2$. It is thus invertible because $(\tilde{S} + \tilde{A})x = 0$ implies $x^\top \tilde{S} x = 0$ (the skew symmetry of $\tilde{A}$ implies $x^\top \tilde{A} x = 0$), which is zero only for $x = 0$ by the definiteness of $\tilde{S}$. $\qquad\square$

Example with 2D rigid transformations

A 2D rigid transformation can be parameterized by $T = (\theta, t_1, t_2)$, where $\theta \in]-\pi, \pi]$ is the angle of the rotation of SO(2) $\simeq S_1$, and $t = [t_1, t_2] \in \mathbb{R}^2$ is the translation vector. We consider the following example of three rigid transformations proposed in [67, p. 31] to show that left- and right-invariant Riemannian means were different:

- $T_1 = (\pi/4, -\sqrt{2}/2, \sqrt{2}/2)$,
- $T_2 = (0, \sqrt{2}, 0)$,
- $T_3 = (-\pi/4, -\sqrt{2}/2, -\sqrt{2}/2)$.

A left-invariant Fréchet mean can also be computed explicitly in this case thanks to the simple form taken by the corresponding geodesics. The analogous right-invariant Fréchet mean can be computed by inverting the data, computing their left-invariant mean, and then inverting this Fréchet mean. The biinvariant mean can be computed with the above formula. This yields (after a number of simple but tedious algebraic manipulations):

- Left-invariant Fréchet mean $(0, 0, 0)$,
- Biinvariant mean
  $(0, (\sqrt{2} - \frac{\pi}{4})/(1 + \frac{\pi}{4}.(\sqrt{2} + 1)), 0) \simeq (0, 0.2171, 0)$,
- Right-invariant Fréchet mean $(0, \sqrt{2}/3, 0) \simeq (0, 0.4714, 0)$.

As expected, the mean rotation angle is exactly the same in all cases. But the mean translations are different, and the biinvariant mean is located nicely *between* the left- and right-invariant Fréchet means. This is quite intuitive, since the biinvariant mean can be looked upon as an in-between alternative with regard to left- and right-invariant Fréchet means.

5.6 The stationary velocity fields (SVF) framework for diffeomorphisms

Nonlinear registration aims at maximizing the geometrical similarity of anatomical images by optimizing the spatial deformations that are acting on them. In this process, deformation fields quantify the anatomical changes as local changes of coordinates. Thus deformations represent a powerful and rich geometrical object for the statistical analysis of motion and differences across organs.

In the context of medical image registration, *diffeomorphic registration* restricts the set of possible spatial transformations to diffeomorphisms. There is a rich mathematical background for the estimation and analysis of deformations that brings key properties to the analysis of medical images. Diffeomorphic registration was introduced with the "Large Deformation Diffeomorphic Metric Mapping (LDDMM)" framework [78,13], which parameterizes deformations with the flow of *time-varying velocity fields* $v(x, t)$ with a right-invariant Riemannian metric, as described in Chapter 4. In view of reducing computational and memory costs of LDDMM, [8] subsequently proposed to restrict this parameterization to the subset of diffeomorphisms parameterized by the flow of *stationary velocity fields* (SVFs). This setting is of particular methodological interest, since the flow associated with an SVF is a one-parameter subgroup, and we can thus take advantage of the properties of the associated Lie algebra to develop efficient and flexible computational tools. We further review the main aspects of SVF-based image registration with a particular focus on the computational schemes arising from the one-parameter subgroup properties.

5.6.1 Parameterizing diffeomorphisms with the Flow of SVFs

Before investigating in depth the computational aspects of SVF-based registration, in this section we illustrate the theoretical background and rationale of the SVF framework. To work in a well-posed space of deformations, we need to specify the space on which the Lie algebra is modeled. This is the role of the regularization term of the SVF registration algorithms [82,34] or of the spline parameterization of the SVF in [10,61]: this regularization restricts the Lie algebra to sufficiently regular velocity fields. A sufficiently powerful Hilbert metric is usually chosen to model the Lie Algebra. The flow of these stationary velocity fields and their finite composition generates a subgroup of all diffeomorphisms, which is the group we consider. Up to now, the theoretical framework is very similar to the LDDMM setting: if we model the Lie algebra on the same admissible Hilbert space as LDDMM, then all the diffeomorphisms generated by the one-parameter subgroups (the exponential of SVFs) also belong to the LDDMM group. As in finite dimension, the affine geodesics of the CCS connection (group geodesics) are metric-free. Thus, these group geodesics generally differ from the Riemannian geodesics of LDDMM.

However, it is well known that the above construction generates a group that is significantly larger than the space covered by single group exponentials. Although our affine connection space is geodesically complete (all geodesics can be continued for all time without hitting a boundary), there is no Hopf–Rinow theorem in affine geometry that can ensure that any two points can be joined by a geodesic. Thus, in general, not all the elements of the group may be reached by a one-parameter subgroup. An example in finite dimension that we have already seen is $SL(2, \mathbb{R})$ (two-dimensional square matrices with unit determinant), where elements with trace less than -2 cannot be reached by any one-parameter subgroup. In the image registration context this is generally not a problem since all the possible diffeomorphisms of the group are not as likely and we are only interested in admissible anatomical transformations. Another potential problem is that, contrarily to the finite dimension, the exponential map is not in general a diffeomorphism from a neighborhood of zero in the Lie algebra onto a neighborhood of the identity in the infinite-dimensional group. For instance, there exist diffeomorphisms in every neighborhood of the identity in $\mathrm{Diff}^s(\mathcal{M})$ that are not exponentials of an H^s vector field. A classical example of the nonsurjectivity of the exponential map is the function $f_{n,\epsilon}(\theta) = \theta + \pi/n + \epsilon \sin^2(n\theta)$ in $\mathrm{Diff}(\mathbb{S}^1)$ [57]. This function cannot be reached by any one-parameter subgroup, but can be made as close as we want to the identity by dimensioning ϵ and n. However, such deformations are very unlikely in our applications since the norm of the kth derivative $\| f_{n,\epsilon} \|_{H^k}$ is increasing as k goes to infinity. Regularity is indeed a critical issue in image registration. Thus it may be a good idea to actually exclude this type of diffeomorphisms from the space under consideration

In practice there is also an issue with the discretization of the flow of velocity fields: we inevitably have a spatial discretization of the velocity fields (and of the deformations) on a grid. For LD-DMM methods, there is an additional temporal discretization of the time-varying velocity fields by a fixed number of time steps. These discretizations intrinsically limit the frequency of the deformations and prevent very high spatial frequency diffeomorphisms to be reached both by the SVF and by the discrete LDDMM frameworks. Chapter 13 of this book provides an insight on such numerical issues in LDDMM, whereas Chapter 15 builds on this low-pass behavior to explicitly limit the deformation frequency. These limitations remain to be compared to those of the SVFs.

5.6.2 SVF-based setting: properties and algorithm

In SVF-based methods the deformation $\phi = \exp(v)$ is parameterized by the Lie group exponential of a smooth SVF $v : \Omega \to \mathbb{R}^3$ defined by the ODE

$$\frac{\partial \phi(x,t)}{\partial t} = v(\phi(x,t)) \tag{5.16}$$

with initial condition $\phi(x,0) = x$. This ODE defines a one-parameter subgroup $\phi_t(x) = \phi(x,t)$ since $\phi_{s+t}(x) = \phi(x,s)\,\phi(x,t) = \phi(x,s+t)$. The Lie group exponential is obtained at the parameter value $t = 1$, that is, $\exp(v) = \phi(x) = \phi(x,1)$. The one-parameter subgroup structure is the key element of the SVF setting, as it provides an efficient way to tackle important computational problems in image registration, such as:

- the numerical integration of spatial vector fields (computing the exponential),
- the efficient inversion of spatial transformations,
- the stable computation of differential quantities and quantification of volume changes,
- the composition of spatial transformations.

We illustrate in this section the related schemes proposed in the literature.

5.6.2.1 Exponential of an SVF

The one-parameter subgroup property guarantees that the exponential operation can be efficiently implemented as the composition of transformations:

$$\exp(v) = \phi(x, 1) = \phi(x, \tfrac{1}{2}) \, \phi(x, \tfrac{1}{2}) = \exp(v/2) \exp(v/2). \qquad (5.17)$$

This property is at the core of the generalization of the "scaling and squaring" integration scheme from matrices to SVF [8]. As a result, the ODE (5.16) can be effectively computed as the iterative composition of successive exponentials (Algorithm 5.1).

Algorithm 5.1 Scaling and squaring for the Lie group exponential.

---

1. Scaling step: choose n so that $2^{-n}v$ is "small".
2. Compute a first approximation:
   $\phi_0(x) \leftarrow \exp(2^{-n}v)(x) \approx x + 2^{-n}v(x)$.
3. Squaring step: For $k = 1$ to n do $\phi_k \leftarrow \phi_{k-1} \, \phi_{k-1}$.

The initial integration step (Step 2 of Algorithm 5.1) is a sensitive step affecting the quality of the integration. This issue was investigated, for example, in [24], where different integration schemes and initial approximations strategy were benchmarked in terms of integration accuracy and computation time. Among the tested methods, optimal performances were obtained with Runge–Kutta and exponential integrator methods [62]. Moreover, computing the transformation $\phi_k(x_i) = \phi_{k-1}(\phi_{k-1}(x_i))$ at the image grid point x_i in the squaring step (Step 3 of Algorithm 5.1) involves a resampling since $\phi_{k-1}(x_i)$ is in general not at an exact grid point. The numerical accuracy of this step is critical. For instance, trilinear interpolation can easily be nondiffeomorphic for large deformations.

5.6.2.2 Inversion of spatial transformations

Given a diffeomorphism ϕ, the computation of its inverse requires the estimation of a spatial transformation ϕ^{inv} such that

$\phi(\phi^{inv}(x)) = x$ and $\phi^{inv}(\phi(x)) = x$. In general, this is performed using a least-squares optimization minimizing the error over the domain. In the SVF setting, such a computation can be performed through very simple algebraic manipulations on the related SVF parameters. Indeed, the one-parameter subgroup properties guarantee $\phi^{inv} = \phi(x, -1)$, since $\phi(x, 1)\phi(x, -1) = \phi(x, 0) = e$, and vice versa. Thus the diffeomorphism $\phi = \exp(v)$ parameterized by the SVF v has the inverse $\phi^{inv} = \exp(-v)$ parameterized by the SVF $-v$.

5.6.2.3 Computing differential quantities

The quantification of the amount of warping ϕ applied at each voxel by the dense deformation field is usually locally derived from the Jacobian matrix $d\phi = \nabla\phi^\top$ of the deformation in terms of determinant, log-determinant, trace, and the right Cauchy–Green strain tensor $d\phi^\top d\phi$. An index of volume change over an anatomical region Ω can be obtained by integrating the change of volume of all elements in the region of interest or by computing the flux that is going inward or outward of this region.

Integration of the Jacobian determinant in the region of interest

This is an average measure of *volume change*. The computation of the Jacobian matrix $d\phi$ is normally performed by spatial differentiation of the transformation by finite differences (Algorithm 5.2).

Algorithm 5.2 Classical computation of the Jacobian determinant by finite differences.

Given a discrete sampling ϕ of the transformation over the image grid space $\{x_i\}$:
1. Compute the Jacobian matrix F via finite differences along coordinates e_k:
   $d\phi_{jk}(x_i) = [\partial_{e_k}\phi(x_i)]_j = (\phi_j(x_i + \delta e_k) - \phi_j(x_i))/\delta,$
   where δ is the discretization step size.
2. Compute $\det(d\phi)$ with the preferred numerical method.

The differentiation by finite differences is however usually highly sensitive to the spatial noise and completely depends on the size of the discrete space-sampling. This can create instabilities in case of large deformations leading to incorrect Jacobian determinant estimation. This limitation is elegantly overcome in the SVF framework using a variation of the scaling and squaring method for the Lie group exponential. In fact, the (log-)Jacobian can be reliably estimated by finite differences for the *scaled* velocity field $v/2^n$ and then recursively computed thanks to the additive property of the one-parameter subgroups and by applying the chain rule (Algorithm 5.3).

Algorithm 5.3 Jacobian matrix and log-Jacobian determinant with scaling and squaring.

Given a deformation $\phi = \exp(v)$:
1. Scaling step: Choose n so that $2^{-n}v$ is "small".
2. Compute the first approximation (dv is computed using finite differences):
   $\phi_0 = \exp(2^{-n}v) \approx \mathrm{Id} + 2^{-n}v$ and $d\phi_0 \approx \mathrm{Id} + 2^{-n}dv$.
   $LD_0 = \log \det(d\phi_0) = \mathrm{Tr}(\log(d\phi_0)) \approx \mathrm{Tr}(2^{-n}dv)$.
3. Squaring step: For $k = 1$ to n do:
   $\phi_k = \phi_{k-1}\phi_{k-1}$ and $d\phi_k = (d\phi_{k-1}\phi_{k-1})\, d\phi_{k-1}$
   $LD_k = \log \det(d\phi_k) = LD_{k-1} \circ \phi_{k-1} + LD_{k-1}$.

With this scheme, the Jacobian determinant is therefore evaluated accordingly to the exponential path and is consistent with the definition of diffeomorphisms parameterized by the one-parameter subgroup. Moreover, the log-Jacobian determinant is defined in terms of the divergence of the velocity, and by definition the value of the corresponding Jacobian determinant is always strictly positive. This property implies that the evaluation preserves the diffeomorphic formulation and is therefore robust to the discretization approximations. For instance, in case of large deformations, the sampling of the deformation field in the image grid space may introduce spurious folding effects (e.g. in presence of an unequal distribution of the vectors around a sink), thus leading to an incorrect negative Jacobian estimation with direct estimation, whereas it would be still correctly defined with the present method. We should be careful that the estimation of the full Jacobian matrix $d\phi$ with this method is numerically less stable than the log-Jacobian as we need to resample and multiply many matrices that are very small deviations from the identity.

Flux of the deformation field across the boundary of the region

We can also derive a volume change index by comparing the volume enclosed by the deformed surface relatively to the original one. This is related to the flux of the velocity field across the boundary of the region $\delta\Omega$. Nevertheless, a direct computation of the flux is usually hindered by its high sensitivity to the localization and orientation of the boundaries. This limitation led to the development of surrogate intensity-based measures of the flux [25,76]. However, the properties of the SVF framework enables us to derive a stable and efficient numerical scheme. Following [49], formula (5.16) leads to the following relationship:

$$\int_\Omega \log(\det(d\phi(x, 1)))d\Omega = \int_0^1 \text{flux}_{\partial\Omega}(v \circ \phi(x, t)) \, dt. \qquad (5.18)$$

This formula shows that the spatial integration of the log-Jacobian determinant of the deformation over the region of interest is equal to the flux of the velocity field across the corresponding boundary, integrated along the path described by the exponential map. Formula (5.18) consistently computes the flow of the vector field during the evolution described by the SVF parameterization, and measures the flux of a vector field over a surface (right side of (5.18)) by scalar integration of the log-Jacobian determinant in the enclosed volume (left side of (5.18)). Moving from the surface to the volume integration simplifies and robustifies the measure of the flux by attenuating the segmentation errors (and relative erroneous boundary detection). This also allows us to deal with uncertainties in the region of interest, for instance, by integration on probabilistic masks. The difference between the Jacobian and the log-Jacobian analysis becomes clear: the former quantifies volume changes, whereas the latter quantifies the shift of the boundaries (given by the average regional log-Jacobian determinant).

5.6.2.4 *Composing transformations parameterized by SVF*

The Baker–Campbell–Hausdorff (BCH) formula (Theorem 5.6) was introduced in the SVF diffeomorphic registration in [15] and provides an explicit way to compose diffeomorphisms parameterized by SVFs by operating in the Lie algebra only. More specifically, if v, u are SVFs, then $\exp(v)\exp(u) = \exp(w)$ with

$$w = BCH(v, u) = v + u + \frac{1}{2}[v, u] + \frac{1}{12}[v, [v, u]] - \frac{1}{12}[u, [v, u]] + \cdots.$$

In this formula the Lie bracket of vector fields $[v, u]$ is the derivative of u in the direction of the flow of v: $[v, u] = dv\,u - du\,v = \partial_u v - \partial_v u$. Here the Lie algebra of diffeomorphisms is by convention the algebra of right-invariant vector fields instead of the traditional left-invariant ones used in finite-dimensional Lie groups. This explains why this bracket is the opposite of the one of Section 5.3.1 (see comments in [82,15]).

For a small u, the computation can be truncated at any order to obtain an approximation for the composition of diffeomorphisms.

For this reason, the BCH is a key tool for the development of efficient gradient-based optimization algorithms. Keeping the description of our deformations within the Lie algebra significantly simplifies the optimization of the SVF parameters via gradient descent in the log-Demons algorithm.

5.6.3 SVF-based diffeomorphic registration with the log-demons

Inspired by the idea of encoding diffeomorphisms with the flow of SVF [8], several SVF-based nonlinear image registration algorithms were concurrently proposed [80,15,10,82,81,34,61]. Among them, the (log)-Demons registration algorithm [80–82] found a considerable interest in the medical image registration community. Successful application to several clinical problems include [70,53,52,75]. This setting is particularly appealing since it leads to a computationally effective and flexible registration scheme leveraging on the mathematics and numerics of SVF. We illustrate in this section the SVF properties presented in Section 5.6.2 within the log-Demons registration framework.

Image similarity in the log-demons

Given a pair of images $I, J : \mathbb{R}^3 \mapsto \mathbb{R}$, we aim at estimating an SVF v parameterizing diffeomorphically the spatial correspondences that minimize the functional $Sim[I, J, v]$. For example, if the similarity is the log-likelihood of a Gaussian intensity error (the *sum of squared differences* criterion, SSD), we may have $Sim[I, J, v] = \|I - J \circ \exp(-v)\|_{L_2}^2$, or $Sim[I, J, v] = \|I \circ \exp(v) - J\|_{L_2}^2$ depending on the choice of the reference image. The SVF formulation easily allows us to symmetrize the similarity term to make it independent of the choice of the reference image. For example, [82] proposed unbiased correspondences by averaging the forward and backward correspondences $v = \frac{1}{2}(u + w)$ separately estimated from the SSD functional on both sides: $Sim_{forw}[I, J, u] = \|I \circ \exp(u) - J\|_{L_2}^2$ and $Sim_{back}[I, J, w] = \|I - J \circ \exp(-w)\|_{L_2}^2$. Although the symmetrization comes straightforwardly from the SVF parameterization of the deformations, the strategy requires twice the optimization of the correspondence terms and can be computationally costly when extended to similarity terms more complex than the standard SSD.

To address this issue, [49] proposed a symmetric criterion optimizing at the half-way space, were both images are resampled simultaneously. This can be easily formulated within the SVF framework thanks to the inverse property by considering the resampled images $I \circ \exp(v/2)$ and $J \circ \exp(-v/2)$. For instance, the standard

SSD can be symmetrized as follows:

$$SSD_{[\text{sym}]}(I, J, v) = \|I \circ \exp(v/2) - J \circ \exp(-v/2)\|_{L_2}^2.$$

More complex similarity functionals, such as the local correlation coefficient (LCC), were easily extended to symmetric criteria using this formulation [49].

Regularization of SVF parameters

To prevent overfit, image registration usually considers a regularization term $Reg(v)$ aiming at promoting the spatial regularity of the solution. Several regularization functionals have been proposed in the literature to promote specific mechanistic constraints, such as diffusion properties $Reg(v) = \|dv\|_{L_2}^2$, incompressibility $Reg(v) = \|\text{Tr}(dv)\|_{L_2}^2$ [53,54], or more complex terms involving the penalization of the (potentially infinite) high-order derivative terms of the SVF [17].

However, instead of adding the regularization to the similarity term as classically done in image registration, it was observed in [18] that introducing an auxiliary variable for the correspondences with a coupling term in the demons criterion was providing a more efficient optimization. In the log-demons framework this amounts to parameterize the image correspondences by the flow of an SVF v_c and the coupling term by

$$Aux(v_c, v) = \|v_c - v\|_{L_2}^2 \approx \|BCH(v_c, -v)\|_{L_2}^2$$
$$= \|\log(\exp(v_c)\exp(-v))\|_{L_2}^2.$$

Then the criterion optimized by the log-demons is

$$E(v, v_c, I, J) = \tfrac{1}{\sigma_i^2} Sim(I, J, v_c) + \tfrac{1}{\sigma_x^2} Aux(v_c, v) + \tfrac{1}{\sigma_T^2} Reg(v). \quad (5.19)$$

5.6.4 Optimizing the log-demons algorithm

The interest of the auxiliary variable is to decouple a nonlinear and nonconvex optimization into two optimizations that are respectively local and quadratic. The classical criterion is obtained at the limit when the typical scale of the error σ_x^2 between the transformation and the correspondences tends to zero. The minimization of (5.19) is alternatively performed with respect to the SVF parameters v_c and v in two steps:

- *Matching.* The correspondence energy $E_{\text{corr}}(v, v_c, I, J) = \tfrac{1}{\sigma_i^2} Sim(I, J, v_c) + \tfrac{1}{\sigma_x^2} Aux(v_c, v)$ is minimized to find a (nonregularized) SVF v_c that best puts into correspondence the two images. The optimization of this nonconvex energy is usually performed via gradient descent, Gauss–Newton, or Levenber–Marquardt methods. Thanks to the quadratic formulation of the auxiliary term in v_c, the correspondence energy update can be efficiently computed with respect to standard similarity functionals Sim, such as the sum of squared differences (SSD), or the local correlation coefficient (LCC). In particular, the Taylor expansion of the similarity with respect to the variation δu of v_c leads to a closed form with a second-order Newton-like gradient descent scheme

$$\delta u = \left(\|\Lambda\|^2 + \frac{1}{Sim(I,J,v_c)} \frac{\sigma_i^2}{\sigma_x^2} \right)^{(-1)} \Lambda,$$

where Λ is the gradient of $E_{\mathrm{corr}}(v, v_c, I, J)$ with respect the update δu [49].

- *Regularization.* The functional $E_{\mathrm{reg}}(v, v_c) = \frac{1}{\sigma_x^2} Aux(v_c, v) + \frac{1}{\sigma_T^2} \mathrm{Reg}(v)$ is optimized with respect to v. Following [53], formulating the term Reg with infinite-dimensional isotropic differential quadratic forms (IDQFs, [17]) leads to a closed form for the regularization step: the optimal v is obtained using a Gaussian convolution $v = G_\sigma * v_c$, where σ is a parameter of the IDQF. Thus this regularization step can be solved explicitly and very efficiently.

5.7 Parallel transport of SVF deformations

Modeling the temporal evolution of the tissues of the body is an important goal of medical image analysis, for instance, to understand the structural changes of organs affected by a pathology or to study the physiological growth during the life span. This requires to analyze and compare the anatomical differences in time series of anatomical images of different subjects. The main difficulty is to compare across individuals the transformation parameters describing the anatomical changes over time (longitudinal deformations) within each subject.

Comparison of longitudinal deformations can be done in different ways, depending on the analyzed feature. For instance, the scalar Jacobian determinant of longitudinal deformations represents the associated local volume change and can be compared by scalar resampling in a common reference frame via intersubject registration. This simple transport of scalar quantities is the basis of the classical tensor-based morphometry techniques [11, 74]. However, transporting the Jacobian determinant is not sufficient to reconstruct a deformation in the template space.

If we consider vector-values characteristics of deformations instead of scalar quantities, the transport is not uniquely defined anymore. For instance, a simple method of transport consists in *reorienting* the longitudinal intrasubject displacement vector field by the Jacobian matrix of the subject-to-reference deformation. Another intuitive method uses the *transformation conjugation* (change of coordinate system) to compose the longitudinal intrasubject deformation with the subject-to-reference one [73]. As pointed out in [14], this method relies on the inverse consistency of the intersubject deformations, which can raise numerical problems for large deformations. Among these normalization methods, the *parallel transport* of longitudinal deformations is arguably a more principled tool in the diffeomorphic registration setting thanks to its differential geometric background.

5.7.1 Continuous and discrete parallel transport methods

In computational anatomy, the parallel transport along geodesics of diffeomorphisms with a right-invariant metric has been initially proposed in the LDDMM context by [84]. This work builds upon the idea of approximating the parallel transport by Jacobi fields [5]. An application of this framework can be found in [72] for the study of hippocampal shape changes in Alzheimer's disease. Although representing a rigorous implementation of the parallel transport, this framework is generally computationally intensive. Moreover, the formulation is quite specific to LDDMM geodesics, and it is not evident to extend it to a general computational scheme in affine spaces.

In the context of SVF-based registration, [46] provided explicit formulas for the parallel transport with respect to the standard Cartan–Schouten connections (left, right, and symmetric) in the case of *finite-dimensional Lie groups*. Although further investigations are needed to better understand the generalization to infinite dimensions, practical examples of parallel transport of longitudinal diffeomorphisms with respect to the Cartan–Schouten connections demonstrated that it was an effective approach to transport SVFs. However, experiments showed that the numerical implementation plays a central role in the stability and accuracy of the different transport methods. For instance, the left and symmetric Cartan transports appear to be less stable than the right one due to the need of computing high-order differentials.

The practical implementation of continuous transport methods requires a precise knowledge of connection underlying the space geometry. This is not always simple, especially in the image registration setting. Moreover, the parallel transport involves the computation of high-order derivatives, which in practice may introduce numerical issues. In particular, differential operations are particularly sensitive to the discretization of energy functionals and operators on the image grid.

The complexity and limitations deriving from the direct computation of continuous parallel transport methods can be alleviated when considering *discrete approximations*. Inspired by the work of the theoretical physicist Alfred Schild, the *Schild's Ladder* was proposed in [59] as a scheme for performing the parallel transport through the construction of geodesic parallelograms. The interest of the Schild's ladder resides in the generality of its formulation, since it only requires to compute geodesics. This means in particular that this type of parallel transport remains consistent with the numerical scheme used to compute the geodesics. Indeed, although the geodesics on the manifold are not sufficient to recover all the information about the geometric properties of the space, such as the torsion of the connection, it was shown in [42] that Schild's ladder approximates the parallel transport with respect to the symmetric part of the connection of the space at the first order.

5.7.2 Discrete ladders for the registration of image sequences

Let $\{I_i\}$ $(i = 1, \ldots, n)$ be a time series of images with the baseline I_0 as reference. The longitudinal deformation from I_0 to I_i can be computed with image registration, in our case encoded with SVFs. Our goal is to transport these registration parameters to a template image T_0 to produce a follow-up image T_i that transforms the image sequence $I_0, \ldots, I_i$ to the corresponding sequence $T_0, \ldots, T_i$ in the reference space. To relate geodesics between images to geodesics in the diffeomorphism group, here we assume that all images belong to the orbit $\mathbb{I}$ of the template (or of any other image of the sequence) and that our registration algorithm provides an exact matching. These are of course simplifying assumptions whose impact needs to be evaluated in practice. In particular, we know that the registration is never perfect as the regularization term always prevents from achieving a perfect image match.

Nevertheless, this assumption allows us to model the image space $\mathbb{I}$ as the quotient of the group of diffeomorphisms by the isotropy group of the template (this is the set of deformations that leaves the template image unchanged). This construction endows the image space $\mathbb{I}$ with an invariant affine structure. We assume here that the affine manifold $(\mathbb{I}, \nabla)$, which is produced, is a geodesic orbit space [1,63] where all geodesics are homogeneous i.e. orbits of one-parameter subgroups of deformations: $I(t) = I \circ \exp(tv)$ for $I \in \mathbb{I}$. This idealized setting is perfectly aligned with the SVF-based registration methodology.[1]

5.7.2.1 Schild's ladder

In the medical image registration domain, [48,46] was the first to adapt Schild's ladder to SVF-based diffeomorphic image registration. Schild's ladder transports a vector along a curve through the construction of geodesic parallelograms. One step of the ladder is illustrated in Fig. 5.1. The corresponding algorithm in our idealized image space model $\mathbb{I}$ is described in Algorithm 5.4.

It is interesting that the Schild's ladder implementation appeared to be more stable in practice than the closed-form expression of the symmetric Cartan–Schouten parallel transport on group geodesics of diffeomorphisms. The reason is probably the inconsistency of numerical schemes used for the computation of the geodesics and for the transformation Jacobian in the implementation of this exact parallel transport formula.

Algorithm 5.4 Schild's ladder for the transport of a longitudinal deformation.

Let I_0 and I_1 be a series of (two) images, and T_0 a reference frame.
1. Compute the geodesic $\gamma(s)$ in the space $\mathbb{I}$ connecting I_1 and T_0 and define the midpoint $I_{1/2} = \gamma(1/2)$.
2. Compute the geodesic $\rho(s)$ from I_0 to $I_{1/2}$ and shoot twice along this geodesic to define the transported follow-up image $T_1 = \rho(2)$.
3. The transported SVF $\log_{T_0}(T_1)$ is obtained by registering the images T_0 and T_1.

This scheme requires the computation of two logarithms/registrations (from I_1 to T_0 and from I_0 to $I_{1/2}$) and can thus be computationally expensive when transporting multiple images. Moreover, the transport of time series of $\{I_i\}$ images is not defined with respect to the same baseline-to-reference curve, since the midpoint $I_{1/2}$ depends on the follow-up image I_i (see Fig. 5.1). This issue is critical because it may introduce inconsistencies in practice. These problems may be tackled by modifying the Schild's ladder to lead to a novel scheme, the pole ladder.

---

[1] The study of this construction remains to be mathematically substantiated. It is notably complexified by the infinite dimension. However, we believe that this idealized setting is a good metaphor anyway because it provides an extraordinary simplifying framework to explain the parallel transport on images.

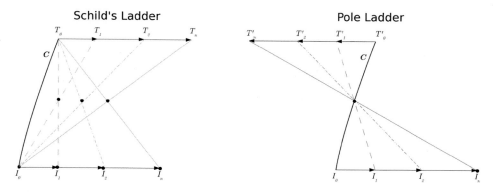

Figure 5.1. Geometrical schemes in the Schild's ladder and in the pole ladder. By using the curve C as diagonal, the pole ladder requires the computation of half times of the geodesics (blue (dark gray in print version)) required by the Schild's ladder (red (mid gray in print version)) (Figure adapted from [47]).

5.7.2.2 Pole ladder

The pole ladder is a modified version of the Schild's ladder based on the observation that if the curve along which we want to transport is itself a geodesic, then it can be used as one of the diagonals of the geodesic parallelogram. In this case constructing the ladder for image time series requires the computation of a new diagonal of the parallelogram only and is defined with respect to the same reference (Fig. 5.1). The resulting ladder is therefore analogous to the Schild's one, with the difference of explicitly using as a diagonal the geodesic C that connects I_0 and T_0 (Algorithm 5.5).

Algorithm 5.5 Pole ladder for the transport of a longitudinal deformation.

Let I_0 and I_1 be a series of (two) images, and T_0 a reference frame.
1. Compute the geodesic $C(s)$ in the space $\mathbb{I}$ connecting I_0 and T_0 and define the midpoint $I_{1/2} = C(1/2)$.
2. Compute the geodesic $\gamma(t)$ from I_1 to $I_{\frac{1}{2}}$ and shoot twice along this geodesic to define the transported image $T_1 = \gamma(2)$.
3. The transported SVF is the inverse of velocity field registering T_0 to $p(1) = T_1'$.

5.7.2.3 Theoretical accuracy: pole ladder is a third-order scheme

So far, Schild's and pole ladder methods were shown to be first-order approximations of the Riemannian parallel transport. Building on a BCH-type formula on affine connection spaces, the behavior of one pole ladder step was recently established up to order 5 [68]. In Lie groups we have seen that the BCH formula provides an expansion of the composition of two group exponentials in the Lie algebra, $BCH(v, u) = \log(\exp(v)\,\exp(u))$. In general affine connection manifolds a somewhat similar formula can be established based on the curvature instead of the Lie bracket: the double exponential $\exp_x(v, u) = \exp_y(\Pi_x^y u)$ corresponds to a first geodesic shooting from the point x along the vector v, followed by a second geodesic shooting from $y = \exp_x(v)$ along the parallel transport $\Pi_x^y u$ of the vector u. [29] has shown that the Taylor expansion of the log of this composition $h_x(v, u) = \log_x(\exp_x(v, u))$ is

$$
\begin{aligned}
h_x(v, u) =\,& v + u + \frac{1}{6}R(u, v)v + \frac{1}{3}R(u, v)u \\
&+ \frac{1}{12}\nabla_v R(u, v)v + \frac{1}{24}(\nabla_u R)(u, v)v \\
&+ \frac{5}{24}(\nabla_v R)(u, v)u + \frac{1}{12}(\nabla_u R)(u, v)u + O(\|u\|^5 + \|v\|^5).
\end{aligned}
$$

When applied to pole ladder reformulated using geodesic symmetry, we find that the error on one step of pole ladder to transport the vector u along the geodesic segment $[I_0, T_0] = [\exp_{I_{1/2}}(-v/2), \exp_{I_{1/2}}(v/2)]$ (all quantities being parallel translated at the midpoint $I_{1/2}$) is

$$
\begin{aligned}
&\Pi_{T_0}^{I_{1/2}}\text{pole}(u) - \Pi_{I_0}^{I_{1/2}}u \\
&\quad = \frac{1}{48}\left((\nabla_v R)(u, v)(5u - v) + (\nabla_u R)(u, v)(v - 2u)\right) + O(\|v + u\|^5).
\end{aligned}
$$

It is remarkable that the scheme is of order three in general affine connection spaces with a symmetric connection, much higher than expected. Moreover, the fourth-order error term vanishes in affine symmetric spaces since the curvature is covariantly constant in these spaces. In fact, we can prove that all error terms vanish in a convex normal neighborhood of an affine connection space: one step of pole ladder realizes a transvection, which is an exact parallel transport (provided that geodesics and midpoints are computed exactly) [68]. The scheme is even globally exact in Riemannian symmetric manifolds. These properties make pole ladder a very attractive alternative for parallel transport in more general affine or Riemannian manifolds. In particular, pole ladder is exact for SVF: $\Pi^v(u) = \log(\exp(v/2)\exp(u)\exp(-v/2))$ (see Fig. 5.2), as already noted in [47].

5.7.2.4 Effective ladders on SVF-deformations

Despite the straightforward formulation, Algorithms 5.4 and 5.5 require multiple evaluations of geodesics in the space of diffeomorphisms, thus resulting in high computational cost. Moreover, since an exact matching is practically impossible, the implementation of the ladders through multiple image registrations may lead to important approximations of the parallel transport. For instance, the definition of $I_{1/2}$ using the forward deformation from I_0 or the backward one from T_0 may provide significantly different results. Finally, numerical approximations introduced by exponential and logarithm maps can introduce errors that can propagate during the iteration of the ladder. For all of these reasons, it is desirable to reformulate the above schemes using only transformations to obtain a computationally efficient and numerically stable framework.

Within the SVF framework, the transport can be very effectively approximated using the BCH formula for compositions [47]. The BCH approximation of the above exact parallel transport of a deformation $\exp(u)$ along a geodesic parameterized by the SVF v is obtained by

$$\Pi^v_{BCH}(u) \simeq u + [v/2, u] + \frac{1}{2}[v/2, [v/2, u]] + HOT. \qquad (5.20)$$

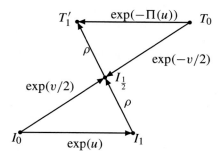

Figure 5.2. Ladder with the one-parameter subgroups. The transport $\exp(\Pi(u))$ is the deformation $\exp(v/2)\exp(u)\exp(-v/2)$. Reprinted by permission from Springer Nature, Journal of mathematical Imaging and Vision, Efficient Parallel Transport of Deformations in Time Series of Images: From Schild's to Pole Ladder by Marco Lorenzi, Xavier Pennec, January 2013.

To gain even more efficiency and numerical stability, we can derive an iterative scheme for the computation of formula (5.20), inspired by the one-parameter subgroup properties of SVF. To provide a sufficiently small vector in the computation of the conjugate, we observe that

$$\exp(v)\exp(u)\exp(-v)$$
$$= \exp\left(\frac{v}{n}\right)\ldots\exp\left(\frac{v}{n}\right)\exp(u)\exp\left(-\frac{v}{n}\right)\ldots\exp\left(-\frac{v}{n}\right).$$

The parallel transport can then be recursively computed by iterating the ladder over small geodesics parameterized by v/n:

1. Scaling step: find n such that v/n is small.
2. Iterate n times the ladder step: $u \leftarrow u + [\frac{v}{n}, u] + \frac{1}{2}[\frac{v}{n}, [\frac{v}{n}, u]]$.

We note that this method preserves the original "ladder" formulation, operated along the intersubject geodesic $\exp(tv)$. In fact, it iterates the construction of the ladder along the path $\exp(v)$ over small steps of size v/n.

5.7.3 Longitudinal analysis of brain deformations in Alzheimer's disease

We illustrate in this section an application of pole ladder to the estimation of a group-wise model of the longitudinal changes in a group of patients affected by Alzheimer's disease (AD). In this disease, the brain atrophy, which is measurable in time sequences of magnetic resonance images (MRI), was shown to strongly correlate with cognitive performance and neuropsychological scores and characterizes the progression from preclinical to pathological stages [26]. For this reason, the development of reliable atlases of the pathological longitudinal evolution of the brain is of great importance for improving the understanding of the pathology. Tackling this problem requires the development of frameworks allowing the comparison across individuals of the atrophy trajectory measured through nonrigid registration.

A preliminary approach to the groupwise analysis of longitudinal morphological changes in AD consists in performing the longitudinal analysis after normalizing the anatomical images to a template space. A key issue here is the different nature of the changes occurring at the intrasubject level, reflecting the individual's atrophy over time and the changes across different subjects, which are usually of larger magnitude and not related to specific biological process. To improve the quantification of the longitudinal dynamics, the intrasubject changes should be modeled at the individual level and only subsequently transported in the common reference for statistical analysis. For this reason, the parallel transport of longitudinal deformations is an ideal tool for the comparison of longitudinal trajectories, allowing statistical analysis of

the longitudinal brain changes in a common reference frame. We
further summarize the findings of [47].

Data analysis and results [47]

Images corresponding to the baseline I_0 and the one-year
follow-up I_1 scans were selected for 135 subjects affected by
Alzheimer's disease. For each subject i, the pairs of scans were
rigidly aligned. The baseline was linearly registered to an unbiased
reference template, and the parameters of the linear transformation were applied to I_1^i. Finally, for each subject, the longitudinal
changes were measured by nonlinear registration using the LCC-
Demons algorithm [49].

The resulting deformation fields $\phi_i = \exp(v_i)$ were transported
with the pole ladder (BCH scheme) in the template reference
along the nonlinear subject-to-template deformation. The group-
wise longitudinal progression was modeled as the mean of the
transported SVFs v_i. The areas of significant longitudinal changes
were investigated by one-sample t-test on the group of log-
Jacobian scalar maps corresponding to the transported deformations to detect the areas of measured expansion/contraction
significantly different from zero.

For comparison, the one-sample t-statistic was tested on the
individual's longitudinal log-Jacobian scalar maps warped into the
template space along the subject-to-template deformation. This
is the classical transport used in tensor-based morphometry studies [11].

Fig. 5.3 illustrates the mean SVF of the transported one-year
longitudinal trajectories. The field flowing outward of the ventricles indicates a pronounced enlargement. Moreover, we notice an
expansion in the temporal horns of the ventricles and a consistent
contracting flow in the temporal areas. The same effect can be statistically quantified by evaluating the areas where the log-Jacobian
maps are significantly different from zero. The areas of significant
expansion are located around the ventricles and spread in the CSF,
whereas a significant contraction is appreciable in the temporal
lobes, hippocampi, parahippocampal gyrus, and in the posterior
cingulate. The statistical result is in agreement with that provided
by the simple scalar interpolation of the individual's longitudinal
log-Jacobian maps. In fact, we do not experience any substantial
loss of localization power by transporting SVFs instead of scalar
log-Jacobian maps. However, by parallel transporting we preserve
also the multidimensional information of the SVFs, which potentially leads to more powerful voxel-by-voxel comparisons than
those obtained with univariate tests on scalars. For instance, we
were able to show statistically significant different brain shape

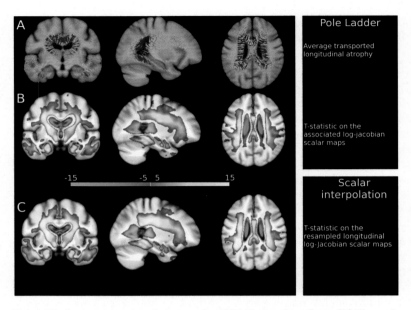

Figure 5.3. One year structural changes for 135 Alzheimer's patients. (A) Mean of the longitudinal SVFs transported in the template space with the pole ladder. We notice the lateral expansion of the ventricles and the contraction in the temporal areas. (B) T-statistic for the corresponding log-Jacobian values significantly different from 0 ($p < 0.001$ FDR corrected). (C) T-statistic for longitudinal log-Jacobian scalar maps resampled from the subject to the template space. Blue color (dark gray in print version): significant expansion, Red color (mid gray in print version): significant contraction (Figure reproduced from [47]).

evolutions depending on the level of $A\beta_{1-42}$ protein in the CSF, which could be presymptomatic of Alzheimer's disease [52]. More generally, a normal longitudinal deformation model allows us to disentangle normal aging component from the pathological atrophy even with one time point only per patient (cross-sectional design) [50].

The SVF describing the trajectory transported in a common template can also be decomposed into local volume changes and a divergence-free reorientation pattern using Helmholtz' decomposition [51]. This allows us to consistently define anatomical regions of longitudinal brain atrophy in multiple patients, leading to improved measurements of the quantification of the longitudinal hippocampal and ventricular atrophy in AD. The method provided best performing results during the MIRIAD atrophy challenge for the regional atrophy quantification in the brain, with a favorable comparison with respect to state-of-art approaches [20].

5.8 Historical notes and additional references

A large part of the body of sections 5.2 and 5.3 is based on the standard books on Riemannian manifolds [43,22,28]. Most parts related to the Cartan connection are taken from the book of Helagson [33], which is the absolute reference for Lie groups. However, notations and a number of coordinate-free formulations are taken from more modern books on differential geometry and Lie groups. Among them, [71] is certainly one of the clearest expositions, especially for the affine setting (Chapters 1 to 6). On the link between left- or right-invariant geodesics on infinite-dimensional Lie groups and mechanics, the presentation of Kolev [44] is really enlightening.

The barycentric definition of biinvariant means on Lie groups based on one-parameter subgroups was developed during the PhD of Vincent Arsigny [6] and in the research report [7]. In this preliminary work, the "group geodesics" were simply defined as left translations of one-parameter subgroups without further justification. [69] extended this work by reformulating and rigorously justifying "group geodesics" as the geodesics of the canonical Cartan–Schouten connections. This allows better distinguishing the properties that are related to the connection itself (biinvariance) from those that are related to the definition of the mean as an exponential barycenter in an affine connection space.

References

1. Dmitri Alekseevsky, Andreas Arvanitoyeorgos, Riemannian flag manifolds with homogeneous geodesics, Transactions of the American Mathematical Society 359 (8) (2007) 3769–3789.
2. Marc Araudon, Xue-Mei Li, Barycenters of measures transported by stochastic flows, Annals of Probability 33 (4) (2005) 1509–1543.
3. Marc Arnaudon, Espérances conditionnelles et C-martingales dans les variétés, in: M. Yor, J. Azema, P.A. Meyer (Eds.), Séminaire de Probabilités XXVIII, in: Lect. Notes in Math., vol. 1583, Springer-Verlag, 1994, pp. 300–311.
4. Marc Arnaudon, Barycentres convexes et approximations des martingales continues dans les variétés, in: M. Yor, J. Azema, P.A. Meyer (Eds.), Séminaire de Probabilités XXIX, in: Lect. Notes in Math., vol. 1613, Springer-Verlag, 1995, pp. 70–85.
5. Vladimir Igorevich Arnol'd, Mathematical Methods of Classical Mechanics, Springer, 1979.
6. Vincent Arsigny, Processing Data in Lie Groups: an Algebraic Approach. Application to Non-Linear Registration and Diffusion Tensor MRI, Thèse de sciences (phd thesis), École Polytechnique, November 2006.

7. Vincent Arsigny, Xavier Pennec, Nicholas Ayache, Bi-Invariant Means in Lie Groups. Application to Left-Invariant Polyaffine Transformations, Research report rr-5885, INRIA Sophia-Antipolis, April 2006.

8. Vincent Arsigny, Olivier Commowick, Xavier Pennec, Nicholas Ayache, A log-Euclidean framework for statistics on diffeomorphisms, in: Proc. of the 9th International Conference on Medical Image Computing and Computer Assisted Intervention (MICCAI'06), Part I, in: LNCS, vol. 4190, 2–4 October 2006, pp. 924–931, PMID: 17354979.

9. Vincent Arsigny, Olivier Commowick, Nicholas Ayache, Xavier Pennec, A fast and log-Euclidean polyaffine framework for locally linear registration, Journal of Mathematical Imaging and Vision 33 (2) (2009) 222–238.

10. John Ashburner, A fast diffeomorphic image registration algorithm, NeuroImage 38 (1) (2007) 95–113.

11. John Ashburner, Karl J. Friston, Voxel-based morphometry – the methods, NeuroImage 11 (6) (2000) 805–821.

12. Martin Bauer, Martins Bruveris, Peter W. Michor, Uniqueness of the Fisher–Rao metric on the space of smooth densities, ArXiv e-prints, November 2014.

13. Mirza Faisal Beg, Michael I.M.I. Miller, Alain Trouvé, Laurent Younes, Computing large deformation metric mappings via geodesic flows of diffeomorphisms, International Journal of Computer Vision 61 (2) (2005) 139–157.

14. Mathias Bossa, Ernesto Zacur, Salvador Olmos, On changing coordinate systems for longitudinal tensor-based morphometry, in: Proc. of Spatio Temporal Image Analysis Workshop (STIA 2010), 2010, p. 44.

15. Matias Bossa, Monica Hernandez, Salvador Olmos, Contributions to 3D diffeomorphic atlas estimation: application to brain images, in: Nicholas Ayache, Sébastien Ourselin, Anthony Maeder (Eds.), Proc. of Medical Image Computing and Computer-Assisted Intervention (MICCAI 2007), in: LNCS, vol. 4792, Springer-Verlag, 2007, pp. 667–674.

16. Peter Buser, Hermann Karcher, Gromov's Almost Flat Manifolds, Astérisque, vol. 81, Société Mathématique de France, 1981.

17. Pascal Cachier, Nicholas Ayache, Isotropic energies, filters and splines for vector field regularization, Journal of Mathematical Imaging and Vision 20 (3) (2004) 251–265.

18. Pascal Cachier, Eric Bardinet, Didier Dormont, Xavier Pennec, Nicholas Ayache, Iconic feature based nonrigid registration: the PASHA algorithm, in: Special Issue on Nonrigid Registration, Computer Vision and Image Understanding 89 (2–3) (Feb.–March 2003) 272–298.

19. Elie Cartan, Jan Arnoldus Schouten, On the geometry of the group-manifold of simple and semi-simple groups, Proceedings Akad. Wekensch, Amsterdam 29 (1926) 803–815.

20. David M. Cash, Chris Frost, Leonardo O. Iheme, Devrim Ünay, Melek Kandemir, Jurgen Fripp, Olivier Salvado, Pierrick Bourgeat, Martin Reuter, Bruce Fischl, Marco Lorenzi, Giovanni B. Frisoni, Xavier Pennec, Ronald K. Pierson, Jeffrey L. Gunter, Matthew L. Senjem, Clifford R. Jack, Nicolas Guizard, Vladimir S. Fonov, D. Louis Collins, Marc Modat, M. Jorge Cardoso, Kelvin K. Leung, Hongzhi Wang, Sandhitsu R. Das, Paul A. Yushkevich, Ian B. Malone, Nick C. Fox, Jonathan M. Schott, Sebastien Ourselin, Assessing atrophy measurement techniques in dementia: results from the MIRIAD atrophy challenge, NeuroImage 123 (December 2015) 149–164.
21. José Manuel Corcuera, Wilfrid S. Kendall, Riemannian barycentres and geodesic convexity, Mathematical Proceedings of the Cambridge Philosophical Society 127 (1999) 253–269.
22. Manfredo do Carmo, Riemannian Geometry. Mathematics, Birkhäuser, Boston, Basel, Berlin, 1992.
23. Michel Emery, Gabriel Mokobodzki, Sur le barycentre d'une probabilité dans une variété, in: M. Yor, J. Azema, P.A. Meyer (Eds.), Séminaire de Probabilités XXV, in: Lect. Notes in Math., vol. 1485, Springer-Verlag, 1991, pp. 220–233.
24. Sebastiano Ferraris, Marco Lorenzi, Pankaj Daga, Marc Modat, Tom Vercauteren, Accurate small deformation exponential approximant to integrate large velocity fields: application to image registration, in: Proceedings of the IEEE Conference on Computer Vision and Pattern Recognition Workshops, 2016, pp. 17–24.
25. Peter A. Freeborough, Nick C. Fox, The boundary shift integral: an accurate and robust measure of cerebral volume changes from registered repeat MRI, IEEE Transactions on Medical Imaging 16 (5) (1997) 623–629.
26. Giovanni B. Frisoni, Nick C. Fox, Clifford R. Jack Jr, Philip Scheltens, Paul M. Thompson, The clinical use of structural MRI in Alzheimer's disease, Nature Reviews Neurology 6 (2) (2010) 67.
27. Jean Gallier, Logarithms and square roots of real matrices, arXiv:0805.0245[math], May 2008.
28. Sylvestre Gallot, Dominique Hulin, Jacques Lafontaine, Riemannian Geometry, 2nd edition, Springer-Verlag, 1993.
29. Aleksei Vladimirovich Gavrilov, Algebraic properties of covariant derivative and composition of exponential maps, Matematicheskie Trudy 9 (1) (2006) 3–20.
30. Roger Godement, Introduction à la Théorie des Groupes de Lie, Tomes I et II, Publications Mathématiques de L'Université Paris, vol. VII, 1982.
31. David Groisser, Newton's method, zeroes of vector fields, and the Riemannian center of mass, Advances in Applied Mathematics 33 (2004) 95–135.
32. Ernst Hairer, Christian Lubich, Gerhard Wanner, Geometric Numerical Integration: Structure Preserving Algorithm for Ordinary Differential Equations, Springer Series in Computational Mathematics, vol. 31, Springer, 2002.

33. Sigurdur Helgason, Differential Geometry, Lie Groups, and Symmetric Spaces, Academic Press, 1978.
34. Monica Hernandez, Matias Bossa, Salvador Olmos, Registration of anatomical images using paths of diffeomorphisms parameterized with stationary vector field flows, International Journal of Computer Vision 85 (2009) 291–306.
35. Nicholas J. Higham, The scaling and squaring method for the matrix exponential revisited, SIAM Journal on Matrix Analysis and Applications 26 (4) (January 2005) 1179–1193.
36. Sheung Hun Cheng, Nicholas J. Higham, Charles S. Kenney, Alan J. Laub, Approximating the logarithm of a matrix to specified accuracy, SIAM Journal on Matrix Analysis and Applications 22 (4) (2001) 1112–1125.
37. Arieh Iserles, Hans Z. Munthe-Kaas, Syvert P. Norsett, Antonella Zanna, Lie-group methods, Acta Numerica 9 (2000) 215–365.
38. Wilfrid S. Kendall, Convexity and the hemisphere, Journal of the London Mathematical Society 43 (2) (1991) 567–576.
39. Wilfrid S. Kendall, The propeller: a counterexample to a conjectured criterion for the existence of certain harmonic functions, Journal of the London Mathematical Society 46 (1992) 364–374.
40. Charles S. Kenney, Alan J. Laub, Condition estimates for matrix functions, SIAM Journal on Matrix Analysis and Applications 10 (1989) 191–209.
41. Boris A. Khesin, Robert Wendt, The Geometry of Infinite Dimensional Lie Groups, Ergebnisse der Mathematik und ihrer Grenzgebiete. 3. Folge / A Series of Modern Surveys in Mathematics, vol. 51, Springer, 2009.
42. Arkady Kheyfets, Warner A. Miller, Gregory A. Newton, Schild's ladder parallel transport procedure for an arbitrary connection, International Journal of Theoretical Physics 39 (12) (2000) 2891–2898.
43. Wilhelm Klingenberg, Riemannian Geometry, Walter de Gruyter, Berlin, New York, 1982.
44. Boris Kolev, Groupes de Lie et mécanique, http://www.cmi.univ-mrs.fr/~kolev/, 2007, Notes of a Master course in 2006–2007 at Université de Provence.
45. Serge Lang, Algebra, 3rd rev. ed., Graduate Texts in Mathematics, Springer, 2002, corr. 4th printing edition, 2004.
46. Marco Lorenzi, Xavier Pennec, Geodesics, parallel transport & one-parameter subgroups for diffeomorphic image registration, International Journal of Computer Vision 105 (2) (November 2013) 111–127.
47. Marco Lorenzi, Xavier Pennec, Efficient parallel transport of deformations in time series of images: from Schild's to pole ladder, Journal of Mathematical Imaging and Vision 50 (1–2) (2014) 5–17.
48. Marco Lorenzi, Nicholas Ayache, Xavier Pennec, Schild's ladder for the parallel transport of deformations in time series of images, in: G. Szekely, H. Hahn (Eds.), IPMI – 22nd International Conference on Information Processing in Medical Images, vol. 6801, Kloster Irsee, Germany, July 2011, Springer, 2011, pp. 463–474, Honorable Mention (runner-up) for the Erbsmann Award.

49. Marco Lorenzi, Nicholas Ayache, Giovanni B. Frisoni, Xavier Pennec, LCC-Demons: a robust and accurate symmetric diffeomorphic registration algorithm, NeuroImage 81 (1) (2013) 470–483.

50. Marco Lorenzi, Xavier Pennec, Giovanni B. Frisoni, Nicholas Ayache, Disentangling normal aging from Alzheimer's disease in structural MR images, Neurobiology of Aging (September 2014).

51. Marco Lorenzi, Nicholas Ayache, Xavier Pennec, Regional flux analysis for discovering and quantifying anatomical changes: an application to the brain morphometry in Alzheimer's disease, NeuroImage 115 (July 2015) 224–234.

52. Marco Lorenzi, Giovanni B. Frisoni, Nicholas Ayache, Xavier Pennec, Mapping the effects of $A\beta_{1-42}$ levels on the longitudinal changes in healthy aging: hierarchical modeling based on stationary velocity fields, in: G. Fichtinger, A. Martel, T. Peters (Eds.), Medical Image Computing and Computer-Assisted Intervention – MICCAI 2011, in: LNCS, vol. 6893, Springer, Heidelberg, Sep. 2011, pp. 663–670.

53. Tommaso Mansi, Xavier Pennec, Maxime Sermesant, Hervé Delingette, Nicholas Ayache, iLogDemons: a demons-based registration algorithm for tracking incompressible elastic biological tissues, International Journal of Computer Vision 92 (1) (2011) 92–111.

54. Kristin McLeod, Adityo Prakosa, Tommaso Mansi, Maxime Sermesant, Xavier Pennec, An incompressible log-domain demons algorithm for tracking heart tissue, in: Oscar Camara, Ender Konukoglu, Mihaela Pop, Kawal Rhode, Maxime Sermesant, Alistair Young (Eds.), Statistical Atlases and Computational Models of the Heart. Imaging and Modelling Challenges, vol. 7085, Springer, Berlin, Heidelberg, 2012, pp. 55–67.

55. Alberto Medina, Groupes de Lie munis de pseudo-métriques de Riemann bi-invariantes. Séminaire de géométrie différentielle 1981–1982, 1982.

56. Alberto Medina, Philippe Revoy, Algèbres de Lie et produit scalaire invariant, Annales Scientifiques de l'Ecole Normale Supérieure 18 (3) (1985) 553–561.

57. John Milnor, Remarks on infinite-dimensional Lie groups, in: Relativity, Groups and Topology, Les Houches, 1984, pp. 1009–1057.

58. Nina Miolane, Xavier Pennec, Computing bi-invariant pseudo-metrics on Lie groups for consistent statistics, Entropy 17 (4) (April 2015) 1850–1881.

59. Charles W. Misner, Kip S. Thorne, John Archibald Wheeler, Gravitation, W.H. Freeman and Company, 1973.

60. Maher Moakher, Means and averaging in the group of rotations, SIAM Journal on Matrix Analysis and Applications 24 (1) (January 2002) 1–16.

61. Marc Modat, Gerard R. Ridgway, Pankaj Daga, Manuel Jorge Cardoso, David J. Hawkes, John Ashburner, Sébastien Ourselin, Log-Euclidean free-form deformation, in: Proc. of SPIE Medical Imaging 2011, SPIE, 2011.

62. Cleve Moler, Charles Van Loan, Nineteen dubious ways to compute the exponential of a matrix, twenty-five years later, SIAM Review 45 (1) (2003) 3–49.

63. Yurii G. Nikonorov, Evgenii Dmirtievich Rodionov, Viktor Vladimirovich Slavskii, Geometry of homogeneous Riemannian manifolds, Journal of Mathematical Sciences 146 (6) (November 2007) 6313–6390.

64. Xavier Pennec, L'incertitude dans les problèmes de reconnaissance et de recalage – Applications en imagerie médicale et biologie moléculaire, Phd thesis, Ecole Polytechnique, December 1996.

65. Xavier Pennec, Computing the Mean of Geometric Features – Application to the Mean Rotation, Research Report RR-3371, INRIA, March 1998.

66. Xavier Pennec, Intrinsic statistics on Riemannian manifolds: basic tools for geometric measurements, Journal of Mathematical Imaging and Vision 25 (1) (2006) 127–154, a preliminary appeared as INRIA RR-5093, January 2004.

67. Xavier Pennec, Statistical Computing on Manifolds for Computational Anatomy, Habilitation à diriger des recherches, Université Nice Sophia Antipolis, December 2006.

68. Xavier Pennec, Parallel transport with pole ladder: a third order scheme in affine connection spaces which is exact in affine symmetric spaces, arXiv:1805.11436[cs, math], May 2018.

69. Xavier Pennec, Vincent Arsigny, Exponential barycenters of the canonical Cartan connection and invariant means on Lie groups, in: Frederic Barbaresco, Amit Mishra, Frank Nielsen (Eds.), Matrix Information Geometry, Springer, May 2012, pp. 123–168.

70. Jean-Marc Peyrat, Hervé Delingette, Maxime Sermesant, Xavier Pennec, Registration of 4D time-series of cardiac images with multichannel diffeomorphic demons, in: D. Metaxas, L. Axel, G. Fichtinger, G. Székely (Eds.), Medical Image Computing and Computer-Assisted Intervention – MICCAI 2008, in: LNCS, vol. 5242, Springer, Heidelberg, Sep. 2008, pp. 972–979.

71. Mikhail Mikhailovich Postnikov, Geometry VI: Riemannian Geometry, Encyclopedia of Mathematical Sciences, Springer, 2001.

72. Anqi Qiu, Laurent Younes, Michael I. Miller, John G. Csernansky, Parallel transport in diffeomorphisms distinguishes the time-dependent pattern of hippocampal surface deformation due to healthy aging and the dementia of the Alzheimer's type, NeuroImage 40 (1) (2008) 68–76.

73. Anil Rao, Raghavendra Chandrashekara, Gerardo I. Sanchez-Ortiz, Raad Mohiaddin, Paul Aljabar, Joseph V. Hajnal, Basant K. Puri, Daniel Rueckert, Spatial transformation of motion and deformation fields using nonrigid registration, IEEE Transactions on Medical Imaging 23 (9) (2004) 1065–1076.

74. William R. Riddle, Rui Li, J. Michael Fitzpatrick, Susan C. DonLevy, Benoit M. Dawant, Ronald R. Price, Characterizing changes in mr images with color-coded Jacobians, Magnetic Resonance Imaging 22 (6) (2004) 769–777.

75. Christof Seiler, Xavier Pennec, Mauricio Reyes, Geometry-aware multiscale image registration via OBBTree-based polyaffine log-demons, in: G. Fichtinger, A. Martel, T. Peters (Eds.), Medical Image Computing and Computer-Assisted Intervention – MICCAI 2011, in: LNCS, vol. 6893, Springer, Heidelberg, Sep. 2011, pp. 631–638.
76. Stephen M. Smith, Nicola De Stefano, Mark Jenkinson, Paul M. Matthews, Normalized accurate measurement of longitudinal brain change, Journal of Computer Assisted Tomography 25 (3) (2001) 466–475.
77. Shlomo Sternberg, Lectures on Differential Geometry, Prentice Hall Mathematics Series, Prentice Hall Inc., 1964.
78. Alain Trouvé, Diffeomorphisms groups and pattern matching in image analysis, International Journal of Computer Vision 28 (3) (1998) 213–221.
79. H. Turner Laquer, Invariant affine connections on Lie groups, Transactions of the American Mathematical Society 331 (2) (1992) 541–551.
80. Tom Vercauteren, Xavier Pennec, Aymeric Perchant, Nicholas Ayache, Non-parametric diffeomorphic image registration with the Demons algorithm, in: Nicholas Ayache, Sébastien Ourselin, Anthony Maeder (Eds.), Medical Image Computing and Computer-Assisted Intervention – MICCAI 2007, Springer, Berlin, Heidelberg, 2007, pp. 319–326.
81. Tom Vercauteren, Xavier Pennec, Aymeric Perchant, Nicholas Ayache, Diffeomorphic demons: efficient non-parametric image registration, NeuroImage 45 (1) (March 2009) S61–S72.
82. Tom Vercauteren, Xavier Pennec, Aymeric Perchant, Nicholas Ayache, Symmetric Log-domain diffeomorphic registration: a Demons-based approach, in: D. Metaxas, L. Axel, G. Fichtinger, G. Szekely (Eds.), Proc. of Medical Image Computing and Computer-Assisted Intervention – MICCAI 2008, vol. 5241, Springer, Heidelberg, Sep. 2008, pp. 754–761.
83. Michael Wüstner, A connected Lie group equals the square of the exponential image, Journal of Lie Theory 13 (2003) 307–309.
84. Laurent Younes, Jacobi fields in groups of diffeomorphisms and applications, Quarterly of Applied Mathematics (2007) 113–134.
85. Milos Zefran, Vijai Kumar, Christopher Croke, Metrics and connections for rigid-body kinematics, The International Journal of Robotics Research 18 (2) (February 1999) 243–258.

Statistics on manifolds and shape spaces

6

Object shape representation via skeletal models (s-reps) and statistical analysis

Stephen M. Pizer[a,d], **Junpyo Hong**[a,d], **Jared Vicory**[a,d],
Zhiyuan Liu[a,d], **J.S. Marron**[a,d], **Hyo-young Choi**[a,e],
James Damon[a,e], **Sungkyu Jung**[c,e], **Beatriz Paniagua**[a,e],
Jörn Schulz[b,e], **Ankur Sharma**[a,e], **Liyun Tu**[a,e], **Jiyao Wang**[a,e]

[a]*UNC, Chapel Hill, NC, United States.* [b]*Arctic University of Norway, Tromsø, Norway.* [c]*Seoul National University, Seoul, Republic of Korea*

6.1 Introduction to skeletal models

There are many ways to represent an anatomic object or object tuple, entities in three dimensions. These representations can be categorized into those that describe the object in terms of its geometric features and those that describe it in terms of a deformation of space from an atlas containing the object. Here we will be describing a representation via geometric object features.

Which geometric features are useful to capture in the representation? Many describe only boundary geometry, given by the boundary locations and/or boundary normal directions and/or boundary curvature features. Boundary normal directions and curvatures have been shown to be particularly important shape properties. But for the many objects that have the form of a bent slab, there is one additional set of features that intuitively seems important, *object widths* as they vary along the slab. The skeletal models are the only ones that explicitly capture object widths as well as boundary locations and normal directions. As laid out later in this chapter, comparisons of models according to two capabilities suggest that skeletal models are particularly strong; these capabilities are their power for classification and in providing prior probabilities to support segmentation.

As illustrated in Fig. 6.1, skeletal models for objects are best understood as formed by a skeleton with the same topology as the

[d]Principal coauthors of this chapter.
[e]Contributors of important material to this chapter.

Riemannian Geometric Statistics in Medical Image Analysis
https://doi.org/10.1016/B978-0-12-814725-2.00014-5

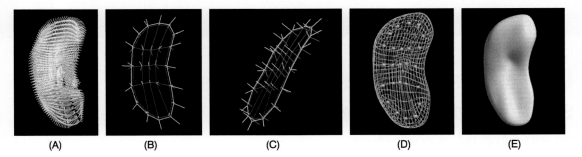

(A)   (B)   (C)   (D)   (E)

Figure 6.1. A skeletal model for a hippocampus. (A) Densely sampled spokes. (B, C) The computer representation of an s-rep, coarsely sampled spokes, from two points of view. The grid of green lines (mid gray in print version) connect vertices whose locations are interior skeletal points, each repeated to be on both sides of the folded skeletal surface. The yellow lines (light gray in print version) connect vertices whose locations are on the skeletal fold. The line segments proceeding from the skeletal fold points are fold spokes. The magenta line (dark gray in print version) segments proceeding from the interior skeletal points on one side of the object are interior spokes on that side. The cyan line (gray in print version) segments proceeding from the interior skeletal points on the other side of the object are also interior spokes. (D) The computer representation and the s-rep's implied boundary shown as a wire mesh. (E) The boundary implied by the s-rep.

object boundary, together with a vector function on the skeleton with the following properties: the tail of each vector is on the skeleton, and the tip of each vector is on the object boundary, and the set of all such vectors have no crossings within the object and fill the object interior. We call these vectors "spokes". The skeleton is a collapsed form of the object; it is folded onto itself such that except at the folds, at least and typically two places on the skeleton are at the same location. That is, the two spokes emanating from these places share tails; together each spoke pair captures the object width there. Also, the spoke tips cover the whole boundary, and the spoke directions capture boundary directions. Although such skeletons exist and are useful for both 2D and 3D objects, we focus here on the ones in 3D.

The earliest form of skeletal models was "medial". Whereas there were many variants (see Chapter 1 of [2]), the one due to Blum [1] was largely settled upon, and the mathematics of the Blum medial loci were deeply developed (especially, see Chapters 2 and 3 of [2]). The basic properties of the Blum representation are the following:

1. For slab-like objects, most skeletal points have two spokes whose tails are at that point and for which the two spokes have equal lengths, making the skeleton exactly centered between two opposing boundary points and making the common length a half-width of the object;

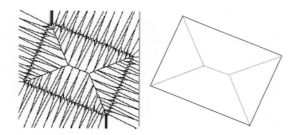

Figure 6.2. Left: A bushy Blum medial axis of a rectangle with boundary noise (from G. Székely, Chapter 6 of [2]). The desired medial axis consists only of the five blue line (light gray in print version) segments shown in the right figure within the noise-free rectangle; the remainder of the lines shown interior to the noisy rectangle are the unwanted bushy components of the computed axis.

2. At the tip of each spoke it is orthogonal to the object boundary: it captures the boundary position and normal.
3. Skeletal branches occur where three spokes share a tail point. The topology of the skeleton of 3D objects also has more complicated skeletal points (see Giblin and Kimia [2], Chapter 2).

However, when the input boundary has details, the Blum skeleton ("medial axis") is extremely bushy (Fig. 6.2). The variability in this branching across cases makes that object representation very challenging for object shape statistics. Moreover, pruning the representation was found to be fraught [2], and the locus of spoke tips from the pruned axis containing only intuitively essential branching could not succeed in giving a reasonably accurate approximation to an input object's boundary.

Thus Damon and Pizer [3] developed a more general, more flexible form of skeletal model and its mathematics (Chapter 3 of [2]). This model was named the "s-rep"; this chapter describes the s-rep and its mathematics and statistics. By only penalizing, rather than preventing, deviations from the medial properties of a) precisely matching the input boundary, b) having spokes that are precisely orthogonal to the input boundary, and c) having interior spokes that have exactly the same length as their partners proceeding to the other side from the same skeletal point, the s-rep could imply a boundary that accurately fits the input boundaries while containing only essential branching. Indeed, so many anatomic objects could be represented with no branching whatsoever that only limited work has been done to describe essentially branched objects with s-reps.

For a population of instances of an object, it is desirable to have correspondence between interior locations across instances. This first requires the same branching structure, second, correspon-

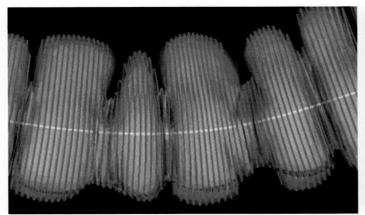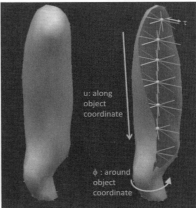

Figure 6.3. Left: A section of the large intestine represented as a generalized cylinder [4]. The center curve is the axis of the generalized cylinder, and the blue curves (dark gray in print version) orthogonal to the axis show the cross-sections of the generalized cylinder. Right: A discrete s-rep with tubular topology, implying the boundary shown in the left half of the panel.

dence of the fold curves, and third, correspondence within the respective skeletal sheets.

While the discussion so far has been for slab-like objects that have the topology of a sphere, objects with other topologies can be also usefully represented with skeletal models. In particular, objects that have the topology of a cylinder without its top and bottom, sometimes called "generalized cylinders", are also usefully represented skeletally (Fig. 6.3). In these objects the skeleton is formed by collapsing the quasitubular structure to a space curve that is infinitesimally dilated to a tube. In this structure, here again, there is one spoke per skeletal point, and the spokes fill the object and do not cross in the object interior.

6.2 Computing an s-rep from an image or object boundary

The almost innumerable algorithms for transforming an object boundary into its Blum medial axis fall into a few categories, summarized in Chapters 4–7 of [2]. There you will find an algorithm in each category that the authors deemed to be the best at the time that book was written. The categories are 1) computing shocks of a grassfire boundary evolution; 2) computing skeletons that are lists of voxels using discrete methods, for example, via the distance transform; and 3) using the Voronoi diagram to compute

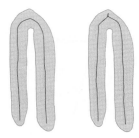

Figure 6.4. Bent bar with branching medial axis. Left: with intuitive axis; right: with approximate Blum medial axis.

skeletons. These algorithms face in common the problem that the function from object boundaries to skeletal loci is ill-conditioned; that is, it turns small errors into large ones and in particular produces bushy skeletons that need pruning. This is problematic because of the failure to have found adequate methods for pruning.

What is needed are algorithms for finding a skeleton that recognize only the specific branching of the object that is essential to its shape. For example (Fig. 6.4), a tube with a smooth bend going around 180 degrees to become parallel close to itself would have a single curvilinear skeleton unlike the medial skeleton that has a branch at the bend.

One algorithm for extracting a quasimedial skeleton with this trait works on images and generates nonbranching skeletons by using the properties that height ridges generically do not branch [5]. These images can be those with high contrast at object boundaries or can be signed pseudodistance images, in which the voxel values are zero at the boundary, negative on the inside of the object, positive outside it, and monotonic in magnitude of distance from the object boundary. The idea is to consider probing the image via a primitive (Fig. 6.5) that responds strongly when it is consistent with medial behavior. Specifically, the probe is a function of image position (the candidate medial position x), spoke length (r), and the directions of two spokes ($\underline{\theta_1}, \underline{\theta_2}$); thus in 3D images the probe is eight-dimensional. The probe measures the evidence that at the two spoke tips the image is boundary-like in the spoke directions. Applying the probe produces a scalar measurement $M(\underline{x}, r, \theta_1, \theta_2)$ in an eight-dimensional non-Euclidean Riemannian manifold. In this algorithm a medial locus of dimension k (e.g., 2 for a slab-like object or 1 for a generalized cylinder) is a k-dimensional height ridge of M called a "core".

These cores [7] proved to be particularly powerful for finding blood vessels in noisy 3D medical images [8,9]. Fridman also showed they could support finding blood vessel branches by ex-

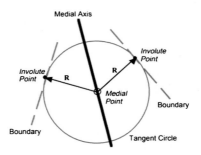

Figure 6.5. Medial strength probe (copied from [6]). x is the position labeled "Medial Point". θ_1 and θ_2 respectively give the directions of the two spoke vectors of length $\overline{R}$ (called "r" in the text) proceeding from the medial point to the involute points, at which the object boundary is sensed with tangent direction (the dashed lines) perpendicular to the vectors.

ploring the behavior of the function M, and he demonstrated this property as well for slab-like branches on slab-like objects.

However, cores had several problems. The algorithms for computing them worked by ridge following, and like all such algorithms, initializing the ridge was not easy, and the ridges could break in areas where the medial evidence is weak, where they would change into height saddles.

Reflecting that transforming boundaries into skeletal structures mapped small errors into large ones, it became clear that the inverse process (skeletal model mapped to the boundary) would be far preferable, as it would map large errors into small ones. Thus the approach that we have adopted was born: fitting a skeletal model with fixed branching topology into boundary data. This has proven to have adequate stability to allow a variety of uses, presented later in this chapter.

The s-reps that we invented have developed through a number of computer representations. In the medial literature it has been traditional to think of the skeletal surface of an object as a bounded surface (in 3D; a curve in 2D) with two spokes from all locations except for branch and surface-end locations; in early incarnations of the s-rep this was how it was represented in the computer. However, as illustrated in Fig. 6.6, it is notably clearer and more generalizable to think of the skeleton as being a folded surface produced by collapsing the two sides of an object onto each other, with each location on that folded surface having a single spoke. In this view the end points in the traditional view have become the fold. Thus, other than at the fold, two skeletal points are at the same location, but the skeleton has the same topology as the object being represented. Mathematically, the s-rep is writ-

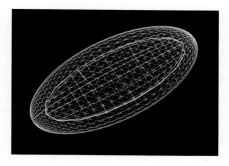

Figure 6.6. An ellipsoid and its skeleton, formed by collapsing the ellipsoid with respect to its principal axis of shortest length. The doubled ellipse shown by the top side in orange (mid gray in print version) and the bottom side in yellow (light gray in print version) actually share locations; the slight offset is used in this visualization to allow you see the two ellipses.

ten as follows: Let u parameterize the boundary of the object being represented. Then the s-rep $m(u) = (p(u), S(u))$ is also parameterized by u, where $p(u) = (x(u), y(u), z(u))$ is the skeleton, and $S(u)$ is the spoke emanating from the skeletal point $p(u)$. Moreover, $S(u) = (U(u), r(u))$, where the unit vector U is the spoke direction, and r is the spoke length.

In the computer representation the skeleton and its spokes are spatially sampled (see Fig. 6.1, where strictly the dense spokes are interpolated from the coarse spokes in the computer representation) into a sparse version that we also refer to as "the discrete s-rep". Such a computer representation implies a continuous s-rep by the use of a spoke interpolation method supported by the mathematics of skeletal structures due to Damon (Chapter 3 in [2]); see Section 6.3.

Yushkevich [10] developed a useful alternative form in which the interpolation is built in through the use of an explicit analytic representation; this is done via the use of a specialized spline on (x, y, z, r). Like all splines, this one is represented by spline coefficients that can be understood as control "points". Although this form of skeletal representation of 3D objects has found important medical application where physical modeling of anatomic objects is desirable, for statistical applications, it has not been shown to be competitive with our s-reps based on skeletal sampling.

6.3 Skeletal interpolation

To fit an s-rep to an object boundary, the spokes must be dense enough. Thus the skeletal surface and the spokes from it must be interpolated from the sparse representation that we use (Fig. 6.1). Skeletal interpolation is also needed to display the boundary implied by the s-rep. Spokes on a skeletal surface follow the skeletal geometry of each spoke direction living abstractly on a 2-sphere and each log of spoke length living in a Euclidean space. That is, spokes live in a curved abstract space. Moreover, the fact that the s-rep is approximately medial places soft constraints on that space. We have shown that actually using that geometry is necessary to ensure that the interpolated s-rep is usable.

It would probably be mathematically best to interpolate the skeletal surface and the spokes in a single interpolation. However, for simplicity, Vicory [11] divided this into a skeletal surface interpolation operation and a spoke interpolation on the interpolated skeletal surface.

The skeletal surface interpolation method uses standard polynomial-based methods. One idea would use the property that the normal to the skeletal surface can be expected to be in a direction near the difference of the spoke directions; this is a fact in the medial case. Since our skeletal representations are only quasimedial, this would have to be done via a penalty, that is, soft constraint, on the angles of the paired spokes to the skeletal surface being computed, and to date we have not used this approach.

Our method for spoke interpolation depends on first interpolating the spoke directions U and then interpolating the spoke lengths r. Our experience shows that this tack is preferable because we have found a good way to interpolate the directions and have found that the overall result is then very robust against approximation errors in the spoke length interpolation.

Let the skeletal surface be parameterized by (u_1, u_2), where both parameters are integers at the corners of a quadrilateral in the grid on which the discrete s-rep is specified. Thus the discrete s-rep gives both r and U at these quadrilateral corners. Consider interpolation of the spoke directions U at any point $p(u_1, u_2)$ within any grid quadrilateral on the skeletal surface. Our plan for interpolation of r is based on a second-order Taylor series, for which we need not only the spoke directions U but also their first- and second-order derivative values[1] U_{u_i} and U_{u_i, u_i} for $i = 1, 2$ at arbitrary points in the quadrilateral. Spoke directions live on the unit 2-sphere $\mathbb{S}^2$. Thus, the sort of finite difference calculations that must be used to compute U at our discrete skeletal points should be done on the sphere. These calculations are done by representing the discrete spokes U as unit quaternions and thus its derivatives with respect to u_i as derivatives on the sphere. Using

---

[1] Subscripted variables refer to directional derivatives in the direction of the subscript.

these derivatives, Vicory applies the squad method of interpolating quaternions to estimate the spoke direction U at an arbitrary point interior to a quadrangle of discrete points by fitting Bezier curves to the quaternions on the surface of the sphere. This approximation allows the computation of not only the U values but also their directional derivatives of both first and second orders in either u_1 or u_2.

Given the ability to evaluate U and its derivatives in a quadrilateral, we need to interpolate the r values in a way consistent with skeletal geometry. Spokes can be written $S = rU$. The derivatives of the spoke at a skeletal location p with respect to a step in direction v in either of the two orthogonal directions u_1 or u_2 must follow $S_v = rU_v + r_vU$, from which it follows that $r_v = S_v \cdot U$. Also, $S_{vv} \cdot U = (S_v)_v \cdot U = r_{vv} + rU_{vv} \cdot U$. From this a Taylor series in the length d of a small step in direction v together with three forward-distance derivative approximations yields $r(p + dv) = \frac{1}{2}(S(p) + S(p + 2dv)) \cdot U(p + dv) - \frac{d^2}{2}(S(p) \cdot U_{vv}(p))$. Because the same mathematics works using a Taylor series in the backward direction about $p + 2dv$, for symmetry and to reduce approximation error, the results of the two versions should be averaged, yielding the final formula as

$$r(p + dv) = U(p + dv) \cdot \left(\frac{1}{2}(S(p) + S(p + 2dv))\right)$$
$$- \frac{d^2}{4}(S(p) \cdot U_{vv}(p) + S(p + 2dv) \cdot U_{vv}(p + 2dv)).$$

(6.1)

This formula allows computing the spoke half-way between two horizontally adjacent quadrilateral corners and using successive subdivision with it by halving as many times as necessary to get the desired small spacing in u_1. Applying the same method separably (on the results) in the u_2 direction yields a spoke at any successively subdivided point within the quadrilateral. Finally, since the method gives different results when you apply it first in u_2 and then in u_1, we compute using both orders and average the results.

At a skeletal fold, the skeletal surface's lack of smoothness prevents direct application of the aforementioned method. We solve this problem by first dilating the fold curve into a tube with very narrow radius. We then find where the spoke at the fold curve intersects the tube. Then we use the method for smooth surfaces to compute the continuation of the spoke from the smooth surface of the tube to the object boundary.

6.4 Skeletal fitting

After trying many approaches, the best ways we have found to fit an s-rep to the given boundary of a particular object is to initialize a process with a reference s-rep appropriate to the object, to map that s-rep via boundary correspondences to the target, and then to complete the process by a refinement of the mapped s-rep.

Two methods for initialization have been created. The newer form [12] involves using an ellipsoidal reference object; this is attractive both because no user-chosen reference object is needed and because the ellipsoid has a mathematically known unbranching *medial* representation with a folded flat ellipse as the skeletal surface. The method uses mean-curvature flow on the input object boundary in small steps until it approaches closely enough to an ellipsoid, from which a sampled s-rep can be derived. The small steps allow the establishment of correspondence between points on the boundary before a step and those after a step. Then the boundary correspondences for each step, together with correspondences at the skeletal fold, can be used in reverse to obtain a thin-plate-spline transformation from the after-flow state to the before-flow state. The skeletal fold correspondences are computed from the normal and the radius of curvature at the corresponding crest points. The small-step transformations can be composed and applied to the ellipsoidal s-rep's spoke tips (boundary points) and tails (skeletal points) to yield an initialized s-rep in the original object.

This method is new, so it has been shown to work for only a few objects, namely the relatively blob-shaped hippocampus (see Fig. 6.7), the thin-width lateral ventricle, and the narrowing-shaped caudate nucleus (for which a special primitive to handle the cusp-end has been designed [12]), the parotid gland, and the rather complicated-shaped mandible. Objects with sharp points or crests, such as the mandible, need special attention to avoid some of the mesh tiles becoming too small. Alternative means of mapping the ellipsoid's s-rep back to the original object should perform faster.

This method establishes a correspondence among a population of objects as follows. After the mean curvature flow, each of the objects is mapped to an ellipsoid, the geometric means of the corresponding principal radii can be computed, and each object's ellipsoid can be mapped to the mean ellipsoid by the implied expansion of its three principal radii. Thereby, the sampled s-rep of the mean ellipsoid (Fig. 6.7) can be mapped to each object, after which each object's sampled s-rep can be deformed back to its original object.

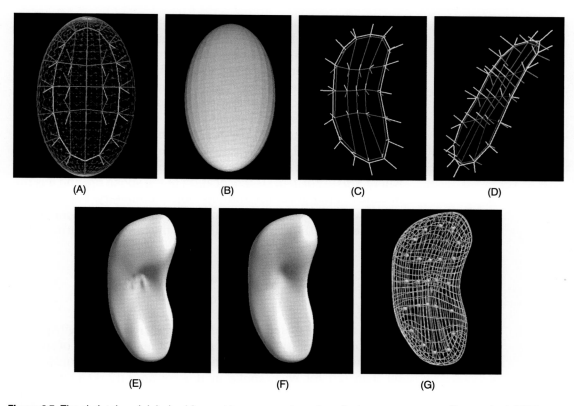

Figure 6.7. The skeletal model derived from a hippocampus boundary via the mean curvature flow method. (A) The ellipsoid s-rep from which the hippocampus s-rep is derived, together with a wire-mesh showing the ellipsoid, and (B) its implied boundary. (C,D): The fitted hippocampus s-rep from two points of view. The interior skeletal points are grid vertices in green (dark gray in print version). Magenta (gray in print version) and cyan (light gray in print version) spokes emanate from them. The yellow curve (white in print version) is the fold, with fold spokes emanating from it. (E) The implied boundary of the s-rep after initial fitting. (F) The implied boundary of the refined s-rep. (G) The refined s-rep showing both the implied boundary as a wire mesh and the s-rep itself.

The older form of initialization involves producing s-rep fits for many instances of an object and then taking the reference model to be their backwards mean, as described in Section 6.6. In this form we have found that a deformation of the reference object boundary into the target object boundary can be calculated by the thin-shell demons method of Zhao [13] (preceded by a similarity transformation), which yields a transformation of the boundary locations with correspondence that can be generalized to 3D using thin-plate splines and then applied to the tails and tips of the reference s-rep.

For both methods of initializing an object's s-rep, refinement of the initialized model is done by optimization of a penalty measuring the deviation of the s-rep from the medial ideal. The penalty is the integral over the spokes of a weighted sum of three terms, one measuring the fit of each original and interpolated spoke tip to the target object boundary, another measuring how orthogonal the spoke tip is to the boundary, and the third measuring how mathematically proper the model is at that spoke tip, that is, how stable the model is against spoke crossing in the object interior. The measure of fit integrates $|d(p(u) + r(u)U(u))|$ over the spokes, where $p(u) + r(u)U(u)$ is the location of the spoke tip, and d is the distance of that location from the object boundary. The measure of spoke-to-boundary orthogonality is 1 minus the cosine of the angle between the spoke direction and the boundary normal, that is,

$$1 - \frac{U(u) \cdot \nabla d(p(u) + r(u)U(u))}{|\nabla d(p(u) + r(u)U(u))|}. \tag{6.2}$$

The measure of stability against spoke crossing heavily penalizes spoke crossing and slightly penalizes near-crossing of spokes. In particular, the spoke-crossing test devised by Damon (Chapter 3 in [2]) for each spoke in the continuous skeletal model, namely, $1 - \det(r S_{\text{rad}}) > 0$, is used as the argument of the penalty weight, where S_{rad} is what Damon calls the radial shape operator. This operator is analogous to the familiar shape operator from differential geometry, which is a 2×2 matrix that, when applied to a small step $\underline{\Delta B} = av + bw$ on a surface B whose tangent plane is spanned by the frame (v, w), yields the change of the surface normal for that step, also represented in the frame (v, w). Analogously, the radial shape operator is also a 2×2 matrix that, when applied to a small step $\underline{\Delta p} = av + bw$ on the skeletal surface, yields the component of the spoke direction change ΔU in the skeletal surface for that step, also represented in the frame (v, w). The matrix S_{rad} is computed from derivatives in the orthogonal directions v and w, respectively, of the spoke direction U; as described in Section 6.3, this is computed by quaternion derivatives on the sphere.

In some cases it is useful to combine the spoke crossing penalty with a penalty for nonuniformity of the discrete spoke positions on the skeletal surface. In particular, the penalty can be monotonic with the size of the difference between each interior discrete skeletal position and the average of those positions at adjacent grid positions.

6.5 Correspondence

In producing statistics on any geometric representation of a training population, and in particular for s-reps, correspondence of the primitives is important. For s-reps, two methods for producing correspondence have been developed. The first depends on starting the fitting of each object in the population from the same reference model or related reference models, such as the ellipsoids in the method described in Section 6.4. This already produces useful correspondence. Somewhat improved correspondence, according to a measure of entropy among the object s-reps (see Section 6.7.2), can be obtained by the method developed by Tu et al. [11], who maximized the geometric entropy (the probability distribution is tightened) with an additional entropy term in the objective function that encourages uniformity of the spokes within each object in the population.

Tu (Fig. 15) showed that when correspondence optimization was applied, measures of specificity and of generalization on s-rep-implied boundary points (see Section 6.7.3) were improved. But also there was an improvement as compared to the method of Cates et al. [14], where the boundary points' entropy is directly optimized by the same entropy-based method that the s-reps method was modeled after. We take this improvement as a value-added of including features of object width and spoke direction in addition to boundary point location.

6.6 Skeletal statistics

The major scientific challenges in modern medical image analysis arise at the population level and are addressed using random samples drawn from the population of interest. For a given skeletal configuration (discrete s-rep), the set of all possible skeletal models is called the *shape space*, and the sampling process is understood via a probability distribution on that space. Statistical analysis is then used to infer underlying population properties from the available sample.

Because, as described in Section 6.6.1.3, the s-rep shape space is naturally represented as typically hundreds of Euclidean variables (3D locations of atoms plus log spoke lengths) and of angles on respective spheres $\mathbb{S}^2$, sufficiently general probability distributions are most naturally considered as being defined on the corresponding Riemannian manifold (or even a Finslerian manifold).

There are a number of approaches to statistical analysis of data objects lying on a Riemannian manifold, which have led to varying degrees of success. One class of these has been called *extrinsic*;

see [15] for a good introduction and overview. The key idea is to treat data on the manifold as points in the embedded Euclidean space, do statistical analysis there, and project the results back to the manifold. Another class of approaches is *intrinsic* analysis, which aims to more directly incorporate the curved manifold nature of the data space into the analysis. Here we discuss several intrinsic approaches that are commonly used in the analysis of s-rep data. For more detailed discussion in this direction, see [16].

The intrinsic statistical methods that we will discuss all involve Gaussian probability distributions. Some methods try to apply Gaussians directly on the manifold; we will call these *directly Gaussian methods*. Others map the manifold to another Euclidean manifold in which Gaussians are used; we will call these *Gaussian via Euclideanization methods*. For example, in producing statistics on LDDMM deformations understood as geodesic paths according to a complicated metric on a very high-dimensional manifold, we might try to accomplish this directly or try to Euclideanize by mapping each path to a still very high but much lower dimensional space of momenta and then do Gaussian analysis on the space of momenta, which is arguably a cotangent space [17].

Our methods of statistics on s-reps fall into the category of Gaussian via Euclideanization methods.[2] They work by using PCA-like methods to produce scores that frequently can be treated as measured via a Euclidean norm, then doing Gaussian analysis on the space of these scores, and finally mapping the results of the Gaussian analysis back onto the original manifold.

We first discuss methods for estimation of the probability distribution on s-reps, and later we discuss methods for classification via s-reps.

6.6.1 Probability distribution estimation

6.6.1.1 Tangent plane statistical analysis methods

The first generation of methods is intrinsic analogs of PCA for the analysis of Riemannian manifold data. A manifold is a surface in the ambient space that is smooth in the sense of having an approximating hyperplane (in the sense of shrinking neighborhoods) at every point. In this spirit Fletcher [18] first proposed a directly Gaussian method that he called *Principal Geodesic Analysis* (PGA). Here ordinary PCA, which we now call forward PCA (see our later discussion of backward PCA), is generalized to the manifold via geodesics. The zero-dimensional approximation is the point on the manifold minimizing the sum of squared geodesic

[2]The following is appropriately modified material from our previous paper [16] reprinted here by permission of the copyrighter.

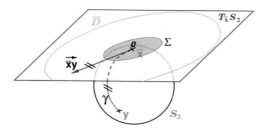

Figure 6.8. Tangent plane statistical analysis (by permission from X. Pennec).

distances from the sample data points to it (the Fréchet mean); the one-dimensional approximation is the curve on the manifold through the Fréchet mean minimizing the sum of squared geodesic distances from the sample data points to it; and so on.

Because computing these geodesic distances is often unwieldy or worse, Fletcher [19] proposed an approach using Euclideanization. This is based on the plane that is tangent at the Fréchet mean (Fig. 6.8). The data on the surface of the manifold are represented as points in the tangent plane using the *Log map*. PCA is then performed there, and the resulting eigenvectors and summarized data are mapped back into the manifold using the *Exponential map*. The corresponding scores give a type of Euclideanization.

Although much useful shape analysis has been done using tangent plane methods, large gains in statistical efficiency have been realized through the development of more sophisticated Gaussian via Euclideanization methods. The reason for this can be understood from the S^2 example shown in Fig. 6.9. The blue points (dark gray in print version) are a sample of S^2 directions for a single spoke in the bladder-prostate-rectum simulator model of [20]. Note that these data points tend to lie along a circle, so their Fréchet mean lies near the center of the circle. Thus the data appear as a circle when they are mapped into the tangent plane using the Log map.

Hence, although the data are essentially *one-dimensional* in nature (since they just follow a single small circle), the PGA requires *two* components (because the projections again follow a circle) to appropriately describe the variation in the data. A data representation living in two dimensions is much less statistically efficient than a one-dimensional representation in the sense that modeling with higher-dimensional probability distributions is less efficient. This has motivated a search for more statistically efficient approaches to the statistical analysis of data lying on a manifold.

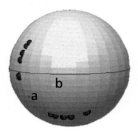

Figure 6.9. Set of locations of a single spoke generated by an s-rep simulator model. Shows that important s-rep modes of variation follow small circles, whose variation is poorly captured by tangent plane analysis. The orange point (light gray in print version), marked by 'b' is the Fréchet mean, which captures the center of the data less well than the red point (mid gray in print version), marked by 'a', which is the backward mean (see Section 6.6.1.2).

The first of the methods recognizing that the data are on a sphere and principally lie on a subsphere of that sphere is *Principal Nested Spheres* (PNS), motivated and described in Section 6.6.1.2. Extension of this to more complicated manifolds, such as the polyspheres central to s-rep shape representations, is given in Section 6.6.1.3. Section 6.6.1.4 discusses a yet more efficient approach to polysphere analysis involving a high-dimensional spherical approximation followed by a PNS analysis.

6.6.1.2 Principal nested spheres

In the case of data lying in a high-dimensional sphere $\mathbb{S}^k$ embedded in $\mathbb{R}^{k+1}$ a useful intrinsic version of PCA is Principal Nested Spheres (PNS) [21]. The central idea is to iteratively find a nested (through dimension) series of subspheres, each of which provides an optimal fit to the data (Fig. 6.10). In particular, at each step the dimension of the approximation is reduced by 1, finding the subsphere that best fits the data in the sense of minimum sum of squared residuals, measured using geodesic arc length along the surface of the sphere. In the case of $\mathbb{S}^2$, as shown in Fig. 6.9, PNS corresponds to the use of a polar coordinate representation carefully chosen with its pole at the correct place on the sphere.

The signed residuals are also saved as PNS scores for that component. The concatenation of these scores over the dimensions becomes the PNS Euclideanization of each data point. The advantages of this approach are statistical efficiency (in terms of a lower-dimensional scores representation, as illustrated in Fig. 6.9) and tractability, since each lower-dimensional manifold is determined by the imposition of a single (usually easy to find) constraint. Note that when the PNS scores are modeled as a Gaussian distribution,

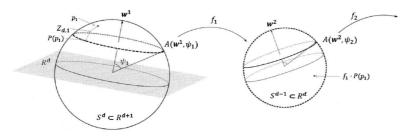

Figure 6.10. An optimal small subsphere, geodesic distances $(Z_{d,1})$ forming scores, and projections onto the subsphere (by permission from S. Jung).

the induced probability distribution on the shape manifold will keep the property of unimodality and will generally have a roughly Gaussian shape as long as the spread along the manifold is not too large.

One reason that PNS was an important statistical landmark is that it motivated the more general idea of *Backward PCA* as a general paradigm for finding principal components in non-Euclidean data contexts. The full generality of this idea can be found in [22]. A key concept is that the general utility of backward PCA follows from thinking of PCA in terms of a nested series of constraints. Backward tends to be easier to work with because from that viewpoint, the constraints can be found sequentially, instead of needing to know the full set and then sequentially relaxing them. As noted in [22], this idea is seen to generate (or to have the potential to generate) useful analogs of PCA in a variety of other non-Euclidean settings such as on other manifolds, for Nonnegative Matrix Factorization, and for Manifold Learning.

The example shown in Fig. 6.9 also shows that the Fréchet mean, shown as the orange point (light gray in print version), marked by 'b' in the figure, can be a poor choice of center in that it may not be representative of the data in the sense that it lies outside the cloud of data points. A more representative notion of center is the *backward mean*, shown as the red point (mid gray in print version), marked by 'a' in the figure. This backward mean is an intrinsic mean that is much more representative of the data in that example than the Fréchet mean. Generally this is computed by taking one more step in PNS. In this last step the best fitting point, that is, zero-dimensional sphere, to the $\mathbb{S}^1$ approximations of the data, is found. In particular, the backward mean is the Fréchet mean of the rank 1 circular representation of the data, which can then be viewed as the best backward rank 0 approximation. So in Fig. 6.9 the backward mean falls on the circle determined by the data, whereas the forward mean (the Fréchet mean) falls far from that circle.

A fundamental observation of [23] is that both the backward methods (e.g., PNS), which were explicitly described in [22], and forward methods such as PGA rely upon greedy sequential searches (in opposite directions). That motivated a simultaneous fitting approach called *barycentric subspaces*, which are affine combinations (a generalization of Fréchet, Karcher, or exponential weighted averages where negative weights allow appropriate extrapolation) of a set of *reference points*. These methods are described in detail elsewhere in this book.

6.6.1.3 Composite principal nested spheres

Pizer et al. [3] proposed extending PNS to manifolds that involve products of spheres, such as those for both boundary point distribution models and s-reps, using the idea of Composite Principal Nested Spheres (CPNS). The idea here is to first develop the PNS representation (Euclideanization) for each spherical component and then concatenate these, together with Euclidean components, into a large Euclidean representation. This would then be followed by PCA on the result.

In the case of s-reps, the spheres in question are one $\mathbb{S}^2$ for each spoke direction and a high-dimensional sphere for the scaled and centered skeletal points. The Euclidean variables are the log spoke lengths and the log scale of the object. The sphere for the n scaled skeletal points, of dimension $3n - 4$, arises from centering each skeleton on its center of mass and then scaling each point $\underline{x}_i$ by the object scale $\gamma = (\sum_{i=1}^{n} |\underline{x}_i|^2)^{\frac{1}{2}}$.

Of importance is the commensuration between the components before applying the PCA. Hong et al. [24] designed an experiment to determine the most reasonable commensuration on the Euclideanized features, more precisely, on the object scale and the sphere-resident features derived from the centered and normalized skeletal points. First, the features were transformed to be in the same units. In our case the log-transformed version of the scale factor γ (i.e., $\bar{\gamma} \log \frac{\gamma}{\bar{\gamma}}$) had units of millimeters. On the other hand, radians (unitless values θ_i for each of the dimensions of the unit sphere) are the units for the Euclideanized shape features derived by PNS from the 2-spheres on which the spoke directions live and from the high-dimensional unit sphere on which the scaled skeletal point tuple for each case lives. Thus we multiplied each PNS-derived feature by $\bar{\gamma}$ to put them into units of distance. The problem then is to determine the factor to commensurate the feature capturing scale with the PNS-derived features. We determined that factor by creating a new population that would have a nonvarying shape consistent with those in the original population and a scale variation that was the same as those in the original population. To do this, we formed the new population by applying the measured log-transformed γ values for each case to the object of median scale that was then scaled to have $\gamma = 1$. By comparing the total variances of the original and created populations, respectively, we could determine the correct commensuration factor between $\bar{\gamma} \log \frac{\gamma}{\bar{\gamma}}$ and the Euclideanized features from PNS, namely, $\bar{\gamma}\theta_i$. The experiment concluded that the correct commensuration factor was 1.0 up to sample variation. This idea of separately treating scale can be used for problems of commensuration of other types of variation. In particular, the geometric mean $\bar{r}_i$ of the ith spoke's lengths is used to commensurate PNS-derived features from its spoke directions.

6.6.1.4 Polysphere PCA

Data spaces that are products of spheres, such as the skeletal model spaces of Section 6.6.1.3, have been called polyspheres in [25]. That paper goes on to propose a new method, *Polysphere PCA*. This allows a Euclideanization provided by a more flexible modeling of the dependence between features than that achieved by CPNS's PCA on the geometric properties Euclideanized one by one. This potential improvement is achieved through a distortion of carefully selected angles on each sphere component to map the polysphere data onto a high-dimensional sphere and then using PNS on that. This has the advantage relative to CPNS that the PNS is done on a single sphere rather than sphere by sphere, which potentially better captures nonlinear dependence. It has the disadvantage that except near the mean the mapping to the sphere rather severely distorts distances on the manifold. On one population of skeletal shape data this approach has been shown to give a lower-dimensional probability distribution representation than is available from CPNS. However, our initial unpublished results comparing classification via Polysphere Euclideanization vs. PNS sphere by sphere Euclideanization [26] suggest that difficulties of Polysphere Euclideanization in separate commensuration for each geometric property can counteract its potential advantages in improved Euclideanization. This holds even when the radius of the various spheres is taken as the geometric means of their entity sizes (length for spokes, scale for skeletal point sequences).

6.6.2 Classification

A major analytic task when working with populations of shape data is statistical *classification* (also called *discrimination*). For

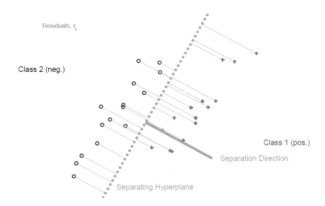

Figure 6.11. The idea of the separation direction determined from SVM or DWD (each method will determine a somewhat different separation direction).

this task, training data with known class labels is given and is used to develop a classification rule for assigning new data to one of the classes. For Euclidean data objects, there are many methods available; see [27] for a good overview.

The most common methods for classification are based on Euclidean spaces. Particularly widely used these days is the method called support vector machines (SVM); see, for example, [28] for detailed discussion. SVM is based on optimizing the gap in feature space between the training cases in the two classes. A more statistically efficient method called Distance-Weighted Discrimination (DWD), still in a Euclidean feature space, was developed [29]. Its efficiency derives from using all of the training data, not just those near the gap. Both SVM and DWD yield a direction in feature space that optimally separates the classes (Fig. 6.11). Classification then involves projecting the feature tuple onto the separation direction and deriving the class or the class probability from the resulting scalar value.

Use of DWD with data objects lying in a manifold is often done by Euclideanizing the object features and then applying DWD to the result. We call this *Discriminative PNS* (DPNS). As shown in [24], DPNS can improve classification accuracy over using the object features directly in DWD.

Section 6.7 lays out the details of the applications in which the benefits of s-reps statistics have been shown. In brief, diagnostic classifications of two brain structures in two diseases have been shown to be improved by s-reps over boundary point representations, high-quality segmentations by posterior optimization of multiple organs in both CT and 3D ultrasound have been produced using shape priors based on s-reps, and useful hypothesis testing by locality and by s-rep feature has been demonstrated.

6.7 How to compare representations and statistical methods

Given all of the different shape representations discussed in Section 6.2, the analytic approaches discussed in Sections 6.3 and 6.4, and the statistical methods discussed in Section 6.5, an important issue is their comparison. One basis for this is knowledge of how they work, which can lead to sensible choices in a wide variety of shapes. But it is also interesting to consider quantitative bases for comparison, which is done in this section.[3]

6.7.1 Classification accuracy

When a data set is naturally grouped into two (or perhaps more) subsets, for example, pathology vs. normal controls, various methods can be compared on the basis of *classification accuracy*. The classification problem starts with a group of labeled data called the *training set*, and the goal is to develop a rule for classifying new observations. Classification accuracy is simply the rate of correct classifications, either for an independent test set or using some variation of the cross-validation idea. See [27] for access to the large literature on classification.

6.7.2 Hypothesis testing power

A related approach to comparing shape methodologies, again based on two well-labeled subgroups in the data, is to construct a formal hypothesis test for the difference between the groups. Quantification of the difference then follows from the level of statistical significance, allowing a different type of comparison of the relative merits of various approaches to the analysis. This was done to good effect in [30]. The most important contribution there was a technique for dealing in a nonpessimistic way with high positive correlation that always occurs among geometric properties at nearby points on an object. The methods shown in that paper involve commensurating the various local geometric properties by transforming them to standard Gaussian probabilities. The methods not only work for a test on significance on the whole

---

[3]Much of this section appeared previously in [16]; reprinted here by permission of the copyrighter.

shape description but also for correcting for multiple tests when testing significance geometric property by geometric property.

6.7.3 Specificity, generalization, and compactness

In object statistics work in medicine, two common measures of the quality of a probability distribution derived from data via its eigenmodes are specificity and generalization [31].

Specificity is a measure of how well the estimated probability distribution represents only valid instances of the object. It is computed as the average distance between sample objects randomly generated in the computed shape space and their nearest members of the data.

Generalization is a measure of how close new instances of the object are to the probability distribution estimated from the training cases that do not include the new instance. It is calculated by computing an average over the training cases of the distance of that training case to the shape space specified by eigenmodes, where those eigenmodes are produced using all but the left out training case. That distance is computed as between the left out shape and its projection onto that shape space.

Both specificity and generalization are measured in units of geometric object property differences, where example geometric properties are boundary locations, boundary normal directions, or skeletal spoke directions. In our use of the specificity and generalization measures for s-rep based probability distributions reported in Section 6.8.4, the distances only use the corresponding boundary locations and are not based on the additional features of the full s-rep. In particular, for specificity, the measure is the boundary-location-based distance between a random object from the shape space over s-reps to the training object that is nearest according to the boundary location-based distance. For specificity, the measure is the boundary-location-based distance between a training object and its projection onto the shape space over s-reps.

Compactness is a measure that quantifies how tight a probability distribution is. Two measures of compactness that are often used are the entropy of the distribution and the determinant of its covariance matrix (total variance).

6.7.4 Compression into few modes of variation

The Euclidean PCA decomposition of data into modes of variation is also frequently understood from a signal processing viewpoint. In that case a signal that is actually generated from few dimensions is modified by noise. Noise is high dimensional by definition of having energy across the spectrum. PCA provides a data-driven basis (in the sense of linear algebra) that puts as much of the low-dimensional signal as possible into a few basis elements with largest variance. Many of the gains in statistical efficiency, such as those discussed in Section 6.4, can be understood as providing better signal compression in these terms.

However, this analogy fails in the presence of shape signals, which tend to be widely spread across the PCA spectrum in Euclidean data. In particular, the standard Euclidean assumption of all of the signal being present in the first few eigenvalues is usually misleading because nonlinear shape signals tend not to lie within a Euclidean space of low dimension, so that both signal and noise typically spread power among many eigenvalues. The result is that very noisy data can be measured to require fewer eigenmodes to achieve a given fraction of total variance than less noisy data. Hence standard *dimension reduction* approaches, based on "total signal power" or "percent of variation explained", are usually inappropriate.

Yet there is still a natural desire to think in terms of *effective dimensionality*, that is, the concept that the true underlying signal has much less variation than is present in noisy data. Ideas based in *random matrix theory* are promising avenues for research in this direction. See [32] for a good discussion of using this powerful theory in the context of Euclidean PCA. The first important part of this theory is the asymptotic probability distribution of the full collection of eigenvalues under a pure noise model, called the Marčenko–Pastur distribution [33]. The second part is the corresponding limiting distribution of the largest eigenvalue, called the Tracy–Widom distribution [34].

As yet, little development of Marčenko–Pastur theory for data on curved manifolds appears to have been done. An exception is unpublished research in progress by Choi, Pizer, and Marron. That work is studying analogs of limiting distributions of eigenvalues in the case of PNS. Eigenvalues are defined in terms of sums of squares of scores, that is, of the energy measured along the manifold surface. Careful study has revealed appropriate scale factor modifications that take the curvature of the space appropriately into account. These yield variations of the Marčenko–Pastur distribution, which, as illustrated in Fig. 6.12, are seen to effectively fit simulated data on the high-dimensional sphere very well. Both panels are Q-Q plots showing quantiles of the theoretical Marčenko–Pastur distribution on the vertical axis as a function of quantiles of the empirical distributions on the horizontal axis. A good distributional approximation is indicated by the points lying close to the red (gray in print version) 45 degree line.

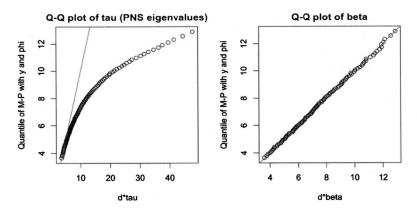

Figure 6.12. Q-Q plots showing poor goodness of fit of the Marčenko–Pastur distribution to the raw PNS eigenvalues in the left panel and good fit to the rescaled eigenvalues in the right panel. The data consists of simulated Gaussian noise on a $d = 1000$-dimensional tangent plane projected to the unit sphere with sample size $n = 100$. The notation "tau" refers to PNS eigenvalues, and the notation "beta" refers to the rescaled version.

6.8 Results of classification, hypothesis testing, and probability distribution estimation

A good approach to comparing shape analysis methods is to study their impact when used for various applications. This section reviews some recent work,[4] with many specific applications of the above ideas.

6.8.1 Classification of mental illness via hippocampus and caudate s-reps

Hong et al. [24] compared boundary point distribution models (PDMs) vs. s-reps and Euclideanization vs. direct Euclidean analysis of the ambient space coordinate values in classifying a hippocampus as to whether it was from a typical individual (control) or from a first-episode schizophrenic. The hippocampus was represented using a 3×8 skeletal grid (on each side of the skeleton), and the analysis was done using 238 schizophrenics and 56 controls. They showed that, according to areas under the Receiver Operating Characteristic curve (ROC) [35], Euclideanizing boundary PDMs produced better classification than without Euclideaniza-

[4]Much of parts 1–4 of this section appeared previously in [16]; reprinted here by permission of the copyrighter.

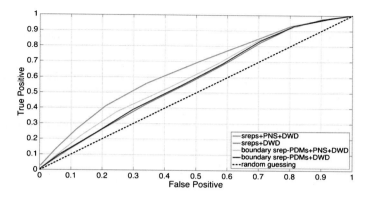

Figure 6.13. ROCs for classifying hippocampi as to schizophrenia vs. typical using s-reps and PDMs, each with original features and their Euclideanized counterparts.

Table 6.1 AUCs for classifying hippocampi or caudate nuclei between individuals having experienced a first schizophrenic behavioral episode and controls. The classifications compared are based on s-reps, respectively for row 1) s-reps analyzed using PNS Euclideanization, 2) s-reps analyzed without Euclideanization, 3) spoke end boundary points analyzed using PNS Euclideanization, 4) spoke end boundary points analyzed without Euclideanization, and 5) pure random guessing.

Methods	Hippocampus AUC	Caudate AUC
s-reps + PNS + DWD	0.72	0.75
s-reps + DWD	0.67	–
Boundary s-rep PDMs + PNS + DWD	0.70	0.72
Boundary s-rep PDMs + DWD	0.67	–
Random guessing	0.50	0.50

tion and that Euclideanized s-reps produced better classification than either of the boundary-based analyses (Fig. 6.13 and Table 6.1). In Table 6.1, as well as Tables 6.2, 6.3, "AUC" stands for the area under the ROC (the measure of classification quality), "PNS" stands for Euclideanization by Principal Nested Spheres, and "DWD" stands for the Euclidean classification method used, Distance-Weighted Discrimination.

As also shown in Table 6.1, similar results were obtained on the same population of subjects for the caudate nucleus that was represented using 4 × 8 grid of skeletal points.

Table 6.2 AUCs for classifying hippocampi or caudate nuclei between children at high risk for Autism Spectrum Disorder actually developing autism symptoms and those not developing autism symptoms. The classifications compared are based on s-reps, respectively, for row 1) s-reps analyzed using PNS Euclideanization, 2) s-reps analyzed without Euclideanization, 3) spoke end boundary points analyzed using PNS Euclideanization, 4) spoke end boundary points analyzed without Euclideanization, 5) s-rep-implied volume only, and 6) pure random guessing.

Methods	Hippocampus AUC	Caudate AUC
s-reps + PNS + DWD	0.6400	0.5708
s-reps + DWD	0.6123	0.5419
Boundary s-rep PDMs + PNS + DWD	0.6062	0.5400
Boundary s-rep PDMs + DWD	0.6050	0.5365
Global volume + DWD	0.5560	0.5372
Random guessing	0.5000	0.5000

Hong et al. [24] also showed the usefulness of displaying the variation of the object along the vector in the Euclideanized feature space passing through the pooled mean and in the separation direction (see Fig. 6.11) of the classes (Fig. 6.14).

Hong [12] further evaluated s-reps for the classification of autism vs. controls via hippocampal or caudate shape imaged via MRI for at-risk subjects at the age of 6 months. That is, the classification was between babies who would show autistic behavioral symptoms two years later and those who would not. The hippocampus was represented using a 3×8 skeletal grid (on each side of the skeleton), and the caudate nucleus was represented using a 4×8 skeletal grid (on each side of the skeleton). The analysis was done using 49 subjects who eventually displayed autistic symptoms and 149 who did not display such symptoms.

Similarly to Table 6.1, Table 6.2 shows that 1) s-reps analyzed with PNS yield notably better classification than with boundary points; 2) much less gain in classification quality occurs when the s-reps are not Euclideanized; 3) little gain in classification quality occurs when the boundary points are not Euclideanized; and 4) at least for the hippocampus, global volume gives inferior classification relative to any of the shape representations.

Hong's results above were on unrefined s-reps. In yet unpublished work Wang [36] has shown that when the analysis is repeated on those s-reps after refinement, the same AUC value is obtained. That is, the measure of the classification neither increases nor decreases.

Table 6.3 AUCs for classifying between children at high risk for Autism Spectrum Disorder actually developing autism symptoms and those not developing autism symptoms. The classifications compared are based on hippocampi or caudate nucleus s-reps, respectively, for 1) temporal shape differences at 6 months and 12 months, 2) 6-month shapes, 3) 12-month shapes, and 4) pure random guessing.

Methods	Hippocampus AUC	Caudate AUC
Temporal difference s-reps + PNS + DWD	0.5427	0.5041
6-month s-reps + PNS + DWD	0.6400	0.5087
12-month s-reps + PNS + DWD	0.5837	0.5605
Random guessing	0.5000	0.5000

Figure 6.14. Boundaries implied by s-reps of hippocampi: Left: at pooled mean −2 standard deviations in the separation direction for classification between first episode schizophrenics and controls. Right: at pooled mean +2 standard deviations in that separation direction. The shape change between these can be particularly noted by the changed bending in the right third of the hippocampus.

Finally, Hong [12] showed how to better skeletally represent an object like the caudate nucleus that approximately ends at a cusp of zero width. He developed a new primitive that represents one end of the s-rep narrowing to a cusp. That primitive consists simply of the location of the cusp and the tangent direction of the cusp. He showed how to interpolate a skeleton of an object with the grid s-rep augmented by the new primitive and how to fit such a skeleton to caudate nuclei. When these new skeletons were used for the caudate classification in the autism data, the AUC (in the upper-right entry of Table 6.2) became 0.587; that is, it added 0.016 to the AUC derived from the s-rep without the cusp primitive.

For all these area under the ROC measurements, we would wish error bars. Unfortunately, it is not known how to compute error bars for this measurement when it is made with repeated hold-outs, which results in complicated correlations among the values for different holdouts. Our group is researching what other measurements might allow the computation of error bars. At present, all we can say is that consistently across two anatomic objects and two diseases the addition of the object width and direction features provided by s-rep spokes increases the area under the ROC in classifications by a few hundredth values. Lest one feel this is a small difference, note that it is around $\frac{3}{4}$ of the difference in AUC between random guessing and classification using global volume of the object.

Looking at the classification results together, we see that for boundary point representation, PNS Euclideanization makes only a small improvement in AUC, but for s-reps, it makes a notable improvement in AUC. Moreover, using s-reps to capture not only location information but also object widths and spoke directions consistently yields notable improvement in AUC over using locational information alone.

6.8.2 Hypothesis testing via s-reps

Schulz et al. [30] demonstrated the ability to test hypotheses on shape variation between two objects using s-rep features. They showed how to do not only global hypothesis tests but also GOP (geometric object property)-by-GOP and location-by-location tests. The method involved a modification of the statistical technique of permutation tests in a way that recognizes that means benefit from being backward means and that GOP differences need to use a metric appropriate for curved manifolds. As discussed in Section 6.7.2, this work reported a new method for compensating the notable correlations of these GOPs. With this approach they were able to analyze which locations on hippocampi of first-episode schizophrenics had statistically significant GOP differences from controls and which GOPs had those statistically significant differences. Thus they found important shape differences between the classes.

6.8.3 Shape change statistics

Vicory [37] studied statistics on the change of object shape between two stages. Realizing that statistics on change requires transporting each object pair such that the starting object was at a fixed place on the manifold of objects, he solved this problem by pooling all $2n$ objects in the n shape pairs in the training set, producing a polar system by PNS on the pool of GOP tuples, Euclideanizing each object according to that polar system and then producing Euclidean (ordinary) differences between the Euclideanized features of each pair.

Vicory [37] studied this method in two applications. The first was on ellipsoids that were randomly bent and/or twisted. The GOPs in this study were the boundary point coordinates provided by spherical harmonic analysis. His findings with simulated data produced from random samples from a single transformation type were as follows: 1) Analysis either with or without Euclideanization yielded a single correct eigenmode. 2) Analysis with Euclideanization allowed more accurate estimation of an object bending or twisting angle. 3) When the mode of variation was visualized, the object moved more naturally than using PCA alone. He also found that when the simulated data came from random bending cascaded with twisting, both types of analysis yielded two modes of variation, but Euclideanization allowed a more correct estimate of the relative variances and mean deformations, which were closer to the expected deformations than their PCA-alone counterparts.

Vicory's second test was on prostates segmented from MRI and the same prostate within 3D transrectal ultrasound; the latter was deformed by the ultrasound transducer (discussed in more detail in Section 6.8.5). The shape-change eigenmodes were used as a shape space within which to segment the prostate from the ultrasound image, given the patient's prostate shape derived from his MRI. The geometric object properties he used were the skeletal points, spoke lengths, and spoke directions from fitted s-reps. He found that using the shape-change space resulting from Euclideanization followed by subtraction yielded more accurate segmentations than when a shape space was formed by s-rep feature differences applied to the mean of the prostates in the training MRIs and then applying CPNS to the resulting objects. For a target segmentation using that superior method, it was necessary to form an ultrasound-relevant starting prostate s-rep from which the optimization over the shape-change shape space would be computed. That initialized s-rep in the ultrasound image was computed by starting with the patient's in-MRI prostate s-rep and then applying to it (adding in the Euclideanized form) the mean prostate s-rep difference between the ultrasound-based prostates and their corresponding MRI prostates.

Recently Hong has applied this shape-change Euclideanization approach to two classes of pairs of shapes, at two different ages, namely 6 and 12 months. For each anatomic object he analyzed, he pooled all his objects for children at both 6 months and 12 months to yield a Euclideanization. Then he analyzed shape changes via this Euclideanization to determine how informative shape differences in the hippocampus and caudate nucleus were, respectively, between children at high risk for autism who do not develop autistic symptoms and those at high risk who do develop such symptoms. However, as shown in Table 6.3 (from [12]), the classification based on the shape difference provides poorer classification than either of the classifications of 6-month and

12-month shapes. As previously noted, in that table "AUC" stands for the area under the ROC (the measure of classification quality), "PNS" stands for Euclideanization by Principal Nested Spheres, and "DWD" stands for the Euclidean classification method used, Distance-Weighted Discrimination.

6.8.4 Correspondence evaluation via entropy minimization

The basic idea of correspondence optimization is to consider all reparameterizations of each object in a population and to find the reparameterization of each that produce the tightest estimated probability distribution. The notion of reparameterizing an object representation is to apply a diffeomorphism on the boundary surface or skeletal surface while leaving the object geometrically the same. For a spatially sampled object boundary, that is a fancy way of saying how to shift the respective sample points along the boundary. For example, if an object of spherical topology is understood as a smooth one-to-one mapping from the unit sphere boundary to the object boundary, the shifting of where each sphere point maps to on the object is a reparameterization [38,39]. For s-reps, the shifting is of spokes along the skeletal surface.

The tightness of a probability distribution can be measured in many ways, but the ones that have turned out to be the most effective are based on information theory. Taylor and his team [40] pioneered a form based on minimum description length (MDL) and an almost equivalent form based on entropy was developed in Whitaker's laboratory [14]. In these works objects represented according to the specified parameterization were used, and the population of GOPs derived from these parameterizations was fitted by a Gaussian distribution. Then the entropy of this Gaussian is minimized over all object reparameterizations while also penalizing irregularity of the discrete object samples (points on a boundary or spokes on a skeleton).

The entropy of an n-dimensional Gaussian is given by

$$n\left(\frac{1}{2}\ln\left(2\pi + 1\right)\right.$$

$$\left. + \text{ the mean of the logarithms of the principal variances}\right).$$

A difficulty is that when the idea is applied to a probability distribution estimated from data by a PCA or PCA-like method that involves Euclideanization, the successive sorted principal variances get successively smaller and eventually are dominated by noise in the data. Thus each logarithm of these small principal variances is very large in magnitude, so these noise-induced principal variances dominate the population principal variances in the entropy calculation. Cates et al. [14] dealt with this problem by adding a small constant to each principal variance. Tu et al. [41] dealt with it by cutting off the series when the ratio of the principal variance to the total variance fell below a certain threshold.

Cates et al. [14] showed that entropy minimization for GOPs that were a boundary point distribution could yield improvements in hypothesis testing significances. In their work boundary points were slid along the boundary to minimize entropy. Tu et al. [41] developed the same idea for s-reps, whereby the skeletal spokes were slid along the skeletal surface to minimize entropy. They showed (Fig. 6.15) the result that, according to the measures described in Section 6.5 on a training set of hippocampi, when the s-rep-based correspondence method was applied, the boundary points at the ends of the spokes had better (lower) values of the statistical properties, specificity and generalization (see Section 6.7.3), than when the Cates boundary point shifting method was applied. This result is surprising and arguably indicative of the strength of s-reps because the object comparisons used in measuring specificity and generalization were based on boundary point distributions, so we might have expected that optimization directly of boundary point shiftings, that is, the Cates method, would be superior.

6.8.5 Segmentations by posterior optimization

An important application of shape statistics is *segmentation* in medical images, where the goal is to find the region of an image occupied by an object such as a particular organ. A series of successive improvements in shape analysis resulting in improved image segmentation can be found in [42,18,43,44,3,45,37].

For many years, Pizer, Chaney, et al. (Chapter 9 in [2]) worked on the segmentation of male pelvis organs from CT to aid radiation treatment planning for prostate cancer. Their method involved an earlier form of s-reps and used them in both terms of a posterior optimization approach, slightly modified to make the log prior and log likelihood terms have the same variance. In the log prior (shape statistics) term the s-rep statistics of each organ was used, and in the log likelihood (statistics of the match between the image and the object geometry) intensity-derived features at positions implied by interpolated s-rep spokes were used to produce statistics by PCA. This method was taken over by a spinoff company, Morphormics, now part of Accuray, Inc. With further

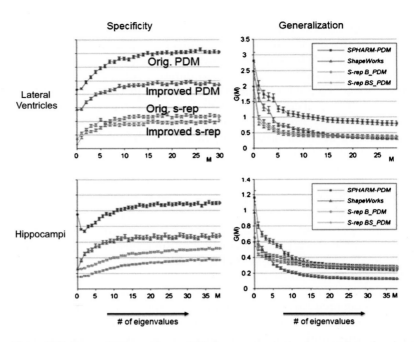

Figure 6.15. Generalization and specificity improvements due to s-rep-based and PDM-based correspondence optimization. Smaller values indicate better performance. At the left of each panel all the curves are in the same order as is marked in the upper left panel.

modifications of the method by Morphormics, the evaluations of the method showed it to be superior to various competitors [46] and were brought into broad clinical use.

In another segmentation application Vicory [37] worked on extracting the prostate from 3D transrectal ultrasound (TRUS), in which the intrarectal probe deforms the adjacent prostate. The method was given the shape of that patient's prostate in an MR image that did not have the ultrasound probe in place. His term measuring the match between the image and the object geometry in the objective function that he optimized involved intensity and as well 48 texture features. It classified each pixel according to that 49-tuple, with the result being the probability p(inside) that the pixel was inside the prostate (see the left panel of Fig. 6.16). Then his term measuring the match between the image and the object geometry for paired regions, respectively, inside and outside a particular patch within the s-rep-implied boundary was

$$\sum_{\text{patches } i} \left[(\rho_i^{\text{in}} - \rho_i^{\text{out}}) - \left| \rho_i^{\text{in}} + \rho_i^{\text{out}} - 1 \right| \right],$$

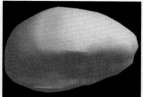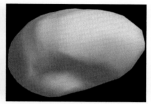

Figure 6.16. Left: an example of the p(inside) image of a prostate derived from a 3D TRUS image; Middle: the prostate before the shape change; Right: the resulting prostate segmentation from the 3D TRUS image, i.e., after the shape change.

where ρ_i^{in} and ρ_i^{out} are the average p(inside) values for the regions inside and outside the ith patch, respectively. Each patch was a quadrilateral centered at an s-rep spoke tip and extending halfway to the adjacent spoke in each of the two cardinal directions of the skeletal surface grid of points. Thus it used the correspondence across prostates provided by the s-rep.

Vicory's log prior used the shape change statistics method described in Section 6.8.3, namely, on the change between the prostate s-rep in the patient's MRI and that in the patient's 3D TRUS image. It was intended that this method should be followed by a local refinement step, but this refinement was never studied. Nevertheless, even without refinement the method's segmentations (see Fig. 6.16) were competitive with others that had been proposed (e.g., [47,48]).

6.9 The code and its performance

The code for fitting an s-rep with a skeletal surface to an object boundary, s-rep visualization, and s-rep statistics (via PNS) is becoming part of Slicer Shape AnaLysis Toolbox (SlicerSALT) [49, 50], a web-resident toolkit that was first announced at MICCAI 2018. While the previous versions of code for these purposes were hard to understand and use, the version in the toolkit is designed for clarity of use and modification. Moreover, the computer representation of the s-rep used in that toolkit is more generalizable and closer to the mathematics than the "legacy representation" used in the previous versions of the code. In the SlicerSALT s-rep code [51] automatic fitting an s-rep to an object boundary takes approximately 5 to 10 minutes. In that code the input object is given as a triangle mesh, but extension to representations of the input object in the form of a binary image or in the form of a signed distance-to-boundary image are anticipated.

The generalizations of s-reps that will ultimately be included in the SlicerSALT package will also include generalized cylinders, that is, quasitubular objects that are well represented by a skeletal curve rather than a surface.

The s-rep code in SlicerSALT is for single objects, but we have ongoing research on multiobject models, that is, models that do not simply concatenate the s-reps of individual objects but also capture s-rep-derived geometry on the relations between the objects [52]. Because objects can slide along each other, this is a challenging problem, yet one we are making progress on.

Some objects have essential branching of the skeletal surface. The branches represent essential protrusions or essential indentations. Because so many anatomic objects can be represented by s-reps without branching, there has been little work on those with essential branching. That little work on s-reps for objects with protrusions or indentations has treated each branch as having its own s-rep and has provided a way for the branch to be additively (for a protrusion) or subtractively (for an indentation) connected to the parent s-rep [53]. Yushkevich and his colleagues have worked on branching with their cm-reps [54].

6.10 Weaknesses of the skeletal approach

Although s-reps have been shown to be a powerful representation for applications using shape statistics, some objects for which statistics are needed are not suitably represented by a skeletal model. These include objects that need variable skeletal topology, for example, that vary with some instances of a skeletal surface becoming so narrow that they approach a curve. They also presently include objects with variation in the branching arrangement, for which tree statistics would need to be combined with that on the skeletal descriptions of the branches; methods of tree statistics, although of great interest, are still under development [55–58].

Open questions on s-reps include:

1. quantitative comparisons between Yushkevich's cm-reps and s-reps;
2. the production of statistical methods on s-reps that work directly on the polysphere manifold;
3. the use of other statistical analysis techniques such as Fletcher's Bayes [59] or Sommer's Brownian motion-induced Gaussians [60] in s-rep applications;
4. improvements in the representation of generalized cylinders ("quasitubes") via s-reps and doing statistics thereon.

Acknowledgments

We are grateful to Martin Styner for useful conversations and for providing brain MRI data, IBIS for providing brain MRI data, and the editors of this book for helpful suggestions in the writing.

References

1. H. Blum, A transformation for extracting new descriptors of shape, Models for Perception of Speech and Visual Forms 1967 (1967) 362–380.
2. K. Siddiqi, S. Pizer, Medial Representations: Mathematics, Algorithms and Applications, vol. 37, Springer Science & Business Media, 2008.
3. S.M. Pizer, S. Jung, D. Goswami, J. Vicory, X. Zhao, R. Chaudhuri, et al., Nested sphere statistics of skeletal models, in: Innovations for Shape Analysis, Springer, 2013, pp. 93–115.
4. R. Ma, Q. Zhao, R. Wang, J.N. Damon, J. Rosenman, S.M. Pizer, Generalized Cylinder Deformation for Visualization of a Tube Interior, Tech. Rep., University of North Carolina at Chapel Hill, Department of Computer Science, 2018.
5. J. Damon, Properties of ridges and cores for two-dimensional images, Journal of Mathematical Imaging and Vision 10 (2) (1999) 163–174.
6. R. Katz, et al., Form Metrics for Interactive Rendering Via Figural Models of Perception, Ph.D. thesis, University of North Carolina at Chapel Hill, 2002.
7. B.S. Morse, S.M. Pizer, D.S. Fritsch, Robust Object Representation Through Object-Relevant Use of Scale, Medical Imaging 1994: Image Processing, vol. 2167, International Society for Optics and Photonics, 1994, pp. 104–116.
8. S.R. Aylward, E. Bullitt, Initialization, noise, singularities, and scale in height ridge traversal for tubular object centerline extraction, IEEE Transactions on Medical Imaging 21 (2) (2002) 61–75.
9. Y. Fridman, S.M. Pizer, S. Aylward, E. Bullitt, Extracting branching tubular object geometry via cores, Medical Image Analysis 8 (3) (2004) 169–176.
10. P.A. Yushkevich, H. Zhang, Continuous medial representation for anatomical structures, IEEE Transactions on Medical Imaging 25 (12) (2006) 1547–1564.
11. L. Tu, J. Vicory, S. Elhabian, B. Paniagua, J.C. Prieto, J.N. Damon, et al., Entropy-based correspondence improvement of interpolated skeletal models, Computer Vision and Image Understanding 151 (2016) 72–79.
12. J. Hong, Classification of Neuroanatomical Structures Based on Non-Euclidean Geometric Object Properties, Ph.D. thesis, University of North Carolina at Chapel Hill, 2018.

13. Q. Zhao, J. Price, S.M. Pizer, M. Niethammer, R. Alterovitz, J.G. Rosenman, Surface registration in the presence of missing patches and topology change, in: MIUA, 2015, pp. 8–13.

14. J. Cates, P.T. Fletcher, M. Styner, M. Shenton, Shape modeling and analysis with entropy-based particle systems, in: Biennial International Conference on Information Processing in Medical Imaging, Springer, 2007, pp. 333–345.

15. V. Patrangenaru, L. Ellingson, Nonparametric Statistics on Manifolds and Their Applications to Object Data Analysis, CRC Press, 2015.

16. G. Zheng, S. Li, G. Szekely, Statistical Shape and Deformation Analysis: Methods, Implementation and Applications, Academic Press, 2017.

17. M. Vaillant, M.I. Miller, L. Younes, A. Trouvé, Statistics on diffeomorphisms via tangent space representations, NeuroImage 23 (2004) S161–S169.

18. P.T. Fletcher, S.M. Pizer, S. Joshi, Statistical Variability in Nonlinear Spaces: Application to Shape Analysis and DT-MRI, Citeseer, 2004.

19. P.T. Fletcher, C. Lu, S.M. Pizer, S.Joshi, Principal geodesic analysis for the study of nonlinear statistics of shape, IEEE Transactions on Medical Imaging 23 (8) (2004) 995–1005.

20. J.Y. Jeong, Estimation of Probability Distribution on Multiple Anatomical Objects and Evaluation of Statistical Shape Models, Ph.D. thesis, University of North Carolina at Chapel Hill, 2009.

21. S. Jung, I.L. Dryden, J. Marron, Analysis of principal nested spheres, Biometrika 99 (3) (2012) 551–568.

22. J. Damon, J. Marron, Backwards principal component analysis and principal nested relations, Journal of Mathematical Imaging and Vision 50 (1-2) (2014) 107–114.

23. X. Pennec, Barycentric subspaces and affine spans in manifolds, in: International Conference on Networked Geometric Science of Information, Springer, 2015, pp. 12–21.

24. J. Hong, J. Vicory, J. Schulz, M. Styner, J. Marron, S.M. Pizer, Non-Euclidean classification of medically imaged objects via s-reps, Medical Image Analysis 31 (2016) 37–45.

25. B. Eltzner, S. Jung, S. Huckemann, Dimension reduction on polyspheres with application to skeletal representations, in: International Conference on Networked Geometric Science of Information, Springer, 2015, pp. 22–29.

26. A. Sharma, Euclideanization of s-reps via Discriminative Principal Nested Spheres (DPNS) vs. Polysphere Nested Deformed Spheres (PDNS), Tech. Rep., University of North Carolina at Chapel Hill, Department of Computer Science, 2018.

27. R.O. Duda, P.E. Hart, D.G. Stork, Pattern Classification, John Wiley & Sons, 2012.

28. B. Schölkopf, A.J. Smola, F. Bach, et al., Learning With Kernels: Support Vector Machines, Regularization, Optimization, and Beyond, MIT Press, 2002.

29. J.S. Marron, M.J. Todd, J. Ahn, Distance-weighted discrimination, Journal of the American Statistical Association 102 (480) (2007) 1267–1271.
30. J. Schulz, S.M. Pizer, J.S. Marron, F. Godtliebsen, Non-linear hypothesis testing of geometric object properties of shapes applied to hippocampi, Journal of Mathematical Imaging and Vision 54 (1) (2016) 15–34.
31. R.H. Davies, Learning Shape: Optimal Models for Analysing Natural Variability, University of Manchester, Manchester, 2002.
32. J. Yao, S. Zheng, Z. Bai, Sample Covariance Matrices and High-Dimensional Data Analysis, Cambridge University Press, 2015.
33. V.A. Marčenko, L.A. Pastur, Distribution of eigenvalues for some sets of random matrices, Mathematics of the USSR. Sbornik 1 (4) (1967) 457.
34. C.A. Tracy, H. Widom, On orthogonal and symplectic matrix ensembles, Communications in Mathematical Physics 177 (3) (1996) 727–754.
35. J.A. Hanley, B.J. McNeil, The meaning and use of the area under a receiver operating characteristic (roc) curve, Radiology 143 (1) (1982) 29–36.
36. J. Wang, Z. Liu, J. Hong, S.M. Pizer, Hippocampus Classification via Refined vs. Initially Fit s-reps, Tech. Rep., University of North Carolina at Chapel Hill, Department of Computer Science, 2019.
37. J. Vicory, Shape Deformation Statistics and Regional Texture-Based Appearance Models for Segmentation, Ph.D. thesis, The University of North Carolina at Chapel Hill, 2016.
38. S. Kurtek, E. Klassen, Z. Ding, M.J. Avison, A. Srivastava, Parameterization-invariant shape statistics and probabilistic classification of anatomical surfaces, in: Biennial International Conference on Information Processing in Medical Imaging, Springer, 2011, pp. 147–158.
39. C. Brechbühler, G. Gerig, O. Kübler, Parametrization of closed surfaces for 3D shape description, Computer Vision and Image Understanding 61 (2) (1995) 154–170.
40. R.H. Davies, C.J. Twining, T.F. Cootes, J.C. Waterton, C.J. Taylor, A minimum description length approach to statistical shape modeling, IEEE Transactions on Medical Imaging 21 (5) (2002) 525–537.
41. L. Tu, M. Styner, J. Vicory, S. Elhabian, R. Wang, J. Hong, et al., Skeletal shape correspondence through entropy, IEEE Transactions on Medical Imaging 37 (1) (2018) 1–11.
42. S.M. Pizer, S. Joshi, P.T. Fletcher, M. Styner, G. Tracton, Segmentation of single-figure objects by deformable m-reps, in: International Conference on Medical Image Computing and Computer-Assisted Intervention, Springer, 2001, pp. 862–871.
43. M. Rao, J. Stough, Y.Y. Chi, K. Muller, G. Tracton, S.M. Pizer, et al., Comparison of human and automatic segmentations of kidneys from CT images, IEEE Transactions on Medical Imaging 61 (3) (2005) 954–960.

44. K. Gorczowski, M. Styner, J.Y. Jeong, J. Marron, J. Piven, H.C. Hazlett, et al., Statistical shape analysis of multi-object complexes, in: Computer Vision and Pattern Recognition, 2007, CVPR'07, IEEE Conference on, IEEE, 2007, pp. 1–8.
45. J. Vicory, M. Foskey, A. Fenster, A. Ward, S.M. Pizer, Prostate segmentation from 3DUS using regional texture classification and shape differences, in: Symposium on Statistical Shape Models & Applications, in: Citeseer, 2014, p. 24.
46. (now Accuray Inc) MI, Morphormics technology overview white paper, avaialble on www.morphormics.com, 2008, until 2012.
47. C. Garnier, J.J. Bellanger, K. Wu, H. Shu, N. Costet, R. Mathieu, Prostate segmentation in HIFU therapy, IEEE Transactions on Medical Imaging 30 (3) (2011) 792–803.
48. W. Qiu, J. Yuan, E. Ukwatta, Y. Sun, M. Rajchl, A. Fenster, Prostate segmentation: an efficient convex optimization approach with axial symmetry using 3-D TRUS and MR images, IEEE Transactions on Medical Imaging 33 (4) (2014) 947–960.
49. J. Vicory, L. Pascal, P. Hernandez, J. Fishbaugh, J. Prieto, M. Mostapha, et al., Slicersalt: shape analysis toolbox, in: International Workshop on Shape in Medical Imaging, Springer, 2018, pp. 65–72.
50. Slicersalt, http://salt.slicer.org/. (Accessed 5 May 2019).
51. Shape analysis via skeletal models in slicersalt, https://github.com/KitwareMedical/SlicerSkeletalRepresentation/blob/master/SrepModule-Tutorial-Visualizer.pdf, 2019.
52. J. Damon, E. Gasparovic, Modeling multi-object configurations via medial/skeletal linking structures, International Journal of Computer Vision 124 (3) (2017) 255–272.
53. Q. Han, et al., Proper Shape Representation of Single Figure and Multi-Figure Anatomical Objects, Ph.D. thesis, University of North Carolina at Chapel Hill, 2008.
54. A.M. Pouch, S. Tian, M. Takebe, J. Yuan, R. Gorman Jr, A.T. Cheung, et al., Medially constrained deformable modeling for segmentation of branching medial structures: application to aortic valve segmentation and morphometry, Medical Image Analysis 26 (1) (2015) 217–231.
55. B. Aydın, G. Pataki, H. Wang, E. Bullitt, J.S. Marron, et al., A principal component analysis for trees, Annals of Applied Statistics 3 (4) (2009) 1597–1615.
56. P. Bendich, J.S. Marron, E. Miller, A. Pieloch, S. Skwerer, Persistent homology analysis of brain artery trees, Annals of Applied Statistics 1 (1) (2016) 198.
57. D. Shen, H. Shen, S. Bhamidi, Y. Muñoz Maldonado, Y. Kim, J.S. Marron, Functional data analysis of tree data objects, Journal of Computational and Graphical Statistics 23 (2) (2014) 418–438.
58. S. Skwerer, E. Bullitt, S. Huckemann, E. Miller, I. Oguz, M. Owen, et al., Tree-oriented analysis of brain artery structure, Journal of Mathematical Imaging and Vision 50 (1-2) (2014) 126–143.
59. M. Zhang, T. Fletcher, Probabilistic principal geodesic analysis, in: Advances in Neural Information Processing Systems, 2013, pp. 1178–1186.

60. S. Sommer, Anisotropic distributions on manifolds: template estimation and most probable paths, in: International Conference on Information Processing in Medical Imaging, Springer, 2015, pp. 193–204.

Efficient recursive estimation of the Riemannian barycenter on the hypersphere and the special orthogonal group with applications

Rudrasis Chakraborty, Baba C. Vemuri
University of Florida, CISE Department, Gainesville, FL, United States

7.1 Introduction

Manifold-valued data have gained much importance in recent times due to their expressiveness and ready availability of machines with powerful CPUs and large storage. For example, these data arise as *diffusion tensors* (manifold of symmetric positive definite matrices) [1,2], *linear subspaces* (the Grassmann manifold) [3–8], *column orthogonal matrices* (the Stiefel manifold) [3, 9–11], *directional data* and *probability densities* (the hypersphere) [12–15], and others. A useful method of analyzing manifold-valued data is to compute statistics on the underlying manifold. The most popular statistic is a *summary* of the data, that is, *the* Riemannian barycenter (Fréchet mean, FM) [16–18], Fréchet median [19,20], and so on.

FM computation on Riemannian manifolds has been an active area of research for the past few decades. Several researchers have addressed this problem, and we refer the reader to [21,18, 22,23,19,24–27]. In most of these works, the authors relied on the standard gradient descent-based iterative computation of the FM, which suffers from two major drawbacks in an online computation setting: (1) for each new sample, it has to compute the new FM from scratch, and (2) it requires the entire input data to be stored to estimate the new FM. Instead, an *incremental* that is, a recursive technique can address this problem more efficiently with respect to time/space utility. In this age of massive and continuous streaming data, samples are often acquired incrementally. Hence, also from the applications perspective, the desired algo-

Riemannian Geometric Statistics in Medical Image Analysis
https://doi.org/10.1016/B978-0-12-814725-2.00015-7

rithm should be *recursive/inductive* to maximize computational efficiency and account for availability of data, requirements that are seldom addressed in more theoretically oriented fields.

Recently, several incremental mean estimators for manifold-valued data have been reported [28–31,5,32]. Sturm [29] presented an incremental mean, the so-called *inductive mean*, and proved its convergence to the true FM for all nonpositively curved (NPC) spaces. In [33] the authors showed several algorithms (including a recursive algorithm) for FM computation for data residing in CAT(0) spaces, which are NPC. They also demonstrated several applications of the same to computer vision and medical imaging. Further, in [31] an incremental FM computation algorithm along with its convergence and applications was presented for a population of symmetric positive definite (SPD) matrices. Recently, Lim [30] presented an inductive FM to estimate the weighted FM of SPD matrices. The convergence analysis in all of these works is applicable only to the samples belonging to NPC spaces, and hence their convergence analysis does not apply to the case of the manifolds with positive sectional curvature, which are our "objects" of interest in this chapter. Arnaudon et al. [34] present a stochastic gradient descent algorithm for barycenter computation of probability measures on Riemannian manifolds under some conditions. Their algorithm is quite general as it is applicable both to nonpositively and positively curved Riemannian manifolds.

In this work we present a novel incremental FM estimator (*iFME*) of a set of samples on two Riemannian manifolds of positive sectional curvature, that is, the hypersphere and the special orthogonal group. Data samples from either of these aforementioned manifolds are very commonly encountered in medical imaging, computer vision, and computer graphics. To mention a few, the directional data that are often encountered in image processing and computer vision are points on the unit 2-sphere $\mathbb{S}(2)$ [12]. Further, 3×3 rotation matrices can be parameterized by unit quaternions, which can be represented by points on the projective space $\mathcal{P}(3)$, i.e. couples of points and their antipodal point on the three-dimensional unit sphere $\mathbb{S}(3)$ [15]. Also, any probability density function, for example, orientation distribution function (ODF) in diffusion magnetic resonance imaging (MRI) [14], can be represented as points on the positive quadrant of a unit Hilbert sphere [35,13].

7.2 Riemannian geometry of the hypersphere

The hypersphere is a constant positive curvature Riemannian manifold that is commonly encountered in numerous application problems. Its geometry is well known, and here we will simply present (without derivations) the closed-form expressions for the Riemannian Exponential and Log maps as well as the geodesic between two points on it. Further, we also present the well-known square root parameterization of probability density functions (PDFs), which allows us to identify them with points on the unit Hilbert sphere. This will be needed in representing the probability density functions, namely, the ensemble average propagators (EAPs) derived from diffusion MRI, as points on the unit Hilbert sphere.

Without loss of generality we restrict the analysis to PDFs defined on the interval $[0, T]$ for simplicity: $\mathcal{P} = \{p : [0, T] \to \mathbb{R} \mid \forall s, p(s) \geq 0, \int_0^T p(s)ds = 1\}$. In [26], the Fisher–Rao metric was introduced to study the Riemannian structure of a statistical manifold (the manifold of probability densities). For a PDF $p \in \mathcal{P}$, the Fisher–Rao metric is defined as $\langle v, w \rangle = \int_0^T v(s)w(s)p(s)ds$ for $v, w \in T_p\mathcal{P}$. The Fisher–Rao metric is invariant to reparameterizations of the functions. To facilitate easy computations when using Riemannian operations, the square root density representation $\psi = \sqrt{p}$ was used in [13], which was originally proposed in [36,37] and further developed from geometric statistics view point in [38]. The space of square root density functions is defined as $\Psi = \{\psi : [0, T] \to \mathbb{R} \mid \forall s, \psi(s) \geq 0, \int_0^T \psi^2(s)ds = 1\}$. As we can see, Ψ forms a convex subset of the unit sphere in a Hilbert space. Then, the Fisher–Rao metric can be written as $\langle v, w \rangle = \int_0^T v(s)w(s)ds$ for tangent vectors $v, w \in T_\psi\Psi$. Given any two functions $\psi_i, \psi_j \in \Psi$, the geodesic distance between these two points is given in closed form by $d(\psi_i, \psi_j) = \cos^{-1}(\langle \psi_i, \psi_j \rangle)$. The geodesic at ψ with a direction $\mathbf{v} \in T_\psi\Psi$ is defined as $\Gamma(t) = \cos(t)\psi + \sin(t)\frac{\mathbf{v}}{\|\mathbf{v}\|}$. The Riemannian exponential map can then be expressed by $\mathsf{Exp}_\psi(\mathbf{v}) = \cos(\|\mathbf{v}\|)\psi + \sin(\|\mathbf{v}\|)\frac{\mathbf{v}}{\|\mathbf{v}\|}$, where $\|\mathbf{v}\| \in [0, \pi)$. The Riemannian inverse exponential map is then given by $\mathsf{Log}_{\psi_i}(\psi_j) = u \cos^{-1}(\langle \psi_i, \psi_j \rangle)/\sqrt{\langle u, u \rangle}$, where $u = \psi_j - \langle \psi_i, \psi_j \rangle \psi_i$. Note that, for the rest of this chapter, we will assume that the data points are within a geodesic ball of radius less than the *injectivity radius* so that the Riemannian exponential is unique, and hence there always exists the corresponding inverse exponential map. We can define the geodesic between ψ_i and ψ_j by $\Gamma_{\psi_i}^{\psi_j}(t) = \cos(t)\psi + \sin(t)\frac{\mathbf{v}}{\|\mathbf{v}\|}$, where $\mathbf{v} = \mathsf{Log}_{\psi_i}(\psi_j)$ and $t \in [0, 1]$. We will use the term geodesic to denote *the shortest geodesic* between two points.

Using the geodesic distance provided previously, we can define the Fréchet mean (FM) [16,17] of a set of points on the hypersphere as the minimizer of the sum of squared geodesic distances (the so-called Fréchet functional). Let $\mathcal{B}(\mathbf{x}, \rho)$ be the geodesic ball centered at $\mathbf{x}$ with radius ρ, that is, $\mathcal{B}(\mathbf{x}, \rho) = \{\mathbf{y} \in \mathbb{S}(k) | d(\mathbf{x}, \mathbf{y}) < \rho\}$. Authors in [39,18] showed that for any $\mathbf{x} \in S_k$ and for data samples in $\mathcal{B}(\mathbf{x}, \frac{\pi}{2})$, the minimizer of the Fréchet functional exists and is unique. For the rest of this chapter, we will assume that this condition is satisfied for any given set of points $\{\mathbf{x}_i\} \subset \mathbb{S}(k)$. For more details on Riemannian geometry of the sphere, we refer the reader to Chapter 2 of [40] and references therein.

7.3 Weak consistency of *iFME* on the sphere

In this section we present a detailed proof of convergence of our recursive estimator on the $\mathbb{S}(k)$. The proposed method is similar in "spirit" to the incremental arithmetic mean update in the Euclidean space; given the old mean $\mathbf{m}_{n-1}$ and the new sample point $\mathbf{x}_n$, we define the new mean $\mathbf{m}_n$ as the weighted mean of $\mathbf{m}_{n-1}$ and $\mathbf{x}_n$ with the weights $\frac{n-1}{n}$ and $\frac{1}{n}$, respectively. From a geometric viewpoint, this corresponds to the choice of the point on the geodesic between $\mathbf{m}_{n-1}$ and $\mathbf{x}_n$ with the parameter $t = \frac{1}{n}$, that is, $\mathbf{m}_n = \Gamma_{\mathbf{m}_{n-1}}^{\mathbf{x}_n}(1/n)$.

Formally, let $\mathbf{x}_1, \mathbf{x}_2, \cdots, \mathbf{x}_N$ be a set of N samples on the hypersphere $\mathbb{S}(k)$, all of which lie inside a geodesic ball of radius $\frac{\pi}{2}$. The incremental FM estimator (denoted by *iFME*) $\mathbf{m}_n$ with the given nth sample point $\mathbf{x}_n$ is defined by

$$\mathbf{m}_1 = \mathbf{x}_1, \tag{7.1}$$

$$\mathbf{m}_n = \Gamma_{\mathbf{m}_{n-1}}^{\mathbf{x}_n}\left(\frac{1}{n}\right), \tag{7.2}$$

where $\Gamma_{\mathbf{m}_{n-1}}^{\mathbf{x}_n}$ is the shortest geodesic path from $\mathbf{m}_{n-1}$ to $\mathbf{x}_n$ $(\in S_k)$, and $\frac{1}{n}$ is the weight assigned to the new sample point (in this case the nth sample), which is henceforth called the *Euclidean weight*. In the rest of this section we will show that if the number of given samples N tends to infinity, then the *iFME* estimates will converge to the expectation of the distribution from which the samples are drawn. *Note that the geometric construction steps in the proof given further are not needed to compute the iFME; these steps are only needed to prove the weak consistency of iFME.*

Our proof is based on the idea of projecting the samples $\mathbf{x}_i$ on the sphere to the tangent plane using the gnomonic projection [15] and performing the convergence analysis on the projected samples $\tilde{\mathbf{x}}_i$ in this linear space, instead of performing the analysis on the hypersphere. We take advantage of the fact that the geodesic curve between any pair of points on the hemisphere is projected to a straight line in the tangent space at the anchor point (in this case, without loss of generality, assumed to be the north pole) via the gnomonic projection. A figure depicting the gnomonic projection is shown in Fig. 7.1. Despite the simplifica-

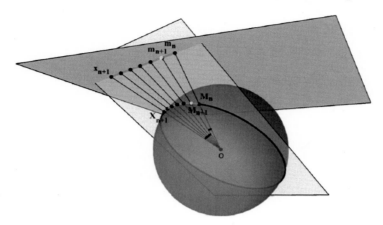

Figure 7.1. Gnomonic projection.

tions used in the statistical analysis of the *iFME* estimates on the hypersphere using the gnomonic projection, there is one important obstacle that must be considered. Without loss of generality, suppose the true FM of the input samples $\{\mathbf{x}_i\}$ is the north pole. Then it can be shown through counter examples that:

- The use of Euclidean weights $\frac{1}{n}$ to update the *iFME* estimates on $\mathbb{S}(k)$ does *not* necessarily correspond to the same weighting scheme between the old arithmetic mean and the new sample in the projection space, that is, the tangent space.

This fact can be illustrated using two sample points on a unit circle (S_1), $\mathbf{x}_1 = (\cos(\pi/6), \sin(\pi/6))^t$ and $\mathbf{x}_2 = (\cos(\pi/3), \sin(\pi/3))^t$, whose intrinsic mean is $\mathbf{m} = (\cos(\pi/4), \sin(\pi/4))^t$. Then the midpoint of the gnomonic projections of $\mathbf{x}_1$ and $\mathbf{x}_2$, which are denoted by $\tilde{\mathbf{x}}_1$ and $\tilde{\mathbf{x}}_2$, is $\hat{\mathbf{m}} = \frac{\tan(\pi/3)+\tan(\pi/6)}{2} = 1.1547 \neq \tan(\pi/4) = \tilde{\mathbf{m}}$ (see Fig. 7.2).

For the rest of this section, without loss of generality, we assume that the FM of N given samples is located at the north pole. Since the gnomonic projection space is anchored at the north pole, this assumption leads to significant simplifications in our convergence analysis. However, a similar convergence proof can be developed for any arbitrary location of the FM, with the tangent (projection) space anchored at the location of this mean.

In what follows we prove that the use of Euclidean weights $w_n = \frac{1}{n}$ to update the incremental FM on the hypersphere corresponds to a set of weights in the projection space, denoted henceforth by t_n, for which the weighted incremental mean in the tangent plane

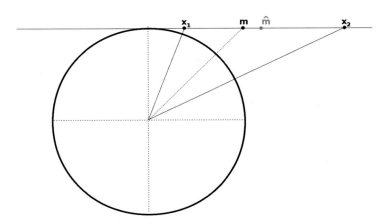

Figure 7.2. Illustration of the counterexample.

converges to the true FM on the hypersphere, which in this case is the point of tangency.

Theorem 7.1 (Angle Bisector Theorem). *[41] Let $\mathbf{m}_n$ and $\mathbf{m}_{n+1}$ denote the iFME estimates for n and n + 1 given samples, respectively, and $\mathbf{x}_{n+1}$ denotes the (n + 1)th sample. Further, let $\tilde{\mathbf{m}}_n$, $\tilde{\mathbf{m}}_{n+1}$, $\tilde{\mathbf{x}}_{n+1}$ be the corresponding points in the projection space. Then*

$$t_n = \frac{\|\tilde{\mathbf{m}}_n - \tilde{\mathbf{m}}_{n+1}\|}{\|\tilde{\mathbf{x}}_{n+1} - \tilde{\mathbf{m}}_{n+1}\|} = \frac{\|\tilde{\mathbf{m}}_n\|}{\|\tilde{\mathbf{x}}_{n+1}\|} \times \frac{\sin(d(\mathbf{m}_n, \mathbf{m}_{n+1}))}{\sin(d(\mathbf{m}_{n+1}, \mathbf{x}_{n+1}))}, \qquad (7.3)$$

where d is the geodesic distance on the hypersphere.

Assumption. *For the rest of this section, we will assume that the input samples $\{\mathbf{x}_i\}$ are within the geodesic ball $\mathcal{B}(\mathbf{x}, \rho)$, where $0 < \rho < \pi/2$, for some $\mathbf{x} \in S_k$. This is needed for the uniqueness of the FM on the hypersphere (see [42]).* □

Then we bound t_n with respect to the radius ρ.

Lemma 7.1 (Lower and Upper Bounds for t_n). *With the same assumptions made as in Theorem 7.1, we have the following inequality:*

$$\frac{\cos(\rho)}{n} \leq t_n \leq \frac{1}{\cos(\rho)^3 n}. \qquad (7.4)$$

Proof. Lower Bound To prove this lower bound for t_n, we find the lower bounds for each fraction on the right-hand side of Eq. (7.3). The first term reaches its minimum value if $\mathbf{m}_n$ is located at the north pole and $\mathbf{x}_{n+1}$ is located on the boundary of the geodesic ball $\mathcal{B}(\mathbf{x}, \rho)$. In this case, $\|\tilde{\mathbf{m}}_n\| = 1$ and $\|\tilde{\mathbf{x}}_{n+1}\| = \frac{1}{\cos(\rho)}$. This implies that

$$\frac{\|\tilde{\mathbf{m}}_n\|}{\|\tilde{\mathbf{x}}_{n+1}\|} \geq \cos(\rho). \tag{7.5}$$

Next, note that based on the definition of *iFME*, this second fraction in (7.3) can be rewritten as $\frac{\sin(d(\mathbf{m}_n, \mathbf{m}_{n+1}))}{\sin(d(\mathbf{m}_{n+1}, \mathbf{x}_{n+1}))} = \frac{\sin(d(\mathbf{m}_n, \mathbf{m}_{n+1}))}{\sin(nd(\mathbf{m}_n, \mathbf{m}_{n+1}))} = \frac{1}{U_{n-1}(\cos(d(\mathbf{m}_n, \mathbf{m}_{n+1})))}$, where $U_{n-1}(x)$ is the Chebyshev polynomial of the second kind [43]. For any $x \in [-1, 1]$, the maximum of $U_{n-1}(x)$ is reached when $x = 1$, for which $U_{n-1}(1) = n$. Therefore $U_{n-1}(x) \leq n$ and $\frac{1}{U_{n-1}(x)} \geq \frac{1}{n}$. This implies that

$$\frac{\sin(d(\mathbf{m}_n, \mathbf{m}_{n+1}))}{\sin(nd(\mathbf{m}_{n+1}, \mathbf{m}_{n+1}))} = \frac{1}{U_{n-1}(\cos(d(\mathbf{m}_n, \mathbf{m}_{n+1})))} \tag{7.6}$$
$$\geq \frac{1}{n}.$$

Inequalities (7.5) and (7.6) complete the proof. $\qquad\square$

Note that as ρ tends to zero, $\cos(\rho)$ converges to one, and this lower bound tends to $\frac{1}{n}$, which is the case for the Euclidean space.

Proof. Upper Bound First, the upper bound for the first term in (7.3) is reached when $\mathbf{m}_n$ is on the boundary of geodesic ball and $\mathbf{x}_{n+1}$ is given at the north pole. Therefore

$$\frac{\|\tilde{\mathbf{m}}_n\|}{\|\tilde{\mathbf{x}}_{n+1}\|} \leq \frac{1}{\cos(\rho)}. \tag{7.7}$$

Finding the upper bound for the sin term however is quite involved. Note that the maximum of the angle between $\mathbf{m}_n$ and $\mathbf{x}_{n+1}$ at the center of the $\mathbb{S}(k)$, denoted by α, is reached when $\mathbf{m}_n$ and $\mathbf{x}_{n+1}$ are both on the boundary of the geodesic ball, that is, $\alpha \leq 2\rho$. Therefore $\rho \in [0, \frac{\pi}{2})$ implies that $\alpha \in [0, \pi)$. Further we show in the next lemma that the following inequality holds for any $\alpha \in (0, \pi)$:

$$\frac{\sin(\frac{n\alpha}{n+1})}{\sin(\frac{\alpha}{n+1})} \geq n\cos^2(\frac{\alpha}{2}) = n\cos^2(\rho). \tag{7.8}$$

From (7.7) and (7.8) the result follows. $\qquad\square$

Lemma 7.2.

$$\frac{\sin(\frac{n\alpha}{n+1})}{\sin(\frac{\alpha}{n+1})} \geq n\cos^2(\frac{\alpha}{2}) \tag{7.9}$$

for any $\alpha \in (0, \pi)$.

Proof. Let $f = \sin(n\theta) - n\cos^2(\frac{n+1}{2}\theta)\sin(\theta)$, $\theta \in (0, \alpha/(n+1))$, $\alpha \in (0, \pi)$, $n \geq 1$, and $f_\theta = n\cos(n\theta) + 2n\cos(\frac{n+1}{2}\theta)\sin(\theta)\sin(\frac{n+1}{2}\theta)(\frac{n+1}{2}) - n\cos^2(\frac{n+1}{2}\theta)\cos(\theta)$. As $\theta \in (0, \pi/(n+1))$, by solving the above equation we get $\theta = 0$. But $f_{\theta\theta}|_{\theta=0} = 0$. Hence we check $f_{\theta\theta\theta}$: $f_{\theta\theta\theta}|_{\theta=0} = -n^3 + 1.5n(n+1)^2 + n > 0$, $n \geq 1$. So, at $\theta = 0$, f has a minimum where $\theta \in (0, \alpha/(n+1))$ and $f|_{\theta=0} = 0$. Thus $f \geq 0$ as $n \geq 1$. Since, for $\theta \in (0, \alpha/(n+1))$, $\sin(\theta) > 0$, $\frac{f}{\sin(\theta)} \geq 0$ $\frac{f}{\sin(\theta)} = \frac{\sin(n\theta)}{\sin(\theta)} - n\cos^2(\frac{n+1}{2}\theta)$. Hence $\frac{\sin(n\theta)}{\sin(\theta)} - n\cos^2(\frac{n+1}{2}\theta) \geq 0$. Then by substituting $\theta = \alpha/(n+1)$ we get $\frac{\sin(\frac{n\alpha}{n+1})}{\sin(\frac{\alpha}{n+1})} \geq n\cos^2(\frac{\alpha}{2})$. This completes the proof. $\square$

Thus far we have shown analytical bounds for the sequence of weights t_n in the projection space corresponding to Euclidean weights on the sphere (Eq. (7.4)). We now prove the convergence of *iFME* estimates to the expectation of distribution from which the samples are drawn as the number of samples tends to infinity.

Theorem 7.2 (Unbiasedness). *Let (σ, ω) denote a probability space with probability measure ω. A vector-valued random variable $\tilde{\mathbf{x}}$ is a measurable function on σ taking values in $\mathbf{R}^k$, that is, $\tilde{\mathbf{x}}: \sigma \to \mathbf{R}^k$. The distribution of $\tilde{\mathbf{x}}$ is the push-forward probability measure $dP(\tilde{\mathbf{x}}) = \tilde{\mathbf{x}}^*(\sigma)$ on $\mathbf{R}^k$. The expectation is defined by $E[\tilde{\mathbf{x}}] = \int_\sigma \tilde{\mathbf{x}} d\omega$. Let $\tilde{\mathbf{x}}_1, \tilde{\mathbf{x}}_2, \ldots$ be i.i.d. samples drawn from the distribution of $\tilde{\mathbf{x}}$. Also, let $\tilde{\mathbf{m}}_n$ be the incremental mean estimate corresponding to the nth given sample $\tilde{\mathbf{x}}_n$, which is defined by: (i) $\tilde{\mathbf{m}}_1 = \tilde{\mathbf{x}}_1$, (ii) $\tilde{\mathbf{m}}_n = t_n\tilde{\mathbf{x}}_n + (1-t_n)\tilde{\mathbf{m}}_{n-1}$. Then, $\tilde{\mathbf{m}}_n$ is an unbiased estimator of the expectation $E[\tilde{\mathbf{x}}]$.*

Proof. For $n = 2$, $\tilde{\mathbf{m}}_2 = t_2\tilde{\mathbf{x}}_2 + (1-t_2)\tilde{\mathbf{x}}_1$, and hence $E[\tilde{\mathbf{m}}_2] = t_2 E[\tilde{\mathbf{x}}] + (1-t_2)E[\tilde{\mathbf{x}}] = E[\tilde{\mathbf{x}}]$. By induction hypothesis we have $E[\tilde{\mathbf{m}}_{n-1}] = E[\tilde{\mathbf{x}}]$. Then $E[\tilde{\mathbf{m}}_n] = t_n E[\tilde{\mathbf{x}}] + (1-t_n)E[\tilde{\mathbf{x}}] = E[\tilde{\mathbf{x}}]$, hence the result. $\square$

Theorem 7.3 (Weak Consistency). *Let $Var[\tilde{\mathbf{m}}_n]$ denote the variance of the nth incremental mean estimate (defined in Theorem 7.2) with $\frac{\cos(\rho)}{n} \leq t_n \leq \frac{1}{\cos(\rho)^3 n}$ for $\phi \in [0, \pi/2)$. Then there exists $p \in (0, 1]$ such that $\frac{Var[\tilde{\mathbf{m}}_n]}{Var[\tilde{\mathbf{x}}]} \leq (n^p \cos^6(\rho))^{-1}$.*

First note that $Var[\tilde{\mathbf{m}}_n] = t_n^2 Var[\tilde{\mathbf{x}}] + (1-t_n)^2 Var[\tilde{\mathbf{m}}_{n-1}]$. Since $0 \leq t_n \leq 1$, we can see that $Var[\tilde{\mathbf{m}}_n] \leq Var[\tilde{\mathbf{x}}]$ for all n. Besides, for each n, the maximum of the right-hand side is achieved when t_n attains either its minimum or maximum value. Therefore we need to prove the theorem for the following two values of t_n: (i) $t_n = \frac{\cos(\rho)}{n}$ and (ii) $t_n = \frac{1}{n\cos^3(\rho)}$. These two cases will be proved in Lemmas 7.3 and 7.4, respectively.

Lemma 7.3. *Suppose the same assumptions as in Theorem 7.2 are made. Further, let $t_n = \frac{1}{n\cos^3(\rho)}$ for all n and all $\rho \in [0, \pi/2)$. Then $\frac{Var[\tilde{\mathbf{m}}_n]}{Var[\tilde{\mathbf{x}}]} \leq (n\cos^6(\rho))^{-1}$.*

Proof. For $n = 1$, $Var[\tilde{\mathbf{m}}_1] = Var[\tilde{\mathbf{x}}]$, which yields the result, since $\cos(\rho) \leq 1$. Now assume by induction that $\frac{Var[\tilde{\mathbf{m}}_{n-1}]}{Var[\tilde{\mathbf{x}}]} \leq (n-1) \times \cos^6(\rho))^{-1}$. Then

$$
\begin{aligned}
\frac{Var[\tilde{\mathbf{m}}_n]}{Var[\tilde{\mathbf{x}}]} &= t_n^2 + (1-t_n)^2 \frac{Var[\tilde{\mathbf{m}}_{n-1}]}{Var[\tilde{\mathbf{x}}]} \leq t_n^2 + (1-t_n)^2 \frac{1}{(n-1)\cos^6(\rho)} \\
&\leq \frac{1}{\cos^6(\rho)n^2} + (1 - \frac{1}{\cos^3(\rho)n})^2 \times \frac{1}{(n-1)\cos^6(\rho)} \\
&\leq \frac{1}{\cos^6(\rho)n^2} + (1 - \frac{1}{n})^2 \times \frac{1}{(n-1)\cos^6(\rho)} \\
&= \frac{1}{\cos^6(\rho)n^2} + \frac{n-1}{n^2\cos^6(\rho)} = \frac{1}{n\cos^6(\rho)}. \qquad \square
\end{aligned}
$$

Lemma 7.4. *Suppose the same assumptions as in Theorem 7.2. Further, let $t_n = \frac{\cos(\rho)}{n}$ for all n and all $\phi \in [0, \pi/2)$. Then $\frac{Var[\tilde{\mathbf{m}}_n]}{Var[\tilde{\mathbf{x}}]} \leq n^{-p}$ for some $0 < p \leq 1$.*

Proof. For $n = 1$, $Var[\tilde{\mathbf{m}}_n] = Var[\tilde{\mathbf{x}}]$, which yields the result, since $\cos(\rho) \leq 1$. Now assume by induction that $\frac{Var[\tilde{\mathbf{m}}_{n-1}]}{Var[\tilde{\mathbf{x}}]} \leq (n-1)^{-p}$. Then

$$
\begin{aligned}
\frac{Var[\tilde{\mathbf{m}}_n]}{Var[\tilde{\mathbf{x}}]} &= t_n^2 + (1-t_n)^2 \frac{Var[\tilde{\mathbf{m}}_{n-1}]}{Var[\tilde{\mathbf{x}}]} \leq t_n^2 + (1-t_n)^2 \frac{1}{(n-1)^p} \\
&\leq \frac{\cos^2(\rho)}{n^2} + \frac{(n-\cos(\rho))^2}{n^2} \times \frac{1}{(n-1)^p} \\
&= \frac{(n-1)^p \cos^2(\rho) + \cos^2(\rho) - 2n\cos(\rho) + n^2}{n^2(n-1)^p}.
\end{aligned}
$$

Now it suffices to show that the numerator of this expression is not greater than $n^{2-p}(n-1)^p$. In other words,

$$
(n-1)^p \cos^2(\rho) + \cos^2(\rho) - 2n\cos(\rho) + n^2 - n^{2-p}(n-1)^p \leq 0. \tag{7.10}
$$

This quadratic function in $\cos(\rho)$ is less than zero when

$$
n\left(\frac{1 - (n-1)^{p/2}\sqrt{(\frac{n-1}{n})^p + \frac{1}{n^p} - 1}}{1 + (n-1)^p} \right)
$$

$$\leq \cos(\rho) \leq n \left(\frac{1 + (n-1)^{p/2}\sqrt{(\frac{n-1}{n})^p + \frac{1}{n^p}} - 1}{1 + (n-1)^p} \right). \qquad (7.11)$$

The inequality on the right is satisfied for all values of the cos function. Besides, it is easy to see that the function on the left-hand side is increasing w.r.t. $n > 1$ and hence attains its minimum when $n = 2$. This implies that

$$1 - \sqrt{2^{1-p} - 1} \leq \cos(\rho)$$
$$\Rightarrow \rho \leq \cos^{-1}(1 - \sqrt{2^{1-p} - 1}) \qquad (7.12)$$
$$\Rightarrow 0 < p \leq 1 - log_2[(1 - \cos(\rho))^2 + 1].$$

Note that $p > 0$ for all $\rho < \pi/2$. $\qquad\qquad\qquad\square$

Proof. Convergence Equipped with the previous two results, it is easy to see that for all $\rho \in [0, \pi/2)$, there exists p satisfying $0 < p \leq 1$ such that
- If $t_n = \frac{\cos(\rho)}{n}$, then $\frac{\text{Var}[\tilde{\mathbf{m}}_n]}{\text{Var}[\tilde{\mathbf{x}}]} \leq \frac{1}{n^p} \leq \frac{1}{n^p \cos^6(\rho)}$, because $\cos(\rho) \leq 1$.
- If $t_n = \frac{1}{n \cos^3(\rho)}$, then $\frac{\text{Var}[\tilde{\mathbf{m}}_n]}{\text{Var}[\tilde{\mathbf{x}}]} \leq \frac{1}{n \cos^6(\rho)} \leq \frac{1}{n^p \cos^6(\rho)}$, because $p \leq 1$.

These two pieces together complete the proof of convergence. $\quad\square$

The inequality in Theorem 7.3 implies that as $n \to \infty$, for any $\rho \in [0, \pi/2)$, the variance of *iFME* estimates in the projection space tends to zero. Besides, when ρ approaches $\pi/2$, the corresponding power of n and $\cos(\rho)$ become very small, hence the rate of convergence gets slower. Note that instead of the weighting scheme used here (i.e., in the spirit of incremental mean in Euclidean space), we can choose a different weighting scheme that is intrinsic to the manifold (i.e., as a function of curvature) to speed up the convergence rate.

Now we will show that our proposed recursive FM estimator has a linear convergence rate.

Theorem 7.4 (Convergence rate). *Let* $\mathbf{x}_1, \ldots, \mathbf{x}_N$ *be the samples on* $\mathbb{S}(k)$ *drawn from any distribution. Then algorithm* (7.2) *has a linear convergence rate.*

Proof. Let $\mathbf{x}_1, \ldots, \mathbf{x}_N$ be the samples drawn from a distribution S_k. Let $\mathbf{m}$ be the FM of $\{\mathbf{x}_i\}$. Then, using the triangle inequality, we have

$$
\begin{aligned}
d(\mathbf{m}_k, \mathbf{m}) &\leq d(\mathbf{m}_{k-1}, \mathbf{m}_k) + d(\mathbf{m}_{k-1}, \mathbf{m}) \\
&= \frac{1}{k} d(\mathbf{m}_{k-1}, \mathbf{x}_k) + d(\mathbf{m}_{k-1}, \mathbf{m})
\end{aligned}
$$

$$\leq \quad \frac{1}{k}\left(d(\mathbf{m}_{k-1},\mathbf{m}) + d(\mathbf{x}_k,\mathbf{m})\right) + d(\mathbf{m}_{k-1},\mathbf{m}).$$

Hence

$$\frac{d(\mathbf{m}_k,\mathbf{m})}{d(\mathbf{m}_{k-1},\mathbf{m})} \leq \left(1 + \frac{1}{k} + \frac{d(\mathbf{x}_k,\mathbf{m})}{k\, d(\mathbf{m}_{k-1},\mathbf{m})}\right).$$

Now, since $d(\mathbf{m}_{k-1},\mathbf{m})$ and $d(\mathbf{x}_k,\mathbf{m})$ are finite as $\{\mathbf{x}_i\}$ are within a geodesic ball of radius $< \pi/2$, as $k \to \infty$, $\frac{d(\mathbf{m}_k,\mathbf{m})}{d(\mathbf{m}_{k-1},\mathbf{m})} \leq 1$. But the equality holds only if $\mathbf{m}$ lies on the geodesic between $\mathbf{m}_{k-1}$ and $\mathbf{x}_k$. Let $l < \infty$, and let $\mathbf{m}$ lie on the geodesic between $\mathbf{m}_{k-1}$ and $\mathbf{x}_k$ for some $k > l$. As $\mathbf{m}$ is fixed, using induction, we can easily show that $\mathbf{m}$ cannot lie on the same geodesic for all $k > l$. Hence $\frac{d(\mathbf{m}_k,\mathbf{m})}{d(\mathbf{m}_{k-1},\mathbf{m})} < 1$, and the convergence rate is linear. $\square$

7.4 Experimental results

We now evaluate the effectiveness of the *iFME* algorithm, compared to the nonincremental counterpart *FME*, for computing the FM of a finite set of samples on the sphere (northern hemisphere not including the equator). For *FME*, we used a gradient descent technique to minimize the sum of squared geodesic distances cost function. We report the results for samples drawn from a Log-Normal distribution (with mean at the north pole and the variance set to 0.2) on the upper hemisphere. A set of random samples are drawn from the distribution and incrementally input to both *iFME* and *FME* algorithms. The computation time needed for each method to compute the sample FM and the error were recorded for each new sample incrementally introduced. In all the experiments the computation time is reported for execution on a 3.3 GHz desktop with a quadcore Intel $i7$ processor and 24 GB RAM. The error is defined by the geodesic distance between the estimated mean (using either *iFME* or *FME*) and the expectation of the input distribution. Because of the randomness in generating the samples, we repeated this experiment 100 times for each case, and the mean execution time and the error for each method are shown.

The performances of *iFME* and *FME* are evaluated with respect to the execution time and error and are illustrated in Fig. 7.3. From these plots we can clearly see that *iFME* performs almost equally good in terms of error/accuracy but takes comparatively very less execution time.

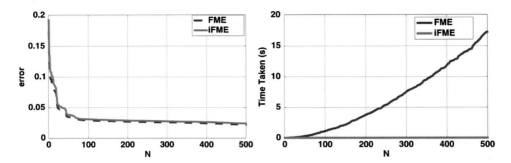

Figure 7.3. Time and error comparisons of *iFME* and *FME*.

7.5 Application to the classification of movement disorders

In this section we use an exact-PGA (exact principal geodesic analysis) algorithm presented in [44], which is applicable to data residing on a hypersphere. We will call this the *ePGA* algorithm. We will also use the tangent PCA (tPCA) algorithm presented in [45] for diffusion tensor fields as a comparison. This algorithm consists of (1) computing the FM of the input data, (2) projecting each data point to the tangent space at the FM using the Riemannian *log*-map, (3) performing standard PCA in the tangent plane, and (4) projecting the result (principal vectors) back to the manifold using the Riemannian exponential map.

In the *ePGA* algorithm we will use *iFME* to compute the FM and make use of the parallel transport operation on the hypersphere. For completeness, we now present the *ePGA* algorithm from [44] and used here.

The projection algorithm/step in the above algorithm has an analytic expression for manifolds with constant sectional curvature, that is, for hypersphere and hyperbolic space. Here we will present the projection algorithm.

Note that the parallel transport operation on the hypersphere can be expressed in analytic form. The formula for parallel transporting $\mathbf{u} \in T_{\mathbf{n}}\mathbb{S}(k)$ from $\mathbf{n}$ to $\mathbf{m}$ is given by

$$
\begin{aligned}
\mathbf{w} &= \Gamma_{\mathbf{n}\to\mathbf{m}}(\mathbf{p}) \\
&= \left(\mathbf{p} - \mathbf{v}\left(\frac{\mathbf{v}^t\mathbf{p}}{\|\mathbf{v}\|^2}\right)\right) + \frac{\mathbf{v}^t\mathbf{p}}{\|\mathbf{v}\|^2}\left(\mathbf{n}\left(-\sin(\|\mathbf{v}\|)\|\mathbf{v}\|\right) + \mathbf{v}\cos(\|\mathbf{v}\|)\right),
\end{aligned}
$$

where $\mathbf{v} = Log_{\mathbf{n}}\mathbf{m}$. We refer the reader to [44] for details of the *ePGA* algorithm.

Algorithm 7.1 The ePGA algorithm on manifold $\mathcal{M}$.

1: Given dataset $X = \{x_1, \cdots, x_N\} \in \mathcal{M}$, and $1 \leq L \leq dim(\mathcal{M})$

2: Compute the FM μ of X [42]

3: Set $k \leftarrow 1$

4: Set $\{\bar{x}_1^0, \cdots, \bar{x}_n^0\} \leftarrow \{x_1, \cdots, x_N\}$

5: **while** $k \leq L$ **do**

6:     Solve $\mathbf{v}_k = \text{argmax}_{\|\mathbf{v}\|=1, \mathbf{v} \in T_\mu M, \mathbf{v} \in V_{k-1}^\perp} \frac{1}{N} \sum_{j=1}^{N} d^2(\mu, \Pi_{\mathbb{S}(k)}(x_j))$.

7:     Project $\{\bar{x}_1^{k-1}, \ldots, \bar{x}_N^{k-1}\}$ to a k codimension one submanifold Z of M, which is orthogonal to the current geodesic subspace.

8:     Set the projected points to $\{\bar{x}_1^k, \ldots, \bar{x}_N^k\}$

9:     $k \leftarrow k + 1$

10: **end while**

Algorithm 7.2 Algorithm for projecting the data points to a codimension one submanifold.

1: *Input*: a data point $x_i \in \mathbb{S}(n)(\mathbb{H}(n))$, a geodesic submanifold defined at μ and $\mathbf{v} \in T_\mu S_n(T_\mu H_n)$, and $y(\mathbf{v}, x_i)$, which is the projection of ψ on to the geodesic submanifold.

2: *Output*: $\bar{x}_i$, which is the projection of the data point x_i to a subspace $\mathbb{S}(n)$ $(\mathbb{H}(n))$, which is orthogonal to the current geodesic submanifold.

3: Step 1. Evaluate the tangent vector $\mathbf{v}_i \in T_{y(\mathbf{v}, x_i)}\mathbb{S}(n)$ $(T_{y(\mathbf{v}, x_i)}\mathbb{H}(n))$ directed toward x_i using the Inverse Exponential Map. It is clear that $\mathbf{v}_i$ is orthogonal to $\mathbf{v}$.

4: Step 2. Parallel transport $\mathbf{v}_i$ to μ. Let $\mathbf{v}_i^\mu$ denote the parallel transported vector. The geodesic submanifold defined by μ and $\mathbf{v}_i^\mu$ is orthogonal to geodesic submanifolds obtained from the previous steps in Algorithm 7.1.

5: Step 3. Set $\bar{x}_i \leftarrow y(\mathbf{v}_i^\mu, x_i)$

The dataset for classification consists of high angular resolution diffusion image (HARDI) scans from (1) healthy controls, patients with (2) Parkinson's disease (PD), and (3) essential tremor (ET). We aim to automatically discriminate between these three classes using features derived from the HARDI data. This dataset consists of 25 controls, 24 PD, and 15 ET images. The HARDI data were acquired using a 3T Phillips MR scanner with the following parameters: $TR = 7748$ ms, $TE = 86$ ms, b-values: 0, 1000 $\frac{\text{s}}{\text{mm}^2}$, 64 gradient directions, and voxel size = $2 \times 2 \times 2\,\text{mm}^3$.

Authors in [46] employed DTI-based analysis using scalar-valued features to address the problem of movement disorder classification. Later in [47] a PGA-based classification algorithm was proposed using Cauchy deformation tensors (computed from a nonrigid registration of patient scans to a HARDI control atlas), which are SPD matrices. In the next subsection we develop classification method based on (1) Ensemble Average Propagators (EAPs) derived from HARDI data within an ROI and (2) shapes of the ROI derived from the input population. Using a square root density parameterization [48], both features can be mapped to points on an unit Hilbert sphere, where the proposed *iFME* in conjunction with the *ePGA* method is applicable.

Classification results using the ensemble average propagator as features: To capture the full diffusional information, we chose to use the ensemble average propagator (EAP) at each voxel as our feature in the classification. We compute the EAPs using the method described in [49] and use the square root density parameterization of each EAP. This way the full diffusion information at each voxel is represented as a point on the unit Hilbert sphere.

We now present the classification algorithm, which is a combination of *ePGA*-based reduced representation and a nearest-neighbor classifier. The input to the *ePGA* algorithm are EAP features in this case. The input HARDI data are first rigidly aligned to the atlas computed from the control (normal) group, then EAPs are computed in a 3-D region of interest (ROI) in the midbrain. Finally, the EAP field extracted from each ROI image is identified with a point on the product manifold (the number of elements in the product is equal to the number of voxels in the ROI) of unit Hilbert spheres. This is in spirit similar to the case of the product manifold formalism in [45,47].

A set of 10 control, 10 PD, and 5 ET images are randomly picked as the test set, and the rest of the images are used for training. Also, classification is performed using *ePGA*, tPCA, and the standard PCA and is repeated 300 times to report the average accuracy. The results using EAP features are summarized in Table 7.2. It is evident that the accuracy of *ePGA* is better than that of the tPCA, whereas both methods are considerably more accurate than the standard PCA, as they account for the nonlinear geometry of the sphere.

Classification results using the shape features: In this section we evaluated the *ePGA* algorithm based on shape of the Substantia Nigra region in the given brain images for the task of movement disorder classification. We first collected random samples (point) on the boundary of each 3-D shape and applied the

Table 7.1 Classification results from *ePGA*, tPCA, and PCA.

| | Results using shape features | | | | | | | | |
| | Control vs. PD | | | Control vs. ET | | | PD vs. ET | | |
	ePGA	tPCA	PCA	ePGA	tPCA	PCA	ePGA	tPCA	PCA
Accuracy	94.5	93.0	67.3	91.4	90.1	75.7	88.1	87.6	64.6
Sensitivity	92.3	91.0	52.0	87.5	86.2	80.1	84.7	82.4	58.4
Specificity	96.8	95.0	82.7	96.3	94.1	71.3	94.2	92.8	70.8

Table 7.2 Classification results from *ePGA*, tPCA, and PCA.

| | Results using EAP features | | | | | | | | |
| | Control vs. PD | | | Control vs. ET | | | PD vs. ET | | |
	ePGA	tPCA	PCA	ePGA	tPCA	PCA	ePGA	tPCA	PCA
Accuracy	93.7	93.5	59.8	92.8	91.3	70.2	92.4	90.9	66.0
Sensitivity	93.1	91.8	48.3	90.7	89.7	79.8	86.2	84.7	56.3
Specificity	96.9	95.2	71.3	93.1	92.9	60.6	98.7	97.1	75.7

Schrödinger distance transform (SDT) technique in [50] to represent each shape as a point on the unit hypersphere. The size of the ROI for the 3-D shape of interest was set to $28 \times 28 \times 15$, and the resulting samples lie on an S_{11759} manifold. Then we used *ePGA* for classification. The results reported in Table 7.1 depict the accuracy gained in classification when using *ePGA* compared to tPCA. Evidently, *ePGA* yields a better classification accuracy.

7.6 Riemannian geometry of the special orthogonal group

The set of all $n \times n$ orthogonal matrices is denoted by $\mathrm{O}(n)$, that is, $\mathrm{O}(n) = \{X \in \mathbf{R}^{n \times n} | X^T X = I_n\}$. The set of orthogonal matrices with determinant 1, denoted by the special orthogonal group $\mathfrak{so}(n)$, forms a compact subset of $\mathrm{O}(n)$. As $\mathfrak{so}(n)$ is a compact Riemannian manifold, by the Hopf–Rinow theorem it is also a geodesically complete manifold [51]. Its geometry is well understood, and we recall a few relevant concepts here and refer the reader to [51] for details. The manifold $\mathfrak{so}(n)$ has a Lie group structure, and the corresponding Lie algebra is defined as $\mathfrak{so}(n) = \{W \in$

$\mathbf{R}^{n \times n} | W^T = -W\}$. In other words, $\mathfrak{so}(n)$ (the set of Left invariant vector fields with associated Lie bracket) is the set of $n \times n$ antisymmetric matrices. The Lie bracket $[,]$, operator on $\mathfrak{so}(n)$, is defined as the commutator, that is, $[U, V] = UV - VU$ for $U, V \in \mathfrak{so}(n)$. Now we can define a Riemannian metric on $\mathfrak{so}(n)$ as follows: $\langle U, V \rangle_X = trace\left(U^T V\right)$ for $U, V \in T_X \mathfrak{so}(n)$, $X \in \mathfrak{so}(n)$. Note that it can be shown that this is a biinvariant Riemannian metric. Under this biinvariant metric, now we define the Riemannian exponential and inverse exponential maps as follows. Let $X, Y \in \mathfrak{so}(n)$, $U \in T_X \mathfrak{so}(n)$. Then the Riemannian inverse exponential map is defined as

$$\mathsf{Log}_X(Y) = X \log(X^T Y), \tag{7.13}$$

and the Riemannian exponential map is defined as

$$\mathsf{Exp}_X(U) = X \exp(X^T U), \tag{7.14}$$

where exp and log are the matrix exponential and logarithm, respectively. Due of the computational complexity of matrix exponential, we may instead choose to use the Riemannian retraction map as follows. Given $W \in \mathfrak{so}(n)$, the Cayley map is a conformal mapping $\mathrm{Cay} : \mathfrak{so}(n) \to \mathfrak{so}(n)$ defined by $\mathrm{Cay}(W) = (I_n + W)(I_n - W)^{-1}$. Using the Cayley map, we can define the Riemannian retraction map as, $\mathsf{Ret}_X : T_X \mathfrak{so}(n) \to \mathfrak{so}(n)$ by $\mathsf{Ret}_X(W) = \mathrm{Cay}(W)X$. Using the Riemannian exponential (retraction) and inverse exponential map, we can define the geodesic on $\mathfrak{so}(n)$ as $\Gamma_X^Y(y) = \mathsf{Exp}\left(t\mathsf{Log}_X(Y)\right)$.

7.7 Weak consistency of *iFME* on $\mathfrak{so}(n)$

In this section we present a detailed proof of convergence of our recursive estimator on $\mathfrak{so}(n)$. Analogous to our FM estimator on $\mathbb{S}(k)$, we first define the FM estimator on $\mathfrak{so}(n)$ and then prove its consistency.

Formally, let $X_1, \ldots, X_N$ be a set of N samples on $\mathfrak{so}(n)$, all of which lie inside a geodesic ball of an appropriate radius such that FM exists and is unique. The *iFME* estimate M_n of the FM with the nth given sample X_n is defined by

$$M_1 = X_1, \tag{7.15}$$
$$M_n = \Gamma_{M_{n-1}}^{X_n}\left(\frac{1}{n}\right), \tag{7.16}$$

where $\Gamma_{M_{n-1}}^{X_n}$ is the shortest geodesic path from M_{n-1} to X_n ($\in \mathfrak{so}(n)$). In what follows we will show that as the number of given samples N tends to infinity, the *iFME* estimates will converge to the expectation of the distribution from which the samples are drawn.

Theorem 7.5. *Let $X_1, X_2, \ldots, X_N$ be i.i.d. samples drawn from a probability distribution on $\mathfrak{so}(n)$. Then the inductive FM estimator (iFME) M_N of these samples converges to M as $N \to \infty$, where M is the expectation of the probability distribution.*

Proposition 7.1. *Any arbitrary element of $\mathfrak{so}(n)$ can be written as the composition of planar rotations in the planes generated by the n standard orthogonal basis vectors of $\mathbb{R}^n$.*

Proof. Let $X \in \mathfrak{so}(n)$. Observe that $\log(X) \in \mathfrak{so}(n)$. Further, $\log(X)$ is a skew-symmetric matrix. Let $U = \log(X)$. Then U_{ij} is the angle of rotation in the plane formed by the basis vectors $\mathbf{e}_i$ and $\mathbf{e}_j$ for all $i = 1, \ldots, n$ and $j = i + 1, \ldots, n$. $\qquad\square$

By Proposition 7.1 we can express X as a product of $n(n-1)/2$ planar rotation matrices. Each planar rotation matrix can be mapped onto $\mathbb{S}(n-1)$, hence there exists a mapping $F : \mathrm{SO}(n) \to \underbrace{\mathbb{S}(n-1) \times \cdots \times \mathbb{S}_{n-1}}_{n(n-1)/2 \text{ times}}$. Let us denote this product space of hyperspheres by $\mathfrak{O}(n-1, \frac{n(n-1)}{2})$. Then F is a embedding of $\mathrm{SO}(n)$ in $\mathfrak{O}(n-1, \frac{n(n-1)}{2})$. Notice that as this product space has $n(n-1)/2$ components, we will use two indices (i, j) to denote a component. Hence, given $X \in \mathrm{SO}(n)$, the (i, j)th component of $F(X)$ has ith and jth entries $\cos(\theta_{ij})$ and $\sin(\theta_{ij})$, respectively, and the rest of the $n - 2$ entries are zero. Here θ_{ij} is the planar rotation angle in the plane spanned by $\mathbf{e}_i$ and $\mathbf{e}_j$. The following propositions allow us to prove that $\mathrm{SO}(n)$ is a submanifold of $\mathfrak{O}(n-1, \frac{n(n-1)}{2})$.

To do that, we will first use the Log-Euclidean metric on $\mathrm{SO}(n)$ defined as follows: Given $X, Y \in \mathrm{SO}(n)$, the metric $d(X, Y) = \frac{1}{2}\| \log(X) - \log(Y) \|_F$. Notice that this metric is adjoint invariant, as $\| Z \log(X) Z^T - Z \log(Y) Z^T \|_F = \| \log(X) - \log(Y) \|_F$ for some $Z \in \mathrm{SO}(n)$.

The following proposition shows that F is an isometric mapping using the product ℓ_2 arc-length metric on $\mathfrak{O}(n-1, \frac{n(n-1)}{2})$.

Proposition 7.2. *F is an isometric mapping from $\mathrm{SO}(n)$ to $\mathfrak{O}(n - 1, \frac{n(n-1)}{2})$.*

Proof. Given $X, Y \in \mathrm{SO}(n)$, let $F(X)_{ij}$ and $F(Y)_{ij}$ be the (i, j)th entries of $F(X)$ and $F(Y)$, respectively. Let $F(X)_{ij} = \left(0 \cdots, 0, \cos(\theta_{ij}^X), 0, \cdots, 0, \sin(\theta_{ij}^X), 0, \cdots, 0\right)^t$ and $F(Y)_{ij} =$

$\left(0, \dots, 0, \cos(\theta_{ij}^Y), 0, \dots, 0, \sin(\theta_{ij}^Y), 0, \dots, 0\right)^t$. Then $F(X)_{ij}, F(Y)_{ij} \in S_{n-1}$, and hence $d\left(F(X)_{ij}, F(Y)_{ij}\right) = |\theta_{ij}^X - \theta_{ij}^Y|$. Thus the (i, j)th entry of $\log(X) - \log(Y)$ is the signed distance $d\left(F(X)_{ij}, F(Y)_{ij}\right)$. This concludes the proof. $\square$

It is easy to see that the Γ_X^Y from X to Y is given by

$$\Gamma_X^Y(t) = \exp\left(\log(X) + t\left(\log(Y) - \log(X)\right)\right).$$

In the following propositions we will show that F maps Γ_X^Y to the (shortest) geodesic from $F(X)$ to $F(Y)$ for any $X, Y \in \mathsf{SO}(n)$.

Proposition 7.3. *The shortest geodesic between* $\mathbf{x} = (0, \dots, 0, \cos(\theta_1), 0, \dots, 0, \sin(\theta_1), 0, \dots, 0)^t$ *and* $\mathbf{y} = (0, \dots, 0, \cos(\theta_2), 0, \dots, 0, \sin(\theta_2), 0, \dots, 0)^t$ *is given by*

$$\Gamma_{\mathbf{x}}^{\mathbf{y}}(t) = ((0, \dots, 0, \cos\left((1-t)\theta_1 + t\theta_2\right)), 0, \dots, 0,$$
$$\sin\left((1-t)\theta_1 + t\theta_2\right), 0, \dots, 0)^t.$$

Proof. From spherical geometry we know that given $\mathbf{x}, \mathbf{y} \in S_{n-1}$, the shortest geodesic is given by

$$\Gamma_{\mathbf{x}}^{\mathbf{y}}(t) = \frac{1}{\sin(\theta)}\left(\sin(t\theta)\mathbf{x} + \sin((1-t)\theta)\mathbf{y}\right),$$

where $\theta = d(\mathbf{x}, \mathbf{y})$. Now, given the hypothesis: $\theta = |\theta_2 - \theta_1|$, observe that, for $t \in [0, 1]$, $\Gamma_{\mathbf{x}}^{\mathbf{y}}(t)$ is the unique point on S_{n-1} such that $d\left(\Gamma_{\mathbf{x}}^{\mathbf{y}}(t), \mathbf{x}\right) = t|\theta_2 - \theta_1|$ and $d\left(\Gamma_{\mathbf{x}}^{\mathbf{y}}(t), \mathbf{y}\right) = (1-t)|\theta_2 - \theta_1|$. Substituting

$$\Gamma_{\mathbf{x}}^{\mathbf{y}}(t) = ((0, \dots, 0, \cos\left(t\theta_1 + (1-t)\theta_2\right)), 0, \dots, 0,$$
$$\sin\left(t\theta_1 + (1-t)\theta_2\right), 0, \dots, 0)^t,$$

we conclude the proof. $\square$

Theorem 7.6. $\mathsf{SO}(n)$ *is a geodesic submanifold of* $\mathfrak{O}(n-1, \frac{n(n-1)}{2})$.

Proof. Given $X, Y \in \mathsf{SO}(n)$ and $t \in [0, 1]$, the shortest geodesic is given by $\Gamma_X^Y(t) = \exp\left(\log(X) + t\left(\log(Y) - \log(X)\right)\right)$. Now observe that

$$F(X)_{ij} = (0, \dots, 0, \cos(\theta_1), 0, \dots, 0, \sin(\theta_1), 0, \dots, 0)^t,$$

where $\theta_1 = \log(X)_{ij}$, and

$$F(Y)_{ij} = (0, \dots, 0, \cos(\theta_2), 0, \dots, 0, \sin(\theta_2), 0, \dots, 0)^t,$$

where $\theta_2 = \log(Y)_{ij}$. By Proposition 7.3,

$$\log\left(F\left(\Gamma_X^Y(t)\right)\right) = (0, \ldots, 0, \cos(\theta), 0, \ldots, 0, \sin(\theta), 0, \ldots, 0)^t,$$

where $\theta = (1-y)\theta_1 + t\theta_2$. This concludes our proof. $\qquad\square$

We are now ready to prove Theorem 7.6.

Proof. (Proof of Theorem 7.6). To show weak consistency of our proposed estimator on $\{X_i\} \subset \mathsf{SO}(n)$, it is sufficient to show the weak consistency of our estimator on $\{F(X_i)\} \subset \mathfrak{O}(n-1, \frac{n(n-1)}{2})$. A proof of the weak consistency of our proposed FM estimator on hypersphere has been shown in Section 7.3. Note that the distance d on $\mathfrak{O}(n-1, \frac{n(n-1)}{2})$ is given by

$$d\left((\mathbf{x}_1, \ldots, \mathbf{x}_m), (\mathbf{y}_1, \ldots, \mathbf{y}_m)\right) = \|d(\mathbf{x}_i, \mathbf{y}_i)\|_2, \qquad (7.17)$$

where, on the RHS, d is the distance on S_{n-1}, and $m = n(n-1)/2$. We can easily show that the FM on $\mathfrak{O}(n-1, \frac{n(n-1)}{2})$ can be found from the FM of each component. Thus we can trivially extend the proof of the weak consistency of S_{n-1} to $\mathfrak{O}(n-1, \frac{n(n-1)}{2})$, which in turn proves the weak consistency on $\mathsf{SO}(n)$. $\qquad\square$

7.8 Experimental results

We now evaluate the effectiveness of the *iFME* algorithm, compared to the nonincremental counterpart *FME*, for computing the FM of a finite set of samples synthetically generated on SO_n. We report the results for samples randomly drawn from a Log-Normal distribution on SO_{20} with expectation I_{20} (I denotes the identity matrix) and variance 0.25. The computation time needed by each method for computing the sample FM and the error were recorded for each new sample incrementally introduced. The error is defined by the geodesic distance between the estimated mean (using either *iFME* or the *FME*) and the expectation of the input distribution. Because of the randomness in generating the samples, we repeated this experiment 100 times for each case, and the mean time consumption and the error for each method are shown.

From the comparison plots in Fig. 7.4 we can see that *iFME* is very competitive in accuracy and much more efficient in execution time. We also present a comparison plots in Fig. 7.5 depicting the execution time taken by both the algorithms to achieve a prespecified error tolerance (with respect to the expectation of the distribution from which the samples are drawn). This plot suggests that to achieve a prespecified tolerance, *iFME* needs far less

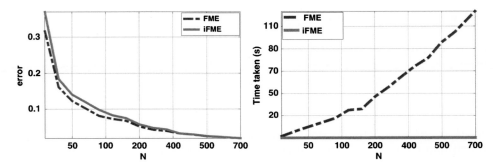

Figure 7.4. Time and error comparisons of *iFME* and *FME*.

execution time compared to *FME*. Once again, all the time comparisons were performed on a 3.3 GHz desktop with quadcore Intel $i7$ processor and 24 GB RAM.

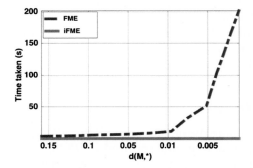

Figure 7.5. Error tolerance comparison of *iFME* and *FME*.

We now present an application to the atlas construction problem. Results on toy images taken from the MPEG-7 database using the proposed recursive FM computation technique are shown. Note that to compute the atlas, it is required to align the image data whose atlas we seek prior to computing the average. In this context we use the computationally efficient technique proposed in [52]. This technique involves picking an arbitrary reference image data set and aligning all the data to this reference. Then the alignment transformations between the reference and the rest of the images in the population are averaged. It was shown that this average transformation when applied to the chosen reference yields the atlas. For further details on this technique, we refer the reader to [52].

Two toy images were taken from the MPEG-7 database, and for each of these images, we generated four rotated images (highlighted in orange (mid gray in print version) in Fig. 7.6) and then computed the "mean image" (or atlas) of these rotated images (highlighted in red (dark gray in print version) in Fig. 7.6). The results clearly suggest that our approach gives an efficient way to compute atlas for images with planar rotations.

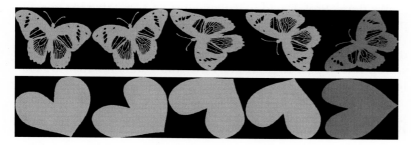

Figure 7.6. Mean images on MPEG-7 toy data.

7.9 Conclusions

In this chapter we presented a recursive estimator for computing the Riemannian barycenter a.k.a. the Fréchet mean of manifold-valued data sets. Specifically, we developed the theory for two well-known and commonly encountered Riemannian manifolds, namely, the hypersphere S_n and the special orthogonal group $SO(n)$. The common approach to estimating the FM from a set of data samples involves the application of Riemannian gradient descent to the Fréchet functional. This approach is not well suited for situations where data are acquired incrementally, that is, in an online fashion. In an online setting the Riemannian gradient descent proves to be inefficient both computationally and storagewise, since it requires computation of the Fréchet functional from scratch and thus requires the storage of all past data. In this chapter we presented a recursive FM estimator that does not require any optimization and achieves the computation of the FM estimate in a single pass over the data. We proved the weak consistency of the estimator for S_n and $SO(n)$. Further, we experimentally demonstrated that the estimator yields comparable accuracy to the Riemannian gradient descent algorithm. Several synthetic data and real-data experiments were presented showcasing the performance of the estimator in comparison to the Riemannian gradient descent technique for the FM computation and PG for the classification experiments with applications in neuroimaging. Our future work will focus on developing an FM estimator that uses intrinsic weights in the incremental updates, which will likely improve the convergence rate of the estimator.

Acknowledgments

We thank Prof. David E. Vaillancourt and Dr. Edward Ofori for providing the diffusion MRI scans of movement disorder patients. We also thank Dr. Xavier Pennec and the anonymous reviewer for their invaluable comments in improving this manuscript. This research was in part supported by the NSF grants IIS-1525431 and IIS-1724174.

References

1. M. Moakher, P.G. Batchelor, Symmetric positive-definite matrices: from geometry to applications and visualization, Visualization and Processing of Tensor Fields (2006) 285–298.
2. X. Pennec, P. Fillard, N. Ayache, A Riemannian framework for tensor computing, International Journal of Computer Vision 66 (1) (2006) 41–66.
3. P. Turaga, A. Veeraraghavan, R. Chellappa, Statistical analysis on Stiefel and Grassmann manifolds with applications in computer vision, in: IEEE Conference on Computer Vision and Pattern Recognition (CVPR), IEEE, 2008, pp. 1–8.
4. S. Hauberg, A. Feragen, M.J. Black, Grassmann averages for scalable robust PCA, in: Proceedings of the IEEE Conference on Computer Vision and Pattern Recognition, 2014, pp. 3810–3817.
5. R. Chakraborty, B.C. Vemuri, Recursive Fréchet mean computation on the Grassmannian and its applications to computer vision, in: IEEE International Conference on Computer Vision (ICCV), 2015, pp. 4229–4237.
6. R. Chakraborty, S. Hauberg, B.C. Vemuri, Intrinsic Grassmann averages for online linear and robust subspace learning, arXiv preprint, arXiv:1702.01005, 2017.
7. C.R. Goodall, K.V. Mardia, Projective shape analysis, Journal of Computational and Graphical Statistics 8 (2) (1999) 143–168.
8. V. Patrangenaru, K.V. Mardia, Affine shape analysis and image analysis, in: 22nd Leeds Annual Statistics Research Workshop, 2003, pp. 57–62.
9. H. Hendriks, Z. Landsman, Mean location and sample mean location on manifolds: asymptotics, tests, confidence regions, Journal of Multivariate Analysis 67 (2) (1998) 227–243.
10. Y. Chikuse, Asymptotic expansions for distributions of the large sample matrix resultant and related statistics on the Stiefel manifold, Journal of Multivariate Analysis 39 (2) (1991) 270–283.
11. R. Chakraborty, B.C. Vemuri, et al., Statistics on the Stiefel manifold: theory and applications, The Annals of Statistics 47 (1) (2019) 415–438.

12. K.V. Mardia, P.E. Jupp, Directional Statistics, vol. 494, John Wiley & Sons, 2009.

13. A. Srivastava, I. Jermyn, S. Joshi, Riemannian analysis of probability density functions with applications in vision, in: IEEE Conf. on Computer Vision and Pattern Recognition (CVPR), 2007, pp. 1–8.

14. D.S. Tuch, T.G. Reese, et al., Diffusion MRI of complex neural architecture, Neuron 40 (5) (2003) 885–895.

15. R. Hartley, J. Trumpf, et al., Rotation averaging, International Journal of Computer Vision 103 (3) (2013) 267–305.

16. M. Fréchet, Les éléments aléatoires de nature quelconque dans un espace distancié, Annales de l'institut Henri Poincaré, vol. 10, Presses Universitaires de France, 1948, pp. 215–310.

17. H. Karcher, Riemannian center of mass and mollifier smoothing, Communications on Pure and Applied Mathematics 30 (5) (1977) 509–541.

18. B. Afsari, Riemannian L^p center of mass: existence, uniqueness, and convexity, Proceedings of the American Mathematical Society 139 (2) (2011) 655–673.

19. M. Arnaudon, F. Barbaresco, L. Yang, Riemannian medians and means with applications to radar signal processing, IEEE Journal of Selected Topics in Signal Processing 7 (4) (2013) 595–604.

20. M. Charfi, Z. Chebbi, M. Moakher, B.C. Vemuri, Bhattacharyya median of symmetric positive-definite matrices and application to the denoising of diffusion-tensor fields, in: Biomedical Imaging (ISBI), 2013 IEEE 10th International Symposium on, IEEE, 2013, pp. 1227–1230.

21. A. Bhattacharya, R. Bhattacharya, Statistics on Riemannian manifolds: asymptotic distribution and curvature, Proceedings of the American Mathematical Society 136 (8) (2008) 2959–2967.

22. D. Groisser, Newton's method, zeroes of vector fields, and the Riemannian center of mass, Advances in Applied Mathematics 33 (1) (2004) 95–135.

23. X. Pennec, Intrinsic statistics on Riemannian manifolds: basic tools for geometric measurements, Journal of Mathematical Imaging and Vision 25 (1) (2006) 127–154.

24. M. Moakher, A differential geometric approach to the geometric mean of symmetric positive-definite matrices, SIAM Journal of Matrix Analysis (SIMAX) 26 (3) (2005) 735–747.

25. R. Bhatia, Matrix Analysis, vol. 169, Springer Science & Business Media, 2013.

26. C.R. Rao, Differential metrics in probability spaces, Differential Geometry in Statistical Inference 10 (1987) 217–240.

27. P. Fletcher, S. Joshi, Riemannian geometry for the statistical analysis of diffusion tensor data, Signal Processing 87 (2) (2007) 250–262.

28. T. Ando, C.K. Li, R. Mathias, Geometric means, Linear Algebra and Its Applications 385 (2004) 305–334.

29. K.T. Sturm, Probability measures on metric spaces of nonpositive, in: Heat Kernels and Analysis on Manifolds, Graphs, and Metric Spaces: Lecture Notes From a Quarter Program on Heat Kernels,

Random Walks, and Analysis on Manifolds and Graphs, vol. 338, April 16–July 13, 2002, Emile Borel Centre of the Henri Poincaré Institute, Paris, France, 2003, p. 357.

30. Y. Lim, M. Pálfia, Weighted inductive means, Linear Algebra and Applications 453 (2014) 59–832.

31. J. Ho, G. Cheng, et al., Recursive Karcher expectation estimators and geometric law of large numbers, in: Proc. of the Conf. on Artificial Intelligence and Statistics (AISTATS), 2013, pp. 325–332.

32. H. Salehian, R. Chakraborty, E. Ofori, D. Vaillancourt, B.C. Vemuri, An efficient recursive estimator of the Fréchet mean on a hypersphere with applications to medical image analysis, Mathematical Foundations of Computational Anatomy (2015).

33. A. Feragen, S. Hauberg, M. Nielsen, F. Lauze, Means in spaces of tree-like shapes, in: Computer Vision (ICCV), 2011 IEEE International Conference on, IEEE, 2011, pp. 736–746.

34. M. Arnaudon, C. Dombry, A. Phan, L. Yang, Stochastic algorithms for computing means of probability measures, Stochastic Processes and Their Applications 122 (4) (2012) 1437–1455.

35. H.E. Cetingul, B. Afsari, et al., Group action induced averaging for HARDI processing, in: IEEE Intl. Symp. on Biomedical Imaging, 2012, pp. 1389–1392.

36. A.P. Dawid, et al., Further comments on some comments on a paper by Bradley Efron, The Annals of Statistics 5 (6) (1977) 1249.

37. J. Burbea, Informative Geometry of Probability Spaces, Tech. Rep., Pittsburgh Univ. PA Center for Multivariate Analysis, 1984.

38. D.C. Brody, L.P. Hughston, Statistical Geometry in Quantum Mechanics, Proceedings - Royal Society. Mathematical, Physical and Engineering Sciences 454 (1998) 2445–2475.

39. W.S. Kendall, Probability, convexity, and harmonic maps with small image I: uniqueness and fine existence, Proceedings of the London Mathematical Society 3 (1990), (2) 371–406.

40. B. Iversen, Hyperbolic Geometry, vol. 25, Cambridge University Press, 1992.

41. G. Amarasinghe, On the standard lengths of angle bisectors and the angle bisector theorem, Global Journal of Advanced Research on Classical and Modern Geometries 1 (1) (2012).

42. B. Afsari, R. Tron, et al., On the convergence of gradient descent for finding the Riemannian center of mass, SIAM Journal on Control and Optimization 51 (3) (2013) 2230–22605.

43. N.J. Sloane, et al., The On-line Encyclopedia of Integer Sequences, 2003.

44. R. Chakraborty, D. Seo, B.C. Vemuri, An efficient exact-PGA algorithm for constant curvature manifolds, in: Proceedings of the IEEE Conference on Computer Vision and Pattern Recognition, 2016, pp. 3976–3984.

45. Y. Xie, B.C. Vemuri, J. Ho, Statistical analysis of tensor fields, in: Medical Image Computing and Computer Aided Intervention (MICCAI), Springer, 2010, pp. 682–689.

46. D. Vaillancourt, M. Spraker, et al., High-resolution diffusion tensor imaging in the substantia nigra of de novo Parkinson disease, Neurology (2009) 1378–1384.
47. H. Salehian, D. Vaillancourt, B.C. Vemuri, IPGA: Incremental Principal Geodesic Analysis With Applications to Movement Disorder Classification, International Conference on Medical Image Computing and Computer-Assisted Intervention (MICCAI), vol. 17, NIH Public Access, 2014, p. 765.
48. J. Sun, Y. Xie, et al., Dictionary learning on the manifold of square root densities and application to reconstruction of diffusion propagator fields, in: Intl. Conf. on Info. Processing in Medical Imaging (IPMI), 2013, pp. 619–631.
49. B. Jian, B.C. Vemuri, A unified computational framework for deconvolution to reconstruct multiple fibers from DWMRI, IEEE Transactions on Medical Imaging (TMI) 26 (2007) 1464–1471, https://doi.org/10.1109/TMI.2007.907552.
50. Y. Deng, A. Rangarajan, S. Eisenschenk, B.C. Vemuri, A Riemannian framework for matching point clouds represented by the Schrödinger distance transform, in: IEEE Conference on Computer Vision and Pattern Recognition, 2014, pp. 3756–3761.
51. S. Helgason, Differential Geometry and Symmetric Spaces, vol. 12, Academic Press, 1962.
52. R. Chakraborty, M. Banerjee, D. Seo, S. Turner, D. Fuller, J. Forder, et al., An efficient recursive algorithm for atlas construction, Mathematical Foundations of Computational Anatomy (2015).

Statistics on stratified spaces

Aasa Feragen[a], Tom Nye[b]

[a]University of Copenhagen, Department of Computer Science, Copenhagen, Denmark. [b]Newcastle University, School of Mathematics, Statistics and Physics, Newcastle upon Tyne, United Kingdom

8.1 Introduction to stratified geometry

The majority of statistical methodology is built on the premise that the data being analyzed lie in a finite-dimensional vector space equipped with the Euclidean L^2 inner product. As seen in the other chapters of this book, there are important applications for which data in fact lie in a smooth manifold and for which work must be done to extend existing "linear" methodology to this new context. Instead, in this chapter we consider a different class of data spaces for which the structure of a smooth manifold is not available everywhere and for which the dimension of the space can vary from point to point. These *stratified spaces* have attracted interest from researchers in recent years, and examples of data lying in stratified spaces include trees [11,25,19], graphs [34], point sets such as persistence diagrams [56], objects invariant to a nontrivial group action (lying in a group quotient space) [43,38], and positive semidefinite matrices [29,55].

We will not give a general formal definition of a stratified space—more details can be found, for instance, in [51]—but instead illustrate the properties of such spaces and associated data analysis largely via examples. Indeed, existing statistical methods in stratified spaces generally make no use at all of the formal definition of a stratified space. This section describes three key toy examples before going on to survey definitions and results from metric geometry, which are necessary to understand the geometry of stratified spaces more generally. Although simple, the toy examples are highly illustrative of the unusual properties of data analysis in stratified spaces. Properties of least squares estimators are considered in more detail in Section 8.2, in particular, by considering the examples introduced in this section. In Sections 8.3 and 8.4 we describe the geometry of two related stratified spaces, the space of evolutionary trees with leaves labeled by a fixed set of species and a space of unlabeled trees. The final section goes be-

Riemannian Geometric Statistics in Medical Image Analysis
https://doi.org/10.1016/B978-0-12-814725-2.00016-9

yond trees to illustrate how other types of data may also be modeled as residing in a stratified space. Examples include graphs, point sets, sequences, and data invariant under nontrivial group actions. Some of these constructions are well known, whereas the others are new, coming with associated open problems.

8.1.1 Examples

Statistical models and estimators on stratified spaces can display strikingly different behavior than intuition suggests from working on linear Euclidean spaces. Many of these properties arise with the following fundamental simple examples.

Example 8.1 (Spiders). The k-spider consists of k copies of the positive real line $\mathbb{R}_{\geq 0}$ glued together at the origin. The metric is the Euclidean metric on each "leg" of the spider, extending in the obvious way to the whole space: given two points x, y on different legs, $d(x, y) = d(x, 0) + d(0, y)$. We use the notation Spider$_k$ to denote the k-spider. It is clear that for $k > 2$, the k-spider does not have the structure of a topological manifold: no chart can be defined at the origin. The set of tangent directions at the origin is not a vector space, but it is in fact a copy of the space itself.

Most of the examples we consider, like the k-spider, are formed by gluing pieces of the Euclidean space or other manifolds together along their boundaries. We will be deliberately informal about the operation of gluing two topological spaces X_1 and X_2, since the geometry of the resulting space does not depend on the technical details for all the examples we consider. However, formally we mean that two subsets of the spaces X_1 and X_2 are identified by a bijection (often an isometry when there are underlying metrics), and we then form the quotient of $X_1 \cup X_2$ where two points are equivalent if and only if they are identified under the bijection.

Example 8.2 (Open books). The open book of dimension $n + 1$ on k pages is Book$_k^n = \mathbb{R}^n \times$ Spider$_k$. The spine of the book is the subset $\mathbb{R}^n \times \{0\}$, and each page of the book is a subset $\mathbb{R}^n \times \mathbb{R}_{\geq 0}$. The metric is the product metric, and so is just the Euclidean metric on each page $\mathbb{R}^n \times \mathbb{R}_{\geq 0}$. The simplest open book has $n = 1$ and $k = 3$ and consists of three half-planes joined along their shared edge. Open books are stratified in the following way: the spine is an n-dimensional manifold that forms the boundary of the k pages, each of which is an $(n + 1)$-dimensional manifold with boundary. Each piece in this decomposition is a *stratum*, and the space consists of several strata glued together along lower-dimensional substrata.

The 3-spider parameterizes a certain set of trees and so forms a *tree space*. Consider the set of rooted trees with 3 leaves, which are labeled bijectively with the set $S = \{A, B, C\}$. There are three possible binary tree topologies and one "star" tree with no internal edges, shown in Fig. 8.1. If we further assume that internal edges are *weighted*, that is, assigned weights or lengths in $\mathbb{R}_{\geq 0}$, then Spider_3 parameterizes the corresponding set of tree objects: each "leg" of the spider corresponds to a different binary tree, and the position along the leg determines the weight assigned to the single internal edge of the tree. If *all* the edges are weighted, then the space is $\mathbb{R}_{\geq 0}^3 \times \text{Spider}_3 \subseteq \text{Book}_3^3$, and so open books parameterize certain sets of trees.

Example 8.3 (Cones). Let $\text{Cone}_{k\pi/2}$ denote the space formed by gluing together k copies of the positive quadrant $\mathbb{R}_{\geq 0}^2$ to form a cone, so that the origin is a common point in each quadrant and forms the point of the cone. An embedding of $\text{Cone}_{5\pi/2}$ in $\mathbb{R}^3$ is shown in Fig. 8.2. On each quadrant of $\text{Cone}_{k\pi/2}$ the metric is Euclidean, and the distance between points in different quadrants is the length of the shortest path between them, where the path consists of straight line segments in each quadrant. In contrast to spiders and open books, each cone $\text{Cone}_{k\pi/2}$ has the structure of a topological manifold. As a stratified space, $\text{Cone}_{k\pi/2}$ can be thought of as containing two strata, the origin and the complement of the origin. (An alternative stratification of $\text{Cone}_{5\pi/2}$ is by

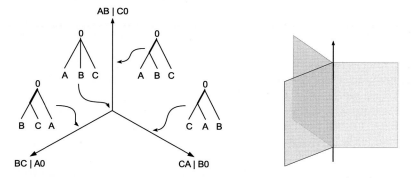

Figure 8.1 The 3-spider and open book. The space Spider_3 (left) consists of three copies of the positive real line joined together at the origin. It parameterizes the set of rooted trees with leaves A, B, C such that the internal edge has a positive weight or length. The position along the axis labeled with the bipartition $AB|C0$, for example, determines the length of the highlighted edge on the corresponding tree. The origin corresponds to a tree obtained by contracting the internal edge to length zero. The open book Book_3^1 is shown on the right.

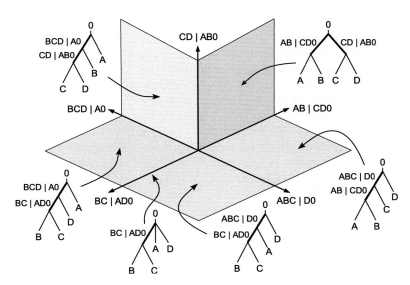

Figure 8.2 The 5-cone. An embedding of $\text{Cone}_{5\pi/2}$ in $\mathbb{R}^3$, annotated to show how the cone parameterizes a certain set of trees with 4 leaves. The space consists of 5 quadrants glued along their edges, where each quadrant corresponds to a different binary tree. Each binary tree has two weighted internal edges, and the weights determine the position within the quadrant. The trees contain 5 different internal edges, labeled as the corresponding axes in $\mathbb{R}^3$. The quadrant boundaries correspond to trees where an edge has been contracted to have zero weight, as shown for the axis $BC|AD0$.

tree topology.) As we will see, a notion of curvature can be defined for certain metric spaces. For $k = 1, 2, 3$, $\text{Cone}_{k\pi/2}$ is nonnegatively curved, whereas for $k > 4$, it is nonpositively curved.

The cone $\text{Cone}_{5\pi/2}$ parameterizes a certain set of trees, as shown in Fig. 8.2. This is a subspace of the space of all leaf-labeled weighted rooted trees on 4 leaves. More details are given in Section 8.3, which describes the *Billera–Holmes–Vogtmann* tree space [11], the space of edge-weighted trees on a fixed set of N labeled leaves. This stratified space has received the most attention to date in terms of the development of statistical methods due to its importance in evolutionary biology and its attractive geometric properties.

All three examples are metric spaces that fail to have the structure of a Riemannian manifold: spiders and open books are not topological manifolds, whereas the metric on any cone is singular at the origin. How then can we analyze data in these spaces or in more general stratified spaces? To answer this question, we recall various definitions and results from metric geometry. The following overview gives the essential background geometry, but a more complete account is given in [12].

8.1.2 Metric spaces

Suppose X is the space in which we want to develop our statistical methodology, and let d be a metric on X. It is easily seen that an arbitrary metric d does not itself give enough structure on X to develop any useful statistics. For example, the metric defined by $d(x, y) = 1$ for all $x \neq y$ and $d(x, x) = 0$ only tells us whether two data points are the same or not and so cannot be used to calculate any useful summary statistics. More structure on the space X is required, and so we consider paths in X and their associated lengths.

Definition 8.1 (Geodesics). A *geodesic* [12] in a metric space (X, d) is a path $\gamma: [0, 1] \to X$ such that for any $t, t' \in [0, 1]$, we have $d(\gamma(t), \gamma(t')) = |t - t'| \cdot d(\gamma(0), \gamma(1))$. The image of a geodesic γ is called a *geodesic segment* in X.

A path $\gamma: [0, 1] \to X$ is *locally geodesic* if there exists $\varepsilon > 0$ such that $d(\gamma(t), \gamma(t')) = |t - t'| \cdot d(\gamma(0), \gamma(1))$ whenever $|t - t'| < \varepsilon$.

Definition 8.2 (Geodesic spaces). (X, d) is called a *geodesic metric space* if there is at least one geodesic path between every pair of points in X. It is *uniquely geodesic* if there is exactly one geodesic between every pair of points.

The existence of geodesics is really fundamental to the development of statistics on a metric space X, just as in the case of Riemannian manifolds. However, it is also useful to assign lengths to arbitrary paths in X.

Definition 8.3 (Path length). If $c : [0, 1] \to X$ is a path in X, then the *length* of c is

$$\ell(c) = \sup_{a=t_0 \leq t_1 \leq \cdots \leq t_n = b} \sum_{i=0}^{n-1} d(c(t_i), c(t_{i+1}))$$

where the supremum is taken over all possible n and partitions of the interval $[0, 1]$. The length of c is taken to be infinite when this expression is unbounded.

The triangle inequality implies that $\ell(c) \geq d(c(a), c(b))$ for any path c. It follows from the definition of a geodesic γ on X that $\ell(\gamma) = d(\gamma(0), \gamma(1))$. Thus a geodesic is a shortest path connecting its endpoints. Conversely, a shortest path can always be parameterized as a geodesic. Many spaces have pairs of points with no shortest connecting path: for example, take $\mathbb{R}^2$ equipped with the Euclidean metric but with the origin removed. A point x cannot be joined to the antipodal point $-x$ by a path of length $2\|x\|$. A metric space (X, d) is called a *length space* if $d(x, y)$ is the infimum of lengths of paths connecting x and y for all $x, y \in X$. The Hopf–Rinow theorem states that any complete locally compact length space (X, d) is a geodesic metric space. The example of $\mathbb{R}^2$ without the origin is a length space, but it does not satisfy the conditions of the Hopf–Rinow theorem as it is not complete.

8.1.3 Curvature in metric spaces

We next turn attention to the idea of curvature in a geodesic metric space. The idea is to look at whether triangles are "fat" or "thin" compared to triangles in Euclidean space. We will denote by $\Gamma(x, y)$ a choice of a geodesic segment between $x, y \in X$. (Of course, if X is uniquely geodesic, then there is exactly one choice of a segment.) Given $p, q, r \in X$, a geodesic triangle $\Delta(p, q, r) \subseteq X$ is a choice of geodesic segments $\Gamma(p, q)$, $\Gamma(q, r)$, $\Gamma(r, p)$. A corresponding flat Euclidean triangle is required to draw comparisons. A triangle $\Delta' = \Delta(p', q', r')$ in $\mathbb{R}^2$ is a comparison triangle if

$$d(p, q) = d(p', q'), \quad d(q, r) = d(q', r'), \quad \text{and} \quad d(r, p) = d(r', p').$$

Such a triangle always exists in $\mathbb{R}^2$ (by applying the triangle inequality to Δ in X) and is unique up to isometries of $\mathbb{R}^2$. Given $x \in X$ on $\Gamma(p, q)$, a comparison point x' in Δ' is a point on $\Gamma(p', q')$ such that

$$d(x, p) = d(x', p') \quad \text{and} \quad d(x, q) = d(x', q').$$

We call (x, x') a *comparison pair* for the edge $\Gamma(p, q)$. We illustrate this in Fig. 8.3.

Geodesic metric spaces with nonpositive curvature play a very prominent role in the theory of statistics on stratified spaces. In order to have a nonpositive curvature, every geodesic triangle must

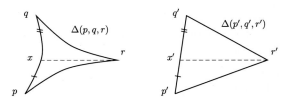

Figure 8.3 Comparison triangles. Comparing triangles in a geodesic metric space (left) and $\mathbb{R}^2$ (right).

be at least as "thin" as its Euclidean comparison triangle. This is made rigorous via the following definition of the so-called CAT(0) inequality.

Definition 8.4. A geodesic triangle $\Delta(p, q, r)$ satisfies the *CAT(0) inequality* if $d(x, r) \leq d(x', r')$ for all comparison pairs (x, x') with $x \in \Gamma(p, q)$ and $x' \in \Gamma(p', q')$, and similarly for all comparison pairs on the other two edges. The geodesic metric space X is a *CAT(0) space* if every geodesic triangle satisfies the CAT(0) inequality.

CAT(0) spaces, and more generally spaces that are locally CAT(0), are often called nonpositively curved spaces. They have a rich geometry, analogous to geometry on Riemannian manifolds, which lends them as very suitable spaces for developing statistical methods. There is an analogous definition of a CAT(κ) space for $\kappa \neq 0$, and these spaces can be thought of as having curvature $\leq \kappa$. Here comparison triangles are constructed not in the plane, but in a model space M_κ. For $\kappa < 0$, M_κ is a scaled version of the hyperbolic plane; for $\kappa > 0$, M_κ is a scaled version of the sphere S^2.

The name CAT(κ) comes from the concatenated initials of Cartan, Alexandrov, and Topogonov, pioneers in defining and understanding the notion of curvature for metric spaces [12]. In contrast, there is a definition of nonnegatively curved geodesic spaces due to Alexandrov [2]: X is nonnegatively curved if every geodesic triangle in the space is at least as "fat" as a comparison triangle in $\mathbb{R}^2$.

Referring back to our fundamental examples, it is straightforward to check that every triangle in a k-spider satisfies the CAT(0) inequality. Any product of two CAT(0) spaces is CAT(0), so since $\mathbb{R}^n$ is CAT(0), it follows that the open book Book_k^n is also CAT(0). More generally, a metric tree (X, d) is a tree where each edge has an isometry to an interval in $\mathbb{R}$, and such spaces are also CAT(0). On the other hand, when $k \leq 3$, the cone $\text{Cone}_{k\pi/2}$ is nonnegatively curved. Triangles in $\text{Cone}_{k\pi/2}$ that do not contain the origin in the interior are easily seen to be Euclidean triangles. However, triangles that wind around the origin have interior angles that add up to $> \pi$ and are "fatter" than Euclidean triangles. The origin is repulsive: the only geodesics that pass through the origin have an end point at the origin. We will consider cones with $k \geq 5$ later.

CAT(0) spaces have many appealing properties that help the development of statistical methods within the spaces. First, they are uniquely geodesic, so every pair of points in a CAT(0) space is joined by a unique geodesic. The geodesic segment $\Gamma(x, y)$ between x and y varies continuously as a function of x, y. Moreover, any locally geodesic path is in fact a geodesic path.

In addition to these attractive properties of geodesics, there is a notion of projection onto closed sets in CAT(0) spaces. If X is a CAT(0) space, then a function $f : X \to \mathbb{R}$ is convex if for any geodesic path $\gamma : I \to X$ parameterized proportional to length, the function $I \to \mathbb{R}$ defined by $t \mapsto f(\gamma(t))$ is convex. Given any $x \in X$, it can be shown that the distance function $d(\cdot, x) : X \to \mathbb{R}$ is convex. Similarly, the function $d(\cdot, \cdot)$ is convex on the product space $X \times X$. Now suppose that $A \subseteq X$ is convex and complete in the induced metric. (A subset $A \subseteq X$ is convex if $\Gamma(x, y) \subseteq A$ for all $x, y \in A$.) Then given any $x \in X$, there is a unique point $\pi(x) \in A$ closest to x:

$$\pi(x) = \operatorname{argmin}_{a \in A} d(a, x).$$

This is called the projection of x onto A. If A is closed but not convex, then a closest point in A to x exists, but it is not necessarily unique.

Cubical complexes are a rich source of examples of CAT(0) spaces and are defined in the following way. Let $I^n \subset \mathbb{R}^n$ be the unit cube $[0, 1]^n$ equipped with the Euclidean metric. The codimension-k faces of I^n correspond to fixing k coordinates on I^n to be either 0 or 1. A cubical complex is a metric space obtained by gluing together cubes (potentially of different dimensions) along their faces: a dimension-k face in one cube can be glued isometrically to one or more dimension-k faces in other cubes. Cubical complexes are thus analogous to simplicial complexes, but each cell is a unit cube rather than a simplex. A cubical complex X can be given a metric as follows. On each cube the metric is the Euclidean metric. More generally, the distance between $x, y \in X$ is defined to be the infimum of the lengths of paths between x and y that are straight line segments within each cube. When X is locally compact, then it is a geodesic metric space by the Hopf–Rinow theorem. Several spaces of trees and networks [11,28,16] are examples of cubical complexes, although the space of networks in [16] is not CAT(0).

Gromov [30] gave a combinatorial condition that specifies when a cubical complex is CAT(0). The condition is defined in terms of the *link* of each vertex in the complex. The link of a vertex v is the set $\{x \in X : d(x, v) = \varepsilon\}$, where $0 < \varepsilon < 1$ is a fixed constant. The link of v can be regarded as an abstract simplicial complex, and Gromov's condition is expressed purely in terms of the combinatorics of this object. Rather than state the condition precisely, we will illustrate it using the example $\mathrm{Cone}_{k\pi/2}$ for $k = 3$ and $k = 5$. The cones $\mathrm{Cone}_{k\pi/2}$ can be constructed as cubical complexes by filling each quadrant with an infinite array of 2-cubes (unit squares). For $k = 3$, the link of the origin consists of three quarter-circular arcs forming a loop. In order to be CAT(0), Gromov's condition states that the link must contain the 2-simplex bounded by this loop, but it does not, so the condition fails, and Cone$_{3\pi/2}$ is not CAT(0). On the other hand, when $k = 5$, the link of the origin consists of a loop formed from 5 quarter-circular arcs. Gromov's condition states that any simplex whose one-dimensional faces (quarter-circular arcs) are in the link must itself be in the link. Since the loop consists of 5 arcs rather than 3, it does not bound any 2-simplex, and so Gromov's condition is satisfied for the origin. It also holds for the other vertices in the cubical complex, and so Cone$_{5\pi/2}$ is CAT(0). We will consider Gromov's condition again when describing evolutionary tree space, but we next turn attention to least squares estimators.

8.2 Least squares models

In Euclidean space standard statistical methods, such as computation of sample means, linear regression, and principal component analysis, can be formulated as problems that minimize a least squares modeling error. Least squares errors generalize easily to metric spaces and have therefore been popular for building statistical models both on manifolds and metric spaces. In stratified spaces, however, least squares statistics have surprising and potentially unwanted properties [32,24].

8.2.1 Least squares statistics and stickiness

In this section we suppose that X is a geodesic metric space. Given a finite dataset $\{x_1, \ldots, x_n\} \subset X$, its Fréchet mean is defined as the point minimizing the sum of squared distances to the data points [36]:

$$\bar{x} = \operatorname{argmin}_{x \in X} \sum_{i=1}^{n} d(x_i, x)^2. \tag{8.1}$$

However, in stratified spaces, Fréchet means can be *sticky* [32]:

Definition 8.5 (Stickiness of Fréchet mean). The Fréchet mean $\bar{x}$ of a finite sample $\{x_1, \ldots, x_n\} \subset X$ is *sticky* if any sufficiently small perturbations $\{x_1', \ldots, x_n'\}$ of the sample also have mean $\bar{x} = \bar{x}'$.

An example [32] of a sticky Fréchet mean can be found on the 3-spider, as illustrated in Fig. 8.4. Three unit point masses are positioned on the 3-spider, one on each leg of the spider and unit

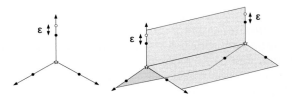

Figure 8.4 Sticky means and principal components. *Left:* The Fréchet mean (star-shaped point) of the dataset consisting of the black points on Spider$_3$ is sticky. *Right:* On the open book, the first principal component (the line connecting the two star-shaped endpoints) of the dataset consisting of the black points sticks to the spine of the book.

distance from the origin. These are shown as black dots in the figure. When one of the point masses is moved by distance ε away from the origin, the Fréchet mean (shown by a star on the figure) remains at the origin until $\varepsilon = 1$, at which point it moves on to the upper leg in Fig. 8.4 for $\varepsilon > 1$. In fact, the mean remains at the origin for all sufficiently small perturbations of the point masses. For more general stratified spaces, stickiness implies that the Fréchet means of sampled data tend to be located at lower-dimensional strata where three or more strata are joined, just as for the 3-spider. In the case of tree spaces such lower-dimensional strata correspond to trees where at least one node has degree ≥ 4.

A natural extension of the Fréchet mean is the first principal component. This can be defined if there is a notion of projection onto geodesics or, more generally, onto closed sets. It is denoted $PC1$ and is defined [44,46,21] as the geodesic segment $\gamma_{a_0 b_0}$ minimizing the sum of squared residual distances $E(a, b)$:

$$a_0, b_0 = \operatorname{argmin}_{a,b \in X} E(a, b), \quad \text{where } E(a, b) = \sum_{i=1}^{n} d(x_i, \operatorname{pr}_{\gamma_{ab}}(x_i))^2,$$

and $\operatorname{pr}_{\gamma_{ab}}(x_i)$ denotes the projection of x_i onto γ_{ab}. This definition is analogous to the definition of first principal component on manifolds due to Huckemann et al. [33], except for the restriction to geodesic segments, which is due to the problem of parameterizing geodesic rays in X [44,46,21].

Just like Fréchet means, first principal components can also be sticky:

Definition 8.6 (Stickiness of PC1). The first principal component $PC1$ for a finite sample in X *sticks* to a subset $S \subset X$ if the first principal component of any sufficiently small perturbation $\{x'_1, \ldots, x'_n\}$ of the sample also lies in S.

An example of stickiness for $PC1$ on the open book $\mathbb{R} \times \text{Spider}_3$ is given in Fig. 8.4, and it is a straightforward extension of the sticky mean example on the 3-spider. Here two data points are positioned on each sheet of the book, several units apart parallel to the spine. It is clear that $PC1 \subset S$ where S is the spine of the open book, and the same in fact holds for all small perturbations of the sample.

Stickiness of $PC1$ indicates that, just as for Fréchet means, first principal components in stratified spaces have a tendency to be contained in lower-dimensional strata, even when the data are contained in top-dimensional strata. This creates difficulties in building more advanced statistics: for instance, it is not clear how parallel transport along such principal components might be defined, which has consequences for extending techniques from manifold statistics to the open problem of defining second principal components.

8.2.2 The principal component and the mean

Stickiness is not the only surprising property of least squares statistics in stratified spaces. In Fig. 8.5 we give an example on the open book, where the Fréchet mean does *not* lie on the first principal component. In the figure the Fréchet mean lies on the spine. In the Euclidean space the Fréchet mean always lies on the first principal component; on curved manifolds, this is known not to be the case [33]. This has consequences for the definition and

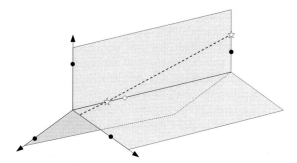

Figure 8.5 The principal component does not contain the mean. Let $\{x_1, x_2, x_3, x_4\}$ consist of the circular points in the figure. The Fréchet mean $\bar{x}$ is the open diamond, which sits on the spine. However, calculations show that $PC1$ is the dotted line segment connecting the two star-shaped points. It extends from the page of the book above the spine onto either of the lower two pages and is therefore not unique. The dotted line can be shown to give a lower least squares error than the geodesic running along the spine.

interpretation of the fraction of variance captured by a principal component, which is frequently used to measure the success of dimensionality reduction via PCA in the Euclidean space [46]. The definition of the fraction of variance relies on the Pythagorean theorem, and this breaks down in almost any non-Euclidean space.

8.3 BHV tree space

Stratified spaces naturally appear in many applications, and among the most investigated so far are spaces of *trees*. Tree spaces can be defined in different ways, leading to different models and geometries, and this chapter will visit two tree spaces in detail. The first, *BHV tree space* [11], assumes that all trees have the same fixed set of labeled leaves. This is a strong modeling assumption, which makes sense for the study of evolutionary trees where it was first defined, but which might be overly restrictive in other applications. The modeling cost does, however, come with strong computational advantages. The second tree space construction, which does *not* assume a fixed set of labeled leaves, will be discussed in Section 8.4.

Phylogenetic trees represent evolutionary relationships between a chosen set of biological species. The leaves of a phylogenetic tree, or *phylogeny*, represent present day species, whereas internal vertices represent speciation events when a population has differentiated into distinct subspecies. The edges in each tree are typically assigned a weight in $\mathbb{R}_{\geq 0}$, which represents the degree of evolutionary divergence along each edge. Trees can be either rooted or unrooted, and we will describe the space of phylogenetic trees in both cases. Phylogenetic trees are usually estimated from incomplete noisy data (often genetic sequence data in present-day organisms), and so it is natural to study distributions on the space of all possible phylogenies relating a fixed set of species. A geometry for this space was first described by Billera, Holmes, and Vogtmann [11], and the corresponding geodesic metric space has become known as the BHV tree space. The BHV tree space has been used to analyze sets of anatomical trees [21,52] and evolutionary trees. This section explains the geometry of the BHV tree space and reviews existing methods for analyzing sets of phylogenetic trees via BHV geometry.

8.3.1 Geometry in BHV tree space

Definition 8.7 (Unrooted phylogenetic tree). Suppose $S = \{1, \ldots, N\}$ is a fixed set of labels. (We sometimes let S be any set with N

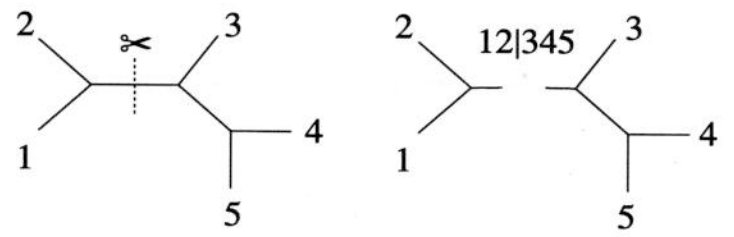

Figure 8.6 Edges and splits. Cutting an edge on a leaf-labeled tree (left) creates a bipartition, or split, of the labels (right). The terms *edge* and *split* are therefore used interchangeably.

elements.) An *unrooted phylogenetic tree* on S is an unrooted tree with N leaves satisfying the following conditions:
1. The leaves are bijectively labeled with the elements of S.
2. The edges are weighted by values in $\mathbb{R}_{\geq 0}$.
3. There are no vertices with degree 2.

Unrooted trees are important in evolutionary biology since it can be difficult to identify the position of the root, which represents a distant ancestor with any certainty. Phylogenetic trees are often represented graphically with edge lengths drawn in proportion to their weights, and so edge weights are often referred to as *lengths*. Any unrooted phylogeny on S contains at most $2N - 3$ edges, with the upper bound being attained when every nonleaf vertex has degree 3. Such trees are called *resolved* or *bifurcating* trees. However, trees can contain $< 2N - 3$ edges, in which case one or more vertices have degree > 3. These trees are called *unresolved*. The edges containing the leaves are called *pendant edges*. Conversely, *internal edges* and *internal vertices* are, respectively, edges that do not end in a leaf and vertices with degree ≥ 3. The collection of all unrooted phylogenies on S is denoted $\mathcal{U}_N$.

A *split* is a bipartition of S or, in other words, a decomposition of S as a union of two disjoint subsets $S = A \cup A^c$. Splits are often written using, for example, the notation 12|345 to represent $\{1, 2, 3, 4, 5\} = \{1, 2\} \cup \{3, 4, 5\}$. Given a tree $x \in \mathcal{U}_N$ and an edge e in x, cutting e disconnects x and yields a bipartition of the leaves, and so every edge is associated with a unique split. In fact, on labeled trees, edges and splits are entirely equivalent, as shown in Fig. 8.6, and so we will use the terms interchangeably in this section. The splits represented by a tree are called its *topology*. Equivalently, the topology of $x \in \mathcal{U}_N$ can be thought of as an unweighted *combinatorial tree*. Two splits $A|A^c$ and $B|B^c$ are called *compatible* if there exists at least one tree containing both splits. Examples of incompatible splits are easy to construct: 12|345 is not compatible with 13|245 since the corresponding edges cannot coexist in any tree. It can be shown that $A|A^c$ and $B|B^c$ are compatible if one of the sets $A \cap B$, $A \cap B^c$, $A^c \cap B$, $A^c \cap B^c$ is empty. Arbitrary sets of splits do not generally correspond to tree topologies due to incompatibility. The following theorem, due to Buneman [14], characterizes tree topologies.

Theorem 8.1 (Splits-equivalence theorem). *Any set of pairwise compatible splits that contains the splits* $\{1\}|\{1\}^c, \ldots, \{N\}|\{N\}^c$ *determines an unweighted tree on S.*

To describe the BHV tree space, we first consider the pendant edges. These are present in all trees, and so an unrooted tree space can be written as a product

$$\mathcal{U}_N = \mathbb{R}^N_{\geq 0} \times \mathrm{BHV}_N$$

where BHV_N parameterizes the internal edge lengths and topologies of unrooted trees on S. At this stage it is convenient to consider rooted trees on S formally. *Rooted* phylogenetic trees are defined in the same way as unrooted phylogenies, except that they contain a unique vertex labeled as the root. The root vertex has degree ≥ 2, with degree exactly 2 in fully resolved trees. By attaching an additional leaf labeled 0 to the root vertex via an unweighted edge, an unrooted phylogeny is obtained, but the leaf set is now labeled $\{0, 1, \ldots, N\}$. It follows that the collection of all rooted phylogenies on $S = \{1, \ldots, N\}$, denoted $\mathcal{T}_N$, is given by

$$\mathcal{T}_N = \mathbb{R}^N_{\geq 0} \times \mathrm{BHV}_{N+1}.$$

The space BHV_N can be described either by an embedding into a high-dimensional Euclidean space or, equivalently, by an intrinsic construction, and we consider both approaches. There are $M = 2^{N-1} - 1$ possible splits of S, of which $M - N$ correspond to internal edges on trees. To embed BHV_N in Euclidean space, we order these splits arbitrarily and then associate the ith split σ_i with the standard basis vector e_i in $\mathbb{R}^{M-N}$ for $i = 1, \ldots, M - N$. Every point $x \in \mathrm{BHV}_N$ can be represented by its vector of internal edge weights $\sum_i \lambda_i(x)e_i$ where

$$\lambda_i(x) = \begin{cases} \text{weight of split } \sigma_i \text{ in } x & \text{if } x \text{ contains } \sigma_i, \text{ or} \\ 0 & \text{if } \sigma_i \text{ is not contained in } x. \end{cases}$$

Arbitrary vectors in $\mathbb{R}^{M-N}$ do not generally correspond to trees, as arbitrary collections of splits do not give valid tree topologies. In fact there are $(2N - 5)!! = 1 \times 3 \times 5 \times \cdots \times (2N - 5)$ fully resolved unrooted topologies on N leaves, so the fully resolved trees occupy $(2N - 5)!!$ copies of $\mathbb{R}^{N-3}_{\geq 0}$ in $\mathbb{R}^{M-N}$. Hence the number of topologies and the dimension of the ambient space grow exponentially in N, whereas the local dimension of tree space grows linearly. The space BHV_4, corresponding to the unrooted trees on 4 leaves or (equivalently) rooted trees on 3 leaves has $M = 7$ different splits, and the embedding into $\mathbb{R}^{M-N} = \mathbb{R}^3$ consists of the three positive orthogonal axes. In other words, $\text{BHV}_4 = \text{Spider}_3$ as illustrated in Fig. 8.1.

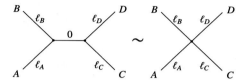

Figure 8.7 Trees are equivalent when zero weight splits are removed. Illustration of the equivalence relation in Eq. (8.2). Here A, B, C, D are subtrees, and ℓ_A, ℓ_B, ℓ_C, ℓ_D are the associated edge lengths. The internal edge in the tree on the left has length zero. The equivalence relation similarly applies when there are arbitrarily many subtrees either side of an internal edge.

Although the embedding into $\mathbb{R}^{M-N}$ can be used to give a complete description of the geometry of BHV_N, it is not useful computationally due to the sparsity of vectors representing trees. Instead, BHV_N can be constructed intrinsically in terms of an equivalence relation in the following way [42]. This description differs in some ways from the original BHV paper [11], but the explicit use of an equivalence relation and quotient makes the construction comparable to that for unlabeled trees in Section 8.4. The collection of trees $\mathcal{O}_T$ with some fixed fully resolved topology T can be parameterized by $\mathbb{R}_{\geq 0}^{N-3}$ by associating each internal edge in the topology with a coordinate axis. In fact we equip $\mathcal{O}_T$ with the induced Euclidean metric so that $\mathcal{O}_T \cong \mathbb{R}_{\geq 0}^{N-3}$ is an isometry. The same notation is used when T is unresolved: $\mathcal{O}_T \cong R_{\geq 0}^k$ when T contains k internal edges. Each set of trees $\mathcal{O}_T$ is called an *orthant*, and if T is fully resolved, then $\mathcal{O}_T$ is a *maximal orthant*. The BHV tree space is constructed by taking the disjoint union of all orthants and quotienting by an equivalence relation:

$$\text{BHV}_N = \bigcup_T \mathcal{O}_T \Big/ \sim, \qquad (8.2)$$

where the union is taken over all possible topologies. The equivalence relation $\sim$ is defined in Fig. 8.7. Under the relation, trees are identified if and only if they are identical modulo the presence of splits with zero weight. Thus, when an edge is contracted to length zero, it can equivalently be removed from the tree.

The equivalence relation glues orthants together to form BHV_N. Orthants corresponding to unresolved topologies are contained in the equivalence classes of elements contained in the boundary of maximal orthants. Maximal orthants are glued at their codimension-1 boundaries in a relatively simple way. If a single internal edge in a tree with fully resolved topology T is contracted to length zero and removed from the tree, then the result is a vertex of degree 4. There are then three possible ways to add in an extra edge to give a fully resolved topology, including the original topology T, so each codimension-1 face of $\mathcal{O}_T$ is glued to two other maximal orthants at their boundaries. It follows that near codimension-1 boundaries, BHV_N locally resembles Book_3^{N-4}. On the other hand, the tree containing no internal edges, called the *star tree*, corresponds to the origin in every set $\mathcal{O}_T$.

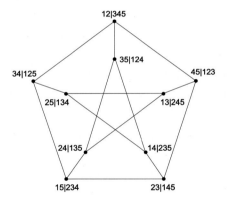

Figure 8.8 The Petersen graph. Vertices are drawn as dots, and other edge crossings do not correspond to graph vertices. Each vertex is labeled with a split and corresponds to the codimension-1 boundary between three quadrants in BHV_5. Each edge corresponds to the quadrant in BHV_5 comprising trees whose two internal edges are determined by the two splits at either end of the edge.

For $N = 5$, the embedding of BHV_5 into $\mathbb{R}^{M-N} = \mathbb{R}^{10}$ is difficult to visualize, but the intrinsic construction is more accessible. There are 15 different maximal orthants defined on 10 different internal splits. The graph representing attachments between codimension-1 faces of maximal orthants is a 3-valent graph with 10 vertices (one for each split) and 15 edges (one for each orthant) called the Petersen graph, illustrated in Fig. 8.8. Assuming that the graph is equipped with unit edge lengths, points on the graph are in one-to-one correspondence with the points in BHV_5 whose two internal edge weights sum to a fixed nonzero constant. In entirety, BHV_5 is the cone of the Petersen graph or, in other words, the set of rays (copies of $\mathbb{R}_{\geq 0}$) joined at their common origin and in one-to-one correspondence with points on the graph. The rays passing through a fixed edge of the Petersen graph form the quadrant associated with that edge. As shown by Fig. 8.8, the graph contains various cycles of length 5, each of which corresponds to an arrangement of 5 quadrants resembling Fig. 8.2. Similarly, in neighborhoods of vertices of the Petersen graph, the cone resembles $Book_3^1$.

It is straightforward to see that BHV_N is a cubical complex: each maximal orthant is an infinite array of unit $(N-3)$-cubes, and the structure of the complex is determined by the way cubes are glued together at their boundaries according to the unresolved trees they represent. Since each cube is glued to a finite number of other cubes, the space is locally compact, and the Hopf–Rinow theorem implies that BHV_N is a geodesic metric space. Billera, Holmes, and Vogtmann [11] proved that BHV_N is CAT(0) by showing that Gromov's condition for cubical complexes holds, as discussed in Section 8.1. Gromov's condition corresponds exactly to the condition that pairwise compatible collections of splits determine valid tree topologies, as established in Theorem 8.1. Since BHV_N is CAT(0), the product spaces $\mathcal{T}_N$ and $\mathcal{U}_N$ of rooted and unrooted trees are also CAT(0).

By definition, if two points $x, y \in BHV_N$ lie in the same orthant, then the geodesic segment $\Gamma(x, y)$ between them is simply the straight line segment within the orthant. When the points x, y lie in different orthants, the geodesic comprises straight line segments in different orthants joining x to y. Along each geodesic, x is continuously deformed into y by contracting and expanding various edges. One possibility for the geodesic between points in different orthants is that it consists of the straight line segment from x to the origin and then the straight line segment from the origin to y. This is the path given by contracting all internal edges in x to length zero, to give the star tree, followed by expanding out all the edges in y. This is called the *cone path* between x and y. Cone paths are geodesics for certain points $x, y \in BHV_N$, and the length of the cone path provides an upper bound on the length of the geodesic segment $\Gamma(x, y)$. Geodesics on $\mathcal{T}_N$ and $\mathcal{U}_N$ are the obvious trivial product between the geodesics in $\mathbb{R}_{\geq 0}^N$ for the pendant edges and the geodesics in BHV_N.

Fig. 8.9 shows three geodesics in $\mathcal{T}_4$. All three occupy orthants on a single copy of $Cone_{5\pi/2}$, and the figure shows the different types on geodesic that can occur on $\mathcal{T}_4$. Depending on the endpoints, some geodesics are cone paths, in which case there is a "kink" at the origin. Examples like this on $\mathcal{T}_4$ and $\mathcal{U}_5$ give the impression that unresolved topologies are isolated points along geodesics. Fig. 8.10 gives an example in $\mathcal{U}_6$ where this is not the case. Geodesics on $\text{Cone}_{5\pi/2}$ can be thought of via a physical analogy. Suppose you construct an object like the squares in Fig. 8.9 out of some rigid board. A piece of elastic string can be stretched between any two points on this object. The string acts to minimize its length and gives an approximate geodesic. As you move the end-points of the string around, it is easy to see that it will tend to catch on the origin, so that the geodesic is a cone-path. In fact, this is a characteristic of tree space caused by the non-

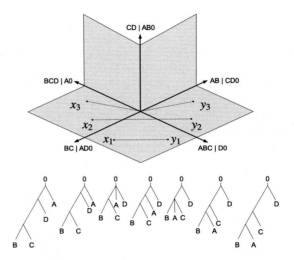

Figure 8.9 Geodesics on $\mathcal{T}_4$. Three geodesics drawn in a copy of $\text{Cone}_{5\pi/2}$ within tree space (dashed lines). The geodesic $\Gamma(x_1, y_1)$ is the line segment in one orthant. $\Gamma(x_2, y_2)$ traverses three orthants by expanding and contracting edges: representative trees along the geodesic are shown below. The geodesic $\Gamma(x_3, y_3)$ is a cone path: both internal edges are contracted to length zero with alternative edges then expanding out.

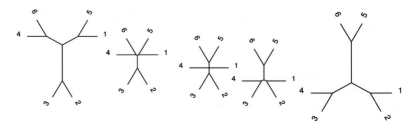

Figure 8.10 Trees along a geodesic in $\mathcal{U}_6$. The unresolved topology displayed by the central tree is not an isolated point along the geodesic: the section of the geodesic in the corresponding nonmaximal orthant has length strictly greater than zero.

positive curvature: geodesics have a tendency to move through high-codimension regions.

Whereas the existence and uniqueness of geodesics on tree space follow as a result of BHV_N being CAT(0), it took a number of years following the original paper by Billera–Holmes–Vogtmann for a computationally efficient algorithm for constructing geodesics to emerge. Given the exponential number of orthants in tree space, computing geodesics could potentially be nonpolynomial. However, Owen and Provan [47] developed a remarkable $O(N^4)$ algorithm for constructing geodesics, which forms the basis of most of the methods described further. It operates by finding a maximum flow on a certain bipartite graph whose two vertex sets correspond to the splits in the two trees being connected. It can be thought of via the physical analogy of "tightening the string" between two points, like the example on the cone above, where the imaginary string is initiated as a cone path.

Before turning attention to existing statistical methodology in BHV tree space, we mention generalizations and related spaces. In the BHV tree space, edges are assigned positive weights. However, arbitrary values in $\mathbb{R}$ or even elements of some vector space can also be used as the set of possible edge weights [26]. In this case, orthants are replaced with products of vector spaces, glued together at points where vectors are zero.

Retaining the assumption that edge weights are positive reals, three spaces related to the BHV tree space have been studied. The first is the subspace of trees for which the sum of all edge lengths is some fixed constant [61]. This space is also CAT(0), but it is not a cubical complex; as yet, there is no exact algorithm for computing geodesics. Another space of trees of interest to biologists comprises equidistance trees, namely rooted phylogenies for which all leaves are at the same distance from the root. Gavryushkin and Drummond [28] considered two different geometries on this space, one of which consists of a CAT(0) cubical complex. Finally, Devadoss and Petti [16] have described a space of certain phylogenetic networks, which are generalizations of trees. This is a cubical complex, but it is not CAT(0).

8.3.2 Statistical methodology in BHV tree space

Throughout this section we assume that $D = \{x_1, \ldots, x_n\}$ is a sample of trees in either $\mathcal{T}_N$ or $\mathcal{U}_N$.

8.3.2.1 Fréchet mean and variance

Although biologists have defined and computed the mean of a sample D in a variety of ways, it is natural to consider the Fréchet mean $\bar{x}$ of D, defined in Eq. (8.1). If d is the largest distance between two points in D, and r is the distance between the origin and the furthest point, then any x that minimizes the Fréchet variance lies in the ball centered at the origin and with radius $d + r$. As the tree space is CAT(0), the Fréchet function $\sum_i d(x, x_i)^2$ is convex in x and so attains a unique minimum within this ball. It follows that the Fréchet sample mean of D exists and is unique.

An algorithm originally due to Sturm [54], later extended and modified by other authors [9,42], has been used for computing the Fréchet mean and variance in the BHV tree space. The algorithms work in an iterative way, maintaining some estimate μ of $\hat{x}$. At each iteration a data point x_i is selected either deterministically or by sampling from D, the geodesic from the current estimate μ to x_i is constructed, and μ is replaced with a point a certain proportion along this geodesic. Although the algorithms are guaranteed to converge to $\bar{x}$, convergence can be slow in practice. Bačák's algorithms [9] are able to incorporate a weight for each data point in D and can also be used to compute sample medians. Methods for minimizing the Fréchet function within a fixed orthant by making use of the local differentiable structure have also been developed [53]. Owen and Brown [13] have carried out a simulation study to investigate behavior of the Fréchet mean for samples from particular distributions of interest to biologists.

Asymptotic results have also been established for the Fréchet mean in a tree space under the limit of increasing sample size [6, 5]. These reflect the "stickiness" of the estimator, as described in Section 8.2. The asymptotic distribution of the sample mean consists of various Gaussian distributions on orthants, and in some situations nonmaximal orthants can have strictly positive mass corresponding to stickiness.

An example of a mean tree computed with the Sturm algorithm [54,42] is shown in Fig. 8.11. Here the tree is formed by the centerlines passing through the tubular airway tree in the lung, segmented from chest CT scans [40], as originally presented in [21]. To model the airway trees using the BHV tree space, they are labeled using the automatic airway labeling algorithm of [22, 26], and the tree is cut off below the segment branches. Each branch of the tree is represented by five equidistant 3D landmark points, leading to 15-dimensional edge attributes (which is an easy extension of the BHV tree space, as remarked on p. 317). The mean was computed from 8016 airway trees from the Danish Lung Cancer Screening Trial [49].

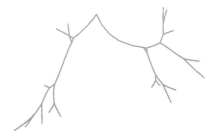

Figure 8.11. The mean airway centerline tree computed from a population of 8016 labeled airway centerline trees.

Note that the mean tree does not have any nodes with degree higher than 3. This indicates that the mean tree sits in the top-dimensional orthant of the BHV tree space and that it does not display sticky behavior. This lack of stickiness indicates that the population of trees is topologically relatively homogeneous but does *not* mean that the airway trees all have the *same* topology; actually, the dataset contains 1385 distinct topologies. However, about a third of the airway trees are contained in the 10 most frequent topologies, and more than 800 topologies only contain a single tree. Moreover, given the relatively fixed structure of airway trees, we expect different topologies to be quite similar to each other. These facts together explain why the mean airway tree is *not* sticky.

8.3.2.2 Principal component analysis

Principal component analysis (PCA) is a widely used method for exploratory analysis and dimension reduction of high-dimensional data sets. It operates by identifying the main directions or modes of variation in a sample of vectors by eigen-decomposition of the associated sample covariance matrix. As such, it inherently relies on the linear structure of the sample space, but the analysis can be reexpressed in a number of different, though equivalent, ways. In particular, PCA is equivalent to fitting affine subspaces to the data in such a way as to minimize the sum of the squared distances of the data points from their projections onto each subspace. In a Euclidean space this amounts to finding the Fréchet mean (the zeroth-order component), then a line of best fit to the data (the first principal component), then a plane of best fit, and so on. In a Euclidean space the affine subspaces are necessarily nested, so, for example, the first principal geodesic passes through the Fréchet mean.

A best-fit geodesic is a natural analog in tree space to the Euclidean first principal component. Nye [44] first considered PCA in tree space, presenting an algorithm for constructing geodesics of best fit, constrained to pass through some choice of mean tree. The algorithm works by firing geodesics forward from the mean with a greedy search to identify the optimal direction in which to fire. Golden ratio search is used to project data points onto candidate geodesics. The class of geodesics explored by this approach as candidates is limited by the constraint of passing through a given fixed mean, and as shown in Section 8.2.2, in a tree space the principal geodesic does not necessarily contain the Fréchet mean. Furthermore, in a tree space it is more natural to consider finite geodesic segments rather than infinitely long geodesic lines as principal components, since many infinite lines can share the same best-fit geodesic determined by the data. As an extreme example, consider the situation where all the data points are tightly clustered within the interior of a maximal orthant. Conventional PCA could be used to construct a principal line within the orthant, but there would be many ways to extend this beyond the orthant into tree space. In view of this, Feragen et al. [21] fitted finite geodesics to data by searching over geodesic segments whose end points were taken from the data set D. Examples can be constructed where such geodesics fit poorly in comparison to an unconstrained geodesic [62]. The constraint on the end points was subsequently dropped [46] by employing a stochastic search algorithm to vary the end points in tree space and search for the geodesic segment of best fit.

Construction of higher-dimensional objects in a tree space to act as analogs of Euclidean principal components proved challenging. For example, the convex hull of three points in a tree space, a natural candidate for a second-order principal component, can have dimension strictly greater than 2. Examples of convex hulls in a tree space with "wrong" dimension in comparison to a Euclidean space were first constructed by Sean Skwerer (personal communication). Details of a similar example based on his construction can be found in [45]. As an alternative to the convex hull, Nye et al. [45] considered the locus of the weighted Fréchet mean of three given points as the weights vary over the standard simplex. Also known as *barycentric subspaces* [50], these objects have the correct dimension, although they are not necessarily convex. It is possible that other analogs of PCA could be developed in a tree space in the future, for example, with different objects playing the role of higher-dimensional components, potentially a nested version of PCA, or via some probabilistic model.

Figure 8.12. Airway trees sampled at 5 equidistant locations along the first principal component of the 8016 airway centerline trees, as computed in [21].

Fig. 8.12 shows five sampled trees along the first principal component of the same 8016 airway centerline trees as used in Fig. 8.11. The principal component was computed using the algorithm from [21]. We see the airways from two different views to emphasize the development throughout the principal component, which appears to capture breathing motion. Note that some of the trees along the principal component *do* contain a single node of degree 4, which indicates that the principal component partly runs along a codimension-1 stratum in the BHV tree-space.

8.3.2.3 Other approaches

The preceding methods all rely on least squares estimation, but a few methods have been developed in the BHV tree space that take a different approach. First, Weyenberg et al. [59,58] used Gaussian kernels in a tree space to identify outliers in data sets. Gaussian kernels have density functions of the form $f(x) \propto \exp(d(x, x_0)^2/\sigma^2)$ where $d(\cdot, \cdot)$ is the BHV metric, x_0 is a point in a tree space representing the mode of the distribution, and σ is a dispersion parameter. The normalizing constant for these kernels is challenging to compute, and various computational approximations were employed. Second, Willis [60] developed analysis via projection onto a tangent space based at the Fréchet mean by an analog of the Riemannian log-map. Here the log-map is used to represent trees as points in a vector space in which existing Euclidean statistical methods can be applied. In [52] a set of brain artery trees were mapped to points in the BHV tree space, and the data set was analyzed by a variety of methods, including construction of the Fréchet mean, multidimensional scaling, and minimal spanning trees. Finally, Chakerian and Holmes [15] presented a method for evaluating how close a data set comes to lying on a tree within a tree space (a "tree of trees") in addition to various methods based on multidimensional scaling.

8.4 The space of unlabeled trees

Although the BHV tree space has the advantage of CAT(0) geometry and polynomial-time algorithms for computing geodesics, it comes with the assumption that all trees have the same labeled set of leaves. In many applications, including most anatomical trees, this assumption does not hold. In this section we review the space of unlabeled trees (tree-like shapes) as defined in [25]. Versions of this space have been used to study airway trees from human lungs [25], blood arteries on the surface of the heart [31], and neuronal trees [19].

As we will see further, the geometry of the space of unlabeled trees is more complicated than the geometry of the BHV tree space. Among other things, geodesics are not generally unique, and the curvature is not generally bounded. As a result, most research has so far gone into algorithms or heuristics for computing geodesics [25,31,19] and analysis that only requires geodesics or their lengths, such as labeling [31], clustering, and classification [19]. Heuristic "means" have been proposed in place of the Fréchet mean [20], but these are not exact. To study more complex statistics, a better understanding of tree space geometry is needed. This section contributes to that by giving a thorough definition of the space of unlabeled trees and linking its geodesics to geodesics in BHV tree space. We use this link to prove that for two points sampled from a natural class of probability distributions, their connecting geodesic is almost surely unique. Such uniqueness of geodesics is important for geometric statistical methods to be well-defined.

8.4.1 What is an unlabeled tree?

Unlabeled trees are represented as pairs $(T, \mathbf{x})$ consisting of a *combinatorial tree* T and a *branch attribute map* $\mathbf{x}$, where T plays a role similar to the tree topology in Section 8.3. A combinatorial tree is a triple $T = (V, E, r)$ where V is a vertex set, E is an edge set such that the resulting graph is connected and does not have cycles, and $r \in V$ is a designated root vertex. Edges are undirected, so that the vertex pairs (u, v) and (v, u) define the same edge in E. Given an edge $e \in E$, any other edge $e' \in E$ on the path from e to r is said to be *above* e. If e' is above e, then we say that e is *below* e'. Parent, child, and sibling relationships between edges can be similarly defined using the root.

A branch attribute map is a mapping $\mathbf{x} \colon E \to A$ associating with each edge $e \in E$ an edge attribute $\mathbf{x}(e) \in A$, where A is called the edge attribute space. In all our applications, A will contain a 0 element, which represents a *contracted* branch. Through contracted

Figure 8.13 The supertree and the effect of 0-**valued edge attributes.** The supertree T must be large enough to span all trees of interest. It can represent smaller trees using 0-valued attributes to represent contracted branches. This allows representation of higher-order vertices but also results in multiple equivalent representations of unlabeled trees, as shown on the right.

branches we can represent many different unlabeled trees using the same combinatorial tree, and we can also represent higher-order vertices using a binary combinatorial tree as in Fig. 8.13. This leads us to define *minimal* representations of unlabeled trees: A representation $(T, \mathbf{x})$ with combinatorial tree $T = (V, E, r)$ is *minimal* if $\mathbf{x}(e) \neq 0$ for all $e \in E$. Given an unlabeled tree representation $(T, \mathbf{x})$, we denote by $(\hat{T}, \hat{\mathbf{x}})$ its minimal representation with $\hat{T} = (\hat{V}, \hat{E}, \hat{r})$ and $\hat{\mathbf{x}} = \mathbf{x}|\hat{E}$, where $\hat{T}$ is obtained from T by contracting all edges that have 0 attribute.

An unlabeled tree is *spanned* by the combinatorial tree T if it can be represented as a pair $(T, \mathbf{x})$. Two unlabeled trees $(T_0, \mathbf{x}_0)$ and $(T_1, \mathbf{x}_1)$ are *equivalent*, denoted $(T_0, \mathbf{x}_0) \sim (T_1, \mathbf{x}_1)$, if for their minimal representations $(\hat{T}_0, \hat{\mathbf{x}}_0)$ and $(\hat{T}_1, \hat{\mathbf{x}}_1)$, there exists a tree isomorphism $\phi \colon \hat{T}_0 \to \hat{T}_1$ such that if $\phi_{\hat{E}} \colon \hat{E}_0 \to \hat{E}_1$ is the restriction of ϕ to edges, then $\hat{\mathbf{x}}_1 \circ \phi_{\hat{E}} = \hat{\mathbf{x}}_0$. Finally, we define an *unlabeled tree* as an equivalence class $x = [(T, \mathbf{x})]$.

In some applications, such as retinal vessels [41] or coronary arteries [31], the tree might actually reside on a surface and therefore have a natural planar order. This can be encoded by requiring the tree isomorphism ϕ to be an isomorphism of ordered trees, resulting in ordered unlabeled trees.

Example 8.4 (Edge attributes). The edge attribute space A can be designed to encode application-dependent branch properties. The branch length is encoded using $A = \mathbb{R}_{\geq 0}$, and to encode branch geometry via landmarks (Fig. 8.14), set $A = (\mathbb{R}^N)^n$. Here a branch is described by n landmark points $x(e) = (x^0, x^1, x^2, \dots, x^n)$ $\in \{0\} \times (\mathbb{R}^N)^n$. The first landmark is typically translated to the origin $(x^0 = 0)$ and left out of the analysis. Branch geometry can also be encoded via curves, giving $A = C^r(I, \mathbb{R}^N)$, the family of C^r curves. A version of this is used in [19].

Most results in this chapter assume that A is a finite-dimensional vector space (or its positive orthant) with metric given by the Euclidean norm.

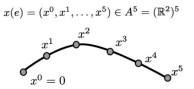

$$x(e) = (x^0, x^1, \ldots, x^5) \in A^5 = (\mathbb{R}^2)^5$$

Figure 8.14 Branch geometry via landmarks. A simple model for branch geometry is obtained by representing the edge e by a set of n equidistant landmark points $x(e) \in (\mathbb{R}^N)^n$.

Definition 8.8 (The space of unlabeled trees). Fix a (possibly infinite) binary combinatorial tree T that is sufficiently large to span all the unlabeled trees of interest; we will henceforth refer to T as the *supertree*; see Fig. 8.13. The space

$$X = \prod_{e \in E} A = \{\mathbf{x} \colon E \to A\}$$

of all branch attribute maps $\mathbf{x}$ on E contains all possible representations $(T, \mathbf{x})$ of unlabeled trees spanned by T. As shown in Fig. 8.13, some unlabeled trees have multiple representations (T, x), and we construct the space of trees spanned by T as the quotient of X with respect to the equivalence $\sim$ defined before:

$$\mathfrak{X} = X/\sim.$$

This definition covers both a space of *ordered* unlabeled trees and a space of *unordered* unlabeled trees, as accounted for in the definition of the equivalence $\sim$.

The identifications made by the equivalence induce singularities in the tree space $\mathfrak{X}$. The metric on X induces a quotient metric [12] on $\mathfrak{X}$, called the *QED metric* (short for quotient Euclidean distance, as the original metric used on X was Euclidean).

As opposed to the BHV tree space, not much is known about the geometry of $\mathfrak{X}$. The following theorem summarizes what we *do* know.

Theorem 8.2. (Geometry and topology of $\mathfrak{X}$ [25]).
  i) *The tree space $\mathfrak{X}$ with the QED metric is a contractible complete proper geodesic space.*
  ii) *At generic points $x \in \mathfrak{X}$, the tree space $\mathfrak{X}$ is locally $CAT(0)$.*
  iii) *There exist $x_0, x_1 \in \mathfrak{X}$ with more than one geodesic connecting them.* □

Due to the far more complex geometry of $\mathfrak{X}$, the computational tools and statistics in $\mathfrak{X}$ are far less developed than in the BHV tree space. Computing geodesics is NP complete [23], but some heuristics have appeared [31].

8.4.2 Geodesics between unlabeled trees

In this section we describe a previously unpublished relation between BHV geodesics and QED geodesics, which hints at a potential algorithm for computing or approximating geodesics in $\mathfrak{X}$. Additionally, we use this relation to prove the almost sure uniqueness of geodesics between pairs of points in $\mathfrak{X}$. Throughout the section, we will analyze an unlabeled tree $x \in \mathfrak{X}$ via its minimal representation $(\hat{T}, \hat{\mathbf{x}})$ with minimal combinatorial tree $\hat{T} = (\hat{V}, \hat{E}, \hat{r})$.

8.4.2.1 Mappings, geodesics, and compatible edges

A tree space geodesic from x_0 to x_1 in $\mathfrak{X}$ carries with it an identification of subsets of the corresponding edge sets $\hat{E}_0$ and $\hat{E}_1$. A *mapping* [10] between $\hat{T}_0$ and $\hat{T}_1$ is defined as a subset $M \subset \hat{E}_0 \times \hat{E}_1$ such that for any two $(a, b), (c, d) \in M \subset \hat{E}_0 \times \hat{E}_1$, we have

 i) $a = c$ if and only if $b = d$, and

 ii) a is an ancestor of c if and only if b is an ancestor of d.

The mapping M identifies subsets of $\hat{E}_0$ and $\hat{E}_1$ in the sense that if the pair of edges $(a, b) \in \hat{E}_0 \times \hat{E}_1$ is in the subset $M \subset \hat{E}_0 \times \hat{E}_1$, then the edge a from $\hat{T}_0$ is identified with the edge b from $\hat{T}_1$. In view of this, condition i) is a 1–1 identification condition on the edges; the edge a from $\hat{T}_0$ can only be identified with a single edge in $\hat{T}_1$ and vice versa. Condition ii) ensures that when all unidentified edges are contracted, the identification is a tree isomorphism between $\hat{T}_0$ and $\hat{T}_1$.

Given two trees $x_0, x_1 \in \mathfrak{X}$ and a mapping M between their minimal combinatorial trees $\hat{T}_0$ and $\hat{T}_1$, we say that a pair of unmapped edges $(e_0, e_1) \in \hat{E}_1 \times \hat{E}_2 \setminus M$ are *compatible* with M if $M \cup (e_0, e_1)$ is also a mapping between $\hat{T}_0$ and $\hat{T}_1$. A single unmapped edge $e_0 \in \hat{E}_0 \setminus \mathrm{pr}_{\hat{E}_0} M$ is *compatible* with the mapping M if $\hat{T}_1$ can be transformed into a tree $\hat{T}_1'$ by adding a zero-attributed edge e_1' so that $M \cup (e_0, e_1')$ is a mapping between $\hat{T}_0$ and $\hat{T}_1'$. Compatibility with M of a single unmapped edge $e_1 \in \hat{E}_1 \setminus \mathrm{pr}_{\hat{E}_1} M$ is defined analogously.

A path $\gamma : [0, 1] \to \mathfrak{X}$ from $x_0 = \gamma(0)$ to $x_1 = \gamma(1)$ naturally induces a mapping $M \subset \hat{E}_0 \to \hat{E}_1$: If the edge $a \in \hat{E}_0$ is identified with the edge $b \in \hat{E}_1$ by the path γ as illustrated in Fig. 8.15, then $(a, b) \in M$, and vice versa. The *unmapped edges compatible with the mapping* are edges that do not "disturb" the shortest path as-

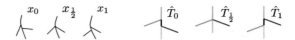

Figure 8.15 Incompatible edge. A geodesic γ from x_0 to x_1 induces a mapping between the minimal combinatorial trees $\hat{T}_0$ and $\hat{T}_1$ as indicated by colors. The black edges are unmapped and incompatible with the mapping. In γ the black edge from $\hat{T}_1$ cannot appear until the black edge from $\hat{T}_0$ has been contracted.

sociated with M, where length is measured with respect to the QED metric. In the shortest path from x_0 to x_1 associated with M such edges will appear or disappear at one of the geodesic endpoints, shrinking to or growing from 0 at constant speed throughout the path. The *unmapped edges incompatible with the mapping* are edges from $\hat{T}_0$ that, in the shortest path associated with M, will have to disappear before other edges from $\hat{T}_1$ can appear, or edges from $\hat{T}_1$ that cannot appear before other edges from $\hat{T}_0$ have disappeared. See Fig. 8.15 for an example.

In the QED metric the order and speed of edge deletions and additions in a tree space path affect the length of the path. In particular, a path will, when possible, be shorter if it continuously performs two branch deformations simultaneously rather than first performing one and then the other. Thus, to find a QED geodesic, it is not enough to know which branches will be identified and which branches appear and disappear throughout the geodesic. That is, it is not enough to know the mapping. We also need to know at which point in the geodesic the branches will appear/disappear.

8.4.2.2 Link between QED geodesics and BHV geodesics

Consider two unlabeled trees x_0 and x_1, and let $\gamma : [0, 1] \to \mathfrak{X}$ be a geodesic from x_0 to x_1 with mapping $M \subset \hat{E}_0 \times \hat{E}_1$ between the minimal representations $\hat{T}_0$ and $\hat{T}_1$.

Definition 8.9 (Subtrees spanned by a mapping). The subtrees $\tilde{x}_0$ and $\tilde{x}_1$ spanned by the mapping M are the subtrees of x_0 and x_1 obtained by removing all edges *below* the edges from $\hat{T}_0$ and $\hat{T}_1$ that appear in M. More precisely, $\tilde{x}_0 = (\tilde{T}_0, \tilde{\mathbf{x}}_0)$, where $\tilde{T}_0 = (\tilde{V}_0, \tilde{E}_0, \tilde{r}_0 = \hat{r}_0)$, is the combinatorial tree obtained by keeping all those vertices and edges from $\hat{T}_0$ that are found on the path from the root $\hat{r}_0$ to some edge in $\text{pr}_{\hat{E}_0}(M)$. The branch attribute mapping is defined by the restriction $\tilde{\mathbf{x}}_0 = \hat{\mathbf{x}}_0|\tilde{E}_0$. The subtree $\tilde{x}_1$ of x_1 is defined similarly. The remaining edges are collected in residual edge sets $R_i = \hat{E}_i \setminus \tilde{E}_i$, and attributed residual edge sets $r_i = (R_i, \mathbf{x}_i|R_i)$, $i = 0, 1$. See Fig. 8.16.

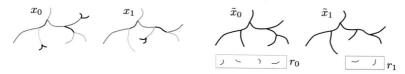

Figure 8.16 Subtrees spanned by a mapping. The mapping indicated on the left spans the subtrees $\tilde{x}_0$ and $\tilde{x}_1$ shown on the right, leaving the residual edge sets r_0 and r_1.

We now show that there is a leaf labeling of the subtrees $\tilde{x}_0$ and $\tilde{x}_1$ spanned by the mapping M, such that the geodesic γ decomposes as a product of a BHV geodesic between the leaf-labeled $\tilde{x}_0$ and $\tilde{x}_1$, and constant-speed interpolations between the origin and the attributed residual sets r_0 and r_1, respectively.

Consider M as a subset of $\tilde{E}_0 \times \tilde{E}_1$; then M is a mapping from $\tilde{T}_0$ to $\tilde{T}_1$. Each leaf in $\tilde{T}_0$ is mapped to a leaf in $\tilde{T}_1$, so by arbitrarily labeling the leaves in $\tilde{T}_0$ there is a labeling of the leaves in $\tilde{T}_1$ with the same labels, which is consistent with the mapping: If $(a, b) \in M$ where a and b are both leaves, then b is given the same label as a. The trees $\tilde{T}_0$ and $\tilde{T}_1$ might contain nodes of order 2, in which case a labeled "ghost" leaf with zero attribute is added at the node to raise its order. It may be necessary to add the corresponding ghost edges and leaves in the other tree as well. Assume that the number of leaves in $\tilde{T}_0$ and $\tilde{T}_1$ is N; now the trees $\tilde{T}_0$ and $\tilde{T}_1$ can be considered as trees in the BHV tree space $\mathcal{T}_N$ (with edge attribute set A; see p. 317). The geodesic γ restricts to a map $\tilde{\gamma} : [0, 1] \to \mathcal{T}_N$ which takes $\tilde{x}_0$ to $\tilde{x}_1$; this is a geodesic in $\mathcal{T}_N$:

Theorem 8.3. *A geodesic $\gamma : [0, 1] \to \mathfrak{X}$ from x_0 to x_1 in $\mathfrak{X}$ decomposes as a BHV geodesic between $\tilde{x}_0$ and $\tilde{x}_1$, and Euclidean geodesics from r_0 to 0 and from 0 to r_1. In particular:*

i)   All edges in R_0 and R_1 are compatible with the mapping M.

ii) All leaves in $\tilde{T}_0$ are mapped with leaves in $\tilde{T}_1$.

iii) The map $\tilde{\gamma} = pr_{\mathcal{T}_N} \circ \gamma$ is a geodesic in the BHV space $\mathcal{T}_N$.

iv) Denote by $\mathfrak{R}_0 = \prod_{R_0} A$ and $\mathfrak{R}_1 = \prod_{R_1} A$; now $pr_{\mathfrak{R}_i} \circ \gamma : [0, 1] \to \mathfrak{R}_i$ for $i = 1, 2$ are constant-speed parameterizations of straight lines in $\mathfrak{R}_i$, the first from r_0 to 0 and the second from 0 to r_1.

For the proof, we need the following well-known lemma on product geodesics.

Lemma 8.1. [12, Chapter I, Proposition 5.3] *Let A and B be geodesic metric spaces, and let $A \times B$ have the metric $d^2 ((a_1, b_1), (a_2, b_2)) = d_A^2 (a_1, a_2) + d_B^2 (b_1, b_2)$. Now a path $\gamma : [0, 1] \to A \times B$ is a geodesic if and only if it is a product of geodesics $\gamma_A : [0, 1] \to A$ and $\gamma_B : [0, 1] \to B$, that is, $\gamma = (\gamma_A, \gamma_B) : [0, 1] \to A \times B$.* $\qquad \square$

We are now ready to prove Theorem 8.3.

Proof. (Proof of Theorem 8.3) i) This holds because R_i consists of subtrees rooted at leaves in $\tilde{T}_i$, and such subtrees can be mapped onto ghost subtrees in the other tree. ii) This follows from the definition of a mapping: A leaf e_0 in $\tilde{T}_0$ cannot be mapped to a nonleaf edge e_1 in $\tilde{T}_1$, whereas some other edge e_0' in $\tilde{T}_0$ is mapped to the child of e_1 in $\tilde{T}_1$. iii)–iv) The geodesic γ must necessarily correspond to some path μ in $\mathcal{T}_N \times \mathfrak{R}_0 \times \mathfrak{R}_1$, and the length of γ in $\mathfrak{X}$ is the same as the length of μ in $\mathcal{T}_N \times \mathfrak{R}_0 \times \mathfrak{R}_1$. Reversely, for any other path $\tilde{\mu}$ in $\mathcal{T}_N \times \mathfrak{R}_0 \times \mathfrak{R}_1$, there is a corresponding path γ' in $\mathfrak{X}$ of the same length. Thus the geodesic γ must correspond to a geodesic μ in $\mathcal{T}_N \times \mathfrak{R}_0 \times \mathfrak{R}_1$. However, a geodesic in $\mathcal{T}_N \times \mathfrak{R}_0 \times \mathfrak{R}_1$ consists precisely of a BHV geodesic in $\mathcal{T}_N$ and straight Euclidean lines in $\mathfrak{R}_0$ and $\mathfrak{R}_1$ by Lemma 8.1. $\square$

The significance of Theorem 8.3 is that it hints at an algorithm for computing QED geodesics by searching over all possible leaf labelings of the two unlabeled trees $x_0, x_1 \in \mathfrak{X}$. For each leaf mapping, we can compute the corresponding BHV geodesic between the corresponding $\tilde{x}_0, \tilde{x}_1$ and the interpolation between the corresponding attributed residual edge sets. Combining these, we can form the corresponding path in $\mathfrak{X}$, where the shortest possible such path is indeed the geodesic. Although such an algorithm is still NP complete due to the search over all possible leaf labelings, we might be able to utilize heuristics for tree matching to reduce the search space in practice.

8.4.3 Uniqueness of QED geodesics

Although we have just seen that geodesics in $\mathfrak{X}$ decompose into products of BHV geodesics and Euclidean interpolations in $\mathfrak{R}_1$ and $\mathfrak{R}_2$, this does *not* indicate that $\mathfrak{X}$ is a product of $\mathcal{T}_N$ and a Euclidean space. The leaf-number N for $\mathcal{T}_N$, the assignment of leaf labels, and the residual spaces $\mathfrak{R}_1$ and $\mathfrak{R}_2$ all on the two unlabeled trees x_0 and x_1. Nevertheless, we can use the previous result to prove uniqueness results for geodesics in $\mathfrak{X}$. First, note that such geodesics in $\mathfrak{X}$ are not *generally* unique:

Example 8.5. Consider the simple case of the tree space spanned by the combinatorial tree T with two edges rooted at the root vertex, representing two geometric trees x_0 and x_1 with one edge each and with branch attributes $\mathbf{x}_0(e_1) = (0, 1) \in \mathbb{R}^2$ and $\mathbf{x}_1(e_2) = (1, 0)$. There are now two geodesics from x_0 to x_1 in $\mathfrak{X}$: one that maps the two edges onto each other and one that does not.

However, we show that for a natural family of probability distributions, two independently sampled trees almost surely have a unique connecting geodesic.

Any measure μ on X can be pushed forward to a measure $\mu_\sharp(Y) = \mu(\phi^{-1}(Y))$ on $\mathfrak{X}$ through the quotient map $\pi \colon X \to \mathfrak{X}$. Thus in the case where the edge attribute space A is a Euclidean space (or orthant), we can endow $\mathfrak{X}$ with the push-forward of the Lebesgue measure on X. We now state the main theorem of this section.

Theorem 8.4 (Main theorem). *Assume that the edge attribute space A is Euclidean or a Euclidean orthant, and let f be any probability density distribution on $\mathfrak{X}$ with respect to the push-forward of the Lebesgue measure on X. If x_0 and x_1 are independently sampled from f, then with probability 1, there is a unique geodesic connecting x_0 and x_1.*

Note that in Theorem 8.4 the probability density function f exists whenever the corresponding probability measure is absolutely continuous with respect to the push-forward of the Lebesgue measure, ensuring that positive probability mass does not concentrate on the cut locus where pairs of points can have multiple geodesics.

To prove Theorem 8.4, we need to link unlabeled tree-space geodesics to BHV geodesics by assigning artificial "leaf labels" to select subsets of edges that will play the role of leaves.

Definition 8.10 (Leaf mapping). Given a mapping M between combinatorial trees T_0 and T_1, and subtrees $\tilde{T}_0$ and $\tilde{T}_1$ spanned by the mapping M, define

$$M_L = \{(e_0, e_1) \in M \mid e_0 \text{ is a leaf in } \tilde{T}_0, \text{ and } e_1 \text{ is a leaf in } \tilde{T}_1\}.$$

We call M_L the *leaf mapping* associated with the mapping M (and, when relevant, with the geodesic γ whose mapping is M).

Our proof relies on the following observations.

Lemma 8.2. *Assume that x_0 and x_1 are sampled independently from f, where f is any probability density distribution on $\mathfrak{X}$ with respect to the push-forward of the Lebesgue measure on X.*

  (i) *Note that although every geodesic in $\mathfrak{X}$ induces a mapping M and thus a leaf mapping M_L, there may be several mappings $M_1, \ldots, M_k$, not all associated with geodesics, that give the same leaf mapping M_L.*

  (ii) *For any leaf mapping M_L, there is almost surely a unique shortest path from x_0 to x_1 associated with the leaf mapping*

as follows: The leaf mapping defines leaf-labeled subtrees $\tilde{x}_0$ and $\tilde{x}_1$ of x_0 and x_1, respectively, as before. Associated with the leaf-labeled subtrees $\tilde{x}_0$ and $\tilde{x}_1$, there is a BHV geodesic $\tilde{\gamma}$ and residual spaces $\mathfrak{R}_0$ and $\mathfrak{R}_1$, which give rise to a path γ from x_0 to x_1; this is the shortest possible path from x_0 to x_1 with the given leaf mapping M_L associated with it.

(iii) *There are finitely many possible leaf mappings $(M_L)_i$, $i = 1, \ldots, N$, between the trees x_0 and x_1, which almost surely give rise to N shortest possible paths γ_i from x_0 to x_1 in $\mathfrak{X}$ with that given leaf mapping.*

(iv) *Associated with the $(M_L)_i$ and their associated shortest paths γ_i, there are finitely many possible distances $d_1, \ldots, d_N$ between x_0 and x_1. It is possible that $d_i = d_j$ for different i, j, for instance, if the geodesic is not unique.*

(v) *Among the possible paths γ_i, $i = 1, \ldots, N$, enumerated in (iii), the shortest one(s) will be the geodesic(s) between x_0 and x_1. Among the possible distances d_i in (iv), the smallest distance $\min\{d_1, \ldots, d_N\}$ is the QED distance between the unlabeled trees x_0 and x_1.*

Proof. (i) If the subtrees spanned by the leaf mapping M_L do not have degree 2 vertices, then there is only one (maximal) mapping M with leaf mapping M_L. But if one of the subtrees, say $\tilde{x}_0$, spanned by the mapping *has* a degree 2 vertex, then there may be more than one way to add ghost vertices and edges to obtain a tree whose internal vertices have degree ≥ 3. (ii) If the subtrees spanned by the leaf mapping M_L do not have degree 2 vertices, then there is a unique corresponding geodesic and mapping. If one of the subtrees *has* a degree 2 vertex, then there will only be more than one shortest path (and corresponding mapping) if there are different equal-cost ways of matching the edges adjacent to the degree 2 mapping and the added ghost subtree to the corresponding edges and subtrees in the other tree. This will only happen if permutations of matched edges give the same total difference, which can only happen on a subset of measure 0. (iii) Follows from (ii). (iv) Trivial. (v) Follows from Theorem 8.3. $\square$

In a similar way as Theorem 8.3, we have the following:

Lemma 8.3. *Let γ be a geodesic from x_0 to x_1 in $\mathfrak{X}$ with a corresponding mapping M, and assume that $(e_0, e_1) \in M$, that is, the edge e_0 in $\hat{T}_0$ is matched to the edge e_1 in $\hat{T}_1$ by the geodesic. Let $x_c(e_0)$ denote the child subtree of x_0 rooted at the end of e_0, and let $x_p(e_0)$ denote the remaining subtree of x_0 after removing e_0 and its child subtree $x_c(e_0)$. Similarly for x_1 and e_1. Then γ can also be rep-*

resented as a product

$$\gamma = (\gamma_1, \gamma_2, \gamma_3) \colon I \to \mathfrak{X} \times A \times \mathfrak{X},$$

where γ_1 is the shortest path from $x_c(e_0)$ to $x_c(e_1)$ respecting the restriction of M, γ_2 is the straight line from $\mathbf{x}(e_0)$ to $\mathbf{x}(e_1)$ in A, and γ_3 is the shortest path from $x_p(e_0)$ to $x_p(e_1)$ respecting the restriction of M. In particular, the length of γ in $\mathfrak{X}$ is the same as the length of $(\gamma_1, \gamma_2, \gamma_3)$ in $\mathfrak{X} \times A \times \mathfrak{X}$.

We are now ready to start the proof of Theorem 8.4. Suppose that x_0 is any tree in $\mathfrak{X}$ where no two nonzero edges have the same attribute. Denote by W_{x_0} the set of trees x_1 in $\mathfrak{X}$ such that there are at least two distinct geodesics γ_a and γ_b in $\mathfrak{X}$ connecting x_0 to x_1. If we can show that the set $\mathfrak{X} \setminus W_{x_0}$ is open and dense in $\mathfrak{X}$, then we have proven Theorem 8.4, since the measure on $\mathfrak{X}$ is the push-forward of the Lebesgue measure.

Lemma 8.4. *The complement $\mathfrak{X} \setminus W_{x_0}$ is open.*

First, note that for the set Δ of trees x_1 where at least two branches have identical attributes, its complement $\mathfrak{X} \setminus \Delta$ is open and dense in $\mathfrak{X}$. It is thus enough to show that $\mathfrak{X} \setminus (W_{x_0} \setminus \Delta)$ is open and dense in $\mathfrak{X}$, since the intersection of two open and dense sets is dense, and $\mathfrak{X} \setminus W_{x_0} \supset (\mathfrak{X} \setminus (W_{x_0} \setminus \Delta)) \cap (\mathfrak{X} \setminus \Delta)$.

Next, assume that $x_1 \in W_{x_0} \setminus \Delta$. We are going to show that for any $\varepsilon > 0$ the ball $B(x_1, \varepsilon)$ intersects $\mathfrak{X} \setminus W_{x_0}$. Since $x_1 \in W_{x_0}$, there are two distinct geodesics γ_a and γ_b from x_0 to x_1 in $\mathfrak{X}$. Let M_a and M_b be the corresponding mappings between $\hat{E}_0$ and $\hat{E}_1$, and denote by $\hat{E}_1^a = \mathrm{pr}_{\hat{E}_1}(M_a) \subset \hat{E}_1$ and $\hat{E}_1^b = \mathrm{pr}_{\hat{E}_1}(M_b) \subset \hat{E}_1$ the sets of edges in x_1 identified with some edge in x_0 by γ_a and γ_b, respectively. We divide the proof into two cases.
Case I: $\hat{E}_1^a = \hat{E}_1^b$, and
Case II: $\hat{E}_1^a \neq \hat{E}_1^b$.

Proof of Case I. In this case, since $\gamma_a \neq \gamma_b$, there must be some edge e_1 in $\hat{E}_1^a = \hat{E}_1^b$ onto which two *different* edges e_0^a and e_0^b in $\hat{E}_0$ are mapped by $(M_L)_a$ and $(M_L)_b$, respectively. The two source edges have different edge attributes $\mathbf{x}_0(e_0^a)$ and $\mathbf{x}_0(e_0^b)$ by the assumption of the theorem, and e_1 has edge attribute $\mathbf{x}_1(e_1)$. □

Lemma 8.5. *For any $\varepsilon > 0$, we can find an unlabeled tree x_1' with the same minimal combinatorial tree as x_1 such that $d(x_1, x_1') < \varepsilon$ and the number of geodesics from x_0 to x_1' is at most $p - 1$, where p is the number of geodesics from x_0 to x_1.*

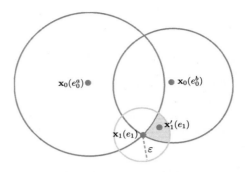

Figure 8.17 Finding x_1'. Since $\mathbf{x}_0(e_0^a) \neq \mathbf{x}_0(e_0^b)$, it is possible to find some $\mathbf{x}_1'$ such that the inequalities in Eqs. (8.3) and (8.4) are satisfied.

Proof. By Lemma 8.2 there are (almost surely) finitely many leaf mappings between x_0 and x_1, denoted $(M_L)_1, \ldots, (M_L)_N$, with corresponding shortest possible paths $\gamma_1, \ldots, \gamma_N$ of lengths $l_1, \ldots, l_N$. We may assume that $l_1 = l_2 = \cdots = l_p < l_{p+1} \leq \cdots \leq l_N$. The length of a geodesic from x_0 to x_1 is thus l_1. Without loss of generality, and possibly swapping a and b, we may assume that $\varepsilon < l_{p+1} - l_1$. As illustrated in Fig. 8.17, since $\varepsilon > 0$, we can find an attribute map $\mathbf{x}_1' : E_1 \to A$ such that $\mathbf{x}_1' | \hat{E}_1 \setminus \{e_1\} = \mathbf{x}_1 | \hat{E}_1 \setminus \{e_1\}$ and

$$\|\mathbf{x}_1'(e_1) - \mathbf{x}_1(e_1)\| < \varepsilon, \tag{8.3}$$

whereas

$$\|\mathbf{x}_0(e_0^a) - \mathbf{x}_1(e_1)\| < \|\mathbf{x}_0(e_0^a) - \mathbf{x}_1'(e_1)\| \text{ and}$$
$$\|\mathbf{x}_0(e_0^b) - \mathbf{x}_1(e_1)\| > \|\mathbf{x}_0(e_0^b) - \mathbf{x}_1'(e_1)\|. \tag{8.4}$$

Denote by x_1' the unlabeled tree whose edge attribute map is $\mathbf{x}'$. Note that the leaf mappings $(M_L)_a$ and $(M_L)_b$ can be transferred to the pair (x_0, x_1') since x_1' has the same tree topology as x_1. This induces two paths γ_a' and γ_b' from x_0 to x_1' that are the shortest possible paths with the corresponding leaf mappings $(M_L)_a$ and $(M_L)_b$. By Lemma 8.3 and Eq. (8.4) the length $l(\gamma_b')$ of γ_b' satisfies

$$l(\gamma_b')^2 = l(\gamma_b)^2 + \|\mathbf{x}_0(e_0^b) - \mathbf{x}_1'(e_1)\|^2 - \|\mathbf{x}_0(e_0^b) - \mathbf{x}_1(e_1)\|^2 < l(\gamma_b)^2,$$

so $l(\gamma_b') < l(\gamma_b)$. Now we see that the shortest path from x_0 to x_1' corresponds to a leaf mapping M_L that also gives a shortest path from x_0 to x_1.

To see this, let γ_c' be the geodesic from x_0 to x_1', with leaf mapping $(M_L)_c$; we then have $l(\gamma_c') \leq l(\gamma_b')$. The leaf mapping $(M_L)_c$ also generates path γ_c from x_0 to x_1 that is the shortest possible with leaf mapping $(M_L)_c$. We now have

$$
\begin{aligned}
l(\gamma_c) &\le l(\gamma_c') + d(x_1', x_1) < l(\gamma_c') + \varepsilon < l(\gamma_c') + (l_{p+1} - l_1) \\
&\le l(\gamma_b') + (l_{p+1} - l_1) \\
&< l(\gamma_b) + (l_{p+1} - l_1) = l_1 + (l_{p+1} - l_1) < l_1 + l_{p+1} - l_1 = l_{p+1},
\end{aligned}
$$

so we must necessarily have $l(\gamma_c) = l_1$, that is, γ_c is a shortest path from x_0 to x_1.

As a consequence, there are no new geodesic-generating leaf mappings between x_0 and x_1', which were not geodesic-generating between x_0 and x_1. Thus the number of shortest paths from x_0 to x_1' is at most $p - 1$, where p is the number of shortest paths from x_0 to x_1. This concludes the proof of Lemma 8.5. $\quad\square$

By repeatedly using Lemma 8.5 we see that for any $\varepsilon > 0$, there is a tree x_1' with $d(x_1, x_1') < \varepsilon$ and a unique geodesic from x_0 to x_1', which proves Case I.

Proof of Case II. We must have $|\hat{E}_1^a| = |\hat{E}_1^b|$ by the definition of a mapping; therefore we may assume (by symmetry) that $e_1 \in \hat{E}_1^a \setminus \hat{E}_1^b$; that is, there exists $e_0 \in \hat{E}_0$ that is identified with $e_1 \in \hat{E}_1^b$ by γ_b, whereas e_0 is not identified with any edge in $\hat{E}_1$ by γ_a. Let $t_0 \in [0, 1]$ be the time at which the zero-attributed edge corresponding to e_1 appears in the geodesic γ_a. Let $x_{t_0}^b(e_0)$ be the attribute associated with the edge mapped from e_0 to e by γ_b at time t_0. Find an attribute map $x_1' \colon \hat{E}_1 \to \mathbb{R}^N$ such that $\mathbf{x}_1'|\hat{E}_1 \setminus \{e_1\} = \mathbf{x}_1|\hat{E}_1 \setminus \{e_1\}$ and $\|\mathbf{x}_1'(e_1) - \mathbf{x}_1(e_1)\| < \varepsilon$, whereas

$$
\|(\mathbf{x}')_{t_0}^a(e_0) - \mathbf{x}_1(e_1)\| < \|\mathbf{x}_{t_0}^a(e_0) - \mathbf{x}_1'(e_1)\| \quad \text{and} \quad \|\mathbf{x}_1(e_1)\| > \|\mathbf{x}_1'(e_1)\|.
$$

Now γ_b' is shorter than γ_a', and, in particular,

$$
\begin{aligned}
l(\gamma_b') &\le d(x_0, x_{b,t_0}) + d(x_{b,t_0}, x_1') < d(x_0, x_{b,t_0}) + d(x_{b,t_0}, x_1) \\
&= d(x_0, x_1) = l(\gamma_b).
\end{aligned}
$$

The second inequality holds by Lemma 8.3. The proof wraps up as in Case I. $\quad\square$

8.5 Beyond trees

A tree space is so far a stratified data space that has seen the most attention, both in theoretical developments and in applications that perform statistical analysis in the stratified space (as opposed to reducing the data to Euclidean features). This is most likely caused in part by the availability of efficient code for computing BHV geodesics [47] and in part the availability of tree-structured data [1].

However, a number of other applications generate data with combinatorial properties that are modeled well using stratified spaces. We further discuss a few examples, some of which have seen some analysis, and some which are yet unexplored.

8.5.1 Variable topology data

Stratified spaces are well suited for modeling data with variable topological structure, as we have already seen in the case of trees. This idea generalizes also to other examples.

Example 8.6 (Graphs). Graph-structured data are often represented using adjacency matrices. An adjacency matrix representing a directed graph with n vertices is an $n \times n$ matrix M such that the entry M_{ij} contains a scalar or vector attribute that describes the directed edge from vertex i to vertex j and the entry M_{ii} describes the vertex i. Undirected graphs are given by symmetric matrices, and graphs with different sizes can be represented as fixed-size $n \times n$ adjacency matrices by entering empty (ghost) vertices described by zero attributes, just like the unlabeled trees from Section 8.4. Such an approach is used by Jain and Obermayer [34], who build a space of attributed graphs as a quotient of the space of adjacency matrices on n vertices, where vertex permutations are factored out. In their graph-space the zero attribute M_{ij} denotes a situation where there is no edge connecting the edges i and j, as in Fig. 8.18(A, top). A similar space of attributed graphs was also studied recently by Kolaczyc et al. [39], reproducing several results from [34].

In the space of attributed graphs from [34] the zero edge attribute corresponds to "no edge", as in Fig. 8.18(A, top). Within such a model, Jain and Obermayer develop theory for statistics and machine learning such as means and medians, clustering, and classification using Lipschitz optimization on the quotient, which is computationally efficient. However, this model does not accommodate continuous edge lengths well: In the case where the "shape" of a graph is simply described by the lengths of edges, we obtain converging sequences as illustrated in Fig. 8.18(B, top), where a sequence of cycles with one decreasing edge converges to a "line" graph with four vertices on it. To accommodate edge lengths, we might prefer a length 0 branch to be a contracted one, as shown in Fig. 8.18(A, bottom). This would imply identification of vertices, which has a drastic impact on the geometry of the space of graphs, which in the top case is a quotient with respect

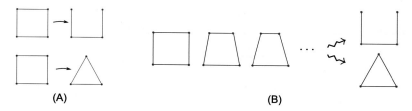

(A)   (B)

Figure 8.18 Challenges when building a space of graphs. Having edge attribute 0 can be used to model either no branch (a, top) or a contracted edge, causing vertices to melt together (A, bottom). This choice drastically affects limits of sequences (B).

to the permutation group as introduced in [34], but which in the bottom case is not.

Another example of variable topology data is given by *point sets*, which can be used to represent a wide variety of data objects.

Example 8.7. A *point set* is a finite set $\{x_1, \ldots, x_n\} \subset X$ of points in a geodesic metric space X. We denote by $\mathcal{P} = \{\{x_1, \ldots, x_n\} \subset X \mid n \in \mathbb{N}\}$ the space of point sets of arbitrary cardinality. Geometric objects can be specified by point clouds or landmark points, where exact correspondence between the point sets for different objects is traditionally required [38]. However, this does not always make sense, for example, if there is occlusion or missing annotations, if the landmark points correspond to nonexistent physical attributes, or if the landmark points represent geometric features such as high curvature, rather than specific physical attributes. Other examples of point set data include objects tracked over time or over different 2D slices of a 3D object. Persistence diagrams [56] are a particular case of point sets, where the points lie above the diagonal in the positive orthant of $\mathbb{R}^2$. In persistence diagrams the diagonal itself represents an arbitrary number of "dummy" points to which points from another persistence diagram can be matched, in effect constituting a quotient space in which all points on the diagonal are identified. Returning to point sets in general, by imposing an order on the point sets we obtain *sequences*, where examples include spike trains, time series, and other discrete signals [3,35].

There are different ways to interpolate between point sets with variable cardinality, and different modeling choices lead to different "point set spaces". In case of occlusion or missing labels it is natural to introduce "dummy" points, which can be matched to points that exist in one object but not in the other. This is similar to the 0 attributed edges in the space of graphs. A different modeling choice could be to allow points to merge together. This would, for instance, make sense when tracking cells over time, which might divide.

In every example encountered in this chapter a data space can be built as follows: Consider data objects belonging to a discrete set of topologies $\mathcal{T} = \{T_i : i \in I\}$. These topologies could be different: different tree topology, different graph structures, different point set cardinality, or something else entirely. Restricting analysis to the set X_i of data objects that have the fixed topology T_i, we apply known techniques: Trees, graphs, and point sets with a fixed topology are represented as fixed-length vectors or matrices, to which standard Euclidean or manifold statistics can be applied. Including all the different topologies in $\mathcal{T}$, we obtain a disjoint union $X = \dot{\bigcup} X_i$ of spaces where different topologies are represented, but where we cannot yet interpolate between points in different subspaces X_i. Ultimately, we interpolate between different topologies by realizing that, as with the trees, the boundary of each fixed-topology stratum X_i consists of data whose topology is a degeneration of the topology found in X_i and thus topologically different. We join the different X_i when their degenerated boundary topologies coincide, just like with the trees in Sections 8.3 and 8.4.

8.5.2 More general quotient spaces

For all the previous examples, different topologies are bridged by identifying different representations of the same degenerated topologies along stratum boundaries. As with trees, this can be thought of as creating a quotient $X/\sim$, where $x \sim x'$ whenever x and x' are two different representations of the same point in two different strata.

This quotient space approach extends beyond topological variation, for example, to the case of symmetric positive definite (SPD) matrices. SPD matrices are frequently encountered data objects representing, for example, diffusion tensors [7,4,27,8,18] or covariance descriptors [57]. Any SPD matrix Σ can be interpreted as the covariance of a centered normal distribution whose shape is characterized by its eigenvalues and whose orientation is characterized by its eigenvectors. Note that whenever all eigenvalues are distinct, the eigenvectors (orientations) are unique up to sign change, whereas when two or more eigenvalues coincide, the eigenvectors are no longer unique (corresponding to rotational symmetry of the normal distribution). This leads to a stratification of the set of eigenspace decompositions of $n \times n$ SPD matrices [29], where the stratification corresponds to the eigenvalue multiplicities.

Both the topologically variable data and the SPD matrices are quotient spaces with respect to equivalences. A particularly well-understood type of equivalence is defined by belonging to the same group action orbit. For instance, Kendall's shape space is a quotient of $(\mathbb{R}^d)^n$ with respect to the group of rotations, translations, and rescaling, and the space of attributed graphs is a quotient of the space of adjacency matrices with respect to the node permutation group. Group quotients appear when we seek invariance with respect to a group action; invariant properties are properties that can be defined on orbits rather than on data points. However, unless the group action is particularly nice (and often it is not), group quotients are not generally smooth. For instance, Kendall's shape space [38] has singularities, and these singularities correspond to changes in the diffeomorphism class of the group orbit at the singularity. Other variants of shape space, such as projective shape space, have also been studied as stratified data spaces [37,48]. When a Lie group acts properly on a smooth manifold, the quotient is a stratified space, stratified by orbit type, and the stratification can be helproofful in understanding the geometric, computational, and statistical properties of the quotient [29].

Although imposing invariants means that one is actually working on a quotient space, geometric statistics is not always phrased as a problem on a quotient. Moreover, when it *has* been phrased as a statistical problem on a quotient, it has not typically been acknowledged that noise in the data might *not* live on the quotient. This is the topic of recent work [43,17], which shows that statistics on quotients can be biased by these modeling choices. It is still unknown whether this can be interpreted through stratified (singular) space geometry.

8.5.3 Open problems

Stratified spaces have many attractive properties from the modeling point of view. They allow continuously bridging different topologies or structures, and they give a way to organize singularities in quotient spaces. However, a number of open problems are still left unanswered. As we have seen in Section 8.2, least squares statistics in stratified spaces exhibit unexpected and possibly unwanted properties due to the singularities in the stratified space. Can we design statistical methods that do not exhibit stickiness or that, perhaps, are sufficiently rich to capture the variation ignored by stickiness? As we have seen in Sections 8.3 and 8.4, computing geodesics is another challenge and thus also an open problem, at least in the case of unlabeled trees. However, the other data types above do not exhibit the hierarchical structure of trees and might therefore prove to be less computationally challenging. A general open challenge is thus to utilize the modeling capabilities of stratified spaces in new applications.

Acknowledgments

The authors wish to thank the editors and the anonymous reviewers for their insightful feedback, which helped greatly improve the quality of the paper. Aasa Feragen was supported by the Lundbeck Foundation, as well as by the Centre for Stochastic Geometry and Advanced Bioimaging, funded by a grant from the Villum Foundation.

References

1. Treebase, a database of phylogenetic knowledge, http:// www.treebase.org.
2. A.D. Aleksandrov, V.N. Berestovskii, I.G. Nikolaev, Generalized Riemannian spaces, Russian Mathematical Surveys 41 (3) (1986) 1.
3. Dmitriy Aronov, Jonathan D. Victor, Non-Euclidean properties of spike train metric spaces, Physical Review E 69 (6) (2004).
4. V. Arsigny, O. Commowick, X. Pennec, N. Ayache, A Log-Euclidean framework for statistics on diffeomorphisms, in: MICCAI, 2006.
5. Dennis Barden, Huiling Le, The logarithm map, its limits and Fréchet means in orthant spaces, arXiv preprint, arXiv:1703.07081, 2017.
6. Dennis Barden, Huiling Le, Megan Owen, Central limit theorems for Fréchet means in the space of phylogenetic trees, Electronic Journal of Probability 18 (25) (2013) 1–25.
7. Peter J. Basser, James Mattiello, Denis LeBihan, MR diffusion tensor spectroscopy and imaging, Biophysical Journal 66 (1) (1994) 259–267.
8. P.G. Batchelor, M. Moakher, D. Atkinson, F. Calamante, A. Connelly, A rigorous framework for diffusion tensor calculus, Magnetic Resonance in Medicine 53 (1) (2005) 221–225.
9. M. Bačák, Computing medians and means in Hadamard spaces, SIAM Journal on Optimization 24 (3) (2014) 1542–1566.
10. Philip Bille, A survey on tree edit distance and related problems, Theoretical Computer Science 337 (1–3) (2005) 217–239.
11. L.J. Billera, S.P. Holmes, K. Vogtmann, Geometry of the space of phylogenetic trees, Advances in Applied Mathematics 27 (4) (2001) 733–767.
12. M.R. Bridson, A. Haefliger, Metric Spaces of Non-positive Curvature, Springer, 1999.
13. D.G. Brown, M. Owen, Mean and variance of phylogenetic trees, arXiv preprint, arXiv:1708.00294, 2017.

14. P. Buneman, The recovery of trees from measures of dissimilarity, in: F.R. Hodson, D.G. Kendall, P. Tautu (Eds.), Mathematics in the Archaeological and Historical Sciences, Edinburgh University Press, Edinburgh, 1971, pp. 387–395.

15. John Chakerian, Susan Holmes, Computational tools for evaluating phylogenetic and hierarchical clustering trees, Journal of Computational and Graphical Statistics 21 (3) (2012) 581–599.

16. Satyan L. Devadoss, Samantha Petti, A space of phylogenetic networks, SIAM Journal on Applied Algebra and Geometry 1 (1) (2017) 683–705.

17. Loïc Devilliers, Stéphanie Allassonnière, Alain Trouvé, Xavier Pennec, Inconsistency of template estimation by minimizing of the variance/pre-variance in the quotient space, Entropy 19 (6) (2017) 288.

18. Ian L. Dryden, Alexey Koloydenko, Diwei Zhou, Non-Euclidean statistics for covariance matrices, with applications to diffusion tensor imaging, Annals of Applied Statistics 3 (3) (September 2009) 1102–1123.

19. Adam Duncan, Eric Klassen, Anuj Srivastava, Statistical shape analysis of simplified neuronal trees, Annals of Applied Statistics 12 (3) (2018) 1385–1421.

20. A. Feragen, S. Hauberg, M. Nielsen, F. Lauze, Means in spaces of tree-like shapes, in: ICCV, 2011.

21. A. Feragen, M. Owen, J. Petersen, M.M.W. Wille, L.H. Thomsen, A. Dirksen, M. de Bruijne, Tree-space statistics and approximations for large-scale analysis of anatomical trees, in: Information Processing in Medical Imaging, in: Lecture Notes in Computer Science, 2013, pp. 74–85.

22. A. Feragen, J. Petersen, M. Owen, P. Lo, L.H. Thomsen, M.M.W. Wille, A. Dirksen, M. de Bruijne, A hierarchical scheme for geodesic anatomical labeling of airway trees, in: Medical Image Computing and Computer-Assisted Intervention (MICCAI) 2012, in: Lecture Notes in Computer Science, 2012, pp. 147–155.

23. Aasa Feragen, Complexity of computing distances between geometric trees, in: Structural, Syntactic, and Statistical Pattern Recognition – Joint IAPR International Workshop, SSPR&SPR 2012, Hiroshima, Japan, November 7–9, 2012. Proceedings, 2012, pp. 89–97.

24. Aasa Feragen, Sean Cleary, Megan Owen, Daniel Vargas, On tree-space PCA, in: Mini-Workshop: Asymptotic Statistics on Stratified Spaces, in: Mathematisches Forschungsinstitut Oberwolfach, vol. 44, 2014, pp. 2491–2495, Report No. 44/2014.

25. Aasa Feragen, Pechin Lo, Marleen de Bruijne, Mads Nielsen, and François Lauze. Toward a theory of statistical tree-shape analysis, IEEE Transactions on Pattern Analysis and Machine Intelligence 35 (8) (2013) 2008–2021.

26. Aasa Feragen, Jens Petersen, Megan Owen, Pechin Lo, Laura Hohwu Thomsen, Mathilde Marie Winkler Wille, Asger Dirksen, Marleen de Bruijne, Geodesic atlas-based labeling of anatomical trees:

application and evaluation on airways extracted from CT, IEEE Transactions on Medical Imaging 34 (6) (2015) 1212–1226.

27. P. Thomas Fletcher, Sarang Joshi, Principal Geodesic Analysis on Symmetric Spaces: Statistics of Diffusion Tensors, 2004, pp. 87–98.

28. Alex Gavryushkin, Alexei J. Drummond, The space of ultrametric phylogenetic trees, Journal of Theoretical Biology 403 (2016) 197–208.

29. David Groisser, Sungkyu Jung, Armin Schwartzman, Geometric foundations for scaling-rotation statistics on symmetric positive definite matrices: minimal smooth scaling-rotation curves in low dimensions, Electronic Journal of Statistics 11 (1) (2017) 1092–1159.

30. M. Gromov, Hyperbolic groups, in: Essays in Group Theory, in: Math. Sci. Res. Inst. Publ., vol. 8, Springer, 1987, pp. 75–263.

31. Mehmet A. Gülsün, Gareth Funka-Lea, Yefeng Zheng, Matthias Eckert, CTA coronary labeling through efficient geodesics between trees using anatomy priors, in: Medical Image Computing and Computer-Assisted Intervention – MICCAI 2014 – 17th International Conference, Boston, MA, USA, September 14–18, 2014, Proceedings, Part II, 2014, pp. 14–18.

32. Thomas Hotz, Stephan Huckemann, Huiling Le, J.S. Marron, Jonathan C. Mattingly, Ezra Miller, James Nolen, Megan Owen, Vic Patrangenaru, Sean Skwerer, Sticky central limit theorems on open books, The Annals of Applied Probability 23 (6) (2013) 2238–2258, 12.

33. S. Huckemann, T. Hotz, A. Munk, Intrinsic shape analysis: geodesic PCA for Riemannian manifolds modulo isometric Lie group actions, Statistica Sinica 20 (1) (2010) 1–58.

34. B.J. Jain, K. Obermayer, Structure spaces, Journal of Machine Learning Research 10 (2009) 2667–2714.

35. Brijnesh J. Jain, Generalized gradient learning on time series, Machine Learning 100 (2) (2015) 587–608.

36. H. Karcher, Riemannian center of mass and mollifier smoothing, Communications on Pure and Applied Mathematics 30 (5) (1977) 509–541.

37. Florian Kelma, Projective Shapes: Topology and Means, PhD thesis, TU Ilmenau, 2017.

38. D.G. Kendall, Shape manifolds, Procrustean metrics, and complex projective spaces, Bulletin of the London Mathematical Society 16 (2) (1984) 81–121.

39. Eric Kolaczyk, Lizhen Lin, Steven Rosenberg, Jackson Walters, Averages of unlabeled networks: geometric characterization and asymptotic behavior, arXiv:1709.02793, 2017.

40. P. Lo, J. Sporring, H. Ashraf, J.J.H. Pedersen, M. de Bruijne, Vessel-guided airway tree segmentation: a voxel classification approach, Medical Image Analysis 14 (4) (2010) 527–538.

41. M.E. Martinez-Perez, A.D. Highes, A.V. Stanton, S.A. Thorn, N. Chapman, A.A. Bharath, K.H. Parker, Retinal vascular tree morphology: a semi-automatic quantification, IEEE Transactions on Biomedical Engineering 49 (8) (2002) 912–917.

42. E. Miller, M. Owen, J.S. Provan, Polyhedral computational geometry for averaging metric phylogenetic trees, Advances in Applied Mathematics 68 (2015) 51–91.
43. Nina Miolane, Susan Holmes, Xavier Pennec, Template shape estimation: correcting an asymptotic bias, SIAM Journal on Imaging Sciences 10 (2) (2017) 808–844.
44. T.M.W. Nye, Principal components analysis in the space of phylogenetic trees, The Annals of Statistics 39 (2011) 2716–2739.
45. T.M.W. Nye, X. Tang, G. Weyenberg, R. Yoshida, Principal component analysis and the locus of the Fréchet mean in the space of phylogenetic trees, Biometrika 104 (2017) 901–922.
46. Tom M.W. Nye, An algorithm for constructing principal geodesics in phylogenetic treespace, IEEE/ACM Transactions on Computational Biology and Bioinformatics 11 (2) (2014) 304–315.
47. M. Owen, J.S. Provan, A fast algorithm for computing geodesic distances in tree space, ACM/IEEE Transactions on Computational Biology and Bioinformatics 8 (1) (2011) 2–13.
48. Victor Patrangenaru, Leif Ellingson, Nonparametric Statistics on Manifolds and Their Applications to Object Data Analysis, 1st edition, CRC Press, Inc., Boca Raton, FL, USA, 2015.
49. J. Pedersen, H. Ashraf, A. Dirksen, K. Bach, H. Hansen, P. Toennesen, H. Thorsen, J. Brodersen, B. Skov, M. Døssing, J. Mortensen, K. Richter, P. Clementsen, N. Seersholm, The Danish randomized lung cancer CT screening trial – overall design and results of the prevalence round, Journal of Thoracic Oncology 4 (5) (May 2009) 608–614.
50. Xavier Pennec, Barycentric subspace analysis on manifolds, Annals of Statistics 46 (6A) (2018) 2711–2746, arXiv:1607.02833.
51. Markus J. Pflaum, Analytic and Geometric Study of Stratified Spaces, Lecture Notes in Mathematics, vol. 1768, Springer, 2001.
52. Sean Skwerer, Elizabeth Bullitt, Stephan Huckemann, Ezra Miller, Ipek Oguz, Megan Owen, Vic Patrangenaru, Scott Provan, J.S. Marron, Tree-oriented analysis of brain artery structure, Journal of Mathematical Imaging and Vision 50 (2014) 126–143.
53. Sean Skwerer, Scott Provan, J.S. Marron, Relative optimality conditions and algorithms for treespace Fréchet means, SIAM Journal on Optimization 28 (2) (2018) 959–988.
54. K.-T. Sturm, Probability measures on metric spaces of nonpositive curvature, Contemp. Math. 338 (2003) 357–390.
55. Asuka Takatsu, Wasserstein geometry of Gaussian measures, Osaka Journal of Mathematics 48 (4) (2011) 1005–1026, 12.
56. K. Turner, Y. Mileyko, S. Mukherjee, J. Harer, Fréchet means for distributions of persistence diagrams, Discrete & Computational Geometry 52 (1) (2014) 44–70.
57. O. Tuzel, F. Porikli, P. Meer, Region covariance: a fast descriptor for detection and classification, in: European Conference on Computer Vision (ECCV), 2006, pp. 589–600.
58. G. Weyenberg, R. Yoshida, D. Howe, Normalizing kernels in the Billera-Holmes–Vogtmann treespace, IEEE/ACM Transactions on Computational Biology and Bioinformatics (2016), https://doi.org/10.1109/TCBB.2016.2565475.

59. Grady Weyenberg, Peter M. Huggins, Christopher L. Schardl, Daniel K. Howe, Ruriko Yoshida, KDEtrees: non-parametric estimation of phylogenetic tree distributions, Bioinformatics 30 (16) (2014) 2280–2287.
60. A. Willis, Confidence sets for phylogenetic trees, Journal of the American Statistical Association (2018).
61. Sakellarios Zairis, Hossein Khiabanian, Andrew J. Blumberg, Raul Rabadan, Genomic data analysis in tree spaces, arXiv preprint, arXiv:1607.07503, 2016.
62. H. Zhai, Principal Component Analysis in Phylogenetic Tree Space, PhD thesis, University of North Carolina at Chapel Hill, 2016.

Bias on estimation in quotient space and correction methods
Applications to statistics on organ shapes

Nina Miolane[a,b], Loic Devilliers[a], Xavier Pennec[a]
[a]*Université Côte d'Azur and Inria, Epione team, Sophia Antipolis, France.*
[b]*Stanford University, Department of Statistics, Stanford, CA, United States*

9.1 Introduction

The shape of a set of points, the shape of a signal, the shape of a surface, or the shape in an image can be defined as the remainder after we have filtered out the position and the orientation of the object [26]. Studying shapes in medical images has many applications. For example, orthopaedic surgeons analyze *bones' shapes* for surgical preplanning [9]. In neuroimaging studying *brain shapes* as they appear in the MRIs facilitates discoveries on disorders like Alzheimer's disease [29].

What do these applications have in common? Position and orientation of the anatomical structures do not matter for the studies' goal: only *shapes* matter. Mathematically, the study analyzes the statistical distributions of *the equivalence classes of the data* under translations and rotations. This amounts to projecting the data in a quotient space.

The most widely used method for summarizing shape data is the computation of the mean shape. Researchers refer to the mean shape with different terms: mean configuration, mean pattern, template, atlas, and so on. We use the term "template" in this chapter. The template is most often computed in practice as a representative of the average of the data equivalence classes. This average is a Fréchet mean in the quotient space, and the corresponding procedure is often called the "max–max algorithm" [1].

We may wonder if the procedure of template estimation is biased. If it is, then inferences in computational anatomy on organ shapes will be too. This chapter uses Riemannian geometry and statistics on quotient spaces to show that a bias is indeed introduced under certain conditions. We illustrate the bias in examples from computational anatomy and present correction methods.

Riemannian Geometric Statistics in Medical Image Analysis
https://doi.org/10.1016/B978-0-12-814725-2.00017-0

9.2 Shapes and quotient spaces

9.2.1 Group actions

Consider three-dimensional MRIs of different brains. The concept of the brains' "shapes" has an intuitive meaning: we can make statements such as "these two shapes look different" or "these two shapes look similar". Computational anatomy seeks to formalize and quantify such statements. Can we give a good *formal definition* of the concept of "shape"? Can we give a good *mathematical representation* of an organ shape? We present a mathematical formalism of shapes by considering the following complementary question: can we give a good representation of what leaves a shape invariant? This section presents the notion of *group actions* as an answer to this question.

Definition 9.1 (Group action of G on a set $\mathcal{M}$). A group (left) action of G on a set $\mathcal{M}$ is a map

$$
\begin{aligned}
\rho : G \times \mathcal{M} &\to \mathcal{M}, \\
(g, x) &\mapsto g.x
\end{aligned}
$$

such that $e.x = x$ for all $x \in \mathcal{M}$, where e is the identity element of G, and $h.(g.x) = (h \circ g).x$ for all $(g, h) \in G^2$ and $x \in \mathcal{M}$. A right group action is defined similarly.

We use the action of $g \in G$ on an object $x \in \mathcal{M}$ to represent a transformation that leaves the shape of x invariant. In other words, x and $g.x$ have the same shape for any $g \in G$.

Definition 9.2 (Lie group action of G on a differentiable manifold $\mathcal{M}$). If G is a Lie group, $\mathcal{M}$ is a differentiable manifold, and ρ is differentiable group action, then ρ is a Lie group action of G on $\mathcal{M}$.

Definitions 9.1–9.2 are illustrated in Examples 9.1–9.4 from computer vision, signal processing, and medical imaging. In these examples we note that several left and right group actions can be defined on the same space $\mathcal{M}$. The space $\mathcal{M}$ itself can be a set, a finite- or infinite-dimensional vector space, or a finite- or infinite-dimensional differentiable manifold. G can be a finite group as well as a finite- or infinite-dimensional Lie group.

Example 9.1 (k landmarks in $\mathbb{R}^d$). A k-tuple of landmarks in d dimensions is a function ϕ from the space of labels $\{1, \dots, k\}$ to the ambient space $\mathbb{R}^d$:

$$
\phi : \{1, \dots, k\} \longmapsto \mathbb{R}^d. \tag{9.1}
$$

Here the space of objects is the space of k-tuples, that is, the space of functions $\mathcal{M} = \mathcal{F}(\{1, \ldots, k\}, \mathbb{R}^d)$, and is finite dimensional. Two groups act on the space of k-tuples $\mathcal{M}$. First, the finite group of permutations $G_1 = \mathfrak{S}$ acts naturally on the space of labels and induces a right action on $\mathcal{M}$. Second, the finite-dimensional Lie group $G_2 = \mathrm{SE}(d)$ of rigid body transformations naturally acts on $\mathbb{R}^d$ and induces a left action on $\mathcal{M}$.

Some authors do not consider the right action on the space of labels and work with $\mathcal{M} = \left(\mathbb{R}^d\right)^k$ equipped with a left action of $G = \mathrm{SE}(d)$, for example, in Kendall analyses [25] or Procrustean analyses [10,15,18].

Example 9.2 (k landmarks in S^d). We can also consider k-tuple of landmarks on hyperspheres. Such k-tuple is a function ϕ from the space of labels $\{1, \ldots, k\}$ to the ambient space S^d:

$$\phi : \{1, \ldots, k\} \longmapsto S^d. \tag{9.2}$$

The space of objects is the space of functions $\mathcal{M} = \mathcal{F}(\{1, \ldots, k\}, S^d)$ and is finite dimensional. Two groups act on the space of k-tuples $\mathcal{M}$. The finite group of permutations $G_1 = \mathfrak{S}$ acts naturally on the space of labels and induces a right action on $\mathcal{M}$. The finite-dimensional Lie group $G_2 = \mathrm{SO}(d + 1)$ of rotations naturally acts on S^d and induces a left action on $\mathcal{M}$.

Example 9.3 (Continuous 1D signals and 2D/3D images). A continuous 1D-signal is a continuous function ϕ from its support $[a, b]$ to $\mathbb{R}$:

$$\phi : [a, b] \longmapsto \mathbb{R}. \tag{9.3}$$

Here the space of objects is the space of functions $\mathcal{M} = \mathcal{F}([a, b], \mathbb{R})$ and is infinite dimensional. Several groups act on the space of 1D signals $\mathcal{M}$. The (infinite-dimensional) group $\mathrm{Diff}([a, b])$ of diffeomorphisms (also called warpings or reparameterizations) of $[a, b]$ induces a right action on $\mathcal{M}$; see Chapter 4. The (finite-dimensional) group of translations and scalings, which naturally acts on $\mathbb{R}$, induces a left action on $\mathcal{M}$ [28]. As another example, a (medical) image is a function ϕ from its domain D to the grey levels $[0, 256]$:

$$\phi : D \longmapsto [0, 256]. \tag{9.4}$$

Here the space of objects is the space of functions $\mathcal{M} = \mathcal{F}(D, [0, 256])$. The group of diffeomorphisms $\mathrm{Diff}(D)$ of the domain D induces a right action on $\mathcal{M}$; see again Chapter 4. Subgroups of $\mathrm{Diff}(D)$ are also often considered, like the LDDMM subgroup, or the rotations or affine transformations [29].

Example 9.4 (Discrete 1D signals and 2D/3D images). A 1D discrete signal with periodic boundary conditions is a function ϕ from the set of N points to $\mathbb{R}$:

$$\phi : \mathbb{Z}/N\mathbb{Z} \longmapsto \mathbb{R}. \qquad (9.5)$$

This can be generalized to discrete 2D or 3D images, where the values are now intensities:

$$\phi : (\mathbb{Z}/N\mathbb{Z})^d \longmapsto \mathbb{R}. \qquad (9.6)$$

When $d = 1$, this is a discrete signal with N points, when $d = 2$, it is a discrete image with $N \times N$ pixels, and when $d = 3$, it is a discrete 3D image with $N \times N \times N$ pixels. The action of translations on the coordinates of pixels is a simplified setting for image registration.

9.2.2 Orbit, isotropy group, quotient space

We consider a set $\mathcal{M}$ equipped with a left action of a group G, denoted $(\mathcal{M}, G, .)$. The action of the group G on $\mathcal{M}$ formalizes the statement "$x \in \mathcal{M}$ and $y \in \mathcal{M}$ have the same shape" through the notion of orbit, which we now define.

Definition 9.3 (Orbit of $x \in \mathcal{M}$). The *orbit of* $x \in \mathcal{M}$ under the action of G, written $[x]$, is defined as

$$[x] = \{g.x \mid g \in G\}. \qquad (9.7)$$

The orbit of $x \in \mathcal{M}$ contains the points of $\mathcal{M}$ reachable with the action of G on x.

Intuitively, the orbit of $x \in \mathcal{M}$ is the set of all objects in $\mathcal{M}$ that have the same shape as x. The relation "having the same shape" defined by $x \sim y : [x] = [y]$ is an equivalence relation whose equivalence classes are the orbits. By properties of the equivalence relations the orbits defined by this action form a partition of $\mathcal{M}$.

An object $x \in \mathcal{M}$ can be left unchanged by the action of an element $g \in G$. Not only the action of g on x does not change the shape of x, but the action does not change the object x at all.

Definition 9.4 (Fixed points of $g \in G$). A point $x \in \mathcal{M}$ is a fixed point of $g \in G$ if

$$g.x = x. \qquad (9.8)$$

Equivalently, we say that g fixes x.

When $x \in \mathcal{M}$ is a fixed point of g, g can be seen as a symmetry of the object shape. When we consider all the elements g that leave the object x unchanged, that is, all the symmetries of x, we define the isotropy group of x.

Definition 9.5 (Isotropy group of $x \in \mathcal{M}$). The isotropy group (or stabilizer) of x, written G_x, is the subgroup of transformations that leaves this element fixed:

$$G_x = \{g \in G \mid g.x = x\}. \tag{9.9}$$

Each isotropy group G_x is a subgroup of G.

Remark 9.1 (Particular case of a Lie group action). If $(\mathcal{M}, G, .)$ is a Lie group action of G on $\mathcal{M}$, then each orbit $[x]$ is a submanifold of $\mathcal{M}$, and each isotropy group is a Lie subgroup of G.

We are interested in studying the shapes of the objects in $\mathcal{M}$, that is, we are interested in studying the orbits of objects.

Definition 9.6 (Quotient space). The set of orbits is called the *quotient space of $\mathcal{M}$ by the action of G*:

$$\mathcal{Q} = \mathcal{M}/G = \{[x] \mid x \in \mathcal{M}\}. \tag{9.10}$$

Intuitively, the quotient space $\mathcal{Q}$ is the space of the shapes of the objects described in $\mathcal{M}$. $\mathcal{Q}$ is sometimes called the shape space.

Remark 9.2 (Terminology). The spaces $\mathcal{M}$ and $\mathcal{Q}$ have different names in the literature. $\mathcal{M}$ can be called the top space, the ambient space, the object space, and so on; $\mathcal{Q}$ can be called the bottom space, the quotient space, the shape space, and so on.

Definitions 9.3, 9.5, and 9.6 are illustrated in Examples 9.5–9.6 and in Fig. 9.1.

Example 9.5 (2 landmarks in the plane $\mathbb{R}^2$). Consider two landmarks in the plane $\mathbb{R}^2$, one red (mid gray in print version) and one black as in Fig. 9.1 (left). The landmarks are initially parameterized each with two coordinates. We then consider that one landmark is fixed at the origin on $\mathbb{R}^2$. Thus the system is now parameterized by the two coordinates of the second landmark only, for example, in polar coordinates (r, θ). We consider the action of the Lie group $SO(2)$ on the second landmark. This action does not change the shape of the system of the two landmarks. The shape of the two landmarks is the distance between them, which is simply r in our notations: the shape is an element of the quotient space $\mathbb{R}^2/SO(2)$.

Fig. 9.1 (left) shows the action of g on the landmark x by a blue arrow (dark gray in print version) and the orbit $[x]$ by a blue dotted circle. The shape space is the space $\mathcal{Q} = \mathbb{R}_+$ of all possible distances between the two landmarks. Every $x \neq (0, 0)$ has isotropy group the identity, and $(0, 0)$ has isotropy group the whole group of 2D rotations.

2 landmarks in the plane $\mathbb{R}^2$ 2 landmarks on the sphere S^2

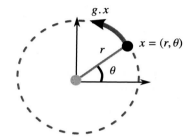   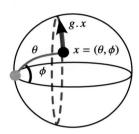

Figure 9.1. Two landmarks, one in red (mid gray in print version) and one in black, in the plane $\mathbb{R}^2$ (left) and on the sphere $\mathbb{S}^2$ (right) described in Examples 9.5–9.6. The blue arrow (dark gray in print version) shows the action of $g \in$ SO(2) on the landmark x, and the blue dotted circle represents the orbit of x.

Example 9.6 (Two landmarks on the sphere $\mathbb{S}^2$). Consider two landmarks on the sphere $\mathbb{S}^2$, one in red (mid gray in print version) and one in black as in Fig. 9.1 (right). One of the landmarks is fixed at a pole of $\mathbb{S}^2$. The system is now parameterized by the two coordinates of the second landmark only, that is, $x = (\theta, \phi)$, where θ is the latitude, and ϕ is the longitude. We consider the action of the Lie group $SO(2)$ on the second landmark. This action does not change the shape of the system of the two landmarks. The shape of the two landmarks is the angle between them, which is simply θ in our notations: the shape is an element of the quotient space $\mathbb{S}^2/SO(2)$.

Fig. 9.1 (right) shows the action of g on the landmark x by a blue arrow (dark gray in print version) and the orbit in $\mathcal{M}$ by a blue dotted circle. The shape space is $\mathcal{Q} = [0, \pi]$, the space of all possible angles between the two landmarks.

9.2.3 Proper and effective group actions

There are different types of group actions, which have different properties. A group action can be proper, effective (or faithful), free, locally free, transitive, regular (or simply transitive or sharply transitive), and so on. We define and consider only proper and effective actions.

Definition 9.7 (Proper group action). A group action of G on $\mathcal{M}$ is proper if the map

$$\varphi \colon G \times \mathcal{M} \to \mathcal{M} \times \mathcal{M}$$
$$(g, x) \to (g.x, x)$$

is proper, that is, the preimage of any compact set is compact.

If G is compact and if the map φ is continuous, then the action of G on $\mathcal{M}$ is proper. A proper action enables to separate points in the quotient space, that is, to separate shapes in the shape space, as shown in the following proposition.

Proposition 9.1. *If the action of G on $\mathcal{M}$ is proper, then every orbit is a closed subset of $\mathcal{M}$, and the quotient space $\mathcal{Q}$ is Haussdorff.*

Definition 9.8 (Effective group action). A group action of G on $\mathcal{M}$ is effective if

$$\cap_x G_x = \{e\}, \tag{9.11}$$

that is, if the only group element that leaves all points fixed is the identity element. An effective group action is also called faithful.

Lastly, we consider the situation where there are no fixed points for any $g \in G$, which is the definition of a free action.

Definition 9.9 (Free group action). A group action of G on $\mathcal{M}$ is free if all isotropy groups are trivial, that is, equal to $\{e\}$.

The actions described in Examples 9.5–9.6 are proper and effective but not free. Even if there are points fixed by all elements of the group, there is no single group element that fixes all points.

9.2.4 Principal and singular orbits

The isotropy group of an object x controls the "size" of its orbit, that is, the amount of objects that have the same shape as x:

Theorem 9.1 (Orbit-stabilizer theorem). *For $x \in \mathcal{M}$, consider the map from G to $\mathcal{M}$ given by $g \mapsto g.x$. Its image is the orbit $[x]$. Besides, the map*

$$G/G_x \;\; \to [x]$$
$$g \circ G_x \;\; \mapsto g.x$$

is well defined and is a bijection.

If $x, y \in \mathcal{M}$ are in the same orbit $[x] = [y]$, then their isotropy groups G_x and G_y are conjugate groups in G, that is, there exists an element $g \in G$ such that $G_x = g \circ G_y \circ g^{-1}$.

Definition 9.10 (Orbit type). The *orbit type* of the orbit $[x]$ is the conjugacy class (H) of the isotropy group G_x.

The "smaller" the isotropy group, the "larger" the orbit and its type: the less symmetries a shape has, the more configurations of objects exist with this shape. The following definition formalizes the notion of ordering that can be defined between isotropy groups and corresponding orbit types.

Definition 9.11 (Partial ordering on isotropy groups and orbit types). If H and K are isotropy subgroups of G, then we denote their isotropy types by (H) and (K), and we say that $(H) \leq (K)$ if and only if H is conjugate to a subgroup of K.

This defines a partial ordering on the set of isotropy groups and orbit types. The "largest" orbit type exists and is unique under the following theorem; see, for example, [4].

Theorem 9.2 (Principal orbit theorem). *Consider a proper Lie group action $(\mathcal{M}, G, .)$ of G on a connected differential manifold $\mathcal{M}$. Then, the smallest orbit type is unique, and the stratum generated by principal orbits is open and dense in $\mathcal{M}$. We denote it $\check{\mathcal{M}}$.*

Under the assumptions of the theorem, we can give the following definitions.

Definition 9.12 (Principal and singular orbits). The principal orbit type is the orbit type with largest isotropy group. We call principal orbits the orbits with principal orbit type. We call singular orbits any other orbits.

We call principal shapes the shapes that correspond to the principal orbits: they are "nondegenerate" shapes. Similarly, singular shapes correspond to singular orbits: they are shapes with symmetries, that is, degenerate shapes. The density of $\check{\mathcal{M}}$ means that there are objects with principal shapes almost everywhere.

The following proposition, which can be found, for example in [4], gives additional properties of sets of orbits with same orbit type and of $\check{\mathcal{M}}$, in particular:

Proposition 9.2. *Consider an isotropy type and the set $\mathcal{N}$ of orbits with this isotropy type. Then $\mathcal{N}$ and $\mathcal{N}/G$ are smooth manifolds. Furthermore, the inclusion $\mathcal{N}/G \to \mathcal{M}/G$ is smooth, and the submersion $\mathcal{N} \to \mathcal{N}/G$ is smooth.*

Under our assumptions, the principal shape space $\check{\mathcal{Q}} = \check{\mathcal{M}}/G$ is a smooth manifold, and $\check{\pi} : \check{\mathcal{M}} \to \check{\mathcal{Q}}$ is a smooth submersion. The space $\check{\mathcal{Q}}$ of nondegenerate shapes is the manifold part of $\mathcal{Q}$.

How do the singular shapes, or singularities of $\mathcal{Q}$, or singular orbits of $\mathcal{M}$, enter the picture? Consider a Lie group action $(\mathcal{M}, G, .)$ of G on a differentiable manifold $\mathcal{M}$. The orbits, principal or singular, can be gathered into a stratification of $\mathcal{M}$ as formalized in the following:

Definition 9.13 (Stratification and orbit type stratification). A *stratification of $\mathcal{M}$* is a locally finite partition of $\mathcal{M}$ by embedded submanifolds called *strata*, required to fit together in a certain way, called the *frontier condition*. The connected components of the *orbit types* form a stratification of $\mathcal{M}$, called the *orbit-type stratification of $\mathcal{M}$*.

The orbit-type stratification induces a stratification of the quotient space.

Proposition 9.3. *The quotient space $\mathcal{Q}$ is a stratified space, where the strata are the connected components of the orbit types.*

Example 9.5 continued (two landmarks in the plane $\mathbb{R}^2$). The principal stratum of $\mathcal{M} = \mathbb{R}^2$ is $\check{\mathcal{M}} = \mathbb{R}^2 \setminus (0, 0)$, which is dense in $\mathbb{R}^2$. Likewise, principal shapes form an open and dense subset $\check{\mathcal{Q}} = \mathbb{R}_+^*$, which is dense in $\mathcal{Q} = \mathbb{R}_+$.

Example 9.6 continued (two landmarks on the sphere $\mathbb{S}^2$). The principal stratum in $\mathcal{M}$ is $\check{\mathcal{M}} = \mathbb{S}^2 \setminus \{(0, 0), (\pi, 0)\}$, which is dense in $\mathbb{S}^2$. The point $(0, 0)$ denotes one pole of $\mathbb{S}^2$, and $(\pi, 0)$ denotes its opposite pole in $\mathbb{S}^2$. In $\mathcal{Q}$ the principal stratum is $\check{\mathcal{Q}} =]0, \pi[$, which is dense in $\mathcal{Q} = [0, \pi]$.

9.2.5 Metric structure

We now formalize and quantify the statement "these shapes are similar". So far, we have not introduced any notion of distance or dissimilarity between objects or shapes. We address this by adding a Riemannian structure on the previous framework.

We consider a vector space or a differentiable manifold $(\mathcal{M}, G, .)$ equipped with a group action. Let $d_{\mathcal{M}}$ be a distance defined on $\mathcal{M}$, that is, a way to quantify the (dis)similarity between shapes. We study below the "compatibility" of this distance with the group action.

Definition 9.14 (G-invariant distance and isometric action). The distance $d_{\mathcal{M}}$ on $\mathcal{M}$ is invariant under the action of the group G on

$\mathcal{M}$ and is called a G-invariant distance if

$$\forall g \in G, \quad \forall x, y \in \mathcal{M} \quad d_\mathcal{M}(x, y) = d_\mathcal{M}(g.x, g.y). \qquad (9.12)$$

The distance between two elements in $\mathcal{M}$ is conserved after an action by the same group element g. Equivalently, the action is said to be isometric with respect to $d_\mathcal{M}$ because it conserves the distances.

The distance $d_\mathcal{M}$ may come from an inner product or a Riemannian metric on $\mathcal{M}$. Intuitively, a G-invariant distance means that the (dis)similarity between two objects does not change if we transform both objects in the same way.

Example 9.5 continued (two landmarks in the plane $\mathbb{R}^2$). Consider the Euclidean plane $(\mathbb{R}^2, \langle\,,\,\rangle)$, where $\langle\,,\,\rangle$ is the canonical inner product. The action of $SO(2)$ is isometric with respect to the distance induced by $\langle\,,\,\rangle$.

Example 9.6 continued (two landmarks on the sphere $\mathbb{S}^2$). Consider the sphere $(\mathbb{S}^2, \langle\,,\,\rangle)$, where $\langle\,,\,\rangle$ is the Riemannian metric on $\mathbb{S}^2$ induced by the canonical inner product in $\mathbb{R}^3$. The action of $SO(2)$ is isometric with respect to the Riemannian distance induced by $\langle\,,\,\rangle$.

Example 9.4 continued (Discrete 1D signals and 2D/3D images). Consider the space of discrete 1D signals or the space of discrete 2D/3D image with the distance being the sum of the square differences in intensities. The action of translation on coordinates is isometric with respect to this distance.

Remark 9.3 (Particular case of a Hilbert space $(\mathcal{M}, \langle\,,\,\rangle)$). We consider the distance in the Hilbert space $\mathcal{M}$ given by the norm: $d_\mathcal{M}(a, b) = \|a - b\|$. We say that G acts isometrically and linearly on $\mathcal{M}$ if $x \mapsto g.x$ is a linear map that leaves the norm unchanged.

Remark 9.4 (Particular case of a Riemannian manifold $(\mathcal{M}, \langle\,,\,\rangle)$). The Riemannian metric on $\mathcal{M}$ is G-invariant if the differential of its action ρ,

$$d\rho_g : T_x\mathcal{M} \to T_{g.x}\mathcal{M}, \qquad (9.13)$$

leaves the metric $\langle\,,\,\rangle_x$ at x invariant. A G-invariant Riemannian metric induces a G-invariant Riemannian distance.

The distance in $\mathcal{M}$ represents a measure of (dis)similarity between objects. We examine how to turn it into a distance in $\mathcal{Q}$, a measure of (dis)similarity between shapes. A first step in this direction is the concept of registration of objects, also called alignment, which can be formulated using group actions:

Definition 9.15 (Optimal positioning). We say that the point $g.x_1$ is in optimal position to x_2 if

$$d_{\mathcal{M}}(g.x_1, x_2) = \inf_{g \in G} d_{\mathcal{M}}(g.x_1, x_2). \qquad (9.14)$$

Equivalently, we say that the objects x_1 and x_2 are registered (medical imaging terminology, e.g., [38]) or aligned (signal processing terminology, e.g., [28]).

Then a distance on $\mathcal{M}$ induces a distance on the quotient space $\mathcal{Q}$:

Definition 9.16 (Distance on the quotient space $\mathcal{Q}$). Let $d_{\mathcal{M}}$ be a distance on $\mathcal{M}$, and let $(\mathcal{M}, G, .)$ be an isometric action with respect to $d_{\mathcal{M}}$. Then

$$d_{\mathcal{Q}}([x], [y]) = \inf_{g \in G} d_{\mathcal{M}}(g.x, y) \qquad (9.15)$$

is a distance on $\mathcal{Q}$.

Example 9.1 continued (k landmarks in $\mathbb{R}^d$). Consider the case of k-tuples in $\mathbb{R}^d$ with the action of the rigid-body motions SE(d) on $(\mathbb{R}^d)^k$ of Example 9.1. The Euclidean metric on $\mathbb{R}^d$ induces a metric on $(\mathbb{R}^d)^k$, which is invariant for the action of SE(d). This induces the so-called Procrustean distance on the quotient space, which is computed in practice by first registering the k-tuples and then using the distance on $(\mathbb{R}^d)^k$ [10,42]. The Riemannian structure of the quotient space has been studied by Le and Kendall [32].

In practice the distance in $\mathcal{Q}$, that is, the distance between two shapes, is computed by first registering the objects and then using the distance in the ambient space $\mathcal{M}$. The registration is a crucial step as there is no a priori closed-form expression to compute the distance between two points in $\mathcal{Q}$, even if there is one in $\mathcal{M}$. One case where it may be possible is when an isometric section exists.

Definition 9.17 (Global and local isometric sections). Take the canonical projection $\pi : \mathcal{M} \mapsto \mathcal{Q}$ into the quotient space. Let $\mathcal{U}$ be an open subset of $\mathcal{Q}$. A map $s : \mathcal{U} \mapsto \mathcal{M}$ is a *local section* if $\pi \circ s = \text{Id}$. Moreover, we say that s is *isometric* if

$$\forall o, o' \in \mathcal{U}, \quad d_{\mathcal{Q}}(o, o') = d_{\mathcal{M}}\left(s(o), s(o')\right). \qquad (9.16)$$

Then the image $\mathcal{S} = s(\mathcal{U})$ of the open subset $\mathcal{U}$ of the quotient by the section s is a subset of $\mathcal{M}$ with the following property: $d_{\mathcal{M}}(x, y) = d_{\mathcal{Q}}([x], [y])$ for all $x, y \in \mathcal{S}$. Moreover, we say that the section is global if $\mathcal{U} = \mathcal{Q}$.

A global section gives a subset of $\mathcal{M}$ containing a point of each orbit such that all points in $\mathcal{S}$ are registered. A global isometric section rarely exists.

Example 9.7. There exists a global isometric section for Examples 9.5 and 9.6 of the two landmarks in $\mathbb{R}^2$ and $\mathbb{S}^2$: we can compute a closed-form expression for the distance in the respective quotient spaces $\mathbb{R}_+$ and $[0, \pi]$. However, we can show that there is no global isometric section for Example 9.4 of discrete 1D signals and 2D/3D discrete images.

9.3 Template estimation

Differential geometry on quotient spaces, introduced in the previous sections, gives a mathematical framework to analyze algorithms in medical imaging and computational anatomy. We consider the algorithms of template estimation. Intuitively, a template of a given population is a prototype of this population. In medical imaging for example, a template of a data base of brain images is a brain image representing a reference anatomy. The template shows the prototype shape of the brain population under study.

Various methods exist to compute a template from a given database; see [10] for templates of landmarks or [12] for brain templates. A first practice was to select one object from the database as the template. If the shape of the selected object is far from the population mean shape, then the template is necessarily biased toward this specific data point. Thus the template fails at being a prototype of the population. Therefore researchers have developed other algorithms to compute the template. We investigate here the computation of the template as a Fréchet mean in the quotient space.

9.3.1 Generative model

The template represents a prototype of the data. Here we formally define it as a parameter of a generative model. We have a sample $\{X_i\}_{i=1}^n$ of size n, which can be sets of landmarks, curves, images, and so on. Each element of the sample is interpreted as a noisy observation of the template up to a group action that does not change the template's shape, for example, the action of a repositioning or a reparameterization [1,5,6,8,28]. We further present common generative models, first, for data in a Hilbert space and then for data in a Riemannian manifold.

Observations in a Hilbert space

Let $(\mathcal{M}, \langle\,,\,\rangle, G, .)$ be a (potentially infinite-dimensional) Hilbert space with a group action. The generative model of the data is defined as

$$X = g \cdot y_0 + \epsilon, \tag{9.17}$$

where $y_0 \in \mathcal{M}$ is the template, g is a random transformation in G, and ϵ is a random variable that represents a standardized noise in $\mathcal{M}$ with null mean $\mathbb{E}(\epsilon) = 0$ and finite variance $\mathbb{E}(\|\epsilon\|^2) < \infty$. We assume that g and ϵ are independent random variables.

Example 9.5 continued (two landmarks in the plane $\mathbb{R}^2$). The generative model of the landmark in the 2D plane writes in Cartesian coordinates as

$$(x, y) = R_\theta \cdot (0, r_0) + \epsilon = r_0(\cos\theta, \sin\theta) + \epsilon,$$

where $y_0 = (0, r_0)$ is the template, the 2D rotation matrix R_θ of rotation angle θ is a random variable in $SO(2)$, and ϵ is the noise in $\mathbb{R}^2$.

Observations in a finite-dimensional Riemannian manifold

Let $(\mathcal{M}, \langle\,,\,\rangle, G, .)$ be a finite-dimensional Riemannian manifold with a group action. By $\mathrm{Exp}_p(u)$ we denote the Riemannian exponential of u at point p. The generative model of the data is defined as

$$X = \mathrm{Exp}_{g \cdot y_0}(\epsilon), \tag{9.18}$$

where $y_0 \in \mathcal{M}$ is the template, $g \in G$ is a random transformation, and ϵ is a random variable in the tangent space $T_{g \cdot y}\mathcal{M}$, which represents the noise. We assume that g and ϵ are independent random variables. We assume the noise to be isotropic Gaussian of standard deviation σ in each coordinate on the tangent space $T_{g \cdot y}\mathcal{M}$.

Example 9.6 continued (two landmarks on the sphere $\mathbb{S}^2$). The generative model writes in latitude and longitude coordinates as

$$(\lambda, \phi) = R_\theta \cdot (y_0, 0) + \epsilon = (y_0, \theta) + \epsilon, \tag{9.19}$$

where $y_0 = (y_0, 0)$ is the template, the random 2D rotation matrix R_θ is a random variable in $SO(2)$, and ϵ is the noise.

An alternative generative model where the noise is added before the group action can also be considered for data belonging respectively to a Hilbert space and to a Riemannian manifold:

$$X = g.(y_0 + \epsilon) \quad \text{resp.} \quad X = g.\text{Exp}_{t_0}(\epsilon). \quad (9.20)$$

A model without noise $X = g.y_0$ can be found in [28].

9.3.2 An iterative estimation procedure

The template $y_0 \in \mathcal{M}$ is defined as a parameter of the generative model. We now describe the usual procedure of template estimation [1,5,6,8,21,28], which is given in Algorithm 9.1. Let $(\mathcal{M}, \langle , \rangle, G, .)$ be a Hilbert space or a finite-dimensional Riemannian manifold equipped with a group action of G. Data are generated from the generative model described in the previous subsection. The template estimate is initialized with one of the observed data $\hat{y} = X_1$. Then the procedure iterates two steps (i) and (ii) until the convergence of the template estimation.

Algorithm 9.1 Template estimation.

Input: Observed data $\{X_i\}_{i=1}^{n}$, convergence threshold δ

Initialization: $k = 0$ and $\hat{y}_0^{(0)} = X_1$

Repeat:

- (i) Registration: $\forall i \in \{1, ..., n\}, \hat{g}_i = \underset{g \in G}{\text{argmin}} \, d_{\mathcal{M}}(\hat{y}_0^{(k)}, g.X_i),$

- (ii) Fréchet mean computation:
  $\hat{y}_0^{(k+1)} = \underset{y \in \mathcal{M}}{\text{arg min}} \, \sum_{i=1}^{n} d_{\mathcal{M}}(y, \hat{g}_i.X_i)^2$

- $k \leftarrow k + 1$

until convergence: $d_{\mathcal{M}}(\hat{y}_0^{(k)}, \hat{y}_0^{(k-1)}) < \delta$

Output: $\hat{y}_0^{(k)}$.

Step (i) is the registration of each object X_i to the current template. We assume that each minimizer $\hat{g}_i$ exists and is reached by (i). In practice this is the case where G is compact. Step (ii) is the computation of the Fréchet mean of the registered data $\hat{g}_i.X_i$. We assume that the minimizer $\hat{y}_0^{(k+1)}$ exists and is reached in (ii). In practice this is the case for low levels of noise σ in the generative model, as the registered data $\hat{g}_i.X_i$ will end up being concentrated on a small neighborhood of $\mathcal{M}$ [13]. The procedure described in Algorithm 9.1 is sometimes called the "max–max procedure".

Example 9.5 continued (two landmarks in the plane $\mathbb{R}^2$). Let x_1, x_2, x_3 be three objects in $\mathbb{R}^2$ in Fig. 9.2 (left). Step (i) filters out the position or parameterization component, that is, the coordinate on the orbit. The objects x_1, x_2, x_3 are projected in the shape space $\mathcal{Q}$ using the blue arrows (dark gray in print version). Then the Fréchet mean is computed in Step (ii).

Example 9.6 continued (two landmarks on the sphere $\mathbb{S}^2$). Similarly, Fig. 9.2 shows Steps (i) and (ii) of the template estimation procedure for a sample of size 3, where each element is a set of two landmarks on the sphere $\mathbb{S}^2$.

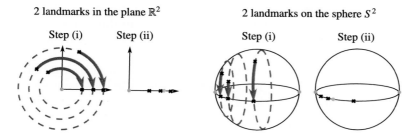

Figure 9.2. Steps (i)–(ii) of template estimation. The three black plus signs in $\mathbb{R}^2$ (left) or $\mathbb{S}^2$ (right) represent the three data. The three dotted blue curves (dark gray in print version) are their orbits. In Step (i) the data are registered. The three black crosses in $\mathbb{R}_+$ (positive x-axis) (left) or $[0, \pi]$ (right) represent the registered data. In Step (ii) the Fréchet mean of the registered data is computed and shown in orange (light gray in print version).

9.3.3 Convergence to the Fréchet mean in the quotient space

We consider the convergence of the iterative procedure of template estimation, described in Algorithm 9.1, as the number of iterations $k \to +\infty$. The procedure decreases at each step the following cost, which is bounded below by zero:

$$\text{Cost}(g_1, \dots, g_n, y) = \sum_{i=1}^{n} d_{\mathcal{M}}^2(y, g \cdot X_i). \tag{9.21}$$

Under the assumptions that both steps (i) and (ii) reach their minimizers, we are guaranteed of the convergence to a local minimum.

Proposition 9.4. *We assume that the procedure converges to the global minimum as $k \to +\infty$. Then, the estimate of the template is*

$$\hat{y}_0 = \underset{y \in \mathcal{M}}{\arg\min} \sum_{i=1}^{n} \min_{g \in G} d_{\mathcal{M}}^2(y, g \cdot X_i), \tag{9.22}$$

where we recognize the sample Fréchet mean in the quotient space as in Section 4.6.4 of Chapter 4. Moreover, if the group is finite, then the algorithm converges in a finite number of steps [7].

We recall that the template y_0 is defined as an element of $\mathcal{M}$. Proposition 9.4 shows that the iterative procedure converges to $\hat{y}_0$, which is an element of the quotient space $\mathcal{Q}$. Recovering y_0 is indeed an ill-posed problem. We can only estimate the equivalence class of y_0. In other words, we estimate the shape of the template.

We want to compare $\hat{y}_0$ to the parameter y_0 it was designed to estimate: to this aim, we want y_0 and $\hat{y}_0$ to be in the same space. We assume that there exists a local isometric section s around y_0 and compare $s(\hat{y}_0)$, a representative object of the shape $\hat{y}_0$, to the template y_0 in $\mathcal{M}$. In the following, we write $\hat{y}_0$ or $s(\hat{y}_0)$ indifferently, as well as $\pi(y_0)$ or y_0 indifferently, since the local geometry of $\check{\mathcal{Q}}$ is equivalent to the local geometry of its local isometric section in $\check{\mathcal{M}}$.

9.3.4 Other convergence(s)

We can investigate two other types of convergence in the estimation procedure. First, we consider the convergence in the sample size $n \to +\infty$. The sample Fréchet mean on a manifold converges to the population Fréchet mean set when sample size goes to infinity [44]. Thus we assume that we have an infinite sample, and we consider the population Fréchet mean as the estimator of the template:

$$\hat{y}_0 = \arg\min_{y \in \mathcal{M}} \int \min_{g \in G} d^2_{\mathcal{M}}(y, g.X)\, d\mathcal{M}(X). \tag{9.23}$$

Second, we consider the convergence as the noise level $\sigma \to 0$. When there is no noise, the population Fréchet mean in $\mathcal{Q}$ gives the template shape of the generative model: the estimator gives the parameter it was designed to estimate. There is no bias in the estimation in this case. The next sections investigate what happens when the noise is nonzero, that is, in the context of a real experimental setting.

9.3.5 Bias of the procedure

Consider the template y_0 and a representative of its estimate $\hat{y}_0$. We want to know if the procedure described above has a bias when the noise level $\sigma \neq 0$. The following definition generalizes to Riemannian manifolds the usual definition of a bias $\text{Bias}(\hat{y}_0, y_0) = \mathbb{E}[\hat{y}_0 - y_0]$ in a linear space.

Definition 9.18 (Bias). Consider a Riemannian manifold $(\mathcal{M}, \langle\,,\,\rangle)$ and its Riemannian logarithm Log. Take $y_0 \in \mathcal{M}$ and an estimator $\hat{y}_0^{(n)} \in \mathcal{M}$ of y_0, computed from a sample of size n. We assume that $\hat{y}_0^{(n)}$ is within the injectivity radius of the Riemannian exponential at y_0, so that the Riemannian logarithm at y_0 is well defined. The bias of the estimator $\hat{y}_0^{(n)}$ with respect to the (manifold-valued) parameter y_0 is defined as

$$\text{Bias}(\hat{y}_0^{(n)}, y_0) = \mathbb{E}\left[\text{Log}_{y_0}(\hat{y}_0^{(n)})\right], \tag{9.24}$$

where the expectation is taken over the repeated draws of samples of size n. The asymptotic bias is defined as the bias of the estimator $\hat{y}_0^{(\infty)}$ with respect to the parameter y_0.

From now on we assume that $\hat{y}_0^{(n)}$ converges in probability to a single value $\hat{y}_0^{(\infty)} = \hat{y}_0$ as the sample size goes to infinity. If this value is exactly the original template value y_0, then the estimate is said to be consistent.

Definition 9.19 (Weak consistency). An estimator is weakly consistent if it converges in probability to the parameter it is designed to estimate as the number of data points goes to infinity.

In the following we use the term "consistency" to refer to the "weak consistency". In the general case the estimation $\hat{y}_0$ differs from the original template value y_0. The asymptotic bias

$$\text{Bias}(\hat{y}_0, y_0) = \text{Log}_{y_0}(\hat{y}_0) \tag{9.25}$$

measures how much we would have to shoot from y_0 along a Riemannian geodesic to get the estimated parameter $\hat{y}_0$.

Remark 9.5 (Variance and asymptotic variance). In statistics an estimator is evaluated based on its bias and variance. Since we assumed that the estimator $\hat{y}_0^{(\infty)}$ of the template converges in probability to the value $\hat{y}_0$, the asymptotic variance of the estimator is vanishing:

$$\text{Var}(\hat{y}_0^{(\infty)}) = \lim_{n \to \infty} \mathbb{E}\left[\text{dist}^2(\hat{y}_0^{(n)}, \hat{y}_0)\right] = 0. \tag{9.26}$$

Thus we focus on the asymptotic bias.

9.4 Asymptotic bias of template estimation

We first consider $\mathbb{R}^2$ with the canonical inner product as an example of a finite-dimensional Hilbert space and $\mathbb{S}^2$ with the metric inherited from $\mathbb{R}^3$ as an example of a finite-dimensional Riemannian manifold. We show the asymptotic bias of the template estimation for these special cases before extending to general cases.

9.4.1 Intuition on examples

The special cases of two landmarks on the plane $\mathbb{R}^2$ and on the sphere $\mathbb{S}^2$, introduced in Examples 9.5–9.6, are useful to show the origin of the asymptotic bias of $\hat{y}_0$. We consider a generative model with a Gaussian isotropic noise of standard deviation σ on each coordinate. As long as $\sigma \neq 0$, there is *a bias that comes from the curvature of the orbit of the template.* Fig. 9.3 shows the orbit of the template and the level σ of the Gaussian noise for both examples.

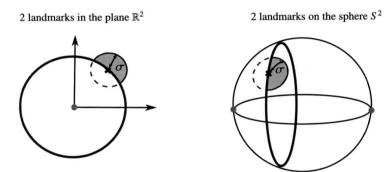

2 landmarks in the plane $\mathbb{R}^2$ 2 landmarks on the sphere S^2

Figure 9.3. Geometric origin of the bias. The extrinsic curvature of the template orbit creates the asymptotic bias. The blue curves (dark gray in print version) represent the respective template orbits. The balls of radius σ represent the level of the Gaussian noise distribution. The grey-colored areas represent the noise distribution that generates data "outside" the orbit of y_0, that is, on the orbit side that is the furthest away from the closest singularity.

Example 9.5 continued (two landmarks in the plane $\mathbb{R}^2$). Fig. 9.3 (left) shows that the probability of generating an observation X_i outside the shape orbit of the template is greater than the probability of generating it inside: the grey area in the black circle is larger than the white area. When the data are registered and projected in the shape space, there will be more registered data that are greater than the template. Their expected value, which is the template estimator, will therefore be greater than the template: there is a bias of the estimator with respect to the parameter it is designed to estimate.

Fig. 9.4 (left) shows the bias of $\hat{y}_0$ with respect to y_0 as a function of σ. Increasing the noise level σ takes the estimate $\hat{y}_0$ away from

y_0. The estimate is driven away from 0: it goes to ∞ as $\sigma \to \infty$. It can be shown numerically that the bias varies as σ^2 around $\sigma = 0$.

Example 9.6 continued (two landmarks on the sphere $\mathbb{S}^2$). Fig. 9.3 (right) shows that if the template shape orbit is defined by a constant $\theta < \pi/2$, then the probability of generating an observation X_i "outside" it, that is, with $\theta_i > \theta$, is greater than the probability of generating it "inside". When the data are registered and projected in the shape space, there will be more registered data that are greater than the template θ, and again, their expected value will also be greater than the template. Conversely, if the template is $\theta > \pi/2$, then the phenomenon is inverted: there will be more registered data that are smaller than the template. The average of these registered data will also be smaller than the template. Finally, if the template shape orbit is the great circle defined by $\theta = \pi/2$, then the probability of generating an observation X_i on the left is the same as the probability of generating an observation X_i on the right. In this case the registered data will be well balanced around the template $\theta = \pi/2$, and their expected value will be $\pi/2$: there is no asymptotic bias in this particular case.

Fig. 9.4 (right) shows the bias of $\hat{y}_0$ with respect to y_0 as a function of σ. Increasing the noise level σ takes the estimate $\hat{y}_0$ away from y_0. It is repulsed from 0 and π: it goes to $\pi/2$ as $\sigma \to \pi$, and the probability distribution becomes uniform on the sphere in this limit. It can be shown numerically that the bias varies as σ^2 around $\sigma = 0$.

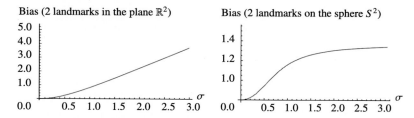

Figure 9.4. Asymptotic bias on the template estimate $\hat{y}_0$ with respect to the noise level σ for $r = 1$ (left) and $\theta = 1$ (right). The bias is quadratic near $\sigma = 0$. Increasing σ takes the estimate $\hat{y}_0$ away from the singularities of $\mathcal{Q}$.

9.4.2 Bias on quotient of finite-dimensional Riemannian manifold

In this section we use geometry of quotient spaces to prove the origin of the bias observed in the special cases above. Consider a finite-dimensional manifold with an isometric proper effective action of a finite-dimensional Lie group $(\mathcal{M}, \langle \,, \, \rangle, G, .)$. The data X_i are generated in $\mathcal{M}$ through the model (9.18): $X = \mathrm{Exp}_{g \cdot y_0}(\epsilon)$, where g and ϵ are independent random variables. We assume that the template y_0 is in the principal stratum of $\mathcal{M}$, that is, $y_0 \in \check{\mathcal{M}}$, and that there exists a local isometric section[1] around y_0. We assume that the noise ϵ is a random variable with isotropic Gaussian distribution of standard deviation σ in each coordinate of the tangent space $T_{g \cdot y_0}\mathcal{M}$.

We show that there is an asymptotic bias on the template shape estimation under these assumptions. We proceed in two steps. The template shape estimate is the Fréchet mean of the observations projected in the quotient space. Thus we first compute the distribution of the observations in the quotient space Q; see Theorem 9.3. Then we compute the estimator $\hat{y}_0$ as the expectation of the distribution in Q and compare it with the parameter y_0 to get the bias, see Theorem 9.4.

Theorem 9.3 (Induced probability density on $\mathcal{Q}$ [34]). *Under the above assumptions, the probability density function f on the $[X_i]$, $i = 1, \ldots, n$, in the asymptotic regime on an infinite number of observations $n \to +\infty$ has the following Taylor expansion around the noise level $\sigma = 0$:*

$$f(z) \quad = \frac{1}{C_\mathcal{Q}(\sigma)} \exp\left(-\frac{d^2_{\mathcal{M}}(y_0, z)}{2\sigma^2}\right)\left(F_0(z) + \sigma^2 F_2(z) + \mathcal{O}(\sigma^4) + \Xi(\sigma)\right),$$

where z denotes a point in $\check{\mathcal{M}}$ belonging to a local isometric section around y_0. In this expression, $C_\mathcal{Q}(\sigma)$ is the integration constant of the Gaussian. Then, for a fixed z, Ξ is a function of σ that decreases exponentially as $\sigma \to 0$. F_0 and F_2 are functions of z involving the local geometry of $\check{\mathcal{M}}$ around each $z \in \check{\mathcal{M}}$.

The expression of f is obtained by locally integrating the probability distribution function of the observations in $\mathcal{M}$ along the orbits; see [34] for the proof. Thus f is the probability density function on $\check{\mathcal{Q}}$, that is, the probability density of the object shapes associated with the generative model. Moreover, we have $d^2_{\mathcal{M}}(y_0, z) = d^2_{\mathcal{Q}}([y_0], [z])$ for $d_{\mathcal{M}}(z, y_0) \leq r$.

Consider now that $\hat{y}_0$ is computed with the template estimation procedure presented in this section. This means that $\hat{y}_0$ is the expectation of the distribution f. The following theorem computes its Riemannian logarithm from the parameter y_0, that is, the asymptotic bias of the template shape estimation.

[1]This technical assumption due to the structure of the proof currently limits the application range of the bias analysis of this section. We conjecture that is can be notably softened.

Theorem 9.4 (Asymptotic bias [34]). *Under the above assumptions, in the regime of an infinite number of observations $n \to +\infty$, the asymptotic bias of the template shape estimator $\hat{y}_0$ with respect to the parameter y_0 has the following Taylor expansion around the noise level $\sigma = 0$:*

$$Bias(\hat{y}_0, y_0) = -\frac{\sigma^2}{2} H(y_0) + \mathcal{O}(\sigma^3) + \epsilon(\sigma), \qquad (9.27)$$

where H is the mean curvature vector of the template's orbit, which represents the extrinsic curvature of the orbit in $\check{\mathcal{M}}$, and ϵ is a function of σ that decreases exponentially as $\sigma \to 0$.

The proof of this result can be found in [34]. This expression of the bias generalizes the quadratic behavior observed in the examples in Fig. 9.4. The asymptotic bias has a geometric origin: it comes from the extrinsic curvature of the template orbits; see Fig. 9.3.

The results are valid when $\mathcal{M}$ is a finite-dimensional manifold and G is a finite-dimensional Lie group. Some interesting examples belong to the framework of infinite-dimensional manifold with infinite-dimensional Lie groups. This is the case for the LD-DMM framework on images [22]. Therefore it is important to extend these results to the infinite-dimensional case. The next subsection presents results for (infinite-dimensional) Hilbert spaces.

9.4.3 Bias on quotient of (in)finite-dimensional Hilbert space

Consider a Hilbert space with a linear and isometric group action $(\mathcal{M}, \langle , \rangle, G, .)$. We assume that the data are generated with the model $X = g.(y_0 + \epsilon)$, where $y_0 \in \mathcal{M}$ is a template, and ϵ is an independent noise. We define the random variable $Y = y_0 + \epsilon$.

When we are in a Hilbert space $\mathcal{M}$ of infinite dimension, it does not make sense to take an isotropic Gaussian variable defined as a Gaussian noise on each coordinate with a parameter σ. Therefore we have to proceed differently to control the noise level: we consider a standardized noise η with zero mean and unit variance ($\mathbb{E}(\eta) = 0$ and $\mathbb{E}(\|\eta\|^2) = 1$) and scale it with the standard deviation τ: $\epsilon = \tau\eta$. Then the observable variable is assumed to be

$$X = g.y_0 + \epsilon = g.y_0 + \tau\eta.$$

When $\mathcal{M}$ is a linear space of finite dimension k, an isotropic Gaussian of parameter σ on each coordinate has the standard deviation $\tau = \sqrt{k}\sigma$. Therefore σ and τ are two equivalent measures of the noise level, which is added as far as we remain in finite dimension.

Theorem 9.5 (Sufficient condition leading to a bias). *Let G be a group acting isometrically and linearly on a Hilbert space $\mathcal{M}$, and let $X = g.(y_0 + \epsilon)$ be a random variable in $\mathcal{M}$ with $E(\|X\|^2) < +\infty$. We pose $Y = y_0 + \epsilon$ with $E(Y) = y_0 \neq 0$. If*

$$\mathbb{P}\left(d_Q([y_0], [Y]) < \|y_0 - Y\|\right) > 0, \tag{9.28}$$

then $[y_0]$ is not a Fréchet mean of $[X]$ in $Q = \mathcal{M}/G$. The max–max template estimation procedure is inconsistent.

Notice that here the linearity assumption is crucial. For instance, this does not hold with translations. In practice it is easy to fulfill the condition given by (9.28). For instance, a Gaussian noise fulfills this condition as soon as the template is not a fixed point under the group action. We have also the following proposition.

Proposition 9.5. *Let G be a group acting isometrically and linearly on a Hilbert space $\mathcal{M}$, and let Y be a random variable in $\mathcal{M}$ with $\mathbb{E}(\|Y\|^2) < +\infty$. Assume $Y = y_0 + \epsilon$, where $y_0 \neq 0$ and $\mathbb{E}(\epsilon) = 0$. We suppose that $[y_0]$ is a submanifold of $\mathcal{M}$ with tangent space $T_{y_0}[y_0]$ at y_0. If*

$$\mathbb{P}(\epsilon \notin T_{y_0}[y_0]^\perp) > 0, \tag{9.29}$$

then (9.28) is fulfilled, and the template estimation is inconsistent.

For a consistent estimation, we need the support of the noise to be included into a proper linear space of $\mathcal{M}$. This is a severe restriction.

Asymptotic bias for a very large noise

As τ tends to infinity, we have the following a behavior of the bias.

Theorem 9.6. *Let G be a group acting isometrically and linearly on a Hilbert space $\mathcal{M}$. We assume that the support of the noise ϵ is not included in the set of fixed points under the group action. Let $X = g.y_0 + \tau\epsilon$ be the observable variable. If the Fréchet mean of $[X]$ exists, then the asymptotic has the following asymptotic behavior as the noise level τ tends to infinity:*

$$Bias(\hat{y}_0, y_0) = \sigma K + o(\tau) \quad as \quad \tau \to +\infty, \tag{9.30}$$

where $K = \sup_{\|v\|=1} \mathbb{E}\left(\sup_{g \in G} \langle v, g.\epsilon \rangle\right) \in (0, 1]$ is a constant that depends only on the standardized noise and on the group action. In particular, K does not depend on the template.

9.5 Applications to statistics on organ shapes

The procedure of template shape estimation has an asymptotic bias: even with an infinite number of observations, the estimator does not converge to the parameter it was designed to estimate. We show in this section how the results of Section 9.4 impact the analysis of landmarks and brain shapes.

9.5.1 Shapes defined by landmarks

We first consider landmark shapes and mention the theory introduced by Kendall in the 1980s [25]. Kendall considered shapes of k labeled landmarks in $\mathbb{R}^d$ and assumed that data were observed directly in the quotient space. Thus the framework of Section 9.4 does not apply in this context: such studies do not consider that the data are observed with noise in the space of landmarks $(\mathbb{R}^d)^k$ and then projected in the shape space. The generative model is different, and the question of the bias that we investigate in this chapter is not raised in this context.

However, Section 9.4 applies directly to Procrustean analyses of landmark shapes [10,15,18] that consider observations in the space of landmarks. Data are projected in the shape space by an "alignment" or "registration" step. In this literature the bias has been observed in different settings depending on the assumptions defining the shape, as described further.

Different types of Procrustean analyses

Procrustean analyses that relate to the framework of Section 9.4 are called "generalized" Procrustean analyses. The original orthogonal Procruste problem was to find the rotation minimizing the residuals between two matrices [41] (other solutions for that problem were proposed with different names [23,36]). "Ordinary" Procrustean analysis is the problem of registering a set of matrices to a reference matrix chosen in advance. "Generalized" Procrustean analysis refers to the problem of group-registration of a set of matrices using the max–max algorithm, that is, Algorithm 9.1, which is also called the alternation framework in this literature [19,43].

Then, the terminology depends on the group of transformations G used to register the matrices. If only rotation matrices are used, then this is orthogonal Procrustean analysis. If rotations, translations, and scalings (i.e., similarities) are used, then this is called "extended orthogonal" Procrustean analysis. The setting that relates to the isometric action framework of Section 9.4 is the use of rotations and translations only.

A distinction has been made in this literature between "shape" and "form" (or size-and-shape) to help determining which group of transformation G is used for registration. "Form" relates to the quotient of the object by rigid – transformations only. "Shape" denotes the quotient of the object by similarities. Kendall shape spaces refer to "shape": the scalings are quotiented by constraining the size of the landmark set to be 1.

Note that the estimation of the mean form or shape, that is, the group of transformations used to register the objects, can be distinct from the group used in the generative model. If there is no scaling in the generative model and we estimate the mean form, then we get the partial Procrustes estimate of form. If there is some scaling in the generative model and we estimate the mean form, we get the full Procrustes estimate of shape [27]. The partial estimate of shape can also be considered.

Mean form and mean shape for 2D/3D landmarks

Existing results on bias for shapes of landmarks in 2D and 3D first confirm the findings of Section 9.4, but also give intuition to prove bias results in settings not covered in Section 9.4.

We first consider the Gaussian noise assumption on the landmarks in 2D and 3D. The partial Procrustes estimate of the mean "form" through generalized Procrustean analysis was known to be inconsistent, as shown in [31] with a reducto ad absurdum proof. Section 9.4 provides a geometric interpretation of this fact while extending the results for landmarks in higher dimensions. The full Procrustes estimate of the mean "shape" through generalized Procrustean analysis was known to be consistent for shapes of landmarks in 2D and 3D [30,31]. This result goes beyond the setting of Section 9.4 and shows that there can be no bias for a nonisometric action in this specific case.

Now we relax the Gaussian noise assumption on the landmarks. We investigate if there is bias in other noise settings. For landmarks in 2D and under isotropic noise model (nonnecessarily Gaussian), the full Procrustes estimate of shape is proven to be consistent [27]. Under the isotropic Gaussian noise model, the partial Procrustes estimator of form is inconsistent, but its shape is correct. Bias thus appears only in the size of the estimate and is shown to be of order σ^2. Then, for nonisotropic errors, the full Procrustes estimate need not be consistent and can be arbitrarily inconsistent for high level of noise. This analysis gives an excellent line of work to extend the results of Section 9.4 to other noise settings.

9.5.2 Brain images

We turn in this section to shapes of brains as shown in medical images and especially in MRIs. We show how Section 9.4 can be applied to gather intuition about bias of brain template estimation.

Brain template

Computing a brain template is often the first step in neuroimaging studies. The template is often called an atlas in this literature. In general, the brain template is used as a standardized 3D coordinate frame where the subject brains can be compared. The subjects are then characterized by their *spatial diffeomorphic deformations from the template*; see Chapter 4. These deformations may then serve in a statistical analysis of the subject shapes [3] where the normal and pathological variations of the subjects with respect to the template are quantified. In other words, the template serves as prior knowledge of the brain anatomy [33]. It should be representative of the population under study, thus avoiding bias in subsequent statistical analyses.

Such an "unbiased" template is often constructed by performing an iterative averaging of intensities and deformations [17,20, 21] in the spirit of Algorithm 9.1: the brain template can be interpreted as an instance of a Fréchet mean in a quotient space; see Section 4.6.2 of Chapter 4. We can gain insight about its statistical properties using the intuition developed in this chapter and quantify its asymptotic bias, locally on the brain template image.

Spatial bias on the brain template image

We produce maps showing the local asymptotic bias with a color code superimposed on the original tridimensional brain template image, as shown in Fig. 9.5. We call these maps the *asymptotic bias maps*. A green color (light gray in print version) indicates a low asymptotic bias for a given brain region, and a red color (dark gray in print version) indicates a high asymptotic bias on another brain region. These maps are computed by leveraging the geometric understanding of this chapter to quantify the bias on the brain image through the following heuristic.

Section 9.4 shows that the asymptotic bias of the template estimate $\hat{y}_0$ depends on the noise level σ at the scale of a distance d to the singularity of the space. The variables d and σ depend on the topology of the brain template image level sets and can be expressed using the Morse–Smale complex of the image [35]. The indicator quantifying the local asymptotic bias is expressed in a logarithmic scale as

$$\mathrm{SNR}_{\mathrm{dB}} = 10 \log_{10}\left[\left(\frac{d}{\sigma}\right)^2 \right]. \qquad (9.31)$$

The scale is thus in dB, as the decibel is the logarithmic unit that expresses the ratio of two values of a physical quantity. This unit emphasizes that the quantification of the asymptotic bias depends on a signal-to-noise ratio (SNR). Indeed, we can consider that the signal is d, which is the template distance to a singularity, and the "noise" is σ, the intersubject variability after registration. The lower the SNR on a given brain region, the larger the local asymptotic bias on the brain template on that brain region.

We compute several local asymptotic bias maps for the same brain template; see (C)–(D)–(E) on Fig. 9.5. The difference between the maps is a threshold used to compute the asymptotic bias, which is increased from (C) to (E) [35]. The threshold corresponds to the intensity scale at which we look at the images. It controls the brain regions spatial scale. Increasing the threshold makes more and more regions appear, and these regions are smaller and smaller as well as more and more biased: they become colored in orange–red (mid–dark gray in print version) on Fig. 9.5 (C)–(E).

The interpretation with respect to neuroimaging is the following. Each map of Fig. 9.5 (C)–(D)–(E) represents the asymptotic bias of the brain template we would obtain if we were constraining the image level set topology complexity at a given intensity scale. The local asymptotic bias maps show smaller regions, in orange–red, where the estimated template brain structures are small with respect to the subject variability in the database. In these orange–red regions it is not reasonable to have a sharply defined template, because the estimated "anatomical" structures may have appeared by chance, by registration of noise between the different subjects. In other words, the maps reveal brain regions where the assumption of a unique anatomy in the subject population may break down.

9.6 Bias correction methods

The bias of the template shape estimation impacts analysis of organ shapes in medical imaging and computational anatomy. We now investigate how to correct for the bias. A first correction would be to change the estimate of the template, moving away from the Fréchet mean in the quotient space. This is, for instance, what is

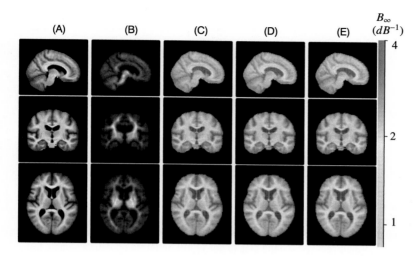

Figure 9.5. Local asymptotic bias maps of the brain template computed from the OASIS database [39]. (A) Template. (B) Template whitened by the intersubject variability. (C) Local asymptotic bias maps for a threshold = 1.3, (D) for threshold = 2, (E) for threshold = 4 (dimensionless). Reprinted by permission from Society for Industrial and Applied Mathematics: Nina Miolane, Susan Holmes, and Xavier Pennec. Topologically constrained template estimation via Morse–Smale complexes controls its statistical consistency. SIAM Journal on Applied Algebra and Geometry 2(2) (2018) 348–375.

provided by the maximum likelihood template estimation techniques or Bayesian mixed effect models [2]. This is beyond the scope of this chapter. Here we present methods to quantify the bias in the Fréchet mean estimate and to correct it when it is sufficiently important.

9.6.1 Riemannian bootstrap

Procedures to correct the asymptotic bias on the template estimate are described in [34]. They rely on the bootstrap principle, more precisely on a parametric bootstrap, which is a general Monte Carlo based resampling method that enables us to estimate the sampling distributions of estimators [11]. We focus here on one of the methods, called the iterative bootstrap (Algorithm 9.2), and we refer to [34] for the other method, called the nested bootstrap.

Algorithm 9.2 starts with the usual (biased) template estimate $\hat{y}_0$ (see Fig. 9.6 (A)) and iteratively improves it. At each iteration we correct $\hat{y}_0$ with a better approximation of the bias. First, we generate bootstrap data by using $\hat{y}_0$ as the template shape of the gener-

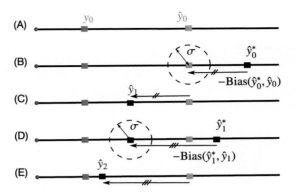

Figure 9.6. Algorithm 9.2 Iterative bootstrap procedure on the example of 2 landmarks in the plane as $n \to +\infty$. (A) Initialization, (B) generate bootstrap sample from $\hat{y}_0$ and compute the corresponding estimate $\hat{y}_0^*$, compute the bias $\hat{y}_0 - \hat{y}_0^*$, (C) correct $\hat{y}_0$ with the bias to get $\hat{y}_1$, (D) generate bootstrap sample from $\hat{y}_1$ and iterate as in (B), (E). Get $\hat{y}_2$, and so on. Reprinted by permission from Society for Industrial and Applied Mathematics: Nina Miolane, Susan Holmes, Xavier Pennec. Template shape estimation: correcting an asymptotic bias. SIAM Journal on Imaging Sciences, Society for Industrial and Applied Mathematics 10(2) (2017) 808–844.

ative model. We perform the template estimation procedure with the Fréchet mean in the quotient space. This gives an estimate $\hat{y}_0^*$ of $\hat{y}_0$. The bias of $\hat{y}_0^*$ with respect to $\hat{y}_0$ is $\text{Bias}(\hat{y}_0^*, \hat{y}_0)$. It gives an estimation $\widehat{\text{Bias}(\hat{y}_0, y_0)}$ of the bias $\text{Bias}(\hat{y}_0, y_0)$; see Fig. 9.6 (B). We correct $\hat{y}_0$ by this approximation of the bias. This gives a new estimate $\hat{y}_1$; see Fig. 9.6 (C). We recall that the bias $\text{Bias}(\hat{y}_0, y_0)$ depends on y_0; see Theorem 9.4. $\hat{y}_1$ is closer to the template y_0 than $\hat{y}_0$. Thus the next iteration gives a better estimation $\text{Bias}(\hat{y}_1^*, \hat{y}_1)$ of $\text{Bias}(\hat{y}_0, y_0)$. We correct the initial $\hat{y}_0$ with this better estimation of the bias, and so on. The procedure is written formally for a general manifold $\mathcal{M}$:

In Algorithm 9.2, $\Pi_{x_1}^{x_2}$ denotes the parallel transport from $T_{x_1}\mathcal{M}$ to $T_{x_2}\mathcal{M}$ along a geodesic. For linear spaces like $\mathbb{R}^2$ in the plane example, we have $\text{Log}_{x_1} x_2 = \overrightarrow{x_1 x_2}$, $\text{Exp}_{x_1}(u) = x_1 + u$, and the parallel transport is the identity $\Pi_{x_1}^{x_2}(u) = u$. For general manifolds, the parallel transport $\Pi_{x_1}^{x_2}(u)$ can be approximately computed using the Schild ladder [14] or more accurately using the pole ladder [37] (see Chapter 5 of this book). In constant curvature spaces-like spheres the pole ladder is even exact in one step [40].

Algorithm 9.2 is a fixed-point iteration $y_{k+1} = F(y_k)$, where

$$F(x) = \text{Exp}_{\hat{y}_0}(-\Pi_x^{\hat{y}_0}(\text{Bias})) \qquad \text{and:} \quad \text{Bias} = \text{Log}_x \hat{x}. \qquad (9.32)$$

Algorithm 9.2 Riemannian iterative bootstrap.

Input: Objects $\{X_i\}_{i=1}^n$, noise variance σ^2, convergence threshold δ

Initialization:

$\hat{y}_0 = \text{Fréchet}(\{[X_i]\}_{i=1}^n)$

$k \leftarrow 0$

Repeat:

- Generate bootstrap sample $\{X_i^{(k)*}\}_{i=1}^n$ from $\mathcal{N}_M(y_k, \sigma^2)$
- $\widehat{y_k} = \text{Fréchet}(\{[X^{(k)*}]_i\}_{i=1}^n)$ $\text{Bias}_k = \text{Log}_{y_k}\widehat{y_k}$
- $\hat{y}_k = \text{Exp}_{\hat{y}_0}\left(-\Pi_{\hat{y}_k}^{\hat{y}_0}(\text{Bias}_k)\right)$
- $y_{k+1} \leftarrow \hat{y}_k$
- $k \leftarrow k+1$

until convergence: $||\text{Log}_{\hat{y}_{k+1}}\hat{y}_k|| < \delta$

Output: $\hat{y}_k$

In a linear setting we have simply $F(x) = \hat{y}_0 - \overrightarrow{x\hat{x}}$. We can show that F is a contraction and that the template shape y_0 is the unique fixed point of F; see [34] for details. Thus the procedure converges to y_0 in the case of an infinite number of observations $n \to +\infty$.

The bootstrap methods work for any type of data but may be computationally expensive as the estimation procedure is performed at each step of the bootstrap. These methods also depend on how confident we are in the generative model. As such, we can consider alternatives to correct the bias.

9.6.2 Brain images: topologically constrained template

We present a correction method that can specifically be applied to the case of brain images presented in Section 9.5.

Constrain the topology to control the bias

In Section 9.5 each map of Fig. 9.5 (C)–(D)–(E) represents the asymptotic bias of the brain template we would obtain if we were constraining the level sets of the image to have a specific topology of increasing complexity. On the one hand, a complex topology implies an important asymptotic bias on the template, which may not represent faithfully the brain anatomy shared by the subjects in the database. On the other hand, a topology that is too simple has no chance of representing a brain anatomy at all. If we want to look at small brain structures, then have to allow for some precision in the topology.

Which topology shall we choose in this trade-off of asymptotic unbiasedness versus image sharpness? If the local intensity of the computed template is below the noise, then there is no hope to compute a consistent template. If the noise is of the same order of magnitude as the signal, then the template may estimate the noise instead of the signal. Thus we choose an threshold that expresses the limit situation where signal (intensity on the brain image) and noise are of the same order of magnitude. In practice this threshold is between -1 and 0 dB [35].

Applying topological denoising on the brain template's

We have decided on the complexity of the brain template topology. This topology can be enforced by applying a topological denoising step in the template estimation procedure [16,24]. By doing so we enforce the asymptotic bias to be below a threshold. Such a control of the brain template bias enables us to build a template in which the topological denoising step has blurred the image where the sharply defined brain template does not make sense as a representative of the shared brain anatomy [35].

We could be interested in a brain template that would be sharp *and* unbiased. In this case we could consider dropping the assumption of a unique brain anatomy expressed by a unique template y_0 in the generative model. We could consider multiple templates by expressing the generative model as a mixture model. Further work is needed to investigate the construction of a stratified template, which would add a new stratification every time a region asymptotic bias crosses the threshold $B_\infty \sim 1$ dB.

9.7 Conclusion

This chapter has introduced tools of Riemannian geometry to study the properties of template shape estimation in medical imaging. The study of consistency and asymptotic bias that was presented summarizes the results of several works. In particular, Table 9.1 recaps the contents of the Theorems 9.3–9.6 taken from these works, with their main differences.

In both analyses, the fixed point of the group actions plays a fundamental role. The fixed points are the "worse" singularities of the space in the sense that their isotropy group is the whole acting group. They are responsible for the curvature of the orbits as shown in the Riemannian manifold case, and they play a role in the hypothesis on the noise support in the Hilbert case.

Nonisometric actions are often encountered in the literature. However, obtaining results in this setting is much more difficult

Table 9.1 Summary of the mathematical results presented in this chapter.

	Work in [7,8]	Work in [34]
Top space $\mathcal{M}$	Hilbert space	Finite-dimensional manifold
Noise ϵ	Sufficient condition	Gaussian noise
Quantification (noise level)	Taylor expansion for $\sigma \to +\infty$ and bounds	Taylor expansion for $\sigma \to 0$ with orbit's geometry

since the distances are now changed by the action of the group. As a consequence, we cannot define a priori a quotient distance anymore. However, for Hilbert spaces, it is still possible to define the classical loss function

$$F(m) = \mathbb{E}\left(\inf_{g \in G} \| g.m - X \|^2 \right).$$

In this setting we can show that the template used to generate the variable X does not minimize this function F, at least when the noise level σ is large enough [7]. Future works could probably improve this result.

We have also presented specific examples of template computations in which bias appears, as well as methods to correct it. Computations of templates have been used in the medical imaging literature for at least 15 years. In particular, in neuroimaging computing the template is often the first step of a study, and understanding the associated bias is key. Still, a biased template can be seen as an indication that the assumption of a unique template, for example, a unique brain anatomy within the population, should be relaxed. In further work we will investigate the estimation of a mixture of templates or stratified templates and how this may allow us to reduce the bias.

Acknowledgment

This work was partially supported by the National Science Foundation, grant NSF DMS RTG 1501767.

References

1. Stéphanie Allassonnière, Yali Amit, Alain Trouvé, Towards a coherent statistical framework for dense deformable template

estimation, Journal of the Royal Statistical Society 69 (1) (2007) 3–29.

2. Stéphanie Allassonnière, Stanley Durrleman, Estelle Kuhn, Bayesian mixed effect atlas estimation with a diffeomorphic deformation model, SIAM Journal on Imaging Sciences 8 (3) (2015) 1367–1395.

3. John Ashburner, Chloe Hutton, Richard Frackowiak, Ingrid Johnsrude, Cathy Price, Karl Friston, Identifying global anatomical differences: deformation-based morphometry, Human Brain Mapping 6 (5–6) (1998) 348–357.

4. Dmitri Alekseevsky, Andreas Kriegl, Mark Losik, Peter W. Michor, The Riemannian geometry of orbit spaces. The metric, geodesics, and integrable systems, Publicationes Mathematicae Debrecen 62 (2003).

5. Jeremie Bigot, Benjamin Charlier, On the consistency of Fréchet means in deformable models for curve and image analysis, Electronic Journal of Statistics (5) (2011) 1054–1089.

6. Jeremie Bigot, Sebastien Gadat, A deconvolution approach to estimation of a common shape in a shifted curves model, Annals of Statistics 38 (4) (2010) 2422–2464.

7. Loïc Devilliers, Stéphanie Allassonnière, Alain Trouvé, Xavier Pennec, Inconsistency of template estimation by minimizing of the variance/pre-variance in the quotient space, Entropy 19 (6) (2017) 288.

8. Loïc Devilliers, Stéphanie Allassonnière, Alain Trouvé, Xavier Pennec, Template estimation in computational anatomy: Fréchet means in top and quotient spaces are not consistent, SIAM Journal on Imaging Sciences 10 (3) (2017) 1139–1169.

9. Hugo Darmanté, Benoit Bugnas, Regis Bernard De Dompsure, Laurent Barresi, Nina Miolane, Xavier Pennec, Fernand de Peretti, Nicolas Bronsard, Analyse biométrique de lánneau pelvien en 3 dimensions – à propos de 100 scanners, Revue de Chirurgie Orthopédique et Traumatologique 100 (7) (2014) S241.

10. Ian L. Dryden, Kanti V. Mardia, Statistical Shape Analysis, John Wiley & Sons, New York, 1998.

11. Bradley Efron, Bootstrap methods: another look at the jackknife, Annals of Statistics 7 (1) (1979) 1–26.

12. Alan C. Evans, Andrew L. Janke, D. Louis Collins, Sylvain Baillet, Brain templates and atlases, NeuroImage 62 (2) (2012) 911–922.

13. Michel Émery, Gabriel Mokobodzki, Sur le barycentre d'une probabilité dans une variété, Séminaire de probabilités de Strasbourg 25 (1991) 220–233.

14. Jürgen Ehlers, Felix A.E. Pirani, Alfred Schild, Republication of: the geometry of free fall and light propagation, General Relativity and Gravitation 44 (6) (2012) 1587–1609.

15. John C. Gower, Garmt B. Dijksterhuis, Procrustes Problems, Oxford Statistical Science Series, vol. 30, Oxford University Press, Oxford, UK, January 2004.

16. David Gunther, Alec Jacobson, Jan Reininghaus, Hans-Peter Seidel, Olga Sorkine-Hornung, Tino Weinkauf, Fast and memory-efficient topological denoising of 2d and 3d scalar fields, IEEE Transactions on Visualization and Computer Graphics 20 (12) (2014) 2585–2594.

17. Alexandre Guimond, Jean Meunier, Jean-Philippe Thirion, Average brain models: a convergence study, Computer Vision and Image Understanding 77 (2) (2000) 192–210.
18. Colin Goodall, Procrustes methods in the statistical analysis of shape, in: Procrustes Methods in the Statistical Analysis of Shape Journal of the Royal Statistical Society, Series B, Methodological 53 (2) (1991) 285–339.
19. John C. Gower, Generalized Procrustes analysis, Psychometrika 40 (1975) 33–51.
20. Mehdi Hadj-Hamou, Marco Lorenzi, Nicholas Ayache, Xavier Pennec, Longitudinal analysis of image time series with diffeomorphic deformations: a computational framework based on stationary velocity fields, Frontiers in Neuroscience (2016).
21. Sarang Joshi, Brad Davis, Matthieu Jomier, Guido Gerig, Unbiased diffeomorphic atlas construction for computational anatomy, NeuroImage 23 (2004) 151–160.
22. Shantanu Joshi, David Kaziska, Anuj Srivastava, Washington Mio, Riemannian structures on shape spaces: a framework for statistical inferences, in: Statistics and Analysis of Shapes, Modeling and Simulation in Science, Engineering and Technology, Birkhäuser, Boston, 2006, pp. 313–333.
23. Richard M. Johnson, The minimal transformation to orthonormality, Psychometrika 31 (1966) 61–66.
24. Alec Jacobson, Tino Weinkauf, Olga Sorkine, Smooth shape-aware functions with controlled extrema, Computer Graphics Forum (Proc. SGP) 31 (5) (2012) 1577–1586.
25. David G. Kendall, The diffusion of shape, Advances in Applied Probability 9 (3) (1977) 428–430.
26. David G. Kendall, Shape manifolds, Procrustean metrics, and complex projective spaces, Bulletin of the London Mathematical Society 16 (2) (1984) 81–121.
27. John T. Kent, Kanti V. Mardia, Consistency of Procrustes estimators, Journal of the Royal Statistical Society, Series B, Statistical Methodology 59 (1) (1997) 281–290.
28. Sebastian A. Kurtek, Anuj Srivastava, Wei Wu, Signal estimation under random time-warpings and nonlinear signal alignment, in: J. Shawe-taylor, R.s. Zemel, P. Bartlett, F.c.n. Pereira, K.q. Weinberger (Eds.), Advances in Neural Information Processing Systems 24 (2011) 675–683.
29. Marco Lorenzi, Nicholas Ayache, Xavier Pennec, Regional flux analysis for discovering and quantifying anatomical changes: an application to the brain morphometry in Alzheimer's disease, NeuroImage 115 (2015) 224–234.
30. Huiling Le, On the consistency of Procrustean mean shapes, Advances in Applied Probability 30 (1) (1998) 53–63.
31. Subhash Lele, Euclidean distance matrix analysis (EDMA): estimation of mean form and mean form difference, Mathematical Geology 25 (1993) 573–602.

32. Huiling Le, David G. Kendall, The Riemannian structure of Euclidean shape spaces: a novel environment for statistics, Annals of Statistics 21 (3) (1993) 1225–1271.
33. Michael I. Miller, Gary E. Christensen, Yali Amit, Ulf Grenander, Mathematical textbook of deformable neuroanatomies, Proceedings of the National Academy of Sciences 90 (24) (1993) 11944–11948.
34. Nina Miolane, Susan Holmes, Xavier Pennec, Template shape estimation: correcting an asymptotic bias, SIAM Journal on Imaging Sciences 10 (2) (2017) 808–844.
35. Nina Miolane, Susan Holmes, Xavier Pennec, Topologically constrained template estimation via Morse–Smale complexes controls its statistical consistency, SIAM Journal on Applied Algebra and Geometry 2 (2) (2018) 348–375.
36. Charles I. Mosier, Determining a simple structure when loadings for certain tests are known, Psychometrika (1939) 149–162.
37. Marco Lorenzi, Xavier Pennec, Parallel transport with pole ladder: application to deformations of time series of images, in: Geometric Science of Information: First International Conference, GSI 2013, Proceedings, Paris, France, August 28–30, 2013, Springer, Berlin, Heidelberg, 2013, pp. 68–75.
38. J.B. Antoine Maintz, Max A. Viergever, An overview of medical image registration methods, in: Symposium of the Belgian Hospital Physicists Association (SBPH-BVZF), 1996, Tech. report.
39. Daniel S. Marcus, Tracy H. Wang, Jamie Parker, John G. Csernansky, John C. Morris, Randy L. Buckner, Open access series of imaging studies (OASIS): cross-sectional mri data in young, middle aged, nondemented, and demented older adults, Journal of Cognitive Neuroscience 19 (2007) 1498–1507.
40. Xavier Pennec, Parallel transport with pole ladder: a third order scheme in affine connection spaces which is exact in affine symmetric spaces, ArXiv e-prints, arXiv:1805.11436, 2018.
41. Peter H. Schönemann, A generalized solution of the orthogonal Procrustes problem, Psychometrika 31 (1966) 1–10.
42. Christopher G. Small, The Statistical Theory of Shape, Springer Series in Statistics, Springer, New York, 1996.
43. Jos M.F. Ten Berge, Orthogonal Procrustes rotation for two or more matrices, Psychometrika 42 (1977) 267–276.
44. Herbert Ziezold, On Expected Figures and a Strong Law of Large Numbers for Random Elements in Quasi-Metric Spaces, Springer, Netherlands, Dordrecht, 1977, pp. 591–602.

Probabilistic approaches to geometric statistics

Stochastic processes, transition distributions, and fiber bundle geometry

Stefan Sommer

University of Copenhagen, Department of Computer Science, Copenhagen, Denmark

10.1 Introduction

When generalizing Euclidean statistical concepts to manifolds, it is common to focus on particular properties of the Euclidean constructions and select those as the defining properties of the corresponding manifold generalization. This approach appears in many instances in *geometric statistics*, statistics of manifold-valued data. For example, the Fréchet mean [9] is the minimizer of the expected square distance to the data. It generalizes its Euclidean counterpart by using this least-squares criterion. Similarly, the principal component analysis (PCA) constructions discussed in Chapter 2 use the notion of linear subspaces from Euclidean space, generalizations of those to manifolds, and least-squares fit to data. Although one construction can often be defined via several equivalent characterizations in the Euclidean situation, curvature generally breaks such equivalences. For example, the mean value and PCA can in the Euclidean situation be formulated as maximum likelihood fits of normal distributions to the data resulting in the same constructions as the least-squares definitions. On curved manifolds the least-squares and maximum likelihood definitions give different results. Fitting probability distributions to data implies a shift of focus from the Riemannian distance as used in least-squares to an underlying probability model. We pursue such probabilistic approaches in this chapter.

The probabilistic viewpoint uses the concepts of likelihood-functions and parametric families of probability distributions. Generally, we search for a family of distributions $\mu(\theta)$ depending on the parameter θ with corresponding density function $p(\cdot; \theta)$, from which we get a likelihood $\mathcal{L}(\theta; y) = p(y; \theta)$. With independent observations $y_1, \ldots, y_N$, we can then estimate the parameter by setting

$$\hat{\theta}_{\text{ML}} = \text{argmax}_\theta \prod_{i=1}^{N} \mathcal{L}(\theta; y_i), \qquad (10.1)$$

giving a sample maximum likelihood (ML) estimate of θ or, when a prior distribution $p(\theta)$ for the parameters is available, the maximum a posteriori (MAP) estimate

$$\hat{\theta}_{\text{MAP}} = \text{argmax}_\theta \prod_{i=1}^{N} \mathcal{L}(\theta; y_i) p(\theta) . \qquad (10.2)$$

We can, for example, let the parameter θ denote a point m in M, and let $\mu(\theta)$ denote the normal distribution centered at m, in which case θ_{ML} is a *maximum likelihood* mean. This viewpoint transfers the focus of manifold statistics from least-squares optimization to constructions of natural families of probability distributions $\mu(\theta)$. A similar case arises when progressing beyond the mean to modeling covariance, data anisotropy, and principal components. The view here shifts from geodesic sprays and projections onto subspaces to the notion of covariance of a random variable. In a sense, we hide the complexity of the geometry in the construction of $\mu(\theta)$, which in turn implies that constructing such distributions is not always trivial.

Throughout the chapter, we will take inspiration from and refer to the standard Euclidean linear latent variable model

$$y = m + Wx + \epsilon \qquad (10.3)$$

on $\mathbb{R}^d$ with normally distributed latent variable $x \sim \mathcal{N}(0, \text{Id}_r), r \leq d$ and isotropic noise $\epsilon \sim \mathcal{N}(0, \sigma^2 \text{Id}_d)$. The marginal distribution of y is normal $y \sim N(m, \Sigma)$ as well with mean m and covariance $\Sigma = WW^T + \sigma^2 \text{Id}_d$. This simple model exemplifies many of the challenges when working with parametric probability distributions on manifolds: 1) Its definition relies on normal distributions with isotropic covariance for the distribution of x and ϵ. We describe two possible generalizations to manifolds of these, the Riemannian Normal law and the transition density of the Riemannian Brownian motion. 2) The model is additive, but on manifolds addition is only defined for tangent vectors. We handle this fact by defining probability models infinitesimally using stochastic differential equations. 3) The marginal distribution of y requires a way to translate the directions encoded in the matrix W to directions on the manifold. This can be done both in the tangent space of m,

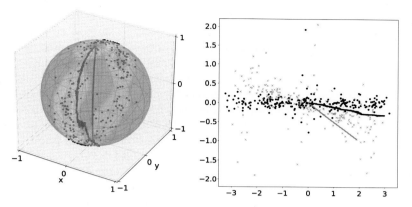

Figure 10.1. (Left) Samples (black dots) along a great circle of $\mathbb{S}^2$ with added minor variation orthogonal to the circle. The sphere is colored by the density of the distribution, the transition density of the underlying stochastic process. (Right) Red crosses (gray in print version): Data mapped to the tangent space of the north pole using the standard tangent principal component analysis (PCA) linearization. Variation orthogonal to the great circle is overestimated because the curvature of the sphere lets geodesics (red (gray in print version) curve and line) leave high-density areas of the distribution. Black dots: Corresponding linearization of the data using the infinitesimal probabilistic PCA model [34]. The black curve represents the expectation over samples of the latent process conditioned on the same observation as the red (gray in print version) curve. The corresponding path shown on the left figure clearly is attracted to the high-density area of the distribution contrary to the geodesic. The orthogonal variation is not overestimated, and the Euclidean view provides a better representation of the data variability.

by using fiber bundles to move W with parallel transport, by using Lie group structure, or by referring to coordinate systems that in some cases have special meaning for the particular data at hand.

The effect of including all these points is illustrated in Fig. 10.1. The linear Euclidean view of the data produced by tangent space principal component analysis (PCA) is compared to the linear Euclidean view provided by the infinitesimal probabilistic PCA model [34], which transports covariance parallel along the manifold. Because the infinitesimal model does not linearize to a single tangent space and because of the built-in notion of data anisotropy, infinitesimal covariance, the provided Euclidean view gives a better representation of the data variability.

We start in section 10.2 by discussing two ways to pursue construction of $\mu(\theta)$ via density functions and from transition distributions of stochastic processes. We exemplify the former with the probabilistic principal geodesic analysis (PPGA) generalization of manifold PCA, and the later with maximum likelihood means and an infinitesimal version of probabilistic PCA. In section 10.3, we discuss the most important stochastic process on manifolds, the Brownian motion, and its transition distribution, both in the Riemannian manifold case and when Lie group structure is present. In section 10.4, we describe aspects of fiber bundle geometry necessary for the construction of stochastic processes with infinitesimal covariance as pursued in section 10.5. The fiber bundle construction can be seen as a way to handle the lack of global coordinate system. Whereas it touches concepts beyond the standard set of Riemannian geometric notions discussed in chapter 1, it provides intrinsic geometric constructions that are very useful from a statistical viewpoint. We use this in section 10.6 to define statistical concepts as maximum likelihood parameter fits to data and in section 10.7 to perform parameter estimation. In section 10.8, we discuss advanced concepts arising from fiber bundle geometry, including interpretation of the curvature tensor, sub-Riemannian frame-bundle geometry, and examples of flows using additional geometric structure present in specific models of shape.

We aim with the chapter for providing an overview of aspects of probabilistic statistics on manifolds in an accessible way. This implies that mathematical details on the underlying geometry and stochastic analysis are partly omitted. We provide references to the papers where the presented material was introduced in each section, and we include references for further reading by the end of the chapter. The code for the presented models and parameter estimation algorithms discussed in this chapter are available in the Theano Geometry library https://bitbucket.com/stefansommer/theanogeometry, see also [16,15].

10.2 Parametric probability distributions on manifolds

We here discuss two ways of defining families of probability distributions on a manifold: directly from a density function, or as the transition distribution of a stochastic process. We exemplify their use with the probabilistic PGA generalization of Euclidean PCA and an infinitesimal counterpart based on an underlying stochastic process.

10.2.1 Probabilistic PCA

Euclidean principal component analysis (PCA) is traditionally defined as a fit of best approximating linear subspaces of a given dimension to data, either by maximizing variance

$$\hat{W} = \text{argmax}_{W \in O(\mathbb{R}^r, \mathbb{R}^d)} \sum_{i=1}^{N} \| W W^T y_i \|^2 \qquad (10.4)$$

of the centered data $y_1, \ldots, y_N$ projected to r-dimensional subspaces of $\mathbb{R}^d$ represented here by orthonormal matrices $W \in O(\mathbb{R}^r, \mathbb{R}^d)$ of rank r or by minimizing residual errors

$$\hat{W} = \text{argmin}_{W \in O(\mathbb{R}^r, \mathbb{R}^d)} \sum_{i=1}^{N} \| y_i - W W^T y_i \|^2 \qquad (10.5)$$

between the observations and their projections to the subspace. We see that fundamental for this construction is the notion of linear subspace, projections to linear subspaces, and squared distances. The dimension r of the fitted subspace determines the number of principal components.

PCA can however also be defined from a probabilistic viewpoint [37,29]. The approach is here to fit the latent variable model (10.3) with W of fixed rank r. The conditional distribution of the data given the latent variable $x \in \mathbb{R}^r$ is normal

$$y|x \sim N(m + Wx, \sigma^2 I). \qquad (10.6)$$

With x normally distributed $\mathcal{N}(0, \text{Id}_r)$ and noise $\epsilon \sim \mathcal{N}(0, \sigma^2 \text{Id}_d)$, the marginal distribution of y is $y \sim N(m, \Sigma)$ with $\Sigma = W W^T + \sigma^2 \text{Id}_d$.

The Euclidean principal components of the data are here interpreted as the conditional distribution $x|y_i$ of x given the data y_i. From the data conditional distribution, a single quantity representing y_i can be obtained by taking expectation $x_i := \mathbb{E}[x|y_i] = (W^T W + \sigma^2 I)^{-1} W^T (y_i - m)$. The parameters of the model m, W, σ can be found by maximizing the likelihood

$$\mathcal{L}(W, \sigma, m; y) = |2\pi \Sigma|^{-\frac{1}{2}} e^{-\frac{1}{2}(y-m)^T \Sigma^{-1}(y-m))}. \qquad (10.7)$$

Up to rotation, the ML fit of W is given by $\hat{W}_{\text{ML}} = \hat{U}_r (\hat{\Lambda} - \sigma^2 \text{Id}_d)^{1/2}$, where $\hat{\Lambda} = \text{diag}(\hat{\lambda}_1, \ldots, \hat{\lambda}_r)$, $\hat{U}_r$ contains the first r principal eigenvectors of the sample covariance matrix of y_i in the columns, and $\hat{\lambda}_1, \ldots, \hat{\lambda}_r$ are the corresponding eigenvalues.

10.2.2 Riemannian normal distribution and probabilistic PGA

We saw in chapter 2 the Normal law or Riemannian normal distribution defined via its density

$$p(y; m, \sigma^2) = C(m, \sigma^2)^{-1} e^{-\frac{\text{dist}(m,y)^2}{2\sigma^2}} \qquad (10.8)$$

with normalization constant $C(m, \sigma^2)$ and the parameter σ^2 controlling the dispersion of the distribution. The density is given with respect to the volume measure $d\mathcal{V}_g$ on $\mathcal{M}$, so that the actual distribution is $p(\cdot; m, \sigma^2) d\mathcal{V}_g$. Because of the use of the Riemannian distance function, the distribution is at first sight related to a normal distribution $N(0, \sigma^2 \text{Id}_d)$ in $T_m\mathcal{M}$; however, its definition with respect to the measure $d\mathcal{V}_g$ implies that it differs from the density of the normal distribution at each point of $T_m\mathcal{M}$ by the square root determinant of the metric $|g|^{\frac{1}{2}}$. The isotropic precision/concentration matrix $\sigma^{-2}\text{Id}_d$ can be exchanged with a more general concentration matrix in $T_m\mathcal{M}$. The distribution maximizes the entropy for fixed parameters (m, Σ) [26].

This distribution is used in [39] to generalize Euclidean PPCA. Here the distribution of the latent variable x is normal in $T_m\mathcal{M}$, x is mapped to $\mathcal{M}$ using Exp_m, and the conditional distribution $y|x$ of the observed data y given x is Riemannian normal $p(y; \text{Exp}_m x, \sigma^2) d\mathcal{V}_g$. The matrix W models the square root covariance $\Sigma = WW^T$ of the latent variable x in $T_m\mathcal{M}$. The model is called probabilistic principal geodesic analysis (PPGA).

10.2.3 Transition distributions and stochastic differential equations

Instead of mapping latent variables from $T_m\mathcal{M}$ to $\mathcal{M}$ using the exponential map, we can take an infinitesimal approach and only map infinitesimal displacements to the manifold, thereby avoiding the use of Exp_m and the implicit linearization coming from the use of a single tangent space. The idea is to create probability distributions as solutions to stochastic differential equations, SDEs. In Euclidean space, SDEs are usually written on the form

$$dy(t) = b(t, y(t))dt + a(t, y(t))dx(t), \qquad (10.9)$$

where $a : \mathbb{R} \times \mathbb{R}^d \to \mathbb{R}^{d \times d}$ is the diffusion field modeling the local diffusion of the process, and $b : \mathbb{R} \times \mathbb{R}^d \to \mathbb{R}^d$ models the deterministic drift. The process $x(t)$ of which we multiply the infinitesimal increments $dx(t)$ on a is a semimartingale. For our purposes, we can assume that it is a standard Brownian motion, often written $W(t)$ or $B(t)$. Solutions to (10.9) are defined by an integral equation that discretized in time takes the form

$$y(t_i) = y(0) + \sum_{j=1}^{i-1} b(t_j, y(t_j))(t_{j+1} - t_j) + a(t_j, y(t_j))(x(t_{j+1}) - x(t_j)) \,.$$

(10.10)

This is called an Itô equation. Alternatively, we can use the Fisk–Stratonovich solution

$$y(t_i) = y(0) + \sum_{j=1}^{i-1} b(t_j^*, y(t_j^*))(t_{j+1} - t_j) + a(t_j^*, y(t_j^*))(x(t_{j+1}) - x(t_j))$$

(10.11)

where $t_j^* = (t_{j+1} - t_j)/2$, that is, the integrand is evaluated at the midpoint. Notationally, Fisk–Stratonovich SDEs, often just called Stratonovich SDEs, are distinguished from Itô SDEs by adding $\circ$ in the diffusion term $a(t, y(t)) \circ dx(t)$ in (10.9). The main purpose here of using Stratonovich SDEs is that solutions obey the ordinary chain rule of differentiation and therefore map naturally between manifolds.

A solution $y(t)$ to an SDE is a t-indexed family of probability distributions. If we fix a time $T > 0$, then the transition distribution $y(T)$ denotes the distribution of endpoints of sample paths $y(\omega)(t)$, where ω is a particular random event. We can thus generate distributions in this way and set $\mu(\theta) = y(T)$, where the parameters θ now control the dynamics of the process via the SDE, particularly the drift b, the diffusion field a, and the starting point y_0 of the process.

The use of SDEs fits the differential structure of manifolds well because SDEs are defined infinitesimally. However, because we generally do not have global coordinate systems to write up an SDE as in (10.9), defining SDEs on manifolds takes some work. We will see several examples of this in the sections below.

Particularly, we will define an SDE that reformulates (10.3) as a time-sequence of random steps, where the latent variable x will be replaced by a latent process $x(t)$, where the covariance W will be parallel transported over $\mathcal{M}$. This process will again have parameters (m, W, σ). We define the distribution $\mu(m, W, \sigma)$ by setting $\mu(m, W, \sigma) = y(T)$, and we then assume that the observed data $y_1, \ldots, y_N$ have marginal distribution $y_i \sim \mu(m, W, \sigma)$. Note that $y(T)$ is a distribution, whereas $y_i, i = 1, \ldots, N$, denote the data.

Let $p(y_i; m, W, \sigma)$ denote the density of the distribution $\mu(m, W, \sigma)$ with respect to a fixed measure. As in the PPCA situation, we then have a likelihood for the model

$$\mathcal{L}(m, W, \sigma; y_i) = p(y_i; m, W, \sigma), \tag{10.12}$$

and we can optimize for the ML estimate $\hat{\theta} = (\hat{m}, \hat{W}, \hat{\sigma})$. Again, similarly to the PPCA construction, we get the generalization of the principal components by conditioning the latent process on the data: $x_{i,t} := x(t)|y(T) = y_i$. The picture here is that among all sample paths $y(\omega)(t)$, we single out those hitting y_i at time T and consider the corresponding realizations of the latent process $x(\omega)(t)$ a representation of the data.

Fig. 10.1 displays the result of pursuing this construction compared to tangent space PCA. Because the anisotropic covariance is now transported with the process instead of being tied to a single tangent space, the curvature of the sphere is in a sense incorporated into the model, and the linear view of the data $x_{i,t}$, particularly the endpoints $x_i := x_{i,T}$, provide an improved picture of the data variation on the manifold.

Below, we will make the construction of the underlying stochastic process precise and present other examples of geometrically natural processes that allow for generating geometrically natural families of probability distributions $\mu(\theta)$.

10.3 The Brownian motion

In Euclidean space the normal distribution $N(0, \mathrm{Id}_d)$ is often defined in terms of its density function. This view leads naturally to the Riemannian normal distribution or the normal law (10.8). A different characterization [10] is as the transition distribution of an isotropic diffusion processes, the heat equation. Here the density is the solution to the partial differential equation

$$\partial_t p(t, y) = \frac{1}{2} \Delta p(t, y), \ y \in \mathbb{R}^k, \tag{10.13}$$

where $p : \mathbb{R} \times \mathbb{R}^k \to \mathbb{R}$ is a real-valued function, Δ is the Laplace differential operator $\Delta = \partial_{y^1}^2 + \cdots + \partial_{y^k}^2$. If (10.13) is started at time $t = 0$ with $p(y) = \delta_m(y)$, that is, the indicator function taking the value 1 only when $y = m$, the time $t = 1$ solution is the density of the normal distribution $N(m, \mathrm{Id}_k)$. We can think of a point-sourced heat distribution starting at m and diffusing through the domain from time $t = 0$ to $t = 1$.

The heat flow can be characterized probabilistically from a stochastic process, the Brownian motion $B(t)$. When started at

m at time $t = 0$, a solution p to the heat flow equation (10.13) describes the density of the random variable $B(t)$ for each t. Therefore, we again regain the density of the normal distribution $N(m, \mathrm{Id}_k)$ as the density of $B(1)$. The heat flow and the Brownian motion view of the normal distribution generalize naturally to the manifold situation. Because the Laplacian is a differential operator and because the Brownian motion is constructed from random infinitesimal increments, the construction is an infinitesimal construction as discussed in section 10.2.3.

Whereas in this section we focus on aspects of the Brownian motion, we will later see that solutions $y(t)$ to the SDE $dy(t) = W dB(t)$ with more general matrices W in addition allows modeling covariance in the normal distribution, even in the manifold situation, using the fact that in the Euclidean situation, $y(1) \sim N(m, \Sigma)$ when $\Sigma = WW^T$.

10.3.1 Brownian motion on Riemannian manifolds

A Riemannian metric g defines the Laplace–Beltrami operator Δ_g that generalizes the usual Euclidean Laplace operator used in (10.13). The operator is defined on real-valued functions by $\Delta_g f = \mathrm{div}_g \mathrm{grad}_g f$. When $e_1, \ldots, e_d$ is an orthonormal basis for $T_y M$, it has the expression $\Delta_g f(y) = \sum_{i=1}^d \nabla_y^2 f(e_i, e_i)$ when evaluated at y similarly to the Euclidean Laplacian. The expression $\nabla_y^2 f(e_i, e_i)$ denotes the Hessian ∇_y^2 evaluated at the pair of vectors (e_i, e_i). The heat equation on $\mathcal{M}$ is the partial differential equation defined from the Laplace–Beltrami operator by

$$\partial_t p(t, y) = \frac{1}{2} \Delta_g p(t, y), \; y \in \mathcal{M}. \tag{10.14}$$

With initial condition $p(0, \cdot)$ at $t = 0$ being the indicator function $\delta_m(y)$, the solution is called the heat kernel and written $p(t, m, y)$ when evaluated at $y \in M$. The heat equation again models point sourced heat flows starting at m and diffusing through the medium with the Laplace–Beltrami operator now ensuring that the flow is adapted to the nonlinear geometry. The heat kernel is symmetric in that $p(t, m, y) = p(t, y, m)$ and satisfies the semigroup property

$$p(t + s, m, y) = \int_{\mathcal{M}} p(t, m, z) p(s, z, y) \, dV_g(z).$$

Similarly to the Euclidean situation, we can recover the heat kernel from a diffusion process on $\mathcal{M}$, the Brownian motion. The Brownian motion on Riemannian manifolds and Lie groups with a Riemannian metric can be constructed in several ways: Using charts, by embedding in a Euclidean space, or using left/right invariance as we pursue in this section. A particular important construction here is the Eells–Elworthy–Malliavin construction of Brownian motion that uses a fiber bundle of the manifold to define an SDE for the Brownian motion. We will use this construction in section 10.4 and through the rest of the chapter.

The heat kernel $p(t, m, y)$ is related to a Brownian motion $x(t)$ on $\mathcal{M}$ by its transition density, that is,

$$\mathbb{P}_m(x(t) \in C) = \int_C p(t, m, y) \, d\mathcal{V}_g(y)$$

for subsets $C \subset \mathcal{M}$. If $\mathcal{M}$ is assumed compact, it can be shown that it is stochastically complete, which implies that the Brownian motion exists for all time and that $\int_{\mathcal{M}} p(t, m, y) \, d\mathcal{V}_g(y) = 1$ for all $t > 0$. If $\mathcal{M}$ is not compact, the long time existence can be ensured by, for example, bounding the Ricci curvature of $\mathcal{M}$ from below; see, for example, [7]. In coordinates, a solution $y(t)$ to the Itô SDE

$$dy(t)^i = b(y(t))dt + \sqrt{g(y(t))^{-1}}^i \, dB(t) \tag{10.15}$$

is a Brownian motion on $\mathcal{M}$ [13]. Here $B(t)$ is a Euclidean $\mathbb{R}^d$-valued Brownian motion, the diffusion field $\sqrt{g(y(t))^{-1}}$ is a square root of the cometric tensor $g(y(t))^{ij}$, and the drift $b(y(t))$ is the contraction $-\frac{1}{2}g(y(t))^{kl}\Gamma(y(t))_{kl}$ of the metric and the Christoffel symbols $\Gamma_{kl}{}^i$. Fig. 10.2 shows sample paths from a Brownian motion on the sphere $\mathbb{S}^2$.

10.3.2 Lie groups

With a left-invariant metric on a Lie group G (see chapter 1), the Laplace–Beltrami operator takes the form $\Delta f(x) = \Delta(L_y f)(y^{-1}x)$ for all $x, y \in G$. By left-translating to the identity the operator thus needs only be computed at $x = e$, that is, at the Lie algebra $\mathfrak{g}$. Like the Laplace–Beltrami operator, the heat kernel is left-invariant [21] when the metric is left-invariant. Similar invariance happens in the right-invariant case.

Let $e_1, \ldots, e_d$ be an orthonormal basis for $\mathfrak{g}$, so that $X_i(y) = (L_y)_*(e_i)$ is an orthonormal set of vector fields on G. Let $C^i{}_{jk}$ denote the structure coefficients given by

$$[X_j, X_k] = C^i{}_{jk} X_i, \tag{10.16}$$

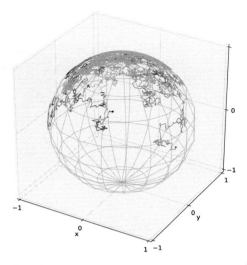

Figure 10.2. Sample paths $x(\omega)(t)$ of a standard Browian motion on the sphere $\mathbb{S}^2$.

and let $B(t)$ be a standard Brownian motion on $\mathbb{R}^d$. Then the solution $y(t)$ of the Stratonovich differential equation

$$dy(t) = -\frac{1}{2}\sum_{j,i} C^j{}_{ij} X_i(y(t))dt + X_i(y(t)) \circ dB(t)^i \qquad (10.17)$$

is a Brownian motion on G. Fig. 10.3 visualizes a sample path of $B(t)$ and the corresponding sample of $y(t)$ on the group SO(3). When the metric on $\mathfrak{g}$ is in addition Ad-invariant, the drift term vanishes leaving only the multiplication of the Brownian motion increments on the basis.

The left-invariant fields $X_i(y)$ here provide a basis for the tangent space at y that in (10.17) is used to map increments of the Euclidean Brownian motion $B(t)$ to T_yG. The fact that X_i are defined globally allows this construction to specify the evolution of the process at all points of G without referring to charts as in (10.15). We will later on explore a different approach to obtain a structure much like the Lie group fields X_i but on general manifolds, where we do not have globally defined continuous and nonzero vector fields. This allows us to write the Brownian motion globally as in the Lie group case.

10.4 Fiber bundle geometry

In the Lie group case, Brownian motion can be constructed by mapping a Euclidean process $B(t)$ to the group to get the pro-

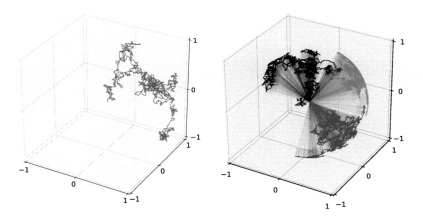

Figure 10.3. (Left) Sample path $B(\omega)(t)$ of a standard Brownian motion on $\mathbb{R}^3$. (Right) The corresponding sample path $y(\omega)(t)$ of the SO(3)-valued process (10.17) visualized by the action of rotation $y.(e_1, e_2, e_3)$, $y \in$ SO(3) on three basis vectors e_1, e_2, e_3 (red/green/blue) (gray/light gray/dark gray in print version) for $\mathbb{R}^3$.

cess $y(t)$. This construction uses the set of left- (or right)-vector fields $X_i(y) = (L_y)_*(e_i)$ that are globally defined and, with a left-invariant metric, orthonormal. Globally defined maps from a manifold to its tangent bundle are called sections, and manifolds that support sections of the tangent bundle that at each point form a basis for the tangent space are called parallelizable, a property that Lie groups possess but not manifolds in general. The sphere $\mathbb{S}^2$ is an example: The hairy-ball theorem asserts that no continuous nowhere vanishing vector fields exist on $\mathbb{S}^2$. Thus we have no chance of finding a set of nonvanishing global vector fields, not to mention a set of fields constituting an orthonormal basis, which we can use to write an SDE similar to (10.17).

A similar issue arises when generalizing the latent variable model (10.3). We can use the tangent space at m to model the latent variables x, map to the manifold using the Riemannian exponential map Exp_m, and use the Riemannian Normal law to model the conditional distribution $y|x$. However, if we wish to avoid the linearization implied by using the tangent space at m, then we need to convert (10.3) from using addition of the vectors x, W, and ϵ to work infinitesimally, to use addition of infinitesimal steps in tangent spaces, and to transport W between these tangent spaces. We can achieve this by converting (10.3) to the SDE

$$dy(t) = W dx(t) + d\epsilon(t) \qquad (10.18)$$

started at m, where $x(t)$ is now a Euclidean Brownian motion, and $\epsilon(t)$ is a Euclidean Brownian motion scaled by σ. The latent process $x(t)$ here takes the place of the latent variable x in (10.3) with $x(1)$ and x having the same distribution $N(0, \mathrm{Id}_d)$. We write $x(t)$ instead of $B(t)$ to emphasize this. Similarly, the noise process $\epsilon(t)$ takes the place of ϵ with $\epsilon(1)$ and ϵ having the same distribution $N(0, \sigma^2 \mathrm{Id}_d)$. In Euclidean space, the transition distribution of this SDE will be equal to the marginal distribution of y in (10.3), that is, $y_1 \sim N(m, \Sigma)$ and $\Sigma = WW^T + \sigma^2 \mathrm{Id}_d$. On the manifold we however need to handle the fact that the matrix W is defined at first only in the tangent space $T_m M$. The natural way to move W to tangent spaces nearby m is by parallel transport of the vectors constituting the columns of W. This reflects the Euclidean situation where W is independent of $x(t)$ and hence spatially stationary. However, parallel transport is tied to paths, so the result will be a transport of W that is now different for each sample path realization of (10.18). This fact is beautifully handled with the Eells–Elworthy–Malliavin [6] construction of Brownian motion. We outline this construction below. For this, we first need some important notions from fiber bundle geometry.

10.4.1 The frame bundle

A fiber bundle over a manifold M is a manifold E with a map $\pi : E \to M$, called the projection, such that for sufficiently small neighborhoods $U \subset M$, the preimage $\pi^{-1}(U)$ can be written as a product $\pi^{-1} \simeq U \times F$ between U and a manifold F, the fiber. When the fibers are vector spaces, fiber bundles are called vector bundles. The most commonly occurring vector bundle is the tangent bundle TM. Recall that a tangent vector always lives in a tangent space at a point in M, that is, $v \in T_y M$. The map $\pi(v) = y$ is the projection, and the fiber $\pi^{-1}(y)$ of the point y is the vector space $T_y M$, which is isomorphic to $\mathbb{R}^d$.

Consider now basis vectors $W_1, \ldots, W_d$ for $T_y M$. As an ordered set $(W_1, \ldots, W_d)$, the vectors are in combination called a frame. The frame bundle $F\mathcal{M}$ is a fiber bundle over M such that the fibers $\pi^{-1}(y)$ are sets of frames. Therefore a point $u \in F\mathcal{M}$ consists of a collection of basis vectors $(W_1, \ldots, W_d)$ and the base point $y \in M$ of which $W_1, \ldots, W_d$ make up a basis for $T_y M$. We can use the local product structure of frame bundles to locally write $u = (y, W)$ where $y \in M$ as $W_1, \ldots, W_d$ are the basis vectors. Often, we denote the basis vectors in u just $u_1, \ldots, u_d$. The frame bundle has interesting geometric properties, which we will use through the chapter. The frame bundle of $\mathbb{S}^2$ is illustrated in Fig. 10.4.

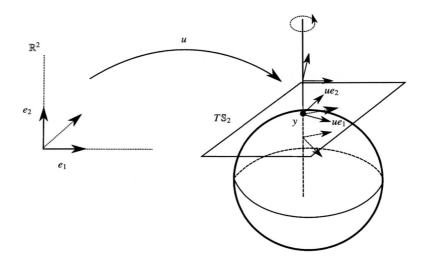

Figure 10.4. The frame bundle $F\mathbb{S}^2$ of the sphere $\mathbb{S}^2$ illustrated by its representation as the principal bundle $\mathrm{GL}(\mathbb{R}^2, T\mathbb{S}^2)$. A point $u \in F\mathbb{S}^2$ can be seen as a linear map from $\mathbb{R}^2$ (left) to the tangent space $T_x\mathbb{S}^2$ of the point $y = \pi(u)$ (right). The standard basis (e_1, e_2) for $\mathbb{R}^2$ maps to a basis (u_1, u_2), $u_i = ue_i$ for $T_y\mathbb{S}^2$ because the frame bundle element u defines a linear map $\mathbb{R}^2 \to T_y\mathbb{S}^2$. The vertical subbundle of the tangent bundle $TF\mathbb{S}^2$ consists of derivatives of paths in $F\mathbb{S}^2$ that only change the frame, that is, $\pi(u)$ is fixed. Vertical vectors act by rotation of the basis vectors as illustrated by the rotation of the basis seen along the vertical line. The horizontal subbundle, which can be seen as orthogonal to the vertical subbundle, arises from parallel transporting vectors in the frame u along paths on $\mathbb{S}^2$.

10.4.2 Horizontality

The frame bundle, being a manifold, itself has a tangent bundle $TF\mathcal{M}$ with derivatives $\dot{u}(t)$ of paths $u(t) \in F\mathcal{M}$ being vectors in $T_{u(t)}F\mathcal{M}$. We can use the fiber bundle structure to split $TF\mathcal{M}$ and thereby define two different types of infinitesimal movements in $F\mathcal{M}$. First, a path $u(t)$ can vary solely in the fiber direction meaning that for some $y \in M$, $\pi(u(t)) = y$ for all t. Such a path is called vertical. At a point $u \in F\mathcal{M}$ the derivative of the path lies in the linear subspace $V_uF\mathcal{M}$ of $T_uF\mathcal{M}$ called the vertical subspace. For each y, $V_uF\mathcal{M}$ is a d^2-dimensional manifold. It corresponds to changes of the frame, the basis vectors for T_yM, while the base point y is kept fixed. $F\mathcal{M}$ is a $(d + d^2)$-dimensional manifold, and the subspace containing the remaining d dimensions of $T_uF\mathcal{M}$ is in a particular sense separate from the vertical subspace. It is therefore called the horizontal subspace $H_uF\mathcal{M}$. Just as tangent vectors in $V_uF\mathcal{M}$ model changes only in the frame keeping y fixed, the horizontal subspace models changes of y keeping, in a sense, the frame fixed. However, frames are tied to tangent spaces, so we need to define what is meant by keeping the frame fixed. When $\mathcal{M}$ is equipped with a connection ∇, being constant along paths is per definition having zero acceleration as measured by the connection. Here, for each basis vector u_i, we need $\nabla_{\dot{y}(t)} u_i(t) = 0$ when $u(t)$ is the path in the frame bundle and $y(t) = \pi(u(t))$ is the path of base points. This condition is exactly satisfied when the frame vectors $u_i(t)$ are each parallel transported along $y(t)$. The derivatives $\dot{u}(t)$ of paths satisfying this condition make up the horizontal subspace of $T_{y(t)}\mathcal{M}$. In other words, the horizontal subspace of $TF\mathcal{M}$ contains derivatives of paths where the base point $y(t)$ changes, but the frame is kept as constant as possible as sensed by the connection.

The frame bundle has a special set of horizontal vector fields $H_1, \ldots, H_d$ that make up a global basis for $HF\mathcal{M}$. This set is in a way a solution to defining the SDE (10.18) on manifolds: Although we cannot in the general situation find a set of globally defined vectors fields as we used in the Euclidean and Lie group situation to drive the Brownian motion (10.17), we can lift the problem to the frame bundle where such a set of vector fields exists. This will enable us to drive the SDE in the frame bundle and then subsequently project its solution to the manifold using π. To define H_i, take the ith frame vector $u_i \in T_y\mathcal{M}$, move y infinitesimally in the direction of the frame vector u_i, and parallel transport each frame vector u_j, $j = 1, \ldots, d$, along the infinitesimal curve. The result is an infinitesimal displacement in $TF\mathcal{M}$, a tangent vector to $F\mathcal{M}$, which by construction is an element of $HF\mathcal{M}$. This can be done for any $u \in F\mathcal{M}$ and any $i = 1, \ldots, d$. Thus we get the global set of horizontal vector fields H_i on $F\mathcal{M}$. Together, the fields H_i are linearly independent because they model displacement in the direction of the linearly independent vectors u_i. In combination the fields make up a basis for the d-dimensional horizontal spaces $H_{\pi(u)}F\mathcal{M}$ for each $u \in F\mathcal{M}$.

For each $y \in \mathcal{M}$, $T_y\mathcal{M}$ has dimension d, and with $u \in F\mathcal{M}$, we have a basis for $T_y\mathcal{M}$. Using this basis, we can map a vector $v \in \mathbb{R}^d$ to a vector $uv \in T_y\mathcal{M}$ by setting $uv := u_i v^i$ using the Einstein summation convention. This mapping is invertible, and we can therefore consider the $F\mathcal{M}$ element u a map in $\mathrm{GL}(\mathbb{R}^d, T\mathcal{M})$. Similarly, we can map v to an element of $H_u F\mathcal{M}$ using the horizontal vector fields $H_i(u)v^i$, a mapping that is again invertible. Combining this, we can map vectors from $T_y\mathcal{M}$ to $\mathbb{R}^d$ and then to $H_u F\mathcal{M}$. This map is called the horizontal lift $h_u : T_{\pi(u)}\mathcal{M} \to H_u F\mathcal{M}$. The inverse of h_u is just the push-forward $\pi_* : H_u F\mathcal{M} \to T_{\pi(u)}\mathcal{M}$ of the projection π. Note the u dependence of the horizontal lift: h_u is a linear isomorphism between $T_{\pi(u)}\mathcal{M}$ and $H_u F\mathcal{M}$, but the mapping will change with different u, and it is not an isomorphism between the bundles $T\mathcal{M}$ and $HF\mathcal{M}$ as can be seen from the dimensions $2d$ and $2d + d^2$, respectively.

10.4.3 Development and stochastic development

We now use the horizontal fields $H_1, \ldots, H_d$ to construct paths and SDEs on $F\mathcal{M}$ that can be mapped to $\mathcal{M}$. Keep in mind the Lie group SDE (10.17) for Brownian motion where increments of a Euclidean Brownian motion $B(t)$ or $x(t)$ are multiplied on an orthonormal basis. We now use the horizontal fields H_i for the same purpose. We start deterministically. Let $x(t)$ be a C^1 curve on $\mathbb{R}^d$ and define the ODE

$$\dot{u}(t) = H_i(u(t))\dot{x}^i(t) \tag{10.19}$$

on $F\mathcal{M}$ started with a frame bundle element $u_0 = u$. By mapping the derivative of $x(t)$ in $\mathbb{R}^d$ to $TF\mathcal{M}$ using the horizontal fields $H_i(u(t))$ we thus obtain a curve in $F\mathcal{M}$. Such a curve is called the development of $x(t)$. See Fig. 10.5 for a schematic illustration. We can then directly obtain a curve $y(t)$ in $\mathcal{M}$ by setting $y(t) = \pi(u(t))$, that is, removing the frame from the generated path. The development procedure is often visualized as rolling the manifold $\mathcal{M}$ along the path of $x(t)$ in the manifold $\mathbb{R}^d$. For this reason, it is denoted "rolling without slipping". We will use the letter x for the curve $x(t)$ in $\mathbb{R}^d$, u for its development $u(t)$ in $F\mathcal{M}$, and y for the resulting curve $y(t)$ on $\mathcal{M}$.

The development procedure has a stochastic counterpart: Let now $x(t)$ be an $\mathbb{R}^d$-valued Euclidean semimartingale. For our purposes, $x(t)$ will be a Brownian motion on $\mathbb{R}^d$. The stochastic development SDE is then

$$du(t) = H_i(u(t)) \circ dx^i(t) \tag{10.20}$$

using Stratonovich integration. In the stochastic setting, $x(t)$ is sometimes called the driving process for $y(t)$. Observe that the development procedure above, which was based on mapping differentiable curves, here works for processes that are almost surely nowhere differentiable. It is not immediate that this works, and arguing rigorously for the well-posedness of the stochastic development employs nontrivial stochastic calculus; see, for example, [13].

The stochastic development has several interesting properties: (1) It is a mapping from the space of stochastic paths on $\mathbb{R}^d$ to M, that is, each sample path $x(\omega)(t)$ gets mapped to a path $y(\omega)(t)$ on $\mathcal{M}$. It is in this respect different from the tangent space linearizations, where vectors, not paths, in $T_m M$ are mapped to points in M.

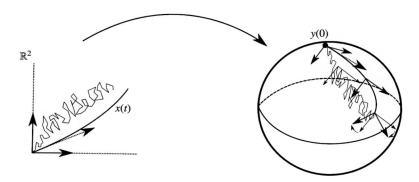

Figure 10.5. Development and stochastic development maps $\mathbb{R}^d$-valued curves and processes to curves and processes on the manifold using the frame bundle. Starting at a frame bundle element u with $y = \pi(u)$, the development maps the derivative of the curve $x(t)$ using the current frame $u(t)$ to a tangent vector in $H_{u(t)}\mathcal{M}$. These tangent vectors are integrated to a curve $u(t)$ in $F\mathcal{M}$ and a curve $y(t) = \pi(u(t))$ on $\mathcal{M}$ using the ODE (10.19). As a result, the starting frame $u(t)$ is parallel transported along $y(t)$. The construction works as well for stochastic processes (semimartingales): the thin line illustrates a sample path. Note that two curves that do not end at the same point in $\mathbb{R}^d$ can map to curves that do end at the same point in $\mathcal{M}$. Because of curvature, frames transported along two curves on $\mathcal{M}$ that end at the same point are generally not equal. This rotation is a result of the holonomy of the manifold.

(2) It depends on the initial frame u_0. In particular, if $\mathcal{M}$ is Riemannian and u_0 orthonormal, then the process $y(t)$ is a Riemannian Brownian motion when $x(t)$ is a Euclidean Brownian motion. (3) It is defined using the connection of the manifold. From (10.20) and the definition of the horizontal vector fields we can see that a Riemannian metric is not used. However, a Riemannian metric can be used to define the connection, and a Riemannian metric can be used to state that u_0 is, for example, orthonormal. If $\mathcal{M}$ is Riemannian, stochastically complete and u_0 orthonormal, we can write the density of the distribution $y(t)$ with respect to the Riemannian volume, that is, $y(t) = p(t; u_0) \, d\mathcal{V}_g$. If $\pi(u_0) = m$, then the density $p(t; u_0)$ will then equal the heat kernel $p(t, m, \cdot)$.

10.5 Anisotropic normal distributions

Perhaps most important for the use here is that (10.20) can be seen as a manifold generalization of the SDE (10.18) generalizing the latent model (10.3). This is the reason for using the notation $x(t)$ for the driving process and $y(t)$ for the resulting process on the manifold: $x(t)$ can be interpreted as the latent variable, and $y(t)$ as the response. When u_0 is orthonormal, then the marginal distribution of $y(1)$ is normal in the sense of equaling the transition distribution of the Brownian motion just as in the Euclidean case where $W = \text{Id}$ and $\sigma = 0$ results in $y \sim N(m, \text{Id})$.

We start by discussing the case $\sigma = 0$ of (10.3), where W is a square root of the covariance of the distribution of y in the Euclidean case. We use this to define a notion of infinitesimal covariance for a class of distributions on manifolds denoted anisotropic normal distributions [32,35]. We assume for now that W is of full rank d, but W is not assumed orthonormal.

10.5.1 Infinitesimal covariance

Recall the definition of covariance of a multivariate Euclidean stochastic variable X: $\text{cov}(X^i, X^j) = \mathbb{E}[(X^i - \bar{X}^i)(X^j - \bar{X}^j)]$, where $\bar{X} = \mathbb{E}[X]$ is the mean value. This definition relies by construction on the coordinate system used to extract the components X^i and X^j. Therefore it cannot be transferred to manifolds directly. Instead, other similar notions of covariance have been treated in the literature, for example,

$$\text{cov}_m(X^i, X^j) = \mathbb{E}[\text{Log}_m(X)^i \, \text{Log}_m(X)^j]$$

defined in [26]. In the form expressed here, a basis for $T_m \mathcal{M}$ is used to extract components of the vectors $\text{Log}_m(X)$. Here we take a different approach and define a notion of infinitesimal covariance in the case where the distribution y is generated by a driving stochastic process. This will allow us to extend the transition distribution of the Brownian motion, which is isotropic and has trivial covariance, to the case of anisotropic distributions with nontrivial infinitesimal covariance.

Recall that when $\sigma = 0$, the marginal distribution of y in (10.3) is normal $N(m, \Sigma)$ with covariance $\Sigma = W W^T$. The same distribution appears when we take the stochastic process view and use W in (10.18). We now take this to the manifold situation by starting the process (10.20) at a point $u = (m, W)$ in the frame bundle. This is a direct generalization of (10.18). When W is an orthonormal basis, the generated distribution is the transition distribution of a Riemannian Brownian motion. However, when W is not orthonormal, the generated distribution becomes anisotropic. Fig. 10.6 shows density plots of the Riemannian normal distribution and a Brownian motion both with $W = 0.5\text{Id}_d$, and an anisotropic distribution with $W \not\propto \text{Id}_d$.

We can write up the likelihood of observing a point $y \in M$ at time $t = T$ under the model,

$$\mathcal{L}(m, W; y) = p(T, y; m, W), \qquad (10.21)$$

Figure 10.6. (Left) Density of the Normal law or Riemannian normal distribution with isotropic variance 0.5. (center) Density of a Brownian motion with isotropic variance 0.5 (stopped at $T = 0.5$). (Right) Density of a Brownian motion with variance 0.5 in one direction and 0.1^2 in the orthogonal direction corresponding to $W = \text{diag}(\sqrt{(.5)}, 0.1)$.

where $p(t, y; m, W)$ is the time t-density at the point $y \in \mathcal{M}$ of the generated anisotropic distribution $y(t)$. Without loss of generality, the observation time can be set to $T = 1$ and skipped from the notation. The density can only be written with respect to a base measure, here denoted μ_0, such that $y(T) = p(T; m, W)\mu_0$. If $\mathcal{M}$ is Riemannian, then we can set $\mu_0 = d\mathcal{V}_g$, but this is not a requirement: The construction only needs a connection and a fixed base measure with respect to which we define the likelihood.

The parameters of the model, m and W, are represented by one element u of the frame bundle $F\mathcal{M}$, that is, the starting point of the process $u(t)$ in $F\mathcal{M}$. Writing θ for the parameters combined, we have $\theta = u = (m, W)$. These parameters correspond to the mean m and covariance $\Sigma = WW^T$ for the Euclidean normal distribution $N(m, \Sigma)$. We can take a step further and *define* the mean for such a distribution to be x as we pursue below. Similarly, we can *define* the notion of infinitesimal square root covariance of $y(T)$ to be W.

10.5.2 Isotropic noise

The linear model (10.3) includes both the matrix W and isotropic noise $\epsilon \sim N(0, \sigma^2 I)$. We now discuss how this additive structure can be modeled, including the case where W is not of full rank d.

We have so far considered distributions resulting from a Brownian motion analogues of isotropic normal distributions and seen that they can be represented by the frame bundle SDE (10.20). The fundamental structure is that u_0 being orthonormal spreads the infinitesimal variation equally in all directions as seen by the Riemannian metric. There exists a subbundle of $F\mathcal{M}$ called the orthonormal frame bundle $O\mathcal{M}$ that consists of only such orthonormal frames. Solutions to (10.20) will always stay in $O\mathcal{M}$ if

$u_0 \in O\mathcal{M}$. We here use the symbol R for elements of $O\mathcal{M}$ to emphasize their pure rotation, not the scaling effect. We can model the added isotropic noise by modifying the SDE (10.20) to

$$dW(t) = H_i(W(t)) \circ dx(t)^i + H_i(R(t)) \circ d\epsilon(t)^i \, ,$$
$$dR(t) = h_{R(t)}(\pi_*(dW)),$$

(10.22)

where the flow now has both the base point and covariance component $W(t)$ and a pure rotation $R(t)$ component serving as basis for the noise process $\epsilon(t)$. As before, we let the generated distribution on $\mathcal{M}$ be $y(t) = \pi(W(t))$, that is, $W(t)$ takes the place of $u(t)$.

Elements of $O\mathcal{M}$ differ only by a rotation, and since $\epsilon(t)$ is a Brownian motion scaled by σ, we can exchange $R(t)$ in the right-hand side of $dW(t)$ by any other element of $O\mathcal{M}$ without changing the distribution. Computationally, we can therefore skip $R(t)$ from the integration and instead find an arbitrary element of $O\mathcal{M}$ at each time step of a numerical integration. This is particularly important when the dimension d of the manifold is large because $R(t)$ has d^2 components.

We can explore this even further by letting W be a $d \times r$ matrix with $r \ll d$, thus reducing the rank of W similar to the PPCA situation (10.6). Without addition of the isotropic noise, this would in general result in the density $p(\cdot; m, W)$ being degenerate, just as the Euclidean normal density function requires full rank covariance matrix. However, with the addition of the isotropic noise, $W + \sigma R$ can still be of full rank even though W has zero eigenvalues. This has further computational advantages: If we instead of using the frame bundle $F\mathcal{M}$, let W be an element of the bundle of rank r linear maps $\mathbb{R}^r \to T\mathcal{M}$ so that $W_1, \ldots, W_r$ are r linearly independent basis vectors in $T_{\pi(W)}\mathcal{M}$, and if we remove $R(t)$ from the flow (10.22) as described before, then the flow now lives in a $(d + rd)$-dimensional fiber bundle compared to the $d + d^2$ dimensions of the full frame bundle. For low r, this can imply a substantial reduction in computation time.

10.5.3 Euclideanization

Tangent space linearizations using the Exp_m and Log_m maps provide a linear view of the data y_i on $\mathcal{M}$. When the data are concentrated close to a mean m, this view gives a good picture of the data variation. However, as data spread grows larger, curvature starts having an influence, and the linear view can provide a progressively distorted picture of the data. Whereas linear views of a curved geometry will never give truly faithful picture of the data, we can use a generalization of (10.3) to provide a linearization that integrates the effect of curvature at points far from m.

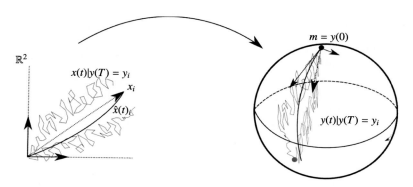

Figure 10.7. Euclideanization using stochastic development: (right) The data point y_i (red dot (dark gray dot in print version)) defines the conditioned process $y(t)|y(T) = y_i$ illustrated by sample paths on the manifold. (left) The antidevelopment of this process $x(t)|y(T) = y_i$ is illustrated by sample paths in the Euclidean space. Note that the Euclidean process $x(t)|y(T) = y_i$ need not end at the same point in $\mathbb{R}^d$ (this will generally only happen if M is Euclidean). The Euclidean process can be summarized into the expected path $\bar{x}(t)_i$ (thick curve left). This path can again be summarized by its endpoint x_i, which is a single vector (dashed arrow left). Contrary to tangent space linearizations, the fact that the process visits all points of the manifold integrates curvature into this vector. It is thus not equivalent to $\mathrm{Log}_m(y_i)$.

The standard PCA dimension-reduced view of the data is writing $W = U\Lambda$, where Λ is the diagonal matrix with the eigenvalues $\lambda_1, \ldots, \lambda_r$ of W in the diagonal. In PPCA this is used to provide a low-dimensional representation of the data from the data conditional expectation $x|y_i$. This can be further reduced to a single data descriptor $x_i := \mathbb{E}[x|y_i]$ by taking expectation, and then we obtain an equivalent of the standard PCA view by displaying Λx_i.

In the current probabilistic model, we can likewise condition the latent variables on the data to get a Euclidean entity describing the data. Since the latent variable is now a time-dependent path, the result of the conditioning is a process $x(t)|y(T) = y_i$ where the conditioning is on the response process hitting the data at time T. This results in a quite different view of the data as illustrated in Fig. 10.7 and exemplified in Fig. 10.1: as in PPCA, taking expectation, we get

$$\bar{x}(t)_i = \mathbb{E}[x(t)|y(T) = y_i]. \tag{10.23}$$

To get a single data descriptor, we can integrate $d\bar{x}(t)_i$ in time to get the endpoint $x_i := \int_0^T d\bar{x}(t)_i dt = \bar{x}(T)_i$. From the example in Fig. 10.1 we see that this Euclideanization of the data can be quite different compared to tangent space linearization.

10.6 Statistics with bundles

We now use the generalization of (10.3) via processes, either in the Lie algebra (10.17) of a group or on the frame bundle (10.20), to do statistics of manifold data. We start with ML estimation of mean and infinitesimal covariance by fitting anisotropic normal distributions to data, then progress to describing probabilistic PCA, a regression model, and estimation schemes.

10.6.1 Normal distributions and maximum likelihood

Considering the transition distribution $\mu(\theta) = y(T)$ of solutions $u(t)$ to (10.20) projected to the manifold $y(t) = \pi(u(t))$ started at $\theta = u = (m, W)$ a normal distribution with infinitesimal covariance $\Sigma = WW^T$, we can now define the sample maximum likelihood mean $\hat{m}_{\mathrm{ML}}$ by

$$\hat{m}_{\mathrm{ML}} = \mathrm{argmax}_m \prod_{i=1}^{N} \mathcal{L}(m; y_i) \qquad (10.24)$$

from samples $y_1, \ldots, y_N \in \mathcal{M}$. Here, we implicitly assume that W is orthonormal with respect to a Riemannian metric. Alternatively, we can set

$$\hat{m}_{\mathrm{ML}} = \mathrm{argmax}_m \max_W \prod_{i=1}^{N} \mathcal{L}(m, W; y_i), \qquad (10.25)$$

where we simultaneously optimize to find the most likely infinitesimal covariance. The former definition defines $\hat{m}_{\mathrm{ML}}$ as the starting point of the Brownian motion with transition density making the observations most likely. The latter includes the effect of the covariance, the anisotropy, and because of this it will in general give different results. In practice the likelihood is evaluated by Monte Carlo sampling. Parameter estimation procedures with parameters $\theta = (m)$ or $\theta = (m, W)$ and sampling methods are the topic of section 10.7.

We can use the likelihood (10.21) to get ML estimates for both the mean x and the infinitesimal covariance W by modifying (10.25) to

$$(\hat{m}_{ML}, \hat{W}_{ML}) = \hat{u}_{ML} = \mathrm{argmax}_u \prod_{i=1}^{N} \mathcal{L}(u; y_i) . \qquad (10.26)$$

Note the nonuniqueness of the result when estimating the square root W instead of the covariance $\Sigma = WW^T$. We discuss this point from a more geometric view in section 10.8.4.

10.6.2 Infinitesimal PPCA

The latent model (10.22) is used as the basis for the infinitesimal version of manifold PPCA [34], which we discussed in general terms in section 10.2.3. As in Euclidean PPCA, r denotes the number of principal eigenvectors to be estimated. With a fixed base measure μ_0, we write the density of the distribution generated from the low-rank plus noise system (10.22) as $\mu(m, W, \sigma) = p(T; m, W, \sigma)\,dV_g$ and use this to define the likelihood $\mathcal{L}(m, W, \sigma; y)$ in (10.12). The major difference in relation to (10.26) is now that the noise parameter σ is estimated from the data and that W is of rank $r \leq d$.

The Euclideanization approach of section 10.5.3 gives equivalents of Euclidean principal components by conditioning the latent process on the data $x_i := x(t)|y(T) = y_i$. By taking expectation this can be reduced to a single path $\bar{x}(t)_i := \mathbb{E}[x(t)|y(T) = y_i]$ or a single vector $x_i := \bar{x}(T)_i$.

The model is quite different from constructions of manifold PCA [11,14,31,5,27] that seek subspaces of the manifold having properties related to Euclidean linear subspaces. The probabilistic model and the horizontal frame bundle flows in general imply that no subspace is constructed in the present model. Instead, we can extract the parameters of the generated distribution and the information present in the conditioned latent process. As we discuss in section 10.8.1, the fact that the model does not generate subspaces is fundamentally linked to curvature, the curvature tensor, and nonintegrability of the horizontal distribution in $F\mathcal{M}$.

10.6.3 Regression

The generalized latent model (10.3) is used in [17] to define a related regression model. Here we assume observations (x_i, y_i), $i = 1, \ldots, N$, with $x_i \in \mathbb{R}^d$ and $y_i \in \mathcal{M}$. As in the previous models, the unknown is the point $m \in \mathcal{M}$, which takes the role of the intercept in multivariate regression, the coefficient matrix W, and the noise variance σ^2. Whereas the infinitesimal nature of the model that relies on the latent variable being a semimartingale makes it geometrically natural, the fact that the latent variable is a process implies that its values in the interval $(0, T)$ are unobserved if x_i is the observation at time T. This turns the construction into a missing data problem, and the values of $x(t)$ in the unobserved interval $(0, T)$ needs to be integrated out. This can be pursued by combining bridge sampling as described below with matching of the sample moments of data with moments of the response variable y defined by the model [18].

10.7 Parameter estimation

So far we have only constructed models and defined parameter estimation as optimization problems for the involved likelihoods. It remains to discuss how we can actually estimate parameters in concrete settings. We describe here three approaches: (1) using a least-squares principle that incorporates the data anisotropy; this model is geometrically intuitive, but it only approximates the true density in the limit as $T \to 0$. (2) Using the method of moments where approximations of low-order moments of the generated distribution is compared with the corresponding data moments. (3) Using bridge sampling of the conditioned process to approximate transition density functions with Monte Carlo sampling.

10.7.1 Anisotropic least squares

The Fréchet mean (see Chapter 2) is defined from the least-squares principle. Here we aim to derive a similar least-squares condition for the variables $\theta = m$, $\theta = (m, W)$, or $\theta = (m, W, \sigma)$. With this approach, the inferred parameters $\hat{\theta}$ will only approximate the actual maximum likelihood estimates in a certain limit. Although only providing an approximation, the least-squares approach is different from Riemannian least-squares, and it is thereby both of geometric interest and gives perspective on the bridge sampling described later.

Until now we have assumed the observation time T to be strictly positive or simply $T = 1$. If instead we let $T \to 0$, then we can explore the short-time asymptotic limit of the generated density. Starting with the Brownian motion, the limit has been extensively studied in the literature. For the Euclidean normal density, we know that $p_{N(m, T\mathrm{Id})}(y) = (2\pi T)^{-\frac{d}{2}} \exp(-\frac{\|y-m\|^2}{2T})$. In particular, the density obeys the limit $\lim_{T \to 0} T \log p_{N(m, T\mathrm{Id})}(y) = -\frac{1}{2}\|y - m\|^2$. The same limit occurs on complete Riemannian manifolds with $\mathrm{dist}(m, y)^2$ instead of the norm $\|y - m\|^2$ and when y is outside the cut locus $C(m)$; see, for example, [13]. Thus, minimizing the squared distance to data can be seen as equivalent to maximizing the density, and hence the likelihood, for short running times of the Brownian motion specified by small T.

It is shown in [35] that there exists a function $d_Q : F\mathcal{M} \times \mathcal{M} \to \mathbb{R}$ that, for each $u \in F\mathcal{M}$, incorporates the anisotropy modeled in u in a measurement of the closeness $d_Q(u, y)$ of $m = \pi(u)$ and y. Like the Riemannian distance, which is defined as the minimal length or energy between curves linking two points in $\mathcal{M}$, d_Q is defined using curves in $F\mathcal{M}$ from u to the fiber $\pi^{-1}(y)$ over y but now with energy weighted by a matrix Σ^{-1}:

$$d_Q(u, y) = \min_{u(t), u(0)=u, \pi(u(1))=y, \dot{u}(t) \in HF\mathcal{M}} \int_0^1 \dot{u}(t)^T \Sigma^{-1}(t) \dot{u}(t) dt \,.$$

$$(10.27)$$

Here $\Sigma(t)^{-1} = (u(t)^{-1})^T u(t)^{-1}$ is the precision matrix of the infinitesimal covariance modeled in the frames $u(t)$. The horizontality requirement $\dot{u}(t) \in HF\mathcal{M}$ implies that the inner product defined by $\Sigma(t)^{-1}$ is parallel transported along with $u(t)$. The anisotropy is thus controlled by starting with a possibly nonorthonormal frame u_0. We motivate this distance further from a geometric viewpoint in sections 10.8.2 and 10.8.3.

It is important here to relate the short-time $T \to 0$ asymptotic limit with the Euclidean normal density with covariance Σ. In the Euclidean case, the density is $p_{N(m,T\Sigma)}(y) = |2\pi T\Sigma|^{-\frac{1}{2}}$ $\exp(-\frac{(y-m)^T \Sigma^{-1}(y-m)}{2T})$ and, as above, $\lim_{T \to 0} T \log p_{N(m,T\Sigma)}(y) = -\frac{1}{2}(y-m)^T \Sigma^{-1}(y-m)$. In the nonlinear situation using the Σ^{-1} weighted distance d_Q, $\lim_{T \to 0} T \log p_{\mu(m,W)}(y) = -\frac{1}{2}d_Q(u,y)^2$. From this we can generalize the Fréchet mean least-squares principle to

$$\hat{\theta} = (\hat{m}, \hat{W}) = \mathrm{argmin}_{u \in F\mathcal{M}} \sum_{i=1}^N d_Q\left(u, q^{-1}(y_i)\right)^2 - \frac{N}{2} \log(\det_g u),$$

$$(10.28)$$

where $\log(\det_g u)$ denotes the Riemannian determinant of the frame u. This term corresponds to the log-determinant in the Euclidean density $p_{N(m,\Sigma)}$, and it acts to regularize the optimization that would otherwise increase W to infinity and reduce distances accordingly; $\hat{m}$ can be seen as an anisotropically weighted equivalent of the Fréchet mean.

10.7.2 Method of moments

The method of moments compares low-order moments of the distribution with sample moments of the data. This can be used for parameter estimation by changing the parameters of the model to make the distribution and sample moments match as well as possible. The method of moments does not use the data likelihood, and it is dependent on ability to compute the moments in an appropriate space, for example, by embedding $\mathcal{M}$ in a larger Euclidean space.

To compare first- and second-order moments, we can set up the cost function

$$S(\mu(\theta), \langle y \rangle_1, \langle y \rangle_2) = c_1 \| \langle \mu(\theta) \rangle_1 - \langle y \rangle_1 \|^2 + c_2 \| \langle \mu(\theta) \rangle_2 - \langle y \rangle_2 \|^2, \tag{10.29}$$

where $\langle \mu(\theta) \rangle_1$ and $\langle y \rangle_1$ denote the first-order moments of the distribution $\mu(\theta)$ and the sample moments of the data $y_1, \ldots, y_N$, respectively, and similarly for the second-order moments $\langle \mu(\theta) \rangle_2$ and $\langle y \rangle_2$, and $c_1, c_2 > 0$ are weights. If $\mathcal{M}$ is embedded in a larger Euclidean space, then the norms in (10.29) can be inherited from the embedding space norm. The optimal values of θ can then be found by minimizing this cost.

This approach is used in [18] to estimate parameters in the regression model. The method of moments can be a computationally more lightweight alternative to the bridge sampling discussed further. In addition, the method can be a relatively stable approach because of the implicit regularization provided by only matching entities, here moments, that are averaged over the entire dataset. This is in contrast to the least-squares approach and the bridge sampling that estimate by evaluating d_Q or the likelihood on individual samples, and where averaging is done afterward, for example, by using averaged gradients when optimizing parameters. The moments $\langle \mu(\theta) \rangle_1$ and $\langle \mu(\theta) \rangle_2$ can be approximated by sampling from the model or by approximation of the Fokker–Planck equation that governs the time evolution of the density; see, for example, [1].

10.7.3 Bridge sampling

At the heart of the methods discussed in this chapter are the data conditional latent processes $x(t)|y(T) = y_i$. We now describe methods for simulating from this conditioned process to subsequently approximate expectation of functions over the conditioned process and the transition density function.

Stochastic bridges arise from conditioning a process to hit a point at a fixed time; here $t = T$. Fig. 10.8 exemplifies the situation with samples from a Brownian bridge on $\mathbb{S}^2$. Denoting the target point v, the expectation over the bridge process is related to the transition density $p(T, v; m)$ of the process by

$$\mathbb{E}_{x(t)|x(T)=v}[f(x(t))] = \frac{\mathbb{E}_{x(t)}[f(x(t))\mathbf{1}_{x(T)=v}]}{p(T, v; m)}, \tag{10.30}$$

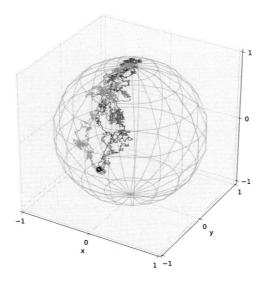

Figure 10.8. Five sample paths from a Brownian bridge on $\mathbb{S}^2$ started at the north pole and conditioned on hitting a fixed point $v \in \mathbb{S}^2$ (black point) at time $T = 1$.

assuming that $p(T, v; m)$ is positive. Here $\mathbf{1}$ is the indicator function. Setting $f(x(t)) = 1$, we can write this as

$$p(T, v; m) = \frac{\mathbb{E}_{x(t)}[\mathbf{1}_{x(T)\in dv}]}{dv} \tag{10.31}$$

for an infinitesimal volume dv containing v. The transition density thus measures the combined probability mass of sample paths $x(\omega)(t)$ with $x(\omega)(T)$ near v. However, from the right-hand side of (10.31), we cannot directly get a good approach to computing the transition density and thereby the likelihood by sampling from $x(t)$ because the probability of $x(t)$ hitting dv is arbitrarily small.

Instead, we will use an approach to evaluate the conditional expectation $\mathbb{E}_{x(t)|x(T)=v}[f(x(t))]$ by drawing samples from the bridge process and approximate the expectation by Monte Carlo sampling. We will see that this provides us with an effective way to evaluate the density $p(T, v; m)$. It is generally hard to simulate directly from the bridge process $x(t)|x(T) = v$. One exception is the Euclidean Brownian motion, where the bridge satisfies the SDE

$$dy(t) = -\frac{y(t) - v}{T - t}dt + dW(t) . \tag{10.32}$$

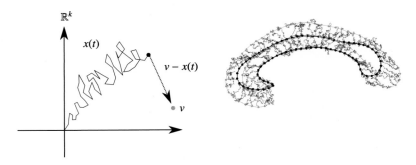

Figure 10.9. (Left) The guided processes (10.34) modifies the original process $x(t)$ by addition of a scalar multiple of the term $v - x(t)$ (dotted arrow), the difference between the time t value $x(t)$ and the target v, to force the modified process $y(t)$ to hit v a.s. (Right) Scheme (10.34) applied to generate a sample from the bridge process (blue curve (dark gray in print version) of each landmark) between two corpora callosa shapes (red (light gray in print version)/black landmark configurations) represented as points in $\mathbb{R}^{156}$ with the non-Euclidean landmark metric described in Chapter 4 and section 10.8.5.

More generally, an arbitrary SDE (10.9) can be modified to give a bridge process by addition of an extra drift term:

$$dy(t) = b(t, y(t))dt + a(t, y(t))a(t, y(t))^T \nabla \log p(T - t, v; y(t))$$
$$+ a(t, y(t))dW(t) . \tag{10.33}$$

This SDE could be used to simulate sample paths if it was not for the fact that it involves the gradient of the transition density $p(T - t, v; y(t))$ from the current value $y(t)$ of the process to v. This transition density gradient generally does not have an explicit or directly computable form; indeed, our goal is to find a way to compute the transition density, and it is thus not feasible to use (10.33) computationally.

To improve on this situation, Delyon and Hu [4] proposed to use the added term from the Brownian bridge (10.32) instead of the gradient of the log-transition density giving an SDE of the form

$$dy(t) = b(t, y(t))dt - \frac{y(t) - v}{T - t}dt + a(t, y(t))dW(t) . \tag{10.34}$$

The drift term is illustrated in Fig. 10.9. Solutions $y(t)$ to (10.34) are not in general bridges of the original process. Instead, they are called guided processes. However, under certain conditions, the most important being that the diffusion field a is invertible, $y(t)$ will hit v at time T a.s., and the law of the conditioned process $x(t)|x(T) = v$ and the guided processes $y(t)$ will be absolutely continuous with respect to each other with explicit Radon–Nikodym derivative φ. This implies that we can compute expectation over the bridge processes by taking the expectation of the guided process $y(t)$ and correcting by factoring in φ:

$$\mathbb{E}_{x(t)|x(T)=v}[f(x(t))] = \frac{\mathbb{E}_{y(t)}[f(y(t))\varphi(y(t))]}{\mathbb{E}_{y(t)}[\varphi(y(t))]} \,. \qquad (10.35)$$

Establishing this identity requires a nontrivial limiting argument to compare the two processes in the limit as $t \to T$, where the denominator $T - t$ in the guiding term in (10.34) approaches zero. As an additional consequence, Delyon and Hu and later Papaspiliopoulos and Roberts [28] write the transition density as the product of the Gaussian normal density and the expectation over the guided process of the correction factor:

$$p(T, v; m) = \sqrt{\frac{|A(T, v)|}{(2\pi T)^d}} e^{-\frac{\|a(0,m)^{-1}(m-v)\|^2}{2T}} \mathbb{E}_{y(t)}[\varphi(y(t))] \qquad (10.36)$$

with $A(t, x) = (a(t, x)^{-1})^T a(t, x)$. See also [36], where guided bridges are produced in a related way by using an approximation of the true transition density to replace $p(T - t, v; y(t))$ in (10.33). The Delyon and Hu approach can be seen as a specific case of this where $p(T - t, v; y(t))$ is approximated by the transition density of a Brownian motion.

10.7.4 Bridge sampling on manifolds

Extending the simulation scheme to general manifolds directly is nontrivial and the subject of ongoing research efforts. The fundamental issue is finding appropriate terms to take the role of the guiding term in (10.34) and controlling the behavior of such terms near the cut locus of the manifold. Here we instead sketch how the Delyon and Hu approach can be used in coordinates. This follows [30], where the approach is used for simulating from the Brownian motion on the landmark manifold described in chapter 4.

We assume that we have a chart covering the manifold up to a set of measure zero, and here we ignore the case where the stochastic process crosses this set. We take as an example the Riemannian Brownian motion with the coordinate process (10.15). Using the approach of Delyon and Hu, we get the guided processes

$$dy(t) = b(y(t))dt - \frac{y(t) - v}{T - t}dt + \sqrt{g(y(t))^{-1}}dB(t) \,. \qquad (10.37)$$

For the analysis in Delyon and Hu, we need the cometric $g(y(t))^{-1}$ and its inverse, the metric $g(y(t))$, to be bounded, whereas the drift coming from the Christoffel symbols can be unbounded or replaced by a bounded approximation. Then using (10.36), we get the expression

$$p(T, v; m) = \sqrt{\frac{|g(v)|}{(2\pi T)^d}} e^{\frac{-(m-v)^T g(m)^{-1}(m-v)}{2T}} \mathbb{E}_{y(t)}[\varphi(y)(t)] \, .$$

This process is in coordinates and thus gives the density with respect to the Lebesgue measure on $\mathbb{R}^d$. We get the corresponding density with respect to dV_g on $\mathcal{M}$ by removing the $\sqrt{|g(v)|}$ term:

$$p(T, v; m) = (2\pi T)^{-\frac{d}{2}} e^{\frac{-(m-v)^T g(m)^{-1}(m-v)}{2T}} \mathbb{E}_{y(t)}[\varphi(y)(t)] \, . \qquad (10.38)$$

The expectation $\mathbb{E}_{y(t)}[\varphi(y(t))]$ has no closed-form expression in general. Instead, it can be approximated by Monte Carlo sampling by simulating processes (10.37) finitely many times and averaging the computed correction factors $\varphi(y(t))$.

With the machinery to approximate the likelihood in place, we can subsequently seek to optimize the likelihood with respect to the parameters θ. This can be done directly by computing the gradient with respect to θ of (10.38). This is a relatively complex expression to take derivatives of by hand. Instead, automatic differentiation methods can be used such as pursued in the Theano Geometry library, which we used to produce the examples in this chapter. This brings us to the following stochastic gradient descent algorithm for parameter estimation by bridge sampling, where we iteratively update the parameter estimate θ_l:

Algorithm 10.1 Parameter estimation from samples $y_1, \ldots, y_N \in \mathcal{M}$.

---

for $l = 1$ *until convergence* **do**

    for $i = 1$ *to N* **do**

        sample J paths from guided process $y_{\theta_l}(t)$ hitting y_i with parameters θ_l

        compute correction factors $\varphi_{\theta_l,i}^j$

    end

    $\mathcal{L}_{\theta_l}(y_1, \ldots, y_N) \leftarrow (2\pi T)^{-\frac{d}{2}} \prod_{i=1}^N e^{\frac{-(m-y_i)^T g(m)^{-1}(m-y_i)}{2T}} \left(\frac{1}{J} \sum_{j=1}^J \varphi_{\theta_l,i}^j\right)$

    $\theta_{l+1} = \theta_l + \epsilon \nabla_{\theta_l} \mathcal{L}_{\theta_l}(y_1, \ldots, y_N)$

end

10.8 Advanced concepts

Here we give more detail on some of the concepts that result from using a fiber bundle structure to model data variation on manifolds. In particular, we discuss how the Riemannian curvature tensor can be expressed directly as the vertical variation of frames resulting from the nonclosure of the bracket of horizontal vector fields. We then define a sub-Riemannian geometry on the frame bundle that has a notion of most probable paths as geodesics, and we discuss how to geometrically model the actual infinitesimal covariance matrix as compared to the square root covariance we have used so far. Finally, we give two examples of flows using special geometric structure, namely flows in the phase space of the landmark manifold.

Many of the concepts presented here are discussed in more detail in [35,33].

10.8.1 Curvature

The curvature of manifold is most often given in terms of the curvature tensor $R \in \mathcal{T}_1^3(\mathcal{M})$, which is defined from the connection; see chapter 1. Let now $u \in FM$ be a frame considered as an element of $\mathrm{GL}(\mathbb{R}^d, T_{\pi(u)}\mathcal{M})$. We use this identification between $T_{\pi(u)}\mathcal{M}$ and $\mathbb{R}^d$ to write the curvature form Ω:

$$\Omega(v_u, w_u) = u^{-1}R(\pi_*(v_u), \pi_*(w_u))u , \quad v_u, w_v \in TFM .$$

Note that Ω takes values in $\mathfrak{gl}(n)$: It describes how the identity map $u^{-1}u : \mathbb{R}^d \to \mathbb{R}^d$ changes when moving around an infinitesimal parallelogram determined by the tangent vectors $\pi_*(v_u)$ and $\pi_*(w_u)$ with u kept fixed. It is thus vertical valued: It takes values in VFM. This can be made precise by employing an isomorphism ψ between $FM \times \mathfrak{gl}(n)$ and VFM given by $\psi(u, v) = \frac{d}{dt}u\exp(tv)|_{t=0}$ using the Lie group exponential exp on $\mathrm{GL}(\mathbb{R}^d)$; see, for example, [19].

Now using the horizontal–vertical splitting of TFM and ψ, we define a $\mathfrak{gl}(n)$-valued vertical one-form $\omega : TFM \to \mathfrak{gl}(n)$ by

$$\omega(v_u) = 0 \text{ if } v_u \in HFM$$
$$\omega(v_u) = \psi^{-1}(v_u) \text{ if } v_u \in VFM . \tag{10.39}$$

Here ω represents the connection via the horizontal–vertical splitting by singling out the vertical part of a TFM vector and representing it as an element of $\mathfrak{gl}(n)$ [13]. Using ω, we have

$$\omega([H_i, H_j]) = -\Omega(H_i, H_j), \tag{10.40}$$

and we see that the curvature form measures the vertical component of the bracket $[H_i, H_j] = H_i H_j - H_j H_i$ between horizontal vector fields. In other words, a nonzero curvature implies that the bracket between horizontal vector fields is nonzero.

As a consequence, nonzero curvature implies that it is impossible to find a submanifold of $F\mathcal{M}$ that has its tangent space being the span of the horizontal vector fields: For this to happen, the horizontal vector fields would need to present an integrable distribution by the Frobenius theorem, but the condition for this is exactly that the bracket between vector fields in this distribution must be closed. This is the reason why the infinitesimal PPCA model described here does not generate submanifolds of $F\mathcal{M}$ or $\mathcal{M}$ as in the Euclidean case.

10.8.2 Sub-Riemannian geometry

A sub-Riemannian metric acts as a Riemannian metric except that it is not required to be strictly positive definite: It can have zero eigenvalues. We now define a certain sub-Riemannian metric on $F\mathcal{M}$ that can be used to encode anisotropy and infinitesimal covariance. First, for $u \in F\mathcal{M}$, define the inner product $\Sigma(u)$ on $T_{\pi(u)}\mathcal{M}$ by

$$\Sigma(u)^{-1}(v, w) = \langle u^{-1}(v), u^{-1}(w) \rangle_{\mathbb{R}^d}, \qquad v, w \in T_{\pi(u)}M . \quad (10.41)$$

Note how u^{-1} maps the tangent vectors v, w to $\mathbb{R}^d$ before the standard Euclidean inner product is applied. To define an inner product on $TF\mathcal{M}$, we need to connect this to tangent vectors in $TF\mathcal{M}$. This is done using the pushforward of the projection π giving the inner product

$$g_u(v, w) = \Sigma(u)^{-1}(\pi_* v, \pi_* w).$$

This metric is quite different compared to a direct lift of a Riemannian metric to the frame bundle because of the application of u^{-1} in (10.41). This is a geometric equivalent of using the precision matrix Σ^{-1} as an inner product in the Gaussian density function. Here it is instead applied to infinitesimal displacements. Note that g_u vanishes on $VF\mathcal{M}$ because $\pi_*(v) = 0$ for $v \in VF\mathcal{M}$. The inner product is therefore only positive definite on the horizontal subbundle $HF\mathcal{M}$.

For a curve $u(t) \in F\mathcal{M}$ for which $\dot{u}(t) \in HF\mathcal{M}$, we define the sub-Riemannian length of $u(t)$ by

$$l(u(t)) = \int_0^1 \sqrt{g_{u(t)}(\dot{u}(t), \dot{u}(t))} dt.$$

If $\dot{u}$ is not a.e. horizontal, then we define $l(u) = \infty$; l defines a sub-Riemannian distance, which is equivalent to the distance d_Q in section 10.7.1. Extremal curves are called sub-Riemannian geodesics. A subclass of these curves are the normal geodesics that can be computed from a geodesic equation as in the Riemannian case. Here we represent the sub-Riemannian metric as a map $\tilde{g} : TF\mathcal{M}^* \to HF\mathcal{M} \subseteq TF\mathcal{M}$ defined by $g_u(w, \tilde{g}(\xi)) = (\xi | w)$, $\forall w \in H_u F\mathcal{M}, \xi \in TF\mathcal{M}^*$ and define the Hamiltonian

$$H(u, \xi) = \frac{1}{2} \xi(\tilde{g}_u(\xi)).$$

In canonical coordinates the evolution of normal geodesics is then governed by the Hamiltonian system

$$\dot{u}^i = \frac{\partial H}{\partial \xi_i}(u, \xi), \qquad \dot{\xi}_i = -\frac{\partial H}{\partial u^i}(u, \xi) \qquad (10.42)$$

10.8.3 Most probable paths

The concept of path probability and maximizing path probability needs careful definitions because of the fact that sample paths of semimartingales are a.s. nowhere differentiable. It is therefore not possible to directly write up an energy for such paths using derivatives and to maximize such an energy. Instead, Onsager and Machlup [8] defined a notion of path-probability as the limit of progressively smaller tubes around smooth paths γ. Here we let $\mu_\epsilon^M(\gamma)$ be the probability that a process $x(t)$ stays within distance ϵ from the curve γ, that is,

$$\mu_\epsilon^M(\gamma) = P\left(\text{dist}(x(t), \gamma(t)) < \epsilon, \forall t \in [0, 1]\right).$$

The most probable path is the path that maximizes $\mu_\epsilon^M(\gamma)$ as $\epsilon \to 0$.

For a Riemannian Brownian motion, Onsager and Machlup showed that

$$\mu_\epsilon^M(\gamma) \propto \exp\left(\frac{c}{\epsilon^2} + \int_0^1 L_\mathcal{M}(\gamma(t), \dot{\gamma}(t))dt\right) \qquad (10.43)$$

as $\epsilon \to 0$, where $L_\mathcal{M}$ is the Onsager–Machlup functional

$$L_\mathcal{M}(\gamma(t), \dot{\gamma}(t)) = -\frac{1}{2}\|\dot{\gamma}(t)\|_g^2 + \frac{1}{12} S_g(\gamma(t)),$$

where S_g is the scalar curvature. Notice the resemblance with the usual Riemannian energy except for the added scalar curvature

Figure 10.10. Geodesics (black curves) and most probable paths (blue) for a driving Brownian motion on the sphere $\mathbb{S}^2$ from the north pole (red dot (dark gray in print version)) to a point on the southern hemisphere (blue dot (light gray in print version)). Left: isotropic process; center and right: processes with covariance visualized by the frame (arrows) at the north pole and the ellipses. The parallel transport of the frame along the most probable paths is plotted. The sphere is colored by an approximation of the generated transition density. It can be clearly seen how increasing anisotropy interacts with curvature to give most probable paths that are not aligned with geodesics. Intuitively, the most probable paths tend to stay in high-density areas on the northern hemisphere before taking the "shorter" low-probability route to the target point on the southern hemisphere.

term. Intuitively, this term senses the curvature of the manifold as the radii of the tubes around γ approaches zero.

Turning to the mapping of Euclidean processes to the manifold via the frame bundle construction, [32,35,33] propose to define the path probability of a process $y(t)$ on $\mathcal{M}$ that is a stochastic development of a Brownian motion $x(t)$ on $\mathbb{R}^d$ by applying the Onsager–Machlup functional to the processes $x(t)$. The path probability is thus measured in the Euclidean space. Extremal paths in this construction are called the most probable paths for the driving semimartingale, which in this case is $x(t)$. Because the scalar curvature term of $L_{\mathcal{M}}$ is zero in the Euclidean space, we identify the curves as

$$\text{argmin}_{y(t),y(0)=m,y(1)=y} \int_0^1 -L_{\mathbb{R}^n}(x(t), \tfrac{d}{dt}x(t))dt \ .$$

The function turns out to be exactly the sub- Riemannian length defined in the previous section, and the most probable paths for the driving semimartingale therefore equal geodesics for the sub-Riemannian metric g_u. In particular, Hamiltonian equations (10.42) characterize the subclass of normal geodesics. Fig. 10.10 illustrates such curves, which are now extremal for the anisotropically weighted metric.

10.8.4 Bundles without rotation

When modeling infinitesimal covariance, the frame bundle in a sense provides an overspecification because $u \in FM$ represents square root covariances $\sqrt{\Sigma}$ and not Σ directly. Multiple such square roots can represent the same Σ. To remedy this, we can factorize the inner product $\Sigma^{-1}(u)$ above through the bundle Sym^+ of symmetric positive definite covariant 2-tensors on M. We have

$$FM \xrightarrow{\Sigma^{-1}} \mathrm{Sym}^+ M \xrightarrow{q} M,$$

and $\Sigma^{-1}(u)$ can now directly be seen as an element of Sym^+. The polar decomposition theorem states that Sym^+ is isomorphic to the quotient $FM/O(\mathbb{R}^d)$ with $O(\mathbb{R}^d)$ being orthogonal transformations on $\mathbb{R}^d$. The construction thus removes the rotation from FM that was the over-specification representing the square root covariance. The fiber bundle structure and horizontality that we used on FM descend to Sym^+. In practice we can work on Sym^+ and FM interchangeably. It is often more direct to write SDEs and stochastic development on FM, which is why we generally prefer this instead of using Sym^+.

10.8.5 Flows with special structure

We have so far created parametric families of probability distribution on general manifold using stochastic processes, either the Brownian motion or stochastic developments of Euclidean semimartingales. Here we briefly mention other types of processes that use special structure of the underlying space and that can be used to construct distributions for performing parameter estimation. We focus on three cases of flows of the LDDMM landmark manifold discussed in chapter 4.

The landmark geodesic equations with the metric discussed in Chapter 4 are usually written in the Hamiltonian form

$$\dot{\mathbf{q}}^i = \frac{\partial H}{\partial \mathbf{p}_i}(\mathbf{q}, \mathbf{p}), \qquad \dot{\mathbf{p}}_i = -\frac{\partial H}{\partial \mathbf{q}^i}(\mathbf{q}, \mathbf{p}), \qquad (10.44)$$

with the position coordinates $\mathbf{q} = (q_1, \dots, q_n)$ of the n landmarks, the momentum coordinates $\mathbf{p}$, and the Hamiltonian $H(\mathbf{q}, \mathbf{p}) = \mathbf{p}^T K(\mathbf{q}, \mathbf{q})\mathbf{p}$. We can use this phase-space formulation to introduce noise that is coupled to the momentum variable instead of only affecting the position equation, $\mathbf{q}$, as pursued so far.

A construction for this is given by Trouvé and Vialard [38] by adding noise in the momentum variable with position and momentum dependent infinitesimal covariance

$$dq^i = \frac{\partial H}{\partial \mathbf{p}_i}(\mathbf{q}, \mathbf{p}), \qquad d\mathbf{p}_i = -\frac{\partial H}{\partial \mathbf{q}^i}(\mathbf{q}, \mathbf{p})dt + \epsilon^i(\mathbf{q}, \mathbf{p})dx(t), \quad (10.45)$$

where $x(t)$ is a Brownian motion on $\mathbb{R}^{nd}$. Similarly, Marsland and Shardlow define the stochastic Langevin equations

$$dq^i = \frac{\partial H}{\partial \mathbf{p}_i}(\mathbf{q}, \mathbf{p}), \qquad d\mathbf{p}_i = -\lambda\frac{\partial H}{\partial \mathbf{q}^i}(\mathbf{q}, \mathbf{p}) - \frac{\partial H}{\partial \mathbf{q}^i}(\mathbf{q}, \mathbf{p})dt + \epsilon dx^i(t).$$

$$(10.46)$$

In both cases the noise directly affects the momentum.

A related but somewhat different model is the stochastic EPDiff equation by Arnaudon et al. [1]. Here a family of fields $\sigma_1, \ldots, \sigma_J$ is defined on the domain Ω where the landmark reside, and noise is multiplied on these fields:

$$d\mathbf{q}_i = \frac{\partial H}{\partial \mathbf{p}_i}dt + \sum_{l=1}^{J}\sigma_l(\mathbf{q}_i) \circ dx(t)^l,$$

$$d\mathbf{p}_i = -\frac{\partial H}{\partial \mathbf{q}_i}dt - \sum_{l=1}^{J}\frac{\partial}{\partial \mathbf{q}_i}(\mathbf{p}_i \cdot \sigma_l(\mathbf{q}_i)) \circ dx(t)^l.$$

$$(10.47)$$

Here the driving Brownian motion $x(t)$ is $\mathbb{R}^J$-valued. Notice the coupling to the momentum equation by the derivative of the noise fields. The stochasticity is in a certain sense compatible with the geometric construction that is used to define the LDDMM landmark metric. In particular, the momentum map construction [2] is preserved, and the landmarks equations are extremal for a stochastic variational principle

$$S(\mathbf{q}, \mathbf{p}) = \int H(\mathbf{q}, \mathbf{p})\, dt + \sum_{i}\int \mathbf{p}_i \cdot \left(\circ d\mathbf{q}_i + \sum_{l=1}^{J}\sigma_l(\mathbf{q}_i) \circ dx(t)^l\right).$$

$$(10.48)$$

Bridge sampling on these processes can be pursued with the Delyon and Hu approach, and this can again be used to infer parameters of the model. In this case, the parameter set includes parameters for the noise fields σ_i. However, the diffusion field is in this case in general not invertible as was required by the guidance scheme (10.34). This necessitates extra care when constructing the guiding process [1]. Bridge simulation for the Trouvé–Vialard and Marsland–Shardlow models (10.45) and (10.46) can be pursued with the simulation approach of Schauer and van der Meulen; see [3].

In these examples, the Euclidean structure of the landmark domain Ω is used in defining the SDEs by using either the coordinates on the momentum variable in (10.45) and (10.46) or by using the noise fields σ_i on Ω in the stochastic EPDiff case (10.48). In the latter example, the construction is furthermore related to the representation of the landmark space as a homogeneous space arising from quotienting a subgroup of the diffeomorphism group $\text{Diff}(\Omega)$ by the isotropy group of the landmarks. On this subgroup of $\text{Diff}(\Omega)$, there exists an SDE driven by the right-invariant noise defined by σ_i. Solutions of this SDE project to solutions of (10.47). A further interpretation of the fields σ_i is that they represent noise in Eulerian coordinates, and they thereby use the Eulerian coordinate frame for defining the infinitesimal covariance.

In all cases the parameters θ can be estimated from observed landmark configurations $\mathbf{q}_1, \ldots, \mathbf{q}_N$ by maximum likelihood. The parameters θ can specify the starting conditions $(\mathbf{q}_0, \mathbf{p}_0)$ of the process, the shape and position of σ_i, and even parameters for the Riemannian metric on the landmark space.

10.9 Conclusion

The aim of the chapter is to provide examples of probabilistic approaches to manifold statistics and ways to construct parametric families of probability distributions in geometrically natural ways. We pursued this using transition distributions of several stochastic processes: the Riemannian Brownian motion, Brownian motion on Lie groups, anisotropic generalizations of the Brownian motion by use of stochastic development, and finally flows that use special structure related to the particular space, the shape space of landmarks. We have emphasized the role of infinitesimal covariance modeled by frames in tangent spaces when defining SDEs and stochastic processes. In the Lie group setting, left-invariant vector fields provided this basis. In the general situation, we lift to the frame bundle to allow use of the globally defined horizontal vector fields on $F\mathcal{M}$.

As illustrated from the beginning of the chapter in Fig. 10.1, probabilistic approaches can behave quite differently from their least-squares counterparts. We emphasized the coupling between covariance and curvature both visually and theoretically, the latter with the link between curvature and nonclosedness of the horizontal distribution, sub-Riemannian geodesics, and most probable paths for the driving semimartingales.

Finally we used the geometric and probabilistic constructions to describe statistical concepts such as the maximum likelihood mean from the Brownian motion, and maximum likelihood mean and infinitesimal covariance, and we provided ways of optimizing the parameters using bridge sampling.

The theoretical development of geometric statistics is currently far from complete, and there are many promising directions to be explored to approach as complete a theory of geometric statistics as is available for linear statistics. The viewpoint of this chapter is that probabilistic approaches play an important role in achieving this.

10.10 Further reading

Here we provide a few useful example references for background information and further reading.

An introduction to general SDE theory can be found in [25]. Much of the frame bundle theory, stochastic analysis on manifolds using frame bundles, and theory of Brownian motion on manifolds can be found in [13]. See also [7] for details on stochastic analysis on manifolds. Brownian motion on Lie groups is, for example, covered in [20]. Diffusions on stratified spaces is described in the works [23,24] by Tom Nye.

The relation between the horizontal subbundle and curvature can be found in the book [19]. Sub-Riemannian geometry is covered extensively in [22]. The stochastic large deformation model in [1] builds on the stochastic variational method of Holm [12].

References

1. Alexis Arnaudon, Darryl D. Holm, Stefan Sommer, A geometric framework for stochastic shape analysis, Foundations of Computational Mathematics (July 2018).
2. M. Bruveris, F. Gay-Balmaz, D.D. Holm, T.S. Ratiu, The momentum map representation of images, arXiv:0912.2990, December 2009.
3. Joris Bierkens, Frank van der Meulen, Moritz Schauer, Simulation of elliptic and hypo-elliptic conditional diffusions, arXiv:1810.01761 [math, stat], October 2018.
4. Bernard Delyon, Ying Hu, Simulation of conditioned diffusion and application to parameter estimation, Stochastic Processes and Their Applications 116 (11) (November 2006) 1660–1675.
5. Benjamin Eltzner, Stephan Huckemann, Kanti V. Mardia, Torus principal component analysis with an application to RNA structures, arXiv:1511.04993 [q-bio, stat], November 2015.
6. David Elworthy, Geometric aspects of diffusions on manifolds, in: Paul-Louis Hennequin (Ed.), École D'Été de Probabilités de Saint-Flour XV–XVII, 1985–87, Number 136, in: Lecture Notes in Mathematics, Springer, Berlin, Heidelberg, 1988, pp. 277–425.

7. Michel Emery, Stochastic Calculus in Manifolds, Universitext, Springer Berlin Heidelberg, Berlin, Heidelberg, 1989.

8. Takahiko Fujita, Shin-ichi Kotani, The Onsager–Machlup function for diffusion processes, Journal of Mathematics of Kyoto University 22 (1) (1982) 115–130.

9. M. Frechet, Les éléments aléatoires de nature quelconque dans un espace distancié, Annales de L'Institut Henri Poincaré 10 (1948) 215–310.

10. U. Grenander, Probabilities on Algebraic Structures, John Wiley and Sons, 1963.

11. Stephan Huckemann, Thomas Hotz, Axel Munk, Intrinsic shape analysis: geodesic PCA for Riemannian manifolds modulo isometric lie group actions, Statistica Sinica 20 (1) (January 2010) 1–100.

12. Darryl D. Holm, Variational principles for stochastic fluid dynamics, Proceedings - Royal Society. Mathematical, Physical and Engineering Sciences 471 (2176) (April 2015).

13. Elton P. Hsu, Stochastic Analysis on Manifolds, American Mathematical Soc., 2002.

14. Sungkyu Jung, Ian L. Dryden, J.S. Marron, Analysis of principal nested spheres, Biometrika 99 (3) (January 2012) 551–568.

15. Line Kühnel, Stefan Sommer, Alexis Arnaudon, Differential geometry and stochastic dynamics with deep learning numerics, Applied Mathematics and Computation 356 (1 September 2019) 411–437.

16. Line Kuhnel, Stefan Sommer, Computational anatomy in Theano, in: Mathematical Foundations of Computational Anatomy (MFCA), 2017.

17. Kühnel Line, Stefan Sommer, Stochastic development regression on non-linear manifolds, in: Information Processing in Medical Imaging, in: Lecture Notes in Computer Science, Springer, Cham, June 2017, pp. 53–64.

18. Kühnel Line, Stefan Sommer, Stochastic development regression using method of moments, in: Geometric Science of Information, in: Lecture Notes in Computer Science, Springer, Cham, November 2017, pp. 3–11.

19. Ivan Kolář, Jan Slovák, Peter W. Michor, Natural Operations in Differential Geometry, Springer Berlin Heidelberg, Berlin, Heidelberg, 1993.

20. Ming Liao, Lévy Processes in Lie Groups, Cambridge University Press, Cambridge, New York, 2004.

21. Zoltán Magyar, Heat kernels on Lie groups, Journal of Functional Analysis 93 (2) (October 1990) 351–390.

22. Richard Montgomery, A Tour of Subriemannian Geometries, Their Geodesics and Applications, American Mathematical Soc., August 2006.

23. T.M.W. Nye, M.C. White, Diffusion on some simple stratified spaces, Journal of Mathematical Imaging and Vision 50 (1) (September 2014) 115–125.

24. Tom M.W. Nye, Convergence of random walks to Brownian motion on cubical complexes, arXiv:1508.02906 [math, q-bio], August 2015.

25. Bernt Øksendal, Stochastic Differential Equations: An Introduction With Applications, Springer Science & Business Media, 2003.

26. Xavier Pennec, Intrinsic statistics on Riemannian manifolds: basic tools for geometric measurements, Journal of Mathematical Imaging and Vision 25 (1) (2006) 127–154.

27. Xavier Pennec, Barycentric subspace analysis on manifolds, arXiv:1607.02833 [math, stat], July 2016.

28. Omiros Papaspiliopoulos, Gareth O. Roberts, Importance sampling techniques for estimation of diffusion models, in: Statistical Methods for Stochastic Differential Equations, Chapman & Hall/CRC Press, 2012.

29. Sam Roweis, EM algorithms for PCA and SPCA, in: Proceedings of the 1997 Conference on Advances in Neural Information Processing Systems 10, NIPS '97, MIT Press, Cambridge, MA, USA, 1998, pp. 626–632.

30. Stefan Sommer, Alexis Arnaudon, Line Kuhnel, Sarang Joshi, Bridge simulation and metric estimation on landmark manifolds, in: Graphs in Biomedical Image Analysis, Computational Anatomy and Imaging Genetics, in: Lecture Notes in Computer Science, Springer, September 2017, pp. 79–91.

31. Stefan Sommer, Horizontal dimensionality reduction and iterated frame bundle development, in: Geometric Science of Information, in: LNCS, Springer, 2013, pp. 76–83.

32. Stefan Sommer, Anisotropic distributions on manifolds: template estimation and most probable paths, in: Information Processing in Medical Imaging, in: Lecture Notes in Computer Science, vol. 9123, Springer, 2015, pp. 193–204.

33. Stefan Sommer, Anisotropically weighted and nonholonomically constrained evolutions on manifolds, Entropy 18 (12) (November 2016) 425.

34. Stefan Sommer, An infinitesimal probabilistic model for principal component analysis of manifold valued data, arXiv:1801.10341 [cs, math, stat], January 2018.

35. Stefan Sommer, Anne Marie Svane, Modelling anisotropic covariance using stochastic development and sub-Riemannian frame bundle geometry, Journal of Geometric Mechanics 9 (3) (June 2017) 391–410.

36. Moritz Schauer, Frank van der Meulen, Harry van Zanten, Guided proposals for simulating multi-dimensional diffusion bridges, Bernoulli 23 (4A) (November 2017) 2917–2950.

37. Michael E. Tipping, Christopher M. Bishop, Probabilistic principal component analysis, Journal of the Royal Statistical Society. Series B 61 (3) (January 1999) 611–622.

38. Alain Trouve, François-Xavier Vialard, Shape splines and stochastic shape evolutions: a second order point of view, Quarterly of Applied Mathematics 70 (2) (2012) 219–251.

39. Miaomiao Zhang, P.T. Fletcher, Probabilistic principal geodesic analysis, in: NIPS, 2013, pp. 1178–1186.

On shape analysis of functional data

Ruiyi Zhang, Anuj Srivastava
Florida State University, Tallahassee, FL, United States

11.1 Introduction

The problem of shape analysis of objects is very important with applications across all areas. Specifically, the shape analysis of curves in Euclidean spaces is important with widespread applications in biology, computer vision, and medical image analysis. For instance, the functionality of biological objects, such as proteins, RNAs, and chromosomes, is often closely related to their shapes, and we would like statistical tools for analyzing such shapes to understand their functionalities. These tools include metrics for quantifying shape differences, geodesics to study deformations between shapes, shape summaries (including means, covariances, and principals components) to characterize shape population, and statistical shape models to capture shape variability. Consequently, a large number of mathematical representations and approaches have been developed to analyze shapes of interest. Depending on their goals, these representations can differ vastly in their complexities and capabilities.

Shape analysis naturally involves elements of differential geometry of curves and surfaces. In the appendix we summarize some concepts and notions from differential geometry that are useful in any approach to shape analysis. Specifically, we introduce the concepts of a Riemannian metric, geodesics, group actions on manifolds, quotient spaces, and equivalence relations using orbits. We also provide some simple examples to illustrate them to a reader not familiar with these concepts. Given these items, we can layout a typical approach to shape analysis. A typical framework for shape analysis takes the following form. We start with a mathematical representation of objects—as vectors, matrices, or functions—and remove certain shape-preserving transformations termed as preprocessing. The remaining transformations, the ones that cannot be removed as preprocessing, as removing by forming group actions and quotient spaces.

David Kendall [10] provided one of the earliest formal mathematical frameworks for quantifying shapes. In this framework we start with a finite set of points, termed *landmarks*, that represent an object and removes the effects of certain transformation groups, namely rigid motions and global scaling, to reach final shape representations. As depicted in Fig. 11.1, the

Riemannian Geometric Statistics in Medical Image Analysis
https://doi.org/10.1016/B978-0-12-814725-2.00019-4

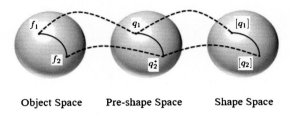

Object Space   Pre-shape Space   Shape Space

Figure 11.1. A general framework of shape analysis: a mathematical representation leads to a preshape space that further results in the shape space.

key idea is to remove two groups via preprocessing—remove translation group by centering landmarks and remove size group by rescaling landmark vector—and reach a constrained space called the *preshape space*. The remaining transformation, the rotation in this case, is removed by forming orbits under this group action, or equivalence classes, and imposing a metric on this quotient space of orbits. We introduce the concepts of equivalence relations, group actions, orbits, and quotient spaces in the Appendix. A number of prominent researchers have subsequently developed this framework into a rich set of statistical tools for practical data analysis [3,17,11,6].

One of the most important challenges in shape analysis is *registration*. Registration stands for densely matching points across objects and using this registration for comparing shapes and developing shape models. Historically, some approaches presume that objects are already perfectly registered, whereas some other approaches use off-the-shelf methods to preregister before applying their own shape analysis. Whereas a presumption of perfect registration is severely restrictive, the use of registration as a preprocessing step is also questionable, especially when the metrics for registration have no bearing on the metrics used in ensuing shape analysis and modeling. A better solution, one that has gained recognition over the last few years, is an approach called *elastic shape analysis*. Here we incorporate a solution for performing registration along with the process of shape comparisons, thus resulting in a unified framework for registration, shape comparisons, and analysis. The key idea here is to endow the shape space with an elastic Riemannian metric that has an appropriate invariance under the action of the registration group (and other nuisance groups). Whereas such elastic metrics are somewhat complicated to be of use directly, especially for analyzing large datasets, there is often a square-root transformation that simplifies them into the standard Euclidean metric. This point of view is the main theme of this chapter.

In this chapter we focus on the problem of shape analysis of curves in Euclidean spaces and provide an overview of this problem area. This setup includes, for example, shape analysis of planar curves that form silhouettes of objects in images or shape analysis of space curves representing complex biomolecular structures, such as proteins and chromosomes. A particular case of this problem is when we restrict to curves in $\mathbb{R}$, that is, we analyze shapes of real-valued functions on a fixed interval. This fast growing area in statistics, called *functional data analysis* [16], deals with modeling and analyzing data, where observations are functions over intervals. The use of elastic Riemannian metrics and square-root transformations for curves was first proposed by [22,23] although this treatment used complex arithmetic and was restricted to planar curves. Later on, [15] presented a family of elastic metrics that allowed for different levels of elasticity in shape comparisons. Joshi et al. [9] and Srivastava et al. [19] introduced a square-root representation, slightly different from that of Younes, which was applicable to curves in any Euclidean space. Subsequently, several other elastic metrics and square-root representations, each representing a different strength and limitation, have been discussed in the literature [25,1,2,12,24]. In this chapter we focus on the framework of [9] and [19] and demonstrate that approach using a number of examples involving functional and curve data.

We mention in passing that such elastic frameworks have also been developed for curves taking values on nonlinear domains also, including unit spheres [26], hyperbolic spaces [5,4], the space of symmetric positive definite matrices [27], and some other manifolds. Additionally, elastic metrics and square-root representations have also been used to analyze shapes of surfaces in $\mathbb{R}^3$. These methods provide techniques for registration of points across objects, as well as comparisons of their shapes, in a unified metric-based framework. For details, we refer the reader to a text book by [8] and some related papers [7,21,13].

11.2 Registration problem and elastic approach

Using a formulation similar to Kendall's approach, we provide a comprehensive framework for comparing shapes of curves in Euclidean spaces. The key idea here is to study curves as (continuous) parameterized objects and to use parameterization as a tool for registration of points across curves. Consequently, this introduces an additional group, namely the re-parameterization group, which is added in the representation and needs to be removed using the notion of equivalence class and quotient spaces.

11.2.1 The $\mathbb{L}^2$ norm and associated problems

As mentioned earlier, the problem of registration of points across curves is important in comparisons of shapes of curves. To formalize this problem, let Γ represent all boundary-preserving diffeomorphisms of

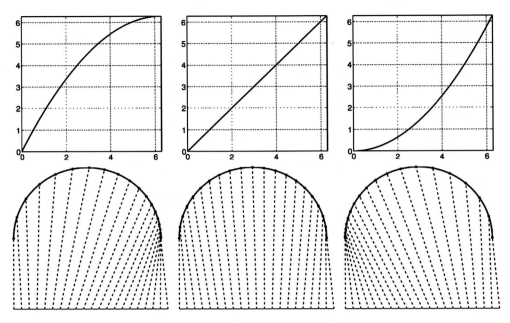

Figure 11.2. An illustration of reparameterization of an open curve. This figure is taken from [18].

[0, 1] to itself. Elements of Γ play the role of re-parameterization (and registration) functions. Let $\mathcal{F}$ be the set of all absolutely continuous parameterized curves of the type $f : [0, 1] \rightarrow \mathbb{R}^n$. For any $f \in \mathcal{F}$ and $\gamma \in \Gamma$, the composition $f \circ \gamma$ denotes a reparameterization of f. Note that both f and $f \circ \gamma$ go through the same set of points in $\mathbb{R}^n$ and thus have exactly the same shape. Fig. 11.2 shows an example of reparameterization of a semi-circular curve f. The top row shows three γ's, and the bottom row shows the corresponding parameterizations of f. For any $t \in [0, 1]$ and any two curves $f_1, f_2 \in \mathcal{F}$, the points $f_1(t)$ and $f_2(t)$ are said to be *registered* to each other. If we re-parameterize f_2 by γ, then the registration of $f_1(t)$ changes to $f_2(\gamma(t))$ for all t. In this way the reparameterization γ controls registration of points between f_1 and f_2. On one hand, reparameterization is a nuisance variable since it preserves the shape of a curve but, and on the other hand, it is an important tool in controlling registration between curves.

To register two curves, we need an objective function that evaluates and quantifies the level of registration between them. A natural choice will use the $\mathbb{L}^2$ norm, but it has some unexpected pitfalls as described next. Let $\|f\|$ represent the $\mathbb{L}^2$ norm, that is, $\|f\| = \sqrt{\int_0^1 |f(t)|^2 dt}$, of a curve f, where $|\cdot|$ inside the integral denotes the ℓ^2 norm of a vector. The $\mathbb{L}^2$ norm provides the most commonly used Hilbert structure in functional data analysis. Despite its popularity, there are problems with this metric.

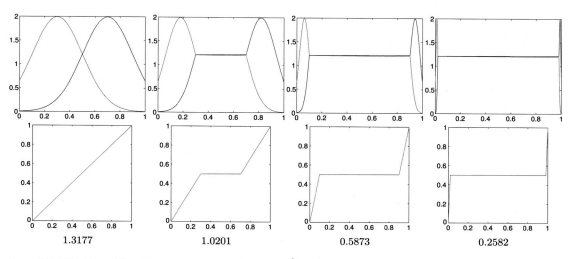

Figure 11.3. Pinching of functions f_1 and f_2 to reduce the $\mathbb{L}^2$ norm between them. In each column we show $f_1 \circ \gamma$, $f_2 \circ \gamma$ (top panel), γ (bottom panel), and the value of $\|f_1 \circ \gamma - f_2 \circ \gamma\|$ below them.

The main problem is that as an objective function for registration, it leads to a degeneracy, called the *pinching effect*. In other words, if we try to minimize $\|f_1 - f_2 \circ \gamma\|$ over γ, this quantity can be made infinitesimally small despite f_1 and f_2 being very different functions. Fig. 11.3 shows a simple example to illustrate this idea using scalar functions on $[0, 1]$. The top left panel of the figure shows to functions f_1, f_2 that agree at only one point $t = 0.5$ in the domain. We design a sequence of piecewise-linear time-warping functions γs (shown in the bottom row) that increasingly spend time at $t = 0.5$ from left to right, resulting in the steady decrease in the $\mathbb{L}^2$ norm $\|f_1 \circ \gamma - f_2 \circ \gamma\|$. Continuing this process, we can arbitrarily decrease the $\mathbb{L}^2$ norm between two functions, irrespective of the other values of these functions. Thus an optimization problem of the type $\inf_{\gamma \in \Gamma} \|f_1 - f_2 \circ \gamma\|$ has degenerate solutions. This problem is well recognized in the literature [16,14], and the most common solution used to avoid pinching is to penalize large warpings using roughness penalties. More precisely, we solve an optimization problem of the type

$$\inf_{\gamma \in \Gamma} \left(\|f_1 - f_2 \circ \gamma\|^2 + \lambda \mathcal{R}(\gamma) \right), \qquad (11.1)$$

where $\mathcal{R}(\gamma)$ measures the roughness of γ. Examples of $\mathcal{R}$ include $\int \dot{\gamma}(t)^2 \, dt$, $\int \ddot{\gamma}(t)^2 \, dt$, and so on. The role of $\mathcal{R}$ is to discourage large time warpings. By large we mean γs whose first or second derivatives have high norms.

Whereas this solution helps avoid the pinching effect, it often also restricts alignment of functions. Since it reduces the solution space for warping functions, it can also inhibit solutions that correctly require large deformations. Fig. 11.4 shows an example of this problem using two functions f_1 and f_2 shown in the top left panel. In this example we use the first order penalty ($\int \dot{\gamma}(t)^2 \, dt$) in Eq. (11.1) and study several properties of the resulting solution—does to align the functions well, is the solution symmetric in the functions f_1 and f_2, does it have pinching effect, and how sensitive is the solution to the choice of λ? In each row, for a certain value of λ, we first obtain an optimal value of γ in Eq. (11.1). Then, to study the symmetry of the solution, we swap f_1 and f_2 and solve this optimization again. Finally, we compose the two resulting optimal warping functions. If the composition is a perfect identity function $\gamma_{id}(t) = t$, then the solution is called *inverse consistent* (and symmetric), otherwise not. In the first row, where $\lambda = 0$, we see that the solution is inverse consistent, but there is substantial pinching, as expected. As we increase λ (shown in the second row), the level of pinching is reduced, but the solution also shows a small inconsistency in the forward and backward solutions. In the last row, where λ is large, the pinching effect is gone, but inverse inconsistency has increased. Also, due to increased penalty, the quality of alignment has gone down too. This discussion also points an obvious limitation of methods involving penalty terms. We need to decide which type of penalty and how large λ should be used in real situations. In contrast to the penalized $\mathbb{L}^2$ approach, the elastic approach described in this chapter results in the solution shown in the bottom row. This solution is inverse consistent, rules out the pinching effect (and does not need any penalty or choice of λ), and achieves an excellent registration between the functions. Additionally, the computational cost is very similar to the penalized $\mathbb{L}^2$ approach.

Lack of invariance under $\mathbb{L}^2$ norm

To study the shape of curves, we need representations and metrics that are invariant to rigid motions, global scale, and reparameterization of curves. The biggest challenge comes from the last group since it is an infinite-dimensional group and requires closer inspection. To understand this issue, take an analogous task of removing the rotation group in Kendall's shape analysis, where each object is represented by a set of landmarks. Let $X_1, X_2 \in \mathbb{R}^{n \times k}$ represent two sets of landmarks (k landmarks in $\mathbb{R}^n$), and let $SO(n)$ be the set of all rotations in $\mathbb{R}^n$. To (rotationally) align X_2 to X_1, we solve for a Procrustes rotation according to $\text{argmin}_{O \in SO(n)} \|X_1 - OX_2\|_F$, where $\|\cdot\|_F$ denotes the Frobenius norm of matrices. In other words, we keep X_1 fixed and rotate X_2 into a configuration that minimizes the Frobenius norm between them. The choice of Frobenius norm is important because it satisfies the following property:

$$\|X_1 - X_2\| = \|OX_1 - OX_2\| \text{ for all } X_1, X_2 \in \mathbb{R}^{n \times k}, \ O \in SO(n) \, .$$
$$(11.2)$$

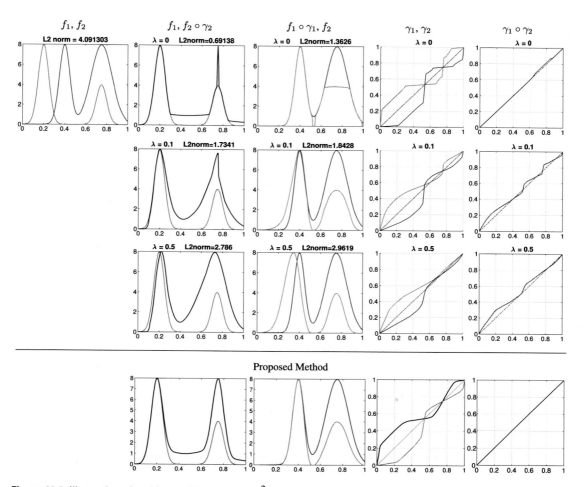

Figure 11.4. Illustration of problems with penalized $\mathbb{L}^2$ norm in registering functions using time warpings: pinching effect, asymmetry of solutions, and need to balance matching with penalty. The bottom row shows the proposed method that avoids all three problems.

If this property was not satisfied, we would not be able to perform Procrustes rotation. In mathematical terms we say that the action of $SO(n)$ on $\mathbb{R}^{n\times k}$ is by *isometries* under the Frobenius norm or that the metric is *invariant* under the rotation group action. (Please refer to the Appendix for a proper definition of isometry under group actions.) A similar approach is needed for performing registration and removing the reparameterization group in the case of functions and curves. However, it is easy to see that $\|f_1 - f_2\| \neq \|f_1 \circ \gamma - f_2 \circ \gamma\|$ in general. In fact, Fig. 11.3 already provides an example of this inequality. Since $\mathbb{L}^2$ norm is not preserved under identical reparameterizations of curves, it is not suitable for use in registration and shape analysis. Thus we seek a new metric to accomplish registration and shape analysis of curves.

11.2.2 SRVFs and curve registration

Now we describe an elastic approach that addresses these issues and provides a fundamental tool for registration and shape analysis of curves.

As earlier, let $\mathcal{F}$ be the set of all absolutely continuous parameterized curves in $\mathbb{R}^n$, and let Γ be the same of all reparameterization functions. Define the square-root velocity function (SRVF) [19,18] of f as a mathematical representation of f given by

$$q(t) = \begin{cases} \dfrac{\dot{f}(t)}{\sqrt{|\dot{f}(t)|}}, & |\dot{f}(t)| \neq 0, \\ 0, & |\dot{f}(t)| = 0. \end{cases} \tag{11.3}$$

In case of $n = 1$ this expression simply reduces to $q(t) = \text{sign}(\dot{f}(t)) \times \sqrt{|\dot{f}(t)|}$. Here are some important properties associated with this definition.

- If f is absolutely continuous, as assumed, then q is square integrable, that is, $\|q\| < \infty$.
- This transformation from f to q is invertible up to a constant, with the inverse given by $f(t) = f(0) + \int_0^t q(s)|q(s)|\,ds$. In fact the mapping $f \mapsto (f(0), q)$ is a bijection between $\mathcal{F}$ and $\mathbb{R} \times \mathbb{L}^2([0,1], \mathbb{R}^n)$.
- If f is reparameterized by $\gamma \in \Gamma$ to result in $f \circ \gamma$, the SRVF change from q to $(q \circ \gamma)\sqrt{\dot{\gamma}} \overset{\Delta}{=} (q \star \gamma)$. In other words, the action of Γ on $\mathbb{L}^2$ is given by $q \star \gamma$. Also, if a curve is rotated by a matrix $O \in SO(n)$, then its SRVF gets rotated by the same matrix O, that is, the SRVF of a curve Of is given by Oq.
- The length of the curve f, given by $L[f] = \int_0^1 |\dot{f}(t)|\,dt$, is equal to the $\mathbb{L}^2$ norm of its SRVF q, that is, $L[f] = \|q\|$.
- The most important property of this representation is preservation of the $\mathbb{L}^2$ norm under time warping or reparameterization, that is,

$$\|q_1 - q_2\| = \|(q_1 \star \gamma) - (q_2 \star \gamma)\|, \quad \forall q_1, q_2 \in \mathbb{L}^2([0,1], \mathbb{R}^n),\ \gamma \in \Gamma. \tag{11.4}$$

We already know that $\mathbb{L}^2$ norm is preserved under identical rotation, that is, $\|q_1 - q_2\| = \|Oq_1 - Oq_2\|$.

In view of the invariant property, this representation provides a proper setup for registration of functional and curve data.

Definition 11.1 (Pairwise registration). Given two curves $f_1, f_2 \in \mathcal{F}$ and their SRVFs $q_1, q_2 \in \mathbb{L}^2([0,1], \mathbb{R}^n)$, we define their registration to be the optimization problem

$$\inf_{\gamma \in \Gamma, O \in SO(n)} \|q_1 - O(q_2 \star \gamma)\| = \inf_{\gamma \in \Gamma, O \in SO(n)} \|q_2 - O(q_1 \star \gamma)\| . \quad (11.5)$$

We make a few remarks about this registration formulation.

1. **No Pinching**: Firstly, this setup does not have any pinching problem. A special case of the isometry condition is that $\|q \star \gamma\| = \|q\|$ for all q and γ. In other words, the action of Γ on $\mathbb{L}^2$ is norm preserving. Thus pinching is not possible in this setup.

2. **No Need for a Penalty Term**: Since there is no pinching, we do not have to include any penalty term in this setup. Therefore there is no inherent problem about choosing the relative weight between the data term and the penalty term. However, if we need to control the time warping or registration, beyond the basic formulation, we can still add an additional penalty term as desired.

3. **Inverse Symmetry**: As stated in Eq. (11.5), the registration of f_1 to f_2 results in the same solution as the registration of f_2 to f_1. The equality between the two terms in that equation comes from fact that $SO(n)$ and Γ are groups, and the isometry condition is satisfied (Eq. (11.4)).

4. **Invariance to Scale and Translation**: We can show that the optimizer in Eq. (11.5) does not change if either function is changed using positive scaling or translation, that is, we can replace any $f_i(t)$ with $af_i(t) + c$ for any $a \in \mathbb{R}_+$ and $c \in \mathbb{R}^n$, and the solution does not change. This is an important requirement for shape analysis since shape is invariant to these transformations. The solution is invariant to translation because the SRVF q_i is based on the of the curve f_i and because

$$\underset{\gamma \in \Gamma}{\mathrm{arginf}} \|q_1 - (q_2 \star \gamma)\| = \underset{\gamma \in \Gamma}{\mathrm{arginf}} \|a_1 q_1 - a_2(q_2 \star \gamma)\|$$

for any $a_1, a_2 \in \mathbb{R}_+$.

5. **Proper Metric**: As described in the next section, the infimum in Eq. (11.5) is a proper metric itself in a quotient space and hence can be used for ensuing statistical analysis. (Please refer to the definition of a metric on the quotient space M/G using an invariant metric on parent space M).

In Eq. (11.5) the optimization over $SO(n)$ is performed using the Procrustes solution:

$$O^* = \begin{cases} UV & \text{if } \det(A) > 0, \\ U \begin{bmatrix} 1 & 0 \\ 0 & -1 \end{bmatrix} V^T & \text{otherwise,} \end{cases}$$

where $A = \int_0^1 q_1(t)q_2^T(t)dt \in \mathbb{R}^{n \times n}$, and $\mathrm{svd}(A) = U\Sigma V^T$. The optimization over Γ is accomplished using the dynamic programming algorithm

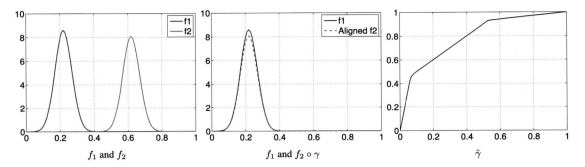

Figure 11.5. Registration of scalar functions using Eq. (11.5).

[20]. The optimization over $SO(n) \times \Gamma$ is performed by iterating between the two individual solutions until convergence.

We present some examples of registration of functions and curves to illustrate this approach. In the case $n = 1$ we do not have any rotation in Eq. (11.5), and one minimizes only over Γ using the dynamic programming algorithm. The last row of Fig. 11.4 shows alignment of two functions studied in that example. It shows alignments of the two functions to each other and the composition of the two γ functions resulting in a perfect identity function (confirming inverse consistency). Note that even though the optimization is performed using SRVFs in $\mathbb{L}^2$ space, the results are displayed in the original function space for convenience. Fig. 11.5 shows another example of registering functions using this approach.

Fig. 11.6 shows a few examples of registration of points along planar curves. In each panel we show the two curves in red (light gray in print version) and blue (dark gray in print version), and optimal correspondences across these curves using black lines, obtained using Eq. (11.5). We can see that the algorithm is successful in matching points with similar geometric features (local orientation, curvature, etc.) despite different locations of matched points along the two curves. This success in registering curves translates into a superior performance in ensuing shape analysis.

11.3 Shape space and geodesic paths

So far we have focused on an important problem of registering curves and functions. Our larger goal, of course, is the shape analysis of these objects, and registration plays an important role in that analysis. Returning to the problem of analyzing shapes, we describe the framework for an elastic shape analysis of Euclidean curves. It is called *elastic* because it incorporates the registration of curves as a part of their shape comparisons.

This framework follows the approach laid out in Fig. 11.1. We will use the SRVF representation of curves, reach a preshape space by removing

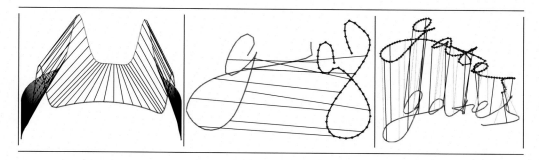

Figure 11.6. Registration of planar curves using Eq. (11.5).This figure is taken from [18].

some nuisance transformations, and form quotient space of that preshape space under the remaining nuisance transformations. Once again, let $\mathcal{F}$ be the set of all absolutely continuous curves in $\mathbb{R}^n$, and let $\mathbb{L}^2$ denote the set of square-integrable curves in $\mathbb{R}^n$. For any $f \in \mathcal{F}$, its length $L[f] = \|q\|$, where q is the SRVF of f. So, if we rescale f to be of unit length, then its SRVF satisfies $\|q\| = 1$. Let $\mathcal{C}$ denote the unit Hilbert sphere inside $\mathbb{L}^2$. $\mathcal{C}$ is called the *preshape space* and is the set of SRVFs representing all unit length curves in $\mathcal{F}$. The geometry of $\mathcal{C}$ is simple, and we can compute distances/geodesics on $\mathcal{C}$ relatively easily. For any two points $q_1, q_2 \in \mathcal{C}$, the distance between them on $\mathcal{C}$ is given by the arc length $d_c(q_1, q_2) = \cos^{-1}(\langle q_1, q_2 \rangle)$. The geodesic path between them is the shorter arc on a great circle given by

$$\alpha : [0, 1] \to \mathcal{C}, \quad \alpha(\tau) = \frac{1}{\sin \theta} \left(\sin((1 - \tau)\theta)q_1 + \sin(\tau\theta)q_2 \right) , \quad (11.6)$$

where $\theta = d_c(q_1, q_2)$.

In representing a unit-length $f \in \mathcal{F}$ by its $q \in \mathcal{C}$ we have removed its translation (since q depends only on the derivatives of f) and its scale. However, the rotation and re-parameterization variabilities are still left in this representation, that is, we can have two curves with exactly the same shape but at different rotations and reparameterizations and thus with nonzero distance between them in $\mathcal{C}$. These transformations are removed using groups actions and equivalence relations, as described next. For any $O \in SO(n)$ and $\gamma \in \Gamma$, $O(f \circ \gamma)$ has the same shape as f. In the SRVF representation we characterize these transformations as actions of product group $SO(n) \times \Gamma$ on $\mathcal{C}$ according to

$$(SO(n) \times \Gamma) \times \mathbb{L}^2 \to \mathbb{L}^2, \quad (O, \gamma) * q = O(q \star \gamma) .$$

This leads to the definition of *orbits* or equivalent classes:

$$[q] = \{O(q \star \gamma) | O \in SO(n), \gamma \in \Gamma\} .$$

Each orbit $[q]$ represents a unique shape of curves. The set of all such orbits forms the *shape space* of curves

$$\mathcal{S} = \mathcal{C}/(SO(n) \times \Gamma) = \{[q] | q \in \mathcal{C}\} .$$

(Once again, we advise the reader not familiar with these ideas to follow the definitions given in the Appendix.)

Definition 11.2 (Shape metric). For any two curves $f_1, f_2 \in \mathcal{F}$, define a metric between their shapes according to

$$d_s([q_1], [q_2]) = \inf_{O \in SO(n), \gamma \in \Gamma} d_c(q_1, O(q_2 \star \gamma)) \quad (11.7)$$

$$= \inf_{O \in SO(n), \gamma \in \Gamma} \cos^{-1}(\langle q_1, O(q_2 \star \gamma) \rangle) . \quad (11.8)$$

The interesting part of this definition is that the process of registration of points across shapes is incorporated in the definition of shape metric. The two computations, registration of curves and comparisons of their shapes, have been unified under the same metric. The optimal deformation from one shape to the other is mathematically realized as a geodesic in the shape space. We can evaluate the geodesic between the shapes $[q_1]$ and $[q_2]$ in $\mathcal{S}$ by constructing the shortest geodesic between the two orbits in $\mathcal{C}$. If $(\hat{O}, \hat{\gamma})$ denote the optimal arguments in Eq. (11.8), then this geodesic is given by

$$\alpha(\tau) = \frac{1}{\sin\theta} \left(\sin((1-\tau)\theta)q_1 + \sin(\tau\theta)\hat{q}_2 \right), \quad \hat{q}_2 = \hat{O}(q_2 \ast \hat{\gamma}).$$

We present some examples of this framework. Fig. 11.7 shows three examples of geodesic paths between given 2D curves. It is clear from these examples that the elastic registration of points across the two curves result in a very natural deformation between them. Similar geometric parts are matched to each other despite different relative sizes across the objects, a clear depiction of stretching and compression needed for optimal matching. Fig. 11.8 shows an example of elastic geodesic between two very simple proteins viewed as curves in $\mathbb{R}^3$.

Shape spaces of closed curves

In case we are interested in shapes of closed curves, we need to restrict to the curves satisfying the condition $f(0) = f(1)$. In this case it is often more natural to choose the domain of parameterization to be $\mathbb{S}^1$, instead of $[0, 1]$. Thus Γ now represents all orientation-preserving diffeomorphisms of $\mathbb{S}^1$ to itself. Under the SRVF representation of f, the closure condition is given by $\int_{\mathbb{S}^1} q(t)|q(t)|dt = 0$. The preshape space for unit-length closed curves is

$$\mathcal{C}^c = \{q \in \mathbb{L}^2(\mathbb{S}^1, \mathbb{R}^n) | \int_{\mathbb{S}^1} |q(t)|dt = 1, \int_{\mathbb{S}^1} q(t)|q(t)|dt = 0\} \subset \mathcal{C} .$$

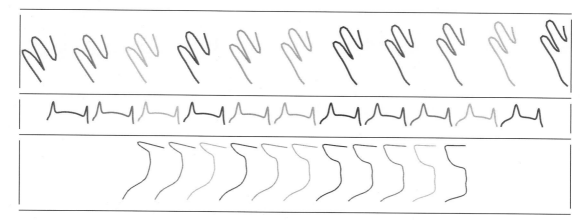

Figure 11.7. Elastic geodesic paths between planar curves, showing that a good registration leads to natural deformations.

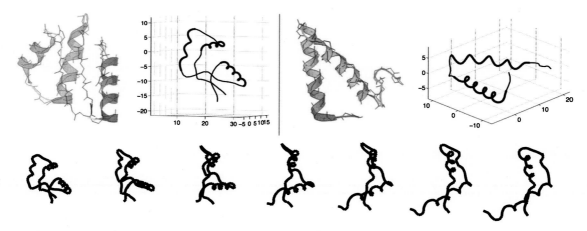

Figure 11.8. Elastic deformation between two proteins. This figure is taken from [18].

An orbit or an equivalence class is defined to be: for $q \in \mathcal{C}^c$, $[q] = \{O(q \star \gamma) | O \in SO(n), \gamma \in \Gamma\}$, and the resulting shape space is $\mathcal{S}^c = \mathcal{C}^c/(SO(n) \times \Gamma) = \{[q] | q \in \mathcal{C}^c\}$. The computation of geodesic paths in $\mathcal{C}^c$ is more complicated as there is no analytical expression similar to Eq. (11.6) is available for $\mathcal{C}^c$. In this case we use a numerical approximation, called *path straightening* [19], for computing geodesics and geodesic distances. Let $d_c(q_1, q_2)$ denote the length of a geodesic path in $\mathcal{C}^c$ between any two curves $q_1, q_2 \in \mathcal{C}^c$. Then the distance between their shapes is given by

$$d_s([q_1], [q_2]) = \inf_{O \in SO(n), \gamma \in \Gamma} d_c(q_1, O(q_2 \star \gamma)). \qquad (11.9)$$

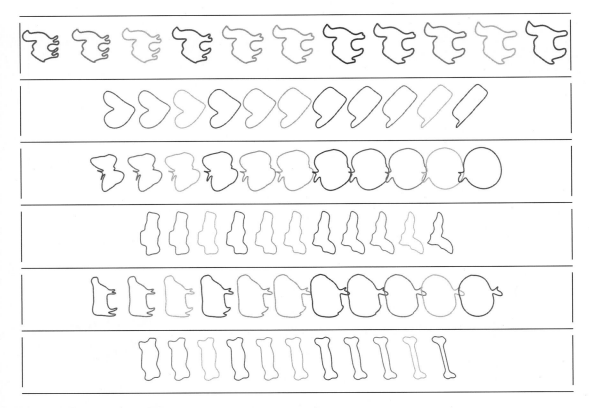

Figure 11.9. Examples of elastic geodesic paths between closed planar curves in $\mathcal{S}^c$.

Fig. 11.9 shows some examples of geodesic between curves taken from the MPEG7 shape dataset.

11.4 Statistical summaries and principal modes of shape variability

Using the mathematical platform developed so far, we can define and compute several quantities that are useful in statistical shape analysis. For example, we can use the shape metric to define and compute a mean or a median shape, as a representative of shapes denoting a population. Furthermore, using the tangent structure of the shape space, we can compute principal modes for variability in a given sample of data. Given mean and covariance estimates, we can characterize underlying shape populations using Gaussian-type distributions on shape spaces.

Definition 11.3 (Intrinsic, Fréchet mean). For a given set of curves $f_1, f_2, \ldots, f_n \in \mathcal{F}$ and the associated shapes $[q_1], [q_2], \ldots, [q_n] \in \mathcal{S}$ (or $\mathcal{S}^c$ if curves are closed), their intrinsic or Fréchet mean is defined as the quantity

$$[\mu] = \operatorname*{argmin}_{[q] \in \mathcal{S}} \sum_{i=1}^{n} d_s^2([q], [q_i])^2 .$$

In other words, the mean is defined to be the shape that achieves minimum of the sum of squared distances to the given shapes. There is a well-known gradient-based algorithm for estimating this mean from given data.

In case of real-valued functions, we can simplify the setup and use it to register and align multiple functions. The basic idea is to use a template to register all the given curves using previous pairwise alignment. A good candidate of the template is a *mean* function defined previously. In the case of unscaled functions the definition of the mean simplifies to

$$[\mu] = \operatorname*{argmin}_{q \in \mathbb{L}^2} \sum_{i=1}^{n} \left(\inf_{\gamma_i \in \Gamma} \|q - (q_i \star \gamma_i)\|^2 \right) .$$

If we fix the optimal warpings to be $\{\gamma_i\}$s, then the solution for the mean reduces to $\mu = \frac{1}{n} \sum_{i=1}^{n} (q_i \star \gamma_i)$. Using this idea, we can write an iterative algorithm for registration of multiple functions or curves.

Multiple alignment algorithm

1. Use Eq. (11.3) to compute SRVFs q_i, $i = 1, \ldots, n$, from the given f_i.
2. Initialize the mean with $\mu = \arg\min_{q_i} \left\| q_i - \frac{1}{n} \sum_{k=1}^{n} q_k \right\|$.
3. For each q_i, solve $\gamma_i = \arg\min_{\gamma \in \Gamma} \|\mu - (q_i \star \gamma)\|$. Compute the aligned SRVFs $\tilde{q}_i = (q_i \star \gamma_i)$.
4. Update $\mu \mapsto \frac{1}{n} \sum_{i=1}^{n} \tilde{q}_i$ and return to step 2 until the change $\left\| \mu - \frac{1}{n} \sum_{i=1}^{n} \tilde{q}_i \right\|$ is small.
5. Map all the SRVFs back to the function space using by $\tilde{f}(t) = f(0) + \int_0^t \tilde{q}(s)|\tilde{q}(s)| \, ds$.

Fig. 11.10 shows an example of registration of multiple functions using this algorithm. The left panel shows a set of simulated functions $\{f_i\}$ that all are bimodal, but their modes differ in the locations and heights. This set forms the input to the algorithm, and the next two panels show the outputs. The middle panel shows the functions $\{\tilde{f}_i\}$ associated with the aligned SRVFs $\{\tilde{q}_i\}$, and the right panel shows the optimal time warping functions $\{\gamma_i\}$. We can see the high quality of registration in matching of peaks and valleys across functions.

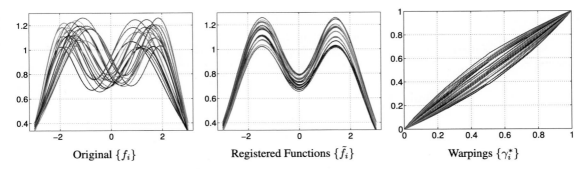

Figure 11.10. Registration of multiple functions by registering each one of them to their mean.

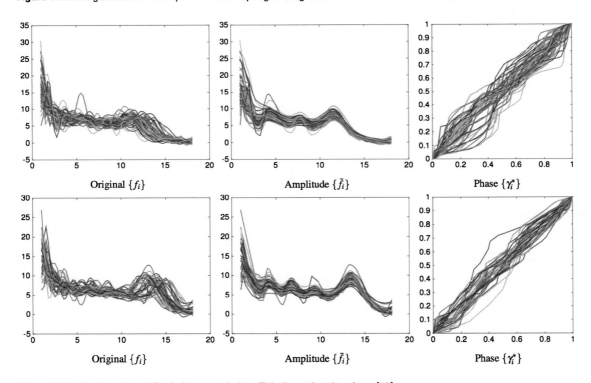

Figure 11.11. Registration of Berkeley growth data. This figure is taken from [18].

Fig. 11.11 shows some more examples of multiple function registration, this time using real data. The two rows of this figure correspond to female (top) and male (bottom) growth curves taken from the famous Berkeley growth dataset. Each curve shows the rate at which the height of an individual changes from the age of one to twelve. Each row shows the original growth rate functions $\{f_i\}$ (left), their registrations $\{\tilde{f}_i\}$ (mid-

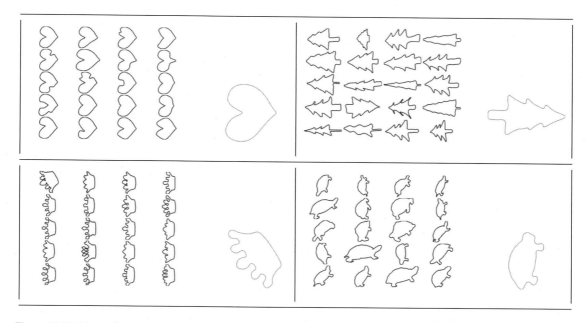

Figure 11.12. Mean shape for a set of closed curves.

dle), and the optimal warpings $\{\gamma_i\}$. The peaks in rate functions, denoting growth spurts, are better matched after registrations and are easier to interpret in the resulting data.

Fig. 11.12 shows some examples of mean shapes computed for a set of given shapes. We can see that the mean shapes are able to preserve main distinguishing features of the shape class while smoothing out the intraclass variabilities.

We can use the shape metric and the flatness of the tangent space to discover principal modes of variability in the given set of shapes. Let $T_{[\mu]}\mathcal{S}$ denote the tangent space to $\mathcal{S}$ at the mean shape $[\mu]$, and let $\exp_{[\mu]}^{-1}([q])$ denote the mapping from the shape space $\mathcal{S}$ to this tangent space using the inverse exponential map. We evaluate this mapping by finding the geodesic α from $[\mu]$ to a shape $[q]$ and then computing the initial velocity of the geodesic, that is, $\exp_{[\mu]}^{-1}([q]) = \dot{\alpha}(0)$. We also call these initial velocities the *shooting vectors*. Let $v_i = \exp_{[\mu]}^{-1}([q_i])$, $i = 1, 2, \ldots, n$, be the shooting vectors from the mean shape to the given shapes. Then performing PCA of $\{v_i\}$ provides the directions of maximum variability in the given shapes and can be used to visualize the main variability in that set. Fig. 11.13 shows three examples of this idea using some leaf shapes. In each panel of the top row we show the set of given leafs and their mean shapes. The bottom row shows the shape variability along the two dominant modes of variability, obtained using PCA in the tangent space. In the bottom plots

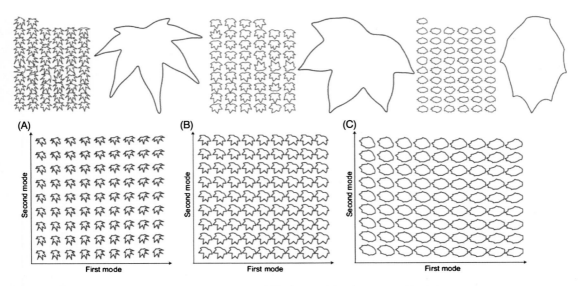

Figure 11.13. Mean (top) and principal modes of variability (bottom) for three sets of leaf shapes.

the two axes represent the two dominant directions, and we can see the variation in shapes as one moves along these coordinates.

11.5 Summary and conclusion

This chapter describes an elastic approach to shape analysis of curves in Euclidean spaces. It focuses on the problem of registration of points across curves and shows that the standard $\mathbb{L}^2$ norm, or its penalized version, has inferior mathematical properties and practical performances. Instead, it uses a combination of SRVFs and $\mathbb{L}^2$ norm to derive a framework for a unified shape analysis framework. Here we register curves and compare their shape in a single optimization framework. We compute geodesic paths, geodesic distances, and shape summarizes using the geometries of shape spaces. These tools can then be used in statistical modeling and analysis of shapes of curves.

Appendix: Mathematical background

We summarize here some background knowledge of algebra and differential geometry with the example of planar shapes represented by k ordered points in $\mathbb{R}^2$, denoted by $X \in \mathbb{R}^{2 \times k}$. Clearly, X and OX, $O \in SO(2)$ have the same shape. That can be defined strictly through the following concepts.

Definition 11.4. A binary relation $\sim$ on a set X is called an **equivalence relation** if it satisfies the following properties: For $x, y, z \in X$,

- $x \sim x$ (reflexivity),
- $x \sim y \Leftrightarrow y \sim x$ (symmetry),
- $x \sim y, y \sim z \Rightarrow x \sim y$ (transitivity).

Definition 11.5. Equivalence class. $[x] = \{y \in X | y \sim x\}$.

Definition 11.6. The **quotient space** of X under equivalence relation $\sim$ is the set of all equivalence classes $[x]$, denoted by $X / \sim$.

Thus the space of planar shapes in the form of discrete points is the quotient space of $\mathbb{R}^{2 \times k} / SO(2)$. To measure the difference between two shapes, we need a proper metric. For $\mathbb{R}^{2 \times k}$, a natural choice is the Euclidean metric, but for a nonlinear manifold, the difference is measured by the length of the shortest path connecting the two shapes, which requires the following definitions.

Definition 11.7. A **Riemannian metric** on differential manifold M is a smooth inner product on the tangent $T_p(M)$ space of M. A differential manifold with a Riemannian metric is called **Riemannian manifold**.

Definition 11.8. Let $\alpha : [0, 1] \to M$ represent a path on a Riemannian manifold M. Then $\frac{d\alpha}{dt}$ represents the velocity at time t. The length of α can be defined as $L[\alpha] = \int_0^1 \sqrt{\langle \frac{d\alpha}{dt}, \frac{d\alpha}{dt} \rangle} dt$. The path connecting two points with shortest length is called the **geodesic** between them. The length of geodesic is a proper metric between the two points.

Example 11.1. The geodesic between $p, q \in \mathbb{R}^n$ is a straight line: $\alpha(\tau) = (1 - \tau)p + \tau q, \tau \in [0, 1]$.

Example 11.2. The geodesic between $p, q \in \mathbb{S}^n \subseteq \mathbb{R}^{n+1}$ is the arc on a great circle: $\alpha(\tau) = \frac{1}{\sin \theta} \left[\sin((1 - \tau)\theta)p + \sin(\tau\theta)q \right], \tau \in [0, 1]$.

For $X \in \mathbb{R}^{2 \times k}$, the fact $\|X\| = \|OX\|$, $O \in SO(2)$, induces two important concepts, group action and isometry.

Definition 11.9. A **Lie group** G is a smooth manifold such that the group operations $G \to G \times G$ defined by $(g, h) \to gh$ and $G \to G$ defined by $g \to g^{-1}$ are both smooth mappings.

The groups appearing in this chapter are all Lie groups.

Definition 11.10. Given a manifold M and a Lie group G, a left group action of G on M is a map $G \times M \to M$, denoted by (g, p), satisfying

1. $(g_1, (g_2, p)) = ((g_1 \cdot g_2), p), \forall g_1, g_2 \in G$ and $p \in M$.

2. $(e, p) = p, \forall p \in M$.

Similarly, we can define the right group action.

Definition 11.11. Given two metric spaces X and Y, a map $f : X \to Y$ is called an **isometry** or distance preserving if $d_X(a, b) = d_Y(f(a), f(b))$ for all $a, b \in X$.

Definition 11.12. A group action of G on a Riemannian manifold M is called isometric if it preserves the Riemannian metric on M, that is, $d(x, y) = d((g, x), (g, y))$ for all $g \in G$ and $x, y \in M$.

Definition 11.13. Given a manifold M, for any $p \in M$, the orbit of p under the action of group G is defined as $[p] = \{g \cdot p | g \in G\}$.

Example 11.3. The rotation group $SO(n)$ acts on $\mathbb{R}^n$ by the action $O * x = Ox$ for all $O \in SO(n)$ and $x \in \mathbb{R}^n$. The orbit of x is the sphere centered at the origin with radius $\|x\|$.

For a planar shape denoted by a $2 \times k$ matrix X, the shape can be identified by an orbit $[X] = \{OX | O \in SO(2)\}$.

Definition 11.14. For group G acting on the manifold M, the quotient space M/G is defined as the set of all orbits of G in M: $M/G = \{[p] | p \in M\}$.

Definition 11.15. If a group action of G on a Riemannian manifold M is isometric and the orbits under G are closed, then we can define a metric on the quotient space M/G as follows:

$$d_{M/G}([p], [q]) = \min_{g \in G} d_M(p, (g, q))$$

We illustrate this idea by an example. Let $\mathbb{R}^{2 \times k}$ be the space of planar shapes of k points with Euclidean metric. Consider the action of rotation group $SO(2)$ on $\mathbb{R}^{2 \times k}$. The metric on the quotient space $\mathbb{R}^{2 \times k}/SO(2)$ is

$$d_{\mathbb{R}^{2 \times k}/SO(2)}([X_1], [X_2]) = \min_{O \in SO(2)} \|X_1 - OX_2\|.$$

The geodesic between two shapes $[X_1]$ and $[X_2]$ is $\alpha(\tau) = (1 - \tau)X_1 + \tau O^* X_2$, where $O^* = \arg\min_{O \in SO(2)} \|X_1 - OX_2\|$, $\tau \in [0, 1]$. If the two shapes are rescaled to be unit length, that is, $\|X_1\| = \|X_2\| = 1$, then the geodesic is the arc on a great circle of the unit sphere $\alpha(\tau) = \frac{1}{\sin(\theta)}[\sin((1 - \tau)\theta)X_1 + \sin(\tau\theta)O^* X_2]$, where $\theta = \arccos(\langle X_1, O^* X_2 \rangle)$, $O^* = \arg\min_{O \in SO(2)} \arccos(\langle X_1, OX_2 \rangle)$.

References

1. M. Bauer, M. Bruveris, P. Harms, J. Møller-Andersen, Second order elastic metrics on the shape space of curves, arXiv preprint, 2015.

2. M. Bauer, M. Bruveris, S. Marsland, P.W. Michor, Constructing reparameterization invariant metrics on spaces of plane curves, Differential Geometry and Its Applications 34 (2014) 139–165.

3. F.L. Bookstein, Morphometric Tools for Landmark Data: Geometry and Biology, Cambridge University Press, 1991.

4. A.L. Brigant, Computing distances and geodesics between manifold-valued curves in the SRV framework, arXiv:1601.02358, 2016.

5. A.L. Brigant, M. Arnaudon, F. Barbaresco, Reparameterization invariant metric on the space of curves, arXiv:1507.06503, 2015.

6. I.L. Dryden, K.V. Mardia, Statistical Shape Analysis, John Wiley & Son, 1998.

7. I.H. Jermyn, S. Kurtek, E. Klassen, A. Srivastava, Elastic shape matching of parameterized surfaces using square root normal fields, in: Proceedings of the 12th European Conference on Computer Vision – Volume Part V, ECCV'12, Springer, Berlin, Heidelberg, 2012, pp. 804–817.

8. I.H. Jermyn, S. Kurtek, H. Laga, A. Srivastava, Elastic shape analysis of three-dimensional objects, in: Synthesis Lectures on Computer Vision, vol. 12, Morgan and Claypool Publishers, 2017.

9. S.H. Joshi, E. Klassen, A. Srivastava, I.H. Jermyn, A novel representation for efficient computation of geodesics between n-dimensional curves, in: IEEE CVPR, 2007.

10. D.G. Kendall, Shape manifolds, Procrustean metrics and complex projective spaces, Bulletin of the London Mathematical Society 16 (1984) 81–121.

11. D.G. Kendall, D. Barden, T.K. Carne, H. Le, Shape and Shape Theory, Wiley, 1999.

12. S. Kurtek, T. Needham, Simplifying transforms for general elastic metrics on the space of plane curves, arXiv, 2018.

13. H. Laga, Q. Xie, I.H. Jermyn, A. Srivastava, Numerical inversion of srnf maps for elastic shape analysis of genus-zero surfaces, IEEE Transactions on Pattern Analysis and Machine Intelligence 39 (12) (2017) 2451–2464.

14. J.S. Marron, J.O. Ramsay, L.M. Sangalli, A. Srivastava, Statistics of time warpings and phase variations, Electronic Journal of Statistics 8 (2) (2014) 1697–1702.

15. W. Mio, A. Srivastava, S. Joshi, On shape of plane elastic curves, International Journal of Computer Vision 73 (3) (2007) 307–324.

16. J.O. Ramsay, B.W. Silverman, Functional Data Analysis, 2nd edn., Springer Series in Statistics, Springer, 2005.

17. C.G. Small, The Statistical Theory of Shape, Springer, 1996.

18. A. Srivastava, E. Klassen, Functional and Shape Data Analysis, Springer Series in Statistics, 2016.

19. A. Srivastava, E. Klassen, S.H. Joshi, I.H. Jermyn, Shape analysis of elastic curves in Euclidean spaces, IEEE Transactions on Pattern Analysis and Machine Intelligence 33 (7) (2011) 1415–1428.

20. A. Srivastava, W. Wu, S. Kurtek, E. Klassen, J.S. Marron, Registration of functional data using Fisher–Rao metric, arXiv:1103.3817v2, 2011.

21. Q. Xie, I. Jermyn, S. Kurtek, A. Srivastava, Numerical inversion of SRNFS for efficient elastic shape analysis of star-shaped objects, in: 2014 European Conference on Computer Vision (ECCV), 2014.

22. L. Younes, Computable elastic distance between shapes, SIAM Journal on Applied Mathematics 58 (1998) 565–586.

23. L. Younes, Optimal matching between shapes via elastic deformations, Journal of Image and Vision Computing 17 (5/6) (1999) 381–389.
24. L. Younes, Elastic distance between curves under the metamorphosis viewpoint, arXiv, 2018.
25. L. Younes, P.W. Michor, J. Shah, D. Mumford, R. Lincei, A metric on shape space with explicit geodesics, Matematica E Applicazioni 19 (1) (2008) 25–57.
26. Z. Zhang, E. Klassen, A Srivastava, Phase-amplitude separation and modeling of spherical trajectories, Journal of Computational and Graphical Statistics 27 (1) (2018) 85–97.
27. Z. Zhang, J. Su, E. Klassen, H. Le, A Srivastava, Rate-invariant analysis of covariance trajectories, Journal of Mathematical Imaging and Vision 60 (8) (2018) 1306–1323.

Deformations, diffeomorphisms and their applications

3

12

Fidelity metrics between curves and surfaces: currents, varifolds, and normal cycles

**Nicolas Charon[a], Benjamin Charlier[b,c], Joan Glaunès[d],
Pietro Gori[e], Pierre Roussillon[f]**

[a]*Johns Hopkins University, Center of Imaging Sciences, Baltimore, MD,
United States.* [b]*IMAG, Univ. Montpellier, CNRS, Montpellier, France.* [c]*Institut
du Cerveau et de la Moëlle Épinière, ARAMIS, Paris, France.* [d]*MAP5,
Université Paris Descartes, Paris, France.* [e]*Télécom ParisTech, LTCI, équipe
IMAGES, Paris, France.* [f]*ENS Cachan, CNRS, Université Paris-Saclay, CMLA,
Cachan, France*

12.1 Introduction

In Chapter 4, following the classical setting proposed by Grenander, metrics on shape spaces were defined through the action of diffeomorphism groups equipped with right-invariant metrics. In particular, the LDDMM framework introduced earlier provides a convenient way to generate diffeomorphic transformations and such right-invariant metrics. In that case the resulting distance between two given shapes is given through the solution of an exact registration problem obtained by optimizing the deformation cost over all possible deformation fields that match the source shape on the target.

This approach, however, only applies if both shapes belong to the same orbit; in other words, if there exists a deformation in the group that can exactly deform one shape on the other. Such an assumption is routinely violated in practical scenarios involving shapes extracted from biomedical imaging data. Indeed, those shapes are typically affected by many other variations including noise, potential topological variations, or segmentation artifacts, all of which are poorly modeled within a pure diffeomorphic setting. From a statistical perspective it is in fact more reasonable to make the computation of shape distances rather as insensitive as possible to those types of perturbations that are not morphologically relevant.

To that end, a standard approach is to relax the exact matching constraint by instead considering inexact registration. Specifically,

Riemannian Geometric Statistics in Medical Image Analysis
https://doi.org/10.1016/B978-0-12-814725-2.00021-2

the original boundary value problem is replaced by the minimization of a composite functional involving a weighted combination of the previous deformation cost and a fidelity or data attachment term between the deformed source shape and the target. The registration problem is thus a priori well posed even for a target outside the orbit of the source shape. The fidelity term and its weight will typically depend on the nature of the shapes (landmarks, images, curves, etc.) as well as the expected noise model and level on the observations. This inexact formulation for LDDMM (as well as for other deformation models) has been very standard in early applications to landmarks [38] or images [6]. In those works fidelity terms consist of the simple Euclidean norm between the landmark positions or the sum of squared differences of the pixel values of the images.

Regarding the construction of fidelity terms, shape spaces of curves, surfaces, and more generally submanifolds of $\mathbb{R}^k$ constitute a particularly challenging case if compared, for instance, to landmarks or images. The main reason is that submanifolds embody a fundamental invariance to reparameterization and thus cannot be a priori treated as labeled point sets like in the situation of landmarks. In concrete applications such shapes are discretized as vertices and meshes. Yet meshes obtained, for example, from different subjects generally do not contain the same number of vertices, and no predefined correspondences exist between them that could provide a straightforward equivalent to Euclidean distances. Many approaches have thus resolved to first extracting and pairing feature points from the two meshes to reduce the problem to registration of the obtained landmarks.

This chapter is dedicated to a particular class of methods providing efficient and robust metrics between submanifolds themselves (discrete or continuous) that completely bypass the need for such preprocessing steps. The primary objective is to get adequate fidelity terms to be embedded into inexact registration frameworks for curves and surfaces. Namely, we seek metrics that are intrinsically independent of a specific shape parameterization or sampling rate that can be evaluated and differentiated directly in competitive computational time and that can compare a large class of objects beyond smooth geometries while being reasonably robust to the aforementioned shape artifacts.

The frameworks presented in this chapter all follow the general philosophy and mathematical ideas introduced in the field of geometric measure theory [1,2,25] in which shapes like submanifolds are basically represented in certain spaces of *generalized measures* such as *currents*, *varifolds*, or *normal cycles*. We further present and compare several of these approaches and computational models, since the earliest work of [30] in this context, by emphasizing the relevance and applicability to shape analysis and computational anatomy. We also point out to the reader that some recent and related works such as [26] have exploited alternative ideas from optimal transport theory for similar purpose. We do not present those works here for the sake of general concision.

12.2 General setting and notations

In the entire chapter and although the mathematical settings readily extend to general submanifolds, we will restrict the presentation to the cases of curves and surfaces embedded in $\mathbb{R}^2$ or $\mathbb{R}^3$ as these constitute the bulk of the applications considered in this book. The methods we introduce can equally deal with smooth curves and surfaces but also piecewise smooth and discrete objects, which are all encompassed by the notion of *rectifiable subsets* in geometric measure theory.

Unless stated otherwise, curves and surfaces are meant in the sense of rectifiable curves and rectifiable surfaces. For the sake of concision and clarity, we will however not introduce in detail the precise definition and properties of rectifiable subsets; the interested reader is referred, for example, to [47]. Instead, here we adopt the following intuitive setting: we will call $\mathcal{M} \subset \mathbb{R}^k$ a rectifiable curve (resp., surface) embedded in the ambient space $\mathbb{R}^k$ with either $k = 2$ or $k = 3$ if for almost every $x \in \mathcal{M}$, there exists a tangent space $T_x\mathcal{M}$ of dimension one (resp., two) of $\mathcal{M}$ at x. This basically allows for the presence of isolated singularities like in a polygonal curve or polyhedral surface. A very important notion for the rest of the chapter will be the orientation. If an orientation of $\mathcal{M}$ is given, that is, the subspaces $T_x\mathcal{M}$ are oriented in a "continuous" way on $\mathcal{M}$, then we will equivalently represent $T_x\mathcal{M}$ by a single unit vector in $\mathbb{S}^{k-1}$, which is either the oriented tangent vector $\vec{t}(x)$ in the case of a curve or the oriented unit normal vector $\vec{n}(x)$ in the case of a surface.

12.3 Currents

The use of currents in computational anatomy has been introduced first to define fidelity metrics between surfaces in [29] and between curves in [31]. These works extend the earlier work on matching distributions [30], which can be seen in turn as a particular case of the currents model, as will be shown later.

12.3.1 Curves and surfaces as currents

Let $\mathcal{M}$ be an oriented shape, that is, a curve in $\mathbb{R}^k$ ($k = 2$ or $k = 3$) or an oriented surface in $\mathbb{R}^3$. As mentioned in Section 12.2, we only assume regularity at almost every point in $\mathcal{M}$, which allows for shapes with or without boundary and possibly several disconnected components and branching parts.

For any continuous vector field $\vec{w} : \mathbb{R}^k \to \mathbb{R}^k$ in the ambient space $\mathbb{R}^k$, we may compute its integral along $\mathcal{M}$, which can be denoted $[\mathcal{M}](\vec{w})$, and writes:

- if $\mathcal{M}$ is a curve,

$$[\mathcal{M}](\vec{w}) := \int_{\mathcal{M}} \langle \vec{w}(x), \vec{t}(x) \rangle d\ell(x); \qquad (12.1)$$

- if $\mathcal{M}$ is a surface,

$$[\mathcal{M}](\vec{w}) := \int_{\mathcal{M}} \langle \vec{w}(x), \vec{n}(x) \rangle dS(x). \qquad (12.2)$$

The application $\vec{w} \to [\mathcal{M}](\vec{w})$ defines a linear mapping between the space of continuous vector fields into $\mathbb{R}$, which characterizes the shape $\mathcal{M}$. This mapping $[\mathcal{M}]$ is called the *current* associated with $\mathcal{M}$. The main advantage of this somewhat abstract setting is viewing shapes as elements of a vector space, allowing us to consider linear combinations of such elements and to define norms, which is the basis of the construction.

Let us define more precisely these notions.

Definition 12.1. A *current* S is a continuous linear mapping $\vec{w} \mapsto S(\vec{w})$ from $C_0(\mathbb{R}^k, \mathbb{R}^k)$ (the space of continuous vector fields of $\mathbb{R}^k$ that vanish at infinity) into $\mathbb{R}$. The *current associated with an oriented shape* $\mathcal{M}$ is the current $[\mathcal{M}]$ defined by formula (12.1) or (12.2) for any $\vec{w} \in C_0(\mathbb{R}^k, \mathbb{R}^k)$.

Let us make a few remarks about this definition. First, the continuity requirement for the linear mapping is equivalent to the existence of a constant C such that the inequality

$$|S(\vec{w})| \leq C \|\vec{w}\|_\infty$$

holds for all $\vec{w} \in C_0(\mathbb{R}^k, \mathbb{R}^k)$. Second, we assume that the vector fields vanish at infinity to get the completeness of the space $C_0(\mathbb{R}^k, \mathbb{R}^k)$ with respect to the infinity norm.

12.3.2 Kernel metrics on currents

The next step defining a tractable distance between currents, which will be used as a data fidelity term. This is done using the framework of reproducing kernel Hilbert spaces (RKHS) [3]. Note that other approaches could be considered such as the finite element framework proposed in [7]. As previously, we first give the main idea before stating precise definitions. The construction starts by the choice of a kernel function $K : \mathbb{R}^k \times \mathbb{R}^k \to \mathbb{R}$. The kernel metric between two shapes $\mathcal{M}_1, \mathcal{M}_2$ is then defined as

$$\langle [\mathcal{M}_1], [\mathcal{M}_2] \rangle_{W'} := \int_{\mathcal{M}_1} \int_{\mathcal{M}_2} K(x, y) \langle \vec{t}_1(x), \vec{t}_2(y) \rangle d\ell_1(x)\, d\ell_2(y) \tag{12.3}$$

for curves or

$$\langle [\mathcal{M}_1], [\mathcal{M}_2] \rangle_{W'} := \int_{\mathcal{M}_1} \int_{\mathcal{M}_2} K(x, y) \langle \vec{n}_1(x), \vec{n}_2(y) \rangle dS_1(x)\, dS_2(y). \tag{12.4}$$

The notation $\langle [\mathcal{M}_1], [\mathcal{M}_2] \rangle_{W'}$ means that the formula defines an inner product between the currents associated with the shapes, as will be detailed in the following definitions. Assuming this point for the moment, we may use the associated norm to define a dissimilarity between two shapes:

$$\begin{aligned} \| [\mathcal{M}_1] - [\mathcal{M}_2] \|_{W'}^2 = &\langle [\mathcal{M}_1], [\mathcal{M}_1] \rangle_{W'} - 2 \langle [\mathcal{M}_1], [\mathcal{M}_2] \rangle_{W'} \\ &+ \langle [\mathcal{M}_2], [\mathcal{M}_2] \rangle_{W'}. \end{aligned} \tag{12.5}$$

To go further and define precisely these notions, we need to use the theory of reproducing kernels for spaces of vector-valued functions. The theory of reproducing kernels was first developed by Aronszajn [3] in the scalar case, which is the most commonly used setting, with applications in many fields such as scattered data interpolation [16] and statistical learning [36]. Shortly after Aronszajn, Laurent Schwartz [53] extended the theory to a more general and abstract setting, including de facto the case of vector-valued functions. Several other works have focused on this case [8,9,14,15,45]. The following definitions and theorem rephrase results found in [46]. We refer to this work for a detailed study. Here we only consider the case of *scalar* kernels for simplicity (but still for vector-valued functions' spaces).

Definition 12.2. Let $K : \mathbb{R}^k \times \mathbb{R}^k \to \mathbb{R}$ and $s \in \mathbb{N}$.
- We say that K is an *s-admissible kernel* if
  1. K is a positive kernel, that is, for all $n \geq 1$ and $x_1, \ldots, x_n \in \mathbb{R}^k$, the $n \times n$ matrix with entries $K(x_i, x_j)$ is a positive semidefinite symmetric matrix.
  2. For all $x \in \mathbb{R}^k$, $K(\cdot, x) \in C_0^{2s}(\mathbb{R}^k \times \mathbb{R}^k, \mathbb{R})$ (i.e., it is of class C^{2s} and vanishes at infinity).

- A Hilbert space W of vector fields $\vec{w} : \mathbb{R}^k \to \mathbb{R}^k$ is called s-admissible if W is continuously embedded in $C_0^s(\mathbb{R}^k, \mathbb{R}^k)$. It is called simply admissible if it is 0-admissible.

Typical examples of such kernels used in applications are the Gaussian kernel $K(x, y) = \exp(\|x - y\|^2/\sigma^2)$ and the Cauchy kernel $K(x, y) = \frac{1}{1+\|x-y\|^2/\sigma^2}$, $x, y \in \mathbb{R}^k$, where $\sigma > 0$ is a fixed scale parameter.

Let us mention that for all material presented here, including the use of the derived discrete formulation for LDDMM registration algorithms, the 0-admissibility (i.e., continuity) assumption is sufficient. However, a stronger 1-admissibility assumption is usually required for some theoretical results to hold for registration problems in the nondiscrete case [27]. This is not an issue at all in practice since usual kernels, such as the Gaussian and Cauchy kernels, have in fact C^∞ regularity, which implies that their corresponding Hilbert space is p-admissible for any p, as ensured by the following theorem.

Theorem 12.1. *([46], Thms. 2.6 and 2.11) Any p-admissible kernel K is associated with a unique p-admissible Hilbert space W of vector fields in $\mathbb{R}^k$ such that*

$$\forall x, \alpha \in \mathbb{R}^k, \ \forall w \in W, \ \langle K(\cdot, x)\alpha, w \rangle_W = \langle w(x), \alpha \rangle.$$

K is called the reproducing kernel of the space W.

Combining Definitions 12.1 and 12.2, we see that by choosing an admissible kernel K we define an admissible Hilbert space W of vector fields such that any current S belongs to its dual space W', since

$$\forall \vec{w} \in W, \qquad |S(\vec{w})| \leq C \|\vec{w}\|_\infty \leq C' \|\vec{w}\|_W.$$

for a certain constant C'. Hence we can consider the canonical inner product in W' between any two currents. Now to derive formula (12.3), let us first rewrite the action of a single current associated with a curve $\mathcal{M}$ on a vector field $\vec{w}$:

$$
\begin{aligned}
[\mathcal{M}](\vec{w}) &= \int_{\mathcal{M}} \langle \vec{w}(x), \vec{t}(x) \rangle \, d\ell(x) \\
&= \int_{\mathcal{M}} \langle K(\cdot, x)\vec{t}(x), \vec{w} \rangle_W \, d\ell(x) \\
&= \left\langle \int_{\mathcal{M}} K(\cdot, x)\vec{t}(x) d\ell(x), \, \vec{w} \right\rangle_W.
\end{aligned}
$$

This shows that $x \mapsto \int_{\mathcal{M}} K(\cdot, x)\vec{t}(x)$ is the unique Riesz representer in W of the current $[\mathcal{M}]$ in W'. This representer is simply a convolution of the tangent bundle of the curve with the kernel. Consequently, considering now two currents $[\mathcal{M}_1]$, $[\mathcal{M}_2]$, we obtain the following expression of their inner product:

$$
\begin{aligned}
\langle [\mathcal{M}_1], [\mathcal{M}_2] \rangle_{W'} &= [\mathcal{M}_1] \left(x \mapsto \int_{\mathcal{M}_2} K(x, y) \vec{t}_2(y) d\ell_2(y) \right) \\
&= \int_{\mathcal{M}_1} \int_{\mathcal{M}_2} K(x, y) \langle \vec{t}_1(x), \vec{t}_2(y) \rangle d\ell_1(x)\, d\ell_2(y).
\end{aligned}
$$

In the case of surfaces, the derivation of Eq. (12.4) is strictly similar.

12.3.3 The discrete model

The computation of the kernel metric (12.3) and (12.4) between shapes requires a discretization of the integrals and unit tangent or normal vectors. In practice shapes are given as meshes: unions of line segments in the case of curves or of triangles in the case of surfaces with connectivity information.

Let us assume that $\mathcal{M}$ is such a mesh, that is, $\mathcal{M}$ is a union of line or triangle elements $f_1, \ldots, f_m$. We will denote f_i^k the vertices of each element f_i with $k = 1, 2$ for curves and $k = 1, 2, 3$ for surfaces. We assume that the orientation is encoded through the ordering of these vertices. We can further define for each element f_i:

- for curves: its center $c_{f_i} = (f_i^1 + f_i^2)/2$, tangent vector $\vec{t}_{f_i} = (f_i^2 - f_i^1)$, length $\ell_{f_i} = \|\vec{t}_{f_i}\|$, and unit tangent vector $\vec{\imath}_{f_i} = \vec{t}_{f_i}/\ell_{f_i}$,
- for surfaces: its center $c_{f_i} = (f_i^1 + f_i^2 + f_i^3)/3$, normal vector $\vec{v}_{f_i} = \frac{1}{2}((f_i^2 - f_i^1) \times (f_i^3 - f_i^1))$, area $S_{f_i} = \|\vec{v}_{f_i}\|$, and unit normal vector $\vec{n}_{f_i} = \vec{v}_{f_i}/S_{f_i}$.

A simple discrete approximation of formula (12.3) is obtained by first writing the double integral as a double sum of double integrals over each pair of triangles and then approximating the values of the kernel $K(x, y)$ by a single value at the centers of the elements. For curves, this reads

$$
\begin{aligned}
&\langle [\mathcal{M}_1], [\mathcal{M}_2] \rangle_{W'} \\
&= \int_{\mathcal{M}_1} \int_{\mathcal{M}_2} K(x, y) \langle \vec{t}_1(x), \vec{t}_2(y) \rangle d\ell_1(x)\, d\ell_2(y) \\
&= \sum_{i=1}^{m_1} \sum_{j=1}^{m_2} \int_{f_{1,i}} \int_{f_{2,j}} K(x, y) \langle \vec{t}_{f_{1,i}}, \vec{t}_{f_{2,j}} \rangle d\ell_1(x)\, d\ell_2(y) \\
&\approx \sum_{i=1}^{m_1} \sum_{j=1}^{m_2} \int_{f_{1,i}} \int_{f_{2,j}} K(c_{f_{1,i}}, c_{f_{2,j}}) \langle \vec{t}_{f_{1,i}}, \vec{t}_{f_{2,j}} \rangle d\ell_1(x)\, d\ell_2(y)
\end{aligned}
$$

$$\approx \sum_{i=1}^{m_1} \sum_{j=1}^{m_2} K(c_{f_{1,i}}, c_{f_{2,j}}) \langle \vec{t}_{f_{1,i}}, \vec{t}_{f_{2,j}} \rangle \ell_{f_{1,i}} \ell_{f_{1,i}}$$

$$= \sum_{i=1}^{m_1} \sum_{j=1}^{m_2} K(c_{f_{1,i}}, c_{f_{2,j}}) \langle \vec{\tau}_{f_{1,i}}, \vec{\tau}_{f_{2,j}} \rangle.$$

A nice characteristic of this approximation is that it corresponds to the exact expression of the inner product in W' when replacing the currents $[\mathcal{M}_1]$, $[\mathcal{M}_2]$ by sums of Dirac functionals (located at the faces centers). More precisely, we can define

$$[\mathcal{M}_1] \approx [\mathcal{M}_1]_d = \sum_{i=1}^{m_1} \delta_{c_{f_{1,i}}}^{\vec{\tau}_{f_{1,i}}} \text{ and } [\mathcal{M}_2] \approx [\mathcal{M}_2]_d = \sum_{j=1}^{m_2} \delta_{c_{f_{2,j}}}^{\vec{\tau}_{f_{2,j}}}, \quad (12.6)$$

where for any $x, \vec{u} \in \mathbb{R}^k$, $\delta_x^{\vec{u}}$ denotes the evaluation functional $\vec{w} \mapsto \langle \vec{w}(x), \vec{u} \rangle$. Using the definition of the reproducing kernel K, we then get exactly that

$$\langle [\mathcal{M}_1]_d, [\mathcal{M}_2]_d \rangle_{W'} = \sum_{i=1}^{m_1} \sum_{j=1}^{m_2} K(c_{f_{1,i}}, c_{f_{2,j}}) \langle \vec{\tau}_{f_{1,i}}, \vec{\tau}_{f_{2,j}} \rangle. \quad (12.7)$$

The approximation in the case of surfaces is again strictly similar and yields

$$\langle [\mathcal{M}_1]_d, [\mathcal{M}_2]_d \rangle_{W'} = \sum_{i=1}^{m_1} \sum_{j=1}^{m_2} K(c_{f_{1,i}}, c_{f_{2,j}}) \langle \vec{v}_{f_{1,i}}, \vec{v}_{f_{2,j}} \rangle. \quad (12.8)$$

The approximation error can be easily computed, either directly from the formula, or using the Dirac currents representation. This is postponed to Section 12.4 since, as we will see, metrics on currents can be viewed as special cases of metrics on varifolds.

12.3.4 Examples of registration using currents metrics

We present here some experiments of diffeomorphic registration of surfaces using kernel metrics on currents as data attachment term. Let us briefly specify the problem: given two shapes $\mathcal{M}_1$, $\mathcal{M}_2$, the registration is performed through the minimization of

$$J(\phi) = \gamma \, d(id, \phi)^2 + \|[\phi(\mathcal{M}_1)] - [\mathcal{M}_2]\|_{W'}^2,$$

where ϕ denotes a one-to-one mapping belonging to a specific group of diffeomorphisms endowed with a right-invariant met-

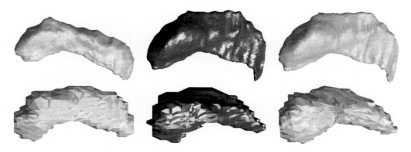

Figure 12.1. Examples of diffeomorphic registrations using kernel metrics on currents. Top row: hippocampal surfaces at high resolution; bottom row: hippocampal surfaces at low resolution. From left to right: source surface, target surface, deformed source.

ric d (see chapter 4). In a discrete setting, assuming that $\mathcal{M}_1$ and $\mathcal{M}_2$ are meshes, $[\phi(\mathcal{M}_1)]$ and $[\mathcal{M}_2]$ are replaced by their discrete approximations, which reduces the problem to a finite-dimensional LDDMM problem. This is tackled down using a geodesic shooting algorithm, optimizing over initial momentum vectors located at vertices of $\mathcal{M}_1$.

Fig. 12.1 shows two examples of registrations of hippocampal cortical surfaces segmented from MRI images as described in [49]; the first one is acquired with high resolution, and the other one with low resolution. Registration was performed using an LDDMM algorithm with kernel metrics on currents as data attachment term. The deformation kernel was chosen to be a sum of four Cauchy kernels with widths $\sigma_V = 10, 5, 2.5, 1.125$ (in mm), whereas the kernel on currents was chosen to be a Cauchy kernel with width $\sigma_W = 1$. To avoid local minima, two registrations with larger scale ($\sigma_W = 20$ and $\sigma_W = 5$) were performed first and used as initializations. As can be noticed in these examples, registrations using currents metrics for such closed shapes perform very well. Currents are also very efficient when dealing with rough or noisy segmentations, as they locally average orientations through the kernel (see Fig. 12.2).

Diffeomorphic registration using currents has been used for several shape analysis applications in medical imaging (see, e.g., [22,44,54]). It has also been the basis for extensions, mainly for template estimation problems [32,43] and methods for analyzing longitudinal datasets [20].

The need for more sophisticated methods like varifolds and normal cycles comes when dealing with shapes presenting singular features like boundaries, branching points, or high curvature points.

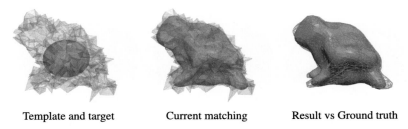

Template and target   Current matching   Result vs Ground truth

Figure 12.2. Registration between a sphere (blue (dark gray in print version)) and a noisy frog (orange (light gray in print version)). The "true" smooth frog surface (red (mid gray in print version) wireframe) is not used to estimate the registration. It is only used to benchmark with the results.

12.4 Varifolds

Despite the clear benefits of kernel-based metrics on currents for the problem of shape comparison, there are two important aspects that are worth emphasizing. First, the current representation and metrics are strongly tied to the orientation given to both shapes. Although it is often not a difficult issue to find proper and consistent orientation like in the case of closed curves or surfaces for example, some cases are much more involved, if not simply ill-posed. A striking example are fiber bundles with potential crossing or tangle, as we illustrate later in Section 12.4.4. Another particularity of currents is the linearity of the representation. As we saw, this can be a strength when (properly oriented) data are corrupted by noise since the resulting oscillations tend to cancel out. However, it can also result in artificial destruction or creation of thin structures, which may be incorrectly equated to noise in this model; cf. [13].

Part of these issues can be addressed through the extended framework of varifolds. Varifolds were introduced in geometric measure theory in the works of [1,2] and first adapted to the context of computational anatomy in [13] as a way to eliminate the previous orientation requirement. In the latest work [39] a little more general framework named oriented varifold was proposed, leading to a class of metrics that can, or not, rely on the orientation and allows us to recover previous frameworks of currents and varifolds as particular cases. We adopt and summarize this latter approach in what follows. Note that, with a slight abuse of vocabulary, we will call here in short a varifold, which corresponds in all rigor to an oriented varifold.

12.4.1 Representation by varifolds

In the same spirit as Section 12.3 we will again characterize curves and surfaces through their effect on certain spaces of test functions. With the notations of Section 12.2:

Definition 12.3. A varifold is a distribution on the product $\mathbb{R}^k \times \mathbb{S}^{k-1}$, namely a continuous linear form on a given space W of smooth test functions $\mathbb{R}^k \times \mathbb{S}^{k-1} \to \mathbb{R}$.

- If $\mathcal{M}$ is an oriented curve, then we associate the varifold $\{\mathcal{M}\} \in W'$ defined for any test function $w \in W$ with the line integral

$$\{\mathcal{M}\}(w) = \int_{\mathcal{M}} w\big(x, \vec{t}(x)\big) d\ell(x). \qquad (12.9)$$

- If $\mathcal{M}$ is an oriented surface, then we associate the varifold $\{\mathcal{M}\} \in W'$ defined for any test function $w \in W$ with the surface integral

$$\{\mathcal{M}\}(w) = \int_{\mathcal{M}} w\,(x, \vec{n}(x))\, dS(x). \qquad (12.10)$$

The product $\mathbb{R}^k \times \mathbb{S}^{k-1}$ can be interpreted as the space of position $\times$ tangent space direction, and formulas (12.9) and (12.10) amount in representing a curve or a surface as the distribution of its points with unit tangent or normal vector attached. We point out that an important difference with currents is that the dependency of w on $\vec{t}$ (or $\vec{n}$) is not anymore constrained to be linear. However, Eqs. (12.9) and (12.10) still rely a priori on an orientation of $\mathcal{M}$. We will see that it is not a necessity if the space of test functions W in the previous definitions is carefully chosen to recover invariance to the choice of orientation. More fundamentally, the actual specification of W is in fact critical and can lead to a wide range of properties of the representations and metrics, as we discuss in the next section.

12.4.2 Kernel metrics

As with currents, we will once again focus on the particular class of test functions given by RKHS. In the context of varifolds, an admissible space W is a Hilbert space continuously embedded in $C_0(\mathbb{R}^k \times \mathbb{S}^{k-1})$, the space of continuous test functions on $\mathbb{R}^k \times \mathbb{S}^{k-1}$ that decay to 0 at infinity. By the standard theory of RKHS such a space is equivalently described by a positive continuous kernel K on $\mathbb{R}^k \times \mathbb{S}^{k-1}$.

In the rest of this section, following the setting of [39], we restrict ourselves to real-valued and separable kernels K, namely,

$$K((x, u), (y, v)) = K_p(x, y) K_s(u, v) \text{ for all } (x, u), (y, v) \in \mathbb{R}^k \times \mathbb{S}^{k-1},$$

where K_p and K_s are continuous positive kernels on $\mathbb{R}^k$ and $\mathbb{S}^{k-1}$, respectively, and such that $K_p(x, y)$ vanish as $\|(x, y)\| \to +\infty$.

With those assumptions, W and its dual W' are Hilbert spaces, and we denote by $\| \cdot \|_{W'}$ the Hilbert norm on W'. Moreover, for any rectifiable curve or surface $\mathcal{M}$, we have that $\{\mathcal{M}\} \in W'$, and then the resulting inner product is

$$\langle \{\mathcal{M}_1\}, \{\mathcal{M}_2\} \rangle_{W'} = \int_{\mathcal{M}_1} \int_{\mathcal{M}_2} K_p(x, y) K_s(\vec{t}_1(x), \vec{t}_2(y)) d\ell(x) d\ell(y)$$

(12.11)

for curves or

$$\langle \{\mathcal{M}_1\}, \{\mathcal{M}_2\} \rangle_{W'} = \int_{\mathcal{M}_1} \int_{\mathcal{M}_2} K_p(x, y) K_s(\vec{n}_1(x), \vec{n}_2(y)) dS(x) dS(y)$$

(12.12)

for surfaces.

Now this gives a new class of candidates for fidelity terms, which we define by

$$d_W(\{\mathcal{M}_1\}, \{\mathcal{M}_2\})^2 = \|\{\mathcal{M}_1\} - \{\mathcal{M}_2\}\|_{W'}^2$$
$$= \|\{\mathcal{M}_1\}\|_{W'}^2 - 2\langle \{\mathcal{M}_1\}, \{\mathcal{M}_2\} \rangle_{W'} + \|\{\mathcal{M}_2\}\|_{W'}^2.$$

(12.13)

In other words this is the "distance" on curves or surfaces induced by the representation of varifolds and the Hilbert metric on W'. Note that since the representation $\{\mathcal{M}\}$ does not depend on a parameterization of $\mathcal{M}$, the quantity $d_W(\mathcal{M}_1, \mathcal{M}_2)$ is independent of the choice of a parameterization for $\mathcal{M}_1$ or $\mathcal{M}_2$. From formulas (12.11) and (12.12) we see that, in essence, such metrics are comparing the relative positions of points $\mathcal{M}_1$ and $\mathcal{M}_2$ through the kernel K_p jointly with the relative direction of their tangent spaces as measured by K_s.

As a side note, $\| \cdot \|_{W'}$ gives a metric on the distribution space W', but d_W may still only result in a pseudodistance as two varifolds $\{\mathcal{M}_1\}$ and $\{\mathcal{M}_2\}$ may coincide in W' even though $\mathcal{M}_1$ and $\mathcal{M}_2$ are distinct. This happens essentially if the space of test functions W is not rich enough. Sufficient conditions on the kernels K_p and K_s to recover a true distance are given in [39], to which we refer for more detail. Similarly, specific regularity conditions are necessary to guarantee the existence of solutions to registration problems involving those fidelity terms.

Remark 12.1. In shape analysis, another usual property of metrics that is very often desired is the *invariance to rigid motions*, namely for all $(R, a) \in O_k \ltimes \mathbb{R}^k$ and all $\mathcal{M}_1, \mathcal{M}_2$,

$$\langle \{R\mathcal{M}_1 + a\}, \{R\mathcal{M}_2 + a\} \rangle_{W'} = \langle \{\mathcal{M}_1\}, \{\mathcal{M}_2\} \rangle_{W'}.$$

Within the setting presented here, this can be satisfied easily by restricting K_p to the class of *radial* kernels $K_p(x, y) = \rho(\|x - y\|^2)$ with $\rho : \mathbb{R}_+ \to \mathbb{R}$ and K_s to the class of *zonal* kernels on $\mathbb{S}^{k-1}$, that is, such that $K_s(\vec{u}, \vec{v}) = \gamma(\langle \vec{u}, \vec{v} \rangle)$ with $\gamma : [-1, 1] \to \mathbb{R}$.

Let us now consider a few specific examples of kernels, which all result in rigid-invariant distances between shapes. For K_p, common choices include Gaussian kernels $K_p(x, y) = e^{-\|x-y\|^2/\sigma^2}$ or Cauchy kernels $K_p(x, y) = \frac{1}{1+\|x-y\|^2/\sigma^2}$, where in both cases σ is a scale parameter that determines the spatial sensitivity of the metric. Sums of kernels with different scales can be also used to define multiscale distances. The choice of the spherical kernel K_s has very important impact on the resulting metric, and we now discuss a few particular cases.

Example 12.1. If $K_s(\vec{u}, \vec{v}) = 1$, then the metric is essentially insensitive to the tangent or normal vectors' components in the two shapes. Equivalently, it can be interpreted as viewing shapes as standard distributions on $\mathbb{R}^k$ and comparing them through the metrics obtained by the single kernel K_p. This exactly corresponds to the simplest model of *measures* introduced in [30] originally to treat point clouds.

Example 12.2. If $K_s(\vec{u}, \vec{v}) = \langle \vec{u}, \vec{v} \rangle$, that is, the restriction of the linear kernel of $\mathbb{R}^k$ to $\mathbb{S}^{k-1}$, then as a particular case, we find the metrics based on currents of formulas (12.3) and (12.4).

Example 12.3. Another possible choice is $K_s(\vec{u}, \vec{v}) = e^{-2\langle \vec{u}, \vec{v} \rangle/\sigma_s^2}$, which is the restriction of a Gaussian kernel of width $\sigma_s > 0$ on $\mathbb{S}^{k-1}$. Such a kernel induces nonlinearity with respect to u and v, which, as we will see, leads to important differences with currents.

Example 12.4. When K_s is chosen to be orientation-invariant, that is, if $K_s(\vec{u}, \vec{v}) = K_s(\vec{u}, -\vec{v}) = K_s(-\vec{u}, \vec{v})$, then interestingly the metric defined by formula (12.11) or (12.12) is completely independent of the orientation given to vectors $\vec{t}(x)$ or $\vec{n}(x)$. In that case orienting $\mathcal{M}_1$ or $\mathcal{M}_2$ is unnecessary, and we can basically select any of the two possible unit vectors at each point x. This leads to the particular class of metrics on varifolds that were considered in [13]. Examples of such symmetric kernels, besides the trivial one of Example 12.1, are $K_s(u, v) = \langle \vec{u}, \vec{v} \rangle^2$, which is known as the Binet kernel on the sphere, and $K_s(\vec{u}, \vec{v}) = e^{-2\langle \vec{u}, \vec{v} \rangle^2/\sigma_s^2}$ (the squared scalar product makes the kernel orientation-invariant).

This framework for constructing fidelity terms also enables simple multiscale registration strategies. One approach, which is used in some of the examples presented previously and further, consists in solving sequentially several registration problems using finer and finer kernel sizes. Another possible approach is to directly combine different scales in the fidelity metric by considering sums of kernels for K_p and/or K_s, which is inspired from a similar idea proposed in the context of multiscale deformation models by [51].

12.4.3 Discrete model

The discrete model for currents' representation and metrics introduced in Section 12.3.3 can be easily adapted to the more general situation of varifolds. Adopting the same notations, given two curve or surface meshes, we can approximate the double integrals in the kernel metrics given by Eqs. (12.11) and (12.12), respectively, as

$$\langle \{\mathcal{M}_1\}, \{\mathcal{M}_2\} \rangle_{W'} \approx \sum_{i=1}^{m_1} \sum_{j=1}^{m_2} K_p(c_{f_{1,i}}, c_{f_{2,j}}) K_s(\vec{t}_{f_{1,i}}, \vec{t}_{f_{2,j}}) \|\vec{\tau}_{f_{1,i}}\| \, \|\vec{\tau}_{f_{2,i}}\|$$

(12.14)

and

$$\langle \{\mathcal{M}_1\}, \{\mathcal{M}_2\} \rangle_{W'} \approx \sum_{i=1}^{m_1} \sum_{j=1}^{m_2} K_p(c_{f_{1,i}}, c_{f_{2,j}}) K_s(\vec{n}_{f_{1,i}}, \vec{n}_{f_{2,j}}) \|\vec{v}_{f_{1,i}}\| \, \|\vec{v}_{f_{2,i}}\|.$$

(12.15)

Note once again that if $K_s(\vec{u}, \vec{v}) = \langle \vec{u}, \vec{v} \rangle$, then we find the same expressions as in Eqs. (12.7) and (12.8). Recall also that the orientation of vectors $\vec{t}_{f_i}$ or $\vec{n}_{f_i}$ depends on the ordering of vertices in each face, which in general needs to be defined consistently across faces. Yet with the orientation-invariant kernels of Example 12.4, orienting the mesh is unneeded as any orientation at each face gives the same value in (12.14) and (12.15).

These discrete formulas can be also interpreted as the varifold inner products between the approximations of $\{\mathcal{M}_1\}$ and $\{\mathcal{M}_2\}$ as finite combinations of Diracs:

$$\{\mathcal{M}_1\} \approx \{\mathcal{M}_1\}_d = \sum_{i=1}^{m_1} \|\vec{v}_{f_{1,i}}\| \, \delta_{(c_{f_{1,i}}, \vec{t}_{f_{1,i}})} \quad \text{and}$$

$$\{\mathcal{M}_2\} \approx \{\mathcal{M}_2\}_d = \sum_{j=1}^{m_2} \|\vec{v}_{f_{2,j}}\| \, \delta_{(c_{f_{2,j}}, \vec{t}_{f_{2,j}})}$$

in the case of curves and with similar equivalent expressions for surfaces. In these equations, a Dirac varifold $\delta_{(x,\vec{u})}$ is the linear functional defined for any $w \in W$ by $\delta_{(x,\vec{u})}(w) = w(x,\vec{u})$. Then, for any polygonal curve or polyhedral surface, we can show (cf. [13] and [39]) that, under the assumptions on kernels introduced in Section 12.4.2 and the extra assumptions that both kernels are C^1, there exists a constant $C \geq 0$ such that

$$\|\{\mathcal{M}\} - \{\mathcal{M}\}_d\|_{W'} \leq C|\mathcal{M}| \max_i \operatorname{diam}(f_i), \qquad (12.16)$$

where $|\mathcal{M}|$ is the total length or area of $\mathcal{M}$, and $\operatorname{diam}(f_i)$ is the diameter of the face f_i. In other words, the approximation error for the varifold norm is controlled by the maximum diameter of the mesh faces and will thus be small if the mesh is sufficiently refined. Similar approximation bounds then follow for the discrete metric formulas of (12.14) and (12.15). In addition, the gradient of the metric and distance with respect to, for example, the vertices' positions in $\mathcal{M}_1$ is easily obtained by simple chain rule differentiation.

12.4.4 Examples and applications

We now illustrate several different properties and potential advantages or downsides of the previous metrics through a few examples of diffeomorphic registration on curves and surfaces. As previously, we rely on the LDDMM model for the deformation framework coupled with general varifold data attachment terms. In all these experiments spatial kernels K_p are chosen Gaussian (we denote by σ the width parameter), and we focus primarily on the effects of the second kernel K_s for which we compare the choices of Examples 12.2, 12.3, and 12.4.

Fig. 12.3 shows a fairly challenging registration experiment on closed curves. With currents (linear kernel), notice the appearance of degenerate structures and the fact that the two humps are not well recovered: this is a downside consequence of the cancellation effect discussed before. It is again very specific to the linearity of this model as these effects do not occur with the two other metrics. Orientation-invariant kernels like the Binet kernel of Example 12.4 still display difficulties in recovering the convoluted double hump by instead creating a single "average" hump. In this particular example where orientation is well-defined and relevant, oriented but nonlinear kernels like the spherical Gaussian of Example 12.3 achieve the most accurate registration as evidenced in the figure.

The previous observations can clearly have impact on registration of real data as well. We show one example among others

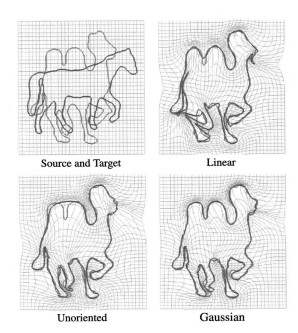

Figure 12.3. Diffeomorphic registration of a template horse (blue (dark gray in print version)) to the target (orange (light gray in print version)). The estimated deformed template is shown for some varifold metrics using various kernels K_S.

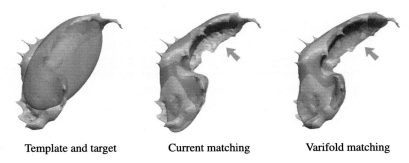

Figure 12.4. Registration between an ellipsoid and a hippocampal surface (left) with the linear kernel (middle) and the Binet kernel (right). The hippocampal surface is segmented from an MRI and contains several segmentation artifacts (spikes).

in Fig. 12.4, where an ellipsoid (blue (dark gray in print version)) is registered on an hippocampal surface segmented from an MRI (orange (light gray in print version)). We compare the estimated registrations using the linear and Binet kernels for the orientation. There are differences to be noticed between the two results, most

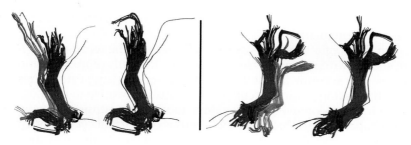

Figure 12.5. Registration of white matter fiber bundles using the Binet kernel for the fidelity term. Two views are shown in which the template is in green (light gray in print version), the target in red (mid gray in print version), and the registered template in blue (dark gray in print version).

notably around the thin part of the hippocampal surface where the overlapping of the registered surface is less accurate in the case of the linear kernel compared to the matching obtained with the Binet kernel (red arrow (mid gray in print version)). This is a clear manifestation of the cancellation of thin shape structures in the representation of currents.

Finally, orientation-invariant fidelity terms can prove very useful in the case of fiber bundle data for which defining an orientation of each fiber that is consistent can be particularly cumbersome and even ill-posed in some situations. We show an example of registration between two white matter fiber tracts in Fig. 12.5 using the unoriented Binet kernel.

Besides these cases, the benefits of oriented or unoriented varifold metrics have also been put to use in several other applications to shape analysis of medical data, which include cortical surfaces [50], complexes of subcortical surfaces [23], or lung vessels [48].

12.5 Normal cycles

Currents and varifolds provide representations for oriented or unoriented shapes that rely on first-order information of the shape (i.e., tangential or normal directions). Depending on the applications, it may be useful to have a second-order model that takes into account the curvature. For this purpose, we define in this section an alternative representation based on *normal cycles*. This is a summary of the work presented in [52].

Rather than the shape itself, the idea of normal cycles is to consider its unit normal bundle, that is, the shape attached with its normal vectors at each point. More precisely, the normal cycle is the current associated with the unit normal bundle. It has been introduced first by Zähle [56] as a generalization of curvatures for sets with singularities.

In this section we propose to briefly present the representation of shapes with normal cycles. We will see that this representation takes into account the boundary of the shapes (e.g., extremities and branching points for curves) and thus is sensitive to topological change. Moreover, it is sensitive to high-curvature regions of the shape. By introducing kernel metrics on normal cycles (as for currents and varifolds) we are once again able to obtain an explicit form for the metric between discrete shapes represented as normal cycles.

12.5.1 Differential forms and currents

Similarly to currents and varifolds, normal cycles are defined through their evaluation on test functions. To define adequate spaces of test functions in that case, we need to recall some notions about differential forms and currents in more general dimensions than the setting of Section 12.3.

Definition 12.4. Let $k \in \mathbb{N}^*$.
- An m-differential form, or simply m-form, is a mapping $x \mapsto \omega(x)$ from $\mathbb{R}^k$ to the space of alternating m-linear forms of $\mathbb{R}^k$.
- An m-current in $\mathbb{R}^k$ is a continuous linear mapping from the space of continuous m-forms to $\mathbb{R}$.

The space of test functions we will consider in the following will be $\Omega_0^{k-1}(\mathbb{R}^k \times \mathbb{S}^{k-1})$, the space of continuous $(k-1)$-differential forms on $\mathbb{R}^k \times S^{k-1}$ vanishing at infinity.

Remark 12.2. For curves in $\mathbb{R}^2$ ($k=2$, $m=1$) or surfaces in $\mathbb{R}^3$ ($k=3$, $m=2$), we can canonically identify an m-differential form to a continuous vector field, and we retrieve the definition given in Section 12.3.

12.5.2 Unit normal bundle and normal cycle

To keep the discussion as simple as possible, we will only consider curves and surfaces in $\mathbb{R}^3$. However, the notion of normal cycles can be generalized to any m-dimensional surface in $\mathbb{R}^k$.

Definition 12.5 (Unit normal bundle and normal cycle). Consider $\mathcal{M}$ a compact C^2 curve or surface (possibly with a boundary).
- The *unit normal bundle* of $\mathcal{M}$ is

$$\mathcal{N}_\mathcal{M} = \{(x, n) \mid x \in \mathcal{M}, \vec{n} \in \text{Nor}(\mathcal{M}, x)\},$$

where $\text{Nor}(\mathcal{M}, x)$ is the set of all the unit normal vectors of $\mathcal{M}$ at point x.

- The *normal cycle* of $\mathcal{M}$, denoted $N(\mathcal{M})$, is the current associated with $\mathcal{N}_{\mathcal{M}}$:

$$N(\mathcal{M})(\omega) := [\mathcal{N}_{\mathcal{M}}](\omega) = \int_{\mathcal{N}_{\mathcal{M}}} \langle \omega(x, \vec{n}), \tau_{\mathcal{N}_{\mathcal{M}}}(x, \vec{n}) \rangle dS(x, \vec{n}),$$

where $\tau_{\mathcal{N}_{\mathcal{M}}}(x, \vec{n})$ is the unit tangent vector to $\mathcal{N}_{\mathcal{M}}$ at point $(x, \vec{n})$, and $\omega \in \Omega_0^{k-1}(\mathbb{R}^k \times \mathbb{S}^{k-1})$.

Remark 12.3. $\mathcal{N}_{\mathcal{M}}$ is a two-dimensional surface in $\mathbb{R}^3 \times \mathbb{S}^2$ independently of the dimensionality of $\mathcal{M}$. Indeed, it can be canonically associated with an ε-expansion of the initial shape for ε small enough. See [52] and the references therein for more detail. Thus the integration over the unit normal bundle is a surface area integration. Hence the notation $dS(x, \vec{n})$ in the definition of normal cycles.

Figure 12.6. Illustration of the unit normal bundle for a regular nonclosed curve in the plane. The curve is in black, the unit normal vectors associated with four points are represented as red arrows (light gray in print version), and the resulting unit normal bundle is represented in blue (mid gray in print version) with its canonical orientation. Note that this representation is only illustrative, as the true normal bundle belongs to the space $\mathbb{R}^2 \times \mathbb{S}^1$ in this case.

The unit normal bundle of a smooth curve with extremities is depicted in Fig. 12.6. Note that extremities have nonnegligible contributions in the normal bundle and thus are taken into account in the normal cycle. This is a major difference with currents or varifolds. Note also that since the unit normal bundle can be depicted as a closed hypersurface (as in Fig. 12.6), it has a canonical orientation that is independent of the orientation of the initial shape.

12.5.3 Normal cycles for discrete curves or surfaces

The unit normal bundle is well-defined for smooth enough sets, specifically sets with positive reach (see [24], section 4). This class of sets encompasses compact C^2 submanifolds with boundary (which we will further refer to as C^2 sets). However, it is a priori not well defined in general for union of C^2 sets as, for instance, with discrete curves or surfaces. Fortunately, it is possible to extend the notion of normal cycles for such sets using the following *additive property*.

Proposition 12.1 (Additive property, [57]). *Consider $\mathcal{M} = \mathcal{M}_1 \cup \mathcal{M}_2$ such that $\mathcal{M}_1$ and $\mathcal{M}_2$ and $\mathcal{M}_1 \cap \mathcal{M}_2$ are C^2 sets (possibly with boundary). Then we can define*

$$N(\mathcal{M}) := N(\mathcal{M}_1) + N(\mathcal{M}_2) - N(\mathcal{M}_1 \cap \mathcal{M}_2).$$

This property allows us to define the normal cycles for shapes that are unions of compact C^2 sets with boundaries. This case encompasses that of discrete curves or surfaces. Such a normal cycle corresponds to a generalized unit normal bundle, which is illustrated in Figs. 12.7 and 12.8.

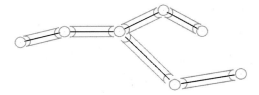

Figure 12.7. Representation of the generalized unit normal bundle of a blue (ligth gray in print version) discrete curve. For curves, we observe two parts for the normal bundle: a cylindrical part (in purple (mid gray in print version)), associated with the edges, and a spherical part (in blue (light gray in print version)) associated with the vertices.

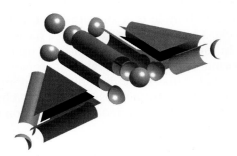

Figure 12.8. Representation of the generalized unit normal bundle of triangles (in black). It comprises three parts: a planar part (in purple (dark gray in print version)) associated with the interior, a cylindrical part (in blue (mid gray in print version)) associated with the edges, and a spherical part (in yellow (light gray in print version)) associated with the vertices.

12.5.4 Kernel metrics on normal cycles

Since normal cycles are currents associated with unit normal bundles, we can again rely on the theory of RKHS presented in Sections 12.3.2 and 12.4.2. It remains to design a scalar kernel K on $\mathbb{R}^3 \times \mathbb{S}^2$ that will be a product of a spatial kernel K_p and a spherical kernel K_s. This has already been presented in Section 12.4.2.

In this framework the inner product between two curves or two surfaces represented as normal cycles takes the form

$$\langle N(\mathcal{M}_1), N(\mathcal{M}_2)\rangle_{W'}$$

$$= \int_{\mathcal{N}_{\mathcal{M}_1}} \int_{\mathcal{N}_{\mathcal{M}_2}} K_p(x, y) K_s(\vec{u}, \vec{v}) \langle \tau_1(x, \vec{u}), \tau_2(y, \vec{v})\rangle dS(x, \vec{u}) dS(y, \vec{v}),$$

$$(12.17)$$

where $\tau_1(x, \vec{u})$ is the tangent vector of the unit normal bundle at point $(x, \vec{u})$. Notice that this expression is true only for compact C^2 curves or surfaces (possibly with boundary). It can be extended to discrete curves or surfaces through the previous additivity property. Let us add a few remarks. First of all, we can notice that this expression is similar for curves or surfaces: the normal bundle is indeed two-dimensional in $\mathbb{R}^3 \times \mathbb{S}^2$, independently of the actual dimension of the shape. Secondly, the contribution of normal vectors through the kernel K_s but also through the tangent vector to the normal bundle τ_1 shows that curvature is taken into account by those metrics in contrast to the previous approaches of currents or varifolds.

The choice of the spherical kernel is mainly driven by the possibility to explicitly compute such inner products between two discrete shapes. With discrete curves, those metrics have been implemented with constant (as in Example 12.1), linear (Example 12.2), or Sobolev kernels (i.e., the reproducing kernel of some Sobolev space on the sphere $\mathbb{S}^2$ that has explicit expansion in the spherical harmonics basis). In the case of surfaces, however, current implementations are restricted to the constant spherical kernel, even though it provides less theoretical guarantees (namely, the space of test functions W is not rich enough to ensure that the associated pseudodistance $d_W(\mathcal{M}, \mathcal{M}') = \|N(\mathcal{M}) - N(\mathcal{M}')\|_{W'}^2$ is a true distance; see again [52] for a precise discussion on these topics).

12.5.5 Discrete inner product

In the case of discrete curves or surfaces, as shown in Fig. 12.8, the unit normal bundle consists of several components: spherical (in green (light gray in print version)) associated with vertices, cylindrical (in red (dark gray in print version)) associated with edges, and for surfaces planar components (in light blue (mid gray in print version)) associated with faces. The expression of the full inner product is greatly simplified thanks to the following result.

Proposition 12.2. *The spherical, cylindrical, and planar components are orthogonal with respect to the kernel metric on normal cycles defined in Section 12.5.4 by formula* (12.17)

Numerical computation involves integrating over the planar, cylindrical, and spherical parts. We approximate the spatial integration as for currents or varifolds. The integration over the normal part is explicitly calculated. For simplicity, here we only express it for the constant spherical kernel ($K_s(\vec{u}, \vec{v}) = 1$); equivalent derivations for linear or Sobolev kernels may be found in [52]. In the case of curves, it reads:

$$\langle N(\mathcal{M}_1), N(\mathcal{M}_2)\rangle_{W'} = \frac{\pi^2}{4} \sum_{i=1}^{m_1} \sum_{j=1}^{m_2} K_p(x_i, y_j)\left\langle \vec{A}_i, \vec{B}_j \right\rangle, \qquad (12.18)$$

where $\vec{A}_i = \sum_k f_k^i/|f_k^i|$ is the sum of the normalized edges with x_i as vertices and oriented outward from x_i. For surfaces,

$$\langle N(\mathcal{M}_1), N(\mathcal{M}_2)\rangle_{W'}$$
$$= \frac{\pi^2}{4} \sum_{i=1}^{n_e} \sum_{j=1}^{m_e} K_p(c_i, d_j)\left\langle \vec{f}_i, \vec{g}_j \right\rangle\left\langle \sum_{\{T|f_i \text{ edge of } T\}} \vec{n}_{T,\vec{f}_i}, \sum_{\{T'|g_j \text{ edge of } T'\}} \vec{n}_{T',\vec{g}_j} \right\rangle$$
$$+ \frac{\pi^2}{4} \sum_{\substack{x_i \text{ vertex} \\ \text{of } \partial\mathcal{M}_1}} \sum_{\substack{y_j \text{ vertex} \\ \text{of } \partial\mathcal{M}_2}} K_p(x_i, y_j)\left\langle \vec{A}_i, \vec{B}_j \right\rangle, \qquad (12.19)$$

where the first double sum is a double loop on the edges (there are n_e edges in $\mathcal{M}$ and m_e in $\mathcal{M}_2$), where $\vec{A}_i = \sum_k f_k^i/|f_k^i|$ is the sum of the normalized edges of the border, with x_i as vertices, and oriented outward from x_i, c_i is the middle of the edge $\vec{f}_i$, $\vec{n}_{T_i,\vec{f}_i}$ is the normal vector of the triangle T_i such that $n_{T_i,\vec{f}} \times \vec{f}_i$ is oriented inward for the triangle T, and B_j is the similar notation as A_i for the triangulation $\mathcal{M}_2$. Note that with the constant normal kernel, the inner product involves only the cylindrical part, that is, quantities associated with the edges of the triangles (and thus with the discrete mean curvature).

Since the expression of the inner product (and thus the metric) is explicit in the discrete case, it is easy to obtain the gradient with respect to the vertices of $\mathcal{M}_1$ by a chain rule.

Remark 12.4. With the linear spherical kernel, the inner product involves the spherical part (associated with the vertices and thus the Gaussian curvature) and the planar part. It is interesting that this planar part corresponds to the inner product obtained from the varifold representation with the Binet spherical kernel introduced in Section 12.4.2.

The crucial difference between normal cycles and currents or varifolds is that any part of the discrete shape has a nonnegligible component in the unit normal bundle and will be taken into account by the metric. Hence there is an explicit term associated with the boundaries of shapes. For registration purpose, this feature will enforce the matching of boundaries, corners, and also of branching points.

12.5.6 Examples and applications

This section aims to illustrate some of the properties of normal cycles.

First, we show an example on curves. The data consist of brain sulcal curves that were automatically segmented and labeled from anatomical magnetic resonance imaging (MRI) brain images, following the method described in [4]. We chose two individuals and six labeled corresponding sulcal curves for each individual. We thank Guillaume Auzias for extracting and providing us the dataset of sulcal curves used in our experiments. The data fit in a box of size $120 \times 140 \times 110$.

The matching is performed with a single deformation but six data attachment terms with normal cycles, one for each pair of corresponding sulci. The details of the registration procedure are specified in Fig. 12.9. The matching is complex since the number of branching points is not necessarily the same for corresponding curves, and two curves to match can be really twisted from one to another. Moreover, the fact that a single deformation is required for the whole brain implies high local variations. In Fig. 12.9 we present the registration with normal cycles and Sobolev normal kernel. The visualization of this three-dimensional configuration is not easy, but the end points and corresponding branching points are well matched when possible (we recall that there is no always a corresponding branching point). Moreover, the registration driven by normal cycles allows complex local deformation (even though it is expensive) to reduce the data attachment term.

In the bottom row we present a zoom on two sulci to showcase the properties of a registration with normal cycles. This specific example shows all the benefits that we can expect from the metric on normal cycles. The natural consideration of the extremities and the branching points provides a convincing registration, even though this implies a deformation with high local variation. This

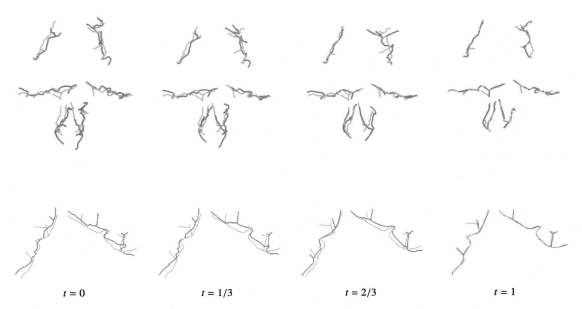

$t = 0$ $t = 1/3$ $t = 2/3$ $t = 1$

Figure 12.9. Top row: registration of blue (dark gray in print version) to orange (light gray in print version) brain sulci. The deformation kernel is a Cauchy kernel of width $\sigma_V = 20$. The data attachment term is normal cycles with a Sobolev kernel of order 3 for K_s and Gaussian spatial kernel for K_p. Bottom row: zoom on the registration of two sulci. Each row shows the evolution of the deformation with time. We can observe that since normal cycles take into account the extremities, the matching is convincing.

is even more striking on the left sulci. The deformation is a good compromise, even though the number of branching points in the source and target is not the same.

As a second real data example, we consider the registration of retinal surfaces, which are shown in Fig. 12.10. Those retina are surfaces in 3D segmented from optical coherence tomography images. The typical size is $8 \times 8\,\text{mm}$, and each retina is sampled with approximately 5000 points. The data acquisition and preprocessing is described in [41]. In our simulations we use a Gaussian deformation kernel K_V with $\sigma_V = 0.6$. All the details of the matching are in Fig. 12.10. These surfaces have boundaries and corners, which will be seen as region with singularities for the kernel metric on normal cycles. This is not the case for the varifolds metric, which makes the registration of the corresponding corners more involved. The matching of the borders is more accurate with normal cycles while providing a much more regular deformation (see Fig. 12.10).

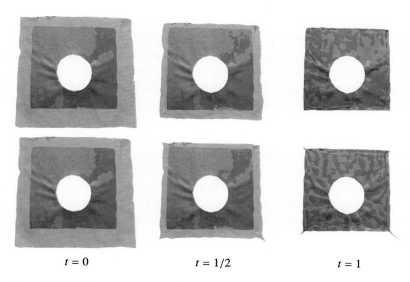

$$t = 0 \qquad\qquad t = 1/2 \qquad\qquad t = 1$$

Figure 12.10. Each row represents the matching of two retina surfaces in 3D with kernel metric on normal cycles (top) and varifolds (bottom). The target shape is in orange (light gray in print version), and the source shape is in blue (dark gray in print version). Each shape has 5000 points. For the varifolds metric, the geometric kernel is Gaussian. The kernel K_s is $K_s(\vec{u}, \vec{v}) = \langle \vec{u}, \vec{v} \rangle^2$ as in Example 12.4, so that no additional parameter is involved. The same parameters are used for each data attachment term. K_V is a Gaussian kernel with $\sigma_V = 0.6$.

12.6 Computational aspects

12.6.1 Fast kernel computations

The metrics presented in this chapter all use embeddings of shapes in some RKHS. Such "kernel methods" are convenient tools as they allow us to define simple yet intuitive distances between shapes by choosing meaningful kernels tailored to particular applications. Moreover, kernel methods lead to natural and efficient discrete approximations of the continuous models, which are amenable to treat real datasets.

As we have seen in the previous sections, the considered metrics are then defined based on the inner product resulting from the RKHS structure. The explicit formulas (12.7), (12.8), or (12.14), (12.15), or (12.18), (12.19) of these various inner products all involve computations of the form

$$S = \sum_{i=1}^{m_1} \sum_{j=1}^{m_2} F_{i,j}, \qquad (12.20)$$

where $F_{i,j}$ are real numbers depending (possibly nonlinearly) on some known quantities such as points position (the variables $c_{f_i} \in \mathbb{R}^k$) or tangent space orientation (variables $\vec{\tau}_{f_i}, \vec{v}_{f_i} \in \mathbb{R}^k$), and so on. Computing a single $F_{i,j}$ in (12.20) requires, in general, several operations such as kernel evaluations. It yields to a total computational complexity of $O(m_1 m_2)$ to evaluate a single distance between two shapes (m_1 and m_2 being the number of segments/triangles in the shapes). This quadratic complexity is one of the main obstacles to apply kernel-based distances on real data. Indeed, many practical cases involve data where m_1 and m_2 can reach an order of magnitude up to 10^7 or more.

There are two main strategies to efficiently perform computations of kernel-based distances: "brute force" exact computations using parallel architectures and methods computing an approximate value of S but with a much lower complexity (typically quasilinear instead of quadratic). We discuss some possible methods in the remainder of this section.

12.6.1.1 Exact computations

By exact computations here we e mean that all $F_{i,j}$ are evaluated up to the machine precision before computing the full double sum in (12.20). The methods described in this section can be used to compute any kernels.

Linear algebra library

The first natural way to perform exact kernel computations is to use one of the standard linear algebra libraries (such as BLAS, Armadillo, etc.). Every scientific programming language now has bindings to state-of-the-art linear algebra libraries that are able to take advantage of multiple cores in modern central processing unit (CPU).

The basic idea here is to create an array of size $m_1 \times m_2$ containing all values $F_{i,j}$ and perform two summation (reduction) steps. For instance, the current inner product (12.21) may be written in Python as in Fig. 12.11 where, under the hood, numpy calls BLAS optimized library to perform the matrix multiplication and the final reduction step of line 7.

This solution is competitive in term of speed when the sizes m_1 and m_2 of the data at hand are small (up to 10^3 typically as shown Fig. 12.12). The bottleneck is the memory footprint since storing the $m_1 \times m_2$ array M of floating-points numbers (line 6 of Fig. 12.11) may be impossible.

```
1  import numpy as np # load numpy library
2
3  def squared_distances(x, y):# matrix of the squared norms
4    return np.sum((x[:,np.newaxis,:] - y[np.newaxis,:,:]) ** 2, axis=2)
5
6  M = np.exp(-squared_distances(c_f1, c_f2) / (sigma*sigma))
7  S =  np.sum(tau_f1  * (np.matmul(M,tau_f2)) # final results
```

Figure 12.11. An implementation of Gaussian kernel sum (12.21) in Python using numpy.

Graphics processing unit (GPU)

Brute force computations using massively parallel architectures such as GPU are a very efficient way to compute kernel based distances when the sizes m_1 and m_2 are moderate (in the range of 10^3 to 10^6). Using a GPU for very small values of m_1 and m_2 is in general counter productive as there may be some overhead due to memory transfers between the standard memory and the GPU memory. This being said, the performances of an implementation highly depend on the environment and are subject to possible changes in the future.

Some high-level languages allow to execute (transparently for the end-user) the code of Fig. 12.11 on a GPU. Nevertheless, the memory limitations remain the same. In fact, they are even worst as the size of the memory on a GPU is usually much smaller than the standard memory size. In Fig. 12.12 we can see that an Nvidia GPU Tesla P100 with 16 Gb of RAM ran out of memory for $m_1, m_2 > 26000$.

To overcome this problem, it is possible to use a so-called "tile implementation" method. The idea is to divide the computations of the $m_1 m_2$ terms $F_{i,j}$ in small batches (the tiles) and aggregate the results on the fly. In practice the computations of the $F_{i,j}$ and the reduction step are then made on a single batch at a time reducing the amount of memory needed to compute S and without loosing accuracy. The memory architecture of GPUs is particularly well suited for this kind of job as it is possible to use a low latency memory called shared memory. Although this tile implementation is well documented, there is currently few high level libraries that can be used for general matrix multiplications or operations as formula (12.20). A notable exception is keops [12], which is a Cuda/C++ software with Python, Matlab, and R bindings designed to compute operations on kernels. Performances are shown Fig. 12.12.

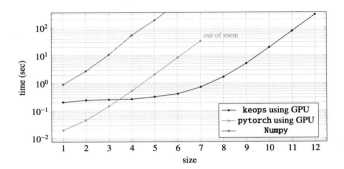

Figure 12.12. Average time to compute 200 Gaussian kernel sums depending on the size. The size increase exponentially: at size i we have $m_1 = 200 \times 2^i$ and $m_2 = 300 \times 2^i$.

12.6.1.2 Approximate methods

Even with a strong parallelized implementation using GPU, exact methods to compute kernel based distances may be impossible to apply when m_1 and m_2 are greater than 10^7. The quadratic complexity being simply too high in this range of values.

We present here two methods that are able to compute an approximated value of S of formula (12.20) with a controlled error in at most a sublinear complexity. Unfortunately, approximation methods may not be used with any general kernel. We will then assume here that the problem has the following form:

$$S = \sum_{i=1}^{m_1} \langle \vec{\tau}_{f_1,i}, [M\vec{\tau}_{f_2}]_i \rangle \text{ where } \begin{cases} M = \left[\rho(\|c_{f_1,i} - c_{f_2,j}\|^2) \right] \in \mathrm{M}_{(m_1,m_2)} \\ \text{and} \\ \vec{\tau}_{f_2} = [\tau_{f_2,j}] \in \mathrm{M}_{(m_2,k)}, \end{cases}$$
(12.21)

where ρ may be a Gaussian or Cauchy function. In formula (12.21), for any $1 \le i \le m_1$, we have denoted $[M\vec{\tau}_{f_2}]_i$ the vector in $\mathbb{R}^k$ whose coordinates are given by the ith row of $[M\vec{\tau}_{f_2}]$. Hence computing S can be done at the price of a convolution (the matrix product $M\vec{\tau}_{f_2}$, which is the costly part) followed by reduction step (the sum over the scalar product in $\mathbb{R}^k$).

Grid method and nonuniform fast Fourier transform (NFFT)

These two methods can be employed to compute approximations of convolutions with radial scalar kernels as used in Eq. (12.21). Both approaches rely on the fact that convolutions can be written as a pointwise product in the frequency domain. The difficulty is that points do not a priori lie on an equispaced grid, and the fast Fourier transform (FFT) cannot be used directly. The idea is then to interpolate the data on a regular grid (first step known as griding step) to be able to apply the FFT for the computation of convolutions (second step). Finally, the results are evaluated at the initial data location (third step). The total cost of the method is then quasilinear in terms of number of points in the shape and grid size. Nevertheless, a major drawback is that the grid size explodes with the dimension of the ambient space limiting the range of applications to $k \leq 3$.

The grid method [17] has been implemented in the software `Deformetrica` [18] for Gaussian kernel and is used to compute current and varifolds norms with Binet kernels. The NFFT can be used for similar tasks, and two possible choices for implementations are [40] and [34].

Fast multipole methods (FMM)

FMM [35] are numerical methods coming from physics to approximate computations involving kernels. Original motivations were to compute numerical solutions of the n-body problem or solutions of some partial differential equations. Although, to the best of the authors' knowledge, these methods are not being currently used in our context, it is worth mentioning FMM as a potential approach to make computations of formulas similar to (12.21) with m_1, m_2 above 10^7 numerically tractable.

The idea of FMM is to perform calculations in a hierarchical way by splitting the ambient space $\mathbb{R}^k$ into adaptive sets of subregions whose sizes depend on the density of points in the space. This partition is then used to make a batch computation of the sum. The evaluation of an admissible kernel in each batch can be approximated with a controlled precision. Finally, the approximated results are aggregated in a divide-and-conquer fashion reducing the overall computational complexity to a sublinear complexity in terms of the number of points. Moreover, the memory needed to perform the overall calculation is also significantly decreased.

Let us finally mention a useful particular case of FMM: the fast Gauss transform [55], which was specifically developed to compute sums of the form (12.21) with Gaussian kernel. FGT can then be used to compute current distances or varifold distances with a Binet kernel on the orientation part.

12.6.2 Compact approximations

The approximation quality of the discrete models presented so far depends on the resolution of the meshes, namely the numbers

m_1 and m_2 (and sizes) of segments and triangles for curves and surfaces, respectively. Due to the use of kernels, those representations may be redundant and thus simplified prior to further processing. To focus the discussion, we will here restrict to the model of currents presented in Section 12.3.

Take as an example a mesh composed of two segments, which can be modeled as two Dirac currents $\delta_{c_1}^{\tau_1}$ and $\delta_{c_2}^{\tau_2}$ as in Eq. (12.6). Using, for instance, a Gaussian kernel with scale parameter σ, we can easily verify that if $\|c_1 - c_2\| \ll \sigma$, then $\delta_{c_1}^{\tau_1} + \delta_{c_2}^{\tau_2}$ can be well approximated for the $\|\cdot\|_{W'}$ norm by the single Dirac $\delta_{\frac{c_1+c_2}{2}}^{\tau_1+\tau_2}$.

Exploiting this idea, we can approximate all the segments in a neighborhood of size σ (or cells for a surface mesh) with a single "average" segment (i.e., point + orientation) modeled as a Dirac current. This representation is less redundant since the resulting Dirac currents are (almost) orthogonal to each other (i.e., the distance between their centers would be greater than σ). In order to be an optimal decomposition, the small set of Diracs should also accurately approximate the original shape.

A greedy approach of this idea is introduced in [19] and based on the *matching pursuit algorithm*. It results in a set of N Dirac currents $\sum_{i=1}^{N} \delta_{x_i}^{\alpha_i}$ that well approximate the original shape composed of m Dirac currents with a very high compression ratio (i.e., $N \ll m$). Each Dirac current locally integrates the redundancy of the data at the scale of σ. An example of this approximation approach is shown in Fig. 12.13, where we employ a white matter fiber tract resulting from a tractography algorithm applied on diffusion MRI. For more information, we refer the reader to [19] and [21].

The previous technique produces a very concise representation that works quite well in practice for both curves and surfaces. However, it accurately approximates only the areas of the shape characterized by a high density of segments (or cells). Moreover, it results in an ensemble of *disconnected* oriented points that do not preserve the original connectivity of the shape. This can complicate the interpretation and impede the studies where the connectivity of the meshes is important as, for instance, when working with white matter fiber bundles. For this reason, the authors in [33] proposed to approximate an ensemble of curves, as a white matter tract, by selecting a small set of *weighted prototypes*. Prototypes are chosen among the curves, and they approximate their neighbors and similar curves. Their weights are related to the number of curves approximated. All curves, prototypes included, are modeled as weighted currents, an extension of the framework of currents. This computational model takes into consideration both the pathway of the curves and the location of their endpoints.

Using the same notation as for currents and calling (a_1, b_1) and (a_2, b_2) the endpoints of two curves $\mathcal{M}_1$ and $\mathcal{M}_2$, respectively, their inner product is

$$\langle [\mathcal{M}_1], [\mathcal{M}_2] \rangle_{W'}$$
$$\approx K_a(a_1, a_2) K_b(b_1, b_2) \sum_{i=1}^{m_1} \sum_{j=1}^{m_2} K_g(c_{f_{1,i}}, c_{f_{2,j}}) \langle \vec{\tau}_{f_{1,i}}, \vec{\tau}_{f_{2,j}} \rangle, \quad (12.22)$$

where K_a, K_b, and K_g are three radial Gaussian kernels. Two curves are thus considered similar if their endpoints are close to each other and if their trajectories are similar. As for currents, a bundle $\mathcal{B}$ of two curves $\mathcal{M}_1$ and $\mathcal{M}_2$ is represented as a sum in the framework $[\mathcal{B}] = [\mathcal{M}_1] + [\mathcal{M}_2]$. If the two curves are similar, then $[\mathcal{B}]$ can be well approximated by $2[\mathcal{M}_1]$ or $2[\mathcal{M}_2]$. Using this idea, an ensemble of similar curves can be represented with a single *weighted prototype*, where the weight is related to the number of curves approximated. A weighted prototype can be visualized as a constant-radius tube, where the curve chosen as prototype is the central axis, and the radius is proportional to the weight (see Fig. 12.13). To find the best prototypes based on the metric of weighted currents, the authors in [33] proposed a greedy approach divided into two steps. They first divide the bundle of curves into smaller subsets, called fascicles, and then select the prototypes in each fascicle independently. Every fascicle is defined as a small subset of curves, which are considered similar in the framework of weighted currents. This subdivision is based on the maximization of a quality function called *modularity*. The selection of prototypes is even in this case based on an iterative algorithm inspired by orthogonal matching pursuit. The main differences with respect to the previous algorithm are that the prototypes are chosen from the original curves, thus preserving the connectivity, and that all parts of the original bundle, even the small fascicles, are well approximated. However, it can only be used with curves but not with surfaces. More details can be found in [33].

12.6.3 Available implementations

Several open-source codes incorporate implementations of the distances that are described in this chapter. We refer to Table 12.1 for a summary of some of these.

Original bundle   **Approximation**

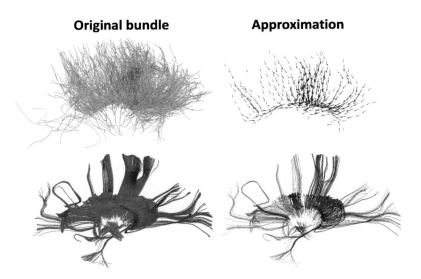

Figure 12.13. Compact approximations of white matter tracts resulting from tractography algorithms applied on diffusion MRI. The first row shows an approximation based on Dirac currents [21]. The second row presents a different tract approximated with weighted prototypes [33].

Table 12.1 **Available implementations of LDDMM registration algorithms described in this chapter. Gauss stands for Gaussian radial kernel, Rad means any radial kernel, Binet is the varifold distance with Binet kernel for K_S. (*) Varifolds in this code are only available as special case of normal cycles, which gives unefficient implementation.**

Name	Language	GPU	Currents		Varifolds		Normal
			Gauss	Rad	Binet	Rad	Cycles
Deformetrica [18]	C++	✓	✓		✓		
FshapesTk [10]	Matlab	✓	✓	✓	✓	✓	
LDDMM/NormalCycles [28]	Matlab	✓	✓	✓	✓(*)		✓
MRICloud [37]	C++	✓	✓				

12.7 Conclusion

In this chapter, we presented different mathematical and numerical models to quantify the discrepancy between two curves or two surfaces. All these approaches rely on embedding shapes into certain distribution or measure spaces on which kernel-based metrics are constructed. We showed that the various possible choices of spaces and kernels provide in turn a large family of fidelity metrics. One important advantage of this framework is its versatility and simplicity of use that allows taking advantage of the properties of one particular metric over another one, tailored to the specific data structure under study.

In particular, we emphasized that metrics based on the model of currents, while requiring a consistent orientation of shapes, provide robustness to certain noisy features in the geometry. Varifolds on the other hand prevent certain undesirable effects of currents like flattening or insensitivity to some thin geometric structures and, with the adequate choice of kernels, can also spare the user from the need to orient the given meshes. Finally, the normal cycle approach leads to a higher-order shape representation with metrics that incorporate comparison of the curvatures. Although it is more costly to compute from a numerical point of view, normal cycles are particularly well-suited for data involving branching structures, complex boundaries, corners, and so on.

In terms of applications, we mainly focused here on the use of such metrics as fidelity terms in LDDMM registration problems, but this framework can be readily combined with other models for inexact registration as, for instance, Sobolev elastic curve matching in the recent work of [5]. It can also be embedded in similar fashion within template/atlas estimation procedures on populations of shapes. As a final note, we also want to emphasize that the interest of these methods goes beyond the sole issue of constructing fidelity terms for those problems. We briefly mentioned in Section 12.6.2 the applications to sparse approximations of shapes. The authors in [39] have also investigated clustering algorithms based on varifold metrics, whereas several works such as [11,42] have proposed extensions of some methods of this chapter for the purpose of joint analysis of shape and function in structuro-functional datasets.

Acknowledgments

Nicolas Charon acknowledges support from the National Science Foundation, through grant no. 1819131.

References

1. W. Allard, On the first variation of a varifold, Annals of Mathematics 95 (3) (1972).
2. F. Almgren, Plateau's Problem: An Invitation to Varifold Geometry, Student Mathematical Library, 1966.
3. N. Aronszajn, Theory of reproducing kernels, Transactions of the American Mathematical Society 68 (1950) 337–404.

4. G. Auzias, O. Colliot, J.A. Glaunès, M. Perrot, J.F. Mangin, A. Trouvé, S. Baillet, Diffeomorphic brain registration under exhaustive sulcal constraints, IEEE Transactions on Medical Imaging 30 (6) (June 2011) 1214–1227.

5. M. Bauer, M. Bruveris, N. Charon, J. Moeller-Andersen, A relaxed approach for curve matching with elastic metrics, in: ESAIM: Control, Optimisation and Calculus of Variations, 2018.

6. M.F. Beg, M.I. Miller, A. Trouvé, L. Younes, Computing large deformation metric mappings via geodesic flows of diffeomorphisms, International Journal of Computer Vision 61 (139–157) (2005).

7. J. Benn, S. Marsland, R. McLachlan, K. Modin, O. Verdier, Currents and finite elements as tools for shape space, ArXiv preprint, 2017.

8. P. Cachier, N. Ayache, Isotropic energies, filters and splines for vector field regularization, Journal of Mathematical Imaging and Vision 20 (3) (May 2004) 251–265.

9. C. Carmeli, E. De Vito, A. Toigo, V. Umanita, Vector valued reproducing kernel Hilbert spaces and universality, Analysis and Applications 8 (01) (2010) 19–61.

10. B. Charlier, N. Charon, A. Trouvé, Fshapestk: the functional shapes toolkit (software), https://github.com/fshapes/fshapesTk/, 2013–2018.

11. B. Charlier, N. Charon, A. Trouvé, The fshape framework for the variability analysis of functional shapes, Foundations of Computational Mathematics 17 (2) (2017) 287–357.

12. B. Charlier, J. Feydy, J.A. Glaunès, Keops (software), https://plmlab.math.cnrs.fr/benjamin.charlier/keops, 2017–2018.

13. N. Charon, A. Trouvé, The varifold representation of non-oriented shapes for diffeomorphic registration, SIAM Journal on Imaging Sciences 6 (4) (2013) 2547–2580.

14. E. De Vito, V. Umanità, S. Villa, An extension of Mercer theorem to matrix-valued measurable kernels, Applied and Computational Harmonic Analysis 34 (3) (2013) 339–351.

15. Fabrice Dodu, Christophe Rabut, Irrotational or divergence-free interpolation, Numerische Mathematik 98 (3) (Sep. 2004) 477–498.

16. J. Duchon, Splines minimizing rotation-invariant semi-norms in Sobolev spaces, in: Walter Schempp, Karl Zeller (Eds.), Constructive Theory of Functions of Several Variables, Springer, Berlin, Heidelberg, 1977, pp. 85–100.

17. S. Durrleman, Statistical Models of Currents for Measuring the Variability of Anatomical Curves, Surfaces and Their Evolution, PhD thesis, Inria Sophia Antipolis, 2009.

18. S. Durrleman, Contributors, Deformetrica (software), www.deformetrica.org, 2009–2018.

19. S. Durrleman, X. Pennec, A. Trouvé, N. Ayache, Statistical models of sets of curves and surfaces based on currents, Medical Image Analysis 13 (5) (2009) 793–808.

20. S. Durrleman, X. Pennec, A. Trouvé, G. Gerig, N. Ayache, Spatiotemporal atlas estimation for developmental delay detection in longitudinal datasets, Medical Image Computing and Computer-Assisted Intervention 12 (Pt 1) (2009) 297–304.

21. S. Durrleman, P. Fillard, X. Pennec, A. Trouvé, N. Ayache, Registration, atlas estimation and variability analysis of white matter fiber bundles modeled as currents, NeuroImage 55 (3) (2011) 1073–1090.

22. S. Durrleman, P. Fillard, X. Pennec, A. Trouvé, N. Ayache, Registration, atlas estimation and variability analysis of white matter fiber bundles modeled as currents, NeuroImage 55 (3) (2011) 1073–1090.

23. S. Durrleman, M. Prastawa, N. Charon, J.R. Korenberg, S. Joshi, G. Gerig, A. Trouvé, Morphometry of anatomical shape complexes with dense deformations and sparse parameters, NeuroImage 101 (2014) 35–49.

24. H. Federer, Curvature measures, Transactions of the American Mathematical Society 93 (1959).

25. H. Federer, Geometric Measure Theory, Springer, 1969.

26. J. Feydy, B. Charlier, F-X. Vialard, G. Peyré, Optimal transport for diffeomorphic registration, Medical Image Computing and Computer Assisted Intervention – MICCAI 2017 (2017) 291–299.

27. J.A. Glaunès, Transport par difféomorphismes de points, de mesures et de courants pour la comparaison de formes et l'anatomie numérique, PhD thesis, Université Paris 13, 2005.

28. J.A. Glaunès, P. Roussillon, Lddmm algorithms using currents and normal cycles (software), http://w3.mi.parisdescartes.fr/~glaunes/LDDMM_Currents_and_NormalCycles.zip, 2014–2018.

29. J.A. Glaunès, M. Vaillant, Surface matching via currents, in: Proceedings of Information Processing in Medical Imaging (IPMI), in: Lecture Notes in Computer Science, vol. 3565(381–392), 2006.

30. J.A. Glaunès, A. Trouvé, L. Younes, Diffeomorphic matching of distributions: a new approach for unlabelled point-sets and sub-manifolds matching, IEEE Computer Society Conference on Computer Vision and Pattern Recognition 2 (2004) 712–718.

31. J.A. Glaunès, A. Qiu, M.I. Miller, L. Younes, Large deformation diffeomorphic metric curve mapping, International Journal of Computer Vision 80 (3) (2008) 317–336.

32. Joan Glaunès, Sarang Joshi, Template estimation from unlabeled point set data and surfaces for computational anatomy, in: X. Pennec, S. Joshi (Eds.), Proc. of the International Workshop on the Mathematical Foundations of Computational Anatomy (MFCA-2006), 1st of October 2006, pp. 29–39.

33. P. Gori, O. Colliot, L. Marrakchi-Kacem, Y. Worbe, F. De Vico Fallani, M. Chavez, C. Poupon, A. Hartmann, N. Ayache, S. Durrleman, Parsimonious approximation of streamline trajectories in white matter fiber bundles, IEEE Transactions on Medical Imaging 35 (12) (2016) 2609–2619.

34. L. Greengard, J.-Y. Lee, Accelerating the nonuniform fast Fourier transform, SIAM Review (2004) 443.

35. L. Greengard, V. Rokhlin, A fast algorithm for particle simulations, Journal of Computational Physics 135 (2) (1987) 280–292.

36. T. Hofmann, B. Schölkopf, A.J. Smola, Kernel methods in machine learning, The Annals of Statistics 36 (3) (2008) 1171–1220.

37. S. Jain, D. Tward, D. Lee, A. Kolasny, T. Brown, T. Ratnanather, M. Miller, L. Younes, Computational anatomy gateway: leveraging XSEDE computational resources for shape analysis, in: Proceedings of the 2014 Annual Conference on Extreme Science and Engineering Discovery Environment, XSEDE '14, 2014, pp. 54:1–54:6.

38. S.C. Joshi, M.I. Miller, Landmark matching via large deformation diffeomorphisms, IEEE Transactions on Image Processing 9 (8) (2000) 1357–1370.

39. I. Kaltenmark, B. Charlier, N. Charon, A general framework for curve and surface comparison and registration with oriented varifolds, in: The IEEE Conference on Computer Vision and Pattern Recognition (CVPR), July 2017.

40. J. Keiner, S. Kunis, D. Potts, Using NFFT 3 – a software library for various nonequispaced fast Fourier transforms, ACM Transactions on Mathematical Software (2009) 2013–2037.

41. S. Lee, N. Fallah, F. Forooghian, A. Ko, K. Pakzad-Vaezi, A.B. Merkur, A.W. Kirker, D.A. Albiani, M. Young, M.V. Sarunic, M.F. Beg, Comparative analysis of repeatability of manual and automated choroidal thickness measurements in nonneovascular age-related macular degeneration, Investigative Ophthalmology & Visual Science 54 (4) (2013) 2864–2871.

42. S. Lee, N. Charon, B. Charlier, K. Popuri, E. Lebed, P.R. Ramana, M. Sarunic, A. Trouvé, M.F. Beg, Atlas-based shape analysis and classification of retinal optical coherence tomography images using the functional shape (fshape) framework, Medical Image Analysis 35 (2017) 570–581.

43. J. Ma, M.I. Miller, L. Younes, A Bayesian generative model for surface template estimation, Journal of Biomedical Imaging 2010 (January 2010) 16:1–16:14.

44. C. McGann, E. Kholmovski, J. Blauer, S. Vijayakumar, T. Haslam, J. Cates, E. DiBella, N. Burgon, B. Wilson, A. Alexander, M. Prastawa, M. Daccarett, G. Vergara, N. Akoum, D. Parker, R. MacLeod, N. Marrouche, Dark regions of no-reflow on late gadolinium enhancement magnetic resonance imaging result in scar formation after atrial fibrillation ablation, Journal of the American College of Cardiology 58 (2) (2011) 177–185.

45. C.A. Micchelli, M. Pontil, On learning vector-valued functions, Neural Computation 17 (1) (2005) 177–204.

46. M. Micheli, J.A. Glaunès, Matrix-valued kernels for shape deformation analysis, Geometry, Imaging, and Computing 1 (1) (2014) 57–139.

47. F. Morgan, Geometric Measure Theory, a Beginner's Guide, Academic Press, 1995.

48. Y. Pan, G. Christensen, O. Durumeric, S. Gerard, J. Reinhardt, G. Hugo, Current- and varifold-based registration of Lung Vessel and airway trees, in: IEEE Conference on Computer Vision and Pattern Recognition Workshops (CVPRW), 2016, pp. 566–573.

49. J. Ratnanather, T. Brown, H. Trinh, L. Younes, M.I. Miller, S. Mori, M. Albert, Shape analysis of hippocampus and amygdala in BIOCARD, Alzheimer's & Dementia 8 (2012) P63.
50. I. Rekik, G. Li, W. Lin, D. Shen, Multidirectional and topography-based dynamic-scale varifold representations with application to matching developing cortical surfaces, NeuroImage 135 (2016) 152–162.
51. L. Risser, F-X. Vialard, R. Wolz, M. Murgasova, D. Holm, D. Rueckert, Simultaneous multi-scale registration using large deformation diffeomorphic metric mapping, IEEE Transactions on Medical Imaging 30 (10) (2011) 1746–1759.
52. P. Roussillon, J.A. Glaunès, Kernel metrics on normal cycles and application to curve matching, SIAM Journal on Imaging Sciences 9 (2016) 1991–2038.
53. L. Schwartz, Sous-espaces hilbertiens d'espaces vectoriels topologiques et noyaux associés (noyaux reproduisants), Journal D'analyse Mathématique 13 (1) (Dec. 1964) 115–256.
54. M. Vaillant, A. Qiu, J.A. Glaunès, M.I. Miller, Diffeomorphic metric surface mapping in subregion of the superior temporal gyrus, NeuroImage 34 (3) (2007) 1149–1159.
55. C. Yang, R. Duraiswami, N.A. Gumerov, Improved Fast Gauss Transform, Technical report, 2003.
56. M. Zähle, Integral and current representation of Federer's curvature measure, Archiv der Mathematik 23 (1986) 557–567.
57. M. Zähle, Curvatures and currents for unions of set with positive reach, Geometriae Dedicata 23 (1987) 155–171.

13

A discretize–optimize approach for LDDMM registration

Thomas Polzin[a], Marc Niethammer[b,c],
François-Xavier Vialard[d], Jan Modersitzki[a,e]

[a]Institute of Mathematics and Image Computing, University of Lübeck, Lübeck, Germany. [b]Department of Computer Science, University of North Carolina at Chapel Hill, Chapel Hill, NC, United States. [c]Biomedical Research Imaging Center (BRIC), Chapel Hill, NC, United States. [d]Laboratoire d'informatique Gaspard Monge, Université Paris-Est Marne-la-Vallée, UMR CNRS 8049, Champs sur Marne, France. [e]Fraunhofer MEVIS, Lübeck, Germany

13.1 Introduction

The goal of image registration is to establish spatial correspondences between images. Image registration is a challenging but important task in image analysis. In particular, in medical image analysis image registration is a key tool to compare patient data in a common space, to allow comparisons between pre-, inter-, or post-intervention images, or to fuse data acquired from different and complementary imaging devices such as positron emission tomography (PET), computed tomography (CT), or magnetic resonance imaging (MRI) [56].

Image registration is of course not limited to medical imaging, but is important for a wide range of applications; for example, it is used in astronomy, biology/genetics, cartography, computer vision, and surveillance. Consequently, there exists a vast number of approaches and techniques; see, for example, [10,29,31,33,44, 56,65,66,84,87,91,97,109] and references therein.

Optical flow approaches [48,55] are popular and commonly used in computer vision [12,100,72,106,11]. However, computer vision applications typically have different requirements regarding spatial transformations than medical image analysis applications. For example, when processing natural images, objects, such as cars or people, should typically be allowed to move independently of the background. However, in many medical applications it is natural to constrain the sought-for mapping to be bijective or even diffeomorphic. In early days of image registration, transformation models were (and sometimes still are) constricted to

Riemannian Geometric Statistics in Medical Image Analysis
https://doi.org/10.1016/B978-0-12-814725-2.00022-4

rigid mappings, which obviously fulfill this constraint. However, more flexible, for example, deformable, transformation models are required to capture subtle localized changes. Early work on deformable image registration includes variational approaches based on elasticity theory [30,9,6], where a spatial transformation is represented nonparametrically (via a deformation field) and is regularized through an elastic potential function.

The mathematical reason for introducing the regularizer is to ensure solutions of the variational formulation. It may also be interpreted as a penalty for nonelasticity. Elastic registration has been widely and successfully used. However, an elastic regularizer can in general not guarantee that a computed mapping is bijective [23]. To ensure bijectivity, one may add constraints to a registration formulation. Alternatively, one can formulate a registration model that by construction guarantees the regularity of the transformation. Examples for the former approach are [79, 36,37]. While Rohlfing et al. [79] employed an additional penalty term on the determinant of the Jacobian of the transformation that improves transformation regularity but cannot guarantee bijective mappings, Haber and Modersitzki developed similar ideas, but with equality [36] or box constraints [37] thereby guaranteeing bijectivity. Nevertheless, Haber and Modersitzki still use a mathematical model based on linear elasticity theory, which is only appropriate for small deformations. As convex energies, such as the linear elastic potential, result in finite penalties, they are insufficient to guarantee one-to-one maps [13,24]. Therefore Burger et al. [13] used hyperelasticity and quasiconvex functions to obtain a registration model yielding bijective transformations while allowing for large deformations.

Another possibility to ensure diffeomorphic mappings (smooth mappings that are bijective and have a smooth inverse) is to express a transformation implicitly through velocity fields. The intuitive idea is that it is easy to ensure diffeomorphic transformations for small-scale displacements by using a sufficiently strong spatial regularization. Hence a complex diffeomorphic transform can be obtained, capturing large displacements, as the composition of a large or potentially infinite number of small-scale diffeomorphisms. These small-scale diffeomorphisms in turn can be obtained by integrating a static or time-dependent velocity field in time. Early work explored such ideas in the context of fluid-based image registration [23]. In fact, for approaches using velocity fields, the same regularizers as for the small displacement registration approaches (based on elasticity theory or the direct regularization of displacement fields) can be used. However, the regularizer is now applied to one or multiple velocity fields instead of a displacement field, and the transformation is obtained via time-integration of the velocity field.

The solution of the arising problems is computationally expensive, as in the most general case we now need to estimate a spatio-temporal velocity field instead of a static displacement field. Greedy solution approaches as well as solutions based on a stationary velocity field have been proposed to alleviate the computational burden (both in computational cost, but also with respect to memory requirements) [23,1,2,57]. However, these methods in general do not provide all the nice mathematical properties (metric, geodesics, etc.) of the nongreedy large deformation diffeomorphic metric mapping (LDDMM) registration approach [61], which we will explore numerically here.

Various numerical approaches have been proposed for LDDMM, for example, [23,61,96,7]. Traditionally, relaxation formulations [7] have been used to solve the LDDMM optimization problem. Here, one directly optimizes over spatio-temporal velocity fields, ensuring that the velocity field at any given time is sufficiently smooth. The resulting transformation, obtained via time-integration of the spatio-temporal velocity field, is used to deform the source image such that it becomes similar to the target image. Specifically, the LDDMM relaxation formulation is solved via an optimize–discretize approach [7], where a solution to the continuous time optimality conditions for the associated constrained optimization problem (the constraint being the relation between the spatial transformation and the velocity fields) is computed. These optimality conditions are the Euler–Lagrange equations corresponding to the constrained optimization problem and can be regarded as the continuous equivalent of the Karush–Kuhn–Tucker (KKT) [71, p. 321] equations of constrained optimization. To numerically determine a solution fulfilling the Euler–Lagrange equations, one uses an adjoint solution approach, which allows the efficient computation of the gradient of the LDDMM relaxation energy with respect to the spatio-temporal velocity field via a forward/backward sweep. This gradient can then be used within a gradient descent scheme or as the basis of sophisticated numerical solution approaches. Note that the adjoint solution approach is, for example, also at the core of the famous backpropagation algorithm for the training of neural networks [54] or the reverse mode of automatic differentiation [34, pp. 37].[1] For an LDDMM relaxation solution, a geodesic path (fulfilling the Euler–Lagrange equations exactly) is only obtained at convergence [7].

---

[1]Automatic differentiation is heavily used in modern approaches for deep learning to avoid manual computations of adjoint equations altogether.

More recently, shooting approaches like [3,98,70] have been proposed. Again, an optimize–discretize approach is used. Here, instead of numerically solving the Euler–Lagrange equations of the LDDMM energy (which can alternatively be represented via the Euler–Poincaré diffeomorphism equation [62] (EPDiff)), these Euler–Lagrange equations are imposed as a dynamical system, and the LDDMM energy is reformulated as an initial value problem. Hence all paths obtained during the optimization process are by construction geodesics—they may just not be the optimal ones. The price to pay for such a reduced parameterization is that one now optimizes over a second-order partial differential equation that describes the geodesic path. A simple analogy in the one-dimensional Euclidean space is that in relaxation, registration between two points is performed over all possible paths leading at convergence to a straight-line path. On the contrary, for shooting, we already know that the optimal solution should be a straight line, and consequentially optimization is only performed regarding the line slope and y-intercept.

Although the mathematical framework for LDDMM is very appealing, its numerical treatment is not trivial, may lead to non-diffeomorphic transformations, and is highly demanding both in terms of memory and computational costs. As discussed before, current LDDMM solutions are mainly based on optimize–discretize formulations, that is, optimality conditions are derived in continuous space and then discretized [7,62]. Not surprisingly, it is possible that a solution of the discrete equations is an optimizer neither for discrete nor for continuous energy [35].

Hence the goal of this chapter is to develop a discretize–optimize approach for LDDMM, where the starting point is the discretization of the *energy functional*. Consequentially, solutions to the associated optimality conditions are indeed optimizers of the discretized energy. Additionally, we integrate a suitable interpolation operator [51] into the LDDMM framework to reduce computational demands and memory consumption without losing registration accuracy. Furthermore, we use the so-called normalized gradient fields (NGF) distance measure, which is designed to align image edges [38,66]. NGF has been successfully applied to lung CT registration [81,51,74–76,82], which is one of our example applications in Section 13.8.

The chapter is organized as follows. In Section 13.2 the LDDMM concept is introduced, and two approaches [7,45] used for solving the constrained optimization problems are discussed. In Section 13.3 we extend these models, discuss the shooting approach, and formulate them in the context of general distance measures for images. For simplicity, Section 13.4 discusses the discretization of the models in the one-dimensional case. This allows introducing the basic ingredients (grids, regularization, derivatives, transport equation, etc.) required for the 3D formulation in a compact manner. In Section 13.5 we address the discretization and solution of the partial differential equations constraining the LDDMM models (e.g., the transport equations) via Runge–Kutta methods. The extension of the described formalism to 3D is given in Section 13.6. In Section 13.7 details on the numerical optimization and the solution of the optimization problems in a multilevel approach are provided. Afterward, in Section 13.8 we evaluate the performance of the proposed methods and present experimental results. Finally, we conclude the chapter with a discussion of the results and possible extensions in Section 13.9.

13.2 Background and related work

LDDMM is used to automatically establish correspondences between two (or more) given datasets, which are referred to as source and target (fixed and moving or reference and template are also common names). The data typically consist of images, landmarks (point clouds), or surfaces. In the following we restrict ourselves to the registration of three-dimensional images. However, when considering landmarks or surfaces, the main change of the presented approaches would be the data term.

Specifically, LDDMM registration estimates a time- and space-dependent velocity field $v \colon \Omega \times [0, 1] \to \mathbb{R}^3$, which flows the source image I^0 so that it matches as well as possible a target image I^1. Conceptually, the data dimension and the time-horizon are arbitrary,[2] but for ease of presentation, we assume that the data are three-dimensional, the images I^0 and I^1 are compactly supported on a domain $\Omega \subset \mathbb{R}^3$, and the time interval is $[0, 1]$.

Assuming that all structures are visible in the source and target images, after an ideal registration $I^0(\phi_1^{-1}(\mathbf{x})) = I^1(\mathbf{x})$ for all $\mathbf{x} \in \Omega$ for a transformation $\phi \colon \Omega \times [0, 1] \to \mathbb{R}^3$. This is, of course, not feasible in practice, either because there is no perfect structural correspondence or due to the presence of noise that precludes exact matching. Here we use the notation $\phi_t(\mathbf{x}) := \phi(\mathbf{x}, t)$. This notation will be used for all variables depending on space and time. In particular, in this notation the subscript is *not* related to a partial derivative. The sought-for transformation and the velocity fields are related via $\dot{\phi}_t(\mathbf{x}) = v_t(\phi_t(\mathbf{x}))$, $\phi_0(\mathbf{x}) = \mathbf{x}$, where $v_t(\mathbf{x}) := v(\mathbf{x}, t)$ and $\dot{\phi} = \partial_t \phi$. In the remainder of the chapter we will often, for a cleaner

---

[2]Although the spatial dimension is arbitrary, care has to be taken to ensure that the regularization is strong enough to ensure diffeomorphic results.

and more compact notation, omit the spatial argument and assume that equations hold for arbitrary $\mathbf{x} \in \Omega$. Furthermore, if t is not specified, then we assume that equations hold for all $t \in [0, 1]$.

Following the work of Beg et al. [7], a solution of the registration problem is given by a minimizer of the energy

$$
\left.\begin{aligned}
\mathcal{E}^{\text{Beg}}(v, \phi) \quad &:= \text{Reg}(v) + \text{Sim}^{\text{SSD}}(I^0 \circ \phi_1^{-1}, I^1) \\
\text{s.t.} \quad &\dot{\phi}_t = v_t \circ \phi_t, \ \phi_0 = \text{Id}.
\end{aligned}\right\}
\tag{13.1}
$$

The regularizer Reg enforces the smoothness of the velocity fields, and the distance measure (data fit) Sim^{SSD} is used to compute the similarity of the transformed source image $I^0 \circ \phi_1^{-1}$ at $t = 1$ and the target image I^1. The distance measure for images I and J is $\text{Sim}^{\text{SSD}}(I, J) = \frac{1}{2\sigma^2} \int_\Omega (I(\mathbf{x}) - J(\mathbf{x}))^2 \, d\mathbf{x}$ and is called the sum of squared differences (SSD). SSD is only one of many possibilities; see, for example, [66, p. 95]. We discuss further details and choices of distance measures in Section 13.3.4. The regularity of v is encouraged by employing a differential operator L in Reg:

$$
\left.\begin{aligned}
&\text{Reg}(v) := \tfrac{1}{2} \int_0^1 \|v_t\|_L^2 \, dt \text{ with} \\
&\|v_t\|_L^2 := \langle Lv_t, Lv_t \rangle := \int_\Omega v_t(\mathbf{x})^\top L^\dagger L v_t(\mathbf{x}) \, d\mathbf{x},
\end{aligned}\right\}
\tag{13.2}
$$

where $L^\dagger$ is the adjoint operator of L. We use the Helmholtz operator $L := (\gamma \, \text{Id} - \alpha \Delta)^\beta$, $\alpha, \gamma > 0$, and $\beta \in \mathbb{N}$, which is a typical choice [7,45,107]. Here Δ denotes the spatial vectorial Laplacian, and v_t^i, $i = 1, 2, 3$, is the ith component of v at time t:

$$
\Delta v_t(\mathbf{x}) := \begin{pmatrix} \sum_{i=1}^3 \partial_{x_i, x_i} v_t^1(\mathbf{x}) \\ \sum_{i=1}^3 \partial_{x_i, x_i} v_t^2(\mathbf{x}) \\ \sum_{i=1}^3 \partial_{x_i, x_i} v_t^3(\mathbf{x}) \end{pmatrix}.
\tag{13.3}
$$

Standard LDDMM models follow the optimize–discretize approach, that is, optimality conditions are computed for the continuous model through calculus of variations, and the resulting optimality conditions are then discretized. For example, in the derivation by Beg et al. [7] the variation of (13.1) with respect to v is computed resulting in optimality conditions of the form

$$
\left.\begin{aligned}
I_t \quad &:= I^0 \circ \phi_t^{-1}, \\
\lambda_t \quad &= |J_{\tau_t^{-1}}| \lambda_1 \circ \tau_t^{-1}, \\
L^\dagger L v_t + \lambda_t \nabla I_t \quad &= \mathbf{0},
\end{aligned}\right\}
\tag{13.4}
$$

with initial and final conditions

$$I_0 = I^0 \quad \text{and} \quad \lambda_1 = -\frac{1}{\sigma^2}\left(I^0 \circ \phi_1^{-1} - I^1\right), \qquad (13.5)$$

where $\tau_t := \tau(t)$ is the flow for the negative velocity field (with $\tau_1 = \mathrm{Id}$), and I_t is the transformed source image at time t. The adjoint variable $\lambda \colon \mathbb{R}^3 \times [0, 1] \to \mathbb{R}$ is initialized at $t = 1$ with the negative image mismatch (also called residual; see Section 13.3.4 on distance measures) scaled by the weighting factor $\frac{1}{\sigma^2} > 0$, which balances regularizer and distance measure energy. The spatial gradient of the image at time t is referred to as ∇I_t, and the Jacobian of the spatial variables of τ_t^{-1} is $\mathrm{J}_{\tau_t^{-1}}$. Note that the adjoint variable λ is also called the scalar momentum in the literature [98], and the quantity $\lambda \nabla I = m$ is the vector-valued momentum [90]. In fact, the optimality conditions can be written solely with respect to the vector-valued momentum m, resulting in the EPDiff equation; see, for example, [67].

Computing the variation leading to (13.4) and (13.5) in the optimize–discretize framework is rather involved. If the interest is only in I_1, alternatively the flow equation in the form of a transport equation in Eulerian coordinates can be added as a constraint to the optimization problem. This has been proposed by Borzí et al. [8] for optical flow and by Hart et al. [45] for LDDMM. Following [45], the LDDMM formulation then becomes

$$\left.\begin{aligned}
\mathcal{E}^{\mathrm{Hart}}(v, I) &= \mathrm{Reg}(v) + \mathrm{Sim}^{\mathrm{SSD}}(I_1, I^1), \\
\text{s.t.} \quad \dot{I}_t + \nabla I_t^{\top} v_t &= 0, \ I_0 = I^0,
\end{aligned}\right\} \qquad (13.6)$$

with the optimality conditions

$$\left.\begin{aligned}
\dot{I}_t + \nabla I_t^{\top} v_t &= 0, \ I_0 = I^0, \\
\dot{\lambda}_t + \mathrm{div}(\lambda_t v_t) &= 0, \ \lambda_1 = -\frac{1}{\sigma^2}(I_1 - I^1), \\
L^{\dagger} L v_t + \lambda_t \nabla I_t &= \mathbf{0}.
\end{aligned}\right\} \qquad (13.7)$$

The optimality conditions (13.4)–(13.5) and (13.7) are the same, but (13.7) are written directly in terms of the image I and the Lagrange multiplier λ. In practice both formulations are solved by computing the flows ϕ and τ from which the solution of the transport equation (for I) can be obtained by interpolation.[3] The solution for the scalar conservation law/the continuity equation for λ

---

[3]Whereas it is possible to solve the transport equation directly for the images (see Section 13.3.1), it is numerically much easier to solve for ϕ and τ as they will be spatially smooth; see Section 13.3.2.

is obtained by interpolation and local weighting by the determinant of the Jacobian of the transformation.

The advantage of the second optimize–discretize approach (13.6) is that the optimality conditions (13.7) are (relatively) easy to derive and retain physical interpretability. For example, it is immediately apparent that the adjoint to the transport equation is a scalar conservation law. However, great care needs to be taken to make sure that all equations and their boundary conditions are consistently discretized in the optimize–discretize approach. For example, it cannot be guaranteed that for any given discretization, the gradients computed based on the discretized optimality conditions will minimize the overall energy [35]. In particular, these formulations require interpolation steps, which can cause trouble with the optimization, because it is unclear how they should affect a discretized gradient. Furthermore, the flow equations can be discretized in various ways (e.g., by a semi-Lagrangian scheme [7], upwind schemes [45], etc.). But, as these discretizations are not considered part of the optimization, their effect on the gradient remains unclear.

Therefore we follow the discretize–optimize approach in image registration [66, p. 12], which starts out with a discretization of the energy to be minimized and derives the optimality conditions from this discretized representation. Our approach is related to the work by Wirth et al. [101,83] on geodesic calculus for shapes but approaches the problem from an optimal control viewpoint.

In [5] the diffeomorphic matching is phrased as an optimal control problem, which is solved using a discretize–optimize approach. This method is related to the approach we will propose, but instead of matching images, in [5] surfaces and point clouds are registered. Another difference is the use of explicit first-order Runge–Kutta methods (i.e., forward Euler discretization), whereas we are using fourth-order methods (see Section 13.5.1) to fulfill numerical stability considerations. Recently, Mang and Ruthotto [58] also formulated LDDMM registration as an optimal control problem using a discretize–optimize approach. Specifically, they use the Gauss–Newton approach, which improves the convergence rate compared to the L-BFGS method we will apply but requires the solution of additional linear systems. However, the biggest difference between our proposed approach and the approach by Mang et al. [58] is that we use explicit Eulerian discretizations of the partial differential equation constraints of LDDMM via Runge–Kutta methods, whereas Mang et al. [58] use Lagrangian methods. Although such Lagrangian methods are attractive as they eliminate the risk of numerical instabilities and allow for arbitrary time step sizes, they require frequent interpolations and consequentially become computationally demanding. Instead, our formulation operates on a fixed grid and only requires interpolations for the computation of the image distance measure. To avoid numerical instabilities due to too large time-steps, we investigate how an admissible step size can be chosen under easily obtainable estimations for the maximal displacement when using a fourth-order Runge–Kutta method. To illustrate the difference in computational requirements, we note that although in [58] experiments were performed on a compute node with 40 CPUs, the computation for a 3D registration (with a number of voxels per image that is only about 10% of the voxel numbers of the images we are registering) takes between 25 and 120 minutes and thus is two to five times slower than our proposed methods on a single CPU. This dramatic difference in computational effort is most likely due to the tracking of the points/particles in the Lagrangian setting or the required interpolations.

An optimal solution v^* fulfills the optimality conditions (e.g., (13.7)). However, these conditions need to be determined numerically. The classical approach, proposed in [7], is the so-called *relaxation* approach. Here, for a given v, the transport equation for I is solved forward in time and the adjoint equation for λ backward in time. Given I and λ, the gradient of the energy with respect to the velocity v at any point in space and time can be computed, i.e.,

$$\nabla_{v_t}\mathcal{E}(v, I) = L^\dagger L v_t + \lambda_t \nabla I_t, \tag{13.8}$$

which can then, for example, be used in a gradient descent solution scheme. In practice typically the Hilbert-gradient is used [7]

$$\nabla_{v_t}^H \mathcal{E}(v, I) = v_t + (L^\dagger L)^{-1}(\lambda_t \nabla I_t) \tag{13.9}$$

to improve numerical convergence.[4] Upon convergence, a relaxation approach will fulfill the optimality conditions, which describe a geodesic path [7]. Unfortunately, the optimality conditions will in practice frequently not be fulfilled exactly, and the relaxation approach requires optimization over the full spatio-temporal velocity field v, whereas the geodesic path is completely specified by its initial conditions, that is, its initial velocity v_0 and its initial image I_0. This has motivated the development of *shooting* approaches [3,98], where ones optimizes over the initial conditions of the geodesic directly instead of v. The numerical solution is similar to the relaxation approach in the sense that the adjoint system is derived to compute the gradient with respect to the

---

[4]Note that $(L^\dagger L)^{-1}$ amounts to a smoothing operation, and hence the Hilbert gradient is a spatially smoothed gradient.

initial conditions through a forward–backward sweep. Shooting approaches also allow for extensions to the LDDMM registration models, such as LDDMM-based geodesic regression [70].

A common problem with LDDMM is its large memory footprint and the high computational costs. For example, to register lung CT images, run times of up to three hours on a computer with 128 GB of RAM and 32 CPUs have been reported [86]. In particular, for the shooting approaches, several ideas to overcome these problems have been proposed. Marsland and McLachlan [59] and Durrleman et al. [27] use a limited number of control points for LDDMM and observe that the number of control points can be decreased substantially (i.e., much fewer control points than number of pixels or voxels are needed) without greatly impacting the registration result. Zhang et al. [107] exploit the smoothness of the velocities in the Fourier domain. The underlying idea is that the initial velocities of the geodesic shooting are band-limited and therefore can be well approximated by a limited number of elements of a finite-dimensional vector space.

In contrast to the brain MRI or synthetic examples discussed in most LDDMM publications (see, e.g., [7,27,107]), lung registration (our motivating registration application) requires aligning many small spatially distributed salient structures (such as vessels). Hence the spatial discretization for the images cannot be too coarse as it would otherwise risk ignoring these fine structures. We can still reduce computational costs and memory requirements by recognizing that velocity fields will be smooth. Specifically, as we assume that the structures of interest are well dispersed over the whole lung volume, we employ regular grids for the velocity fields (or momenta fields). However, as confirmed in our own previous work [76], velocity fields can be discretized more coarsely (about one quarter of resolution per dimension) than the images themselves due to their inherent smoothness. We thereby obtain a method that aligns images well without losing accuracy compared to higher-resolution approaches while reducing computational costs and memory requirements.

13.3 Continuous mathematical models

In this section we introduce the continuous models that will be solved in a discretize–optimize approach. Fig. 13.1 shows different options. To obtain a consistent discretization for relaxation and shooting, we would ideally like to start from a discretized LDDMM energy, derive the KKT conditions, impose the KKT conditions as a constraint, and then obtain a discretization of the

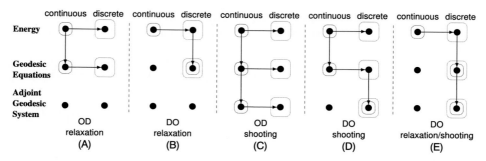

Figure 13.1. Different discretization options for LDDMM. Red (light gray in print version) squares indicate domains of numerical evaluation (all discrete), whereas the blue (dark gray in print version) squares indicate the domain of the optimality conditions. The standard approaches use an optimize–discretize approach. In particular, Beg et al. [7] use the relaxation approach (A), whereas Vialard et al. [98] use the shooting approach (C). An ideal approach would have consistent discretization for relaxation and shooting (E). However, this is difficult due to related requirements on the numerical integration approach. We therefore explore the discretize–optimize variants of relaxation (B) (see Section 13.5.3 and Section 13.5.4) and shooting (D) (see Section 13.5.5) in this chapter. In all discretize–optimize approaches the energy is consistent with the gradient used for optimization, which may not be the case for the optimize–discretize approaches. Furthermore, in shooting approaches the energy gets reformulated via the initial conditions of the geodesic equation, which is enforced and yields the adjoint geodesic system to compute the gradient with respect to the initial conditions.

shooting equations, which is consistent with the relaxation equations (i.e., the KKT equations of the discretized LDDMM energy). However, this is difficult in practice as it would no longer allow the use of explicit time-integration schemes. Instead, we suggest separate discretize–optimize approaches for the relaxation and the shooting formulations of LDDMM. For the discretize–optimize formulation of relaxation, we simply discretize the LDDMM energy including the transport equation constraint. We discuss in Section 13.3.1 the related continuous relaxation energies for the direct transport of images, whereas in Section 13.3.2 the corresponding energies for the transport of maps are considered. Alternatively, for the discretize–optimize approach for the shooting formulation of LDDMM, it is sensible to start with the discretized energy of the continuous shooting model including the associated constraints given by the EPDiff equation, which are described in Section 13.3.3.

In contrast to the methods presented in Section 13.2, we will use a general distance measure in what follows. Specifically, distance measures quantify the similarity of images by assigning a low (scalar) value to image pairs that are similar and a large value to image pairs that are different. Formally, we define the set of gray-value images as $\mathcal{I} := \{I : \Omega \to \mathbb{R}\}$. A distance measure is a mapping $\mathrm{Sim} : \mathcal{I} \times \mathcal{I} \to \mathbb{R}$ [65, p. 55]. We assume that the distance measure is differentiable and that $\nabla_A \mathrm{Sim}(A, B)$ is the derivative with respect to the first image. In Section 13.3.4 we give details of the used distance measures. Next, we describe the models we will use for registration. These are extensions of the methods in Section 13.2 and are called IBR, MBR, and MBS, respectively, where I means image, M map, B based, R relaxation, and S shooting.

13.3.1 Relaxation with transport of images (IBR)

We extend the relaxation model of Hart et al. [45] (see (13.6)) via a general differentiable distance measure Sim. This model is a relaxation model as the optimization is performed with respect to the full spatio-temporal velocity field in $t \in [0, 1]$. This is in contrast to shooting approaches where images (or transformations) are following a flow determined completely by initial conditions at $t = 0$; see Section 13.3.3. We do not explicitly model a transformation ϕ to transform the source image, but directly compute the image mismatch between the modeled image at $t = 1$ ($I(1) = I_1$) and the target image $I^1 \in \mathcal{I}$:

$$\left. \begin{array}{ll} \underset{v}{\arg\min}\, \mathcal{E}_1(v, I) & \text{s.t. } \dot{I}_t + \nabla I_t^\top v_t = 0, \ I_0 = I^0, \\[2mm] \text{with} & \mathcal{E}_1(v, I) = \text{Reg}(v) + \text{Sim}(I_1, I^1). \end{array} \right\} \quad (13.10)$$

13.3.2 Relaxation with transport of maps (MBR)

Typically, the spatial transform ϕ is of interest and needs to be computed, for example, to calculate local volume changes during respiration [95]. This transform can be computed via time-integration of the spatio-temporal velocity field. Hence, in Eulerian coordinates we now advect a deformation map instead of an image. When solving the transport equation this is advantageous because the deformations are smooth by design and thus suffer less from dissipation effects than images.

As our goal is to work with fixed computational grids (i.e., in Eulerian coordinates), we can also write the evolution equation for the inverse map ϕ_1^{-1} in Eulerian coordinates. The inverse transformation ϕ_1^{-1} is required to deform the source image to the coordinate system of the target image (i.e., $I^0 \circ \phi_1^{-1}$; see (13.1)).

The evolution of ϕ_1^{-1} is given by [63].

$$\dot{\phi}_t^{-1} = -J_{\phi_t^{-1}} v_t, \ \phi_0^{-1} = \text{Id}, \quad (13.11)$$

which is nothing else than a set of independent transport equations for the coordinate functions (x, y, and z in 3D). Here, we use the spatial Jacobian ($J_\phi := J_\phi(\mathbf{x}, t) \in \mathbb{R}^{3 \times 3}$) of $\phi = (\phi^1, \phi^2, \phi^3)^\top$, which is defined as

$$J_\phi := \begin{pmatrix} \partial_{x_1}\phi_t^1(\mathbf{x}) & \partial_{x_2}\phi_t^1(\mathbf{x}) & \partial_{x_3}\phi_t^1(\mathbf{x}) \\ \partial_{x_1}\phi_t^2(\mathbf{x}) & \partial_{x_2}\phi_t^2(\mathbf{x}) & \partial_{x_3}\phi_t^2(\mathbf{x}) \\ \partial_{x_1}\phi_t^3(\mathbf{x}) & \partial_{x_2}\phi_t^3(\mathbf{x}) & \partial_{x_3}\phi_t^3(\mathbf{x}) \end{pmatrix}. \tag{13.12}$$

Note, that we used superscripts to refer to the components of vectors such as $\phi(\mathbf{x}, t) \in \mathbb{R}^3$. As the point of view for the time direction of the transformations is arbitrary, we change the notation of the inverse transformation used in [7] (see also (13.1)) for convenience to ϕ. This results in the simplified notation

$$\dot{\phi}_t + J_{\phi_t} v_t = \mathbf{0}, \quad \phi_0 = \text{Id}. \tag{13.13}$$

We use (13.13) as the constraint for the map-based optimization problem:

$$\left. \begin{array}{ll} \underset{v}{\arg\min}\, \mathcal{E}_2(\phi, v) & \text{s.t. } \dot{\phi}_t + J_{\phi_t} v_t = \mathbf{0}, \ \phi_0 = \text{Id}, \\ \text{with} & \mathcal{E}_2(\phi, v) := \text{Reg}(v) + \text{Sim}(I^0 \circ \phi_1, I^1). \end{array} \right\} \tag{13.14}$$

13.3.3 Shooting with maps using EPDiff (MBS)

Recall that the optimality conditions of the relaxation formulation can be written with respect to the vector-valued momentum m only. Hence, instead of obtaining a solution to these optimality conditions at convergence (as done in the relaxation approach), we simply enforce these optimality conditions as constraints in an optimization problem. This is the shooting approach [62,98]. Specifically, if we express these conditions with respect to the momentum, then we obtain the EPDiff equation (abbreviation for the Euler–Poincaré equation on the group of diffeomorphisms) [47, 61,105]

$$\dot{m}_t = -J_{m_t} v_t - m_t \text{div}(v_t) - J_{v_t}^\top m_t, \quad v_t = K m_t. \tag{13.15}$$

Here $m \colon \Omega \times [0, 1] \to \mathbb{R}^3$ is the momentum, and $K = (L^\dagger L)^{-1}$ is a smoothing kernel. This equation describes a geodesic path and fully determines the transformation as it implies an evolution of the velocities v via $v_t = K m_t$. The total momentum will be constant for a geodesic due to the conservation of momentum [104, 98]:

$$\langle K m_0, m_0 \rangle = \langle K m_t, m_t \rangle, \quad t \in [0, 1]. \tag{13.16}$$

If we integrate (13.15) and (13.16) into (13.14), then the minimization problem has the following form:

$$
\left.\begin{array}{l}
\underset{m_0}{\arg\min}\, \mathcal{E}_3(m, \phi, v) \\[4pt]
\text{s.t.} \quad \partial_t\phi + J_\phi v = 0, \ \ \phi_0 = \text{Id}, \\[4pt]
\qquad \partial_t m + J_m v + m\,\text{div}(v) + J_v^\top m = 0, \\[4pt]
\qquad v = Km, \\[4pt]
\text{with } \mathcal{E}_3 := \tfrac{1}{2}\int_0^1 \langle m_t, Km_t\rangle\, \mathrm{d}t + \text{Sim}(I^0 \circ \phi_1, I^1) \\[4pt]
\qquad \overset{(13.16)}{=} \tfrac{1}{2}\langle m_0, Km_0\rangle + \text{Sim}(I^0 \circ \phi_1, I^1).
\end{array}\right\}
\qquad (13.17)
$$

13.3.4 Distance measures

Registration quality depends on the appropriateness of the deformation model and the distance measure. Different distance measures can easily be integrated into LDDMM; see [22,4]. Note that we formulate our models in generality and that the following derivations hold for a large class of differentiable distance measures [66, p. 109]:

$$
\text{Sim}(A, B) := \frac{1}{\sigma^2}\psi(r(A, B)), \qquad (13.18)
$$

where r is the residuum or image mismatch of A and B, and ψ is typically an integral of the residual values. The functions r and ψ are assumed to be at least once differentiable. This is necessary to allow derivative-based optimization, which we are using in our discretize–optimize schemes. Data fidelity and regularity are balanced via the weight $\sigma > 0$, which can be interpreted as the image noise level. We use two different differentiable distance measures in our experiments. The L^2-based distance measure sum of squared differences (SSD) [65, p. 56] is used in most LDDMM publications (see, e.g., [7,45,107]):

$$
\text{Sim}^{\text{SSD}}(A, B) = \frac{1}{2\sigma^2}\int_\Omega (A(\mathbf{x})) - B(\mathbf{x}))^2 \mathrm{d}\mathbf{x}. \qquad (13.19)
$$

Hence $\psi^{\text{SSD}}(r) = \tfrac{1}{2}\int_\Omega r(\mathbf{x})^2 \mathrm{d}\mathbf{x}$, and the residuum is the difference $r^{\text{SSD}}(A, B) = A - B$. As motivated in Section 13.1, we will use the normalized gradient field (NGF) distance measure for the registration of lung CT images. NGF aligns image edges [38,66] and is popular for lung CT registration [81,51,74–76]:

$$
\text{Sim}^{\text{NGF}}(A, B) := \frac{1}{\sigma^2}\int_\Omega 1 - \frac{\langle \nabla A, \nabla B\rangle_\varepsilon^2}{\|\nabla A\|_\varepsilon^2 \|\nabla B\|_\varepsilon^2}\, \mathrm{d}\mathbf{x} \qquad (13.20)
$$

with $\langle \mathbf{u}, \mathbf{v} \rangle_\varepsilon := \varepsilon^2 + \sum_{i=1}^{3} u_i v_i$ and $\|\mathbf{u}\|_\varepsilon^2 := \langle \mathbf{u}, \mathbf{u} \rangle_\varepsilon$ for $\mathbf{u}, \mathbf{v} \in \mathbb{R}^3$. Throughout this chapter we set $\varepsilon = 50$ for lung CT registrations. Rewriting $\mathrm{Sim}^{\mathrm{NGF}}$ with ψ and r yields:

$$\psi^{\mathrm{NGF}}(r) = \int_\Omega 1 - r(\mathbf{x})^2 d\mathbf{x}, \qquad r^{\mathrm{NGF}}(A, B) = \frac{\langle \nabla A, \nabla B \rangle_\varepsilon}{\|\nabla A\|_\varepsilon \|\nabla B\|_\varepsilon}.$$

This concludes the description of the continuous LDDMM models. In the following sections we present their discretization.

13.4 Discretization of the energies

In this section we describe the numerical computation of the continuous energies introduced in Section 13.3. We start with the description of the different regular grids, which are used for discretization of the velocities, images, transformations, et cetera in Section 13.4.1. The discretization of the regularizer and the distance measures is addressed in Section 13.4.2 and Section 13.4.3 respectively.

13.4.1 Discretization on grids

We use regular grids to discretize v, I, ϕ, et cetera in time and space. To properly handle boundary conditions, it is important to discuss on which grid the velocities and images are given. In particular, we choose nodal grids for the velocities v and transformations ϕ and cell-centered grids for the images I. For simplicity, we start with the discretization for the one-dimensional space. We assume that the discrete source and target images have $M \in \mathbb{N}$ values located at equidistant centers of intervals whose union is the closure of the domain $\bar{\Omega} = [\omega_1, \omega_2] \subset \mathbb{R}$. For the nodal grids $n \in \mathbb{N}$, $n \geq 2$ points are used. Details on both types of grids are given, for example, in [66, p. 125].

Fig. 13.2 shows two example grids. The nodal grid is depicted as blue (dark gray in print version) squares, whereas the cell-centered grid is visualized as red (light gray in print version) dots. Note that the number of cells for images and velocities does not need to be equal. In fact, it is the key idea of our approach to speed up computations and reduce memory requirements by discretizing velocity and transformation fields on a lower resolution grid than the images, that is, $n < M$. Consequently, we have different spatial step sizes $h_1^v := \frac{\omega_2 - \omega_1}{n-1}$ and $h_1^I := \frac{\omega_2 - \omega_1}{M}$. As we consider only one dimension first, we will omit the indices and write h^v and h^I. The time axis $[0, 1]$ is discretized for v, ϕ, and I on a nodal grid with N time steps, and accordingly the time step size is $h_t := \frac{1}{N-1}$. The

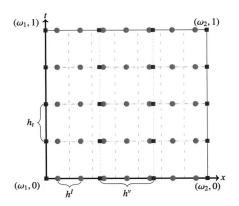

Figure 13.2. Examples for 1D grids for discrete points in time. The image grid points are cell-centered and plotted as red (light gray in print version) circles, whereas the grid points for v and ϕ are nodal and plotted as blue (dark gray in print version) squares. The parameters for these grids are $N = 5$, $M = 7$, and $n = 4$.

resulting nodal grid is $\mathbf{x}^{\mathrm{nd}} \in \mathbb{R}^{nN}$, and the cell-centered image grid is a vector $\mathbf{x}^{\mathrm{cc}} \in \mathbb{R}^{MN}$. The discretized velocity field is then given as $\mathbf{v} := v(\mathbf{x}^{\mathrm{nd}}) \in \mathbb{R}^{n \times N}$. Accordingly, the images are discretized as $\mathbf{I} := I(\mathbf{x}^{\mathrm{cc}}) \in \mathbb{R}^{M \times N}$.

When solving the constraint equations (e.g., the transport equation for images in (13.10)), we need images and velocities discretized at the same resolution. We therefore use a linear grid interpolation (bi/trilinear for 2D/3D data). The appropriate weights are stored in the components of the interpolation matrix $\mathbf{P} \in \mathbb{R}^{M \times n}$. See [51,80] on how to compute the weights and how to implement a matrix-free computation of the matrix–matrix product. By multiplying the velocity matrix $\mathbf{v}$ with the matrix $\mathbf{P}$ we obtain a cell-centered discretization $\mathbf{Pv} \in \mathbb{R}^{M \times N}$, which can be used to transport the intensities located at the image grid points. When solving the adjoint equation of, for example, (13.7), the transposed matrix has to be used to interpolate the derivative of the distance measure to the nodal grid to update the velocities.

13.4.2 Discretization of the regularizer

Two main computations are required to discretize the regularization term. First, we compute the differential operator L, which is based on second derivatives, and its effect on the velocity field to be regularized. Second, we approximate the integral of the regularizer using numerical quadrature. In particular, we use the trapezoidal rule. Here we formulate everything initially in 1D for simplicity and assume Neumann boundary conditions for the velocities v and Dirichlet boundary conditions for the images throughout. The discretized regularizer has the form

$$\text{Reg}^h(\bar{\mathbf{v}}) := \frac{h^v h_t}{2} \bar{\mathbf{v}}^\top \bar{\mathbf{L}}^\top \mathbf{W} \bar{\mathbf{L}} \bar{\mathbf{v}}, \tag{13.21}$$

and we proceed with details on the computation of $\bar{\mathbf{L}}$, $\bar{\mathbf{v}}$, and $\mathbf{W}$.

We use a standard approach to discretize the Helmholtz operator $L = (\gamma \, \text{Id} - \alpha \Delta)^\beta$ with Neumann boundary conditions; see, for example, [92]. The derivatives are approximated with central finite differences. The proper choice of the parameters $\alpha, \gamma > 0$ and $\beta \in \mathbb{N}$ depends on the application and in particular on the spatial dimension $k \in \mathbb{N}$. For instance, to obtain diffeomorphic solutions for $k = 3$, at least $\beta = 2$ is needed [26]. To be more precise, using Sobolev embedding theorems [108, p. 62], the following inequality has to be fulfilled (see [60] and references therein):

$$s > \frac{k}{2} + 1, \tag{13.22}$$

where s is the order of the H^s metric used for the velocity fields v_t, $t \in [0, 1]$. For $\mathbf{v} \in \mathbb{R}^{n \times N}$, the discrete operator is $\mathbf{L} \in \mathbb{R}^{n \times n}$:

$$\mathbf{L} := (\gamma \, \text{Id}_n - \alpha \Delta^{h^v})^\beta, \tag{13.23}$$

where $\text{Id}_n \in \mathbb{R}^{n \times n}$ is the identity matrix, and

$$\Delta^{h^v} := \frac{1}{(h^v)^2} \begin{pmatrix} -1 & 1 & & & \\ 1 & -2 & 1 & & \\ & \ddots & \ddots & \ddots & \\ & & 1 & -2 & 1 \\ & & & 1 & -1 \end{pmatrix} \tag{13.24}$$

is a discrete Laplacian operator. We use a trapezoidal quadrature for integration in space and time. The different weights for inner and outer grid points are assigned by multiplication with the diagonal matrix $\mathbf{W} \in \mathbb{R}^{nN \times nN}$. Kronecker products are used for a compact notation and to compute $\bar{\mathbf{L}} \in \mathbb{R}^{nN \times nN}$, which enables regularization for all time steps at once:

$$\left. \begin{aligned} \mathbf{W} &:= \mathbf{W}_N \otimes \mathbf{W}_n, \\ \mathbf{W}_p &:= \text{diag}(\tfrac{1}{2}, 1, \dots, 1, \tfrac{1}{2}) \in \mathbb{R}^{p \times p}, \\ \bar{\mathbf{L}} &:= \text{Id}_N \otimes \mathbf{L}. \end{aligned} \right\} \tag{13.25}$$

If we use the column-vector representation of $\mathbf{v}$,

$$\bar{\mathbf{v}} := (v_{1,1}, \dots, v_{n,1}, v_{1,2}, \dots, v_{n,2}, \dots, v_{1,N}, \dots, v_{n,N})^\top,$$

and (13.25), then we obtain (13.21) for the discretized regularizer.

13.4.3 Discretization of the distance measures

For simplicity, we only give details of the discretization of the SSD distance measure defined in (13.19). For two discrete one-dimensional images $\mathbf{A} = (a_i)_{i=1}^M$ and $\mathbf{B} = (b_i)_{i=1}^M$ (e.g., the discrete source ($\mathbf{I}^0$) and target ($\mathbf{I}^1$) images), we use a midpoint quadrature to compute the discrete distance measure value

$$\text{Sim}^{h,\text{SSD}}(\mathbf{A}, \mathbf{B}) = \frac{h^I}{2\sigma^2} \sum_{i=1}^M (a_i - b_i)^2 =: \psi(\mathbf{r}). \qquad (13.26)$$

Hence the discrete residual for SSD is $\mathbf{r} := \mathbf{r}(\mathbf{A}, \mathbf{B}) = (a_i - b_i)_{i=1}^M$, and the discrete outer function is given as $\psi(\mathbf{r}) = \frac{h^I}{2\sigma^2} \sum_{i=1}^M r_i^2$. The numerical gradient, which will be needed for numerical optimization, consists of the following derivatives:

$$\nabla \psi(\mathbf{r}) = \frac{h^I}{\sigma^2} \mathbf{r} \in \mathbb{R}^M, \; \partial_i r_j = \delta_{i,j}, \; i, j = 1, \ldots, M. \qquad (13.27)$$

Hence the numerical Jacobian of $\mathbf{r}$ is just the identity matrix, $\nabla_{\mathbf{A}} \mathbf{r} = \text{Id}_M \in \mathbb{R}^{M \times M}$. Based on these results, (13.27), and the chain rule, we obtain the numerical gradient for the distance measure:

$$\nabla_{\mathbf{A}} \text{Sim}^{h,\text{SSD}}(\mathbf{A}, \mathbf{B}) = (\nabla_{\mathbf{A}} \mathbf{r})^\top \nabla \psi(\mathbf{r}) = \frac{h^I}{\sigma^2} \mathbf{r}. \qquad (13.28)$$

We transposed the inner and outer derivative in (13.28) as we assume column vector gradients throughout the chapter. For discretizations of SSD in multiple dimensions or other distance measures, such as NGF, we refer to [66, p. 107].

13.5 Discretization and solution of PDEs

The partial differential equations we need to solve are the transport/advection equation, the EPDiff equation, and the adjoint equations of the models (13.10), (13.14), and (13.17).

The standard LDDMM registrations use semi-Lagrangian methods [7] or upwinding for the solution of the transport equation [45]. In this work semi-Lagrangian methods are not used as they require interpolations at every time step and hence have substantially increased computational costs. Upwinding includes logical switches, which interfere with our model, which requires differentiable constraints. We therefore focus on methods that use central differences to compute spatial derivatives. However, this then requires appropriate schemes for time-integration as, for example, an Euler forward scheme, which is known to be unconditionally unstable in such a case [92] for the solution of the transport equation. An implicit scheme generates stable solutions, but solving many linear equation systems is too expensive for our image registration purposes. As a compromise, we use explicit fourth-order Runge–Kutta methods, which have a sufficiently large stability region (and in particular include part of the imaginary axis) and have acceptable computational requirements; see Section 13.5.1. In Section 13.5.2 we describe how to consistently solve the adjoint equations (e.g., scalar conservation/continuity equations). We then apply these approaches to the IBR (Section 13.5.3), MBR (Section 13.5.4), and MBS (Section 13.5.5) models.

First, consider the one-dimensional transport equation, which is part of the IBR model:

$$\dot{I}_t + (\partial_x I_t)v_t = 0, \quad I_0 = I^0. \tag{13.29}$$

The spatial derivative is approximated with central finite differences and homogeneous Dirichlet boundary conditions are assumed for the images. The matrix to compute the discrete image derivatives is

$$\mathbf{D}_1^I = \frac{1}{2h^I} \begin{pmatrix} 1 & 1 & & & \\ -1 & 0 & 1 & & \\ & \ddots & \ddots & \ddots & \\ & & -1 & 0 & 1 \\ & & & -1 & -1 \end{pmatrix} \in \mathbb{R}^{m \times m}. \tag{13.30}$$

For $t_\ell = \ell h_t \in [0, 1]$, $\ell = 0, \ldots, N - 1$, we approximate the spatial derivative for all image grid points $\mathbf{x}^{\mathrm{cc}}$ as

$$\partial_x I(\mathbf{x}^{\mathrm{cc}}, t_\ell) \approx \mathbf{D}_1^I \mathbf{I}_\ell, \tag{13.31}$$

where $\mathbf{I}_\ell$ is the $(\ell + 1)$th column of $\mathbf{I}$, that is, the image at time t_ℓ.

13.5.1 Runge–Kutta methods

In the following we will use notation that is common in optimal control publications. In particular, $\mathbf{x}$ is not a spatial variable, but it is the state we are interested in, for example, an evolving image or transformation map. Solving the transport equation (13.29) is an initial value problem of the form

$$\dot{\mathbf{x}}(t) = f(\mathbf{x}(t), \mathbf{u}(t)), \quad \mathbf{x}_0 := \mathbf{x}(0) = \mathbf{x}^0, \ t \in [0, 1], \tag{13.32}$$

where $\mathbf{x}(t) \in \mathbb{R}^p$ with initial value $\mathbf{x}_0 = \mathbf{x}^0 \in \mathbb{R}^p$ is the state variable, and $\mathbf{u}(t) \in \mathbb{R}^q$ is an external input called control. The change over time is governed by the right-hand side function $f: \mathbb{R}^p \times \mathbb{R}^q \to \mathbb{R}^p$.

To avoid excessive smoothing when solving (13.29) numerically, we do not use methods that introduce additional diffusion to ensure stability for the Euler forward method such as Lax–Friedrichs [92]. Instead, we use a Runge–Kutta method, which includes at least part of the imaginary axis in its stability region. We can then discretize the spatial derivative of the transport equation using central differences as given in (13.30) and (13.31) while still maintaining numerical stability.

Runge–Kutta methods have been investigated in the context of optimal control, for example, by Hager [39,40]. Since we are dealing with a Hamiltonian system, we would ideally like to pick a symplectic Runge–Kutta scheme [43, p. 179] as proposed for image registration in [59]. Consistent approximations have been explored in [89]. In particular, we are interested in a symplectic symmetric Runge–Kutta scheme [20], which preserves the energy of the system (here the Sobolev norm of the velocity) [85]. Energy-preserving Runge–Kutta methods have been investigated in [19]. The simplest such method is the implicit midpoint method [59, 19]. However, implicit Runge–Kutta methods require the solution of an equation system at every iteration step. Although this can be accomplished by Newton's method or a fixed point iteration, it may compromise the symplectic property [93] and can become computationally costly.

We therefore restrict ourselves to explicit Runge–Kutta methods, which are nonsymplectic, but easy to implement, fast, and (at sufficiently high order) are only mildly dissipative and hence, experimentally, do not lose a significant amount of energy for the short time-periods we are integrating over for image registration.

We restrict the discussion to Runge–Kutta methods with $s \in \mathbb{N}$ stages. See [42, p. 132] for details. In the general case considered now, f has an explicit time dependence $f: [0, 1] \times \mathbb{R}^p \times \mathbb{R}^q \to \mathbb{R}^p$. Given the state variable $\mathbf{x}^0 = \mathbf{x}(t_0) = \mathbf{x}_0 \in \mathbb{R}^p$ with $t_\ell := \frac{\ell}{N-1} = \ell h_t$ and the control $\mathbf{u}_\ell^i \in \mathbb{R}^q$, $\ell = 0, 1, \ldots, N - 1$, $i = 1, \ldots, s$, the evolution of the state over time ($\mathbf{x}_\ell$, $\ell = 1, \ldots, N - 1$) is computed with these methods.

One-step Runge–Kutta methods can be written as [42, p. 134]

$$
\left.
\begin{aligned}
\mathbf{y}_\ell^i &= \mathbf{x}_\ell + h_t \sum_{j=1}^s a_{ij} f(t_\ell + c_j h_t, \mathbf{y}_\ell^j, \mathbf{u}_\ell^j) \\
\mathbf{x}_{\ell+1} &= \mathbf{x}_\ell + h_t \sum_{i=1}^s b_i f(t_\ell + c_i h_t, \mathbf{y}_\ell^i, \mathbf{u}_\ell^i), \\
i &= 1, \ldots, s, \ \ell = 0, \ldots, N - 2.
\end{aligned}
\right\}
\tag{13.33}
$$

Table 13.1 Butcher tableaux of the fourth-order explicit Runge–Kutta methods used in this chapter. For the adjoint system, the matrix $\bar{A}$ with $\bar{a}_{ij} = \frac{b_j a_{ji}}{b_i}$, $i, j = 1, \ldots, s$, is given.

General Butcher tableau	Runge–Kutta 4	Adjoint Runge–Kutta 4
$\dfrac{\mathbf{c}\;\mid\;\mathbf{A}}{\quad\mid\;\mathbf{b}^{\top}}$	$\begin{array}{c\|cccc} 0 & 0 & 0 & 0 & 0 \\ \frac{1}{2} & \frac{1}{2} & 0 & 0 & 0 \\ \frac{1}{2} & 0 & \frac{1}{2} & 0 & 0 \\ 1 & 0 & 0 & 1 & 0 \\ \hline & \frac{1}{6} & \frac{1}{3} & \frac{1}{3} & \frac{1}{6} \end{array}$	$\begin{array}{c\|cccc} 0 & 0 & 1 & 0 & 0 \\ \frac{1}{2} & 0 & 0 & \frac{1}{2} & 0 \\ \frac{1}{2} & 0 & 0 & 0 & \frac{1}{2} \\ 1 & 0 & 0 & 0 & 0 \\ \hline & \frac{1}{6} & \frac{1}{3} & \frac{1}{3} & \frac{1}{6} \end{array}$

According to (13.32) and our definition of f, $\mathbf{x}_{\ell+1} \approx \mathbf{x}(t_{\ell+1})$ is the approximated state, $\mathbf{y}_\ell^i \approx \mathbf{x}(t_\ell + c_i h_t)$ are the intermediate discrete states, and $\mathbf{u}_\ell^i := \mathbf{u}(t_\ell + c_i h_t)$ are the given discrete control variables. The matrix $\mathbf{A} \in \mathbb{R}^{s \times s}$ and the vectors $\mathbf{c}$, $\mathbf{b} \in \mathbb{R}^s$ depend on the chosen Runge–Kutta method. If $c_1 = 0$ and $\mathbf{A}$ is lower triangular, then the Runge–Kutta method is explicit; otherwise, it is implicit [14, p. 98]. In Table 13.1, $\mathbf{A}$, $\mathbf{b}$, and $\mathbf{c}$ are given in the so-called Butcher tableau for the fourth-order Runge–Kutta methods used for solving the state and adjoint equations in this work.

Because all considered constraints can be written in the form of (13.32) and thus do not have an explicit dependence on time, we can simplify (13.33) to

$$\left.\begin{array}{l} \mathbf{y}_\ell^i = \mathbf{x}_\ell + h_t \sum_{j=1}^s a_{ij} f(\mathbf{y}_\ell^j, \mathbf{u}_\ell^j), \\ \mathbf{x}_{\ell+1} = \mathbf{x}_\ell + h_t \sum_{i=1}^s b_i f(\mathbf{y}_\ell^i, \mathbf{u}_\ell^i), \\ i = 1, \ldots, s, \; \ell = 0, \ldots, N-2. \end{array}\right\} \qquad (13.34)$$

13.5.2 Runge–Kutta methods for the adjoint system

As mentioned before, a consistent discretization of the energies and constraints is desirable. Therefore when using Runge–Kutta integrations for time-dependent constraints, we need to compute the adjoint model of the chosen Runge–Kutta integrator. This was worked out by [40]. For completeness, we give the result using our notation. Note that the optimal control problems for the relaxation approaches considered in this chapter are Bolza problems of the form

$$\left.\begin{array}{l} \arg\min_{\mathbf{x}(1),\mathbf{u}} E^{\mathrm{B}}(\mathbf{x}(1), \mathbf{u}) \\ \text{s.t. } \dot{\mathbf{x}}(t) = f(\mathbf{x}, \mathbf{u}), \; \mathbf{x}(0) = \mathbf{x}_0 = \mathbf{x}^0, \\ E^{\mathrm{B}}(\mathbf{x}(1), \mathbf{u}) := C_1(\mathbf{x}(1)) + \int_0^1 C_2(\mathbf{x}(t), \mathbf{u}(t))\mathrm{d}t. \end{array}\right\} \qquad (13.35)$$

Here $C_1 \colon \mathbb{R}^p \to \mathbb{R}$ is only depending on the final state (corresponding to the distance measure in the image registration), and $C_2 \colon \mathbb{R}^p \times \mathbb{R}^q \to \mathbb{R}$ is a cost function depending on all intermediate states and controls (which is the regularization part in LDDMM). In [40] Mayer problems with

$$
\left.
\begin{aligned}
&\arg\min_{\mathbf{x}(1)} E^{\mathrm{M}}(\mathbf{x}(1)) \\
&\text{s.t. } \dot{\mathbf{x}}(t) = f(\mathbf{x}, \mathbf{u}), \ \mathbf{x}_0 = \mathbf{x}(0) = \mathbf{x}^0
\end{aligned}
\right\}
\tag{13.36}
$$

are solved. Mayer and Bolza problems are equivalent as they can be converted into each other [25, p. 159], and hence the results of Hager still apply to our problems. For the sake of a compact notation, we omit the superscripts M and B. Next, we briefly summarize how to obtain the adjoint equations of (13.35); for a complete derivation, see [40].

We introduce the arrays

$$
\mathbf{X} := (\mathbf{x}_\ell)_{\ell=0}^{N-1} \in \mathbb{R}^{p \times N}, \quad \mathbf{Y} := (\mathbf{y}_\ell^i)_{\ell=0,i=1}^{N-1,s} \in \mathbb{R}^{p \times N \times s},
$$
$$
\mathbf{U} := (\mathbf{u}_\ell^i)_{\ell=0,i=1}^{N-1,s} \in \mathbb{R}^{q \times N \times s},
$$

which contain all discrete states, intermediate states, and control variables. Following [40] and given the discretized energy $E(\mathbf{x}_{N-1}, \mathbf{U})$, Eqs. (13.34) are added as constraints through the Lagrangian multipliers

$$
\mathbf{\Lambda} := (\lambda_\ell)_{\ell=1}^{N-1} \in \mathbb{R}^{p \times N-1} \text{ and } \mathbf{\Xi} := (\xi_\ell^i)_{\ell=0,i=1}^{N-2,s},
$$

yielding the Lagrange function

$$
\left.
\begin{aligned}
&\mathfrak{L}(\mathbf{X}, \mathbf{Y}, \mathbf{U}, \mathbf{\Lambda}, \mathbf{\Xi}) \\
&= E(\mathbf{x}_{N-1}, \mathbf{U}) \\
&\quad + \sum_{\ell=0}^{N-2} \Big[\lambda_{\ell+1}^\top \big(\mathbf{x}_{\ell+1} - \mathbf{x}_\ell - h_t \sum_{i=1}^{s} b_i f(\mathbf{y}_\ell^i, \mathbf{u}_\ell^i) \big) \\
&\quad + \sum_{i=1}^{s} (\xi_\ell^i)^\top \big(\mathbf{y}_\ell^i - \mathbf{x}_\ell - h_t \sum_{j=1}^{s} a_{i,j} f(\mathbf{y}_\ell^j, \mathbf{u}_\ell^j) \big) \Big].
\end{aligned}
\right\}
\tag{13.37}
$$

By computing the partial derivatives of (13.37) with respect to $\mathbf{x}_\ell$, $\mathbf{y}_\ell^i$, and $\mathbf{u}_\ell^i$ and substituting

$$
\chi_\ell^i = \lambda_{\ell+1} + \sum_{j=1}^{s} \frac{a_{ji}}{b_i} \xi_\ell^j,
\tag{13.38}
$$

we obtain after some algebra the adjoint system and the gradient with respect to $\mathbf{u}_\ell^i$ as [40]

$$
\left.
\begin{aligned}
\boldsymbol{\lambda}_{N-1} &= -\nabla_{\mathbf{x}} E(\mathbf{x}_{N-1}, \mathbf{U}), \\
\boldsymbol{\chi}_\ell^i &= \boldsymbol{\lambda}_{\ell+1} + h_t \sum_{j=1}^{s} \frac{b_j a_{ji}}{b_i} (\nabla_{\mathbf{x}} f(\mathbf{y}_\ell^j, \mathbf{u}_\ell^j))^\top \boldsymbol{\chi}_\ell^j, \\
\boldsymbol{\lambda}_\ell &= \boldsymbol{\lambda}_{\ell+1} + h_t \sum_{i=1}^{s} b_i (\nabla_{\mathbf{x}} f(\mathbf{y}_\ell^i, \mathbf{u}_\ell^i))^\top \boldsymbol{\chi}_\ell^i, \\
\nabla_{\mathbf{u}_\ell^i} \mathcal{L} &= \nabla_{\mathbf{u}_\ell^i} E - h_t (\nabla_{\mathbf{u}} f(\mathbf{y}_\ell^i, \mathbf{u}_\ell^i))^\top \boldsymbol{\chi}_\ell^i.
\end{aligned}
\right\}
\tag{13.39}
$$

In the case of shooting with the EPDiff equation everything is determined by the initial momentum. Hence the derivatives with respect to $\mathbf{x}_0$ of (13.37) also involve the derivative of E. The partial derivative of (13.37) with respect to the initial condition $\mathbf{x}_0$ can be shown to be

$$
\frac{\partial \mathcal{L}}{\partial \mathbf{x}_0} = \frac{\partial E}{\partial \mathbf{x}_0} - \boldsymbol{\lambda}_1 - h_t \sum_{i=1}^{s} b_i (\nabla_{\mathbf{x}} f(\mathbf{y}_0^i, \mathbf{u}_0^i))^\top \boldsymbol{\chi}_0^i.
\tag{13.40}
$$

The latter part is (formally) the negative of the adjoint variable $\boldsymbol{\lambda}$ evaluated for $\ell = 0$:

$$
\frac{\partial \mathcal{L}}{\partial \mathbf{x}_0} = \frac{\partial E}{\partial \mathbf{x}_0} - \boldsymbol{\lambda}_0.
\tag{13.41}
$$

Note that $\boldsymbol{\lambda}_\ell$ is strictly only defined for $\ell = 1, \ldots, N-1$ and $\boldsymbol{\lambda}_0$ is simply a convenience notation. The adjoint equations given in (13.39) represent a Runge–Kutta method with $\mathbf{b}$ and $\mathbf{c}$ unchanged and $\bar{a}_{ij} = \frac{b_j a_{ji}}{b_i}$. In particular, this implies that an explicit (implicit) Runge–Kutta method yields an explicit (implicit) Runge–Kutta method for the adjoint equations (with time reversed). The adjoint of the considered Runge–Kutta method is also shown in Table 13.1. When applied in reverse time direction, it is identical to the Runge–Kutta method used for the numerical integration of the state. Next, we will explicitly compute the equations for the 1D LDDMM registration using a transport equation on the images (i.e., the IBR model).

13.5.3 Application to the IBR model

The states we are interested in are the discrete images $\mathbf{X} = \mathbf{I} \in \mathbb{R}^{m \times N}$. The control sequence that influences the image transport is the velocity matrix $\mathbf{U} = \mathbf{v} \in \mathbb{R}^{n \times N}$.

For the three-dimensional registration problems we are addressing later, memory consumption cannot be neglected. We therefore propose reducing the number of stored control variables $\mathbf{u}_\ell^i$. We found empirically that $\|\mathbf{v}_\ell - \mathbf{v}_{\ell+1}\|/\|\mathbf{v}_\ell\|$ for all $\ell = 0, \ldots, N - 2$ was small, that is, the velocities v only change marginally over time. Hence we approximate the velocity fields within one Runge–Kutta step as piecewise constant: $\mathbf{u}_\ell^i \approx \mathbf{u}_\ell^1 =: \mathbf{u}_\ell, i = 2, \ldots, s$. This is similar to the classical relaxation approach by Beg et al. [7], where velocities within a time-step are also assumed to be constant, and maps are then computed via a semi-Lagrangian scheme based on these constant velocity fields. Assuming piecewise constant velocity fields for our approach reduces the memory requirement for storing the control variables in $\mathbf{U}$ by a factor s. Empirically, this does not affect the results greatly and still constitutes a possible discretization choice for our discretize–optimize approach. Memory requirements are reduced further by the fact that the update in the last equation of (13.39) now only needs to be computed for one instead of s controls for each time t_ℓ. Additionally, the $\boldsymbol{\chi}_\ell^i$ are then only needed in the update for $\boldsymbol{\lambda}_\ell$ and do not have to be stored for later computations to update the controls as $\boldsymbol{\chi}_\ell^1 = \boldsymbol{\lambda}_\ell$ for the explicit methods considered for numerical integration.

As motivated in Section 13.4.1, n and m might be different, and we use the interpolation matrix $\mathbf{P}$ to change from the $\mathbf{v}$ given on a nodal grid to the resolution of $\mathbf{I}$ that is given on a cell-centered grid. The right-hand side function for our Runge–Kutta method then follows from (13.29) to (13.31):

$$f_1(\mathbf{I}_\ell, \mathbf{v}_\ell) := -\mathrm{diag}(\mathbf{D}_1^I \mathbf{I}_\ell)\mathbf{P}\mathbf{v}_\ell = -(\mathbf{D}_1^I \mathbf{I}_\ell) \odot (\mathbf{P}\mathbf{v}_\ell), \qquad (13.42)$$

where $\odot$ denotes the Hadamard product. The resulting derivatives needed are:

$$\nabla_{\mathbf{I}_\ell} f_1(\mathbf{I}_\ell, \mathbf{v}_\ell) = -\mathrm{diag}(\mathbf{P}\mathbf{v}_\ell)\mathbf{D}_1^I, \qquad (13.43)$$

$$\nabla_{\mathbf{v}_\ell} f_1(\mathbf{I}_\ell, \mathbf{v}_\ell) = -\mathrm{diag}(\mathbf{D}_1^I \mathbf{I}_\ell)\mathbf{P}. \qquad (13.44)$$

The concrete Bolza energy (13.35), that is, the discretized objective function of (13.10), for our problem is given as

$$E_1(\mathbf{I}_{N-1}, \mathbf{v}) := \mathrm{Reg}^h(\bar{\mathbf{v}}) + \mathrm{Sim}^h(\mathbf{I}_{N-1}, \mathbf{I}^1). \qquad (13.45)$$

Taking a closer look at (13.21), we easily compute

$$\nabla_{\mathbf{v}} E_1(\mathbf{I}_{N-1}, \mathbf{v}) = h^v h_t \bar{\mathbf{L}} \mathbf{W} \bar{\mathbf{L}} \bar{\mathbf{v}}. \qquad (13.46)$$

For the update of $\mathbf{v}_\ell$, $\ell = 0, \ldots, N - 1$, the components $\ell n + 1, \ldots, (\ell + 1)n$ of $\nabla_{\mathbf{v}} E_1(\mathbf{I}_{N-1}, \mathbf{v})$ have to be used.

To compute the final adjoint state $\boldsymbol{\lambda}_{N-1} \in \mathbb{R}^m$, the derivative of the discrete distance measure is needed:

$$\boldsymbol{\lambda}_{N-1} = -\nabla_{\mathbf{A}} \mathrm{Sim}^h(\mathbf{I}_{N-1}, \mathbf{I}^1), \qquad (13.47)$$

where $\nabla_A \text{Sim}^h$ denotes the derivative with respect to the first argument of Sim^h.

13.5.4 Application to the MBR model

As a smooth transition at the boundary of the domain is expected for the transformations, we assume homogeneous Neumann boundary conditions. The corresponding matrix to compute the discrete derivative for one component of the transformations given on a nodal grid is

$$\mathbf{D}_1^v = \frac{1}{2h^v} \begin{pmatrix} 0 & 0 & & & \\ -1 & 0 & 1 & & \\ & \ddots & \ddots & \ddots & \\ & & -1 & 0 & 1 \\ & & & 0 & 0 \end{pmatrix} \in \mathbb{R}^{n \times n}. \tag{13.48}$$

The discrete transformation maps $\boldsymbol{\phi} := \phi(\mathbf{x}^{\text{nd}}) \in \mathbb{R}^{n \times N}$ are discretized exactly like the velocities. As before, $\boldsymbol{\phi}_\ell$ is the $(\ell + 1)$th column of $\boldsymbol{\phi}$ and $\ell \in \{0, 1, \ldots, N - 1\}$. To include the full information provided by the images, we will interpolate $\mathbf{I}^0$ linearly using $\mathbf{P}\boldsymbol{\phi}_{N-1}$ and write $\tilde{\mathbf{I}}^0 := \mathbf{I}^0 \circ (\mathbf{P}\boldsymbol{\phi}_{N-1})$ for the resulting image. The discretized objective function of (13.14) then has the following form:

$$E_2(\boldsymbol{\phi}_{N-1}, \mathbf{v}) = \text{Reg}^h(\bar{\mathbf{v}}) + \text{Sim}^h(\tilde{\mathbf{I}}^0, \mathbf{I}^1). \tag{13.49}$$

Prolongating $\boldsymbol{\phi}_{N-1}$ with $\mathbf{P}$ also has an impact on the size of the adjoint variable $\boldsymbol{\lambda} \in \mathbb{R}^{m \times N}$, and the final state is

$$\boldsymbol{\lambda}_{N-1} = -\frac{d}{d\mathbf{P}\boldsymbol{\phi}_{N-1}} \text{Sim}^h(\tilde{\mathbf{I}}^0, \mathbf{I}^1) = -\nabla_A \text{Sim}^h(\tilde{\mathbf{I}}^0, \mathbf{I}^1) \nabla^h \tilde{\mathbf{I}}^0. \tag{13.50}$$

For the second equation, the chain rule was applied yielding the product of the discrete gradient $\nabla^h \tilde{\mathbf{I}}^0 \in \mathbb{R}^m$ and $\nabla_A \text{Sim}^h$.

The discrete right-hand side function f_2 for the transport of the transformation maps is almost identical to (13.42), only the discrete derivatives are changed, and no interpolation is needed:

$$f_2(\boldsymbol{\phi}_\ell, \mathbf{v}_\ell) = -\text{diag}(\mathbf{D}_1^v \boldsymbol{\phi}_\ell)\mathbf{v}_\ell = -(\mathbf{D}_1^v \boldsymbol{\phi}_\ell) \odot \mathbf{v}_\ell. \tag{13.51}$$

The derivatives of (13.51) needed for computing the adjoint equations are:

$$\nabla_{\boldsymbol{\phi}_\ell} f_2(\boldsymbol{\phi}_\ell, \mathbf{v}_\ell) = -\text{diag}(\mathbf{v}_\ell)\mathbf{D}_1^v, \tag{13.52}$$

$$\nabla_{\mathbf{v}_\ell} f_2(\boldsymbol{\phi}_\ell, \mathbf{v}_\ell) = -\text{diag}(\mathbf{D}_1^v \boldsymbol{\phi}_\ell). \tag{13.53}$$

The regularization, which depends on the control variable, in this model (13.49) is the same as (13.45), and hence the partial derivative is equal to (13.46). However, the distance measure depends on the interpolated image $\mathbf{I}_0(\mathbf{P}\boldsymbol{\phi}_{N-1})$, and it is possible that $\boldsymbol{\phi}_{N-1}$ has a lower resolution than $\mathbf{I}_0$. Because the high resolution of the image mismatch (this is essentially the role of the adjoint λ) should be retained during the solution of the adjoint equations, the matrix $\mathbf{P}$ is used to connect Eqs. (13.52) and (13.53) to (13.50). The evolution of λ backward in time is then determined by (13.43) instead of (13.52). Also, before using λ to compute the update for the control $\mathbf{v}$ using (13.53), the grid change has to be undone by computing $\mathbf{P}^\top\lambda$. By doing computations stepwise (i.e., storing only λ_ℓ and $\lambda_{\ell-1}$ on the high image resolution, $\ell = 1, \ldots, N - 1$) and keeping the shorter vectors $\mathbf{P}^\top\lambda_\ell$ the memory requirements can be reduced.

13.5.5 Application to the MBS model using EPDiff

We briefly repeat the constraints of the MBS model:

$$\dot{\phi}_t + \mathrm{J}_{\phi_t}^\top v_t = \mathbf{0}, \ \ \phi_0 = \mathrm{Id}, \tag{13.54}$$

$$\dot{m}_t + \mathrm{J}_{m_t} v_t + m_t \mathrm{div}(v_t) + \mathrm{J}_{v_t}^\top m_t = \mathbf{0}, \tag{13.55}$$

$$v_t = K m_t, \ \ K = (L^\dagger L)^{-1}. \tag{13.56}$$

How (13.54) is solved numerically is described in Section 13.5.4. In 1D the EPDiff equation (13.55) simplifies to

$$\dot{m}_t + (\partial_x m_t) v_t + 2 m_t (\partial_x v_t) = 0. \tag{13.57}$$

Because of (13.56), the momentum m is discretized on the same grid as the velocities. Hence our discrete representation is given on the nodal grid $\mathbf{x}^{\mathrm{nd}}$: $\mathbf{m} = m(\mathbf{x}^{\mathrm{nd}}) \in \mathbb{R}^{n \times N}$, and the matrix $\mathbf{D}_1^v$ is also used for numerical derivation of the momentum.

The adjoint of the discrete differential operator $\mathbf{L}$ defined in (13.23) is the transposed matrix $\mathbf{L}^\top$. As $\mathbf{L}$ is symmetric, $\mathbf{L} = \mathbf{L}^\top$. Furthermore, for a positive weight γ, the matrix $\mathbf{L}$ is positive definite, and we can deduce that $\mathbf{L}^\top\mathbf{L}$ is invertible. We can deduce that the kernel $\mathbf{K} := (\mathbf{L}^\top\mathbf{L})^{-1} \in \mathbb{R}^{n \times n}$ is positive definite and (13.56) can be discretized as $\mathbf{v}_\ell = \mathbf{K}\mathbf{m}_\ell$. Due to the positive definiteness of $\mathbf{K}$, the latter equation system has a unique solution for all $\ell \in \{0, \ldots, N - 1\}$. Note that the equation system $\mathbf{v}_\ell = \mathbf{K}\mathbf{m}_\ell$ can be solved efficiently using the fast Fourier transform; see, for example, [7,107]. The discrete energy for the MBS model can be simplified as the regularizer only depends on the initial momentum (see the last row of (13.17)):

$$E_3(\mathbf{m}, \boldsymbol{\phi}) = \frac{h^v}{2}(\mathbf{m}_0)^\top \mathbf{K}\mathbf{m}_0 + \mathrm{Sim}^h(\tilde{\mathbf{I}}^0, \mathbf{I}^1), \qquad (13.58)$$

where we used again the notation $\tilde{\mathbf{I}}^0 = \mathbf{I}^0 \circ (\mathbf{P}\boldsymbol{\phi}_{N-1})$. The transformations $\boldsymbol{\phi}$ are updated by the following right-hand side function, which is obtained by substituting $\mathbf{v}_\ell = \mathbf{K}\mathbf{m}_\ell$ into (13.51):

$$f_3^1(\boldsymbol{\phi}_\ell, \mathbf{m}_\ell) = -\mathrm{diag}(\mathbf{D}_1^v \boldsymbol{\phi}_\ell)\mathbf{K}\mathbf{m}_\ell. \qquad (13.59)$$

The second discrete right-hand side that is used in the Runge–Kutta method is the discrete version of (13.57), where again $\mathbf{v}_\ell = \mathbf{K}\mathbf{m}_\ell$ is used:

$$f_3^2(\mathbf{m}_\ell) = -\mathrm{diag}(\mathbf{D}_1^v \mathbf{m}_\ell)\mathbf{K}\mathbf{m}_\ell - 2\mathrm{diag}(\mathbf{D}_1^v \mathbf{K}\mathbf{m}_\ell)\mathbf{m}_\ell. \qquad (13.60)$$

Again, for solving the adjoint equations, we need the derivatives. The difference is that we now have two state variables $\boldsymbol{\phi}$ and $\mathbf{m}$ and accordingly two adjoint variables $\boldsymbol{\lambda}^1 := \boldsymbol{\lambda}^\phi \in \mathbb{R}^{n \times N}$ and $\boldsymbol{\lambda}^2 := \boldsymbol{\lambda}^M \in \mathbb{R}^{n \times N}$ with intermediate stages $\boldsymbol{\chi}^{1,i} := \boldsymbol{\chi}^{\phi,i} \in \mathbb{R}^{n \times N}$ and $\boldsymbol{\chi}^{2,i} := \boldsymbol{\chi}^{M,i} \in \mathbb{R}^{n \times N}$, $i = 1, \dots, s$, respectively. We will now summarize the derivatives of the right-hand side function $f_3 = (f_3^1, f_3^2)^\top$ with respect to the state variables $\boldsymbol{\phi}_\ell$ and $\mathbf{m}_\ell$ and omit the function arguments for convenience:

$$\nabla_{\boldsymbol{\phi}_\ell} f_3^1 = -\mathrm{diag}(\mathbf{K}\mathbf{m}_\ell)\mathbf{D}_1^v, \qquad (13.61)$$

$$\nabla_{\mathbf{m}_\ell} f_3^1 = -\mathrm{diag}(\mathbf{D}_v^1 \boldsymbol{\phi}_\ell)\mathbf{K}, \qquad (13.62)$$

$$\nabla_{\boldsymbol{\phi}_\ell} f_3^2 = \mathbf{0}, \qquad (13.63)$$

$$\nabla_{\mathbf{m}_\ell} f_3^2 = -2\mathrm{diag}(\mathbf{D}_1^v \mathbf{K}\mathbf{m}_\ell) - \mathrm{diag}(\mathbf{K}\mathbf{m}_\ell)\mathbf{D}_1^v$$
$$\qquad -2\mathrm{diag}(\mathbf{m}_\ell)\mathbf{D}_1^v \mathbf{K} - \mathrm{diag}(\mathbf{D}_1^v \mathbf{m}_\ell)\mathbf{K}. \qquad (13.64)$$

Contrary to the two models before, we do not need to update our control $\mathbf{u} = \mathbf{v}$ as it is directly available by (13.56), and therefore we do not need to compute $\nabla_{\mathbf{u}} f$. Substituting (13.61)–(13.64) into the adjoint system (13.39) yields:

$$\boldsymbol{\lambda}_\ell^1 = \boldsymbol{\lambda}_{\ell+1}^1 + h_t \sum_{i=1}^s b_i (\nabla_{\boldsymbol{\phi}} f_3^1)^\top \boldsymbol{\chi}_\ell^{1,i}, \qquad (13.65)$$

$$\boldsymbol{\chi}_\ell^{1,i} = \boldsymbol{\lambda}_{\ell+1}^1 + h_t \sum_{j=1}^s \frac{b_j a_{ji}}{b_i} (\nabla_{\boldsymbol{\phi}} f_3^1)^\top \boldsymbol{\chi}_\ell^{1,j}, \qquad (13.66)$$

$$\boldsymbol{\lambda}_\ell^2 = \boldsymbol{\lambda}_{\ell+1}^2 + h_t \sum_{i=1}^s b_i \begin{pmatrix} \nabla_{\mathbf{m}_\ell} f_3^1 \\ \nabla_{\mathbf{m}_\ell} f_3^2 \end{pmatrix}^\top \begin{pmatrix} \boldsymbol{\chi}_\ell^{1,i} \\ \boldsymbol{\chi}_\ell^{2,i} \end{pmatrix}, \qquad (13.67)$$

$$\boldsymbol{\chi}_\ell^{2,i} = \boldsymbol{\lambda}_{\ell+1}^2 + h_t \sum_{j=1}^{s} \frac{b_j a_{ji}}{b_i} \begin{pmatrix} \nabla_{\mathbf{m}_\ell} f_3^1 \\ \nabla_{\mathbf{m}_\ell} f_3^2 \end{pmatrix}^\top \begin{pmatrix} \boldsymbol{\chi}_\ell^{1,j} \\ \boldsymbol{\chi}_\ell^{2,j} \end{pmatrix}. \tag{13.68}$$

The final states of the adjoints $\boldsymbol{\lambda}^1$ and $\boldsymbol{\lambda}^2$ are given by the partial derivatives with respect to the final states $\boldsymbol{\phi}_{N-1}$ and $\mathbf{m}_{N-1}$, respectively:

$$\boldsymbol{\lambda}_{N-1}^1 = -\nabla_{\mathbf{P}\boldsymbol{\phi}_{N-1}} E_3(\mathbf{m},\boldsymbol{\phi}) = -\nabla_{\mathbf{A}} \mathrm{Sim}^h(\tilde{\mathbf{I}}^0, \mathbf{I}^1) \nabla^h \tilde{\mathbf{I}}^0, \tag{13.69}$$

$$\boldsymbol{\lambda}_{N-1}^2 = -\nabla_{\mathbf{m}_{N-1}} E_3(\mathbf{m},\boldsymbol{\phi}) = \mathbf{0}. \tag{13.70}$$

The update of the initial momentum $\mathbf{m}_0$, which is the initial value influencing the complete model via Eqs. (13.54)–(13.56) is given by adapting (13.41):

$$\frac{\partial \mathcal{L}}{\partial \mathbf{m}_0} = \frac{\partial E_3(\mathbf{m},\boldsymbol{\phi})}{\partial \mathbf{m}_0} - \boldsymbol{\lambda}_0^2 = h^v \mathbf{K}\mathbf{m}_0 - \boldsymbol{\lambda}_0^2. \tag{13.71}$$

13.6 Discretization in multiple dimensions

This section generalizes the equations from Section 13.4 and Section 13.5 to multidimensional LDDMM registration problems. Multidimensional formulations can easily be obtained from the one-dimensional representation by defining appropriate discrete operators. We illustrate this here for the three-dimensional case, but the approach is adaptable to arbitrary dimensions. For the computation of distance measures and their derivatives, we refer to [66, p. 95].

13.6.1 Discretization of the regularizer

The number of image voxels per dimension is denoted as M_i, $i = 1, \ldots, 3$, and the number of nodal grid points as n_i. We define the total number of voxels and grid points as

$$M := \prod_{i=1}^{3} M_i, \ n := \prod_{i=1}^{3} n_i. \tag{13.72}$$

The discrete images are thus $\mathbf{I}^0, \mathbf{I}^1 \in \mathbb{R}^M$, and the velocities are discretized as $\mathbf{v} \in \mathbb{R}^{3n \times N}$. Our domain has a box shape: $\bar{\Omega} = [\omega_1, \omega_2] \times [\omega_3, \omega_4] \times [\omega_5, \omega_6] \subset \mathbb{R}^3$. The resulting cell widths are $h_1^I = \frac{\omega_2 - \omega_1}{M_1}$, $h_2^I = \frac{\omega_4 - \omega_3}{M_2}$, $h_3^I = \frac{\omega_6 - \omega_5}{M_3}$ for the images and $h_1^v = \frac{\omega_2 - \omega_1}{n_1 - 1}$, $h_2^v = \frac{\omega_4 - \omega_3}{n_2 - 1}$, $h_3^v = \frac{\omega_6 - \omega_5}{n_3 - 1}$ for the velocities and transformations. For the computation of the regularizer, we need the volume of one cell that is defined as

$$h^v := h_1^v h_2^v h_3^v. \tag{13.73}$$

The construction for the discrete Laplacian is achieved using Kronecker products (see [66, p. 122]):

$$\begin{aligned}\boldsymbol{\Delta} = \ & \text{Id}_{n_3} \otimes \text{Id}_{n_2} \otimes \boldsymbol{\Delta}^{h_1^v} + \text{Id}_{n_3} \otimes \boldsymbol{\Delta}^{h_2^v} \otimes \text{Id}_{n_1} \\ & + \boldsymbol{\Delta}^{h_3^v} \otimes \text{Id}_{n_2} \otimes \text{Id}_{n_1},\end{aligned} \tag{13.74}$$

where $\boldsymbol{\Delta}^{h_i v}$ is the finite difference matrix given in (13.24), which is used to compute the second derivative in the ith dimension of one component of the velocities $\mathbf{v}$. Hence we can write the multidimensional regularization matrix as an extension of (13.23):

$$\mathbf{L} = (\gamma\,\text{Id}_n - \alpha \boldsymbol{\Delta})^\beta \in \mathbb{R}^{n \times n}. \tag{13.75}$$

This makes multiplication of $\mathbf{L}$ with one component of the vector-valued velocities at each discretization time point possible. As in Reg^h, the velocities are integrated over time after multiplication with the Helmholtz operator, and $\mathbf{L}$ has to be multiplied with all components and for all times. We use copies of $\mathbf{L}$ for a short description but do not keep the copies in memory. In fact, as $\mathbf{L}$ is sparse, we implemented the multiplication with $\mathbf{L}$ without building the matrix. The corresponding matrix $\bar{\mathbf{L}}$ is

$$\bar{\mathbf{L}} := \text{Id}_{3N} \otimes \mathbf{L}, \tag{13.76}$$

and the matrix for the proper weighting of cells between grid points that are located at the boundaries of the box is realized as in (13.25), yielding

$$\mathbf{W} := \mathbf{W}_N \otimes \text{Id}_3 \otimes \mathbf{W}_{n_3} \otimes \mathbf{W}_{n_2} \otimes \mathbf{W}_{n_1}. \tag{13.77}$$

The discrete regularization energy is then given by applying the trapezoidal rule:

$$\text{Reg}^h(\bar{\mathbf{v}}) := \frac{h^v h_t}{2} \bar{\mathbf{v}}^\top \bar{\mathbf{L}}^\top \mathbf{W} \bar{\mathbf{L}} \bar{\mathbf{v}}. \tag{13.78}$$

The vector $\bar{\mathbf{v}} \in \mathbb{R}^{3nN}$ is the linearized matrix $\mathbf{v}$, that is, the velocities are stacked up dimension-by-dimension for one time t_ℓ: First, all x-components of the velocities ($\mathbf{v}_\ell^1 \in \mathbb{R}^n$), then all y-components ($\mathbf{v}_\ell^2 \in \mathbb{R}^n$), and finally all z-components ($\mathbf{v}_\ell^3 \in \mathbb{R}^n$) are stored. Then the same is done with the next time point, and so on. In the following equation we summarize this procedure using subvectors $\mathbf{v}_\ell^i$, $i = 1, 2, 3$, $\ell = 0, 1, \ldots, N - 1$, of $\mathbf{v}$:

$$\mathbf{v} := \begin{pmatrix} \mathbf{v}_0^1 & \mathbf{v}_1^1 & \cdots & \mathbf{v}_{N-1}^1 \\ \mathbf{v}_0^2 & \mathbf{v}_1^2 & \cdots & \mathbf{v}_{N-1}^2 \\ \mathbf{v}_0^3 & \mathbf{v}_1^3 & \cdots & \mathbf{v}_{N-1}^3 \end{pmatrix}. \tag{13.79}$$

For the shooting model, the kernel $\mathbf{K}$ is needed. As in the one-dimensional case, it is defined as

$$\mathbf{K} = (\mathbf{L}^\top \mathbf{L})^{-1} \in \mathbb{R}^{n \times n}. \tag{13.80}$$

Note that the matrix $\mathbf{K}$ is not stored, but equation systems are solved to obtain the momentum fields from the velocity fields; see Section 13.5.5.

13.6.2 Integrands and associated gradients for the Runge–Kutta methods

To solve the Runge–Kutta integration (13.34) and in particular the adjoint equations (13.39), the specifications of the right-hand side function f and its derivatives are required. We distinguish here solutions of the transport equation (for a relaxation approach) and direct solutions of the LDDMM optimality conditions (for shooting). In the first case we consider image-based and map-based solutions. As the map-based solution has the advantage that considerably less image artifacts occur during numerical solution of the transport equation (see also Section 13.8.1), we will focus on this adaption for the shooting approach. Additionally, the shooting approach eliminates the dependency on the velocity v as it can be computed from the state variables. To evaluate f and solve the adjoint equations, we will need matrices to numerically compute the first derivative. In three dimensions these matrices are [66, p. 122]:

$$\bar{\mathbf{D}}_1^\square := \mathrm{Id}_3^\circ \otimes \mathrm{Id}_2^\circ \otimes \mathbf{D}_1^\square, \tag{13.81}$$

$$\bar{\mathbf{D}}_2^\square := \mathrm{Id}_3^\circ \otimes \mathbf{D}_2^\square \otimes \mathrm{Id}_1^\circ, \tag{13.82}$$

$$\bar{\mathbf{D}}_3^\square := \mathbf{D}_3^\square \otimes \mathrm{Id}_2^\circ \otimes \mathrm{Id}_1^\circ, \tag{13.83}$$

where the subscripts denote the directions of the partial derivatives (x, y, and z), and $(\square, \circ) \in \{(I, M), (v, n)\}$.

13.6.2.1 IBR model

We start with the discretization of the relaxation approach with transportation of images, that is, model (13.10). This is the simplest case as the state $\mathbf{X}$ corresponds to the vectorized images

$\mathbf{I} = (\mathbf{I}_\ell)_{\ell=0}^{N-1} \in \mathbb{R}^{M \times N}$ only. The control variables are the discretized velocities $\mathbf{v} \in \mathbb{R}^{3n \times N}$. We want to transport the images with all their details and bring the velocities to the image resolution using the trilinear interpolation matrix $\mathbf{P} \in \mathbb{R}^{M \times n}$; see Section 13.4.1 and references therein. With the notation $\mathbf{P}\mathbf{v}_\ell^i =: \hat{\mathbf{v}}_\ell^i$, $i = 1, 2, 3$, $\ell = 0, \ldots, N-1$, the discretized transport equation becomes

$$f_1(\mathbf{I}_\ell, \mathbf{v}_\ell) = -\sum_{i=1}^{3} \mathrm{diag}(\bar{\mathbf{D}}_i^I \mathbf{I}_\ell) \hat{\mathbf{v}}_\ell^i. \tag{13.84}$$

The corresponding derivatives are:

$$\nabla_{\mathbf{I}_\ell} f_1(\mathbf{I}_\ell, \mathbf{v}_\ell) = -\sum_{i=1}^{3} \mathrm{diag}(\hat{\mathbf{v}}_\ell^i) \bar{\mathbf{D}}_i^I, \tag{13.85}$$

$$\nabla_{\mathbf{v}_\ell} f_1(\mathbf{I}_\ell, \mathbf{v}_\ell) = -\mathrm{diag}((\bar{\mathbf{D}}_1^I + \bar{\mathbf{D}}_2^I + \bar{\mathbf{D}}_3^I)\mathbf{I}_\ell)\mathbf{P}. \tag{13.86}$$

For the adjoint system, we need the final state of $\lambda \in \mathbb{R}^{M \times N}$, which is already given in (13.47) but is repeated here for completeness:

$$\lambda_{N-1} = -\nabla_{\mathbf{A}} \mathrm{Sim}^h(\mathbf{I}_{N-1}, \mathbf{I}^1). \tag{13.87}$$

As our objective function is essentially the same as for the one-dimensional case given in (13.45), combining (13.46) and (13.78) yields for the derivative of the regularizer with respect to the velocities:

$$\nabla_{\mathbf{v}} E_1(\mathbf{I}_{N-1}, \mathbf{v}) = h^v h_t \bar{\mathbf{L}} \mathbf{W} \bar{\mathbf{L}} \bar{\mathbf{v}}. \tag{13.88}$$

13.6.2.2 MBR model
In the map-based case we transport all the coordinates (ϕ^1, ϕ^2, ϕ^3) individually, that is, we have as many transport equations as there are spatial dimensions. The discrete transformation maps are ordered as

$$\phi := \begin{pmatrix} \phi_0^1 & \phi_1^1 & \cdots & \phi_{N-1}^1 \\ \phi_0^2 & \phi_1^2 & \cdots & \phi_{N-1}^2 \\ \phi_0^3 & \phi_1^3 & \cdots & \phi_{N-1}^3 \end{pmatrix} \in \mathbb{R}^{3n \times N}. \tag{13.89}$$

Thus ϕ and $\mathbf{v}$ have the same discretization, and the transport equations do not need any further interpolations and hence no matrix/operator $\mathbf{P}$:

$$f_2(\phi_\ell, \mathbf{v}_\ell) = -\begin{pmatrix} \sum_{i=1}^{3} \mathrm{diag}(\bar{\mathbf{D}}_i^v \phi_\ell^1) \mathbf{v}_\ell^i \\ \sum_{i=1}^{3} \mathrm{diag}(\bar{\mathbf{D}}_i^v \phi_\ell^2) \mathbf{v}_\ell^i \\ \sum_{i=1}^{3} \mathrm{diag}(\bar{\mathbf{D}}_i^v \phi_\ell^3) \mathbf{v}_\ell^i \end{pmatrix}. \tag{13.90}$$

The gradients with respect to the state variable $\boldsymbol{\phi}$ for the individual components of (13.90) can be expressed by the Kronecker delta as the transport in the different spatial directions is decoupled:

$$\nabla_{\boldsymbol{\phi}_\ell^l} f_2^j(\boldsymbol{\phi}_\ell, \mathbf{v}_\ell) = -\delta_{j,l} \sum_{i=1}^{3} \mathrm{diag}(\mathbf{v}_\ell^i)\bar{\mathbf{D}}_i^v, \quad j, l = 1, 2, 3. \qquad (13.91)$$

The derivatives with respect to the control variable $\mathbf{v}$ are

$$\nabla_{\mathbf{v}_\ell} f_2(\boldsymbol{\phi}_\ell, \mathbf{v}_\ell) = -\left(\mathrm{diag}(\bar{\mathbf{D}}_j^v \boldsymbol{\phi}_\ell^i)\right)_{i,j=1}^{3}. \qquad (13.92)$$

To complete our adjoint system, we also need the final state of the adjoint variables $\boldsymbol{\lambda}_{N-1}$. Again, we abbreviate the transformed template images as $\tilde{\mathbf{I}}^0 = \mathbf{I}_0 \circ (\bar{\mathbf{P}}\boldsymbol{\phi}_{N-1})$, and $\circ$ denotes trilinear interpolation on the grid $\bar{\mathbf{P}}\boldsymbol{\phi}_{N-1}$. Here the matrix $\bar{\mathbf{P}}$ contains three copies of $\mathbf{P}$ and converts each dimension of $\boldsymbol{\phi}_{N-1}$ to cell-centered points:

$$\bar{\mathbf{P}} = \begin{pmatrix} \mathbf{P} & & \\ & \mathbf{P} & \\ & & \mathbf{P} \end{pmatrix} \in \mathbb{R}^{3\bar{m} \times 3n}. \qquad (13.93)$$

The final state is similar to the one-dimensional case given in (13.50), but each transformation component is treated individually:

$$\boldsymbol{\lambda}_{N-1} = -\mathrm{diag}(\nabla^h \tilde{\mathbf{I}}^0) \begin{pmatrix} \nabla_{\mathbf{A}}\mathrm{Sim}^h(\tilde{\mathbf{I}}^0, \mathbf{I}^1) \\ \nabla_{\mathbf{A}}\mathrm{Sim}^h(\tilde{\mathbf{I}}^0, \mathbf{I}^1) \\ \nabla_{\mathbf{A}}\mathrm{Sim}^h(\tilde{\mathbf{I}}^0, \mathbf{I}^1) \end{pmatrix}. \qquad (13.94)$$

Here $\nabla^h \tilde{\mathbf{I}}^0 \in \mathbb{R}^{3M}$ is the discrete gradient of the image $\tilde{\mathbf{I}}^0 \in \mathbb{R}^M$, where the first M components are the partial derivatives in the x-direction, then the y- and finally the z-directions follow. The arguments given at the end of Section 13.5.4 still apply, and the adjoint equations are solved on the image resolution using the matrix $\mathbf{P}$ appropriately and storing the adjoint only when necessary at high resolution. As the regularization energy is the same as in the image-based model:

$$E_2(\boldsymbol{\phi}_{N-1}, \mathbf{v}) = \mathrm{Reg}^h(\bar{\mathbf{v}}) + \mathrm{Sim}^h(\tilde{\mathbf{I}}^0, \mathbf{I}^1). \qquad (13.95)$$

The derivative with respect to the velocities is also the same:

$$\nabla_{\mathbf{v}} E_2(\boldsymbol{\phi}_{N-1}, \mathbf{v}) = h^v h_t \bar{\mathbf{L}} \mathbf{W} \bar{\mathbf{L}} \bar{\mathbf{v}}. \qquad (13.96)$$

13.6.2.3 MBS model

Instead of solving map-based equations to decouple spatial transformations from the objects to be transported, we can directly solve the EPDiff equation (13.55) with the constraint (13.56) to optimize the discrete energy

$$E_3(\mathbf{m}, \boldsymbol{\phi}) = \frac{h^v}{2} \sum_{i=1}^{3} (\mathbf{m}_0^i)^\top \mathbf{K}\mathbf{m}_0^i + \mathrm{Sim}^h(\tilde{\mathbf{I}}^0, \mathbf{I}^1). \qquad (13.97)$$

To compute the transformed source image, we still need the transformation $\boldsymbol{\phi}$ and thus (13.90) to compute its evolution. The resulting discrete right-hand side function has six components:

$$f_3^j(\boldsymbol{\phi}_\ell, \mathbf{m}_\ell) = -\sum_{i=1}^{3} \mathrm{diag}(\bar{\mathbf{D}}_i^v \boldsymbol{\phi}_\ell^j)\mathbf{K}\mathbf{m}_\ell^i, \qquad (13.98)$$

$$f_3^{j+3}(\mathbf{m}_\ell) = -\sum_{i=1}^{3} \left(\mathrm{diag}(\bar{\mathbf{D}}_i^v \mathbf{m}_\ell^j)\mathbf{K}\mathbf{m}_\ell^i + \mathrm{diag}(\bar{\mathbf{D}}_j^v \mathbf{K}\mathbf{m}_\ell^i)\mathbf{m}_\ell^i \right.$$
$$\left. + \mathrm{diag}(\mathbf{m}_\ell^j)\bar{\mathbf{D}}_i^v \mathbf{K}\mathbf{m}_\ell^i \right) \qquad (13.99)$$

for $j = 1, 2, 3$, where we used $\mathbf{v}_\ell^i = \mathbf{K}\mathbf{m}_\ell^i$, $i = 1, 2, 3$ and $\ell = 0, \dots, N-1$. A useful relation when computing the derivatives of the right-hand side function is

$$\nabla_{\mathbf{m}_\ell^l} \mathbf{v}_\ell^j = \delta_{j,l}\mathbf{K} = \begin{cases} \mathbf{0}, & l \neq j, \\ \mathbf{K}, & l = j. \end{cases} \qquad (13.100)$$

The resulting derivatives of f_3 are

$$\nabla_{\boldsymbol{\phi}_\ell^l} f_3^j = -\delta_{j,l} \sum_{i=1}^{3} \mathrm{diag}(\mathbf{K}\mathbf{m}_\ell^i)\bar{\mathbf{D}}_i^v, \qquad (13.101)$$

$$\nabla_{\mathbf{m}_\ell^l} f_3^j = -\mathrm{diag}(\bar{\mathbf{D}}_l^v \boldsymbol{\phi}_\ell^j)\mathbf{K}, \qquad (13.102)$$

$$\nabla_{\boldsymbol{\phi}_\ell^l} f_3^{j+3} = \mathbf{0}, \qquad (13.103)$$

$$\nabla_{\mathbf{m}_\ell^l} f_3^{j+3} = -\left(\mathrm{diag}(\bar{\mathbf{D}}_i^v \mathbf{m}_\ell^j) + \mathrm{diag}(\mathbf{m}_\ell^l)\bar{\mathbf{D}}_j^v + \mathrm{diag}(\mathbf{m}_\ell^j)\bar{\mathbf{D}}_l^v \right)\mathbf{K}$$
$$- \mathrm{diag}(\bar{\mathbf{D}}_j^v \mathbf{K}\mathbf{m}_\ell^l)$$
$$- \delta_{j,l} \sum_{i=1}^{3} \left(\mathrm{diag}(\bar{\mathbf{D}}_i^v \mathbf{K}\mathbf{m}_\ell^i) + \mathrm{diag}(\mathbf{K}\mathbf{m}_\ell^i)\bar{\mathbf{D}}_i^v \right), \qquad (13.104)$$

for $j, l = 1, 2, 3$.

As we have six state variables $\boldsymbol{\phi}_\ell^1, \boldsymbol{\phi}_\ell^2, \boldsymbol{\phi}_\ell^3$ and $\mathbf{m}_\ell^1, \mathbf{m}_\ell^2, \mathbf{m}_\ell^3$ that are updated using Runge–Kutta methods with the right-hand sides $f_3^1, \ldots, f_3^6$, there are also six adjoint variables $\boldsymbol{\lambda}_\ell^1, \ldots, \boldsymbol{\lambda}_\ell^6$ with intermediate variables $\boldsymbol{\chi}_\ell^{1,i}, \ldots, \boldsymbol{\chi}_\ell^{6,i}$ for $i = 1, \ldots, s$ and $\ell = 0, \ldots, N-1$. The derivatives of f_3, given in (13.101)–(13.104), are used in the adjoint Runge–Kutta system (13.39) to update the adjoint variables. It remains to give a complete description are the final states of the adjoints $\boldsymbol{\lambda}_{N-1}^1, \ldots, \boldsymbol{\lambda}_{N-1}^6$. They are given by the partial derivatives of E_3 with respect to the final states $\boldsymbol{\phi}_{N-1}$ and $\mathbf{m}_{N-1}$, respectively. The first three equations are the same as in (13.94), but we repeat them for completeness, the last $\boldsymbol{\lambda}_{N-1}^4, \boldsymbol{\lambda}_{N-1}^5, \boldsymbol{\lambda}_{N-1}^6$ vanish as the energy depends on the initial momentum and not on the final one:

$$\begin{pmatrix} \boldsymbol{\lambda}_{N-1}^1 \\ \boldsymbol{\lambda}_{N-1}^2 \\ \boldsymbol{\lambda}_{N-1}^3 \end{pmatrix} = -\mathrm{diag}(\nabla^h \tilde{\mathbf{I}}^0) \begin{pmatrix} \nabla_{\mathbf{A}} \mathrm{Sim}^h(\tilde{\mathbf{I}}^0, \mathbf{I}^1) \\ \nabla_{\mathbf{A}} \mathrm{Sim}^h(\tilde{\mathbf{I}}^0, \mathbf{I}^1) \\ \nabla_{\mathbf{A}} \mathrm{Sim}^h(\tilde{\mathbf{I}}^0, \mathbf{I}^1) \end{pmatrix}, \tag{13.105}$$

$$\boldsymbol{\lambda}_{N-1}^j = \mathbf{0}, \; j = 4, 5, 6. \tag{13.106}$$

The update of the initial momentum $\mathbf{m}_0$ that is the initial value influencing the complete model via Eqs. (13.98) and (13.99) is given by adapting (13.41):

$$\frac{\partial \mathcal{L}}{\partial \mathbf{m}_0} = \frac{\partial E_3(\mathbf{m}, \boldsymbol{\phi})}{\partial \mathbf{m}_0} - (\boldsymbol{\lambda}_0^4, \boldsymbol{\lambda}_0^5, \boldsymbol{\lambda}_0^6)^\top = \begin{pmatrix} h^v \mathbf{K} \mathbf{m}_0^1 - \boldsymbol{\lambda}_0^4 \\ h^v \mathbf{K} \mathbf{m}_0^2 - \boldsymbol{\lambda}_0^5 \\ h^v \mathbf{K} \mathbf{m}_0^3 - \boldsymbol{\lambda}_0^6 \end{pmatrix}. \tag{13.107}$$

13.7 Multilevel registration and numerical optimization

A key concept of most image registration algorithms is the registration on multiple levels. By computing solutions to registration problems with images whose resolution is gradually increased the risk of getting stuck in a local minimum is reduced [66, p. 13]. Additionally, the numerical optimization on the coarse levels with images consisting of fewer pixels/voxels is faster but gives a good approximation for the solution on the next level, further reducing runtime.

Because of these two reasons, we also employed a multilevel registration. The number of points in space varied during the multilevel optimization such that the grid spacing was halved on each finer level. After choosing $n_j^1, j = 1, 2, 3$, the number of grid points is hence given as $n_j^i := (n_j^1 - 1)2^{i-1} + 1$. Given images $\mathbf{I}^0, \mathbf{I}^1 \in \mathbb{R}^{M_1 \times M_2 \times M_3}$, smoothed and downsampled versions $\mathbf{I}_i^0, \mathbf{I}_i^1 \in \mathbb{R}^{M_1^i \times M_2^i \times M_3^i}$ with $M_j^i = \lfloor M_j \cdot 2^{-F+i} \rfloor$ were computed for $j = 1, 2, 3$ and $i = 1, \ldots, F$ [66, p. 40]. Problems (13.10), (13.14), and (13.17) were then solved using a coarse-to-fine resolution multilevel strategy with $F \in \mathbb{N}$ levels. For the (bi/tri)linear interpolation, which is needed to compute the transformed source image $\tilde{\mathbf{I}}^0$, we used the Matlab code provided by [66].

The discretization resolution of the velocities, momenta, and transformations can be chosen by the user. One drawback is that (for the 3D lung registration, we are tackling) choosing $n_j^i = M_j^i$ exceeds common memory limitations and results in an extremely expensive solution of the constraint (13.34) and adjoint Eqs. (13.39). As motivated before, by LDDMM design v and ϕ are assumed to be smooth functions, and it is usually not necessary to use a high resolution for $\mathbf{v}$ and $\boldsymbol{\phi}$. This motivates our choice of $n_j^i < M_j^i$.

To maintain accurate registrations, we use all given image information (at the highest resolution) by solving the adjoint equations at image resolution as given in the final adjoint state Eqs. (13.87), (13.94), and (13.105) for the different approaches, respectively. Empirically, $M_j^i \approx 4n_j^i$ worked well for lung CT registrations in our previous work [76]. The appropriate (trilinear) interpolations for the change between grids were realized with $\mathbf{P}$. As mentioned before, $\mathbf{P}$ is sparse but large, but $\mathbf{P}$ does not need to be kept in memory [51,80]. We use matrix *notation* but *implemented* a matrix-free operator following [51,80].

It is useful to start a registration with the result of a preregistration $\boldsymbol{\psi} \in \mathbb{R}^{3n}$. Given a (preferably diffeomorphic) transformation ψ only the initial conditions of the problems (13.10), (13.14), and (13.17) have to be adapted: $I(0) = I^0 \circ \psi$ or $\phi(0) = \psi$, respectively. In discrete notation these equations read $\mathbf{I}_0 = \mathbf{I}^0(\mathbf{P}\boldsymbol{\psi})$ and $\boldsymbol{\phi}_0 = \boldsymbol{\psi} \in \mathbb{R}^{3n}$.

The number of simulated points in time N is very important for the LDDMM registration. From the stability function [41, p. 16] for the explicit Runge–Kutta 4th-order the maximal admissible time step for solving the discrete transport equation can be derived as [73, p. 175]

$$h_t \leq 2\sqrt{2} \left(\sum_{i=1}^{3} \frac{a_i}{h_i} \right)^{-1}, \tag{13.108}$$

where a_i is the expected maximal magnitude of movement in direction x_i. An intermediate temporal step size was determined as

$$\tilde{h}_t = 2.8 \left(\sum_{i=1}^{3} \frac{a_i}{h_i} \right)^{-1}. \qquad (13.109)$$

Using 2.8 instead of $2\sqrt{2}$ adds a safety margin shielding against inaccuracies due to discretization errors. Additionally, as we are interested in integer values N, we compute:

$$N = \left\lceil \tilde{h}_t^{-1} \right\rceil + 1, \; h_t = \frac{1}{N-1}, \qquad (13.110)$$

which results in an even larger safety margin. According to (13.108), the time step has to decrease when the grid step size decreases, and therefore we determine h_t at the finest level ($i = F$). The main difficulty left is the estimation of the maximal motion that occurred to obtain a_i, $i = 1, 2, 3$. However, for typical medical registration scenarios in which we are interested, upper bounds for the motion that should be recovered by the registration are available. In the case of lung CT registration, even from full inspiration to full expiration, the maximal amplitude can be estimated (with a large safety margin) as 100 mm; see [17] for example datasets.

The discretized objective functions (13.45), (13.95), and (13.97) were optimized with an L-BFGS approach [71, p. 176] saving the last 5 iteration vectors for approximation of the inverse Hessian. The maximum number of iterations was set to $k_{\max} = 50$. Additional stopping criteria proposed in [66, p. 78] were used to terminate the optimization on each level. During the optimization, an Armijo line search with parameters $\beta_j = 0.5^{j-1}$, $k_{\max}^{\mathrm{LS}} = 30$, and $c_1 = 10^{-6}$ was used to guarantee a decrease of the objective function [71, p. 33]. The gradients used for the optimization are given in the last equation of (13.39) for the relaxation approaches and in (13.107) for the shooting approach. They are detailed for IBR in Section 13.6.2.1, Section 13.6.2.2, and Section 13.6.2.3 for the IBR, MBR, and MBS models, respectively. Before using the gradients of the relaxation methods for optimization, they are smoothed to obtain the Hilbert gradients (13.9) by N-fold application of $\mathbf{K}$. As $\mathbf{K}^{-1}$ coincides with the second order derivative of Reg^h, this can be viewed as a Newton step only with respect to the regularization term.

The determinant of the Jacobian of the transformation can be used to find singularities (foldings of the grid or grid cells with vanishing volume) or to evaluate whether local volume expansion or contraction occurs. Therefore it is a good criterion to check for local invertibility [24, p. 222] and to find out if the computed transformation is a diffeomorphism. We computed Jacobian determinant values $J_i \in \mathbb{R}$, $i = 1, 2, \ldots, \prod_{\ell=1}^{k} (n_\ell^F - 1)$ on the last registration level F with the dedicated method used for hyperelastic regularization [13] in the FAIR [66] Matlab toolbox.[5] The computed transformation ϕ_{N-1} contained sporadically negative Jacobians for some parameter choices (and thus was not diffeomorphic), which resulted from inaccuracies that occur when solving the transport equation for iterated time steps with the fourth-order Runge–Kutta method. Therefore, we used the obtained velocities $\mathbf{v}$ to compute the final transformation $\varphi \in \mathbb{R}^{3n}$ in a slightly different manner. The fourth-order Runge–Kutta method (13.34) with the right-hand side given in (13.90) was solved for one time step starting from the identity grid $\mathbf{x}^{\text{nd}}$ with varying velocities $\mathbf{v}_{\ell}$ for $\ell = 0, \dots, N-2$ to obtain small deformations φ_{ℓ}. These steps were then concatenated (starting from the preregistration $\boldsymbol{\psi}$) using trilinear interpolation to obtain the total transformation

$$\varphi := \varphi_{N-2} \circ \varphi_{N-3} \circ \cdots \circ \varphi_0 \circ \boldsymbol{\psi}. \qquad (13.111)$$

If each of the transformations $\boldsymbol{\psi}$, φ_{ℓ} for $\ell = 0, \dots, N-2$ is diffeomorphic, then also φ is diffeomorphic [69,50,104]. However, repeated interpolations are time-consuming and difficult to handle when solving the adjoint system consistently. Therefore, during the numerical optimization, the methods presented in Section 13.5 and Section 13.6 are used to estimate the discrete velocity fields $\mathbf{v}$. After the optimization is finished, the final transformation φ is computed within a postprocessing step according to (13.111) to achieve a transformation that is guaranteed to be diffeomorphic.

13.8 Experiments and results

This section shows experimental results on 2D radiographs of hands (Section 13.8.1) and 3D CT lung images (Section 13.8.2).

13.8.1 2D registration of hand radiographs

We illustrate our approach on a 2D dataset. The dataset consists of two 128×128 pixel radiographs of human right hands of two different patients (see Fig. 13.3(A) and Fig. 13.3(F)). The dataset has previously been used in [65] and is part of the FAIR Matlab toolbox [66]. Before applying the LDDMM methods, the images were affinely preregistered using FAIR with SSD distance measure on the coarsest level of the image pyramid. SSD was also used for the LDDMM methods. According to (13.23), H^s regularity with $s > 2$ is necessary for $k = 2$ (and thus $\beta \geq 2$) to guarantee diffeomorphic solutions. However, $s = 2$ is the limit case,

---

[5]Available at https://github.com/C4IR/FAIR.m.

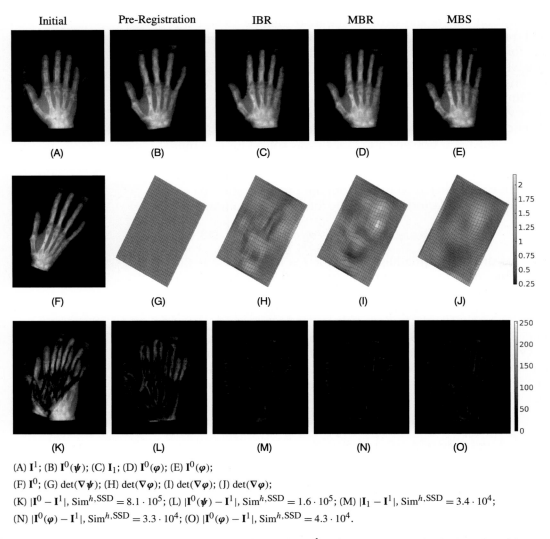

(A) $\mathbf{I}^1$; (B) $\mathbf{I}^0(\boldsymbol{\psi})$; (C) $\mathbf{I}_1$; (D) $\mathbf{I}^0(\boldsymbol{\varphi})$; (E) $\mathbf{I}^0(\boldsymbol{\varphi})$;

(F) $\mathbf{I}^0$; (G) $\det(\nabla\boldsymbol{\psi})$; (H) $\det(\nabla\boldsymbol{\varphi})$; (I) $\det(\nabla\boldsymbol{\varphi})$; (J) $\det(\nabla\boldsymbol{\varphi})$;

(K) $|\mathbf{I}^0 - \mathbf{I}^1|$, $\mathrm{Sim}^{h,\mathrm{SSD}} = 8.1 \cdot 10^5$; (L) $|\mathbf{I}^0(\boldsymbol{\psi}) - \mathbf{I}^1|$, $\mathrm{Sim}^{h,\mathrm{SSD}} = 1.6 \cdot 10^5$; (M) $|\mathbf{I}_1 - \mathbf{I}^1|$, $\mathrm{Sim}^{h,\mathrm{SSD}} = 3.4 \cdot 10^4$;

(N) $|\mathbf{I}^0(\boldsymbol{\varphi}) - \mathbf{I}^1|$, $\mathrm{Sim}^{h,\mathrm{SSD}} = 3.3 \cdot 10^4$; (O) $|\mathbf{I}^0(\boldsymbol{\varphi}) - \mathbf{I}^1|$, $\mathrm{Sim}^{h,\mathrm{SSD}} = 4.3 \cdot 10^4$.

Figure 13.3. Results for the hand examples. First row: Fixed image $\mathbf{I}^1$ and transformed moving images. Second row: Moving image $\mathbf{I}^0$ and Jacobians of the deformation grids. Third row: Absolute differences of fixed and (transformed) moving image. Second column: Results for the affine pre-registration. Third column: Results for the IBR approach. Fourth column: Results for the MBR approach. Fifth column: Results for the MBS approach. The three different LDDMM schemes were applied with the same parameters: $\alpha = 10$, $\beta = 1$, $\gamma = 3$, $\sigma = 1$, $F = 3$ and $m_1^1 = m_2^1 = 32$, $n_1^1 = n_2^1 = 9$, $N = 10$.

and we therefore decided to employ $\beta = 1$. The other parameters were determined empirically and fixed for all three approaches to $\alpha = 10$, $\gamma = 3$, $\sigma = 1$, $F = 3$ and $M_1^1 = M_2^1 = 32$, $n_1^1 = n_2^1 = 9$, $N = 10$. The second column of Fig. 13.3 shows the results of the preregistration. The following columns display the results of the IBR, MBR, and MBS approaches. Properties of the computed transformation maps are most obvious in the Jacobian determinant visualizations in the second row of Fig. 13.3. The shooting approach clearly produces smoother transformations than both relaxation approaches. Furthermore, the volume change for the relaxation approaches is locally quite different indicating that advecting the non-smooth images (via the transport equation) introduces more numerical problems than advecting the comparatively smooth spatial transformations. The resulting distortion in the deformed moving image is apparent when comparing Fig. 13.3(C) and Fig. 13.3(D). In the former oscillations next to sharp edges in the images arise, whereas the latter image has the same quality as the undeformed moving image.

Due to their representational flexibility, the relaxation approaches reach a slightly better image match as visible in the last row in the difference images. In particular the ring and the baby finger of the shooting result lack some width compared to the fixed image and are closer to the width of the fingers in the undeformed source image $\mathbf{I}^0$. The inferior image match is quantified by the three SSD values for the different approaches. These values also indicate that due to the image deterioration induced by the IBR approach, the image match is not as good as with the MBR approach. However, although the differences in image mismatch when comparing IBR and MBR to MBS are relatively small, the difference in transformation field smoothness is remarkable.

13.8.2 3D registration of lung CT data

To demonstrate the suitability of our method for 3D lung CT data, we make use of the publicly available DIR-Lab datasets [16, 17,15]. These datasets were acquired from 20 subjects (with or without pulmonary diseases) during the inhale and exhale phases and are either part of the COPDgene study [77] or 3D volumes from 4DCT scans. The number of voxels per axial slice is 512×512 for all COPD datasets [17] and 4DCT datasets 6 to 10 [16]. For 4DCT datasets 1 to 5 [15], the number of voxels per axial slice is 256×256. Each slice has a thickness of 2.5 mm, and the number of slices ranges between 94 and 135. The axial resolution varies from 0.586 mm $\times$ 0.586 mm to 0.742 mm $\times$ 0.742 mm for the COPD data [17], is 0.97 mm $\times$ 0.97 mm for 4DCT datasets 6 to 10 [16] and ranges from 0.97 mm $\times$ 0.97 mm to 1.16 mm $\times$ 1.16 mm for 4DCT datasets 1 to 5 [15]. Additionally to the images, 300 expert-placed landmarks per image are provided. These landmarks can be used for evaluation of registration accuracy.

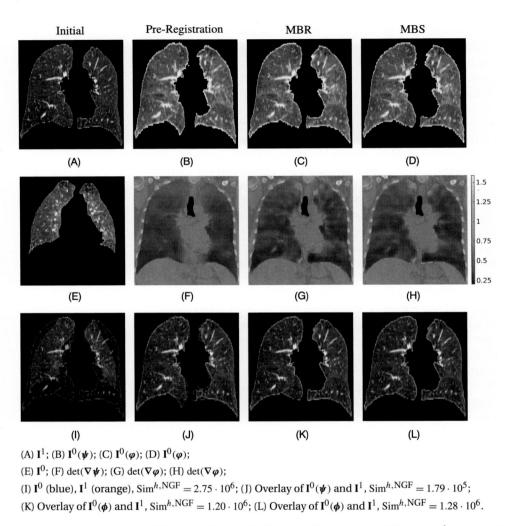

(A) $\mathbf{I}^1$; (B) $\mathbf{I}^0(\boldsymbol{\psi})$; (C) $\mathbf{I}^0(\boldsymbol{\varphi})$; (D) $\mathbf{I}^0(\boldsymbol{\varphi})$;

(E) $\mathbf{I}^0$; (F) $\det(\nabla\boldsymbol{\psi})$; (G) $\det(\nabla\boldsymbol{\varphi})$; (H) $\det(\nabla\boldsymbol{\varphi})$;

(I) $\mathbf{I}^0$ (blue), $\mathbf{I}^1$ (orange), $\text{Sim}^{h,\text{NGF}} = 2.75 \cdot 10^6$; (J) Overlay of $\mathbf{I}^0(\boldsymbol{\psi})$ and $\mathbf{I}^1$, $\text{Sim}^{h,\text{NGF}} = 1.79 \cdot 10^5$;

(K) Overlay of $\mathbf{I}^0(\boldsymbol{\phi})$ and $\mathbf{I}^1$, $\text{Sim}^{h,\text{NGF}} = 1.20 \cdot 10^6$; (L) Overlay of $\mathbf{I}^0(\boldsymbol{\phi})$ and $\mathbf{I}^1$, $\text{Sim}^{h,\text{NGF}} = 1.28 \cdot 10^6$.

Figure 13.4. Exemplary result for the DIR-Lab COPD lung CT dataset 4 [17]. First row: Fixed image $\mathbf{I}^1$ and transformed moving images. Second row: Moving image $\mathbf{I}^0$ and Jacobians of the deformation grids overlaid on the fixed scan. Third row: Overlays of fixed (orange (light gray in print version)) and (transformed) moving image (blue (dark gray in print version)); due to addition of RGB values, aligned structures appear gray or white. Second column: Results for the preregistration. Third column: Results for the MBR approach. Fourth column: Results for the MBS approach. MBR and MBS schemes were applied with the same parameters: $\alpha = 10$, $\beta = 2$, $\gamma = 1$, $\sigma = 0.05$, $F = 3$ and $n_1^1 = n_2^1 = 13$, $n_3^1 = 17$, $N = 9$.

Statistics of the Jacobian of the computed deformation fields are often used to evaluate the plausibility of the registration see, for example, [68] for the application to lung CT registration. There- fore we evaluate the Jacobians for the computed final transformation φ to estimate the reconstructed volume change of local regions of the lung and to assess for unreasonable expansions, contractions, or foldings of lung tissue.

In many clinical applications only information within the lungs is required, for example, for the staging and phenotyping of COPD [32]. Although the motion of the lung induced by respiration is smooth (making LDDMM a suitable registration model), motion discontinuities occur at the interface with the ribcage [88]. These discontinuities interfere with the LDDMM model, although in [78] a modification is presented, which applies special kernels to allow for discontinuous motions. However, as we are only interested in the alignment of the lungs, we generated lung segmentations using the method proposed in [53] and masked the CT scans to remove unnecessary image information. Hence an adaptation of our models is no longer necessary. In addition to the masking the images were cropped such that in each direction approximately 5 mm of margin were retained. For all registrations, the inhale scans were used as target images and the exhale scans as source images.

In the following experiments we used a thin-plate spline (TPS) preregistration. The TPS is based on keypoints acquired with the method in [46], which were also used for the registration of difficult COPD data with remarkably accurate results [82]. However, the TPS preregistration with these keypoints may produce transformations with foldings (i.e., negative Jacobians). Therefore, to ensure that ψ is diffeomorphic, we removed keypoints whose set of six nearest neighbors changes after TPS computation by more than one point, suggesting a violation of topology preservation. This procedure reduced the number of keypoints to approximately one quarter of the original number and results in decreased accuracy of the preregistration; see Table 13.2. The subsequent registration with our LDDMM methods MBR and MBS retained the diffeomorphic property of the estimated transformation, which might not be the case for small deformation methods; see the discussion in [23].

Due to the deteriorated quality of the deformed image of the IBR approach (see Section 13.8.1) and the interest in the volume change and plausibility of the transformation maps, we only applied the MBR and MBS approaches to the 3D lung datasets. We chose NGF as the distance measure, as it has been shown to work well on lung CT data; see Section 13.1. The same model parameters were used for all registrations: $\alpha = 10$, $\beta = 2$, $\gamma = 1$, $\sigma = 0.05$, $\mathbf{n}^1 = (13, 13, 17)^\top$, and $F = 3$. For the estimation of the time step h_t, we need an estimate for the maximal motion that may have occurred, which was denoted as a_i, $i = 1, 2, 3$, in Section 13.7. As the employed preregistration achieves a very good initial alignment and dramatically reduces the maximal motion required, we chose $a_i = 30$, $i = 1, 2, 3$, and the number of time steps according to (13.110).

Registration results for dataset 4 of the COPD datasets are shown as coronal views in Fig. 13.4. The initial unaligned images are shown in the leftmost column; note the differences in noise level and volume for the exhale scan ($\mathbf{I}^0$) and the inhale scan ($\mathbf{I}^1$). The results for the preregistration ψ alone are very good and shown in the second column. Only smaller vessels and some lung boundaries show visually obvious mismatches. Our subsequent LDDMM registrations MBR and MBS, shown in the third and fourth columns, respectively, successfully handle these mismatches and produce visually very similar results. The second row shows that the Jacobian determinant maps for all registration approaches are smooth and positive. The largest volume changes occur near the mediastinum and might be influenced by the beating heart. Taking a closer look at the image of the Jacobian determinants of MBS (Fig. 13.4(H)) reveals that it is smoother than that of MBR (Fig. 13.4(G)) regarding variations in the left-right direction. Both approaches yield very smooth results in the anterior-superior direction. In particular, the lung volume decreases (Jacobian determinant values smaller than 1), which is what we expect during exhalation, which is modeled by our choice of using the inhale phase as the fixed image and the exhale phase as the moving image.

Table 13.2 shows the mean landmark distances for all 20 datasets after MBR and MBS registration and allows for a comparison to reported results of state-of-the-art methods participating in the DIR-Lab benchmark.[6] For the 4DCT data, all compared algorithms achieve similar results regarding landmark accuracy. Results on the DIR-Lab 4DCT data were not reported in the literature for MILO [18], MRF [46], and DIS-CO [82] and are therefore not listed. DIS-CO [82] achieves the best mean landmark distance (also called target registration error (TRE)) on the more challenging COPD data. The second best method regarding TRE is [99] but is closely followed by the MBR and the MBS approaches. The algorithm proposed in [99] does not use lung segmentations for image masking, but its total variation-based regularization allows for sliding motions. However, this also has the drawback that there is no guarantee that the estimated transformations contain no foldings.

The advantage of the MBR and MBS methods (ranking third and fourth regarding TRE) is that they produce transformation

[6]http://www.dir-lab.com/Results.html.

Table 13.2 Mean landmark distances of the 300 landmark pairs after registration with state-of-the-art methods. All values are given in mm and were computed after rounding to the next voxel center.

Case	Initial	Mean landmark distance after registration in mm							
		MILO [18]	MRF [46]	LMP [74]	DIS-CO [82]	isoPTV [99]	Prereg.	MBR	MBS
4DCT1	3.89			0.74		0.76	0.80	0.74	0.76
4DCT2	4.34			0.78		0.77	0.75	0.80	0.82
4DCT3	6.94			0.91		0.90	0.95	0.93	0.95
4DCT4	9.83			1.24		1.24	1.39	1.24	1.31
4DCT5	7.48			1.17		1.12	1.25	1.10	1.11
4DCT6	10.89			0.90		0.85	1.04	0.86	0.87
4DCT7	11.03			0.87		0.80	1.09	0.83	0.88
4DCT8	14.99			1.04		1.34	1.20	1.11	1.10
4DCT9	7.92			0.98		0.92	1.10	0.96	0.93
4DCT10	7.30			0.89		0.82	1.09	0.88	0.90
Average	8.46			0.95		0.95	1.07	0.95	0.96
COPD1	26.34	0.93	1.00	1.21	0.79	0.77	1.15	1.12	0.91
COPD2	21.79	1.77	1.62	1.97	1.46	2.22	2.18	1.49	1.49
COPD3	12.64	0.99	1.00	1.06	0.84	0.82	1.19	0.97	0.96
COPD4	29.58	1.14	1.08	1.64	0.74	0.85	1.32	0.89	0.97
COPD5	30.08	1.02	0.96	1.46	0.71	0.77	1.18	0.79	0.92
COPD6	28.46	0.99	1.01	1.34	0.64	0.86	1.27	0.84	0.92
COPD7	21.60	1.03	1.05	1.16	0.79	0.74	1.32	0.92	0.93
COPD8	26.46	1.31	1.08	1.54	0.77	0.81	1.47	1.03	1.03
COPD9	14.86	0.86	0.79	0.99	0.62	0.83	1.02	0.75	0.73
COPD10	21.81	1.23	1.18	1.39	0.86	0.92	1.51	1.02	1.09
Average	23.36	1.13	1.08	1.38	0.82	0.96	1.36	0.98	1.00
Total Average	15.91	1.13	1.08	1.16	0.82	0.96	1.21	0.96	0.98

maps without foldings or implausible volume changes within the lungs; see Table 13.3. Only two other methods, LMP [74] and DIS-CO [82], can guarantee this regularity, and LMP achieves a worse TRE on the COPD data than both MBR and MBS.

The Jacobians given in Table 13.3 show that the computed transformation field is indeed very smooth, as the standard deviation is small. Furthermore, the mean volume change is well

Table 13.3 Minimum, mean, and standard deviation (SD) of the Jacobian determinant values of the computed transformations $\varphi \in \mathbb{R}^{3\bar{n}}$ restricted to the lung volume. The mean value should be similar to the volume ratio (VR), which was computed as the ratio of exhale lung volume to inhale lung volume using the lung masks.

Case	VR	Min.	MBR Mean ± SD	Min.	MBS Mean±SD
4DCT1	0.91	0.48	0.92±0.10	0.50	0.92±0.10
4DCT2	0.92	0.45	0.92±0.09	0.42	0.92±0.11
4DCT3	0.90	0.47	0.90±0.10	0.52	0.90±0.11
4DCT4	0.86	0.46	0.86±0.15	0.41	0.86±0.16
4DCT5	0.91	0.46	0.92±0.13	0.44	0.92±0.15
4DCT6	0.77	0.42	0.77±0.09	0.44	0.77±0.09
4DCT7	0.82	0.43	0.79±0.09	0.44	0.79±0.09
4DCT8	0.83	0.34	0.80±0.09	0.34	0.80±0.10
4DCT9	0.86	0.46	0.87±0.10	0.42	0.87±0.10
4DCT10	0.86	0.31	0.87±0.13	0.32	0.87±0.14
COPD1	0.62	0.12	0.65±0.15	0.17	0.65±0.14
COPD2	0.73	0.15	0.75±0.24	0.17	0.75±0.25
COPD3	0.80	0.29	0.80±0.13	0.29	0.80±0.14
COPD4	0.49	0.18	0.50±0.12	0.16	0.50±0.12
COPD5	0.49	0.15	0.49±0.11	0.15	0.49±0.11
COPD6	0.62	0.18	0.64±0.16	0.06	0.64±0.16
COPD7	0.75	0.39	0.75±0.11	0.38	0.75±0.12
COPD8	0.58	0.21	0.59±0.13	0.23	0.59±0.13
COPD9	0.73	0.32	0.74±0.12	0.32	0.74±0.13
COPD10	0.61	0.11	0.61±0.12	0.11	0.61±0.13

correlated with the expected volume ratio, and no foldings of the grid occurred as the minimal Jacobian is always positive. To obtain diffeomorphic transformations φ from the previously computed ϕ_{N-1} in the discrete framework, we used the procedure described in Section 13.7. The transformations ϕ_{N-1} and φ show only small differences. The mean value of $\|\phi_{N-1} - \varphi\|_\infty$ computed over all 20 DIR-Lab datasets is 3.15 mm for the MBR method and 5.80 mm for the MBS method.

All experiments were run on a PC with a single 3.4 GHz Intel i7-2600 quad-core CPU, 16 GB of RAM, and Ubuntu 14.04. Runtimes for the MBS approach ranged between 16 and 55 min with an average of 28 min. The peak memory consumption was 4.3 GB over all datasets. Analogously, for MBR, the runtimes ranged between 5 and 24 min with an average of 14 min and a peak memory consumption of 2.1 GB.

13.9 Discussion and conclusion

LDDMM is a popular registration method with nice mathematical properties that has successfully been applied to various applications; see, for example, [64] and references therein. The estimated deformation fields are guaranteed to be diffeomorphic, the deformation paths are geodesics, large displacements can be captured, and LDDMM induces a distance measure on images [7]. These properties, however, come with the drawbacks of a large computational burden, both with respect to runtime and memory consumption.

It is interesting that numerical approaches for LDDMM have not been explored in great depth, and the predominant solution approach is still optimize–discretize via gradient descent as proposed in [7]. Hence we chose to develop discretize–optimize schemes for relaxation and shooting, offering consistent numerical optimizations for the discretized energy, which, as discussed in [35], cannot be guaranteed for optimize–discretize approaches such as [7]. Formulating a discretized energy included the discretization of PDE constraints (mainly transport and scalar conservation equations), which we accomplished via an explicit fourth-order Runge–Kutta method as a good compromise between efficiency and accuracy. We also reduced memory consumption and runtime by representing velocities and transformation maps at lower spatial resolutions compared to the images. This is justified due to the smoothness of velocity fields and transformation maps and still allowed for high-quality registrations. Finally, our proposed methods can also be used with different image similarity measures, and we explored the use of NGF for lung registration.

We demonstrated the characteristics of the proposed registration methods for a two-dimensional registration example of human hand radiographs. This experiment confirmed that the relaxation approaches yield a better image match due to more degrees of freedom compared to the shooting approach, which is much more constrained (solutions are geodesics by construction and not only at absolute convergence) and yields a smoother deformation field.

The methods were also tested on the challenging lung CT datasets provided by DIR-Lab [16,17,15], where we integrated the

NGF distance measure to well align edges located at, for example, vessels and lung boundaries. We compared results based on the distances of 300 expert-annotated landmark pairs per inhale-exhale scan to the state-of-the-art. With an average error of 0.98 mm on the DIR-Lab COPD datasets the relaxation approach achieves the third-best result. The average error is only 0.02 mm higher than for the second-best method [99], which is almost negligible. The shooting approach performs slightly worse with an average landmark distance of 1.00 mm for the COPD datasets whilst yielding desirable smooth transformations. Nevertheless, the relaxation approach may be preferable for registration of lung CT scans from full-inspiration to full-expiration due to its reduced runtime.

In future work an extended evaluation that includes a comparison with publicly available diffeomorphic registration software packages like Deformetrica[7] [28], MRICloud[8] [49], LDDMM with frame-based kernel[9] [94], FshapesTk[10] [21], and Lagrangian LDDMM[11] [58] would be beneficial.

For fast prototyping, the usage of automatic differentiation methods could be employed to derive a DO scheme from a discretized objective function. This has been done, for example, in [52] for shape matching. However, it is an interesting question how the computation time competes with the dedicated methods developed in this chapter. Automatic differentiation is also very popular in the field of machine learning. Recently, deep learning approaches for image registration have been proposed. Yang et al. [102,103] developed such a method for the shooting formulation of LDDMM. To refine the output of the deep-learning approach, it could be used as a fast initialization for a subsequent registration with our discretize–optimize approaches and/or the deep network could be trained based on our LDDMM approaches.

References

1. Vincent Arsigny, Olivier Commowick, Xavier Pennec, Nicholas Ayache, A log-Euclidean framework for statistics on diffeomorphisms, in: Rasmus Larsen, Mads Nielsen, Jon Sporring (Eds.), Medical Image Computing and Computer-Assisted Intervention – MICCAI 2006, Springer, 2006, pp. 924–931.
2. John Ashburner, A fast diffeomorphic image registration algorithm, NeuroImage 38 (1) (2007) 95–113.

[7] http://www.deformetrica.org.
[8] https://mricloud.org/.
[9] http://www.bioeng.nus.edu.sg/cfa/brainmapping.html.
[10] https://github.com/fshapes/fshapesTk/.
[11] https://github.com/C4IR/FAIR.m/tree/master/add-ons/LagLDDMM.

3. John Ashburner, Karl J. Friston, Diffeomorphic registration using geodesic shooting and Gauss–Newton optimisation, NeuroImage 55 (3) (2011) 954–967.

4. Brian B. Avants, Charles L. Epstein, Murray Grossman, James C. Gee, Symmetric diffeomorphic image registration with cross-correlation: evaluating automated labeling of elderly and neurodegenerative brain, Medical Image Analysis 12 (1) (2008) 26–41.

5. Robert Azencott, Roland Glowinski, Jiwen He, Aarti Jajoo, Yipeng Li, Andrey Martynenko, Ronald H.W. Hoppe, Sagit Benzekry, Stuart H. Little, William A. Zoghbi, Diffeomorphic matching and dynamic deformable surfaces in 3D medical imaging, Computational Methods in Applied Mathematics 10 (3) (2010) 235–274.

6. Ruzena Bajcsy, Robert Lieberson, Martin Reivich, A computerized system for the elastic matching of deformed radiographic images to idealized atlas images, Journal of Computer Assisted Tomography 7 (1983) 618–625.

7. Mirza Faisal Beg, Michael I. Miller, Alain Trouvé, Laurent Younes, Computing large deformation metric mappings via geodesic flows of diffeomorphisms, International Journal of Computer Vision 61 (2) (2005) 139–157.

8. Alfio Borzì, Kazufumi Ito, Karl Kunisch, Optimal control formulation for determining optical flow, SIAM Journal on Scientific Computing 24 (3) (2003) 818–847.

9. Chaim Broit, Optimal Registration of Deformed Images, PhD thesis, Computer and Information Science, University of Pensylvania, USA, 1981.

10. Lisa Gottesfeld Brown, A survey of image registration techniques, ACM Computing Surveys 24 (4) (1992) 325–376.

11. Thomas Brox, Jitendra Malik, Large displacement optical flow: descriptor matching in variational motion estimation, IEEE Transactions on Pattern Analysis and Machine Intelligence 33 (3) (2011) 500–513.

12. Andrés Bruhn, Joachim Weickert, Christoph Schnörr, Lucas/Kanade meets Horn/Schunck: combining local and global optic flow methods, International Journal of Computer Vision 61 (3) (2005) 211–231.

13. Martin Burger, Jan Modersitzki, Lars Ruthotto, A hyperelastic regularization energy for image registration, SIAM Journal on Scientific Computing 35 (1) (2013) B132–B148.

14. John C. Butcher, Numerical Methods for Ordinary Differential Equations, 3rd edition, John Wiley & Sons Ltd., Chichester, UK, 2016.

15. Richard Castillo, Edward Castillo, Rudy Guerra, Valen E. Johnson, Travis McPhail, et al., A framework for evaluation of deformable image registration spatial accuracy using large landmark point sets, Physics in Medicine and Biology 54 (7) (2009) 1849–1870.

16. Edward Castillo, Richard Castillo, Josue Martinez, Maithili Shenoy, Thomas Guerrero, Four-dimensional deformable image

registration using trajectory modeling, Physics in Medicine and Biology 55 (1) (2010) 305–327.

17. Richard Castillo, Edward Castillo, David Fuentes, Moiz Ahmad, Abbie M. Wood, et al., A reference dataset for deformable image registration spatial accuracy evaluation using the COPDgene study archive, Physics in Medicine and Biology 58 (9) (2013) 2861–2877.

18. Edward Castillo, Richard Castillo, David Fuentes, Thomas Guerrero, Computing global minimizers to a constrained B-spline image registration problem from optimal l1 perturbations to block match data, Medical Physics 41 (4) (2014) 041904.

19. Elena Celledoni, Robert I. McLachlan, David I. McLaren, Brynjulf Owren, G. Reinout W. Quispel, William M. Wright, Energy-preserving Runge–Kutta methods, ESAIM: Mathematical Modelling and Numerical Analysis 43 (2009) 645–649.

20. Robert P.K. Chan, On symmetric Runge–Kutta methods of high order, Computing 45 (1990) 301–309.

21. Benjamin Charlier, Nicolas Charon, Alain Trouvé, The fshape framework for the variability analysis of functional shapes, Foundations of Computational Mathematics 17 (2) (2017) 287–357.

22. Christophe Chefd'hotel, Gerardo Hermosillo, Olivier Faugeras, Flows of diffeomorphisms for multimodal image registration, in: IEEE International Symposium on Biomedical Imaging – ISBI 2002, IEEE, 2002, pp. 753–775.

23. Gary E. Christensen, Richard D. Rabbitt, Michael I. Miller, Deformable templates using large deformation kinetics, IEEE Transactions on Image Processing 5 (10) (1996) 1435–1447.

24. Philippe G. Ciarlet, Mathematical Elasticity, Volume I: Three-Dimensional Elasticity, Elsevier Science, North-Holland, 1988.

25. Domenico D'Alessandro, Introduction to Quantum Control and Dynamics, Chapman & Hall/CRC, Boca Raton, FL, USA, 2007.

26. Paul Dupuis, Ulf Grenander, Michael I. Miller, Variational problems on flows of diffeomorphisms for image matching, Quarterly of Applied Mathematics 56 (3) (1998) 1–20.

27. Stanley Durrleman, Marcel Prastawa, Guido Gerig, Sarang Joshi, Optimal data-driven sparse parameterization of diffeomorphisms for population analysis, in: Information Processing in Medical Imaging 2011, Springer, Berlin/Heidelberg, 2011, pp. 123–134.

28. Stanley Durrleman, Marcel Prastawa, Nicolas Charon, Julie R. Korenberg, Sarang Joshi, Guido Gerig, Alain Trouvé, Morphometry of anatomical shape complexes with dense deformations and sparse parameters, NeuroImage 101 (2014) 35–49.

29. Bernd Fischer, Jan Modersitzki, Ill-posed medicine – an introduction to image registration, Inverse Problems 24 (2008) 034008.

30. Martin A. Fischler, Robert A. Elschlager, The representation and matching of pictorial structures, IEEE Transactions on Computers 22 (1) (1973) 67–92.

31. J. Michael Fitzpatrick, David L.G. Hill, Calvin R. Maurer Jr, Image registration, in: Jacob Beutel, J. Michael Fitzpatrick, Steven C. Horii, Yongmin Kim, Harold L. Kundel, Milan Sonka, Richard L. Van Metter (Eds.), Handbook of Medical Imaging, Volume 2: Medical Image Processing and Analysis, SPIE, Bellingham, Washington, USA, 2000, pp. 447–514.

32. Craig J. Galbán, Meilan K. Han, Jennifer L. Boes, Komal Chughtai, Charles R. Meyer, et al., Computed tomography-based biomarker provides unique signature for diagnosis of COPD phenotypes and disease progression, Nature Medicine 18 (2012) 1711–1715.

33. A. Ardeshir Goshtasby, Image Registration: Principles, Tools and Methods, Springer, New York, 2012.

34. Andreas Griewank, Andrea Walther, Evaluating Derivatives: Principles and Techniques of Algorithmic Differentiation, 2nd edition, SIAM, Philadelphia, PA, USA, 2008.

35. Eldad Haber, Lauren Hanson, Model Problems in PDE-Constrained Optimization, Technical report, TR-2007-009, Emory University, 2007.

36. Eldad Haber, Jan Modersitzki, Numerical methods for volume preserving image registration, Inverse Problems 20 (5) (2004) 1621–1638.

37. Eldad Haber, Jan Modersitzki, Image registration with a guaranteed displacement regularity, International Journal of Computer Vision 71 (3) (2007).

38. Eldad Haber, Jan Modersitzki, Intensity gradient based registration and fusion of multi-modal images, Methods of Information in Medicine 46 (3) (2007) 292–299.

39. William W. Hager, Rates of convergence for discrete approximations to unconstrained control problems, SIAM Journal on Numerical Analysis 13 (4) (1976) 449–472.

40. William W. Hager, Runge–Kutta methods in optimal control and the transformed adjoint system, Numerische Mathematik 87 (2) (2000) 247–282.

41. Ernst Hairer, Gerhard Wanner, Solving Ordinary Differential Equations II – Stiff and Differential–Algebraic Problems, 2nd edition, Springer, Berlin/Heidelberg, Germany, 1996.

42. Ernst Hairer, Syvert P. Nørsett, Gerhard Wanner, Solving Ordinary Differential Equations I: Nonstiff Problems, Springer, Berlin/Heidelberg, Germany, 1993.

43. Ernst Hairer, Christian Lubich, Gerhard Wanner, Geometric Numerical Integration: Structure-Preserving Algorithms for Ordinary Differential Equations, 2nd edition, Springer, Berlin/Heidelberg, Germany, 2006.

44. Joseph V. Hajnal, Derek L.G. Hill, David J. Hawkes, Medical Image Registration, CRC Press, Boca Raton, FL, USA, 2001.

45. Gabriel L. Hart, Christopher Zach, Marc Niethammer, An optimal control approach for deformable registration, in: Computer Vision and Pattern Recognition Workshops, IEEE, 2009, pp. 9–16.

46. Mattias Paul Heinrich, Heinz Handels, Ivor J.A. Simpson, Estimating large lung motion in COPD patients by symmetric regularised correspondence fields, in: Nassir Navab, Joachim Hornegger, William M. Wells, Alejandro F. Frangi (Eds.), Medical Image Computing and Computer-Assisted Intervention – MICCAI 2015, Springer, 2015, pp. 338–345.

47. Darryl D. Holm, Jerrold E. Marsden, Tudor S. Ratiu, The Euler–Poincaré equations and semidirect products with applications to continuum theories, Advances in Mathematics 137 (1998) 1–81.

48. Berthold K.P. Horn, Brian G. Schunck, Determining optical flow, Artificial Intelligence 17 (1–3) (1981) 185–203.

49. Saurabh Jain, Daniel J. Tward, David S. Lee, Anthony Kolasny, Timothy Brown, J. Tilak Ratnanather, Michael I. Miller, Laurent Younes, Computational anatomy gateway: leveraging XSEDE computational resources for shape analysis, ACM International Conference Proceeding Series (2014) 54:1–54:6.

50. Bilge Karaçalı, Christos Davatzikos, Estimating topology preserving and smooth displacement fields, IEEE Transactions on Medical Imaging 23 (7) (2004) 868–880.

51. Lars König, Jan Rühaak, A fast and accurate parallel algorithm for non-linear image registration using normalized gradient fields, in: International Symposium on Biomedical Imaging – ISBI 2014, IEEE, 2014, pp. 580–583.

52. Line Kühnel, Stefan Sommer, Computational anatomy in Theano, in: Graphs in Biomedical Image Analysis, Computational Anatomy and Imaging Genetics, in: LNCS, vol. 10551, Springer, 2017, pp. 164–176.

53. Bianca Lassen, Jan-Martin Kuhnigk, Michael Schmidt, Stefan Krass, Heinz-Otto Peitgen Lung, Lung Lobe, Segmentation methods at fraunhofer MEVIS, in: Proceedings of the Fourth International Workshop on Pulmonary Image Analysis, 2011, pp. 185–199.

54. Yann LeCun, A theoretical framework for back-propagation, in: David S. Touretzky, Geoffrey Hinton, Terrence J. Sejnowski (Eds.), Proceedings of the 1988 Connectionist Models Summer School, Morgan Kaufmann, 1988, pp. 21–28.

55. Bruce D. Lucas, Takeo Kanade, An iterative image registration technique with an application to stereo vision, in: Proc. Seventh International Joint Conference on Artificial Intelligence, vol. 130, 1981, pp. 674–679.

56. J.B. Antoine Maintz, Max A. Viergever, A survey of medical image registration, Medical Image Analysis 2 (1) (1998) 1–36.

57. Andreas Mang, George Biros, An inexact Newton–Krylov algorithm for constrained diffeomorphic image registration, SIAM Journal on Imaging Sciences 8 (2) (2015) 1030–1069.

58. Andreas Mang, Lars Ruthotto, A Lagrangian Gauss–Newton–Krylov solver for mass- and intensity-preserving diffeomorphic image registration, SIAM Journal on Scientific Computing 39 (5) (2017) B860–B885.

59. Stephen Marsland, Robert McLachlan, A Hamiltonian particle method for diffeomorphic image registration, in: Nico Karssemeijer, Boudewijn Lelieveldt (Eds.), Information Processing in Medical Imaging – IPMI 2007, Springer, Berlin/Heidelberg, 2007, pp. 396–407.

60. Michael I. Miller, Computational anatomy: shape, growth, and atrophy comparison via diffeomorphisms, NeuroImage 23 (Suppl. 1) (2004) S13–S33.

61. Michael I. Miller, Alain Trouvé, Laurent Younes, On the metrics and Euler–Lagrange equations of computational anatomy, Annual Review of Biomedical Engineering 4 (2002) 375–405.

62. Michael I. Miller, Alain Trouvé, Laurent Younes, Geodesic shooting for computational anatomy, Journal of Mathematical Imaging and Vision 24 (2006) 209–228.

63. Michael I. Miller, Laurent Younes, Alain Trouvé, Diffeomorphometry and geodesic positioning systems for human anatomy, Technology 2 (1) (2014) 36–43.

64. Michael I. Miller, Alain Trouvé, Laurent Younes, Hamiltonian systems and optimal control in computational anatomy: 100 years since D'Arcy Thompson, Annual Review of Biomedical Engineering 17 (1) (2015) 447–509.

65. Jan Modersitzki, Numerical Methods for Image Registration, Oxford University Press, New York, 2004.

66. Jan Modersitzki, FAIR: Flexible Algorithms for Image Registration, SIAM, Philadelphia, 2009.

67. David Mumford, Peter W. Michor, On Euler's equation and 'EPDiff', Journal of Geometric Mechanics 5 (3) (2013) 319–344.

68. Keelin Murphy, Bram van Ginneken, Joseph M. Reinhardt, Sven Kabus, Kai Ding, et al., Evaluation of registration methods on thoracic CT: the EMPIRE10 challenge, IEEE Transactions on Medical Imaging 30 (11) (2011) 1901–1920.

69. Oliver Musse, Fabrice Heitz, Jean-Paul Armspach, Topology preserving deformable image matching using constrained hierarchical parametric models, IEEE Transactions on Image Processing 10 (7) (2001) 1081–1093.

70. Marc Niethammer, Yang Huang, François-Xavier Vialard, Geodesic regression for image time-series, in: Gabor Fichtinger, Anne Martel, Terry Peters (Eds.), Medical Image Computing and Computer-Assisted Intervention – MICCAI 2011, Springer, 2011, pp. 655–662.

71. Jorge Nocedal, Stephen Wright, Numerical Optimization, Springer, New York, NY, USA, 2006.

72. Nils Papenberg, Andrés Bruhn, Thomas Brox, Stephan Didas, Joachim Weickert, Highly accurate optic flow computation with theoretically justified warping, International Journal of Computer Vision 67 (2) (2006) 141–158.

73. Thomas Polzin, Large Deformation Diffeomorphic Metric Mappings – Theory, Numerics, and Applications, PhD thesis, University of Lübeck, Institute of Mathematics and Image Computing, 2018.

74. Thomas Polzin, Jan Rühaak, René Werner, Jan Strehlow, Stefan Heldmann, Heinz Handels, Jan Modersitzki, Combining automatic landmark detection and variational methods for lung ct registration, in: Proceedings of the Fifth International MICCAI Workshop on Pulmonary Image Analysis, 2013, pp. 85–96.

75. Thomas Polzin, Jan Rühaak, René Werner, Heinz Handels, Jan Modersitzki, Lung registration using automatically detected landmarks, Methods of Information in Medicine 4 (2014) 250–256.

76. Thomas Polzin, Marc Niethammer, Mattias Paul Heinrich, Heinz Handels, Jan Modersitzki, Memory efficient LDDMM for Lung CT, in: Sebastien Ourselin, Leo Joskowicz, Mert R. Sabuncu, Gozde Unal, William M. Wells (Eds.), Medical Image Computing and Computer-Assisted Intervention – MICCAI 2016, Springer, 2016, pp. 28–36.

77. Elizabeth A. Regan, John E. Hokanson, James R. Murphy, David A. Lynch, Terri H. Beaty, et al., Genetic epidemiology of COPD (COPDGene) study design, COPD 7 (2011) 32–43.

78. Laurent Risser, François-Xavier Vialard, Habib Y. Baluwala, Julia A. Schnabel, Piecewise-diffeomorphic image registration: application to the motion estimation between 3D CT lung images with sliding conditions, Medical Image Analysis 17 (2) (2013) 182–193.

79. Torsten Rohlfing, Calvin R. Maurer Jr., David A. Bluemke, Michael A. Jacobs, Volume-preserving nonrigid registration of MR breast images using free-form deformation with an incompressibility constraint, IEEE Transactions on Medical Imaging 22 (6) (2003) 730–741.

80. Jan Rühaak, Matrix-Free Techniques for Efficient Image Registration and Their Application to Pulmonary Image Analysis, PhD thesis, Jacobs University, Bremen, Germany, 2017.

81. Jan Rühaak, Stefan Heldmann, Till Kipshagen, Bernd Fischer, Highly accurate fast lung CT registration, in: David R. Haynor, Sebastien Ourselin (Eds.), SPIE Medical Imaging 2013: Image Processing, 2013, pp. 86690Y1–86690Y9.

82. Jan Rühaak, Thomas Polzin, Stefan Heldmann, Ivor J.A. Simpson, Heinz Handels, Jan Modersitzki, Mattias Paul Heinrich, Estimation of large motion in lung CT by integrating regularized keypoint correspondences into dense deformable registration, IEEE Transactions on Medical Imaging 36 (8) (2017) 1746–1757.

83. Martin Rumpf, Benedikt Wirth, Discrete geodesic calculus in shape space and applications in the space of viscous fluidic objects, SIAM Journal on Imaging Sciences 6 (4) (2013) 2581–2602.

84. Lars Ruthotto, Jan Modersitzki, Non-linear image registration, in: Otmar Scherzer (Ed.), Handbook of Mathematical Methods in Imaging, Springer, New York, 2015, pp. 2005–2051.

85. Jesús María Sanz-Serna, Runge–Kutta schemes for Hamiltonian systems, BIT Numerical Mathematics 28 (1988) 877–883.

86. Ryo Sakamoto, Susumu Mori, Michael I. Miller, Tomohisa Okada, Kaori Togashi, Detection of time-varying structures by large

deformation diffeomorphic metric mapping to aid reading of high-resolution CT images of the lung, PLoS ONE 9 (1) (2014) 1–11.

87. Otmar Scherzer, Mathematical Models for Registration and Applications to Medical Imaging, Springer, New York, 2006.

88. Alexander Schmidt-Richberg, René Werner, Heinz Handels, Jan Ehrhardt, Estimation of slipping organ motion by registration with direction-dependent regularization, Medical Image Analysis 16 (1) (2012) 150–159.

89. Adam L. Schwartz, Elijah Polak, Consistent approximations for optimal control problems based on Runge–Kutta integration, SIAM Journal on Control and Optimization 34 (4) (1996) 1235–1269.

90. Nikhil Singh, Jacob Hinkle, Sarang C. Joshi, P. Thomas Fletcher, A vector momenta formulation of diffeomorphisms for improved geodesic regression and atlas constructuion, in: 2013 IEEE 10th International Symposium on Biomedical Imaging: From Nano to Macro, San Francisco, 2013, pp. 1219–1222.

91. Aristeidis Sotiras, Christos Davatzikos, Nikos Paragios, Deformable medical image registration: a survey, IEEE Transactions on Medical Imaging 32 (7) (2013) 1153–1190.

92. John C. Strikwerda, Finite Difference Schemes and Partial Differential Equations, 2nd edition, SIAM, Philadelphia, 2004.

93. Xiaobo Tan, Almost symplectic Runge–Kutta schemes for Hamiltonian systems, Journal of Computational Physics 203 (1) (2005) 250–273.

94. Mingzhen Tan, Anqi Qiu, Large deformation multiresolution diffeomorphic metric mapping for multiresolution cortical surfaces: a coarse-to-fine approach, IEEE Transactions on Image Processing 25 (9) (2016) 4061–4074.

95. Nicholas J. Tustison, Tessa S. Cook, Gang Song, James C. Gee, Pulmonary kinematics from image data: a review, Academic Radiology 18 (4) (2011) 402–417.

96. Carole J. Twining, Stephen Marsland, Constructing diffeomorphic representations for the groupwise analysis of nonrigid registrations of medical images, IEEE Transactions on Medical Imaging 23 (2004) 1006–1020.

97. Petra A. van den Elsen, Evert-Jan D. Pol, Max A. Viergever, Medical image matching – a review with classification, IEEE Engineering in Medicine and Biology 12 (1) (1993) 26–39.

98. François-Xavier Vialard, Laurent Risser, Daniel Rueckert, Colin J. Cotter, Diffeomorphic 3D image registration via geodesic shooting using an efficient adjoint calculation, International Journal of Computer Vision 97 (2) (2012) 229–241.

99. Valery Vishnevskiy, Tobias Gass, Gábor Székely, Christine Tanner, Orcun Goksel, Isotropic total variation regularization of displacements in parametric image registration, IEEE Transactions on Medical Imaging 36 (2) (2017) 385–395.

100. Joachim Weickert, Andrés Bruhn, Thomas Brox, Nils Papenberg, A survey on variational optic flow methods for small displacements,

in: O. Scherzer (Ed.), Mathematical Models for Registration and Applications to Medical Imaging, in: Mathematics in Industry, vol. 10, Springer, Berlin, 2006.

101. Benedikt Wirth, Leah Bar, Martin Rumpf, Guillermo Sapiro, A continuum mechanical approach to geodesics in shape space, International Journal of Computer Vision 93 (3) (2011) 293–318.

102. Xiao Yang, Roland Kwitt, Marc Niethammer, Fast predictive image registration, in: International Workshop on Deep Learning and Data Labeling for Medical Applications – LABELS/DLMIA 2016, Springer International Publishing, 2016, pp. 48–57.

103. Xiao Yang, Roland Kwitt, Martin Styner, Marc Niethammer Quicksilver, Fast predictive image registration – a deep learning approach, NeuroImage 158 (2017) 378–396.

104. Laurent Younes, Shapes and Diffeomorphisms, Springer, Berlin/Heidelberg, Germany, 2010.

105. Laurent Younes, Felipe Arrate, Michael I. Miller, Evolutions equations in computational anatomy, NeuroImage 45 (1 Suppl 1) (2009) S40–S50.

106. Christopher Zach, Thomas Pock, Horst Bischof, A duality based approach for realtime TV-l 1 optical flow, in: Fred A. Hamprecht, Christoph Schnörr, Bernd Jähne (Eds.), Joint Pattern Recognition Symposium – DAGM 2007: Pattern Recognition, in: LNCS, vol. 4713, Springer, Berlin, Heidelberg, 2007, pp. 214–223.

107. Miaomiao Zhang, P. Thomas Fletcher, Finite-dimensional lie algebras for fast diffeomorphic image registration, in: Information Processing in Medical Imaging – IPMI 2015, 2015, pp. 249–260.

108. William P. Ziemer, Weakly Differentiable Functions: Sobolev Spaces and Functions of Bounded Variation, 1st edition, Springer Science+Business Media, New York, NY, USA, 1989.

109. Barbara Zitová, Jan Flusser, Image registration methods: a survey, Image and Vision Computing 21 (11) (2003) 977–1000.

Spatially adaptive metrics for diffeomorphic image matching in LDDMM

Laurent Risser[a,c], François-Xavier Vialard[b,c]

[a] Institut de Mathématiques de Toulouse, CNRS, Université de Toulouse, UMR CNRS 5219, Toulouse, France. [b] Laboratoire d'informatique Gaspard Monge, Université Paris-Est Marne-la-Vallée, UMR CNRS 8049, Champs sur Marne, France

14.1 Introduction to LDDMM

14.1.1 Problem definition

The construction of the large deformation diffeomorphic metric mapping (LDDMM) framework is based on a variational setting and the choice of a Riemannian metric. Its goal is to estimate optimal smooth and invertible maps (diffeomorphisms) of the ambient space that represent a mapping between the points of a source image I_S and those of a target image I_T [9,6], see also Chapter 4. This diffeomorphic image registration formalism is particularly adapted to the registration of most 3D medical images, where the hypothesis that organ deformations are smooth is reasonable, and the topology of the represented organs is preserved. Note that this second property is mainly due to the fact that there is no occlusion or out-of-slice motion in such images. Image registration thus takes the form of an infinite-dimensional optimal control problem: Minimize the cost functional

$$\mathcal{J}(\xi) = \frac{1}{2} \int_0^1 \|\xi(t)\|_V^2 \, \mathrm{d}t + S(I_S \circ \varphi^{-1}) \qquad (14.1)$$

under the constraints

$$\partial_t \varphi(t, x) = \xi(t, \varphi(t, x)), \qquad (14.2)$$

$$\varphi(0, x) = x \;\; \forall x \in D. \qquad (14.3)$$

The functional $\mathcal{S}$ represents the similarity measure between the registered images. For grey level images acquired using the same

---

[c] Both authors equally contributed to the chapter.

Riemannian Geometric Statistics in Medical Image Analysis
https://doi.org/10.1016/B978-0-12-814725-2.00023-6

modality (e.g. a pair of MR images), the standard similarity metric is the so-called sum of squared differences between the deformed source image I_S and the target image I_T, that is, $\|I_S \circ \varphi^{-1} - I_T\|_{L^2}^2$, both defined on a domain of the Euclidean space denoted by D. As summarized in Fig. 14.1, constraints (14.2) encode the trajectory of the points $x \in D$: At time $t = 0$ a point x of the source image I_S is naturally at location $\varphi(0, x) = x$. Then its motion at times $t \in [0, 1]$ is defined by the integration of the time-dependent velocity field $\xi(t, x)$. The transformed location of x at time $t = 1$ is finally $\varphi(1, x)$ and corresponds to the mapping of x in the target image I_T.

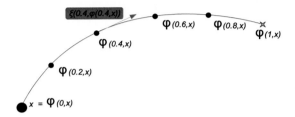

Figure 14.1. Transportation of the point $x \in D$ through the diffeomorphism $\varphi(t, x)$, where D is the domain of the source image I_S. The point $\varphi(1, x)$ is the mapping of x in the target image I_T.

14.1.2 Properties

In Eq. (14.1), V is a Hilbert space of vector fields on a Euclidean domain $D \subset \mathbb{R}^d$. A key technical assumption, which ensures that the computed maps are diffeomorphisms up to the numerical scheme accuracy, is that the inclusion map $V \hookrightarrow W^{1,\infty}(D, \mathbb{R}^d)$, that is, the space of vector fields which are Lipschitz continuous, is continuous. The norm on V controls the $W^{1,\infty}$ norm, and we call such a space V an *admissible* space of vector fields. In particular, these spaces are included in the family of reproducing kernel Hilbert spaces (RKHS) [3] since pointwise evaluations are a continuous linear map, which implies that such spaces are completely defined by their kernel. The kernel, denoted by k in this chapter, is a function from the product space $D \times D$ into $\mathbb{R}^d$ that automatically satisfies the technical assumption mentioned if it is sufficiently smooth. Last, we denote by $K : V^* \to V$ the isomorphism between V^*, the dual of V, and V.

Note that the contributions presented in this chapter build on the flexibility of the RKHS construction not only to accurately match the structure boundaries in the deformed source image $I_S \circ \varphi^{-1}$ and the target image I_T, but also to estimate physiologically plausible final deformation maps φ.

The direct consequence of the *admissible* hypothesis on V is that the flow of a time-dependent vector field in $L^2([0, 1], V)$ is well defined; see [29, Appendix C]. Then the set of flows at time 1 defines a group of diffeomorphisms denoted by $\mathcal{G}_V$; that is, denoting

$$\text{Fl}_1(\xi) = \varphi(1) \text{ where } \varphi \text{ solves } (14.2), \qquad (14.4)$$

define

$$\mathcal{G}_V \stackrel{\text{def.}}{=} \{\varphi(1) : \exists \xi \in L^2([0, 1], V) \text{ s.t. } \text{Fl}_1(\xi)\}, \qquad (14.5)$$

which has been introduced by Trouvé [25]. On this group, Trouvé defines the metric

$$\text{dist}(\psi_1, \psi_0)^2$$

$$= \inf \left\{ \int_0^1 \|\xi\|_V^2 \, dt : \xi \in L^2([0, 1], V) \text{ s.t. } \psi_1 = \text{Fl}_1(\xi) \circ \psi_0 \right\},$$

$$(14.6)$$

under which he proves that $\mathcal{G}_V$ is complete. In full generality very few mathematical properties of this group are known. However, in particular situations, such as where the space V is the space of Sobolev vector fields that satisfy the continuous injection property, then the group is also an infinite-dimensional Riemannian manifold (see [8]). Since the distance (14.6) is right-invariant, it is important to emphasize that for all $\psi_1, \psi_2, \psi_3 \in \mathcal{G}_V$, we have the following property:

$$\text{dist}(\psi_1 \circ \psi_3, \psi_0 \circ \psi_3) = \text{dist}(\psi_1, \psi_0). \qquad (14.7)$$

Instead of formulating the variational problem on the group of diffeomorphisms $\mathcal{G}_V$, it is often possible to rewrite the optimization problem on the space of images. More precisely, the minimization problem is taken to be

$$\mathcal{J}(\xi) = \int_0^1 \|\xi(t)\|_V^2 \, dt + S(I(1)) \qquad (14.8)$$

under the constraints

$$\partial_t I(t, x) + \langle \nabla I(t, x), \xi(t, x) \rangle = 0,$$
$$I(0, x) = I_S(x) \; \forall x \in D.$$

For $S(I(1)) = \epsilon_1 \|I(1) - I_T\|_{L^2}^2$, the sum of squared differences and σ is a positive parameter, and using the Lagrange multiplier rule, we can write the gradient of this functional as

$$\nabla J(\xi) = 2\xi(t) + K(\nabla I(t) P(t)), \qquad (14.9)$$

where $P(t)$ satisfies the continuity equation (the notation div stands for the divergence operator)

$$\partial_t P(t,x) + \text{div}(P\xi) = 0 \qquad (14.10)$$

and the initial condition $P(1) = 2\epsilon_1(I(1) - I_T)$. Therefore Eq. (14.10) has to be solved backward in time from $t = 1$ to $t = 0$. Alternatively, using the solutions of continuity and advection equations in terms of the flow map, it is possible to rewrite the gradient as in (line 12 of) Algorithm 14.1, which will be discussed in Section 14.1.3.

More generally, it is possible to formulate the equivalent variational problem in the case where shapes are deformed rather than images, as, for instance, when registering point clouds or surfaces. Under mild conditions, it is also possible to prove that this approach induces a Riemannian metric on the orbit of the group action in some finite-dimensional cases (see also Chapter 4). We denote by Q the space of objects or shapes on which the deformation group is acting. When Q is an infinite-dimensional Riemannian manifold, the geometric picture is more complicated [5].

We now go back to the optimization problem. By first-order optimality and using again the notation $\mathcal{J}$ for the corresponding but different functional, a solution to formulation (14.1) can be written as

$$\mathcal{J}(P_0) = \frac{1}{2}\int_D K(P_0\nabla I_0)(x)\,P_0(x)\nabla I_0(x)\,\mathrm{d}x + S(I(1)) \qquad (14.11)$$

under the constraints

$$\begin{cases} \partial_t I + \langle \nabla I, \xi \rangle = 0, \\ \partial_t P + \text{div}(P\xi) = 0, \\ \xi + K(P_0\nabla I_0)(x) = 0, \end{cases} \qquad (14.12)$$

with initial conditions $P(t=0) = P_0$ and $I(t=0) = I_0$. The function $P_0 : D \mapsto \mathbb{R}$ is sometimes called the momentum or scalar momentum, and we denoted

$$K(P_0\nabla I_0)(x) = \int_D k(x,y)P_0(y)\nabla I_0(y)\,\mathrm{d}y; \qquad (14.13)$$

in particular, this quantity can be reformulated as an L^2 norm of the quantity $P_0\nabla I_0$ for the square root of the kernel k. Moreover, system (14.12) encodes the fact that the evolution of $I(t)$ is geodesic in the LDDMM setting; see [28]. Therefore this formulation transforms the problem of optimizing on the time-dependent

d-dimensional vector field ξ (sometimes called path-based optimization) into optimizing on a function P_0 defined on the domain D (sometimes called shooting method). At optimality the following fixed point equation has to be satisfied:

$$P(1) + \partial_I S(I(1)) = 0, \qquad (14.14)$$

which can be used in practice for some optimization schemes [1].

14.1.3 Implementation

We now discuss different ideas related to the implementation of the LDDMM framework to register a source image I_S onto a target image I_T. Our discussion specifically builds on [6], where a practical algorithm of LDDMM for image matching was given. We then give hereafter an overview of this algorithm plus different numerical strategies we used to make it work efficiently. Note that our implementation of [6] and the extensions we developed are freely available on sourceforge.[1]

When registering two images, we have first to define a discrete domain on which $\varphi(t, x)$ and $v(t, x)$ are computed, where $\varphi(t, x)$ is the mapping of x at time t through φ, and $v(t, x)$ is the velocity field integrated in time to compute φ. A natural choice is to use a spatial grid defined by the pixel/voxel coordinates of I_S. We denote by $\hat{D}$ this discrete domain and recall that D is the dense image domain. Linear interpolation is recommended to estimate φ and v at point locations in D and outside $\hat{D}$. Note that I_S and I_T may have a different resolution or may not be aligned. We suppose here that they have already been aligned by a rigid deformation and that the final deformation $\varphi(1, x)$ is composed with this deformation to reach the pixel/voxel coordinates of I_T. In our implementation we also used an uniformly sampled grid to discretize t. The grid time step should also be sufficiently small to avoid generating noninvertible deformations when temporally integrating v. About 10 time steps are enough in most applications, but more time steps may be necessary when sharp deformations are computed [18].

We use the following notations to describe the registration algorithm: t_θ, $\theta \in \{1, \ldots, \Theta\}$, are the discrete time points. For each t_θ, several vector fields are required to encode useful deformations based on the diffeomorphism φ: $\boldsymbol{\phi}_{t_j, t_i}(x)$ first transports $x \in \hat{D}$ from time t_i to time t_j through φ. The images I_{S, t_θ} and I_{T, t_θ} also correspond to I_S and I_T transported at time t_θ using $\boldsymbol{\phi}_{0, t_\theta}$ and $\boldsymbol{\phi}_{1, t_\theta}$ respectively. Image registration is then a gradient descent algorithm

---

[1] https://sourceforge.net/projects/utilzreg/.

where v is optimized with respect to I_S, I_T, and the smoothing kernel K as shown Algorithm 14.1.

Algorithm 14.1 Interpreted LDDMM algorithm of [6] to register the images I_S and I_T.

1: {*Initialization*}
2: $\forall \theta \in \{1, \cdots, \Theta\}$ and $\forall x \in \hat{D}$: the velocity $\mathbf{v}(t_\theta, x) = \mathbf{0}$.
3: **repeat**
4:    {*Compute the mappings between $t = 1$ and t_θ*}
5:    **for** $\theta = \Theta - 1 \to 0$ **do**
6:       $\forall x \in \hat{D}$: Compute $\boldsymbol{\phi}_{1,t_\theta}(x)$ and $\boldsymbol{\phi}_{t_\theta,1}(x)$ by temporally integrating $\mathbf{v}$.
7:    **end for**
8:    {*Compute the smooth energy gradients*}
9:    **for** $\theta = 1 \to \Theta$ **do**
10:      $\forall x \in \hat{D}$: Compute $\boldsymbol{\phi}_{0,t_\theta}(x)$.
11:      $\forall x \in \hat{D}$: Compute $I_{S,t_\theta}(x)$ and $I_{T,t_\theta}(x)$.
12:      $\forall x \in \hat{D}$: $\mathbf{u}(t_\theta, x) = \epsilon_1 \left(\text{DetJ}(\boldsymbol{\phi}_{t_\theta,1}(x)) \nabla I_{S,t_\theta}(x)(I_{S,t_\theta}(x) - I_{T,t_\theta}(x)) \right)$ (see Eq. (14.9)).
13:      $\mathbf{u}(t_\theta, .) = K \star \mathbf{u}(t_\theta, .)$.
14:      $\forall x \in \hat{D}$: $\nabla_{\mathbf{v}} E(t_\theta, x) = \mathbf{v}(t_\theta, x) - \mathbf{u}(t_\theta, x)$
15:    **end for**
16:    {*Update* $\mathbf{v}$}
17:    $\forall \theta \in \{1, \cdots, \Theta\}$ and $\forall x \in \hat{D}$: $\mathbf{v}(t_\theta, x) = \mathbf{v}(t_\theta, x) - \epsilon_2 \nabla_{\mathbf{v}} E(t_\theta, x)$
18: **until** Convergence

We can first remark that the mappings $\boldsymbol{\phi}_{1,t_\theta}(x)$ and $\boldsymbol{\phi}_{t_\theta,1}(x)$ are precomputed in the for loop at lines 5–7 of Algorithm 14.1. These mappings are indeed computed once for all and stored by using an Euler method from time t_Θ to time t_0, whereas the mappings $\boldsymbol{\phi}_{0,t_\theta}(x)$ can be computed from time t_0 to time t_Θ in the energy gradients estimation loop.

We also strongly recommend to compute $I_{S,t_\theta}(x)$ and $I_{T,t_\theta}(x)$ by resampling I_S and I_T using $\boldsymbol{\phi}_{0,t_\theta}(x)$ and $\boldsymbol{\phi}_{1,t_\theta}(x)$, respectively. An alternative would be to compute iteratively the deformed images time point after time point, for example, to compute $I_{S,t_\theta}(x)$ using $I_{S,t_\theta-1}(x)$ and $\mathbf{v}(t_\theta - 1, x)$. This strategy would be far less memory consuming than the one we use, but it would also numerically diffuse the image intensities due to the iterative resamplings.

Another remark is that a simple and very efficient technique can be used to speed up the convergence of this registration algorithm. So-called momentum methods [15] are widely known in machine learning to speed up the convergence of gradient descent algorithms in high dimension. At each iteration it simply consists in updating the optimized variables with a linear combination of the current gradients and the previous update. Our (unpublished) experiences have shown that this technique is particularly efficient in image registration where, at a given iteration, the mapping can be already accurate in some regions and inaccurate in other regions.

The most important point to discuss to make the practical use of the LDDMM algorithm clear is that it depends on two parameters ϵ_1 and ϵ_2, respectively the weight in front of the sum of squared differences (see discussion for Eqs. (14.9) and (14.10)) and the step length of the gradient descent. In practice ϵ_1 should be sufficiently large so that $\mathbf{u}(t_\theta, x)$ has much more influence than $\mathbf{v}(t_\theta, x)$ in line 14 of Algorithm 14.1. The vector field $\mathbf{u}(t_\theta, x)$ indeed pushes one image to the other and can be interpreted as a force field. The influence of $\mathbf{v}(t_\theta, x)$ should then be small but not negligible. This term is specific to LDDMM in the medical image registration community and indeed ensures the temporal consistency of the time-dependent deformations. The choice of ϵ_2 is more conventional in a gradient descent algorithm and controls the convergence speed. An empirical technique to tune it was given in [18]: At the first algorithm iteration we compute $v_{max} = \max_{t_\theta, x} ||\nabla_{\mathbf{v}} E(t_\theta, x)||_2$. We then set ϵ_2 equal to $0.5/v_{max}$, where 0.5 is in pixels/voxels, so that the maximum update at the first iteration is half a pixel/voxel. The updates have then a reasonable and automatically controlled amplitude.

14.2 Sum of kernels and semidirect product of groups

14.2.1 Introduction

Hereafter we discuss the work presented in [19,7]. In most applications a Gaussian kernel is used to smooth the deformations. A kernel corresponding to the differential operator $(\mathrm{Id} + \eta \Delta)^k$ for a well-chosen k with a single parameter η may also be used. The Gaussian width σ is commonly chosen to obtain a good matching accuracy. This means that small values, close to the image resolution, are used for σ. We can then wonder what is the effect of this parameter on the structure of the deformation. In [19] we have illustrated the influence of σ on the mapping obtained between two images of the grey matter acquired on a preterm baby at about 36 and 43 weeks of gestational age, as summarized in Fig. 14.2. Let us focus on the (*B-top*) subfigure of Fig. 14.2. The yellow (ligth gray in print version) isoline represents the cortex boundary in a 2D region of interest (ROI) out of a 3D segmented image S_{36}, and the ROI is located in the red square of the (*A-bottom*) subfigure. The grey levels of the same (*B-top*) subfigure also represent the segmented cortex in the same preterm baby but 7 weeks later. It is obvious that the brain became globally larger as the brain and the skull strongly grow at this age. The shapes should be almost translated at the scale of this ROI to capture the amplitude of the deformation. It is important that existing cortex folds also became deeper and new folds appeared, which is normal during brain maturation because the cortex growth is faster than the skull growth. Capturing the folding process requires registering the images at a scale close to the image resolution here. To conclude, the registration of these images requires at a same time a large σ and a small σ. If only a small σ is used, then optimal path (and the optimization process) will lead to physiologically implausible deformations. This is obvious in Fig. 14.2(C), where the brown isoline represents the boundaries of the deformed voxels after registration. In this example the volume of some voxels becomes huge, and other voxels almost disappear. If this deformation was the real one, then the studied brain would have a strongly heterogeneous development in space, which is clearly not realistic. On the contrary, if only a large σ was used, then the optimal path would not capture fine deformations, as shown in Fig. 14.2(D). This justifies the use of multiscale kernels to establish geodesics between such follow-up medical images.

14.2.2 Multiscale kernels

As for the LDDMM model, we recall that the kernel spatially interpolates the rest of the information (i.e., the momentum) to drive the motion of the points where there is no gradient information, for example, in flat image regions. Therefore it is natural to introduce a sum of kernels to fill in the missing information while preserving the physiologically realistic matchings. Therefore more plausible deformations are obtained since the correlation of the motions of the points is higher.

In practice this method works really well, and the mathematical insight for its efficiency is probably the variational interpretation of the sum of kernel, explained hereafter. For simplicity, we only treat the case of a finite set of RKHS Hilbert spaces H_i with kernels k_i and Riesz isomorphisms K_i between H_i^* and H_i for $i = 1, \ldots, n$. For every i, H_i is a subspace of the space of C^1 vector fields on the domain D. Denoting $H = H_1 + \cdots + H_n$, the space of all functions of the form $v_1 + \cdots + v_n$ with $v_i \in H_i$, the norm is

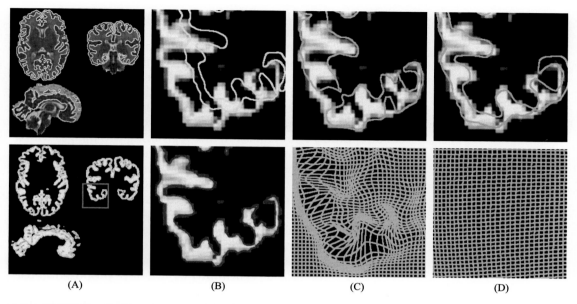

(A) (B) (C) (D)

Figure 14.2. (A) Grey matter extraction of the 3D MR image I_{36} (top) and resulting segmentation S_{36} (bottom). The red square indicates the 2D region of interest shown in (B,C,D). (B) The yellow (ligth gray in print version) and blue (dark gray in print version) isolines represent the cortical surface of S_{36} and S_{43}, respectively. The grey levels are the segmented cortex of S_{43}. (C,D) The brown isolines represent deformed cortical surfaces of S_{36} after LDDMM registration on S_{43} with $\sigma = 1.5$ and $\sigma = 20$, respectively. The grids represent the estimated dense deformations.

defined by

$$\|v\|_H^2 = \inf \left\{ \sum_{i=1}^n \|v_i\|_{H_i}^2 \mid \sum_{i=1}^n v_i = v \right\}. \qquad (14.15)$$

The minimum is achieved for a unique n-tuple of vector fields, and the space H endowed with the norm defined by (14.15) is complete. The result is the following: there exists a unique element $p \in \bigcap_{i=1}^n H_i^*$ for which we have $v_i = K_i p$ and

$$v = \sum_{i=1}^n K_i p, \qquad (14.16)$$

the family $(v_i)_{i=1,\dots,n}$ realizing the (unique) infimum of the variational problem (14.15). Formula (14.15) induces a scalar product on H, which makes H an RKHS, and its associated kernel is $\mathsf{k} := \sum_{i=1}^n \mathsf{k}_i$, where k_i denotes the kernel of the space H_i. This property was written in [3] and is standard in convex analysis. Indeed, note that this property is the particular case of an elementary result in convex analysis, at least in finite dimensions: the convex conjugate of an infimal convolution is equal to the sum of the convex conjugates [20].

Another phenomenon observed in practice is that a better quality of matching is obtained with a sum of kernels than with a single kernel of small width. Although we have no quantitative argument in this direction, we strongly believe that this is due to the convergence of the gradient descent algorithm to local minima. In standard image registration, coarse to fine techniques [11] are ubiquitous. They consist in first registering two images with a strong regularization level and then iteratively decreasing the regularization level when the algorithm has converged at the current scale. At each considered scale, gradient descent-based registration is then likely to be performed in a stable orbit with respect to the compared shape scale. In LDDMM, using the sum of kernels at different scales instead of small scales only may then have a similar effect from an optimization point of view.

Based on the practical implementation of LDDMM for images of [6] and summarized Algorithm 14.1, we have proposed to use smoothing kernels constructed as the sum of several Gaussian kernels [19]. These kernels, denoted by MK, that are the weighted sums of N Gaussian kernels K_{σ_n}, each of them being parameterized by its standard deviation σ_n:

$$
\begin{aligned}
MK(x) &= \sum_{n=1}^{N} a_n K_{\sigma_n}(x) \\
&= \sum_{n=1}^{N} a_n (2\pi)^{-3/2} |\Sigma_n|^{-1/2} \exp\left(-\frac{1}{2} x^T \Sigma_n^{-1} x\right),
\end{aligned}
\tag{14.17}
$$

where Σ_n and a_n are respectively the covariance matrix and the weight of the nth Gaussian function. Each Σ_n is only defined by a characteristic scale σ_n: $\Sigma_n = \sigma_n Id_{\mathbb{R}^d}$. Once this kernel is defined, the registration algorithm is the same as in Algorithm 14.1.

A tricky aspect of this kernel construction for practical applications is however the tuning of their weights a_n. Although the choice of the σ_n has a rather intuitive influence on the optimal deformations, the tuning of the a_n strongly depends on the representation and the spatial organization of the registered shapes at the scales σ_n, $n \in [1, N]$. As described in [19], it depends on: (1) *Representation and spatial organization of the structures*: A same shape can be encoded in various ways. For instance, it can be a binary or a grey-level image. This representation has first a nonlinear influence on the similarity metric (the sum of squared differences in LDDMM) *forces* (unsmoothed gradients) as shown line 12 of Algorithm 14.1. The choice of optimal parameters a_n is even more complicated to do as the spatial relation between the shape structures should also be taken into account when smoothing the forces (line 13 of Algorithm 14.1). (2) *Prior knowledge*: Prior knowledge about the amplitude of the structures displacement at each scale σ_n may be incorporated in a_n.

In [17] we have proposed to semiautomatically tune the a_n as follows:

$$a_n = a'_n / g(K_{\sigma_n}, I_S, I_T),$$

where $g(K_{\sigma_n}, I_S, I_T)$ represents the typical amplitude of the forces when registering I_S to I_T at a scale σ_n. This amplitude is related to (1) and cannot therefore be computed analytically. An empirical technique to tune it is the following: for each K_{σ_n}, the value of $g(K_{\sigma_n}, I_S, I_T)$ can be estimated by observing the maximum update of the velocity field v in a preiteration of registration of I_S on I_T using only the kernel K_{σ_n} with $a_n = 1$. The apparent weights a'_n, $n \in [1, N]$, provide an intuitive control of the amplitude of the displacements and are related to (2). To deform the largest features of I_S and I_T with a similar amplitude at each scale σ_n, the user should tune all the apparent weights a'_n with the same value. Typical results we obtained in [19] on the example of Fig. 14.2 are shown in Fig. 14.3. They make clear the fact that multiscale kernels with automatically tuned a_n following our method efficiently solved the problem we initially described.

14.2.3 Distinguishing the deformations at different scales

It is interesting to remark that the influence of each subkernel of the multiscale kernels we defined can be measured. Distinguishing scale-dependent deformations is indeed useful for further statistical analysis. A first attempt to characterize this influence has been presented in [19] and was strongly developed in [7]. The main contribution of [7] was to formulate the multiscale LDDMM registration with a semidirect product. Registering I_S on I_T is then done by minimizing a registration energy $\mathcal{E}_N$ with respect to the N-tuple $(v_1, \ldots, v_N)$ where each time-dependent velocity field v_n is associated with scale-dependent deformations. Then the minimized energy is

$$\mathcal{E}_N(v_1, \ldots, v_N) = \frac{1}{2} \sum_{n=1}^{N} \int_0^1 \|v_n(t)\|_{H_n}^2 \, dt + \mathcal{S}(I_S, I_T, \varphi), \qquad (14.18)$$

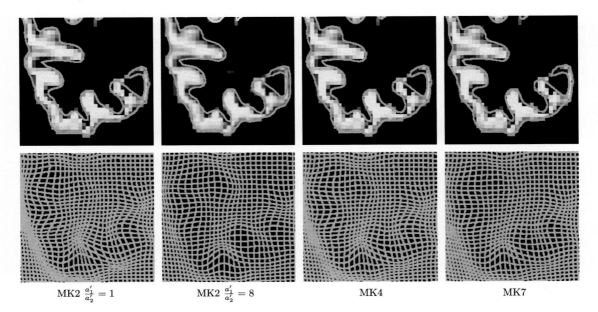

$$\text{MK2 } \tfrac{a'_1}{a'_2} = 1 \qquad \text{MK2 } \tfrac{a'_1}{a'_2} = 8 \qquad \text{MK4} \qquad \text{MK7}$$

Figure 14.3. Registration results obtained on the example of Fig. 14.2 using multiscale kernels. MKN stands for the sum of N kernels. Here MK4 and MK7 were automatically designed with apparent weights a'_i having the same value.

where the space H_n corresponds to the kernel K_{σ_n}, and $\varphi_n(t)$ is defined by

$$\partial_t \varphi_k(t) = \left(v_k(t) + (\mathrm{Id} - \mathrm{Ad}_{\varphi_k(t)}) \sum_{n=k+1}^{n} v_n(t) \right) \circ \varphi_k(t). \qquad (14.19)$$

Here $\mathrm{Ad}_\varphi v$ also denotes the adjoint action of the group of diffeomorphisms on the Lie algebra of vector fields:

$$\mathrm{Ad}_\varphi v(x) = (D\varphi . v) \circ \varphi^{-1}(x) = D_{\varphi^{-1}(x)}\varphi . v(\varphi^{-1}(x)). \qquad (14.20)$$

These equations then allow us to quantify scale-dependent deformations φ_n in the whole deformation φ. We can also sum over all scales to form $v(t) = \sum_{k=1}^{n} v_k(t)$ and compute the flow $\varphi(t)$ of $v(t)$. A simple calculation finally shows that

$$\varphi(t) = \varphi_1(t) \circ \cdots \circ \varphi_n(t) . \qquad (14.21)$$

Results and algorithmic description of the solution for 3D images were given [7]. An illustration of this paper, where the deformations between two brain images were split into 7 scales, is given Fig. 14.4. Note also that in [21] the authors build on these ideas

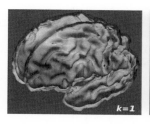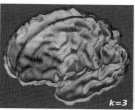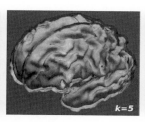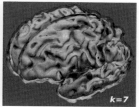

Figure 14.4. Representation of scale-dependent deformations φ_k out of a deformation φ obtained between two brain images using [7]. The colors represent the amplitude of the scale-dependent deformations at the brain surface.

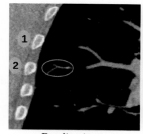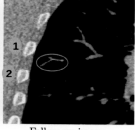

Baseline image   Follow-up image

Figure 14.5. Illustration of the sliding motion at the lung boundary in the coronal view of two CT volumes acquired on the same subject. The motion of the emphasized vessel with respect to ribs 1 and 2 clearly demonstrate the sliding motion at the lung boundary. Images out of the EMPIRE10 challenge [13].

of multiscale kernels and incorporate some sparsity prior. On the other hand, we can extend the space of kernels as done in [24], in which the authors construct multiscale kernels based on wavelet frames and with an apparent improvement of the registration results, although the corresponding group structure interpretation is possibly lost.

14.3 Sliding motion constraints

14.3.1 Introduction

Now we focus on how to model sliding constraints in the LD-DMM formalism. Such constraints are observed, for example, at the lung boundaries, as emphasized in Fig. 14.5. In [18] we have developed a smoothing strategy to solve this problem by using Algorithm 14.1 (of [6]) with specific smoothing properties. The central idea is to predefine different regions of interest Ω^k in the domain Ω of the registered images at the boundary of which discontinuous deformations will be potentially estimated. Note first that these regions of interest are fixed so the source image I_S and the target image I_T should be aligned at the boundaries of the regions Ω^k, which is done in Algorithm 14.1 by using a standard registration strategy with large amount of smoothing. This domain decomposition is illustrated Fig. 14.6.

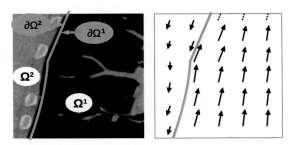

Figure 14.6. *(Left)* Subdivision of the registration domain Ω into Ω^1 (inside the lung) and Ω^2. Subdomain boundaries are represented by $\partial\Omega^1$ and $\partial\Omega^2$. *(Right)* Velocity field **v** which can be obtained in Ω after enforcing sliding conditions in the neighborhoods of $\partial\Omega^1$ and $\partial\Omega^2$.

14.3.2 Methodology

Instead of considering a reproducing kernel Hilbert apace (RKHS) V embedded in $C^1(\Omega, \mathbb{R}^n)$ or $W^{1,\infty}$ as in the previous section, here we use N RKHS of vector fields $V^k \in C^1(\Omega^k, [0,1])$, which can capture sliding motion, that is, with an orthogonal component to the boundary that vanishes at any point of $\partial\Omega^k$. The set of admissible vector fields is therefore defined by $V := \bigoplus_{k=1}^N V^k$, the direct sum of the Hilbert spaces $(V^k)_{k\in[\![1,N]\!]}$. In particular, the norm on V of a vector field $\mathbf{v}_t$ is given by

$$\|\mathbf{v}_t\|_V^2 = \sum_{k=1}^N \|\mathbf{v}_t^k\|_{V^k}^2, \tag{14.22}$$

where $\mathbf{v}_t^k$ is the restriction of $\mathbf{v}_t$ to Ω^k. The flow of any $\mathbf{v} \in L^2([0,1], V)$ is then well defined although the resulting deformations are piecewise diffeomorphic and not diffeomorphic. As a consequence, the deformation is a diffeomorphism on each subdomain and allows for sliding motion along the boundaries.

Now that an admissible RKHS is defined, let us focus on the strategy we used to mimic the Gaussian smoothing of the updates **u** (see line 13 in Algorithm 14.1) with the desired properties. We use the heat equation to smooth **u** in each region Ω^k: $\partial \mathbf{u}/\partial \tau = \Delta \mathbf{u}$, where $\tau \in [0, \Gamma]$ is a *virtual* diffusion time. We denote by $\partial\Omega^k$ the boundaries of Ω^k. Here Γ controls the amount of smoothing. To prevent from information exchange between the different regions, Neumann boundary conditions are additionally modeled at each point x of $\partial\Omega^k$: $\nabla \mathbf{u}(x) \cdot \mathbf{n}(x) = 0$, where $\mathbf{n}(x)$ is normal to $\partial\Omega^k$ at x. Independent Gaussian based convolution in each region Ω^k, would have been a quicker alternative in terms of computations but would not take into account the intrinsic region geometry. Then, to ensure that the orthogonal component to the boundary vanishes at any point of $\partial\Omega^k$, we use a projection strategy of the updates before and after smoothing so that they respect this constraint.

To do so, we consider the vector field $\mathbf{T}$ so that for each point $x \in \Omega$, $x + \mathbf{T}(x)$ is the nearest boundary between two subdomains in a limited neighborhood around the boundaries $\partial\Omega^k$. For the registration of pulmonary images, we empirically use a neighborhood of about $\gamma = 20$ millimeters. Consider a velocity field $\mathbf{w}$ defined on Ω. We use $\mathbf{T}$ to enforce the sliding conditions around $\partial\Omega^k$ by reducing the contributions of $\mathbf{w}(x)$ in the direction of $\mathbf{T}(x)$ when $||\mathbf{T}(x)||_{L^2} < \gamma$:

$$\mathbf{w}(x) = \mathbf{w}(x) - \alpha(x)\mathbf{T}(x)\frac{<\mathbf{w}(x), \mathbf{T}(x)>_{L^2}}{||\mathbf{T}(x)||_{L^2}^2}, \qquad (14.23)$$

where the weight $\alpha(x)$ equals $(\gamma - ||\mathbf{T}(x)||)^2/\gamma$. For numerical stability, $\mathbf{w}(x)$ is set to 0 if $||\mathbf{T}(x)||_{L^2}^2 = 0$. The registration algorithm is then the same as Algorithm 14.1 except line 13, where $\mathbf{u}$ is first projected using Eq. (14.23), then smoothed using the heat (diffusion) equation, and then projected again using Eq. (14.23).

14.3.3 Results and discussion

Results shown in [18] make clear the impact of this strategy compared with standard smoothing kernels. Fig. 14.7 shows the impact of such a piecewise diffeomorphic kernel when registering lung image where a sliding motion is clearly required at the lung boundaries. Note that to make this strategy tractable on large medical images (as in Fig. 14.7), we also coded it in the LogDemons formalism of [26]. This formalism is indeed less memory consuming than LDDMM, as the diffeomorphisms are encoded in stationary velocity fields and not time-dependent ones as in LDDMM. Computational burden would be too high in the LDDMM framework. However, both LogDemons and LDDMM with the proposed sliding motion estimation strategy led to similar results on smaller images.

14.4 Left-invariant metrics

14.4.1 Introduction

In this section, we describe the results obtained in [22,23]. A natural extension of the sum of kernels consists in having a kernel that may depend on the location. However, the right-invariant point of view is meant for a homogeneous material whose properties are translation invariant although this is not required by the theory. In practice the kernel used in diffeomorphic methods has always been chosen to be translationally invariant and isotropic. In LDDMM spatially adaptive or nonisotropic ("direction-dependent") kernels have no obvious interpretation, because the norm is defined in Eulerian coordinates, so that as t varies during the deformation, a fixed point in the source image moves through space, and conversely, a fixed point in space will correspond to different points in the source image. Similarly, the directions in a direction-dependent kernel are defined with respect to Eulerian coordinates, not the coordinates of the moving source image. Nonetheless, spatially adaptive kernels are potentially of great interest in medical applications if they can be made to represent spatially variable (or nonisotropic) deformability of

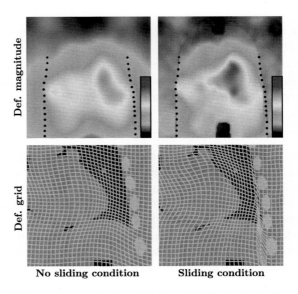

Figure 14.7. Deformation magnitude and deformed grids obtained when registering I_1 to I_5 using LogDemons using sliding motion modeling (S-LogD) or not (LogD MR). Color bar is from 0 to 5 cm. The black dots represent the thoracic cage boundary.

tissue. This is indeed already done in [16] to model sliding conditions between the lungs and the ribs. In this section we present a slightly different registration framework than LDDMM, which naturally supports the use of spatially adaptive kernels.

14.4.2 Methodology

The proposed framework is based on a *left*-invariant metric on the group of deformations, where its name LIDM (left-invariant diffeomorphic metrics) comes from. Left-invariance means that this metric satisfies, in a smooth setting, the following property: For all elements ψ_1, ψ_2, ψ_3 in the group,

$$\text{dist}(\psi_3 \circ \psi_1, \psi_3 \circ \psi_0) = \text{dist}(\psi_1, \psi_0), \qquad (14.24)$$

which is in contrast with formula (14.7). In fact, such a left-invariant metric is based on a choice of norm in the body (Lagrangian) coordinates of the source image. This means that instead of the V norm applied to the spatial velocity defined by (14.12), it is applied to the *convective velocity* $v(t)$ implicitly defined by

$$\partial_t \varphi(t) = d\varphi(t) \cdot v(t), \qquad (14.25)$$

where $d\varphi(t)$ is the spatial derivative of $\varphi(t)$.

It is well known that left- and right-invariant metrics are isometric by the inverse map. Therefore, as expected, we obtain the following result.

Corollary 14.1. *[Equivalence between LIDM and LDDMM] Consider the problem of minimizing*

$$\mathcal{J}_{I_T}(\varphi) = \frac{1}{2} \int_0^1 \|v(t)\|_V^2 \, dt + E(I_S \circ \varphi_1^{-1}, I_T) \qquad (14.26)$$

for $\varphi_0 = Id_\Omega$, and with constraint either

$$\partial_t \varphi_t = d\varphi_t \cdot v_t \qquad \textit{(LIDM constraint)} \qquad (14.27)$$

or

$$\partial_t \varphi_t = v_t \circ \varphi_t \qquad \textit{(LDDMM constraint).} \qquad (14.28)$$

Then
1. *The optimal endpoint φ_1 is the same with either constraint.*
2. *If ϕ_t minimizes $\mathcal{J}$ in LIDM, then $\varphi_t := \phi_{1-t}^{-1} \circ \phi_1$ minimizes $\mathcal{J}$ in LDDMM.*
3. *If φ_t minimizes $\mathcal{J}$ in LDDMM, then $\phi_t := \varphi_1 \circ \varphi_{1-t}^{-1}$ minimizes $\mathcal{J}$ in LIDM.*

Although not surprising, this result gives a mathematical interpretation to the use of spatially adaptive kernels that can be defined using a variational approach. Let us consider, as in the previous section, a family of RKHS $(H_i)_{i=1,...,n}$ and an operator $A : H_1 \oplus \cdots \oplus H_n \mapsto H = H_1 + \cdots + H_n$. On the space H we introduce

$$\|v\|_H^2 = \inf \left\{ \sum_{i=1}^n \|v_i\|_{H_i}^2 \,\middle|\, A(v_1, \ldots, v_n) = v \right\}. \tag{14.29}$$

Using again duality and under mild assumptions, the kernel associated with H is $H^* \ni p \mapsto \sum_{i=1}^n K_i(A^*p)_i \in H$.

Let us give an instance of it in the context of biomedical images. Suppose we have a partition of unity $((\chi_i)_{i=1,...,n})$ of the domain of interest (a manual segmentation of the biological shape) where we have some knowledge of the deformability properties of the shape modeled by the kernel K_i. The map A can be chosen as $\sum_{i=1}^n \chi_i v_i$, and the corresponding kernel is

$$K = \sum_{i=1}^n \chi_i K_i \chi_i. \tag{14.30}$$

This kernel satisfies the embedding condition under mild conditions on the element of the partition of unity $(\chi_i)_{i=1,...,n}$.

14.4.3 Results and discussion

The experiment of Fig. 14.8 is adapted from [22], and it shows registration results for a synthetic example, which includes features at different scales. LIDM shows the results of the registration using a kernel defined accordingly to the partition of unity shown in the figure (two Gaussian kernels with a large σ on the white and a small σ on the black). As expected, it performs better than the sum of kernel because it captures the small scale deformations.

The use of spatially adaptive kernels provably improves the registration results on real data. However, the shortcoming of this approach is that the kernel does not evolve with the deformed shape. For small/medium deformations, it may not be a problem, but it cannot be applied in the case of large deformations. In such a case the kernel has to depend on the shape itself. Such approaches have actually been developed in [30,4,2], where the operator A depends on the shape itself, but developing models for images associated with an efficient implementation remains open.

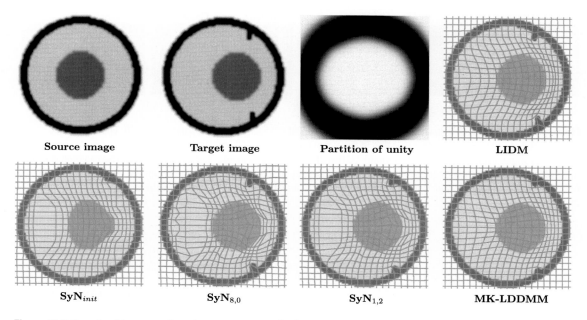

    Source image   Target image   Partition of unity   LIDM

    $\mathbf{SyN}_{init}$ $\mathbf{SyN}_{8,0}$ $\mathbf{SyN}_{1,2}$ **MK-LDDMM**

Figure 14.8. Results of image registration tests on a synthetic example.

14.5 Open directions

14.5.1 Learning the metric

There are two different point of views that can be developed to improve on the results of LDDMM: On the one hand, incorporating mechanical or biological constraints to reproduce more realistic results is what we have described so far in this chapter. On the other hand, it is also natural to learn the metric parameters using data driven methods if no mechanical model is well established for the data of interest. Instead of having a partition of unity drawn by the user, it is also natural to ask whether the smoothing kernel can be learned from data. We summarize here an approach proposed in [27] to learn the parameters from a given population and a given template.

Building on the LIDM model, we aim at designing a set of kernels expressing spatially adaptive metrics. We use (symmetric) positive definite matrices M as a parameterization of this set of kernels. To ensure the smoothness of the deformations, any kernel of this set has to satisfy the constraint that the Hilbert space of vector fields is embedded in the Banach space of C^1 vector fields. To enforce this constraint, we propose the following parameteri-

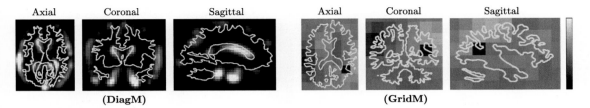

Figure 14.9. Values out of M learnt on 40 subjects of the LONI Probabilistic Brain Atlas (LPBA40). The values are represented at their corresponding location in the template image T. **(DiagM):** Values $M(j,j)$ for $j \in [1, \ldots, N]$. Color bar ranges from 1 (black) to 1.04 (white). **(GridM):** $M(i,j)$ for a fixed i and $j \in [1, \ldots, L]$. The red (mid gray in print version) point corresponds to $i = j$ and has an intensity of 1.03. Color bar ranges from -0.05 (black) to 0.05 (white) for other points. Yellow (ligth gray in print version) curves represent the boundary between white and grey matter in T.

zation:

$$\mathcal{K} = \{\hat{K} M \hat{K} \mid M \text{ SDP operator on } L^2(\mathbb{R}^d, \mathbb{R}^d)\}, \qquad (14.31)$$

where $\hat{K}$ is a spatially homogeneous smoothing kernel (typically Gaussian). Now the variational model consists in minimizing the functional with a positive real β:

$$\mathcal{F}(M) = \frac{\beta}{2} d_{S++}^2 (M, Id) + \frac{1}{N} \sum_{n=1}^{N} \min_v \mathcal{J}_{I_n}(v, M), \qquad (14.32)$$

where M is symmetric. The first term is a regularizer of the kernel parameters so that the minimization problem is well posed. Here, it favors parameterizations of M close to the identity matrix, but other a priori correlation matrix could be used. The term $d_{S++}^2 (Id, M)$ can be chosen as the squared distance on the space of positive definite matrices given by $\| \log(M) \|^2$. Here again other choices of regularizations could have been used such as the log-determinant divergence. This model has been implemented in [27], where a simple method of dimension reduction was used since the matrix M is of size n^2, where n is the number of voxels, and it gave promising results on the 40 subjects of the LONI Probabilistic Brain Atlas (LPBA40). An illustration of the matrix M we computed in this paper is given in Fig. 14.9.

Another possible direction as done in [14] consists in learning the partition of unity $(\chi_i)_{i \in I}$ with some smoothness constraints on the χ_i such as H^1 or TV. Moreover, since there is an interplay in the optimality equations between the gradient of the deformed image and the deformation, it is possible to introduce some information on the regularization of the partition so that it takes into account this interplay.

14.5.2 Other models

From a methodological point of view, the main weakness of the previously presented methods is probably the fact that the metric does not evolve with the shape in Lagrangian coordinates. To make the practical impact of this property clear, assume that a part of the shape follows a fixed volume transformation. In that case the models proposed are clearly unadapted as they cannot incorporate this property. This is why constrained diffeomorphic evolutions have been introduced in the literature [30,2]. Most of the time these constraints are incorporated in Lagrangian coordinates such as in [10]. However, fast computational methods for diffeomorphic image matching are designed in Eulerian coordinates; see, for instance, [31,12]. We propose an Eulerian-based PDE model, which can be seen as a mild modification of the LDDMM framework presented, incorporating the modeling assumption that the metric is naturally image dependent.

The standard formulation of shape-dependent metric registration is similar to the formulation in (14.1) when the norm on the vector field v depends on the current shape I. It is important that it is often possible to preserve the metric property in this type of modification. The manifold Q that we are going to consider consists in augmenting the template image I with a partition of unity $(\chi_i)_{i \in I}$. The definition of the action of φ in the group of diffeomorphisms is as follows:

$$\begin{cases} \varphi \cdot I \overset{\text{def.}}{=} I \circ \varphi^{-1}, \\ \varphi \cdot \chi_i \overset{\text{def.}}{=} \chi_i \circ \varphi^{-1}. \end{cases} \tag{14.33}$$

In other words, we consider the partition of unity as additional images that are advected by the flow. The variational problem is then the following:

$$\min \frac{1}{2} \int_0^1 \|v\|_H^2 \, dt + \mathcal{S}(\varphi \cdot I), \tag{14.34}$$

where the norm is as in Eq. (14.29), that is,

$$\|v\|_H^2 = \inf \left\{ \sum_{i=1}^n \|v_i\|_{H_i}^2 \,\middle|\, v(x) = \sum_{i=1}^n \chi_i(x) v_i(x) \,\forall x \in D \right\}, \tag{14.35}$$

and the flow is defined by

$$\begin{cases} \partial_t \varphi(t, x) = v(t, \varphi(t, x)), \\ \varphi(0, x) = x. \end{cases} \tag{14.36}$$

Alternatively, functional (14.34) can be rewritten using a shape-dependent metric using the Lagrange multiplier method, and it is similar to the constrained evolutions proposed in [30]. The optimality equation can be written as

$$\begin{cases} \dot{I} + \langle \nabla I, v \rangle = 0, \\ \dot{P} + \nabla \cdot (Pv) = 0, \\ \dot{\chi}_i + \langle \nabla \chi_i, v \rangle = 0 \ \forall i = 1, \dots, n, \\ \dot{\lambda}_i + \nabla \cdot (\lambda_i v) = \langle P \nabla I + \lambda_i \nabla \chi_i, v_i \rangle \ \forall i = 1, \dots, n, \\ v = -\sum_{i=1}^{n} \chi_i K_i \chi_i (P \nabla I + \lambda_i \nabla \chi_i). \end{cases} \qquad (14.37)$$

Note that the Lagrange multiplier associated with the partition evolves accordingly to the fourth equation in (14.37), which has a source term on its right-hand side that differs from the optimality equations (14.12).

References

1. John Ashburner, Karl J. Friston, Diffeomorphic registration using geodesic shooting and Gauss–Newton optimisation, NeuroImage 55 (3) (2011) 954–967.
2. S. Arguillère, M. Miller, L. Younes, Diffeomorphic surface registration with atrophy constraints, SIAM Journal on Imaging Sciences 9 (3) (2016) 975–1003.
3. N. Aronszajn, Theory of reproducing kernels, Transactions of the American Mathematical Society 68 (1950) 337–404.
4. S. Arguillere, E. Trélat, A. Trouvé, L. Younes, Shape deformation analysis from the optimal control viewpoint, Journal de Mathématiques Pures et Appliquées 104 (2015).
5. Sylvain Arguillere, Emmanuel Trélat, Alain Trouvé, Laurent Younes, Shape deformation analysis from the optimal control viewpoint, Journal de Mathématiques Pures et Appliquées 104 (2015) 139–178.
6. M. Faisal Beg, Michael I. Miller, Alain Trouvé, Laurent Younes, Computing large deformation metric mappings via geodesic flow of diffeomorphisms, International Journal of Computer Vision 61 (2005) 139–157.
7. Martins Bruveris, Laurent Risser, François-Xavier Vialard, Mixture of kernels and iterated semidirect product of diffeomorphisms groups, Multiscale Modeling & Simulation 10 (4) (2012) 1344–1368.
8. Bruveris Martins, François-Xavier Vialard, On completeness of groups of diffeomorphisms, Journal of the European Mathematical Society 19 (5) (2017) 1507–1544.
9. P. Dupuis, U. Grenander, M.I. Miller, Variational problems on flows of diffeomorphisms for image matching, Quarterly of Applied Mathematics 56 (1998) 587–600.

10. Barbara Gris, Stanley Durrleman, Alain Trouvé, A sub-Riemannian modular approach for diffeomorphic deformations, in: Frank Nielsen, Frédéric Barbaresco (Eds.), Geometric Science of Information, Springer International Publishing, Cham, 2015, pp. 39–47.

11. B.D. Lucas, T. Kanade, An iterative image registration technique with an application to stereo vision, in: Proceedings of the 7th International Joint Conference on Artificial Intelligence – Vol. 2, IJCAI'81, 1981, pp. 674–679.

12. A. Mang, G. Biros, An inexact Newton–Krylov algorithm for constrained diffeomorphic image registration, SIAM Journal on Imaging Sciences 8 (2) (2015) 1030–1069.

13. K. Murphy, B. Van Ginneken, J.M. Reinhardt, S. Kabus, K. Ding, X. Deng, J.P.W. Pluim, et al., Evaluation of registration methods on thoracic CT: the EMPIRE10 challenge, IEEE Transactions on Medical Imaging 30 (10) (2011) 1901–1920.

14. Marc Niethammer, François-Xavier Vialard, Roland Kwitt, Metric Learning for Image Registration, 2018.

15. D.E. Rumelhart, G.E. Hinton, R.J. Williams, Learning representations by back-propagating errors, Nature 323 (6088) (1986) 533–536.

16. Laurent Risser, François-Xavier Vialard, Habib Y. Baluwala, Julia A. Schnabel, Piecewise-diffeomorphic image registration: application to the motion estimation between 3D CT lung images with sliding conditions, Medical Image Analysis 17 (2013) 182–193.

17. L. Risser, F.X. Vialard, M. Murgasova, D.D. Holm, D. Rueckert, Large diffeomorphic registration using fine and coarse strategies. application to the brain growth characterization, in: International Workshop on Biomedical Image Registration (WBIR), in: Lecture Notes in Computer Science, vol. 6204, 2010, pp. 186–197.

18. L. Risser, F.X. Vialard, n.H.Y. Baluwala, J.A. Schnabel, Piecewise-diffeomorphic image registration: application to the motion estimation between 3D CT lung images with sliding conditions, Medical Image Analysis 17 (2) (2012) 182–193.

19. L. Risser, F.-X. Vialard, R. Wolz, M. Murgasova, D.D. Holm, D. Rueckert, Simultaneous multi-scale registration using large deformation diffeomorphic metric mapping, IEEE Transactions on Medical Imaging 30 (10) (2011) 1746–1759.

20. R.T. Rockafellar, R.J-B. Wets, Variational Analysis, vol. 317, Springer Science & Business Media, 2009.

21. Stefan Sommer, Francois Lauze, Mads Nielsen, Xavier Pennec, Sparse multi-scale diffeomorphic registration: the kernel bundle framework, Journal of Mathematical Imaging and Vision 46 (2012) 07.

22. Tanya Schmah, Laurent Risser, François-Xavier Vialard, Left-invariant metrics for diffeomorphic image registration with spatially-varying regularisation, in: Kensaku Mori, Ichiro Sakuma, Yoshinobu Sato, Christian Barillot, Nassir Navab (Eds.), Medical Image Computing and Computer-Assisted Intervention – MICCAI

2013: 16th International Conference, Nagoya, Japan, September 22–26, 2013, Proceedings, Part I, Springer, Berlin, Heidelberg, 2013, pp. 203–210.

23. Tanya Schmah, Laurent Risser, François-Xavier Vialard, Diffeomorphic Image Matching With Left-Invariant Metrics, Springer, New York, NY, 2015, pp. 373–392.

24. Mingzhen Tan, Anqi Qiu, Multiscale frame-based kernels for large deformation diffeomorphic metric mapping, IEEE Transactions on Medical Imaging 37 (10) (2018) 2344–2355.

25. Alain Trouvè, Action de groupe de dimension infinie et reconnaissance de formes (Infinite-dimensional group action and pattern recognition), 1995.

26. Tom Vercauteren, Xavier Pennec, Aymeric Perchant, Nicholas Ayache, Symmetric log-domain diffeomorphic registration: a demons-based approach, in: Int. Conference on Medical Image Computing and Computer Assisted Intervention (MICCAI), in: LNCS, 2008, pp. 754–761.

27. François-Xavier Vialard, Laurent Risser, Spatially-varying metric learning for diffeomorphic image registration: a variational framework, in: Polina Golland, Nobuhiko Hata, Christian Barillot, Joachim Hornegger, Robert Howe (Eds.), Medical Image Computing and Computer-Assisted Intervention – MICCAI 2014: 17th International Conference, Boston, MA, USA, September 14–18, 2014, Proceedings, Part I, Springer International Publishing, Cham, 2014, pp. 227–234.

28. François-Xavier Vialard, Laurent Risser, Daniel Rueckert, Colin J. Cotter, Diffeomorphic 3d image registration via geodesic shooting using an efficient adjoint calculation, International Journal of Computer Vision 97 (2) (Apr. 2012) 229–241.

29. Laurent Younes, Shapes and Diffeomorphisms, Springer, 2010.

30. Laurent Younes, Constrained diffeomorphic shape evolution, Foundations of Computational Mathematics 12 (3) (Jun 2012) 295–325.

31. Miaomiao Zhang, Fletcher P. Thomas, Finite-dimensional Lie algebras for fast diffeomorphic image registration, in: Sebastien Ourselin, Daniel C. Alexander, Carl-Fredrik Westin, Cardoso M. Jorge (Eds.), Information Processing in Medical Imaging, Springer International Publishing, Cham, 2015, pp. 249–260.

Low-dimensional shape analysis in the space of diffeomorphisms

Miaomiao Zhang[a], Polina Golland[b], William M. Wells III[c], Tom Fletcher[d]

[a]Washington University in St. Louis, Computer Science and Engineering, St. Louis, MO, United States. [b]Massachusetts Institute of Technology, Computer Science and Artificial Intelligence Lab, Cambridge, MA, United States. [c]Harvard Medical School, Department of Radiology, Boston, MA, United States. [d]University of Virginia, Departments of Electrical & Computer Engineering and Computer Science, Charlottesville, VA, United States

15.1 Introduction

Statistical shape analysis is an important component of understanding human anatomy from medical images. In particular, the analysis of disease progression via anatomical effects, that is, brain degeneration caused by neurodegenerative disorders, such as Alzheimer's or Huntington's, provides a better understanding of disease mechanisms that could benefit early treatments [13,17]. Developing statistical models with well-defined shape representations such as landmarks [8,4], medial axes [19], and geometric deformations [23,7] forms a core foundation that facilitates advanced imaging research. In this chapter we focus on shapes represented by deformations of a fixed shape, called a template. Such deformation-based shape descriptors explicitly reflect geometric information associated with local structure changes, shrinkage or expansion. Recent shape models, especially for clinical applications, require the deformation to be a diffeomorphism, which guarantees a smooth bijective mapping with a smooth inverse. A typical framework to derive such deformations from population-based images is a deformable template approach that utilizes image registration algorithms, for instance, *large deformation diffeomorphic metric mapping* (LDDMM) endowed with a distance metric on the space of diffeomorphisms [3]. The information of intrapopulation shape variability and interpopulation differences is then provided by computing the statistics of the resulting transformations [11,24,22].

A long-standing challenge of deformation-based statistical shape analysis is the nonlinear and high dimensional nature of the

Riemannian Geometric Statistics in Medical Image Analysis
https://doi.org/10.1016/B978-0-12-814725-2.00024-8

imaging data, typically 128^3 image grid as a shape descriptor for 3D brain MRI scan. This requires large computational resources and careful algorithm design for effective statistical modeling and inferences. To address this problem, data dimensionality reduction methods that extract low-dimensional latent structures from image transformations have been investigated. Due to the complex structure of nonlinear deformations, researchers first performed principal component analysis in the linearized space of diffeomorphisms, for example, time-dependent velocity fields, known as tangent PCA (TPCA) [24]. A Bayesian model of shape variability has been proposed to extract the principal modes after estimating a covariance matrix of transformations [12]. Similar approaches based on alternative parameterizations of diffeomorphisms, such as stationary velocity fields [22] and B-spline deformations [18], were developed until a generalized method principal geodesic analysis (PGA) was invented [11]. In contrast to the methods discussed, PGA estimated the geodesic subspaces by minimizing the sum-of-squared geodesic distances on finite-dimensional manifolds. This enabled factor analysis of diffeomorphisms that treated data variability as a joint inference problem in a probabilistic principal geodesic analysis (PPGA) model [27,28]. All these models were proposed to find a compact low-dimensional space to represent the data. However, their algorithmic inferences are computationally expensive due to the fact that each operation has to be performed numerically on dense image grids in a high-dimensional space.

In this chapter we present a PPGA model [31,32], which effectively estimates the latent subspaces of anatomical shape variability by employing a fast computational method of diffeomorphisms, called FLASH (Fourier-approximated Lie algebras for shooting) [29,30]. Motivated by the low-dimensional representations of diffeomorphisms via bandlimited initial velocity fields introduced in FLASH, we hypothesize that the anatomical shape variability can be effectively characterized by a much more compact parameterization. Our main contributions are listed as follows:

- We define a low-dimensional probabilistic framework of factor analysis in the context of diffeomorphic atlas building.
- We dramatically reduce the computational cost of detecting principal geodesics of diffeomorphisms by employing a bandlimited parameterization in the Fourier space.
- We enforce the orthogonality constraints on the principal modes, which is computationally intractable in high-dimensional models like PPGA [27].

All in-depth derivations of the statistical model and algorithm inferences are provided. Moreover, we perform Markov chain Monte Carlo sampling in the proposed low-dimensional shape space, which is computationally intractable on dense image grids. We report estimated principal modes in the ADNI brain MRI dataset [15] and compare them with the results of the state-of-the-art methods TPCA [24] and PPGA of diffeomorphisms [27,28]. The experimental results show that the low-dimensional statistics encode important features of the data, better capture the group variation, and improve data interpretability with substantially lower computational costs.

15.2 Background

We first briefly review the mathematical background of diffeomorphic atlas building in the LDDMM setting [3] with geodesic shooting [26,25]. More details are also provided in Chapter 4. We then provide a summary of low-dimensional Fourier representation that forms the basis of our method.

Let $J_1, \ldots, J_N$ be the N input images that are assumed to be square-integrable functions defined on a d-dimensional torus domain $\Omega = \mathbb{R}^d/\mathbb{Z}^d$ ($J_n \in L^2(\Omega, \mathbb{R})$, $n \in \{1, \cdots, N\}$), and let $\text{Diff}(\Omega)$ be the space of diffeomorphisms. The problem of diffeomorphic atlas building is to find the template $I \in L^2(\Omega, \mathbb{R})$ and the deformation $\phi_n \in \text{Diff}(\Omega)$ from template I to each input image J_n that minimize the energy function

$$E(\phi_n, I) = \sum_{n=1}^{N} \text{Sim}(J_n, I \circ \phi_n^{-1}) + \text{Reg}(\phi_n), \qquad (15.1)$$

where $\circ$ is the composition operator that resamples I by the inverse of the smooth mapping ϕ_n, $\text{Sim}(\cdot, \cdot)$ denotes a similarity between images such as sum-of-squared difference (SSD), normalized cross correlation (NCC), or mutual information (MI), and $\text{Reg}(\cdot)$ is a regularization term that enforces smoothness of the transformations.

15.2.1 Flows of diffeomorphisms and geodesics

The optimization of the energy function (15.1) over the transformations $\{\phi_n\}$ is challenging due to the nonlinearity of the space of diffeomorphisms. Mathematically, we consider the time-varying deformation $\phi_n(t, x) : t \in [0, 1]$, $x \in \Omega$, to be generated by the integral flow of time-varying velocity field $v_n(t, x) \in V$ in the tangent space of diffeomorphisms at the identity e, denoted as $T_e \text{Diff}(\Omega)$:

$$\frac{d\phi_n(t, x)}{dt} = v_n \circ \phi_n(t, x), \quad \phi_n(0, x) = e.$$

The distance between the identity element and transformation ϕ_n is uniquely determined by a right-invariant Riemannian metric $\| \cdot \|_V$ on the time-dependent velocity fields as

$$\int_0^1 \| v_n(t, x) \|_V \, dt. \tag{15.2}$$

The geodesic is obtained at the minimum of (15.2) by integrating the Euler–Poincaré differential equation (EPDiff) [2,16] with the initial condition of $v_n(t, x)$ at $t = 0$:

$$\frac{\partial v_n}{\partial t} = -\text{ad}_{v_n}^\dagger v_n \tag{15.3}$$
$$= -\mathcal{K}\left[(Dv_n)^T m_n + Dm_n \, v_n + m_n \, \text{div}(v_n) \right],$$

where $\text{ad}^\dagger$ is adjoint to an ad operator on two vector fields, for example, $\text{ad}_v w = Dv \cdot w - Dw \cdot v$, D is the Jacobian matrix, and div is the divergence operator. The operator $\mathcal{K}$ is the inverse of a symmetric positive definite differential operator $\mathcal{L} : V \to V^*$ that maps a velocity field $v_n \in V$ to a momentum vector $m_n \in V^*$ such that $m_n = \mathcal{L}v_n$ and $v_n = \mathcal{K}m_n$. Evaluation of Eq. (15.3) is known as *geodesic shooting* [26,25]. It has been shown that the geodesic shooting algorithm substantially reduces the computational complexity and improves the optimization landscape by only manipulating the initial velocity in the geodesic evolution equation (15.3). Therefore in this chapter we choose to optimize over initial velocities rather than the entire time-dependent velocity fields. With a slight abuse of notation, we set $v_n \triangleq v_n(0, x)$ to represent the initial velocity for the nth image J_n in the remaining sections.

15.2.2 Fourier representation of velocity fields

As demonstrated in FLASH [29], the velocity fields generated by the EPDiff (15.3) can be efficiently captured via a low-dimensional bandlimited representation in the discrete Fourier space. The main idea is that the velocity fields do not develop high frequencies and only a small amount of low frequencies contributes to the transformations (Fig. 15.1). The deformations can be captured in a bandlimited space as accurately as with the original algorithm [3].

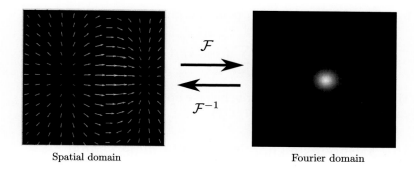

Spatial domain   Fourier domain

Figure 15.1. Velocity fields in spatial and Fourier domain.

Let $f : \mathbb{R}^d \to \mathbb{R}$ be a real-valued function. The Fourier transform $\mathcal{F}$ of f is defined as

$$\mathcal{F}[f](\xi) = \int_{\mathbb{R}^d} f(x) e^{-2\pi i \langle \xi, x \rangle} \, dx, \qquad (15.4)$$

where $x = (x_1, \ldots, x_d)$ is a d-dimensional image coordinate vector, $\xi = (\xi_1, \ldots, \xi_d)$ is a d-dimensional frequency vector, and $\langle \cdot, \cdot \rangle$ denotes the inner product operator. The inverse Fourier transform $\mathcal{F}^{-1}$ of a discretized Fourier signal $\tilde{f}$,

$$\mathcal{F}^{-1}[\tilde{f}](x) = \sum_{\xi} \tilde{f}(\xi) e^{2\pi i \langle \xi, x \rangle}, \qquad (15.5)$$

is an approximation of the original signal f. For vector-valued functions, such as diffeomorphisms ϕ and velocity fields v, we apply the (inverse) Fourier transform to each vector component separately.

Analogously to the definition of a distance metric in (15.2), Zhang and Fletcher [29] developed a new representation of velocity fields entirely in the frequency domain that leads to an efficient computation of diffeomorphisms in a low-dimensional space. In particular, if $\tilde{V}$ is the discrete Fourier space of velocity fields, then for any elements $\tilde{u}, \tilde{v} \in \tilde{V}$, the distance metric at identity is defined as

$$\langle \tilde{u}, \tilde{v} \rangle_{\tilde{V}} = \sum_{\xi} (\tilde{\mathcal{L}} \tilde{u}(\xi), \tilde{v}(\xi)),$$

where $\tilde{\mathcal{L}} : \tilde{V} \mapsto \tilde{V}^*$ is the Fourier transform of a differential operator, for example, a commonly used Laplacian operator $(-\alpha \Delta + e)^c$ with a positive weight parameter α and a smoothness parameter c, and $(\cdot, \cdot)$ is the dot product in the frequency space. The Fourier transform of the Laplacian operator is given by

$$\tilde{\mathcal{L}}(\boldsymbol{\xi}) = \left(-2\alpha \sum_{j=1}^{d} \left(\cos(2\pi\xi_j) - 1\right) + 1\right)^c.$$

The Fourier coefficients of the inverse operator $\mathcal{K} : \tilde{V}^* \mapsto \tilde{V}$ can be easily computed as $\tilde{\mathcal{K}}(\xi) = 1/\tilde{\mathcal{L}}(\xi)$.

15.2.3 Geodesic shooting in finite-dimensional spaces

Since $\mathcal{K}$ is a smoothing operator that suppresses high frequencies, the geodesic evolution equation (15.3) of the time-dependent velocity fields can be computed efficiently as a bandlimited signal in the Fourier space:

$$\frac{\partial \tilde{v}}{\partial t} = -\text{ad}_{\tilde{v}}^\dagger \tilde{v} \qquad\qquad (15.6)$$

$$= -\tilde{\mathcal{K}}\left[(\tilde{D}\tilde{v})^T \star \tilde{m} + \tilde{D}\tilde{m} \star \tilde{v} + \tilde{m} \star \tilde{\nabla} \cdot \tilde{v} \right],$$

where $\tilde{m} = \tilde{\mathcal{L}}\tilde{v}$, $\star$ is the truncated matrix-vector field auto-correlation,[1] and $\tilde{D}\tilde{v}$ is a tensor product $\tilde{D} \otimes \tilde{v}$ with $\tilde{D}(\boldsymbol{\xi}) = i\sin(2\pi\boldsymbol{\xi})$ representing the Fourier frequencies of a central difference Jacobian matrix D. The operator $\tilde{\nabla}\cdot$ is the discrete divergence operator computed as the sum of the Fourier coefficients of the central difference operator $\tilde{D}$ along each dimension, that is, $\tilde{\nabla} \cdot \boldsymbol{\xi} = \sum_{j=1}^{d} i\sin(2\pi\boldsymbol{\xi}_j)$. All computational operations are easy to implement in a truncated low-dimensional space by eliminating the high frequencies. To ensure that $\tilde{f}$ represents a real-valued vector field in the spatial domain, we require $\tilde{f}(\xi_1, \ldots, \xi_d) = \tilde{f}^*(-\xi_1, \ldots, -\xi_d)$, where * denotes the complex conjugate.

Using the inverse Fourier transform defined in (15.5), a time sequence of bandlimited velocity fields in $\tilde{V}$ consequently generates a flow of diffeomorphisms $t \mapsto \phi_t \in \text{Diff}(\Omega)$ in the following way:

$$\frac{d\phi_t}{dt} = \mathcal{F}^{-1}(\tilde{v}_t) \circ \phi_t, \qquad\qquad (15.7)$$

and its inverse mapping ϕ_t^{-1} is computed through

$$\frac{d\phi_t^{-1}}{dt} = -D\phi_t^{-1} \cdot \mathcal{F}^{-1}(\tilde{v}_t). \qquad\qquad (15.8)$$

[1] The autocorrelation operates on zero-padded signals followed by truncating back to the bandlimits in each dimension to guarantee that the output remains bandlimited.

15.3 PPGA of diffeomorphisms

We introduce a generative model for principal geodesic analysis of diffeomorphisms represented in the bandlimited velocity space $\tilde{V}$ with shape variability explicitly encoded as factors of the model.

Let $\tilde{W} \in \mathbb{C}^{p \times q}$ be a matrix in the Fourier space whose q columns ($q < N$) are orthonormal principal initial velocities in a low p-dimensional bandlimited space with unit length, let $\Lambda \in \mathbb{R}^{q \times q}$ be a diagonal matrix of scale factors for the columns of $\tilde{W}$, and let $s \in \mathbb{R}^q$ be a vector of random factors that parameterizes the space of initial velocities. Therefore each initial velocity is generated as $\tilde{v} = \tilde{W} \Lambda s$ (see Fig. 15.2).

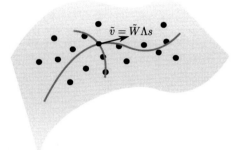

Figure 15.2. Principal geodesic analysis of diffeomorphisms.

For subject $n \in \{1, \ldots, N\}$, we define a prior on the loading coefficient vector s_n to be a Gaussian distribution whose covariance matrix is a combination of the identity matrix e and a matrix $(\tilde{\mathcal{L}} \Lambda \tilde{W}^T \tilde{W} \Lambda)^{-1}$ that ensures the smoothness of the geodesic path, that is,

$$p(s_n \mid \tilde{W}, \Lambda) = \mathcal{N}(s_n; 0, (\tilde{\mathcal{L}} \Lambda \tilde{W}^T \tilde{W} \Lambda)^{-1} + e)$$
$$= \mathcal{N}(s_n; 0, \tilde{\mathcal{L}}^{-1} \Lambda^{-2} + e).$$

The normalizing constant of $p(s_n \mid \tilde{W}, \Lambda)$, including the determinant of the covariance matrix, is computed as

$$(2\pi)^{q/2} |\tilde{\mathcal{L}}^{-1} \Lambda^{-2} + e|^{1/2} = (2\pi)^{q/2} \cdot \prod_{l=1}^{q} \left(\frac{1}{\tilde{\mathcal{L}}(l,l) \Lambda^2(l,l)} + 1 \right),$$

where $l \in \{1, \ldots, q\}$ denote the diagonal element.

Assuming i.i.d. Gaussian noise on image intensities, we obtain the likelihood

$$p(J_n \mid s_n; \; \tilde{W}, \Lambda, I, \sigma) = \mathcal{N}(J_n; \; I \circ \phi_n^{-1}, \sigma^2),$$

where ϕ_n is a deformation that corresponds to the initial velocity $v_n = \mathcal{F}^{-1}[\tilde{W} \Lambda s_n]$ in the spatial domain, that is,

$$\frac{d\phi_n}{dt} = \mathcal{F}^{-1}[\tilde{W} \Lambda s_n] \circ \phi_n, \tag{15.9}$$

and σ^2 is the image noise variance.

Defining $\Theta = \{\tilde{W}, \Lambda, I, \sigma\}$, we employ Bayes' rule to arrive at the posterior distribution of s_n:

$$p(s_n \mid J_n; \; \Theta) \propto p(J_n \mid s_n; \; \Theta) \cdot p(s_n \mid \tilde{W}, \Lambda) \tag{15.10}$$
$$= \mathcal{N}(J_n; \; I \circ \phi_n^{-1}, \sigma^2) \cdot \mathcal{N}(s_n; 0, \tilde{\mathcal{L}}^{-1} \Lambda^{-2} + e).$$

The log posterior distribution of the loading coefficients $s_1, \ldots, s_N$ for the entire image collection therefore is

$$Q \triangleq \log p(s_1, \ldots, s_N \mid J_1, \ldots, J_N; \Theta)$$
$$= \sum_{n=1}^{N} \log p(J_n \mid s_n; \; \Theta) + \log p(s_n \mid \tilde{W}, \Lambda) + \text{const}$$
$$= \sum_{n=1}^{N} -\frac{\|J_n - I \circ \phi_n^{-1}\|_{L^2}^2}{2\sigma^2} - \frac{s_n^T (\tilde{\mathcal{L}}^{-1} \Lambda^{-2} + e) s_n}{2}$$
$$- \frac{dN}{2}(\log \sigma) - \frac{N}{2} \sum_{l=1}^{q} \log(\frac{1}{\tilde{\mathcal{L}}_{ll} \Lambda_{ll}^2} + 1) + \text{const}. \tag{15.11}$$

15.4 Inference

We present two alternative ways to estimate the model parameters, the maximum a posteriori (MAP) and the Monte Carlo expectation maximization (MCEM) that treats the loading coefficients $\{s_1, \ldots, s_N\}$ as latent variables. Both methods require reduced adjoint Jacobi fields in the bandlimited velocity space to compute the gradients.

15.4.1 Reduced adjoint Jacobi fields in bandlimited velocity spaces

Before we develop the adjoint Jacobi field in Fourier space, we first review its definition in the continuous space.

Consider a variation of geodesics $\gamma(s,t) : (-\epsilon, \epsilon) \times [0,1] \to$ Diff(Ω) with $\gamma(s,0) = $ id and $\gamma(0,t) = \phi_t$. Such a variation corresponds to a variation of the initial velocity $\frac{d\gamma}{dt}(s,t)|_{t=0} = v_0 + s\delta v_0$ that produces a "fan" of geodesics (illustrated in Fig. 15.3), where δ denotes a variation on v_0. Taking the derivative of this variation results in a Jacobi field $J(t) = \frac{d\gamma}{ds}(s,t)|_{s=0}$ with its adjoint operator, called adjoint Jacobi field. In this chapter we employ a reduced version of adjoint Jacobi fields [5,14] that equivalently carries all the computations in the Lie algebra. In contrast to the current estimation of LDDMM methods [3,20,25], this reduced adjoint Jacobi field completely decouples the time integration of smooth velocity fields from noisy images, which substantially improves the stability and convergence of the optimization.

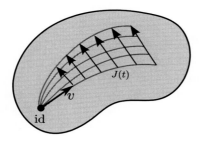

Figure 15.3. Jacobi fields.

Since we are using a right-invariant metric on Diff(Ω), it is natural to formulate the Jacobi field $J(t)$ in the Lie algebra under right invariance. We define a vector field $U(t) \in \tilde{V}$ as the approximated right-invariant Jacobi field $U(t) = v\left(J(t) \circ \phi_t^{-1}\right)$ and a variation of the right-reduced velocity $\tilde{v}$ as $\delta\tilde{v}$. These variables satisfy the following reduced Jacobi equations:

$$\frac{d}{dt}\begin{pmatrix} U \\ \delta\tilde{v} \end{pmatrix} = \begin{pmatrix} \text{ad}_{\tilde{v}} & I \\ 0 & \text{sym}_{\tilde{v}} \end{pmatrix}\begin{pmatrix} U \\ \delta\tilde{v} \end{pmatrix}, \qquad (15.12)$$

where $\text{sym}_{\tilde{v}}\delta\hat{v} = -\text{ad}_{\tilde{v}}^{\dagger}\delta\hat{v} - \text{ad}_{\delta\hat{v}}^{\dagger}\tilde{v}$.

The reduced adjoint Jacobi fields are simply computed by taking the adjoint of the reduced Jacobi equations in (15.12). This results in another set of ordinary differential equations (ODE):

$$\frac{d}{dt}\begin{pmatrix} \hat{U} \\ \delta\hat{v} \end{pmatrix} = \begin{pmatrix} -\text{ad}_{\tilde{v}}^{\dagger} & 0 \\ -I & -\text{sym}_{\tilde{v}}^{\dagger} \end{pmatrix}\begin{pmatrix} \hat{U} \\ \delta\hat{v} \end{pmatrix}, \quad \text{or}$$

$$\frac{d\hat{U}}{dt} = -\text{ad}_{\tilde{v}}^{\dagger}\hat{U}, \quad \frac{d\delta\hat{v}}{dt} = -\hat{U} - \text{sym}_{\tilde{v}}^{\dagger}\delta\hat{v}, \qquad (15.13)$$

where $\hat{U}$ and $\delta\hat{v} \in \tilde{V}$ are auxiliary adjoint variables, and $\mathrm{sym}_{\tilde{v}}^{\dagger}\delta\hat{v} = \mathrm{ad}_{\delta\hat{v}}^{\dagger}\tilde{v} - \mathrm{ad}_{\tilde{v}}\delta\hat{v}$. For more details on the derivation of reduced adjoint Jacobi field equations, see [5,30].

MAP

We use gradient ascent to maximize the log posterior probability (15.11) with respect to the parameters Θ and latent variables $\{s_n\}$.

By setting the derivative of Q with respect to I and σ to zero, we obtain closed-form updates for the atlas template I and noise variance σ^2:

$$I = \frac{\sum_{n=1}^{N} J_n \circ \phi_n |D\phi_n|}{\sum_{n=1}^{N} |D\phi_n|},$$

$$\sigma^2 = \frac{1}{MN} \sum_{n=1}^{N} \|J_n - I \circ \phi_n^{-1}\|_{L^2}^2,$$

where M is the number of image voxels.

To estimate the matrix of principal directions $\tilde{W}$, the scaling factor Λ, and the loading coefficients $\{s_1, \ldots, s_N\}$, we follow the derivations in [29] and first obtain the gradient of Q with respect to the initial velocity $\tilde{v}_n$ as follows:

(i)   Forward integrate the geodesic evolution equation (15.6) to compute time-varying velocity fields $\{\tilde{v}_n\}$ and then follow the flow equation (15.9) to generate a flow of diffeomorphic transformations $\{\phi_n\}$.

(ii)   Compute the gradient $\nabla_{\tilde{v}_n} Q$ at time point $t = 1$ as

$$\delta Q_1 \triangleq [\nabla_{\tilde{v}_n} Q]_{t=1} \tag{15.14}$$

$$= -\tilde{K} \mathcal{F} \left[\frac{1}{\sigma^2}(J_n - I \circ \phi_n^{-1}) \cdot \nabla(I \circ \phi_n^{-1}) \right].$$

(iii)   Backward integrate the gradient (15.14) to $t = 0$ to obtain $\delta Q_0 \triangleq [\nabla_{\tilde{v}_n} Q]_{t=0}$ by using reduced adjoint Jacobi field equations (15.13) with the initial condition $\delta\hat{v}_{t=1} = 0$.

After applying the chain rule, we have the gradient of Q for updating the loading factor s_n:

$$\nabla_{s_n} Q = -\Lambda \tilde{W}^T \delta Q_0 - s_n.$$

The gradients of Q with respect to $\tilde{W}$ and Λ are given as follows:

$$\nabla_{\tilde{W}} Q = -\sum_{n=1}^{N} \delta Q_0 s_n^T \Lambda,$$

$$\nabla_\Lambda Q = -\sum_{n=1}^{N} (\tilde{W} s_n^T \delta Q_0 - \frac{1}{\tilde{\mathcal{L}}\Lambda^2 (\tilde{\mathcal{L}}\Lambda^2 + 1)}).$$

Unlike the PPGA model in the high-dimensional image space [27], we enforce the mutual orthogonality constraint on the columns of $\tilde{W}$ since it is computationally more tractable in the low-dimensional space. There are two natural ways to satisfy this constraint: first is to treat $\tilde{W}$ as a point on the complex Stiefel manifold $V_n(\mathbb{C}^d)$, which is a set of orthonormal n-frames in $\mathbb{C}^d$ [10]. This requires projecting the gradient of $\tilde{W}$ onto the tangent space of $V_n(\mathbb{C}^d)$ and then updating $\tilde{W}$ within a small step along the projected gradient direction. Another way is to use Gram–Schmidt process [6] for orthonormalizing the column vectors of $\tilde{W}$ in a complex inner product space. In practice we employ the latter scheme in our implementation.

MCEM

To treat the loading coefficients $\{s_n\}$ fully as latent random variables, we integrate them out from the posterior distribution (15.11) by using a Hamiltonian Monte Carlo (HMC) method [9] due to the fact that direct sampling is difficult. This scheme includes two main steps:

(i) Draw a random sample of size S of the latent variables $\{s_n\}$ via HMC sampling based on current parameters $\Theta^{(k)}$. Let $s_{jn}, j = 1, \ldots, S$, denote the jth sample for the subject n. A Hamiltonian function $H(\mathbf{s}, \beta) = U(\mathbf{s}) + V(\beta)$ that consists of a potential energy $U(\mathbf{s}) = -\log p(\mathbf{s} \mid J; \Theta)$ and a kinetic energy $V(\beta) = -\log g(\beta)$, where $g(\beta)$ is typically an independent Gaussian distribution on an auxiliary variable β, is constructed to simulate the sampling system. Starting from the current point $(\mathbf{s}, \beta)$, the Hamiltonian function H produces a candidate point $(\hat{\mathbf{s}}, \hat{\beta})$ that is accepted as a new sample with probability

$$p_{\text{accept}} = \min(1, \exp(-U(\hat{\mathbf{s}}) - V(\hat{\beta}) + U(\mathbf{s}) + V(\beta))).$$

The sample mean is taken to approximate the expectation:

$$\Upsilon(\Theta \mid \Theta^{(i)}) \approx \frac{1}{S} \sum_{j=1}^{S} \sum_{n=1}^{N} \log p(s_{jn} \mid J_n; \Theta^{(i)}), \qquad (15.15)$$

where the superscript (i) denotes the current state of the parameter set Θ.

(ii) Maximize the expectation function Υ to update parameters Θ. By setting its derivatives with respect to I and σ^2 to zero we obtain closed-form updates for the atlas template I and noise variance σ^2 as

$$I = \frac{\sum_{j=1}^{S} \sum_{n=1}^{N} I \circ \phi_{jn} |D\phi_{jn}|}{\sum_{j=1}^{S} \sum_{n=1}^{N} |D\phi_{jn}|},$$

$$\sigma^2 = \frac{1}{SMN} \sum_{j=1}^{S} \sum_{n=1}^{N} \| J_n - I \circ \phi_{jn}^{-1} \|_{L^2}^2.$$

Since there is no closed-form update for $\tilde{W}$ and Λ, we use gradient ascent to estimate the principal initial velocity basis $\tilde{W}$ and the scaling matrix Λ. The gradients with respect to $\tilde{W}$ and Λ of (15.15) are given as follows:

$$\nabla_{\tilde{W}} \Upsilon = -\sum_{j=1}^{S} \sum_{n=1}^{N} [\nabla_{\tilde{v}_{jn}} \Upsilon]_{t=0} \, s_{jn}^T \Lambda,$$

$$\nabla_{\Lambda} \Upsilon = -\sum_{j=1}^{S} \sum_{n=1}^{N} (\tilde{W} s_{jn}^T [\nabla_{\tilde{v}_{jn}} \Upsilon]_{t=0} - \frac{1}{\tilde{\mathcal{L}} \Lambda^2 (\tilde{\mathcal{L}} \Lambda^2 + 1)}).$$

15.5 Evaluation

To evaluate the effectiveness of the proposed *low-dimensional principal geodesic analysis* (LPPGA) model, we applied the algorithm to brain MRI scans of 90 subjects from the ADNI study [15], aged from 60 to 90. Fifty subjects have Alzheimer's disease (AD), and the remaining 40 subjects are healthy controls. All MRI scans have the same resolution $128 \times 128 \times 128$ with the voxel size of $1.25 \times 1.25 \times 1.25 \, \text{mm}^3$. All images underwent the preprocessing of skull stripping, downsampling, intensity normalization to [0, 1] interval, bias field correction, and coregistration with affine transformations.

We first estimate a full collection of principal modes $q = 89$ for our model, using $\alpha = 3.0$ and $c = 3.0$ for the differential operator $\tilde{\mathcal{L}}$, which is similar to the settings used in pairwise diffeomorphic image registration [29]. For dimensions of the initial velocity field $\tilde{v}$, we run pairwise image registration with FLASH at different levels of truncated dimension $p = 4^3, 8^3, \ldots, 64^3$ and then choose p at the place where an increased dimension does not improve the image registration energy. The number of time steps for integration in geodesic shooting is set to 10. We initialize the atlas I to be the average of image intensities, Λ to be the identity matrix, s_n to be the all-ones vector, and the principal initial velocity matrix $\tilde{W}$ to be the principal components estimated by TPCA [24] that runs linear PCA in the space of initial velocity fields after atlas building. For the HMC sampling of the MCEM variant of our model, we use the step size of 0.01 for leap-frog integration with 20 units of time discretization in integration of EPDiff equations.

To investigate the ability of our model to capture anatomical variability, we use the loading coefficients $s = \{s_1, \ldots, s_N\}$ as a shape descriptor in a statistical study. The idea is to test the hypothesis that the principal modes estimated by our method are correlated significantly with clinical information such as minimental state examination (MMSE), Alzheimer's disease assessment scale (ADAS), and clinical dementia rating (CDR). We project the transformations that are derived from the estimated atlas I_0 and each individual from a testing dataset with 40 subjects onto the estimated principal modes. We then fit the clinical score MMSE, ADAS, and CDR using a linear regression model on the computed loading coefficients.

We use the previous state of PPGA [27] in a high-dimensional image space and TPCA [24] as two baseline methods. To conduct a fair comparison, we keep all the parameters including regularization and time steps for numerical integration fixed across the three algorithms. To evaluate the model stability, we rerun the entire experiment 50 times on randomly sampled subsets of 50 images.

15.6 Results

Fig. 15.4 reports the total energy (14) averaged over 16 test images for different values of truncated dimension $p = 4^3, 8^3, \ldots, 64^3$. Our method arrives at the same solution at $p = 16^3$ and higher. For the remainder of this section, we use $p = 16^3$ to illustrate the results.

Fig. 15.5 reports the cumulative variance explained by the model as a function of the model size. Both variants of our approach low-dimensional PPGA (LPPGA)-MCEM and LPPGA-MAP achieve higher representation accuracy than the two state-of-the-art baseline algorithms across the entire range of model sizes. This is mainly because that conducting statistical analysis in the low-dimensional space improves the gradient-based optimization landscape, where local minima often occur in a high-dimensional image space. The Monte Carlo sampling of MCEM algorithm further reduces the risk of getting stuck in local minima by allowing random steps away from the current minimal solution.

Table 15.1 reports the number of principal modes required to achieve the same level of shape variation across the entire dataset. Our model LPPGA-MCEM/LPPGA-MAP captures better

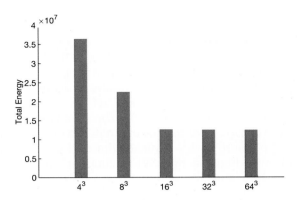

Figure 15.4. Average total energy for different values of the truncated dimension $p = 4^3, 8^3, \ldots, 64^3$.

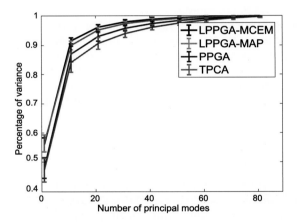

Figure 15.5. Cumulative variance explained by principal modes estimated from our model (LPPGA-MCEM and LPPGA-MAP) and baseline algorithms (PPGA-MAP and TPCA).

shape changes while using fewer principal modes, which also means that our model estimates more compact representation of the image data.

Fig. 15.6 visualizes the first three modes of variation in this cohort by shooting the estimated atlas I along the initial velocities $\tilde{v} = a_i \tilde{W}_i \Lambda_i$ ($a_i = \{-2, -1, 0, 1, 2\}$, $i = 1, 2, 3$). We also show the log determinant of the Jacobian at $a_i = 2$. The first mode of variation clearly reflects that changes in the ventricle size, which is the dominant source of variability in the brain shape. The algorithm estimates standard deviation of the image noise to be $\sigma = 0.02$.

Table 15.1 Number of principal modes that achieves 90% **and** 95% **of total variance.**

Method	90%	95%
LPPGA-MCEM	9	17
LPPGA-MAP	11	20
PPGA-MAP	15	27
TPCA	19	35

Fig. 15.7 reports run time and memory consumption for building the full model of anatomical variability. Our approach LPPGA-MAP offers an order of magnitude improvement in both the run time and memory requirements while providing a more powerful model of variability.

Although the MCEM variant is computationally more expensive than all baseline methods due to the sampling procedure, it provides better statistical analysis of regression (as reported in Table 15.2) than the two baseline algorithms using the first two principal modes. The higher F and R^2 statistics indicate that our approach captures more variation of the MMSE scores than the other models. Another advantage of such Monte Carlo approach is that it provides consistent statistics in noisy case [1] and better model selection.

15.7 Discussion and conclusion

We presented a low-dimensional probabilistic framework for factor analysis in the space of diffeomorphisms. Our model explicitly optimizes the fit of the principal modes to the data in a low-dimensional space of bandlimited velocity fields, which results in (1) better data fitting and (2) dramatically lower computational cost with more powerful statistical analysis. We developed an inference strategy based on MAP to estimate parameters, including the principal modes, noise variance, and image atlas simultaneously. Our model also enables Monte Carlo sampling because of the efficient low-dimensional parameterization. We demonstrated that the estimated low-dimensional latent loading coefficients provide a compact representation of the anatomical variability and yield a better statistical analysis of anatomical changes associated with clinical variables.

This work represents the first step toward *efficient* probabilistic models of shape variability based on high-dimensional diffeomorphisms. There are several avenues for future work to build upon

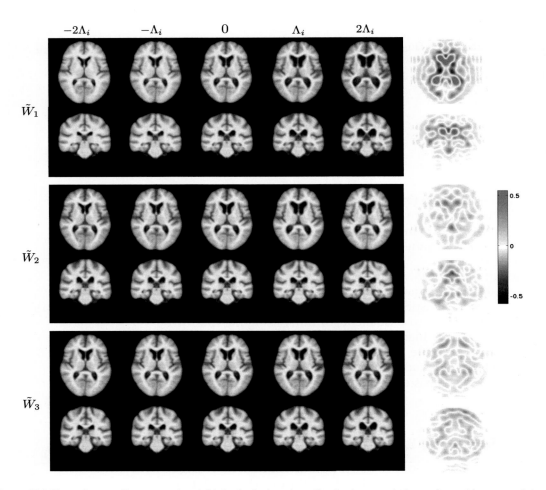

Figure 15.6. Top to bottom: first, second and third principal modes of brain shape variation estimated by our model LPPGA-MCEM for varying amounts of the corresponding principal mode, and log determinant of the transformation Jacobians at $2\Lambda_i$ (regions of expansion in red (mid gray in print version) and contraction in blue (dark gray in print version)). Axial and coronal views are shown.

our model. We will explore Bayesian variants of shape analysis that infer the inherent dimensionality directly from the data by formulating dimensionality reduction with a sparsity prior. Reducing the dimensionality to the inherent modes of shape variability has the potential to improve hypothesis testing, classification, and mixture models. A multiscale strategy like that of [21] can be added to our model to make the inference even faster. Moreover, since Monte Carlo sampling is computationally more tractable in our model, we can automatically estimate the regularization parame-

Table 15.2 Comparison of linear regression models on the first two principal modes for our model (LPPGA-MCEM / LPPGA-MAP) and the baseline algorithms (PPGA and TPCA) on 40 brain MRIs from ADNI.

(a) [MMSE]

Model	Residual	R^2	F	p-value
LPPGA-MCEM	4.42	0.19	21.68	$1.13e^{-5}$
LPPGA-MAP	4.45	0.18	19.47	$2.18e^{-5}$
PPGA	4.49	0.16	17.96	$5.54e^{-5}$
TPCA	4.53	0.14	16.34	$1.10e^{-4}$

(b) [ADAS]

Model	Residual	R^2	F	p-value
LPPGA-MCEM	8.25	0.21	13.14	$1.033e^{-5}$
LPPGA-MAP	8.36	0.19	11.68	$3.20e^{-5}$
PPGA	8.41	0.18	11.10	$5.09e^{-5}$
TPCA	8.65	0.17	10.75	$1.03e^{-4}$

(c) [CDR]

Model	Residual	R^2	F	p-value
LPPGA-MCEM	2.21	0.22	24.78	$3.16e^{-6}$
LPPGA-MAP	2.22	0.20	23.99	$4.37e^{-6}$
PPGA	2.23	0.19	22.92	$6.77e^{-6}$
TPCA	2.25	0.17	21.54	$2.88e^{-5}$

ter jointly with the shape variability model. This eliminates the effort of hand-tuning on parameters and enables uncertainty quantification of the hidden variables. Another interesting avenue is to estimate an even more sharp atlas that has clearer details of brain structures such as sulci. Since the atlas is essentially the average over intensities of all intersubjects, it is possible that structures with relatively large differences across subjects get smoothed out under the spatially invariant smoothness constraints. Therefore developing a spatially varying kernel that penalizes local smoothness is desirable for the problem of atlas estimation.

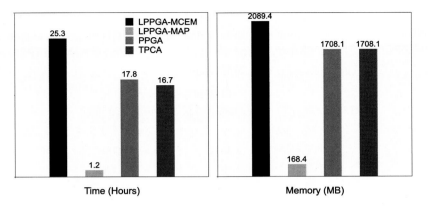

Figure 15.7. Comparison of run time and memory consumption. The implementation employed a message passing interface (MPI) parallel programming for all methods and distributed 90 subjects to 10 processors.

Acknowledgments

This work was supported by NIH NIBIB NAC P41EB015902, NIH NINDS R01NS086905, NIH NICHD U01HD087211, NCIGT NIH P41EB015898, and Wistron Corporation. The data collection and sharing for this project was funded by the ADNI (National Institutes of Health Grant U01 AG024904). All the investigators within the ADNI provided data but did not participate in the analysis or writing of this chapter.

References

1. S. Allassonnière, Y. Amit, A. Trouvé, Toward a coherent statistical framework for dense deformable template estimation, Journal of the Royal Statistical Society, Series B 69 (2007) 3–29.
2. V.I. Arnol'd, Sur la géométrie différentielle des groupes de Lie de dimension infinie et ses applications à l'hydrodynamique des fluides parfaits, Annales de L'Institut Fourier 16 (1966) 319–361.
3. M.F. Beg, M.I. Miller, A. Trouvé, L. Younes, Computing large deformation metric mappings via geodesic flows of diffeomorphisms, International Journal of Computer Vision 61 (2) (2005) 139–157.
4. Fred L. Bookstein, Morphometric Tools for Landmark Data: Geometry and Biology, Cambridge University Press, 1997.
5. F. Bullo, Invariant Affine Connections and Controllability on Lie Groups, Technical Report for Geometric Mechanics, California Institute of Technology, 1995.
6. Ward Cheney, David Kincaid, Linear Algebra: Theory and Applications, The Australian Mathematical Society, vol. 110, 2009.

7. Gary E. Christensen, Richard D. Rabbitt, Michael I. Miller, A deformable neuroanatomy textbook based on viscous fluid mechanics, in: 27th Ann. Conf. on Inf. Sciences and Systems, Citeseer, 1993, pp. 211–216.
8. Timothy F. Cootes, Christopher J. Taylor, David H. Cooper, Jim Graham, et al., Active shape models-their training and application, Computer Vision and Image Understanding 61 (1) (1995) 38–59.
9. S. Duane, A. Kennedy, B. Pendleton, D. Roweth, Hybrid Monte Carlo, Physics Letters B (1987) 216–222.
10. A. Edelman, T.A. Arias, S.T. Smith, The geometry of algorithms with orthogonality constraints, SIAM Journal on Matrix Analysis and Applications 20 (2) (1998) 303–353.
11. P.T. Fletcher, C. Lu, S. Joshi, Statistics of Shape Via Principal Geodesic Analysis on Lie Groups, in: Computer Vision and Pattern Recognition, vol. 1, IEEE, 2003, pp. 1–95.
12. Pietro Gori, Olivier Colliot, Yulia Worbe, Linda Marrakchi-Kacem, Sophie Lecomte, Cyril Poupon, Andreas Hartmann, Nicholas Ayache, Stanley Durrleman, Bayesian Atlas Estimation for the Variability Analysis of Shape Complexes, Medical Image Computing and Computer-Assisted Intervention, vol. 8149, Springer, 2013, pp. 267–274.
13. Guido Gerig, Martin Styner, Martha E. Shenton, Jeffrey A. Lieberman, Shape versus size: improved understanding of the morphology of brain structures, in: Medical Image Computing and Computer-Assisted Intervention, Springer, 2001, pp. 24–32.
14. Jacob Hinkle, P. Thomas Fletcher, Sarang Joshi, Intrinsic polynomials for regression on Riemannian manifolds, Journal of Mathematical Imaging and Vision 50 (1–2) (2014) 32–52.
15. Clifford R. Jack, Matt A. Bernstein, Nick C. Fox, Paul Thompson, Gene Alexander, Danielle Harvey, Bret Borowski, Paula J. Britson, Jennifer L. Whitwell, Chadwick Ward, et al., The Alzheimer's disease neuroimaging initiative (ADNI): MRI methods, Journal of Magnetic Resonance Imaging 27 (4) (2008) 685–691.
16. M.I. Miller, A. Trouvé, L. Younes, Geodesic shooting for computational anatomy, Journal of Mathematical Imaging and Vision 24 (2) (2006) 209–228.
17. Federico Nemmi, Umberto Sabatini, Olivier Rascol, Patrice Péran, Parkinson's disease and local atrophy in subcortical nuclei: insight from shape analysis, Neurobiology of Aging 36 (1) (2015) 424–433.
18. John A. Onofrey, Lawrence H. Staib, Xenophon Papademetris, Semi-supervised learning of nonrigid deformations for image registration, in: International MICCAI Workshop on Medical Computer Vision, Springer, 2013, pp. 13–23.
19. Stephen M. Pizer, Daniel S. Fritsch, Paul A. Yushkevich, Valen E. Johnson, Edward L. Chaney, Segmentation, registration, and measurement of shape variation via image object shape, IEEE Transactions on Medical Imaging 18 (10) (1999) 851–865.
20. N. Singh, J. Hinkle, S. Joshi, P.T. Fletcher, A vector momenta formulation of diffeomorphisms for improved geodesic regression

and atlas construction, in: International Symposium on Biomedial Imaging (ISBI), April 2013.

21. Stefan Sommer, François Lauze, Mads Nielsen, Xavier Pennec, Sparse multi-scale diffeomorphic registration: the kernel bundle framework, Journal of Mathematical Imaging and Vision 46 (3) (2013) 292–308.

22. Andrew Sweet, Xavier Pennec, A log-Euclidean statistical analysis of DTI brain deformations, in: MICCAI 2010 Workshop on Computational Diffusion MRI, 2010.

23. Darcy Wentworth Thompson, et al., On growth and form. On growth and form, 1942.

24. Marc Vaillant, Michael I. Miller, Laurent Younes, Alain Trouvé, Statistics on diffeomorphisms via tangent space representations, NeuroImage 23 (2004) S161–S169.

25. François-Xavier Vialard, Laurent Risser, Daniel Rueckert, Colin J. Cotter, Diffeomorphic 3D image registration via geodesic shooting using an efficient adjoint calculation, International Journal of Computer Vision 97 (2) (2012) 229–241.

26. L. Younes, F. Arrate, M.I. Miller, Evolutions equations in computational anatomy, NeuroImage 45 (1S1) (2009) 40–50.

27. M. Zhang, P.T. Fletcher, Bayesian principal geodesic analysis in diffeomorphic image registration, in: Medical Image Computing and Computer-Assisted Intervention–MICCAI 2014, Springer, 2014, pp. 121–128.

28. M. Zhang, P.T. Fletcher, Bayesian principal geodesic analysis for estimating intrinsic diffeomorphic image variability, Medical Image Analysis (2015).

29. M. Zhang, P.T. Fletcher, Finite-dimensional Lie algebras for fast diffeomorphic image registration, in: Information Processing in Medical Imaging, 2015.

30. M. Zhang, P.T. Fletcher, Fast diffeomorphic image registration via Fourier-approximated Lie algebras, International Journal of Computer Vision (2018).

31. M. Zhang, W.M. Wells III, P. Golland, Low-dimensional statistics of anatomical variability via compact representation of image deformations, in: International Conference on Medical Image Computing and Computer-Assisted Intervention, Springer, 2016, pp. 166–173.

32. M. Zhang, W.M. Wells III, P. Golland, Probabilistic modeling of anatomical variability using a low dimensional parameterization of diffeomorphisms, Medical Image Analysis 41 (2017) 55–62.

Diffeomorphic density registration

Martin Bauer[a], Sarang Joshi[b], Klas Modin[c]

[a] Florida State University, Department of Mathematics, Tallahassee, FL, United States. [b] University of Utah, Department of Bioengineering, Scientific Computing and Imaging Institute, Salt Lake City, UT, United States. [c] Chalmers University of Technology and the University of Gothenburg, Department of Mathematical Sciences, Göteborg, Sweden

16.1 Introduction

Over the last decade image registration has received intense interest, both with respect to medical imaging applications and to the mathematical foundations of the general problem of estimating a transformation that brings two or more given medical images into a common coordinate system [18,22,41,27,39,2,1,13]. In this chapter we focus on a subclass of registration problems referred to as density registration. The primary difference between density registration and general image registration is in how the registration transformation acts on the image being transformed. In density registration the transformation not only deforms the underlying coordinate system, but also scales the image intensity by the local change in volume. In numerous medical imaging applications this is of critical importance and is a fundamental property of the registration problem. The primary motivating clinical application is that of estimating the complex changes in anatomy due to breathing as imaged via 4D respiratory correlated computed tomography (4DRCCT). Given the physical quantitative nature of CT imaging, the natural action of a transformation on a CT image is that of density action: Any local compression induces a corresponding change in local density, resulting in changes in the local attenuation coefficient. We will also see that this difference in action of the transformation on the image being registered has wide ranging implications to the structure of the estimation problem. In this chapter we will study the fundamental geometrical structure of the problem and exemplify its application. The basic outline is as follows: We will first study the abstract mathematical structure of the problem, precisely defining the space of densities and the space of transformation. We will also study the

Riemannian Geometric Statistics in Medical Image Analysis
https://doi.org/10.1016/B978-0-12-814725-2.00025-X

set of transformations that leave the density unchanged. We will see that the explicit characterization of this set of transformations plays a critical role in understanding the geometric structure of the density registration problem. We will then introduce the general (regularized) density matching problem and present efficient numerical algorithms for several specific choices of regularizers. Finally, we will present the before mentioned application to model breathing as imaged via 4D respiratory correlated computed tomography.

16.2 Diffeomorphisms and densities

Let M denote a smooth oriented Riemannian manifold of dimension n with (reference) volume form $\mathrm{d}x$.

Definition 16.1. The space of *smooth densities*[1] on M is given by

$$\mathrm{Dens}(M) = \{\rho \in C^\infty(M) \mid \rho(x) > 0 \quad \forall x \in M\}.$$

The *mass* of a subset $\Omega \subset M$ with respect to $\rho \in \mathrm{Dens}(M)$ is given by

$$\mathrm{Mass}_\rho(\Omega) = \int_\Omega \rho \, \mathrm{d}x.$$

As the focus of the chapter is the registration of densities via transformation, the group $\mathrm{Diff}(M)$ of smooth diffeomorphisms of the manifold plays a central role.

Definition 16.2. The set of diffeomorphisms on M, denoted $\mathrm{Diff}(M)$, consists of smooth bijective mappings $M \to M$ with smooth inverses. This set has a natural group structure by composition of maps. The Lie algebra of $\mathrm{Diff}(M)$ is given by the space $\mathfrak{X}(M)$ of smooth vector fields (tangential if M has a boundary).[2]

The group of diffeomorphisms acts naturally on the space of densities via pullback and pushforward of densities. Indeed, *pullback of densities* is given by

$$\mathrm{Diff}(M) \times \mathrm{Dens}(M) \ni (\varphi, \rho) \mapsto \varphi^*\rho = |D\varphi| \, \rho(\varphi(\cdot)).$$

[1] If M is compact, then $\mathrm{Dens}(M)$ is an infinite-dimensional *Fréchet manifold* [19], that is, a manifold modeled on a Fréchet space. For the purpose of analysis, it is often useful to instead work with the Sobolev completion $\mathrm{Dens}^s(M)$ for a Sobolev index $s > n/2$. $\mathrm{Dens}^s(M)$ is then a *Banach manifold* [25]. The benefit of Banach over Fréchet manifolds is that most standard results from finite dimensions, such as the inverse function theorem, are valid.
[2] If M is compact, then $\mathrm{Diff}(M)$ is a *Fréchet Lie group* [19, § I.4.6], i.e., a Fréchet manifold where the group operations are smooth mappings.

Notice that this is a right action, that is, $(\varphi \circ \eta)^* \rho = \eta^*(\varphi^* \rho)$. The corresponding left action is given by *pushforward of densities*

$$\mathrm{Diff}(M) \times \mathrm{Dens}(M) \ni (\varphi, \rho) \mapsto \varphi_* \rho = (\varphi^{-1})^* \rho$$
$$= |D\varphi^{-1}| \, \rho(\varphi^{-1}(\cdot)).$$

The action of $\mathrm{Diff}(M)$ on densities captures the notion of conservation of mass and is fundamentally different from the standard action of $\mathrm{Diff}(M)$ on functions given by composition (see chapter 4). Indeed, for the density action, we have, for any subset $\Omega \subset M$,

$$\mathrm{Mass}_{\varphi_* \rho}(\varphi(\Omega)) = \mathrm{Mass}_\rho(\Omega),$$

which follows from the change-of-coordinates formula for integrals.

The *isotropy subgroup* of an element $\rho \in \mathrm{Dens}(M)$ is by definition the subgroup of $\mathrm{Diff}(M)$ that leaves the density ρ unchanged. It is given by

$$\mathrm{Diff}_\rho(M) = \{\varphi \in \mathrm{Diff}(M) \mid \varphi_* \rho = \rho\}.$$

The particular case $\rho \equiv 1$ gives the subgroup of volume preserving diffeomorphisms denoted by $\mathrm{SDiff}(M)$. In general, $\varphi \in \mathrm{Diff}_\rho(M)$ implies that φ is *mass preserving with respect to* ρ. In particular, if $\Omega \subset M$, then

$$\mathrm{Mass}_\rho(\Omega) = \mathrm{Mass}_\rho(\varphi(\Omega)).$$

The point of diffeomorphic density registration is to select a template density $\rho_0 \in \mathrm{Dens}(M)$ and then generate new densities by acting on ρ_0 by diffeomorphisms. In our framework we shall mostly use the left action (by pushforward), but analogous results are also valid for the right action (by pullback). One may ask "Which densities can be reached by acting on ρ_0 by diffeomorphisms?" In other words, find the range of the mapping

$$\mathrm{Diff}(M) \ni \varphi \mapsto \varphi_* \rho_0.$$

In the language of group theory it is called the $\mathrm{Diff}(M)$-orbit of ρ_0. This question was answered in 1965 by Moser [31] for compact manifolds: the result is that the $\mathrm{Diff}(M)$-orbit of ρ_0 consists of all densities with the same total mass as ρ_0. This result has been extended to noncompact manifolds [17] and manifolds with boundary [4]. For simplicity, we will only formulate the result in the compact case.

Lemma 16.1 (Moser [31]). *Given $\rho_0, \rho_1 \in \mathrm{Dens}(M)$, where M is a compact manifold without boundary, there exists $\varphi \in \mathrm{Diff}(M)$ such that $\varphi_* \rho_0 = \rho_1$ if and only if*

$$\mathrm{Mass}_{\rho_1}(M) = \mathrm{Mass}_{\rho_0}(M).$$

The diffeomorphism φ is unique up to right composition with elements in $\mathrm{Diff}_{\rho_0}(M)$ or, equivalently, up to left composition with elements in $\mathrm{Diff}_{\rho_1}(M)$.

Since the total mass of a density is a positive real number, it follows from Moser's result that the set of $\mathrm{Diff}(M)$-orbits in $\mathrm{Dens}(M)$ can be identified with $\mathbb{R}_+$. From a geometric point of view, this gives a *fibration* of $\mathrm{Dens}(M)$ as a fiber bundle over $\mathbb{R}_+$ where each fiber corresponds to a $\mathrm{Diff}(M)$-orbit. In turn, Moser's result also tells us that *each orbit in itself* is the base of a principal bundle fibration of $\mathrm{Diff}(M)$. For example, the ρ_0-orbit can be identified with the quotient $\mathrm{Diff}(M)/\mathrm{Diff}_{\rho_0}(M)$ through the projection

$$\pi : \varphi \mapsto \varphi_* \rho_0.$$

See references [29,5] for more details.

Remark 16.1. A consequence of the simple orbit structure of $\mathrm{Dens}(M)$ is that we can immediately check if the registration problem can be solved exactly by comparing the total mass of ρ_0 and ρ_1. Furthermore, there is a natural projection from $\mathrm{Dens}(M)$ to any orbit simply by scaling by the total mass.

In diffeomorphic image registration, where the action on an image is given by composition with a diffeomorphism, the $\mathrm{Diff}(M)$-orbits are much more complicated. Indeed, two generic images almost never belong to the same orbit. The problem of projecting from one orbit to another is ill-posed. On the other hand, because of the principal bundle structure of the space of densities, the exact registration problem of two densities with equal mass is well posed and has a complete geometric interpretation, which we will exploit to develop efficient numerical algorithms.

16.2.1 α-actions

The above mathematical development of diffeomorphisms acting on densities can be further generalized. By parameterizing the action by a positive constant α and define the α-action as follows: The group of diffeomorphisms $\mathrm{Diff}(\Omega)$ acts from the left on densities by the *α-action* via

$$(\varphi, \rho) \mapsto \varphi_{\alpha*}\rho := |D\varphi^{-1}|^\alpha \, \rho \circ \varphi^{-1}, \qquad (16.1)$$

where $|D\varphi|$ denotes the Jacobian determinant of φ.

Remark 16.2. One theoretical motivation to study α-density action is that it enables the approximation of the standard action of $\mathrm{Diff}(M)$ on functions given by composition: formally, $\lim_{\alpha \to 0} \varphi_{\alpha*} I = I \circ \varphi^{-1}$.

From a practical point of view, the motivation for the α-action stems from the fact that CT images do not transform exactly as densities. We will see in section 16.6.1 that for the application of density matching of thoracic CT images, the lungs behave as α-densities for $\alpha < 1$.

Analogous to the standard mass, we define the Mass_{ρ^p} of a subset $\Omega \subset M$ with respect to $\rho \in \mathrm{Dens}^\alpha(M)$ by

$$\mathrm{Mass}_{\rho^p}(\Omega) = \int_\Omega \rho^p \, \mathrm{d}x.$$

With this definition we immediately obtain the analogue of Lemma 16.1 for the α-action and thus also a similar principal fiber bundle picture.

Lemma 16.2. *Given* $\rho_0, \rho_1 \in \mathrm{Dens}(M)$, *where M is a compact manifold, there exists* $\varphi \in \mathrm{Diff}(M)$ *such that* $\varphi_{\alpha*}\rho_0 = \rho_1$ *if and only if*

$$\mathrm{Mass}_{\rho_0^{1/\alpha}}(M) = \mathrm{Mass}_{\rho_1^{1/\alpha}}(M).$$

16.3 Diffeomorphic density registration

In this part we will describe a general (Riemannian) approach to diffeomorphic density registration, that is, the problem of finding an optimal diffeomorphism φ that transports an α-density ρ_0 (source) to an α-density ρ_1 (target). By Moser's result (see Lemma 16.1 and Lemma 16.2) there always exists an infinite-dimensional set of solutions (diffeomorphisms) to this problem. Thus the main difficulty lies in the *solution selection*. Toward this aim, we introduce the regularized *exact α-density registration* problem:

> Given a source density ρ_0 and a target density ρ_1 of the same total $\mathrm{Mass}_{\rho_0^{1/\alpha}}$, find a diffeomorphism φ that minimizes
>
> $$\mathcal{R}(\varphi) \quad \text{under the constraint} \quad \varphi_{\alpha*}\rho_0 = \rho_1. \quad (16.2)$$
>
> Here $\mathcal{R}(\varphi)$ is a regularization term.

Remark 16.3. Note that we have formulated the registration constraint using the left action of the diffeomorphism group, that is, $\varphi_{\alpha*}\rho_0 = \rho_1$. A different approach is to use the right action of

Diff(M) with the constraint $\varphi^{\alpha*}\rho_1 = \rho_0$. These two approaches are conceptually different, as we aim to move the source to target using the left action while one moves the target to source using the right action. The resulting optimal deformations are however equal if the regularization term satisfies $\mathcal{R}(\varphi) = \mathcal{R}(\varphi^{-1})$.

In later sections we will introduce several choices for $\mathcal{R}$ and discuss their theoretical and practical properties. In general, we aim to construct regularization terms such that the corresponding registration problem has the following desirable properties:

1. Theoretical results on the existence and uniqueness of solutions;
2. Fast and stable numerical computations of the minimizers;
3. Meaningful optimal deformations.

Note that the notion of *meaningful* will depend highly on the specific application.

In practice we are sometimes not interested in enforcing the constraint, but are rather interested in a relaxed version of the above problem. Thus we introduce the *inexact density registration* problem:

> Given a source density ρ_0 and a target density ρ_1, find a diffeomorphism φ that minimizes
>
> $$\mathcal{E}(\varphi) = \lambda \, d(\varphi_{\alpha*}\rho_0, \rho_1) + \mathcal{R}(\varphi) \,. \tag{16.3}$$
>
> Here $\lambda > 0$ is a scaling parameter, $d(\cdot, \cdot)$ is a distance on the space of densities (the similarity measure), and $\mathcal{R}(\varphi)$ is a regularization term as before.

Remark 16.4. Note that we do not require the densities to have the same Mass$^{\frac{1}{\alpha}}$ in the inexact density matching framework. For densities that have the same Mass$^{\frac{1}{\alpha}}$, we can retrieve the exact registration problem by considering the inexact registration problem as $\lambda \to \infty$.

On the space of probability densities there exists a canonical Riemannian metric, the Fisher–Rao metric, which allows for explicit formulas of the corresponding geodesic distance: it is given by the (spherical) Hellinger distance. For the purpose of this book chapter, we will often use this distance functional as a similarity measure.

16.4 Density registration in the LDDMM-framework

The LDDMM-framework is based on the idea of using a *right-invariant* metric on the diffeomorphism group to define the regularity measure, that is,

$$\mathcal{R}(\varphi) = \text{dist}(\text{id}, \varphi) \,, \tag{16.4}$$

where $\text{dist}(\cdot, \cdot)$ denotes the geodesic distance of a right-invariant metric on $\text{Diff}(M)$. The resulting framework for inexact registration has been discussed for general shape spaces in chapter 4. Therefore we will keep the presentation in this chapter rather brief. Our focus will be on the geometric picture of the exact registration problem in this setup.

Remark 16.5. In the presentation of chapter 4 right-invariant metrics on $\text{Diff}(M)$ have been defined using the theory of reproducing kernel Hilbert spaces (RKHS). We will follow a slightly different approach and equip the whole group of diffeomorphisms with a weak right-invariant metric; see [12] for a comparison of these two approaches.

From here on we assume that M is equipped with a smooth Riemannian metric g with volume density μ. To define a right-invariant metric on $\text{Diff}(M)$, we introduce the so-called *inertia operator* $A\colon \mathfrak{X}(M) \to \mathfrak{X}(M)$, where $\mathfrak{X}(M)$, the set of smooth vector fields, is the Lie algebra of $\text{Diff}(M)$. We will assume that A is a strictly positive elliptic differential operator, that is, self-adjoint with respect to the L^2 inner product on $\mathfrak{X}(M)$. For simplicity, we will only consider operators A that are defined via powers of the Laplacian of the Riemannian metric g, that is, we will only consider operators of the form

$$A = (1 - \Delta_g)^k \tag{16.5}$$

for some integer k. Here Δ_g denotes the Hodge–Laplacian of the metric g. Most of the results discussed further are valid for a much larger class of (pseudo)differential operators; see [9]. Any such A defines the inner product G_{id} on $\mathfrak{X}(M)$ via

$$G_{\text{id}}(X, Y) = \int_M g\,(AX, Y)\,\mu \,, \tag{16.6}$$

where μ denotes the induced volume density of g. We can extend this to a right-invariant metric on $\text{Diff}(M)$ by right-translation:

$$G_\varphi(h, k) = G_{\text{id}}(h \circ \varphi^{-1}, k \circ \varphi^{-1}) = \int_M g\left(A(h \circ \varphi^{-1}), k \circ \varphi^{-1}\right) \mu \,. \tag{16.7}$$

For an overview on right-invariant metrics on diffeomorphism groups, we refer to [28,12,7,8].

In this framework the exact density registration problem reads as follows.

Given a source density ρ_0 and a target density ρ_1, find a diffeomorphism φ that minimizes

$$\mathrm{dist}(\mathrm{id}, \varphi) \qquad \text{such that } \varphi_{\alpha*}\rho_0 = \rho_1 , \qquad (16.8)$$

where $\mathrm{dist}(\mathrm{id}, \varphi)$ is the geodesic distance on $\mathrm{Diff}(M)$ of the metric (16.7).

Using this particular regularization term provides an intuitive interpretation of the solution selection: we aim to find the transformation that is as close as possible to the identity under the constraint that it transports the source density to the target density.

In the following theorem we present a summary of the geometric picture that underlies the exact registration problem. To keep the presentation simple, we will only consider the case $\alpha = 1$, that is, the standard density action. A similar result can be obtained for general α.

Let π be the projection

$$\pi : \mathrm{Diff}(M) \to \mathrm{Dens}(M) \simeq \mathrm{Diff}_\rho(M)\backslash\mathrm{Diff}(M) \qquad (16.9)$$

induced by the left action of the diffeomorphism group; see Lemma 16.1. By [9] we have the following:

Theorem 16.1. *Let G be a right-invariant metric on $\mathrm{Diff}(M)$ of the form (16.7) with inertia operator A as in (16.5). Then there exists a unique Sobolev-type metric $\bar{G}_\rho$ on $\mathrm{Dens}(M)$ such that the projection π is a Riemannian submersion. The order of the induced metric $\bar{G}$ on $\mathrm{Dens}(M)$ is $k - 1$, where k is the order of the metric G.*

A direct consequence of the Riemannian submersion picture is the following characterization of the solutions of the exact density registration problem.

Corollary 16.1. *Let $\rho(t)$, $t \in [0, 1]$, be a minimizing geodesic connecting the given densities ρ_0 (source) and ρ_1 (target). Then the solution of the exact registration problem is given by the endpoint $\varphi(1)$ of the horizontal lift of the geodesic $\rho(t)$.*

Remark 16.6. This result describes an intriguing geometric interpretation of the solutions of the exact registration problem. Its applicability is however limited to the cases where there exist explicit solutions for the geodesic boundary value problem on the space of probability densities with respect to the metric $\bar{G}$. To our knowledge, the only such example is the so-called optimal information transport setting, which we will discuss in the next section. In the general case the solution of the exact density registration problem requires solving the horizontal geodesic boundary value problem on the group of diffeomorphisms, which is connected to the solution of a nonlinear PDE, the EPDiff equation. Various algorithms have been proposed for numerically solving the optimization problems [10,42,40]. We refer to Chapter 4 for more details.

16.5 Optimal information transport

In this section we describe an explicit way of solving the exact density registration problem. The framework in this section has been previously developed for random sampling from nonuniform arbitrary distributions [6]. For simplicity, we will restrict ourselves to the standard density action, that is, $\alpha = 1$. However, all the algorithms are easily generalized to general α. The specific setting uses deep geometric connections between the Fisher–Rao metric on the space of probability densities and a special right-invariant metric on the group of diffeomorphisms.

Definition 16.3. The *Fisher–Rao metric* is the Riemannian metric on Dens(M) given by

$$G_\rho(\dot\rho, \dot\rho) = \frac{1}{4} \int_M \frac{\dot\rho^2}{\rho}\, dx. \tag{16.10}$$

The main advantage of the Fisher–Rao metric is the existence of explicit formulas for the solution to the geodesic boundary value problem and thus also for the induced geodesic distance:

Proposition 16.1 (Friedrich [14]). *Given $\rho_0, \rho_1 \in$ Dens(M) with the same total mass, the Riemannian distance with respect to the Fisher–Rao metric is given by*

$$d_F(\rho_0, \rho_1) = \arccos\left(\int_M \sqrt{\frac{\rho_1}{\rho_0}}\rho_0\right). \tag{16.11}$$

Furthermore, the geodesic between ρ_0 and ρ_1 is given by

$$\rho(t) = \left(\frac{\sin(1-t)\theta}{\sin\theta} + \frac{\sin t\theta}{\sin\theta}\sqrt{\frac{\rho_1}{\rho_0}}\right)^2 \rho_0, \tag{16.12}$$

where $\theta = d_F(\rho_0, \rho_1)$.

Using formula (16.12) for geodesics, we will construct an almost explicit algorithm for solving an exact density registration problem of the form (16.2). To this end, we need to introduce a suitable regularization term. As in the LDDMM framework (see section 16.4), we will choose it as distance to the identity with respect to a right-invariant Riemannian metric on $\mathrm{Diff}(M)$. However, to exploit the explicit formula (16.12), the right-invariant metric needs to communicate with the Fisher–Rao metric, as we now explain.

Definition 16.4. The *information metric* is the right-invariant Riemannian metric on $\mathrm{Diff}(M)$ given (at the identity) by

$$\bar{G}_{\mathrm{id}}(u, v) = -\int_M \langle \Delta u, v \rangle \, \mathrm{d}x + \sum_{i=1}^k \int_M \langle u, \xi_i \rangle \, \mathrm{d}x \int_M \langle v, \xi_i \rangle \, \mathrm{d}x,$$
(16.13)

where Δu denotes the Laplace–de Rham operator lifted to vector fields, and $\xi_1, \ldots, \xi_k$ are a basis of the harmonic fields on M. The Riemannian distance corresponding to $\bar{G}$ is denoted $d_I(\cdot, \cdot)$. Because of the Hodge decomposition theorem, the metric is independent of the choice of orthonormal basis for the harmonic fields.

Building on work by Khesin, Lenells, Misiolek, and Preston [24], Modin [29] showed that the metric $\bar{G}$ descends to the Fisher–Rao metric on the space of densities. This fundamental property will serve as the basis for our algorithms.

We are now ready to formulate our special density registration problem, called the *optimal information transport problem*:

> ## Optimal information transport (OIT)
>
> Given $\rho_0, \rho_1 \in \mathrm{Dens}(M)$ and a Riemannian metric on M with volume form ρ_0, find a diffeomorphism φ that minimizes
>
> $$\mathcal{E}(\varphi) = d_I(\mathrm{id}, \varphi) = d_F(\rho_0, \varphi_* \rho_0) \qquad (16.14)$$
>
> under the constraint $\varphi_* \rho_0 = \rho_1$.

In general, the formula for $d_I(\mathrm{id}, \varphi)$ is not available explicitly; we would have to solve a nonlinear PDE (the EPDiff equation). However, because of the special relation between d_I and d_F, we have the following result, which is the key to an efficient algorithm.

Theorem 16.2 ([29,5]). *The OIT problem has a unique solution, that is, there is a unique diffeomorphism $\varphi \in \mathrm{Diff}(M)$ minimizing $d_I(\mathrm{id}, \varphi)$ under the constraint $\varphi_* \rho_0 = \rho_1$. The solution is explicitly* *given by $\varphi(1)$, where $\varphi(t)$ is the solution to the problem*

$$\Delta f(t) = \frac{\dot{\rho}(t)}{\rho(t)} \circ \varphi(t),$$
$$v(t) = \nabla(f(t)), \tag{16.15}$$
$$\frac{d}{dt}\varphi(t)^{-1} = v(t) \circ \varphi(t)^{-1}, \quad \varphi(0) = \mathrm{id},$$

and $\rho(t)$ is the Fisher–Rao geodesic connecting ρ_0 and ρ_1:

$$\rho(t) = \left(\frac{\sin(1-t)\theta}{\sin\theta} + \frac{\sin t\theta}{\sin\theta}\sqrt{\frac{\rho_1}{\rho_0}}\right)^2 \rho_0, \quad \cos\theta = \int_M \sqrt{\frac{\rho_1}{\rho_0}}\,\rho_0. \tag{16.16}$$

Based on Theorem 16.2, we now give a semiexplicit algorithm for numerical computation of the solution to the optimal information transport problem. The algorithm assumes that we have a numerical way to represent functions, vector fields, and diffeomorphisms on M and numerical methods for

- composing functions and vector fields with diffeomorphisms,
- computing the ∇ of functions, and
- computing solutions to Poisson's equation on M.

Numerical algorithm for optimal information transport

1. Choose a step size $\varepsilon = 1/K$ for some positive integer K and calculate the Fisher–Rao geodesic $\rho(t)$ and its derivative $\dot{\rho}(t)$ at all time points $t_k = \frac{k}{K}$ using equation (16.16).
2. Initialize $\varphi_0 = \mathrm{id}$. Set $k \leftarrow 0$.
3. Compute $s_k = \frac{\dot{\rho}(t_k)}{\rho(t_k)} \circ \varphi_k$ and solve the Poisson equation

$$\Delta f_k = s_k. \tag{16.17}$$

4. Compute the gradient vector field $v_k = \nabla f_k$.
5. Construct approximations ψ_k to $\exp(-\varepsilon v_k)$, for example,

$$\psi_k = \mathrm{id} - \varepsilon v_k. \tag{16.18}$$

6. Update the diffeomorphism

$$\varphi_{k+1} = \varphi_k \circ \psi_k. \tag{16.19}$$

If needed, we may also compute the inverse by $\varphi_{k+1}^{-1} = \varphi_k^{-1} + \varepsilon v \circ \varphi_k^{-1}$.
7. Set $k \leftarrow k + 1$ and continue from step 3 unless $k = K$.

Although it is possible to use optimal information transport and the algorithm above for medical image registration problems, the results so obtained are typically not satisfactory; the diffeomorphism obtained tends to compress and expand matter instead of moving it (see, e.g., [5, Sec. 4.2]). Another problem is that the source and target densities are required to be strictly positive, which is typically not the case for medical images. In section 16.6 we will develop a gradient flow-based approach, which will lead to much better results for these applications. However, in applications where either the source or the target density is uniform (with respect to the natural Riemannian structure of the manifold at hand), the OIT approach can be very competitive, which yields a natural application for random sampling.

16.5.1 Application: random sampling from nonuniform distribution

In this section we describe an application of OIT to random sampling from nonuniform distributions, that is, the following problem.

> **Random sampling problem**
>
> Let $\rho_1 \in \mathrm{Dens}(M)$. Generate N random samples from the probability distribution ρ_1.

The classic approach to sample from a probability distribution on a higher-dimensional space is to use Markov chain Monte Carlo (MCMC) methods, for example, the Metropolis–Hastings algorithm [20]. An alternative idea is to use diffeomorphic density registration between the density ρ_1 and the standard density ρ_0 from which samples can be drawn easily. Indeed, we can then draw samples from ρ_0 and transform them via the computed diffeomorphism to generate samples from ρ_1. A benefit of transport-based methods over traditional MCMC methods is cheap computation of additional samples; it amounts to drawing uniform samples and then evaluating the transformation. On the other hand, unlike MCMC, transport-based methods scale poorly with increasing dimensionality of M.

Moselhy and Marzouk [30] and Reich [33] proposed to use optimal mass transport (OMT) to construct the desired diffeomorphism φ, thereby enforcing $\varphi = \nabla c$ for some convex function c. The OMT approach implies solving, in one form or another, the heavily nonlinear Monge–Ampere equation for c. A survey of the OMT approach to random sampling is given by Marzouk et al. [26]. Using OIT instead of OMT, the problem simplifies significantly, as the OIT-algorithm only involves solving linear Poisson problems.

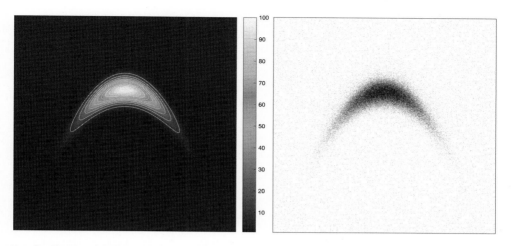

Figure 16.1 Application of OIT to random sampling. (Left) The probability density ρ of (16.20). The maximal density ratio is 100. (Right) 10^5 samples from ρ calculated using our OIT-based random sampling algorithm.

As a specific example, consider $M = \mathbb{T}^2 \simeq (\mathbb{R}/2\pi\mathbb{Z})^2$ with distribution defined in Cartesian coordinates $x, y \in [-\pi, \pi)$ by

$$\rho \sim 3\exp(-x^2 - 10(y - x^2/2 + 1)^2) + 1/10, \qquad (16.20)$$

normalized so that the ratio between the maximum and mimimum of ρ is 100. The resulting density is depicted in Fig. 16.1 (left).

We draw 10^5 samples from this distribution using a MATLAB implementation of our algorithm, available under MIT license at

https://github.com/kmodin/oit-random

The implementation can be summarized as follows. To solve the Poisson problem, we discretize the torus by a 256×256 mesh and use the fast Fourier transform (FFT) to invert the Laplacian. We use 100 time steps. The resulting diffeomorphism is shown as a mesh warp in Fig. 16.2. We then draw 10^5 uniform samples on $[-\pi, \pi]^2$ and apply the diffeomorphism on each sample (applying the diffeomorphism corresponds to interpolation on the warped mesh). The resulting random samples are depicted in Fig. 16.1 (right). Drawing new samples is very efficient. For example, another 10^7 samples can be drawn in less than a second.

16.6 A gradient flow approach

In the optimal information transport described in the previous section the fundamental restriction is that the volume form

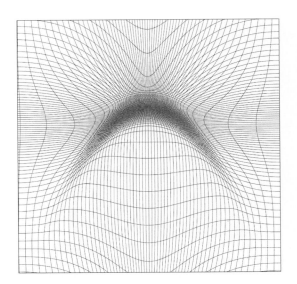

Figure 16.2 Application of OIT to random sampling. The computed diffeomorphism φ_K shown as a warp of the uniform 256×256 mesh (every 4th mesh-line is shown). Notice that the warp is periodic. The ratio between the largest and smallest warped volumes is 100.

of Riemannian metric of the base manifold is compatible with the density being transformed in that it has to be conformally related to the source density ρ_0. In most medical imaging applications this modeling assumption is not applicable. In this section we will develop more general algorithms that relax the requirement for the metric to be compatible with the densities to be registered. We will consider the natural extension of the Fisher–Rao metric to the space of all densities and the case where $dx(\Omega) = \infty$, for which it is given by

$$d_F^2(I_0\,dx,\, I_1\,dx) = \int_\Omega (\sqrt{I_0} - \sqrt{I_1})^2 dx \,. \qquad (16.21)$$

Notice that $d_F^2(\cdot, \cdot)$ in this case is the *Hellinger distance*. For details, see [5].

The Fisher–Rao metric is the unique Riemannian metric on the space of probability densities that is invariant under the action of the diffeomorphism group [7,3]. This invariance property extends to the induced distance function, so

$$d_F^2(I_0\,dx,\, I_1\,dx) = d_F^2(\varphi_*(I_0\,dx),\, \varphi_*(I_1\,dx)) \qquad \forall \varphi \in \mathrm{Diff}(\Omega) \,. \tag{16.22}$$

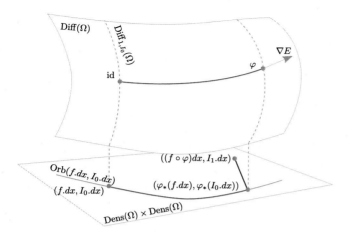

Figure 16.3 Geometry of the density registration problem. Illustration of the geometry associated with the density registration problem. The gradient flow on $\mathrm{Diff}(\Omega)$ descends to a gradient flow on the orbit $\mathrm{Orb}(f\,dx, I_0\,dx)$. When constrained to $\mathrm{Orb}(f\,dx, I_0\,dx) \subset \mathrm{Dens}(\Omega) \times \mathrm{Dens}(\Omega)$, this flow strives to minimize the product Fisher–Rao distance to $((f \circ \varphi)\,dx, I_1\,dx)$.

Motivated by the aforementioned properties, we develop a weighted diffeomorphic registration algorithm for registration of two density images. The algorithm is based on the Sobolev H^1 gradient flow on the space of diffeomorphisms that minimizes the energy functional

$$E(\varphi) = d_F^2(\varphi_*(f\,dx), (f \circ \varphi^{-1})dx) + d_F^2(\varphi_*(I_0\,dx), I_1\,dx). \quad (16.23)$$

This energy functional is only a slight modification of the energy functional studied in [5]. Indeed, if f in the equation is a constant $\sigma > 0$, then (16.23) reduces to the energy functional of Bauer, Joshi, and Modin [5, § 5.1]. Moreover, the geometry described in [5, § 5.3] is valid also for the functional (16.23), and, consequently, the algorithm developed in [5, § 5.2] can be used also for minimizing (16.23). There the authors view the energy functional as a constrained minimization problem on the product space $\mathrm{Dens}(\Omega) \times \mathrm{Dens}(\Omega)$ equipped with the product distance; see Fig. 16.3 and [5, § 5] for details on the resulting geometric picture. Related work on diffeomorphic density registration using the Fisher Rao metric can be found in [37,36].

Using the invariance property of the Fisher–Rao metric and assuming infinite volume, the main optimization problem associated with the energy functional (16.23) is the following.

Given densities $I_0\,dx$, $I_1\,dx$, and $f\,dx$, find $\varphi \in \mathrm{Diff}(\Omega)$ minimizing

$$E(\varphi) = \underbrace{\int_\Omega (\sqrt{|D\varphi^{-1}|} - 1)^2\, f \circ \varphi^{-1}\, dx}_{E_1(\varphi)}$$

$$+ \underbrace{\int_\Omega \left(\sqrt{|D\varphi^{-1}|I_0 \circ \varphi^{-1}} - \sqrt{I_1}\right)^2 dx}_{E_2(\varphi)} . \qquad (16.24)$$

The invariance of the Fisher–Rao distance can be seen with a simple change of variables $x \mapsto \varphi(y)$, $dx \mapsto |D\varphi|dy$, and $|D\varphi^{-1}| \mapsto \frac{1}{|D\varphi|}$. Then, Equation (16.24) becomes

$$E(\varphi) = \int_\Omega (1 - \sqrt{|D\varphi|})^2\, f\, dy + \int_\Omega \left(\sqrt{I_0} - \sqrt{|D\varphi|I_1 \circ \varphi}\right)^2 dy . \qquad (16.25)$$

To better understand the energy functional $E(\varphi)$, we consider the two terms separately. The first term $E_1(\varphi)$ is a *regularity measure* for the transformation. It penalizes the deviation of the diffeomorphism φ from being volume preserving. The density $f\,dx$ acts as a weighting on the domain Ω; that is, change of volume (compression and expansion of the transformation φ) is penalized more in regions of Ω where f is large. The second term $E_2(\varphi)$ penalizes *dissimilarity* between $I_0\,dx$ and $\varphi^*(I_1\,dx)$. It is the Fisher–Rao distance between the initial density $I_0\,dx$ and the transformed target density $\varphi^*(I_1\,dx)$. Because of the invariance (16.22) of the Fisher–Rao metric, this is the same as the Fisher–Rao distance between $I_1\,dx$ and $\varphi_*(I_0\,dx)$.

Solutions to problem (16.24) are *not* unique. To see this, let $\mathrm{Diff}_I(\Omega)$ denote the space of all diffeomorphisms preserving the volume form $I\,dx$:

$$\mathrm{Diff}_I(\Omega) = \{\varphi \in \mathrm{Diff}(\Omega) \mid |D\varphi|\,(I \circ \varphi) = I\}. \qquad (16.26)$$

If φ is a minimizer of $E(\cdot)$, then $\psi \circ \varphi$ for any

$$\psi \in \mathrm{Diff}_{1,I_0}(\Omega) := \mathrm{Diff}_1(\Omega) \cap \mathrm{Diff}_{I_0}(\Omega) \qquad (16.27)$$

is also a minimizer. Notice that this space is not trivial. For example, any diffeomorphism generated by a *Nambu–Poisson vector field* (see [32]), with I_0 as one of its Hamiltonians, will belong to it. A strategy to handle the degeneracy was developed in [5, § 5]: the fact that the metric is descending with respect to the H^1 metric on

Diff(Ω) can be used to ensure that the gradient flow is *infinitesimally optimal*, that is, always orthogonal to the null-space. We employ the same strategy in this paper. The corresponding geometric picture can be seen in Fig. 16.3.

To derive an gradient algorithm to optimize the energy functional the natural metric on the space of diffeomorphisms to use is the H^1-metric due to its intimate link with the Fisher–Rao metric as described previously. The H^1-metric on the space of diffeomorphisms is defined using the Hodge Laplacian on vector fields and is given by

$$G_\varphi^I(U, V) = \int_\Omega \langle -\Delta u, v \rangle dx . \tag{16.28}$$

Due to its connections to information geometry, we also refer to this metric as the *information metric*. Let $\nabla^{G^I} E$ denote the gradient with respect to the information metric defined previously. Our approach for minimizing the functional of (16.25) is to use a simple Euler integration of the time discretization of the gradient flow:

$$\dot{\varphi} = -\nabla^{G^I} E(\varphi). \tag{16.29}$$

The resulting final algorithm is one order of magnitude faster than LDDMM, since we are not required to time integrate the geodesic equations, as is necessary in LDDMM [42].

In the following theorem we calculate the gradient of the energy functional.

Theorem 16.3. *The G^I-gradient of the registration functional* (16.25) *is given by*

$$\nabla^{G^I} E = -\Delta^{-1} \Big(-\operatorname{grad} \big(f \circ \varphi^{-1} (1 - \sqrt{|D\varphi^{-1}|}) \big)$$
$$- \sqrt{|D\varphi^{-1}| I_0 \circ \varphi^{-1}} \operatorname{grad} (\sqrt{I_1}) + \operatorname{grad} \big(\sqrt{|D\varphi^{-1}| I_0 \circ \varphi^{-1}} \big) \sqrt{I_1} \Big) . \tag{16.30}$$

Proof. We first calculate the variation of the energy functional. Therefore let φ_s be a family of diffeomorphisms parameterized by the real variable s such that

$$\varphi_0 = \varphi \quad \text{and} \quad \frac{d}{ds}\Big|_{s=0} \varphi_s = v \circ \varphi. \tag{16.31}$$

We use the following identity derived in [21]:

$$\frac{d}{ds}\Big|_{s=0} \sqrt{|D\varphi_s|} = \frac{1}{2}\sqrt{|D\varphi|}\operatorname{div}(v) \circ \varphi. \tag{16.32}$$

The variation of the first term of the energy functional is

$$\frac{d}{ds}\bigg|_{s=0} E_1(\varphi) = \int_\Omega f(y)(\sqrt{|D\varphi(y)|} - 1)\sqrt{|D\varphi(y)|}\mathrm{div}(v) \circ \varphi(y)dy.$$
(16.33)

We do a change of variables $y \mapsto \varphi^{-1}(x)$, $dy \mapsto |D\varphi^{-1}(x)|dx$, using the fact that $|D\varphi(y)| = \frac{1}{|D\varphi^{-1}(x)|}$:

$$= \int_\Omega f \circ \varphi^{-1}(x)(1 - \sqrt{|D\varphi^{-1}(x)|})\mathrm{div}(v(x))dx \qquad (16.34)$$

$$= \left\langle f \circ \varphi^{-1}(1 - \sqrt{|D\varphi^{-1}|}), \mathrm{div}(v) \right\rangle_{L^2(\mathbb{R}^3)} \qquad (16.35)$$

$$= -\left\langle \mathrm{grad}\left(f \circ \varphi^{-1}(1 - \sqrt{|D\varphi^{-1}|}) \right), v \right\rangle_{L^2(\mathbb{R}^3)} \qquad (16.36)$$

using the fact that the adjoint of the divergence is the negative gradient. For the second term of the energy functional, we expand the square

$$E_2(\varphi) = \int_\Omega I_0(y) - 2\sqrt{I_0(y)I_1 \circ \varphi(y)|D\varphi(y)|} + I_1 \circ \varphi(y)|D\varphi(y)|dy.$$
(16.37)

Now $\int_\Omega I_1 \circ \varphi(y)|D\varphi(y)|dy$ is constant (conservation of mass), so we only need to minimize over the middle term. Then the derivative is

$$\frac{d}{ds}\bigg|_{s=0} E_2(\varphi) = -\int_\Omega 2\sqrt{I_0(y)}\left(\mathrm{grad}\sqrt{I_1}^T v \right) \circ \varphi(y)\sqrt{|D\varphi(y)|}$$
$$- \sqrt{I_0(y)I_1 \circ \varphi(y)|D\varphi(y)|}\mathrm{div}(v) \circ \varphi(y)dy.$$
(16.38)

We do the same change of variables as before:

$$= -\int_\Omega \sqrt{I_0 \circ \varphi^{-1}(x)}\frac{|D\varphi^{-1}(x)|}{\sqrt{|D\varphi^{-1}(x)|}}\left(2\,\mathrm{grad}\sqrt{I_1(x)}^T v(x) \right.$$
$$\left. + \sqrt{I_1(x)}\mathrm{div}(v)(x) \right) \qquad (16.39)$$

$$= -\left\langle 2\sqrt{|D\varphi^{-1}|I_0 \circ \varphi^{-1}}\,\mathrm{grad}\sqrt{I_1}, v \right\rangle_{L^2(\mathbb{R}^3)}$$
$$- \left\langle \sqrt{|D\varphi^{-1}|I_0 \circ \varphi^{-1}I_1}, \mathrm{div}(v) \right\rangle_{L^2(\mathbb{R}^3)} \qquad (16.40)$$

$$= \left\langle -\sqrt{|D\varphi^{-1}|\,I_0 \circ \varphi^{-1}}\, \mathrm{grad}\,\sqrt{I_1}, v \right\rangle_{L^2(\mathbb{R}^3)}$$
$$+ \left\langle \mathrm{grad}\left(\sqrt{|D\varphi^{-1}|\,I_0 \circ \varphi^{-1}}\right)\sqrt{I_1}, v \right\rangle_{L^2(\mathbb{R}^3)}. \quad (16.41)$$

From these equations we conclude that

$$-\Delta(\nabla^{G^I} E) = -\mathrm{grad}\left(f \circ \varphi^{-1}(1 - \sqrt{|D\varphi^{-1}|})\right)$$
$$- \sqrt{|D\varphi^{-1}|\,I_0 \circ \varphi^{-1}}\, \mathrm{grad}\,\sqrt{I_1}$$
$$+ \mathrm{grad}\left(\sqrt{|D\varphi^{-1}|\,I_0 \circ \varphi^{-1}}\right)\sqrt{I_1} \quad (16.42)$$

Since we are taking the Sobolev gradient of E, we apply the inverse Laplacian to the right-hand side of Equation (16.42) to solve for $\nabla^{G^I} E$. □

Remark 16.7. Notice that in the formula for $\nabla^{G^I} E$ we never need to compute φ, so in practice we only compute φ^{-1}. We update this directly via $\varphi^{-1}(x) \mapsto \varphi^{-1}(x + \epsilon \nabla^{G^I} E)$ for some step size ϵ.

16.6.1 Thoracic density registration

We now present an application of the developed theory to the problem of estimating complex anatomical deformations associated with the breathing cycle as imaged via computed tomography (CT) [16]. This problem has wide-ranging medical applications, in particular, radiation therapy of the lung, where accurate estimation of organ deformations during treatment impacts dose calculation and treatment decisions [35,23,38,15]. The current state-of-the-art radiation treatment planning involves the acquisition of a series of respiratory correlated CT (RCCT) images to build 4D (three spatial and one temporal) treatment planning data sets. Fundamental to the processing and clinical use of these 4D data sets is the accurate estimation of registration maps that characterize the motion of organs at risk and the target tumor volumes.

The 3D image produced from X-ray CT is an image of linear attenuation coefficients. For narrow beam X-ray, the linear attenuation coefficient (LAC) for a single material (units cm^{-1}) is defined as $\mu(x) = m\rho(x)$, where m is a material-specific property called the mass attenuation coefficient (units cm^2/g) that depends on the energy of the X-ray beam. The linear attenuation coefficient

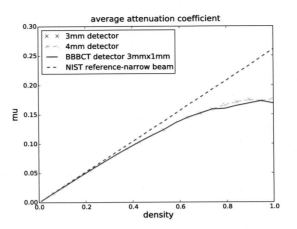

Figure 16.4 Mass$_{\rho^{1/\alpha}}$ **conservation in lung density matching.** Effective LAC from Monte Carlo simulation (solid line) and NIST reference narrow beam LAC (dashed line). The true relationship between effective LAC and narrow beam LAC is nonlinear.

is proportional to the true density and therefore exhibits conservation of mass. Unfortunately, CT image intensities do not represent true narrow beam linear attenuation coefficients. Instead, modern CT scanners use wide beams that yield secondary photon effects at the detector. CT image intensities reflect *effective* linear attenuation coefficients as opposed to the true narrow beam linear attenuation coefficient.

To see the relationship between effective LAC and true narrow beam LAC, we ran a Monte Carlo simulation using an X-ray spectrum and geometry from a Philips CT scanner at various densities of water (since lung tissue is very similar to a mixture between water and air) [11]. The nonlinear relationship between effective LAC and narrow beam LAC relationship is clear (see Fig. 16.4).

If we have conservation of mass within a single subject in a closed system, then we expect an inverse relationship between average density in a region Ω and volume of that region: $D_t = \frac{M}{V_t}$. Here $V_t = \int_{\Omega_t} 1 dx$, $D_t = \int_{\Omega_t} I_t(x) dx / V_t$, Ω_t is the domain of the closed system (that moves over time), and t is a phase of the breathing cycle. This relationship becomes linear in log space with a slope of -1:

$$\ln(D_t) = \ln(M) - \ln(V_t) \qquad (16.43)$$

Our experimental results confirm the Monte Carlo simulation in that lungs imaged under CT do not follow this inverse relationship. Rather, the slope found in these datasets in log space is consistently greater than -1 (see Fig. 16.6). This implies that for real clinical CT data sets, the lung tissue is acted on by an α-density action. Using the isomorphism between α-densities and 1-densities, we estimate the power transformation $I(x) \mapsto I(x)^\alpha$ and estimate the α that yields the best conservation of mass property.

For each subject, we perform a linear regression of the measured LAC density in the homogeneous lung region and the calculated volume in log space. Let $d(\alpha) = \log \left(\int_{\Omega_t} I_t(x)^\alpha dx / \int_{\Omega_t} 1 dx \right)$ (the log density) and $\vec{v} = \log(\int_{\Omega_t} 1 dx)$ (the log volume), where again t is a breathing cycle timepoint. The linear regression then models the relationship in log space as $d(\alpha) \approx a\vec{v} + b$. Let $a_j(\alpha)$ be the slope solved for in this linear regression for the jth subject. To find the optimal α for the entire dataset, we solve

$$\alpha = \arg\min_{\alpha'} \sum_j (a_j(\alpha') + 1)^2, \tag{16.44}$$

which finds the value of α that gives us an average slope closest to -1.

Applying this power function to the CT data allows us to perform our density registration algorithm based on the theory developed. We therefore seek to minimize the energy functional described in the previous section, given by

$$E(\varphi) = d_F^2(\varphi_*(f\,dx), (f \circ \varphi^{-1})dx) + d_F^2(\varphi_*(I_0\,dx), I_1\,dx)) \tag{16.45}$$

$$= \underbrace{\int_\Omega (\sqrt{|D\varphi^{-1}|} - 1)^2 f \circ \varphi^{-1}\,dx}_{E_1(\varphi)}$$

$$+ \underbrace{\int_\Omega \left(\sqrt{|D\varphi^{-1}|I_0 \circ \varphi^{-1}} - \sqrt{I_1}\right)^2 dx}_{E_2(\varphi)}. \tag{16.46}$$

We construct the density $f(x)\,dx$, a positive weighting on the domain Ω, to model the physiology of the thorax: regions where $f(x)$ is high have a higher penalty on nonvolume-preserving deformations and regions where $f(x)$ is low have a lower penalty on nonvolume-preserving deformations. Physiologically, we know that the lungs are quite compressible as air enters and leaves. Surrounding tissue including bones and soft tissue, on the other hand, is essentially incompressible. Therefore our penalty function $f(x)$ is low inside the lungs and outside the body and high elsewhere. For our penalty function, we simply implement a sigmoid function of the original CT image: $f(x) = \text{sig}(I_0(x))$.

Recall the Sobolev gradient calculated in Theorem 16.30 with respect to the energy functional given by

$$\delta E = -\Delta^{-1}\left(-\nabla\left(f \circ \varphi^{-1}(1 - \sqrt{|D\varphi^{-1}|})\right) \right.$$
$$\left. -\sqrt{|D\varphi^{-1}|\,I_0 \circ \varphi^{-1}}\,\nabla(\sqrt{I_1}) + \nabla\left(\sqrt{|D\varphi^{-1}|\,I_0 \circ \varphi^{-1}}\right)\sqrt{I_1} \right).$$

$$(16.47)$$

Then the current estimate of φ^{-1} is updated directly via an Euler integration of the gradient flow [34]:

$$\varphi_{j+1}^{-1}(x) = \varphi_j^{-1}(x + \epsilon \delta E) \qquad (16.48)$$

for some step size ϵ. Since we take the Sobolev gradient, the resulting deformation is guaranteed to be invertible with a sufficiently small ϵ. Also notice that the gradient only depends on φ^{-1}, so there is no need to keep track of both φ and φ^{-1}. The exact numerical algorithm is as follows:

Numerical algorithm for weighted diffeomorphic density registration

Chose $\epsilon > 0$
$\varphi^{-1} \leftarrow id$
$|D\varphi^{-1}| \leftarrow 1$
for $iter = 0 \cdots numiter$ **do**
$\qquad \varphi_* I_0 \leftarrow I_0 \circ \varphi - 1|D\varphi^{-1}|$
$\qquad u \leftarrow -\nabla\left(f \circ \varphi^{-1}(1 - \sqrt{|D\varphi^{-1}|})\right) - \sqrt{|D\varphi^{-1}|\,I_0 \circ \varphi^{-1}}\,\nabla(\sqrt{I_1}) +$
$\qquad \nabla\left(\sqrt{|D\varphi^{-1}|\,I_0 \circ \varphi^{-1}}\right)\sqrt{I_1}\Big)$
$\qquad v \leftarrow -\Delta^{-1}(u)$
$\qquad \varphi^{-1}(y) \leftarrow \varphi^{-1}(y + \epsilon v)$
$\qquad |D\varphi^{-1}| \leftarrow |D\varphi^{-1}| \circ \varphi^{-1} e^{-\epsilon \mathrm{div}(v)}$
end for

The algorithm was implemented using the PyCA package and can be downloaded at

https://bitbucket.org/crottman/pycaapps/src/master/

See the application *Weighted Diffeomorphic Density Registration*.

For the DIR dataset, we solved for the exponent that yields conservation of mass, which yielded $\alpha = 0.60$ giving us the best fit. Without using the exponential fit, the average slope of log density log volume plot was -0.66 (SD 0.048). After applying the exponential to the CT intensities, the average slope is -1.0 (SD 0.054). The

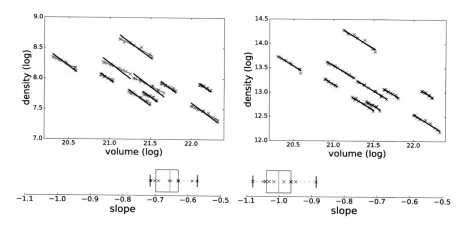

Figure 16.5 Application to lung density matching. Density and volume log–log plots. Upper left: log–log plots without applying the exponential correction for all ten DIR subjects. The best fit line to each dataset is in red (light gray in print version), and the mass-preserving line (slope = −1) is in black. Upper right: log–log plots after applying the exponential correction $I(x)^{\alpha}$ to the CT images. In this plot the best fit line matches very closely to the mass-preserving line. Bottom row: the corresponding box plots of the slopes found in the regression.

log–log plots of all ten patients in the DIR dataset and the box plots of the slope are shown in Fig. 16.5.

For the 30 subject dataset, we solved for $\alpha = 0.52$, which gives us conservation of mass. Without using the exponential fit, the average slope of the log–log plot was −0.59 (SD 0.11).

We applied our proposed weighted density registration algorithm to the first subject from the DIR dataset. This subject has images at 10 timepoints and has a set of 300 corresponding landmarks between the full inhale image and the full exhale image. These landmarks were manually chosen by three independent observers. Without any deformation, the landmark error is 4.01 mm (SD 2.91 mm). Using our method, the landmark error is reduced to 0.88 mm (SD 0.94 mm), which is only slightly higher than the observer repeat registration error of 0.85 mm (SD 1.24 mm).

We implement our algorithm on the GPU and plot the energy and the Fisher–Rao metric with and without applying the deformation. These results are shown in Fig. 16.6. In this figure we show that we have excellent data match, whereas the deformation remains physiologically realistic: inside the lungs there is substantial volume change due to respiration, but the deformation outside the lungs is volume preserving. With a $256 \times 256 \times 94$ voxel dataset, our algorithm takes approximately nine minutes running for four thousand iterations on a single nVidia Titan Z GPU.

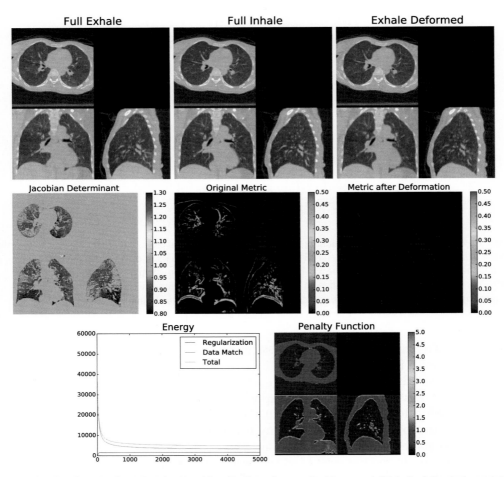

Figure 16.6 Application of to lung density matching. Registration results. Top row: full inhale, full exhale, and the deformed exhale density estimated using our method. Middle row: Jacobian determinant of the transformation, initial Fisher–Rao metric, and Fisher–Rao metric after applying the density action. Notice that outside the lungs the estimated deformation is volume preserving. Bottom row: Energy as a function of iterations, and penalty function.

Acknowledgments

We thank Caleb Rottmann, who worked on the implementation of the weighted diffeomorphic density matching algorithm. We are grateful for valuable discussions with Boris Khesin, Peter Michor, and François-Xavier Vialard.

This work was partially supported by the grant NIH R01 CA169102, the Swedish Foundation for Strategic Research (ICA12-0052), an EU Horizon 2020 Marie Sklodowska-Curie Individual Fellowship (661482), and by the Erwin Schrödinger Institute program: Infinite-Dimensional Riemannian Geometry with Applications to Image Matching and Shape Analysis by the FWF-project P24625.

References

1. John Ashburner, A fast diffeomorphic image registration algorithm, NeuroImage 38 (1) (2007) 95–113.
2. Brian B. Avants, Nicholas J. Tustison, Gang Song, Philip A. Cook, Arno Klein, James C. Gee, A reproducible evaluation of ants similarity metric performance in brain image registration, NeuroImage 54 (3) (2011) 2033–2044.
3. Nihat Ay, Jürgen Jost, Hong Le Van, Lorenz Schwachhöfer, Information geometry and sufficient statistics, The Annals of Statistics (2014).
4. Augustin Banyaga, Formes-volume sur les variétés à bord, L'Enseignement Mathématique 20 (2) (1974) 127–131.
5. M. Bauer, S. Joshi, K. Modin, Diffeomorphic density matching by optimal information transport, SIAM Journal on Imaging Sciences 8 (3) (2015) 1718–1751.
6. M. Bauer, S. Joshi, K. Modin, Diffeomorphic random sampling using optimal information transport, in: F. Nielsen, F. Barbaresco (Eds.), Geometric Science of Information, GSI 2017, in: Lecture Notes in Computer Science, vol. 10589, Springer, Cham, 2017.
7. Martin Bauer, Martins Bruveris, Peter W. Michor, Uniqueness of the Fisher–Rao metric on the space of smooth densities, Bulletin of the London Mathematical Society 48 (3) (2016) 499–506.
8. Martin Bauer, Joachim Escher, Boris Kolev, Local and global well-posedness of the fractional order EPDiff equation on $\mathbb{R}^d$, Journal of Differential Equations 258 (6) (2015) 2010–2053.
9. Martin Bauer, Sarang Joshi, Klas Modin, On geodesic completeness for Riemannian metrics on smooth probability densities, Calculus of Variations and Partial Differential Equations 56 (4) (2017) 113, 18.
10. Mirza Faisal Beg, Michael I. Miller, Alain Trouvé, Laurent Younes, Computing large deformation metric mappings via geodesic flows of diffeomorphisms, International Journal of Computer Vision 61 (2) (2005) 139–157.
11. John M. Boone, J. Anthony Seibert, An accurate method for computer-generating tungsten anode x-ray spectra from 30 to 140 kV, Medical Physics 24 (11) (1997) 1661–1670.
12. Bruveris Martins, François-Xavier Vialard, On completeness of groups of diffeomorphisms, Journal of the European Mathematical Society 19 (2017) 1507–1544, https://doi.org/10.4171/JEMS/698.
13. Brad C. Davis, P. Thomas Fletcher, Elizabeth Bullitt, Sarang Joshi, Population shape regression from random design data, International Journal of Computer Vision 90 (2) (2010) 255–266.
14. Thomas Friedrich, Die Fisher-Information und symplektische Strukturen, Mathematische Nachrichten 153 (1) (1991) 273–296.

15. Sarah E. Geneser, J.D. Hinkle, Robert M. Kirby, Brian Wang, Bill Salter, S. Joshi, Quantifying variability in radiation dose due to respiratory-induced tumor motion, Medical Image Analysis 15 (4) (2011) 640–649.

16. Vladlena Gorbunova, Jon Sporring, Pechin Lo, Martine Loeve, Harm A Tiddens, Mads Nielsen, Asger Dirksen, Marleen de Bruijne, Mass preserving image registration for lung ct, Medical Image Analysis 16 (4) (2012) 786–795.

17. Robert E. Greene, Katsuhiro Shiohama, Diffeomorphisms and volume-preserving embeddings of noncompact manifolds, Transactions of the American Mathematical Society 255 (1979) 403–414.

18. Ulf Grenander, Michael I. Miller, Computational anatomy: an emerging discipline, Quarterly of Applied Mathematics 56 (4) (1998) 617–694.

19. Richard S. Hamilton, The inverse function theorem of Nash and Moser, Bulletin of the American Mathematical Society 7 (1) (1982) 65–222.

20. W. Keith Hastings Monte, Carlo sampling methods using Markov chains and their applications, Biometrika 57 (1) (1970) 97–109.

21. Jacob Hinkle, Sarang Joshi, Idiff: irrotational diffeomorphisms for computational anatomy, in: Information Processing in Medical Imaging, Springer, 2013, pp. 754–765.

22. Sarang Joshi, Brad Davis, Matthieu Jomier, Guido Gerig, Unbiased diffeomorphic atlas construction for computational anatomy, NeuroImage 23 (2004) S151–S160.

23. Paul J. Keall, Sarang Joshi, S. Sastry Vedam, Jeffrey V. Siebers, Vijaykumar R. Kini, Radhe Mohan, Four-dimensional radiotherapy planning for DMLC-based respiratory motion tracking, Medical Physics 32 (4) (2005) 942–951.

24. B. Khesin, J. Lenells, G. Misiołek, S.C. Preston, Geometry of diffeomorphism groups, complete integrability and geometric statistics, Geometric and Functional Analysis 23 (1) (2013) 334–366.

25. Serge Lang, Fundamentals of Differential Geometry, Graduate Texts in Mathematics, vol. 191, Springer, New York, 1999.

26. Youssef Marzouk, Tarek Moselhy, Matthew Parno, Alessio Spantini, Sampling via measure transport: an introduction, in: Roger Ghanem, David Higdon, Houman Owhadi (Eds.), Handbook of Uncertainty Quantification, Springer International Publishing, Cham, 2016.

27. Michael I. Miller, Alain Trouvé, Laurent Younes, On the metrics and Euler–Lagrange equations of computational anatomy, Annual Review of Biomedical Engineering 4 (1) (2002) 375–405.

28. G. Misiołek, S.C. Preston, Fredholm properties of Riemannian exponential maps on diffeomorphism groups, Inventiones Mathematicae 179 (1) (2010) 191–227.

29. Klas Modin, Generalized Hunter–Saxton equations, optimal information transport, and factorization of diffeomorphisms, The Journal of Geometric Analysis 25 (2) (2015) 1306–1334.

30. Tarek A. El Moselhy, Youssef M. Marzouk, Bayesian inference with optimal maps, Journal of Computational Physics 231 (23) (2012) 7815–7850.

31. Jürgen Moser, On the volume elements on a manifold, Transactions of the American Mathematical Society 120 (1965) 286–294.

32. N. Nakanishi, A survey of Nambu–Poisson geometry, Lobachevskii Journal of Mathematics 4 (1999) 5–11 (electronic).

33. Sebastian Reich, A nonparametric ensemble transform method for Bayesian inference, SIAM Journal on Scientific Computing 35 (4) (2013) A2013–A2024.

34. Caleb Rottman, Ben Larson, Pouya Sabouri, Amit Sawant, Sarang Joshi, Diffeomorphic density registration in thoracic computed tomography, in: Sebastien Ourselin, Leo Joskowicz, Mert R. Sabuncu, Gozde Unal, William Wells (Eds.), Medical Image Computing and Computer-Assisted Intervention – MICCAI 2016, Springer International Publishing, Cham, 2016, pp. 46–53.

35. Amit Sawant, Paul Keall, Kim Butts Pauly, Marcus Alley, Shreyas Vasanawala, Billy W. Loo Jr, Jacob Hinkle, Sarang Joshi, Investigating the feasibility of rapid MRI for image-guided motion management in lung cancer radiotherapy, BioMed Research International (2014) 2014.

36. D. Seo, J. Ho, B.C. Vemuri, Computing diffeomorphic paths for large motion interpolation, in: Computer Vision and Pattern Recognition (CVPR), 2013 IEEE Conference on, June 2013, pp. 1227–1232.

37. D.H. Seo, J. Ho, J.H. Traverse, J. Forder, B. Vemuri, Computing diffeomorphic paths with application to cardiac motion analysis, in: 4th MICCAI Workshop on Mathematical Foundations of Computational Anatomy, 2013, pp. 83–94.

38. Yelin Suh, Walter Murray, Paul J. Keall, IMRT treatment planning on 4D geometries for the era of dynamic MLC tracking, Technology in Cancer Research and Treatment 13 (6) (2014) 505–515.

39. Tom Vercauteren, Xavier Pennec, Aymeric Perchant, Nicholas Ayache, Diffeomorphic demons: efficient non-parametric image registration, NeuroImage 45 (1) (2009) S61–S72.

40. François-Xavier Vialard, Laurent Risser, Daniel Rueckert, Colin J. Cotter, Diffeomorphic 3D image registration via geodesic shooting using an efficient adjoint calculation, International Journal of Computer Vision 97 (2) (Apr. 2012) 229–241.

41. Laurent Younes, Shapes and Diffeomorphisms, vol. 171, Springer Science & Business Media, 2010.

42. Laurent Younes, Felipe Arrate, Michael I. Miller, Evolutions equations in computational anatomy, NeuroImage 45 (1, Supplement 1) (2009) S40–S50, Mathematics in Brain Imagingo.

Index